A HISTORY OF THE CATHOLIC CHURCH

a history
of the catholic
church

BY LUDWIG HERTLING, S. J.

Translated from the German by
ANSELM GORDON BIGGS, O.S.B., PH.D.

THE NEWMAN PRESS · WESTMINSTER, MARYLAND
1957

Originally published in Germany as *Geschichte der katholischen Kirche*
by Morus-Verlag, Berlin.

Nihil Obstat: JOANNES A. OETGEN, O.S.B., J.C.L.
    Censor Deputatus

Imprimi Potest: GUALTERUS A. COGGIN, O.S.B., PH.D.
    Coadjutor Abbatis Belmontani

Imprimatur: VINCENTIUS C. TAYLOR, O.S.B., D.D.
    Abbas Nullius Belmontanus

die 21 Aprilis, 1956

TO HIS ALMA MATER

THE CATHOLIC UNIVERSITY OF AMERICA

AND

HIS REVERED MASTER

ALOYSIUS KIERAN ZIEGLER

FROM THE GRATEFUL HEART OF

THE TRANSLATOR

author's foreword

THERE is no lack of presentations of the history of the
Catholic Church. The material of Church History is,
however, so inexhaustible and the interest with which
the various readers approach it is so multiform, that it is always
possible to undertake a new presentation.

In this book an effort is made to provide a readable account
of that history without any critical apparatus. Throughout,
the emphasis is on the interior life of the Church—the Church
in her task of saving souls. For this is the core of Church History. The Church can be understood only when she is considered as a work, or rather as the work, which God has
established for mankind: to find and to show the way to
supernatural salvation. Naturally, there constantly exist re-
ciprocal relations between the Church in her capacity as shep-
herdess of souls and the states and other human communities.
It is among the same human beings and in the same areas with
which the other communities are concerned that the Church
labors to fulfill her task. Culture and economy, wars, dynasties,
states, unceasingly intervene in pastoral endeavors, now pro-
moting, now obstructing. To this extent a "purely religious"

history of the Church is impossible. Just the same, the Church's soul-saving duty will always remain the guiding idea.

At the same time, special attention is devoted to the Church's geographical expansion and hence to historical statistics, a field that is perhaps not sufficiently emphasized in some presentations.

In brief, the content of this book could be described thus: the pervading of humanity by the pastoral institutions of the Church.

LUDWIG HERTLING, S.J.

translator's note

FATHER LUDWIG HERTLING's *Geschichte der katholischen Kirche* is offered to the English-speaking public because of its special merit—its emphasis on the soul-saving work of the Church. The author does not neglect the relations of the Church with governments and her role in the political events of each century, but he is chiefly concerned with her pastoral endeavors and numerical growth. This preoccupation alone would justify the translation. It is hoped that Father Hertling's volume will find a place in undergraduate courses of Church History in colleges and universities and in the homes of the educated laity, as well as in the libraries of seminaries, rectories, and religious houses.

This is Father Hertling's book. Hence, while the translator does not necessarily agree with all details of interpretation, he has either left them inviolate or, in a few cases, has referred the reader to other treatments. A few errors of fact have been corrected; reference is made to such changes by means of footnotes, except when the error was clearly due to an oversight in the proofreading of the foreign text. The German original contains no footnotes. The few citations, mostly in the early chapters, are incorporated into the text, but in the English translation these have been dropped to the bottom of the page. It has been considered worthwhile to amplify the very brief treatment of the American Church in Chapter Sixteen, to bring the pontificate of Pius XII up to date, and to indicate American contributions to the liturgical movement and the most recent restorations in the liturgy. Footnotes make clear the translator's additions. For the most part, the author's statistics have been left untouched.

A bibliography has been added. This is by no means intended to be exhaustive or even adequate. Its main purpose is to indicate some of the principal works on general Church History, works that are comparatively easy of access and that will in turn provide fuller treatment and a more copious bibliography. Except for patrology and papal history, the list does not extend to special fields.

Several persons have rendered valuable assistance to the translator, who takes this opportunity to express his sincere gratitude. His superiors, the Right Reverend Vincent G. Taylor, O.S.B., D.D., Abbot of Belmont Abbey Nullius, and the Very Reverend Walter A. Coggin, O.S.B., Ph.D., Coadjutor to the Abbot, and his confreres, monks of the same abbey, have shown great interest and given encouragement. One of them, the Reverend Boniface Bauer, O.S.B., rendered valuable technical assistance. Miss Mary Ellen Quinn and Mrs. Mary Cook gave generously of their time to prepare the typescript. The translator's former teacher, the Reverend Aloysius K. Ziegler, S.T.D., *archiviste paléographe*, recom-

TRANSLATOR'S NOTE

mended him to The Newman Press and offered important advice. His Excellency, the Most Reverend Bryan J. Mc-Entegart, D.D., LL.D., Titular Bishop of Aradi, graciously accepted the dedication on behalf of the great institution over which he presides. But, most of all, the kindness, suggestions, aid, and sacrifice of his time on the part of a very dear confrere, the Reverend John Oetgen, O.S.B., J.C.L., earn undying thanks. Whatever felicity of expression this English version possesses is due entirely to Father John's deeply appreciated co-operation and inspiration; and the translator's debt extends far beyond this point to every detail of the work.

ANSELM GORDON BIGGS, O.S.B.

Feast of Saint Anselm,
April 21, 1956

contents

A HISTORY OF THE CATHOLIC CHURCH

the founding of the church and her growth in the first three centuries

ROM the theological viewpoint, the Church was founded on the first Good Friday, when Christ, by His Death on the Cross, completed the work of Redemption. The Old Covenant, the period of preparation, ceased to exist then, and the New Order of Salvation began. But from the historical viewpoint one can say that the founding of the Church was a gradual process: it began when Christ called the apostles, selected Peter for the office of "Rock," and instituted the sacraments. It reached completion when the apostles, after the Resurrection, first undertook to carry out the instructions of the Master.

We do not, however, mean that the idea of the Church had gradually developed, as in the case of merely human religious founders, who, moved by varying circumstances, refashioned their ideas until the final result was something quite different from the original plan. In Christ nothing like this is to be found. Each step in the realization of the Kingdom of God on earth was but a partial manifestation of a divine plan complete from the very beginning.

It is not the function of a history of the Church to tell the life of Jesus and to draw a character-sketch of His historical

1

personality, or to give the content of His teaching. The reason is not that the life and teaching of Jesus have no relation to the history of the Church; on the contrary, an exact knowledge of the Gospel is the indispensable key to the understanding of that history. But it may be presumed to be the common property of all educated persons.

Jesus gave to His Kingdom no local cult center, such as the religion of the Israelites possessed from the beginning in the Tabernacle of the Covenant and, later, in the Temple. Instead, He immediately provided for a hierarchy that would be universal. The pious women of Galilee, who took care of Him and His disciples, did not belong to this hierarchy, nor did the wealthy friends in various places, in whose houses He could always count upon a cordial welcome. But expressly chosen by Jesus as His helpers were the seventy-two disciples. They were, so to speak, His men of confidence in the individual villages, and, at the coming of the Master, were sent on ahead to the next localities in order to prepare for His visit.

A special group, the highest in rank, was composed of the Twelve whom Jesus also selected or appointed, and who accompanied Him on all His travels. The word Apostles—that is, emissaries or messengers—did not for the moment correspond to their activity and thus their very title pointed to the future.

The apostles knew that so long as the Master remained with them they were in a period of preparatory training and that their own work lay ahead of them. If they quarreled among themselves in regard to precedence, as the Gospels often relate, no merely childish conceit was the sole reason. The cause lay also in zeal for the task ahead: each wished to secure for himself the greatest possible share in the work yet to come.

We generally represent to ourselves the apostles as not

2

overly bright and the Master's training of them as not particularly fruitful. After the Ascension, the manner in which Peter at once assumed direction in filling the place of the fallen Judas shows that the apostles grasped the meaning of what was occurring. On the other hand, much was still obscure to them, even after the outpouring of the Holy Spirit. A special revelation was needed before Peter agreed to admit heathens to baptism, although this point was clearly contained in the Lord's baptismal command.

At the time of the Ascension the body of believers comprised over 500 souls, for this number witnessed the great appearance of the risen Lord in Galilee. Only a part of these lived in Jerusalem or followed the apostles thither, for we find only 120 gathered in the Cenacle. The first great increase occurred in Jerusalem. After Peter's sermon on the day of Pentecost, 3,000 persons at once received baptism. It seems likely that in this number there were many inhabitants of Jerusalem. A short time later the community counted 5,000 men, and thus, altogether, at least between ten and fifteen thousand. The figure is considerable, if we remember that Jerusalem then had little more than 50,000 inhabitants. The apostles quickly became seriously overburdened with their functions and looked about for helpers. Such assistants of a subordinate rank might already be seen in the "disciples" who buried Ananias and Sapphira; they correspond somewhat to the later porters or *fossores*. In any case, the apostles, by the laying on of hands, now ordained seven deacons (literally, "servants"), who helped with the care of the poor and also acted as preachers or catechists.

DIVISION INTO LOCAL DISTRICTS OF JURISDICTION

At the beginning the apostles directed the community together. And where there were individual Christians or groups of them outside Jerusalem, as in Damascus, nothing is at first heard of local administrators. When, through the efforts of the deacon Philip, a fairly large group was established in Samaria, Peter and John went there in person. Later, when news came of numerous conversions in faraway Antioch, the apostles did not themselves go there, but they sent Barnabas as their official representative. He went to Antioch alone, and summoned Paul thither from Tarsus, but Barnabas was not the local superior nor did he remain constantly in Antioch. He labored there in the service of the apostles. The Christian community had not yet been divided into jurisdictional districts.

Then Paul and Barnabas founded a whole series of communities in Asia Minor and installed local administrators in them. Thus the first step was taken toward dividing the Church into jurisdictional districts, later to be called dioceses. The administrator of the community of Lystra had no authority in Derbe and Iconium. However, these administrators were not yet real diocesan bishops in the present sense, for they ruled temporarily in the place of the founding apostle. As soon as Paul or another apostle came to the community, he immediately assumed charge. The substitution of local administrators for an apostle seems to have been imitated in Palestine and Syria too, although we have no immediate information in this regard.

In the lifetime of the apostles, then, we have a twofold hierarchy, the general and the local. The general jurisdiction was exercised by the apostles conjointly, as at the Council of Jerusalem; or individually, as in the case of Paul, John, and Peter, or through an officially accredited co-worker in the service of an apostle. In the last capacity we can mention, among others, Titus in Crete, Timothy in Ephesus, and possibly Mark in Alexandria. The local jurisdiction was exercised in the lifetime

4

of the apostles and in their stead by local administrators installed by the apostles in particular communities. With the death of the last apostle the general hierarchy disappeared, and the local administrators became real diocesan bishops. The special position of Peter, which did not disappear with his death, and the communion resulting therefrom prevented the Church from breaking up at this juncture into a mere aggregation of independent local churches.

Of course, we should not overestimate the situation that prevailed. The communities were very small. In the first years Jerusalem had more than 10,000 Christians, but in A.D. 70 the city was destroyed, and the community, which had already taken its departure, was dispersed. The other communities, including Corinth, Ephesus, Smyrna, and Philippi, probably numbered a few hundred souls in apostolic times. The hierarchical superiors were humble folk. They knew neither miter nor crosier and in externals were not to be distinguished from the other inhabitants of their city. Furthermore, in late antiquity a local bishop was often only what a pastor is today. But what is of importance is that from the beginning a real hierarchical organization was in existence. Christianity was never a mere spiritual tendency or current nor an enthusiastic mass movement.

THE MONARCHICAL EPISCOPATE

Modern critics have gone to much trouble to discover between the apostles and the later episcopal communities an age of formless mass movement. Accordingly, in non-Catholic theology, they have posed the now classical question: How and when did the "monarchical episcopate" arise? The contention behind this question is clear: Christ did not at all found any Church, but only provided a teaching or ideas. What we call the Church developed, it is maintained, from

5

these ideas but became something quite different from what Christ had intended. Such a theory can be upheld only if the sources are either disregarded or are so twisted that they seem to affirm something else. To begin with, it is very difficult to understand how an unorganized mass could give itself an organization from within, without any outside intervention, and even more how this "development" could have led, in widely separated places, to the same result at the same time. More important still, there is not the slightest bit of information that such unorganized communities ever existed. The sources provide no trace of communities which were governed by a college or *gremium* without a monarchical head, a situation postulated by the theorists of "development" as an intermediate stage. On the contrary, we everywhere find communities with a hierarchical superior. In the letters of Saint Ignatius of Antioch, from the first decade of the second century, there is seen for each community a single bishop, who is aided by priests and deacons. Shortly before this, toward the close of the first century, Clement of Rome, in his letter to the Corinthians, shows himself so clearly as a "monarchical" bishop that many critics conclude that Clement created this office. But he quite definitely did nothing of the sort, for in the Apocalypse, written around A.D. 80, we meet the local administrator of Pergamum, Thyatira, and other cities, addressed as the "angels" of their respective communities; these were certainly particular individuals and not colleges. Furthermore, we have the most ancient episcopal lists of the most important churches—Rome, Antioch, and Alexandria—all reaching back to the apostles themselves. They were drawn up around the middle of the second century for the express purpose of guaranteeing the unbroken succession from the apostles. True, it has been conjectured that the oldest names in these lists are not those of hierarchical superiors but of mere "witnesses of tradition." But what does this mean? The oldest writers who made use of these lists—Irenaeus and others—regarded those mentioned as bishops. The fact that such hypotheses must be resorted to shows how untenable is the whole theory of the gradual origin of the monarchical episcopate.

Another question, but one of secondary importance, is whether all local administrators, including those appointed by Paul and Barnabas in Lystra, Derbe, and other places, possessed episcopal rank from the outset and whether they were the only persons of this rank in the community. Nothing can be determined from their titles. Paul used "presbyter" and "episkopos" as synonyms. Ignatius made a distinction, but Irenaeus occasionally spoke of "presbyters" when he meant bishops. Most probably, at the beginning, when the apostles ordained new officials through the imposition of hands, they invariably imparted the fullness of ordination. Only later was the sacrament, so to speak, divided up, so that the fullness of Orders was no longer imparted in each case, but only to the extent that the function being conferred called for. This would explain, for example, the report, which can be traced to the second century, that Clement was ordained by the Apostle Peter, although he was only Peter's third successor as bishop of Rome; likewise, it would account for the custom existing in Alexandria till the end of the second century that the new bishop was consecrated, not as elsewhere by the neighboring bishops, but by the "presbyters" of the city.[1] In Alexandria, where old customs usually maintained themselves for a long period, all or at least part of the "presbyters" thus possessed the episcopal character till the end of the second century. But

---

[1] In regard to this controverted point, see Jules Lebreton and Jacques Zeiller, *L'église primitive*, Vol. I of *Histoire de l'église depuis les origines jusqu'à nos jours*, published under the direction of Augustin Fliche and Victor Martin (Paris: 1938), pp. 377 f. [English translation: *The History of the Primitive Church*, trans. Ernest C. Messenger, I (New York: 1949), 481 f.] (Translator's note.)

this has nothing to do with the monarchical episcopate. Even today there are large dioceses in which, in addition to the bishop, several priests have received episcopal consecration. In antiquity, as well as today, the administrator of the community was always one.

THE EXPANSION OF CHRISTIANITY

The missionary progress of Christianity is made known to us in its results; almost decade by decade from the time of the apostles, we see the map adding the names of new Christian communities, until at the end of the third century there is scarcely a sizeable locality in the entire Roman Empire where Christians cannot be found. On the other hand, we know very little about the nature and method of this spread of the Faith and less still about the persons who accomplished it.

We know most about the very first beginnings of the expansion, because we possess the Acts of the Apostles, an abundant, vivid, and trustworthy historical source, whose equal can scarcely be found in the rest of ancient literature. But this history is a fragment. Its title does not entirely correspond to its content. In the first twelve chapters, only the deeds and fortunes of Saint Peter are narrated. The account breaks off abruptly with the mysterious sentence, "And he departed, and went to another place." From there till the end, Saint Paul alone is spoken of. Only at the Council of Jerusalem does Peter once more appear. And even the history of Paul comes suddenly to a close with the remark that he remained for two years in his lodging at Rome, where he taught unhindered. Now it is a characteristic of the composition which Luke displays elsewhere, that he apparently digresses suddenly from his subject only to pick up the dropped threads later. It is therefore possible—and the opinion was held in antiquity too—that Luke had the intention of returning to Peter and perhaps of relating the deeds of the other apostles. At any rate, the Acts of the Apostles, apart from the first years, is not a history of the Church, but only of the journeys of the Apostle Paul. Since, in addition, we have the fourteen Epistles of Saint Paul, which also afford us insight into the same subject, the missionary activity of the Apostle of the Gentiles is placed for us in exceedingly bold relief, as though he were not only the most successful, but even the unique propagator of the Faith.

Such, of course, was not the case. We later find everywhere, far from the routes traversed by Paul, Christian communities of equal importance with those established by him. The report that the community in Alexandria was founded by the Evangelist Mark is sufficiently well-attested. But in regard to Rome we do not know who first brought Christianity thither. When Paul reached Rome in the spring of 60, he found an already numerous community. It is striking that the distinguished Roman lady, Pomponia Graecina, changed her manner of life, as Tacitus relates, in the very year when Peter departed from Jerusalem and "went to another place"— in A.D. 43. But the coincidence is not sufficient to prove Saint Peter's presence in Rome at this early date. Of John we know that he eventually established himself in Asia Minor and labored in the churches founded by Paul. Polycarp, bishop of Smyrna, who died a martyr at the middle of the second century, was John's disciple. The grave of the Apostle Philip was shown at Hierapolis in Phrygia toward the end of the second century, but it is uncertain whether he has been confused with the deacon Philip. For the most part, we know practically nothing of the activity and fate of the apostles. The later legends represent them as journeying in known or fabled lands, where they baptized thousands and converted entire kingdoms as the result of stupendous miracles. These legends at least indicate how the Faith could not have spread.

9

We must imagine that the missionary success of the first heralds of the Faith was quite meager, at least in regard to the number of converts. In the individual cities they were seldom able to win more than a few families or small groups of families. For we nowhere find traces of mass conversions, of entire villages or districts which had accepted the Christian Faith. Furthermore, at the beginning of the third century, Origen remarks in his *Homily on Psalm XXXVI:*

> We are not a people. Now in this city, now in that, some are brought to the Faith. But never, since the start of the preaching of the Faith, has an entire race suddenly joined us. It is not with us as with the Jewish people or the Egyptians, that we should be one single stock, but, on the contrary, the Christians gather together individuals from different peoples.[2]

The view of many recent historians that Christianity spread in the manner of an enthusiastic wave is false. Conversions did not result from mass suggestion; each individual knew what he was doing. Only thus can we explain the amazement of the heathens, already expressed by Pliny and later reported by Tertullian, that Christians were found everywhere, without anyone's knowing whence they came.

This modest and quiet manner of expansion makes it difficult for us to know in detail how it happened. Assuredly it occurred principally by means of oral teaching, and to a lesser degree through the spread of the Scriptures. Until about the middle of the second century we hear of wandering prophets or teachers. The philosopher and martyr Justin was such. But it seems that these private preachers of the Faith were not always kindly regarded by the bishops. It is altogether striking that, in the Christian sources into the fourth

[2] Migne, Patrologia Graeca, XII (Paris: 1862), col. 1321.

century and beyond, we are little conscious of missionary purpose or even of missionary enthusiasm. Christians were evidently so accustomed to seeing more and more persons adhere to the Church that they felt no urgent need to open up new roads. Even the writings of the apologists, which were composed directly for the heathens, were not recruiting propaganda. They were content to repel attacks.

PETER IN ROME

In order to mark the future bishops of Rome as his successors in the office of Rock, the personal presence of the Apostle Peter in Rome would not have been absolutely necessary. The theological significance of his geographical presence is at times overstressed by those who affirm it and by those who deny it. The papal primacy as an institution of divine law does not depend on whether Peter was in Rome for a long time or a short time or at all. Historically, however, it is certain that he was in Rome, suffered martyrdom there, and is buried there. Historically considered, this point is really not even a problem, for everything favors it and nothing contradicts it, and for the historian a problem arises only when in his sources he discovers contradictions or facts which cannot be explained by themselves. Nevertheless, the historian, in view of the great historical significance of the fact, may inquire how great is the degree of certainty which it can claim.

The answer to his question is this: the certainty is as great as it can be in the case of a fact for which we possess neither an authentic document nor the undoubted report of an eyewitness, and for which, accordingly, we are dependent upon indirect testimonies. Of these we have so many in regard to Peter's presence in Rome that we can speak of a complete convergence of the sources on this one point.

We have the unmistakable allusion to Peter's martyrdom

11

in Saint John's Gospel (21:19). The later this chapter is dated by the critics, the more striking its witness becomes, for, according to the same critics, no tradition in regard to Peter is supposed to have existed in the second century. We have the letter of Clement, which was almost contemporary with the Fourth Gospel; this letter, written at Rome, treats of things which happened "in our time" and "among us," and it cites the "glorious testimony" of Peter. A few years later, at the beginning of the second century, we have the letter of Saint Ignatius to the Romans; he makes it clear that he does not claim to command them "like Peter and Paul." While he employed the same expression in writing to the churches of Ephesus and Tralles, he omitted in these letters the reference to Peter and Paul, evidently because the princes of the apostles stood in a closer relationship to Rome than to Ephesus and Tralles. We have the tradition in regard to the origin of Saint Mark's Gospel, which Eusebius has preserved from the second-century writers, Papias and Clement of Alexandria. This tradition does not entirely agree, it is true, in details, but it does agree on the point that in Rome Mark acted as Peter's interpreter. The Muratorian Canon, from the second half of the second century, speaks of the *Passio Petri* as of a well-known fact. Furthermore, in the second century we have the express testimony of Dionysius, bishop of Corinth, to the martyrdom of Peter and Paul in Rome; that of Irenaeus to their labors in spreading the Faith; that of Tertullian, who supposes that there is no difference between those whom John baptized in the Jordan and those whom Peter baptized in the Tiber; [3] and finally that of the Roman cleric Caius, who around A.D. 200 offered to show to everyone the "trophies" of the two apostles on the Vatican and on the Via Ostia. Eusebius, who has preserved this testimony, understands by "trophies" the glorious

---

[3] *De Baptismo*, iv (Migne, Patrologia Latina, I [Paris: 1844], col. 1203).

tombs of Peter and Paul, and the context will allow no other meaning.

Independent of all these witnesses is the Roman episcopal list which Irenaeus happened upon. It has come down to us in a very copious tradition, which by no means is derived only from Irenaeus. Throughout, Peter stands at the top of the list.

A particular point which is perhaps not always noticed as it deserves to be is this: Why have the names of Peter and Paul been so joined together that in tradition they always appear united, even in Clement and Ignatius? Such a connection does not derive from the Bible. In the New Testament Peter and Paul are never named in the same breath. Their paths seldom crossed. Modern criticism has even constructed a deep opposition between them and between the two rival forms of Christianity that they respectively personify. How and why, then, did these two names become so joined that for all later time they have represented a proverbial unity? That can have happened only in a place where persons knew of a joint and impressive activity of both apostles. This place can only be Rome. Unless both apostles had given at least their final witness to the Faith in Rome, their two names would never have been united.

Harnack has called attention to a remarkable testimony. In *Contra Celsum* [4] Origen writes: "Phlegon—I believe it is in the thirteenth or fourteenth book of his *Chronicle*—conceded to Christ the knowledge of the future (he is, of course, speaking erroneously of Peter instead of Jesus) and testified that the prophecy had come true." Publius Aelius Phlegon was a freedman of the Emperor Hadrian (117–138), for whom or with whom he composed the great work, the *Olympiads* or *Chronicle*, with all kinds of curious information such as he knew would delight his patron. We no longer have this work and

[4] II, xiv (Migne, Patrologia Graeca, XI [Paris: 1857], cols. 824 f.).

thus do not know what prophecies Phlegon had in mind. What is remarkable, however, is that in Rome at the beginning of the second century a scholarly heathen author could confuse Peter and Jesus. Of course, this does not prove that Peter was in Rome, but only that at the time of Hadrian he was held in the highest esteem by the Roman Christians. But it is just this which the opponents of Peter's presence in Rome have to deny. According to them, in the Rome of the second century Peter was no better known than were Thaddeus and Bartholomew.

Now these testimonies are not contradicted by even one opposing testimony. Never has even one hagiographer named any other place than Rome as the scene of the final activity and death of the two apostles. The only real difficulty is the fact that in all three passages in the New Testament where Paul appears in some connection with Rome—in his Epistle to the Romans, at the close of the Acts of the Apostles, and in his Second Epistle to Timothy—Peter is nowhere mentioned. But from this circumstance the most that can be concluded is, not that Peter was never in Rome, and still less that he did not endure martyrdom there, but that he did not stay in Rome continuously, which, furthermore, is very probably the case.

Independent of this historical evidence, but no less trustworthy, is the archaeological testimony. In archaeology it is regarded as a principle that evidence of an early local cult is sufficient to indicate the existence of the grave and at the same time the fact of martyrdom, unreliable though the later legends of a martyr may be. If this is certain as regards other martyrs, it must also apply in the case of Peter and Paul. Now the archaeological findings at Peter's grave are such as to guarantee that the grave existed at least long before the erection of Constantine's basilica. The most recent excavations under Saint Peter's have clearly shown this. Of course, there is in

Rome still another spot, where, though perhaps there was no tomb, there was a cult center of the apostles, which likewise extends back beyond Constantine. In the excavations made since 1915 under the church of San Sebastiano there has been brought to light a wall which is literally covered with scrawled petitions to the Apostles Peter and Paul. These inscriptions cannot have been made later than the third century, for the place where they are found was filled up when the basilica was built in the early years of the fourth century. Now the cult of a saint away from his tomb was quite unusual in Christian antiquity. Hence, with reference to the old legends, it has been conjectured that the bodies of the apostles were conveyed to San Sebastiano for a short period in the third century. Be that as it may, in any case we have archaeological evidence that Saint Peter had been honored at Rome at an early period as a local saint, and, according to all we know of the customs of Christian antiquity, that was possible only if he was buried in Rome.[5]

There are, of course, those who are not at all satisfied by such a method of proof and who are surprised at the lack of clearer testimony. But these are only the sort who have never clearly grasped on what grounds our entire knowledge of antiquity, even of classical antiquity, is based. In ancient history there are a great many undoubted facts—*e.g.*, that Alexander

---

[5] In regard to the excavations still in progress beneath the Vatican basilica, see *Esplorazioni sotto la Confessione di San Pietro in Vaticano eseguite negli anni 1940–1949. Relazione a cura di B. M. Appollonj Ghetti, A. Ferrua, S.J., E. Josi, E. Kirschbaum, S.J. Appendice numismatica di C. Serafini* (Città del Vaticano: 1951); Eamonn O'Doherty, "The Tomb of Saint Peter," *The American Ecclesiastical Review*, CXXVIII, No. 6 (June, 1953), 438–444; E. Griffe, "La question du transfert des reliques de S. Pierre ad catacumbas," *Bulletin de littérature ecclésiastique*, LIV (1953); J. C. M. Toynbee, "The Shrine of St. Peter and Its Setting," *Journal of Roman Studies*, XLIII (1953); J. Fink, "Archäologie des Petrusgrabes," *Theologische Revue*, L (1954); José Ruysschaert, *Réflexions sur les fouilles vaticanes. Le rapport officiel et la critique. Données archéologiques. Données épigraphiques et littéraires* (Louvain: Extrait de la *Revue d'histoire ecclésiastique*, XLVIII-XLIX [1953-1954]). (Translator's note.)

the Great died in Babylon, that Augustus died in Nola, that the ashes of Trajan were placed in his column—which are not so well-attested as is Peter's grave. It is likewise noteworthy that the authenticity of Paul's grave is not called into question, although the historical evidence for it is the same as for Peter's.

It is a pity that many non-Catholic scholars almost apologize for having to admit, when they finally do, that Peter died in Rome. "It cannot be proved from unquestionable testimonies that Peter was in Rome at all, although one can scarcely avoid the hypothesis." [6] "In the dispute surging through the centuries as to whether Peter came to Rome and suffered martyrdom there, the balance of probability—there is no question of certitude—seems, it is true, to incline to the affirmative side." [7] "I have a very vivid impression that we must reckon with the possibility of Peter's having come to Rome." [8] "Later we hear that Peter, just like Paul, wandered about as a missionary, and on one of these journeys he may have met his death in Rome." [9] All this sounds almost like, "I don't mind, if it must be." One might well ask, "Where in the whole range of our knowledge of antiquity does one move about so nervously?"

THE PAPAL LIST

The oldest surviving list of Roman bishops is found in Irenaeus.[10] It reads as follows:

After the blessed Apostles [Peter and Paul] had founded

6 Gustav Krüger, "Petrus in Rom," *ZNW*, XXXI (1932), 301. This reference and those in footnotes 8 and 9 are reproduced, without verification, from the German original. (Translator's note.)

7 Erich Caspar, *Geschichte des Papsttums*, I (Tübingen: 1930), 1.

8 Goguel, *RNPR*, XVIII (1938), 194.

9 Ad. Jülicher, *Die Religion Jesu und die Anfänge des Christentums*, in Kultur der Gegenwart, hsg. von P. Hinneberg (1922), p. 80.

10 *Adversus Haereses*, III, iii (Migne, Patrologia Graeca, VII [Paris: 1857], cols. 849 ff.).

16

and organized the Church, they entrusted to Linus the liturgy [official responsibility] of the episcopal office. It is he whom Paul mentions in his epistles to Timothy. He was succeeded by Anencletus, after whom Clement was the third following the apostles to hold the episcopal office; he had known the apostles . . . Clement was succeeded by Evaristus, Evaristus by Alexander; then Xystus was installed as the sixth after the apostles, and after him Telesphorus, who rendered a glorious testimony [*i.e.*, was a martyr]. Then followed Hyginus, next Pius, and after him Anicetus. Soter succeeded Anicetus, and now, in the twelfth place after the apostles, Eleutherus has the episcopal office.

This list embraces a period of more than a century. That is not excessively long for the reliable transmission of a series of mere names. Besides, Irenaeus seems not to have been the first to compile the list. The additions of "the third," "the sixth," point to the memory-aids of an oral tradition, and, moreover, we know that, even before Irenaeus, Hegesippus had drawn up a catalogue of the Roman bishops which we no longer possess. The reliability of the list in Irenaeus is doubted by no one.

In the Christian writers of the third century and later, the list keeps turning up and becomes correspondingly longer. Errors are found in it—omissions, transpositions, and distortions of names, which, however, are easily corrected. Thus, for example, in the manuscripts Hyginus appears occasionally as Egenus or Eugenius, and later Zephyrinus as Severinus, Fabianus as Fabius or Flavianus. Generally, the rare name Anencletus is confused, so that many later writers occasionally make two names out of it, a Cletus and an Anacletus. But all of that is of little importance.

17

While the list of the earliest popes is historically certain, it is, nevertheless, only a series of names, not a chronicle. The trustworthy chronology begins only with A.D. 217, the year of the death of Pope Zephyrinus; for the earlier period we have only a few details.

Linus and Anencletus are mere names to us. From Clement I we possess the long Epistle to the community of Corinth. The clergy of Corinth had expelled their bishop, who may have been the Fortunatus appointed by the Apostle Paul. He turned to the Roman bishop, who sent two of his priests to reinstate the deposed prelate and restore order in Corinth. The next three popes, Evaristus, Alexander I, and Xystus I, are, again, only names. About Telesphorus we know from Irenaeus merely that he suffered martyrdom. This is the first martyrdom of a pope about which we have any information. It must have occurred in the reign of Hadrian (117–138). Of Hyginus, Pius I, and Anicetus we know that discussions with Gnostic heretics took place in Rome during their pontificates. Anicetus was the pope whom the aged disciple of the Apostle John, Polycarp, the bishop of Smyrna, visited for a discussion of the celebration of Easter. The question concerned the ritual deviation of the communities of Asia Minor from the practice of the other churches, in particular from the Roman practice. We are casually informed that Soter sent copious alms to the community of Corinth. Eleutherus was the pope whom Irenaeus met when he was sent by the community of Lyon to inquire about the Montanists. Only with his successor, Victor I, does our information begin to become somewhat abundant.

It is striking that so many of these popes bear Greek names. For this reason many hold that the Roman Christian community was for a long period a sort of Greek ethnic colony. A glance at the epigraphy of the city of Rome shows, however, that Greek names were then extremely common, though mainly among slaves and freedmen. Several names of popes, such as Evaristus, Anicetus, and, in the third century, Anterus, are verified as typical servile names. Of Pius I we know from other sources that he was a freedman, though his name is Latin, and the same is true of Callistus I. That need not surprise us. In a Roman freedman it is not necessary to see a pensioned servant. Freedmen actually made up the most industrious part of the population. Commerce and industry lay to a great extent in their hands. In the Roman satire the freedman corresponds rather closely to our *nouveaux riches*. Not that the popes were such, but we nevertheless gain an essential clue as to the social circles in which, for the most part, we must look for the Christians of that day: the old Roman nobility and the official aristocracy contributed few; chiefly they came from the working middle class.

THE GNOSIS

The Gnostics, whose origins go back to the first century, were at first not a separate sect, but rather an intellectual current within the Church. Many highly educated persons who accepted Christianity, especially in the great Greek cultural centers of Antioch and Alexandria, were distressed to find that Christianity was not more complex, that it was too simple and almost vulgar. In antiquity the man of culture could endure any reproach more easily than that of *naïveté*. These academicians did not realize that Christian doctrine is a complex of unchangeable revealed truths. They sought rather to enlarge upon it and establish it after the manner of a philosophical system. That is what the word *Gnosis* is said to mean—a deeper knowledge. Not a practical metaphysic was to issue from it, but quite amazing theosophies and cosmogonies, in which Abstract and Concrete, Time, Silence, Word, God, Abyss, Christ, and Church rolled around confusedly, as in

19

an intricate mythology. We know particular Gnostic systems from Catholic refutations, especially from Irenaeus, who did not assume the task lightly, but we also have fragments of the Gnostics themselves, and even a complete book, the *Pistis Sophia*. Today we are not attracted by this bizarre nonsense, but then the mysterious, mystically sublime tone of these doctrines, far removed from the Christian revelation, apparently exerted over many a fascinating attraction.

Around the middle of the second century there seems to have existed a whole crowd of wandering Gnostic teachers, some of whom practiced mysterious rites and in their secret meetings with their followers celebrated a strange Eucharistic service and indulged in gross immorality. For the Church this activity was a danger. Until after the middle of the second century she could not very effectively oppose the literary flood, because she lacked educated champions. With undaunted persistency, the wandering Gnostic teachers hastened to Rome, not because the Roman Christian community was a promising field of operation for them, but because to possess the Roman *communio* was already clearly regarded as especially worthwhile. We know the names of several—Marcion, Cerdon, Valentine—who were more than once excommunicated by Popes Hyginus and Anicetus. Exclusion from the Christian community was the only weapon that the bishops could then make use of in such cases. Particular small sectarian offshoots, such as the Marcionites, maintained themselves into the fourth century. In Rome two small cemeteries have been found which are thought to have been Gnostic burial places. But as a movement the *Gnosis* was already dead in the third century, chiefly because of the energetic literary reaction on the Catholic side, in which figured Irenaeus of Lyon, Hippolytus of Rome, Clement and Origen of Alexandria, and Tertullian of Carthage, all of whom emphasized, in opposition to the Gnostics, the principle of the apostolic tradition, that is, the character of Christianity as a revelation.

POPE VICTOR I

The dispute in regard to the celebration of Easter still awaited a solution. We are not sufficiently informed as to why the difference concerning the date of Easter was regarded as so serious an inconvenience. Toward the close of the second century, Pope Victor I decided to put an end to the affair. At his suggestion synods were simultaneously held in various regions, and the acts were mutually exchanged. At the beginning of the fourth century, Eusebius saw these acts in the archives of Jerusalem. They are particularly precious, both because they show us which were the most important churches at the end of the second century and because they reveal the nascent metropolitan organization of the Church. Synods were held for Italy in Rome under Victor's presidency, for Gaul in Lyon under Irenaeus, for Pontus (eastern Asia Minor) under the presidency of Palmas, the oldest bishop, for western Asia Minor under Polycrates of Ephesus, for North Syria probably in Edessa, for Palestine in Caesarea. In addition, numerous letters arrived from individual bishops from regions where no synod had been held, e.g., from Bacchyllus of Corinth. It seems that no synod was held in Egypt, because at this time there was only one bishop there, in Alexandria.

All the synodal acts and the letters showed agreement with the Roman method of determining the date of Easter, except for the synod of Ephesus. Eusebius has preserved for us Polycrates' letter to Victor, written in a very haughty tone. In accord with the custom, characteristic of the Church at that time, of proceeding at once to extremes, Victor thereupon excluded from the Church all the bishops of the jurisdiction of Ephesus, to which it seems likely more than one-fourth of

21

all the faithful then belonged. The result was universal consternation. No one denied to the Roman bishop the right to take such a step, but Irenaeus of Lyon made himself the spokesman of public opinion, and in a letter that is still extant exhorted Victor to a more peaceful course. How the affair was settled is unknown, but later Rome and Ephesus were again in communion.

For the entire second century our sources are very meager, and the little we know refers for the most part to Rome and its bishops. Of the provinces we often know not much more than the mere existence of Christian communities in many cities. This lack is due, however, not only to the incompleteness of our tradition but also to the insignificance of the circumstances. The individual Christian communities still had very few members and did not yet live in close union with one another, as they later did. There were still few questions which stirred the entire Church. With the third century this situation changed. Our sources become fuller, so much so that we often know more of the history of the Church in the third century than of the contemporaneous history of the Empire. The Christian literary output almost exceeded that of the pagans. We know Pope Callistus I better than the contemporary Emperor Alexander Severus, and Pope Cornelius and Cyprian, bishop of Carthage, better than Decius, Gallus, and Valerian.

THE SCHOOL OF ALEXANDRIA

In Alexandria, the great center of learned studies and of the book trade of antiquity, there arose toward the close of the second century a sort of Christian Academy, the so-called Catechetical School. In regard to its external organization we know very little, but we are acquainted with a whole list of teachers and scholars, many of whom later became bishops. Nothing survives of the writings of Pantaenus, the founder of the school, but we possess a great quantity of the writings of his successor, Clement, and still more of those of the third master, Origen. Both men stood at the summit of the culture of the day and were especially well-versed in Greek philosophy. In their endeavor to establish the Christian revelation philosophically, both arrived at many erroneous solutions. Origen in particular was later not only vigorously challenged by the Fathers of the Church, but was condemned by councils, notably by the fifth ecumenical council in 553. Even in his lifetime he came into conflict with his bishop and had to leave Alexandria. He went to Caesarea in Palestine, where he laid the ground for a Christian library, which Eusebius later used.

Origen never intended to depart from the teaching of the Church. As a young man he journeyed to Rome, "to see this ancient Church," as Eusebius says—obviously to study the doctrines taught there. After his deposition by the bishop of Alexandria, he sought in a letter to Pope Fabian to prove his orthodoxy.

Origen is the first Christian theologian of really great importance. He is, however, perhaps overrated today by many critics. Without any doubt he has acted as a powerful stimulant on later theologians, but he can by no means be compared with Augustine. In order to arrive at a conclusive judgment on him, we would have to possess all his works, but many of them have been lost.

TERTULLIAN

In the second half of the second century there appeared in Phrygia a prophetico-ascetical movement, which spread even to the West. From its founder, Montanus, the sect was called Montanism. The bishops of Asia Minor denounced it from the beginning; the Roman See reserved its judgment for the time being, and it was Pope Zephyrinus, Victor's successor, who, at the beginning of the third century, excluded the Montanists from the communion of the Church. He thereby aroused the indignation of Tertullian of Carthage, who now broke with the Church and at Carthage founded his own Montanist community.

Tertullian had become a Christian as a mature man around 196 and at once displayed a very prolific literary activity. He wrote in an entirely personal, very expressive Latin, which approached the colloquial speech and is often not easily understood by us. He was the first Christian author to use Latin, which he raised to the rank of a Christian literary language. Tertullian was a thinker and seeker after the manner of Origen. He was quick at repartee, brilliantly witty, and facetious, but his sarcasm was always bitter, regardless of whether he poured it on heathens, heretics, or, in his later years, Catholics. That such a man could join the sect of an ecstatic throng, where he seemed like Saul among the prophets, is explicable only by his personal bitterness. His writings, both the Catholic and the Montanist, remain for us, because of their closeness to life and striking observance of details, an extremely precious source for the knowledge of Christian life at that time.

POPES ZEPHYRINUS AND CALLISTUS I

The disappearance of the Gnostics did not curtail the arrival of Greek teachers at Rome. Victor I, Zephyrinus, and Callistus I condemned several of them because of their unorthodox doctrines. Under Zephyrinus there even occurred a schism, when some of the excommunicated installed an antipope, Natalis. We do not know from whom Natalis received episcopal consecration, but before long he publicly underwent canonical penance before Zephyrinus. More serious was the schism that occurred soon after the death in 217 of Pope

Zephyrinus, for its author was a very important man, the Roman priest Hippolytus.

Hippolytus was the best theologian that the Roman Church then had. He belongs to the great Christian authors of the turn of the second and third centuries, to the group that includes Irenaeus, Clement, Tertullian, and Origen. He wrote in Greek, but most of his numerous works have been lost. To judge from the extant fragments, he published much that was mediocre. He was older than Origen, and when the latter visited Rome he heard Hippolytus preach. Hippolytus did not fail to call the attention of his audience to the presence of the famous Alexandrian. Under Zephyrinus, Hippolytus observed with chagrin how the deacon Callistus, no friend of his, increasingly gained the favor of the pope. According to Hippolytus's own expression, Callistus had completely "taken in" the aged pope. Among other things, Zephyrinus entrusted to the clever deacon, who in his youth had been engaged in banking affairs, the management of the cemetery on the Via Appia, which today still bears his name. When, on the death of Zephyrinus, Callistus became pope, the break occurred. Hippolytus, in his extant libel against Callistus, passes lightly and with amazing silence over the reason for his own withdrawal from the Church. It seems that Callistus called upon him to explain himself in regard to a point of doctrine, and, when the embittered man declined, excommunicated him. But Hippolytus was no Natalis. He gave battle, organized his rival community, and loaded Callistus and the "Callistians" with abuse, charging them with a lax morality and low ideals. Callistus died a martyr on October 14, 222, but the schism continued under his successors, Urban I and Pontian. Only when, in 235, Pontian and Hippolytus were both banished to Sardinia, was the aged schismatic reconciled with the pope. His corpse was brought to Rome, and in his cemetery on the

Via Tiburtina his friends erected a statue to him—a token of respect quite unusual in Christian antiquity. But they were the admirers of Hippolytus the theologian, not of Hippolytus the schismatic. On the base of the statue, which today stands in the Lateran Museum, can be read the titles of all his works; only his libel against Callistus is passed over in eloquent silence. Hippolytus was later highly honored in Rome as a martyr, which he was. Only thus did memory preserve his name. In the fourth century Jerome did not even know who Hippolytus was.

Zephyrinus is the first pope whose burial place we know: the cemetery of Callistus in a mausoleum above the ground. Pontian was buried in the underground papal crypt laid out there by his successor. He is the first pope whose sepulchral inscription has been preserved.

POPE FABIAN

After the brief pontificate of Anterus, the Roman Church was ruled by Fabian, who, according to the extant sources, gave to the Roman clergy a new organization. According to a summary in a letter of his successor, there were then in Rome forty-six priests, seven deacons, seven subdeacons, forty-two acolytes, and fifty-two other inferior clerics. Whether the allotting of the priests to the individual churches of Rome, the so-called *tituli*, goes back to Fabian or is older cannot be determined. The multiplicity of Roman liturgical centers, in contrast to the situation in other cities, where the liturgy was celebrated in only one church, had already been attested by Justin.

Fabian died on January 20, 250, one of the first martyrs of the Decian persecution, and the Roman See remained vacant for more than a year. The three long vacancies which we know of in antiquity—those occurring in 250, 258, and 304—coincide with the last three great persecutions. Otherwise, the Roman bishop was regularly consecrated on the Sunday immediately following the death of his predecessor.

POPE CORNELIUS

When Cornelius was elected in the spring of 251, the persecution was practically at an end. But a schism occurred soon after his accession. The priest Novatian, a clever writer whose book on the Trinity survives, had himself also consecrated bishop and came forward with the claim of founding a reformed Church. He demanded that all who had shown weakness in the recently ended persecution—the *lapsi*, as they were called—be forever excluded from the Church.

The question of the *lapsi* had caused difficulty elsewhere. There were too many of them. Many bishops, as at Antioch, evidently feared that, if they were all absolved in the customary way after having done penance, an unfortunate precedent would have been thereby set for future persecutions. At Carthage, in addition, a special situation existed. It was usual, in the penitential discipline of the age, that the sinner seek for an advocate with the bishop, a sort of rite whereby the humble disposition of penance could find expression. As such advocates, persons showed preference for "confessors," that is, for Christians who had suffered for the Faith in the persecution. In Carthage there was now a group of confessors, who, exulting in their own constancy, no longer distinguished between mediation and absolution, and simply admitted the *lapsi* to communion without the bishop's authorization. Matters went so far that the bishop, Cyprian, excommunicated some of this group, who were causing disturbance in other respects too; among them was the cleric Novatus. Novatus organized a schism and got in touch with Novatian in Rome, oddly enough, for Novatus and Novatian represented com-

27

pletely opposite principles in the penitential question and were at one only in defiance of their respective bishops.

The bishops—Cornelius of Rome, Cyprian of Carthage, Dionysius of Alexandria—took pains, by means of numerous letters, several of which are in existence, to enlighten the other bishops, especially Fabius of Antioch, who at the beginning had hesitated. In this way they succeeded in checking the schismatic movement. The Novatians persisted into the fifth century as a small sect.

THE SACRAMENT OF PENANCE IN ANTIQUITY

Many modern authors steel themselves against understanding the history of the sacrament of penance either for the reason that they start from purely polemical considerations of the question (*e.g.*, when "auricular confession" was instituted), or that they approach the sources with a preconceived pattern of development, as though the penitential discipline had developed by degrees from extreme strictness to extreme mildness, and so forth.

It must first of all be observed that in antiquity penance was something uncommonly frequent. The ecclesiastical writers speak of it constantly. But almost always they speak with a scrupulous reserve, a circumstance that leads many modern critics astray. They continually exhort to a penitential spirit and insist that no sinner need despair, but they do not care to go into particulars, evidently in order not to create in the faithful the feeling that one can confidently sin because all will again be forgiven. They are most fond of speaking in the general context of the economy of salvation: for the baptized person who has again sinned there is one other means of salvation, "a second plank after shipwreck," as Saint Jerome expresses it. From such passages many moderns have concluded that in antiquity sacramental absolution was generally granted only once in life, and this curious notion has invaded numerous manuals of theology. The discussions which were carried on between Cornelius, Cyprian, and other bishops in connection with the problem of the *lapsi* would alone be sufficient to refute this error. In them all possible casuistry is put to use—not only whether, when, and how absolution can be imparted to the *lapsi*, but the distinguishing of the various degrees of guilt. Nowhere does one encounter the difficulty that a person has already previously received absolution and hence is no longer capable of it. But this difficulty would have had to appear, unless the *lapsi* were innocent children.

It is true that before the fourth century the penitential discipline was only to a slight degree regulated by general norms. It was left entirely to the bishop's discretion, and there was as yet no scale of penances. The bishop gave absolution if he believed that the sinner had shown sufficient evidence of repentance. The sinner was considered to have given such proof if he fasted, submitted to the ritual exorcising of penitents in the church, repeatedly asked for absolution, and interested others in interceding for him. If the signs of repentance were especially convincing, as in the case of Natalis, who threw himself at the feet of Pope Zephyrinus in the presence of the assembled community and publicly confessed his guilt, or as in the case of the matron Fabiola, of whom Jerome tells us, then absolution was immediately granted, provided the circumstances permitted. Otherwise, the period of penance usually lasted for some time, until the next Easter or even longer. The *lapsi* of the Decian persecution had to continue in the penitential state for almost two years.

A public confession was not rare in the case of notorious sins and public scandal, and was regarded as a special mark of repentance. But a duty of publicly confessing secret sins never existed. The penitential rites were public, and the penitents

29

even had their own place in the church, but from the fact that a person submitted to the rites no conclusion could be drawn by the rest of the community as to the nature of his moral lapse. It seems that many of the faithful participated in the penitential rites from mere devotion. Of course, a secret confession took place, for the bishop or priest who fixed the length of the period of penance had to know what he was dealing with, but this confession had more the character of a preliminary discussion and lacked ritual form, and thus it is not treated in the sources.

On the whole we must say that, while penance was very frequently practiced, it was not yet studied from the theological viewpoint. It was clear that the Church possessed the power to bind and to loose; but when and how remission actually resulted was hardly considered, and above all the idea of mortal and venial sins was not yet theologically developed. Moreover, the complete lack of norms could lead to arbitrariness. Tertullian's insistence that the three so-called capital sins—murder, idolatry, and adultery—were absolutely unpardonable was, of course, his own particular view, which he first enunciated as a Montanist. Cyprian tells us that individual bishops of his time refused to absolve from sins of impurity. He did not approve their action, but believed that on this point each bishop was responsible to God alone. On the contrary, Origen censures "certain persons," evidently bishops, who pardoned all sins by mere prayer without insisting on a suitable period of penance.

From the end of the fourth century we find a special form of penance, which could be termed "penitential life" or "penitential vow." Those who assumed it were at once absolved, but bound themselves to determined works of penance, including continence, for their lifetime. This penance was esteemed equal to monastic profession, to which was attributed the effect of blotting out sins in the manner of baptism. Of its very nature this penitential vow could not be repeated. The canons of many later councils were concerned with the procedure to be followed in the event that such a penitent again fell into sin. Clerics were not permitted to take the penitential vow. It was not the only form of remission of sins, but was, as it were, the final penance. By holding this penitential vow to be the unique form of sacramental absolution and even projecting it back into the earlier period, in which we find no trace of it, many recent historians have completely obstructed any understanding of the whole history of penance.

THE DISPUTE OVER HERETICAL BAPTISM

In dealing with the *lapsi* and in opposing the schism of Novatian, Pope Cornelius and Cyprian of Carthage were in full agreement. After Cornelius had died in exile, the zealous bishop of Carthage came into serious conflict with the new pope, Stephen I. The controversy arose over the question whether those who turned to the Catholic Church from a sect were to be baptized or not. Cyprian defended the viewpoint that a baptism administered by heretics is no baptism, for "outside the Church there is no salvation." In this general sense the proposition was certainly false, and Cyprian himself admitted that it was a question of an innovation when he was able to appeal to a conciliar decree of one of his predecessors in Carthage. Obviously Cyprian had in mind the African Montanists, whose baptismal formula, at least according to later reports, was really invalid. In Rome, very likely, the concern was with returning Novatians, all of whom had of course been baptized Catholics, for the sect had originated only a few years before.

Although we possess a large quantity of documents, the

31

course of the dispute is not entirely clear. It is certain that Cyprian besieged the pope with documents and embassies to present his side. Stephen seems to have been a blunt jurist who was not disposed to treat the bishop of Carthage differently from other bishops. He would not admit to communion Cyprian's final embassy, which was supposed to hand him conciliar acts signed by ninety African bishops; according to the custom of the day, this procedure signified the ending of diplomatic relations, the exclusion of Cyprian and his followers from the communion of the Roman Church.

Cyprian, for whom the unity of the Church was paramount, was deeply affected. In letters to friends he gave expression to his feelings in passionate complaints. He wrote to Firmilian, bishop of Caesarea in Cappadocia, who replied with a violent denunciation of the pope. It seems that Stephen had sent the same renunciation of communion to Firmilian and had thus excluded him too from the Church.

Unfortunately our sources break off here and we do not know how the dispute was settled. We learn, however, that Dionysius, bishop of Alexandria, exerted himself in behalf of a solution, but he was not sufficiently informed and his mediation came too late. Stephen died in August, 257, at the height of the quarrel. With his successor, Xystus II, Cyprian seems to have been again in agreement. The fact that Cyprian's memory appeared so early in the Roman cult of martyrs likewise indicates that he died at peace with Rome. And we hear nothing more of a break between Rome and Caesarea.

We know only that, in the theological question arising from the dispute, the standpoint of Pope Stephen won out completely, thereby clarifying an important doctrine: the validity of baptism does not depend on the credo of the one baptizing or on his membership in the Church, but on his intention of doing what the Church does. From this it later followed that the validity of the sacraments in general does not depend on the personal worthiness of the minister.

THE DISPUTE OF THE TWO DIONYSII

After a long vacancy of the Roman See caused by the Valerian persecution, the priest Dionysius succeeded the martyred Xystus II. He called his namesake, the bishop of Alexandria, to account for his suspect Christological formulae. Dionysius of Alexandria sought to justify himself, while admitting that he had perhaps not always used happy expressions in his writings; he had, he maintained, not employed the term *homoousios*, used by the pope, which was said to express the consubstantiality of the Son with the Father, because it is not found in Scripture, but on the question he was in full agreement with the pope. Dionysius of Alexandria was not only an outstanding theologian, but above all a great shepherd of souls. His gaze, just as Cyprian's, extended far beyond the boundaries of his diocese. Whereas Cyprian in his zeal wanted to impose his own views on others, Dionysius sought to mediate and establish concord. From him dates that close union with Rome which for almost two centuries was traditional with the bishops of Alexandria.

The period from 260 to 303, from the close of the persecution of Valerian to the outbreak of that of Diocletian, was for the Church an almost undisturbed age of peace. The number of Christians grew. We may estimate it at the beginning of the fourth century as from five to six millions, in the Empire's total population of some fifty millions. Eusebius, who lived at this time, describes how in many places new church buildings were erected, because the old ones became too small. The number of episcopal sees must have reached close to one thousand. Proportionately, most of the Christians were found in North Africa, Egypt, Syria, and Asia Minor, as well as in the great cities, Carthage, Alexandria, Antioch, and especially Rome. Rome, which at the time of Diocletian was declining but still counted 500,000 inhabitants, had a Christian community of more than 50,000, perhaps close to 100,000 souls. Outside the frontiers of the Empire there were at the moment Christian communities only in western Persia. In the last years of the third century Tiridates III, king of Armenia, embraced Christianity. This country, which had only a loose connection with the Empire, can be regarded as the oldest Christian state.

christian life in antiquity

THE UNITY OF THE PRIMITIVE CHURCH: COMMUNION

TODAY, when the pope issues an encyclical letter to the universal Church, he begins: To all patriarchs, archbishops, bishops, and other local ordinaries having peace and communion with the Apostolic See. "Peace and communion" are not merely words that recur constantly in the oldest Christian writings; they embody an idea which is one of the keys to an understanding of the primitive Church.

In the mind of the early Christians communion is the common union of the faithful, of the faithful with the bishops, of the bishops with one another, and of all with the Head, with Christ. The visible sign and at the same time the cause by which this common union is constantly renewed is the Eucharist, the Communion. The sinner is debarred from the Eucharistic Communion and hence from the community of the Church; he is excommunicated. If he does penance, he is again admitted to the Eucharistic union. The guest who comes from a distant church is admitted to Communion, if he brings testimony from his bishop that he belongs to the orthodox communion; otherwise, the Eucharist and hospitality are denied him.

When Polycarp, bishop of Smyrna, journeyed to Rome around the middle of the second century to treat of the Easter

35

question, he reached no agreement with Pope Anicetus; however, as Irenaeus later wrote to Pope Victor I, "Anicetus gave him the Eucharist in the church"; that is, he allowed him to celebrate Mass in the Roman community and give Communion to the clergy and the laity, "and thus they departed from each other in peace." Irenaeus means that common union in the Church, peace and communion, was not broken, despite the continuing difference. We clearly see here that peace denotes something other than identity of opinion or absence of strife. Peace and communion mean a real bond which is not necessarily loosed by an existing controversy, and the sign of this real bond is the Eucharist celebrated together.

In Rome, where the individual priests did not celebrate together with the bishop, but, at least on Sundays, in the titular churches, there existed the custom that the bishop, who offered the Sacrifice first, had acolytes carry to the titular churches consecrated particles which the priests then placed in their respective chalices. This custom is still recalled at Mass in the *"Haec commixtio et consecratio"* following the *"Pax Domini."* Pope Innocent I (401–417) thus explains the practice: "By it they [the priests] feel that on this particular day they are not separated from our communion."

To communicate with heretics meant in antiquity to take the Eucharist with them. Hence, lay persons who were traveling in regions where there was no Catholic church carried the Eucharist with them in order that they might not need to take Communion in an heretical church, for this would have meant to join the community of the heretics. This idea was very concrete: in the fourth century Macedonius, the heretical bishop of Constantinople, had the Catholics who refused to receive Communion from his hand forcibly brought to the altar and their mouths held open, evidently understanding that thus they would enter into his communion, even if they were unwilling. In the fourth century there existed in Asia Minor the little sect of the Messalians who did not believe in the Eucharist. They allowed their members to receive Communion with the Catholics or wherever they wished, because, in their opinion, no common union was thereby effected.

LETTERS OF COMMUNION

When a Christian set out on a journey, he obtained from his bishop a letter of recommendation, a sort of passport, by means of which he was received kindly and lodged gratis wherever he came into a Christian community. This arrangement, which can be traced back to the apostolic period, was advantageous not only for the laity, for example merchants, but for the bishops themselves. They were enabled, without great expense, to send messages and letters throughout the Empire. Only thus can we explain the astonishingly active exchange of letters among the bishops. These passports were termed "letters of peace" or "letters of communion," for they testified that the traveler belonged to the communion and hence could receive the Eucharist. Often they were referred to as *tesserae*, a word which still signifies in Italian any kind of identification card. For this reason, Tertullian calls the entire system *"contesseratio hospitalitatis,"* the "common passport of hospitality."

This institution not only had importance in civic life, so that Julian the Apostate intended to introduce it into his heathen "church," but was also a powerful instrument of the ecclesiastical communion. Every bishop, or at least every larger church, had to keep a list of all bishops who belonged to the communion. The passports of those going on a journey were issued in accordance with this list, and the same list was checked against the passports of arrivals. We can, moreover, observe that each succession to a bishopric was made known

37

to the rest of the churches, and that the bishops, if a heresy or a schism arose, forwarded whole lists of bishops enjoying communion. When, at the beginning of the third century, Pope Zephyrinus excommunicated the Montanists, he did so, as Tertullian says, "by recalling the previously issued letters of peace"; that is, he erased the Montanist communities from the list of orthodox churches enjoying communion. Furthermore, at the beginning of the fifth century Saint Augustine sought to convert the African Donatists, who maintained that they were not schismatics, by calling upon them to issue letters of peace to the most prominent churches in other provinces, which he knew would not be accepted there. In 375 Saint Basil wrote to the community of Neocaesarea, which had embraced Arianism, and enumerated on the map the orthodox communities:

> All these write letters to us and receive letters from us. Hence you can see that we are all of one mind. Whoever, therefore, declines our communion, separates himself from the entire Church. Consider carefully, brethren, with whom you still have communion.

ROME AS THE CENTER OF COMMUNION

In order to prove membership in the Church, one usually argued from the overwhelming majority of the bishops with whom one enjoyed communion; he belongs to the Church who is in communion with almost all bishops or even with a single one who certainly possesses the communion of the rest. But there had to be a definitive criterion by which in cases of doubt one could recognize membership in the communion, and that was communion with the Roman Church. In the fourth century, Optatus, bishop of Mileve in Africa, wrote against the Donatists:

You cannot deny that the first episcopal see has been entrusted to Peter in Rome. On this one see depends the unity of all.

He then enumerated the successors of Peter to his own day, to Damasus I and Siricius:

He is today my colleague [in the episcopal office]; through him the whole world in a single fellowship of communion agrees with me, by means of the system of letters of peace.

Around the same time Ambrose admonished the Emperors Gratian and Valentinian II to see to it that the Roman Church suffered no harm, "for from it the privileges of sacred communion flow to all the others."

This conviction did not originate in the fourth century. In 251 Cyprian called the Roman Church "the See of Peter and the principal church, from which arises the unity of the bishops." Elsewhere he called it "the native soil and the root of the Church." And almost a century earlier Irenaeus had written of the Roman Church: "With this Church all other churches must be in agreement because of its special pre-eminence." This expression, "to be in agreement" (convenire), has not been correctly understood by many commentators. It evidently means nothing else than "to be in communion"; that is, all must belong to the Roman communion. In the same way we must understand the famous and much disputed text of Ignatius of Antioch, in which he called the Roman Church "the president of love"; this "love" (agape) is simply "peace and communion," the common union in peace.

Furthermore, the heathens knew that only he who was in communion with Rome was a legitimate Christian. In 268 Paul of Samosata, bishop of Antioch, was deposed by a synod for his false doctrine and obnoxious conduct. Paul, who not only was very wealthy but was protected by the then powerful king of Palmyra, did not submit and declined to turn over his church and the episcopal residence to his successor. When Emperor Aurelian came to Antioch and put an end to the kingdom of Palmyra, the Christians turned to him for a judicial sentence. Aurelian decided that the property must be handed over to him "to whom the heads of the Christian religion in Italy and the Roman bishop send letters." The Church historian Eusebius, who reports this, calls the decision "perfectly correct."

THE PAPAL PRIMACY IN ANTIQUITY

It is thus clear that the Roman bishop occupied a special position from the earliest time, and this was no merely honorary rank, as many suppose. In the first centuries there was no question of honors and titles and rank. These came into use only in the Byzantine period. Not even the word "pope" was reserved. Cyprian was often called "pope," and the term was applied to various clerics. The pre-eminent position of the Roman bishop was much more real. He was the center of communion. He who was on his list belonged to the Church; he who was erased from his list had ceased to be a member of the Church. Any bishop could suspend communion with another, but only if the universal Church stood behind him, only if he was sure of communion with Rome. The Roman bishop, on the other hand, did not need to appeal to anyone and did not do so. He did not have to refer to the map, like Basil, Athanasius and others. When Victor I excluded the bishops of Asia Minor from his communion, Irenaeus and others regretted this step, but no one challenged the pope's right. When Stephen I broke off communion with Cyprian and more than one hundred bishops of Africa and Asia Minor, the Roman See remained unshaken.

This particular indication of the papal primacy has increased in the course of the centuries. From Anicetus, Victor, Cornelius, and Stephen to Gregory VII, Innocent III, and Boniface VIII the road is long. Comparison again and again misleads many historians into supposing that the popes of antiquity were not yet real "popes." The difference consists mainly in two points: the trappings of sovereignty, which were not acquired until the Middle Ages, when the popes were also temporal princes, and the multiplicity of administrative affairs, which began in the later Middle Ages and attained to a vast expansion only in more recent times. These are secondary roles, which pertain to the pope as head of the Church, it is true, but which do not make him head of the Church. The popes of antiquity were heads of the Church exactly as the pope is today, even if they did not wear the tiara and there were no congregations of cardinals.

One could even find that the papacy's chief function—the office of Rock and the Key to the Kingdom of Heaven—made its appearance almost more frequently than nowadays. The popes of today no longer exclude entire lands and hundreds of bishops from the Church and, in general, resort far more rarely to the *ultima ratio* than did the popes of the early centuries.

LAW AND LOVE

The historical analysis of the concept "peace and communion" shows us clearly that from the beginning the Church was a social structure, not a mere spiritual current, not a crowd of like-minded persons, not a mere league of friendship and love. Among the faithful and among the bishops, who for the most part did not know one another personally and only too frequently were quarreling among themselves, consciousness of unity depended on the conviction of a real bond, which they did not themselves create as in the case of a union for a particular purpose, but which existed independently of them. This real bond, which they expressed by "peace and communion," included a legal as well as a sacramental element. The two were inseparable. The communion is a real society, but by virtue of the sacramental element it differs from every other society found among men. The duty of love flows from the communion, but it is not what the communion constitutes.

No historical development is to be observed in this view of the communion. It is present from the beginning, as when Paul wrote to the Corinthians: "God is trustworthy; by Him you have been called into fellowship with His Son, Jesus Christ our Lord." And John wrote in his First Epistle:

> What we have seen and have heard we announce to you, in order that you also may have fellowship with us, and that our fellowship may be with the Father, and with His Son Jesus Christ. . . . If we say that we have fellowship with Him, and walk in darkness, we lie. . . . But if we walk in the light as He also is in the light, we have fellowship with one another, and the blood of Jesus Christ, His Son, cleanses us from all sin.

It is the same peace that Christ gave to the apostles, the peace which the world cannot give, the *Pax* which the first Christians carved on countless tombstones. "Buried in peace" or simply "In peace," as we read so very often on the inscriptions in the catacombs, does not mean that the deceased is removed from earthly strife. For this, one would not write, "He died in peace," or "He was buried in peace." This peace is rather the communion, the communion of saints, the Church: "He died in the fellowship of the Church and hence belongs now to the Church Triumphant." From the period of a schism in the fourth century we even find "In the legitimate peace," that is, "He died in the legitimate fellowship of the

Church." "In peace" expresses the same idea as when we say nowadays that a person died, "fortified by the holy sacraments of the Church." For in antiquity too the Eucharist stood in the center between peace and communion.

Just as this concept had little reason to develop, so later it hardly disappeared. Today the Church still prays on Corpus Christi: "Mercifully bestow upon Thy Church, O Lord, the gifts of unity and peace, which are mysteriously signified by the offerings presented to Thee."

THE OLDEST TESTIMONIES REGARDING THE EUCHARIST

The Mass has developed from the uniting of two originally separate rites, a service of prayer and instruction and the celebration of the Eucharistic Sacrifice. This is not particularly evident in the so-called Low Mass of today, but it can be seen in the Solemn Pontifical Mass, in which the bishop is at his throne, away from the altar, during the entire Fore-Mass; it is only at the conclusion of the Fore-Mass that he goes in solemn procession to the altar.

The Fore-Mass, with its Scriptural readings, sermon, and common prayer, stems in its basic elements from the synagogue. In the synagogue there were no sacrificial rites; these took place exclusively in the Temple. The Christian Eucharistic celebration, however, is not a continuation of the Temple sacrifices and has nothing in common with them. This feature is peculiar to Christianity from the beginning. Even the apostles celebrated the "Breaking of Bread" neither in the Temple nor in the synagogue, but in a private house, and they did so at a time when the ritual emancipation from the Old Covenant liturgy had not yet been effected.

Whether originally there existed a connection between the ritual "Breaking of Bread" and the so-called "Love Feast" or *agape* cannot be determined. If this was generally the case, their separation must have occurred very quickly, for already in apostolic times the Eucharist was celebrated very early in the morning, whereas the *agape*, so far as we have information on it, took place in the evening. Antiquity did not know the custom of taking a morning meal or breakfast.

The earliest account of the Eucharistic celebration in combination with the service of prayer and instruction is provided in the Acts of the Apostles (20:7–11). Saint Paul was at Troas. The community had gathered in the second story of a house. It was the night between Saturday and Sunday, and many lamps were burning. The express mention of this last point indicates a definite external solemnity. Paul spoke; that is, he read and explained the Scripture till after midnight. "Then he . . . broke bread and ate." After this he again spoke till dawn, when he departed.

The first detailed description of the rite is provided about a century later by Saint Justin Martyr in his first *Apology*, written around 150. This does not mean, however, that for the intervening period there are no testimonies in regard to the Eucharist. It is quite explicitly mentioned by Ignatius of Antioch at the beginning of the second century. Justin wrote for heathens. On Sunday all met together; the "commentaries of the apostles," by which he means the Gospels, and the writings of the prophets were read for as long as time permitted. Then the "president" delivered an exhortation, and after that all stood for prayer, at the end of which the kiss of peace was bestowed. Next began the preparation for the Eucharistic celebration. Bread and a cup containing water and wine were brought to the president, who solemnly accepted them and began the long Eucharistic prayer. This "contains the words of Christ Himself," that is, the words of institution, and "we have been taught that this food is the flesh and the blood of Jesus made man." The Eucharistic prayer concluded

44

with the "Amen" of the people. "Then those whom we call deacons distribute to all present the bread and the wine and water, over which the thanksgiving has been pronounced, and carry them to the absent."

From now on the testimonies become more and more detailed. At the beginning of the third century we find in Hippolytus of Rome a text giving the content of the Eucharistic prayer, in which the words of institution are embedded in the general thanksgiving, just as they are today. Furthermore, the acclamations at the beginning, *"Sursum corda"* and *"Gratias agamus,"* which are only hinted at in Justin, are in their present form in Hippolytus. The text in Hippolytus and that given by later writers was as yet, and for some time, intended only as an example or model. There was still no missal; the celebrant improvised the text each time, but of course within a definite framework. The beginning and the end were fixed, just as were the transition to the words of consecration and these words themselves.

In the earliest period the whole rite, in the form described by Justin, lasted quite a long time, for several hours. Later, it seems, the long readings at the beginning were shortened, and ceremonies were introduced in order to enhance the solemnity of the service. Thus, toward the end of the fourth century, appeared the very impressive dismissals before the beginning of the Eucharistic prayer. All who had no right to be present—catechumens of all grades and penitents—went, group by group, to the altar, received the blessing, and left the church. This was that effort to display reverence in a dramatic manner which led finally throughout the East, and here and there in the West, to the hiding of the priest from the eyes of the faithful during the consecration by means of a curtain or partition. And in the fifth century we find the so-called Discipline of the Secret: writers no longer ventured, out of reverence, to

speak openly of the Eucharist, but made use of various circum-
locutions. In the primitive age persons were not yet so scrupulous.

FREQUENCY OF MASS

In early ages the Eucharist was celebrated only on Sunday.
It is not until the end of the second century that we find the
first indications of Mass on weekdays. Tertullian discusses the
curious difficulty of many of the faithful as to whether one
may attend Mass on a fast day, since by receiving Communion
the fast would be broken! He advises these scrupulous ones
to take the Eucharist home with them and receive it there the
next day: "Thus both precepts are preserved, participation in
the Sacrifice and observance of the fast." [1] From this passage
we see that attendance at Mass without reception of Communion did not take place at that period. Since Sunday could
never be a fasting day, we already have Masses on weekdays.
Probably they were Masses in memory of the dead.

Furthermore, there was but one Mass on Sunday. It was
only in Rome that several priests celebrated at the same time
in the various titular churches. Elsewhere only the bishop
celebrated, attended by the deacons and priests, who did not,
however, recite the Canon with him. This could not be done
because the Canon was not fixed word for word.

From the fourth century the liturgical days on which Mass
was celebrated multiplied, but custom differed widely from
region to region. The Fathers of the Church calmly accepted
such differences, which would greatly disturb us. Augustine
wrote that in many places there is fasting on Saturday, but
not in other places; that in many places the faithful communicate daily, in other places only on specified days; that in

[1] *De Oratione,* xix (Migne, Patrologia Latina, I, cols. 1181 f.).

some churches Mass is offered daily, in others only on Saturday and Sunday or only on Sunday; "one can do all this entirely as one wishes." [2] He finds that, for the individual faithful, this rule alone holds—they should conform to the custom of the place where they are staying; and he adds an admonition which is still valid today:

> If one has seen liturgical customs elsewhere, which he regards as more beautiful or more devotional, he should not, on his return home, maintain that what is done there is incorrect or unlawful, because he has seen it done in another way elsewhere. That is a childish spirit, from which we must preserve ourselves and which we must combat in our faithful.

Only in the fifth century, in the pontificate of Leo I (440–461), do we find the principle enunciated that, because of the larger crowds of people in the Church, several Masses can be celebrated, one after another. Until then we find no trace of this practice, and this seems all the more strange since the old basilicas were on the average very small. We may not judge them by the dimensions of the Constantinian edifices, such as Saint Peter's or the Lateran basilica in Rome, which were splendid buildings rather than churches for the care of souls. In North Africa we have exceedingly numerous remains of ancient Christian basilicas, which have not been distorted by later reconstruction and hence still display the original measurements. They have, moreover, been very painstakingly studied. Many episcopal cities had but a single church of only modest proportions. This lack seriously impeded the care of souls in antiquity. We have every reason to suppose that not nearly all the faithful attended Mass even on Sunday.

[2] *Epistola LIV* (Ad Januarium) (Migne, Patrologia Latina, XXXIII [Paris: 1861], col. 200).

To some extent a substitute for the infrequent celebration
of Mass was offered by the custom of receiving the Eucharist
at home, a practice for which there is evidence in some places
even throughout the fifth century. Basil wrote in the second
half of the fourth century that in his country, Cappadocia, the
faithful communicated four times a week, and only in the
church; he said that there is no objection to the reception of
Communion at home, as this is practiced in all Egypt, for
example, and as was the universal custom in periods of persecution. He answered the objection that there is really no
Communion, no participation, if a person gives himself the
Eucharist alone in his house: after the priest has completed the
Sacrifice, everyone takes part in it who receives the gift from
him, whether it be one portion or several portions, whether
he eats it at once or on the following day.[3] It must be said that
Communion "outside Mass," for which many today feel a
definite repugnance, was a rather frequent occurrence in the
early Christian centuries, and not only under the pressure of
adverse conditions, such as the persecutions.

ORIGIN OF CHRISTIAN PLACES OF WORSHIP

The Christian mysteries are not confined to a definite
place, as was the Jewish worship in the Temple of Jerusalem.
The Sacraments can be dispensed everywhere, and the Mass
itself can be celebrated in a room of a private house or on
shipboard or in the open. That is the reason why Christians
were regarded by the heathens as *athei*. We need not translate
this word as "atheists," as though the heathens meant that the
Christians believed in no deity, but rather as "persons without
religious rites." Around 300 Arnobius wrote: "Above all you
reproach us with not rendering worship, since we neither build

---

3 *Epistola XCIII* (Ad Caesariam) (Migne, Patrologia Graeca, XXXII [Paris: 1857],
cols. 484 f.).

temples nor set up statues of gods nor make altars." At that time there were Christian basilicas everywhere.

The heathen temple was never a place of assembly for a community, whereas from the beginning the Christians needed places in which the community could gather. At first these were dwellings. It was natural that in the same house the same room should always be used and should soon be furnished with equipment, such as choir-screens and lecterns. Architecturally, it would be difficult to determine when the room ceased to be an apartment and began to become a church. But such a room or house could be altered and provided with columns and arcades and apses, so that from the outside it could be recognized as a church. We still have in Rome several examples of basilicas—San Clemente, San Martino ai Monti, and Santi Giovanni e Paolo—which resulted from the reconstruction of private houses in several building periods. At the same time were also built edifices which from the start were intended to serve as places of worship.

This building program has nothing to do with the persecutions. It was not as though the Christians had to be satisfied with using private houses during the persecutions and could begin to construct basilicas only after 313. Eusebius testifies that in the second half of the third century basilicas were built from the ground up in many cities. In Dura-Europos in Mesopotamia a Christian basilica has been unearthed. It is quite small, it is true, but it was constructed before 230, and not as a private house. On the other hand, the conversion of houses into churches took place for a long time after 313.

Many persons like to imagine that in periods of persecution the Christians assembled in the catacombs for common worship. The "Mass in the catacombs" is one of the prominent elements in the unhistorical romances of the martyrs and of early Christianity.

Underground burial places did not exist everywhere by any means, and the Roman catacombs are entirely unsuitable as places of assembly. Scarcely anywhere can space be found in them for accommodating even 100 persons. In the catacombs security was not greater, but rather less, than in the churches of the city, for burial places were known to the police and the public, whereas this was not necessarily true in regard to the places of worship in houses. Furthermore, in all antiquity we have not a single guaranteed report of the celebration of Mass in the catacombs, whereas we are well-informed about Mass in the churches. It was only when, from the fourth century, cemeterial basilicas, such as Santa Agnese and San Lorenzo, were built, that divine worship regularly occurred there, and then not underground. It is possible, however, that burial services, including Mass near the grave, were conducted underground, although we have no trustworthy indications of this.

GROWTH OF LITURGICAL SOLEMNITY

The early Christians loved to adorn in a festive manner the place where the common worship was performed. When the walls were not covered with mosaics or frescoes, as they were to be in a later period, they were hung with colored fabrics. If the basilica had rows of columns, colored curtains were stretched from column to column. Elegant lamps, hanging from the roof, and all sorts of metallic display filled the room. The early Christians were anything but purists in regard to style, and nothing gives so poor an impression of an ancient Christian basilica as an "authentic style basilica," that is, the extremely bare modern restorations.

In the liturgical act itself, on the other hand, practically everything that is today associated with the notion of ceremonies and pomp was lacking in the first centuries. Singing in the sense of melody did not generally appear before the fifth century, but alternating recitation is very old. In the more ancient form the leader of the prayer recited the psalm-verses and, after each verse, the community replied with the same refrain, as in our litanies. At Antioch the so-called antiphonal singing existed in the fourth century and perhaps much earlier. There the men recited a psalm-verse chorally, and the women and children repeated the same verse in the next octave. In Greek music *antiphona* refers to the octave; hence the name. Ambrose introduced this form of singing at Milan toward the end of the fourth century and at the same time John Chrysostom introduced it at Constantinople. The organ came into use only in the Middle Ages. At first the Christians displayed an aversion to incense because it too vividly reminded them of heathen worship. But in the fourth century we find braziers set up in the church to fill the place with the fragrance of incense. The incensing of the altar and of individual objects and persons did not begin until the eleventh century. The Christians were very fond of lights at divine worship, but they used oil lamps rather than candles, for candles too recalled heathen rites. However, from the fourth century candles came into general use, though there were no burning candles on the altar until the eleventh or twelfth century. In stark contrast to the usage of the later period was the lack of any sort of liturgical garment. However, in 403, Saint John Chrysostom, bishop of Constantinople, was accused of vanity by his opponents on the ground that, at divine services, he wore festive dress. In the West the first sure trace of a liturgical garment is found in a council held at Narbonne in 589. Regulations in regard to particular articles of liturgical dress appear first in the Carolingian epoch. There were no church bells in antiquity. The small altar bell came into use only in the twelfth century.

It is not to be supposed that the early Christians strove for

51

dullness and simplicity because of any sort of considerations of style; on the contrary, they did their utmost to give solemnity to their worship. But it must not be forgotten that psychological suppositions were quite different from today. Men of antiquity were much simpler than we are. A symbolical gesture, a movement of the hand, the handing over and accepting of an object, the laying on of hands, the kiss of peace—all these ceremonies immediately impressed them, whereas we must first underline and work out the meaning. Above all, the man of antiquity possessed a much greater susceptibility to the simple spoken word. The entire process of education was aimed, in an extremely one-sided manner, toward speaking and hearing. Listening for hours at a time was a pleasure to any public in antiquity. Hence, the early Christians not only accompanied the sermons with loud applause, even sermons which, when read, seem to us often cold and oversubtle, but they could be deeply affected by merely listening to a sacred text. We have a description of the liturgy of Jerusalem at the end of the fourth century; in it the faithful, at the simple reading of the story of the Passion, broke out into loud sobs, without any effort at drama, and, at the treason of Judas, into cries of anger. Furthermore, the reading did not take place in the vernacular, but in Greek, which most of the congregation understood only imperfectly, so that interpreters must have been active in the church at the same time.

By means of frequent and attentive listening, Christians, even children, often knew much or all of the sacred text from memory. This did not result in boredom, but on the contrary intensified their eagerness to hear. Sermons of the Fathers were occasionally made up almost entirely of scriptural texts woven together; these would make us weary, but then they were a source of enjoyment for the eagerly listening faithful.

Today, with all our technical methods of reading and praying, we are unable to produce such effects.

BAPTISM

In the very earliest period the apostles conferred baptism without requiring any special preparation. But Paul seems not always to have baptized his converts immediately (cf. 1 Cor. 1:14). In the second century we find in Justin a definite time of preparation, with instruction, fasting, and prayer. In Tertullian the name "catechumens" appears. In Hippolytus, at the beginning of the third century, we find the scrutinies, the examination of the candidates in regard to their manner of life. Persons who were engaged in occupations regarded as incompatible with Christianity, such as actors and gladiators, were rejected or deferred. At the same time it is well-established that small children were baptized.

In the fourth century, after the cessation of the bloody persecutions, the abuse of postponing baptism as long as possible increased in Christian families. There were two reasons for this. From the reign of Constantine, all offices and positions were open to Christians, but civic life in general and public life in particular were still so saturated with paganism that it was more convenient to be, not a whole Christian, but only half a Christian. Many, especially those in high station, thus remained perpetual catechumens and had themselves baptized only when in danger of death. The second reason was the increasing severity of the penitential discipline. Hence, baptism, which forgives sin, was delayed at least until one had put behind him the follies of youth. Today we can only marvel that this crying abuse was not firmly combated by zealous and prudent pastors. It penetrated into thoroughly Christian families. Basil, John Chysostom, and Augustine, all of whom had saintly mothers, were baptized only as adults. As a boy,

53

Augustine urgently begged to be baptized in a serious illness, but Saint Monica considered it advisable to wait. Saint Ambrose was not yet baptized when he was elected bishop. The consequence was that many were surprised by death without having received baptism. Inscriptions provide numerous examples of this on graves of catechumens, both children and adults.

However, this abuse had also its good side. Baptism made a deep impression on those who received it at a mature age. Their first contact with the Church was during a period of preparation that was for them especially meaningful, a time that led them with greater appreciation to the impressive rites of baptism. Whoever desired to receive baptism on Easter, the customary time for it, had to give notice of this at the beginning of Lent. Then he had to appear daily in church for the prayers, blessings, and exorcisms, and especially for the catechesis, which was conducted by the bishop personally. This was, so to speak, a retreat of forty days. The baptism itself was very solemn. The ceremonies lasted throughout the entire night between Holy Saturday and Easter Sunday. In the large cities the nocturnal procession from the cathedral to the baptistery and back, in which the entire clergy accompanied the numerous catechumens—there were 3,000 of them at Constantinople in 404—with their sponsors, must have been extremely impressive.

In the same night of Easter the newly baptized received confirmation and, for the first time, Communion. Throughout the entire week of Easter they had to present themselves every day in the church in the white garments they had put on at baptism, until the following "White Sunday," which today still keeps that name.[4] The instructions were continued during

4 In English the Sunday following Easter is usually known as Low Sunday. In German, however, it is called *"Weisser Sonntag,"* an approximation of the liturgical term, *"Dominica in Albis."* The German text thus states that the neophytes wore

these eight days and had as their special object the Eucharist, which had not been treated before baptism. However, this was only a ritual "initiation into the mysteries," for it is hardly to be supposed that grown persons, who had been raised in an entirely Christian environment, would have known nothing at all about the Eucharist.

To this very solemn preparation for the reception of baptism in the fourth century we owe some of the most precious patristic writings, such as the instructions of Saint Cyril of Jerusalem and of Saint Ambrose. Thus, the postponing of baptism unquestionably had salutary results too. We have here a phenomenon similar to that of the nineteenth century's excessive delaying of the First Communion of children. This too was a real abuse and it was zeal for souls that influenced Pius X to put an end to it. But it cannot be denied that at no time were the children more carefully prepared for Communion than in the nineteenth century.

CHARITABLE ACTIVITIES OF THE EARLY CHURCH

As a matter of course, the apostles from the first day devoted themselves to the care of the needy. Without more ado, they regarded this as belonging to their office. The preaching of the Faith was, naturally, their first duty, and when the community in Jerusalem grew so rapidly that the apostles could no longer manage both, they chose helpers, the seven deacons, without, however, relinquishing control of the care of the poor.

This idea remained alive throughout all Christian antiquity. The bishop was so completely the provider for those suffering distress in the community that there were no private works of charity or at least no private initiative. The *Didascalia*, or

their baptismal dress "bis zum Weissen Sonntag, das heute noch davon seinen Namen hat." (p. 45). (Translators' note.)

Church Order, of the third century considered that an injustice was done to the bishop by private almsgiving, as though he were not concerned about the poor. If a case of need reached the ears of an individual, he should report it to the bishop and make his own contributions through the bishop. For his part, the bishop should not give the impression that he was distributing from his own resources, but should let the poor know to whom they owed their relief. Hence, when we hear of pious persons in antiquity who distributed their wealth to the poor, it is usually meant that they turned it over to the Church's fund for the poor.

THE MATRICULARII

Persons regularly supported by the Church were termed *matricularii*, because they were registered on the *matricula* (in Greek, *kanon*) of the Church. They were often referred to as "the widows and orphans," since these were the permanent classes of the needy, but others too belonged—"destitute old persons," as Tertullian says, or such as through misfortune, for example shipwreck, had reached the end of their resources, or, most especially, those who, because of their steadfastness in the Faith under persecution, had fallen into want. From a passage in Hippolytus we learn that the Roman Church around 190 had an exact list of the confessors who were then under sentence of hard labor in Sardinia, and provided regular support for them. In 251 the Roman Church had 1,500 *matricularii*, and Pope Cornelius wrote that the resources took care of all of them. The *Didascalia* recommended that orphans be taken into Christian families and taught a trade. The later Greek revision, the so-called *Apostolic Constitutions*, laid down a sensible principle in regard to the relief of the poor: "[One should procure] work for the able-bodied, [and extend] generosity [only] to him who can no longer work."

Some of the widows were employed for work in the church and in the care of the poor; in the East they were called deaconesses.

From the fourth century special buildings were erected for the *matricularii*—orphanages, poorhouses, inns for traveling Christians who brought letters of communion. These buildings, with their workshops and sheds, usually formed, with the cathedral and the residences of the bishop and clergy, a complex which in the excavated ruins sometimes looks like a small city.

Naturally, the *matricularii* had to be Christians, but otherwise not much distinction was made in the distribution of alms. Tertullian, in keeping with his character, jeered at the heathens, who complained that the revenues of their temples were declining because so many persons were becoming Christians; he felt that the heathen beggars themselves were burden enough without having to bother with their gods as well. Julian the Apostate regarded it as unworthy that the heathen poor received support from the Christians.

In antiquity Christians did not practice charity as a means of propaganda, and even less from a fear of defections and similar anxious motives. Cyprian, in a letter to another bishop, discusses a case of need. It concerned a man who, in order to become a Christian, had to abandon a sinful profession and now declared that he had no means of livelihood. Cyprian stated his willingness to admit him among his *matricularii*, but the man must be content: "He may not expect that we will pay him a wage because he broke with sin; for he has thereby rendered a service, not to us, but rather to himself."

THE RAISING OF FUNDS

The attempt has been made to estimate how much the Roman Church had to spend annually in order to maintain its

1,500 *matricularii* as well as its 150 clerics. The cost of food was, of course, relatively far less in antiquity than it is today even in normal times, but other things, especially clothing, were more expensive. The Roman Church would have needed to have several hundred thousand marks at its disposal, even in the worst days of the persecutions. And yet the great churches, such as Rome and Carthage, always had the means to come to the aid of needy churches elsewhere. Where did this revenue come from?

Its first source was the regular collections from the faithful. Tertullian says that each "gives once a month, or when he wishes, if he wishes at all, and if he can, for no one is forced." Then, the higher clerics were in the habit of turning over to the Church their private property, in return for which the Church undertook to support them. Thus, Cyprian's gardens, which were actually olive orchards and vineyards, came into the possession of the church of Carthage, and Cyprian, when he became bishop, had again to manage his former property. Later, canonical rules in regard to the patrimony of clerics were issued. Thirdly, there was no lack of special gifts on the part of wealthy Christians and also of heathens, even, at times, of friendly officials. The *Didascalia* is much concerned with the question whether such gifts may be accepted from "the evil."

At all events, one obtains the impression that the ecclesiastical administration, especially in the great cities, was always provided with funds. When Marcion entered the Roman clergy in the second century, he brought with him, as customary, his property. When he was unmasked as a heretic and excommunicated, his 200,000 sesterces were returned to him. In the period after Constantine the churches, at least in the large cities, where they were the only charitable institutions, obtained subsidies from the public treasury.

SURVEY OF THE CARE OF SOULS IN ANTIQUITY

Considered as a whole, the Church's pastoral success in the first centuries was very great, though perhaps not in the sense of certain overzealous apologists, who frequently sought to demonstrate that mankind had become essentially "better" through the entry of Christianity into the world. If by "better" is understood an improvement of the average in moral statistics or even an advance in cultural progress, such a betterment of the world by means of the Church, at least in antiquity, is very difficult to prove. Nor is that the Church's task. Her function is to show to individual human beings, and to as many of them as possible, the road to supernatural salvation, the road to heaven. This she performed, and to an amazing degree, especially when one considers the opposition she had to overcome.

In a short time the Church filled the cultural environment in which she had arisen. The spread of the Church was not only geographical; she penetrated all the strata of the society of the age. It is an attractive and, at the same time, instructive pursuit to compile from the inscriptions of the Roman catacombs and from other testimonies the civic occupations of early Christians. In them we find the *vir clarissimus*, Junius Bassus, who, when *Praefectus Urbi* in 359, received baptism on his deathbed; municipal officials, managers of warehouses, and writers; imperial slaves, freedmen, and functionaries, some of them holding positions of great responsibility, such as Marcus Aurelius Prosenes, who, under five emperors, from Marcus Aurelius to Caracalla, managed the imperial private income and died in 217. Sextus Julius Africanus was imperial librarian at the Pantheon under Alexander Severus. There were crowds of lawyers and physicians, a veterinarian, soldiers and officers in all military units; artisans, industrial workers, tradesmen, such as smiths, tanners, stonemasons, painters, ivory carvers, a druggist, a confectioner, a hairdresser, a miner, who, according to his inscription, "worked in all the cemeteries," obviously as an expert; gardeners, fruitgrowers, even old Pollecla, who had a vegetable stand on the Via Nova; dressmakers, silk-merchants, and finally the married couple, Cucumio and Victoria, wardrobe attendants at the Baths of Caracalla. In addition, there are the many, partly pathetic, inscriptions referring to children, and finally those of every rank of the clergy, from the popes down to lectors and *fossores*. The burial inscriptions vary from carefully carved expensive marble slabs to entirely unorthographic scrawls of persons who could scarcely write.

The Church, through her pastoral activity, instructed all these many persons—and there were, in the long run, millions of them—how to end their lives "in peace," in the common fellowship of the saints.

But not all of them were saints in their lifetime. Nothing is more false than that exaggerated notion of the sanctity of the primitive Church, to which, in later centuries, unauthorized reformers loved to refer in order to show that the Church in their own day was degenerate. On the contrary, the Church fought a difficult battle in the care of souls in the first centuries, and she was far from being wholly successful. In antiquity as well as in subsequent times there was cockle among the wheat.

The Church was never able to hold all who had once joined her. Already at the beginning of the second century the heathen Pliny testified that he had, in his judicial investigations, encountered Christians who for years or even decades had not participated in ecclesiastical life. Wickedness has always been found among Christians, and the zealous bishops of antiquity were never satisfied with their flocks. Cyprian,

Gregory Thaumaturgus, and Chrysostom preached exactly like modern Lenten preachers and parish missionaries. The struggle against the depraving exhibitions of the theater and the circus was just as violent in antiquity and had about as little lasting success as today's struggle against immoral entertainments.

Religious life in antiquity was certainly not yet on so high a plane that there could be no further progress beyond it. Many things which were taken for granted in later ages were lacking. Clear theological concepts and, even worse, a precise idea of the Church's teaching office had not yet been arrived at; hence, the incessant heresies and schisms, which could only be damaging to religious life. Pastoral ways and means had not yet been perfected. The churches were too small and too few, the liturgy too long and too infrequent. Even in piety itself real warmth was lacking. Respect for what was holy was very great, but even out of the best writings of the Fathers something similar to a cold breeze often blows against us. Antiquity had no Bernard of Clairvaux, no Francis of Assisi, no Bonaventure, no Gertrude, no Henry Suso, no Francis de Sales, no Teresa. Antiquity did not yet know the loving contemplation of Christ's sufferings or devotion to the Blessed Sacrament. Very wide areas lay as yet uncultivated here. Since antiquity the Church has made progress, tremendous progress, in all fields. That is as it must be. But that does not prevent her cherishing with grateful love the memory of the first centuries, which were her childhood and at the same time her heroic age.

the persecutions

THE FIRST three centuries of the Church's history are
often termed the age of the persecutions or the age of
the martyrs. And justly so, because the bloody persecutions conducted by the Roman state imprint a special stamp on
this period. Around the sublime aspects of history, around
heroic ages, a whole forest of legends always crops up. Because
this has happened with the martyrs of the early centuries, it is
difficult for the historian to draw an accurate picture of actual
occurrences. Not that there is a dearth of sources. From the
age of the persecutions we have quite an abundance of reliable
reports: narratives, letters of eyewitnesses, and judicial
records which acquaint us with absorbing details. The difficulty lies not in these, but in the romantic glorification which
later generations have given to this heroic age. The historian
who investigates the sources critically and wants to describe
things as they happened constantly runs the risk of offending
pious sentiment. This is what happens when he reaches the
conclusion that there were not millions of martyrs and that a
not inconsiderable number of Christians proved to be weak.
It is likewise untrue that the Christians everywhere rushed to
martyrdom with jubilation and enthusiasm. Persecution then,
as later, was always a very bitter and entirely unromantic

affair. The Church has never yearned for persecution and has always rejoiced when it ended.

THE JURIDICAL BASIS

How did it come about that the Roman state assumed such a hostile attitude toward the Christians? We are familiar with the highly developed Roman civil and administrative law. We know that the Roman Empire was at all times extremely tolerant toward cults and religious beliefs of every sort. In the Roman Empire one could worship Jupiter or the Egyptian Isis or the Ephesian Artemis; one could be initiated into the Eleusinian mysteries or the cult of Mithra; one could be an Epicurean philosopher or a skeptic or believe in nothing at all; one could adore the sun or be a Jew. No one was molested, except the Christians. How was this possible?

Many historians think there must have been in Roman penal law some point or other, against which the Christians, from the beginning and by temperament, had offended, so that the persecutions were set in motion by the state, as it were, automatically. In this connection they think first of all of the law of *lèse majesté* in association with the imperial cult. The fact that the Christians rejected the imperial cult on principle would, without more ado, have made them liable to the penalties of the law of *lèse majesté*.

The crime of *lèse majesté* was originally what we term high treason, rebellion, uprising against the authority of the state. The law was quite vague and had been at times extended by certain of the early emperors, notably Tiberius and Domitian, to ridiculous offenses, such as the selling of a garden in which stood a statue of the emperor and similar trivial marks of disrespect to the imperial majesty. It is evident that so elastic a law could be turned against all and each, including the Christians. The question is whether this really happened.

63

Now in all the quite numerous legal proceedings against Christians that we are familiar with, nothing is ever said about the crime of *lèse majesté*. We know, furthermore, that the law of *lèse majesté* was used by the emperors against their personal enemies, senators and others in high station, whom they wished to eliminate, whereas lesser folk were not involved in the very arbitrary extension of this law. The overwhelming majority of the Christian martyrs were lesser folk. Again, Trajan is especially praised for having refused, in contrast to his predecessor, Domitian, to make use of the law of *lèse majesté*, and Trajan is the very emperor who gave to the legal proceedings against Christians their lasting juridical form.

As regards the imperial cult, it is clear that a refusal to participate in it could be interpreted as the crime of *lèse majesté*, but we are not to imagine the imperial cult as a religion or as a regularly recurring act of worship to which all were obliged. Both for the other gods and for the divinity of the reigning emperor or of earlier emperors, for example Augustus, there were priestly colleges which at fixed times had to perform definite acts of worship. To disturb such an act of worship would obviously have been sacrilege. But, as in the case of all exercises of Roman worship, it was unnecessary for any congregation to participate in the imperial cult. Whoever did not have to perform an act of worship *ex officio* could absent himself from it throughout his life without transgressing any law. The private individual was, in regard to Roman worship, in approximately the same situation as he is today in regard to many civic ceremonies, for example, the honoring of the Unknown Soldier or the saluting of the flag. He who does not care to attend can remain at home or go elsewhere. However, the Christians did not object to taking part in such ceremonies through mere presence. The extremely severe moralist Tertullian, in his book *On Idolatry*, discusses such cases thoroughly and decides that a Christian slave can, with a safe conscience, accompany his master to a heathen ceremony. And in a household the Christian guest can witness the performing of a heathen act of worship by the *paterfamilias*. A difficulty arose only when, because of one's position, one was compelled to carry out such acts of worship. Tertullian doubts that a Christian of the governing class can successfully avoid all the reefs of idolatry. Now in the period of the persecutions there were very few Christians in the governing class, at least scarcely any of the many martyrs known to us.

Other historians hold that, by virtue of their own worship, the Christians had made themselves guilty of sacrilege or at least of the crime of performing forbidden rites.

Sacrilege was a definite concept, denoting the violation of a sacred thing, especially of temples, altars, images of the gods, and cemeteries. We know that in the age of the persecutions the Christians always prudently avoided such violations of sanctuaries. Many later legends, of course, attribute such acts to Christian martyrs. As regards forbidden rites, according to the ancient Law of the Twelve Tables all non-Roman rites were forbidden or at least required permission of the government, but this provision had long been obsolete. In the imperial age no law and no authority was concerned about all the countless alien and native cults which were practiced in Rome and throughout the Empire, provided always that they did not disturb the public tranquillity. Besides, the celebration of the Christian mysteries did not seem to the heathens to be acts of worship. The Christians had neither temples nor altars in the customary meaning; they had no statues of gods; they offered neither incense nor sacrificial animals. Public opinion reproached them with being *athei*, "persons without religious rites."

It can also be asked: If there really was in Roman criminal

law a section which the Christians transgressed by virtue of their existence or of their life, so that persecution had to be undertaken automatically, so to speak, by the criminal judge, why then were new edicts, one after another, issued against the Christians for centuries, edicts that differed greatly among themselves in their juridical character?

That historians continue to allow themselves to be deceived into seeking a juridical basis for the persecutions results from their cherishing too high an opinon of the Roman Empire as a state governed by law. As a matter of fact, the Roman *civil* law was of such eminence that almost all modern civilized peoples have gone through its school. In contrast, the Roman *criminal* law was very imperfect, and even more is this true of the Roman law of *procedure*. We need not wonder, then, to find in this so-called flawlessly governed State of Law arbitrariness and even cruelty in the sphere of criminal penalties.

POLITICAL MOTIVES

Still other writers shift the explanation of the persecutions from the juridical to the political sphere, alleging that the Roman Empire felt and had to feel itself threatened in its existence by Christianity; it defended itself as long as it could, but finally the Church became too powerful and thus the Roman Empire perished.

In this interpretation almost everything is false. If the persecutions are understood as a struggle between the Church and the imperial government, their course, in its entirety and in all particulars, shows that, not the Church, but the government was the aggressor. We know, however, that the persecutions, especially in the second century, often proceeded, not from the government, but from the populace. The officials at times had to be almost forced to act. Are we to believe that the people in the provinces, in Lyon, Smyrna, Carthage, Alexandria, were so passionately concerned for the future of the Roman Empire that they therefore demanded the death of their own fellow citizens and countrymen? It is not impossible that the emperors of the last persecution—Diocletian and Galerius—followed political aims, but it cannot be proved. At that time, around 300, the Christians were so numerous that they could have exercised political power, somewhat in the sense of a modern political party, but we nowhere find among them traces of such desires. The Christians never took part in the struggles over the throne and even in the most severe persecutions never made efforts toward anything like self-defense. It is conceivable that Diocletian was apprehensive and wanted to destroy the Christians before they should become too strong. At most this would explain why the persecutions were carried on till after 300, but not why they were begun. For in the time of Nero and Trajan, when there were only a few thousand Christians, no one could have foreseen that the Church would ever become so large. Nero and Trajan would have had to be not only farseeing statesmen but prophets as well.

HATRED AS A MOTIVE

As the only motive that fully explains the start as well as the direction of the persecutions there remains hatred. There is no reason to refuse indignantly to recognize this motive. Hate and love play a prominent role in human history, oftentimes a more important role than rational motives. In all ages, persecutors of Christians have alleged every sort of more or less plausible grounds for their action, but basically it was hatred of the Christian religion and of the Church that drove them. The historian must not close his eyes to such dark sides of the human soul and force himself to seek rational explanations for everything.

67

This does not mean that every individual Roman emperor and, still less, every official who had to deal with the legal proceedings against Christians was moved by personal hatred. There were some among them, perhaps many, who felt themselves to be merely administrative organs and believed they were doing their duty.

THE SOURCES OF ANTI-CHRISTIAN HATRED

Tertullian, who knew well how to express so many ideas in striking formulae, says: "As soon as truth entered the world it aroused hatred and enmity through its mere presence." [1] We should inquire into the deeper causes of this hatred and ask why it again and again assumed new forms and never came to rest.

One thinks first of the Jews. It is not, of course, correct that the Romans originally regarded the Christians as a Jewish sect and had simply transferred to them their aversion for the Jews. Nevertheless, they must have obtained information from the Jews, which could scarcely have been other than hostile. Jews appear later in the capacity of agitators against the Christians, as in the persecution in Smyrna in 156. Tertullian had definite precedents in mind when he wrote that the synagogues were breeding-grounds of persecution.[2]

There likewise come to mind as instigators of hatred all who could feel themselves threatened in their economic existence by Christianity, perhaps not so much the members of the priestly colleges, who were in peaceful possession of their endowments, as the many business people who obtained their livelihood from heathen worship and from everything con-

---

[1] *Apologeticus*, vii (Migne, Patrologia Latina, I, col. 307).

[2] *Adversus Gnosticos Scorpiace*, x (Migne, Patrologia Latina, II [Paris: 1844], col. 143).

nected with it, and the soothsayers, astrologers, school teachers, and philosophers.

However, the attitude of the government must have been of very special influence on public opinion. The average man is for the most part unable to have for long any other view than that of the governing body. Many perhaps thought, "Let the Christians be as they wish; in any case, the government must have its grounds for proceeding so severely against them again and again."

GROUNDS IN THE CHRISTIANS THEMSELVES

No one believes that the Christians actually committed all the horrible deeds ascribed to them by public opinion, but they did other things which antagonized the public. They surrounded their worship with secrecy, which excited hostile curiosity. Tertullian writes that the mob especially delighted in seeking to surprise the Christians during the liturgy.[3] The case of the martyr Tarsicius, who was slain because he refused to give up the Eucharist, is well-authenticated.

Likewise, the quiet spread of Christianity was exasperating. Everywhere one could meet Christians, without knowing where they came from.[4] That the retired, strict lives of the Christians were regarded by many as a silent reproach is clear. Justin narrates a characteristic example. A prominent Roman lady, who, like her husband, had hitherto lived in a very careless manner, became a Christian. She now demanded of her husband conjugal fidelity; otherwise she would separate from him. When the husband could discover no grounds on which to accuse his wife, he denounced as a Christian the catechist who had instructed her in the Faith. Thus was the martyr Ptolemy executed.

3 *Apologeticus, loc. cit.,* col. 308.
4 *Ibid.,* i, cols. 262 f.

FIRST PERIOD OF THE PERSECUTIONS: INDIVIDUAL PROCESSES
BEGINNING OF ANTI-CHRISTIAN LEGISLATION

In the Christian writers of antiquity the Emperor Nero is always named as the author of the persecutions, although even before Nero there were martyrs, at least the deacon Stephen and the Apostle James the Greater. On the other hand, no trace has been found of a formal law issued by Nero. It must have been a question of an instruction to the courts to the effect that the Christians were to be dealt with as notorious criminals. This instruction sufficed for the martyrdoms under Nero himself. According to Tacitus, this was a "huge multitude," but we know only the names of the Apostles Peter and Paul, and we do not know whether executions also occurred outside Rome. In regard to Domitian, we know only that he had his cousin, Flavius Clemens, put to death because of his religion, and banished the latter's wife, Domitilla, to the island of Pontia. Probably there also occurred other martyrdoms under him. As the legal basis, the judicial practice existing since Nero's time was sufficient.

That this was nothing more than a judicial practice we learn from the question sent in 110 or 111 to the Emperor Trajan by Pliny, governor of Bithynia. Naturally, Pliny was acquainted with penal law and criminal proceedings, but he wrote to the emperor that he had never had the opportunity of attending a trial of Christians, and hence did not know how to conduct one. The emperor replied in his celebrated rescript, which thereafter formed the legal basis for all further processes.

TRAJAN'S RESCRIPT

The decisive regulations in Trajan's rescript were these: 1) Christians are not to be sought out, but are to be punished only if a denunciation has been made, and this must not be anonymous; 2) if an accused person declares his unwillingness to be a Christian any longer and proves this by paying homage to the gods, his guilty past will not be held against him because of his change of mind.

The first point corresponds to the Roman penal procedure. In Roman law the function of public accuser or public prosecutor was non-existent. A criminal act might be quite notorious, but the judge was not bound to bring it before his court unless action was taken by a third party. The burden of proof lay with the accuser. Hence, Trajan declared that Christians were to be dealt with according to the usual criminal procedure and that the government was not to take the initiative against them by means of police measures. He took it for granted that to be a Christian was a criminal fact, simply following in this the judicial practice introduced by Nero.

More important is the second point. A Christian who disavows his Faith is to be acquitted. Trajan probably intended by this to be especially mild. His regulation presupposes a certain knowledge of Christianity. A worshiper of Jupiter who presented an offering to the Egyptian Isis or had himself initiated into the Eleusinian mysteries did not thereby cease to be a worshiper of Jupiter. Trajan knew that this was not the case with the Christians. Whoever took part in any non-Christian ceremonies renounced Christianity by this very fact.

It was this special provision that produced the classical martyrdom. For the future the full bulk of the proceedings was concentrated on it. The legal criminal process was extremely simple and hence quite brief. If the accused confessed that he was a Christian, the trial was at an end. What followed was the effort of the judge to make possible an acquittal. He sought to persuade or to force the accused to carry out the required ceremonies. It was in this connection that there sometimes occurred those grotesquely arbitrary and cruel deeds, which were otherwise so foreign to Roman penal procedure and which some recent critics would like to deny, were they not so well-attested. Theodor Mommsen supposed that the whole affair was not a criminal trial but an administrative coercive method. This is incorrect. There was a criminal trial, but it could be finished in five minutes, after which began the measures of coercion, which could last for months.

A sort of duel took place between judge and Christian; the issue depended on which of them held out the longer. According to authentic records we can state that the judge took it as a defeat if the Christian persevered. The Roman judges were generally not bloodthirsty tyrants, and some provincial governors made it their aim not to pass a death sentence during their tenure of office. In his *Ad Scapulam* Tertullian gives a whole series of characteristic examples. A proconsul of the province of Asia commanded the Christians: "You scoundrels, if you really want to die, jump off a cliff or hang yourselves." Cincius Severus, at Thystrus in Africa, suggested to the accused harmless answers, so that he could acquit them. Vespronius Candidus purposely turned over a Christian to the local court as a rebel; the court naturally had to acquit him, because he was not a rebel. Before another judge, Asper, a Christian declared his willingness to offer sacrifice at once. Asper let him go, without waiting for the sacrifice, and explained to his fellow judges that he was sorry such a matter had been brought before him. Evidently such a victory did not interest him.

Saint Augustine, in his *De Civitate Dei*, distinguishes ten persecutions of Christians, based on the pattern of the ten plagues of Egypt. This arrangement, which even today is retained by many historians, does not correspond to the reality of the earlier period. Throughout the entire second century there were no fixed periods of persecution interrupted by periods of peace. A Christian at that time could be brought to trial whenever an accuser could be found. Otherwise, he remained unmolested, unless, as occasionally happened, popular tumults were organized against Christians. Against such illegal persecutions edicts were issued by Hadrian and later by Antoninus Pius, but they seem to have been of little avail.

All this while the Christians lived in public view. Nothing is more false than the popularized notion of "catacomb Christianity," as though the Christians led a sort of underground existence, like timid forest animals or fleeing criminals. The catacombs were not foxholes or places of residence or of assembly, but cemeteries. The Christians lived with their families in their homes and went about their occupations as citizens, and for worship gathered in their modest basilicas in the city.

The Christian philosopher Justin openly conducted a school at Rome. He, like the other apologists, published his writings and addressed his two apologies to the emperors. In the second of these, he writes: "I am waiting for some one to denounce me." The expectation was realized. Only after he had been known for years as a Christian were proceedings instituted against him; we still possess the record.

PARTICULAR MARTYRDOMS OF THE SECOND CENTURY

Of the individual martyrs or groups of martyrs of the second century, the most outstanding was Ignatius, disciple of the apostles and bishop of Antioch. The year of his death is unknown, but it occurred in the reign of Trajan—thus, before 117—and at Rome. While he was being taken there, Ignatius wrote his famous letters, among them one to the Roman Christians, whom he begged to take no steps to prevent his martyrdom. There also took place in the early years of the second century the martyrdom of the aged Simeon, second bishop of Jerusalem, and that of Pope Telesphorus, which is attested by Irenaeus. The execution of Polycarp, bishop of Smyrna, with six companions, seems to belong to the year 156. Concerning it, we possess a circular letter of the community of Smyrna. The martyrdom of Ptolemy, Lucius, and a third Christian at Rome in 160 is told by Justin in his second apology.

Under Marcus Aurelius (161–180) the proceedings against Christians increased in number. Besides Justin, whose death probably occurred in 163, we must mention a group of more than forty Christians at Lyon, with the nonagenarian bishop Pothinus at their head, concerning whom a report by the survivors, containing many moving details, is extant; also, Carpus, Papylas, and Agathonice in Pergamum, of whom we have the official court records; and the twelve martyrs of Scilli in Africa, whose court records also survive. These records are characterized by conciseness and objectivity and differ favorably from the bombast of the later legends of the martyrs. We likewise have genuine acts of the martyrdom of the prominent Apollonius in Rome, which took place in the reign of Commodus, probably in 185.

From the contemporary writers it is clear that the martyrs known to us by name in the second century were by no means the only ones. Just the same, in view of the small size of the Christian communities of that period, we are not to imagine that the number of martyrs was enormous.

SECOND PERIOD: MASS PROCEEDINGS

In the third century the picture of the persecutions changes. Hitherto it was not the imperial government that brought about the great persecutions. Individual judges were responsible for individual executions, after denunciation and under the pressure of public opinion, which in places, as at Lyon and

Smyrna, showed itself very hostile to Christians. In the third century it was the emperors who caused the persecutions on a great scale, whereas the popular mood became more quiet. Private denunciation scarcely occurred. Hence, in the third century one can clearly distinguish between large-scale outbursts of persecution, which were now much more violent, and intervening periods of relative calm.

SEPTIMIUS SEVERUS

In 202 Septimius Severus forbade conversion to Judaism and Christianity. The emperor was a capable ruler and wanted to be just. His advisers were the famous jurists, Papinian, Paulus, and Ulpian. In his unfortunately lost work, *On the Duties of the Proconsul,* Ulpian assembled the laws issued up to that time in regard to Christians. There were, of course, more of them than the few we know. For example, in the acts of Apollonius there is question of an otherwise unknown decree of the Senate against the Christians. All these regulations suffered from the weakness that they regarded the mere fact of being a Christian as a criminal act. Such a defect could not escape so clever a jurist as Ulpian. The decree of 202 was, to be sure, not just, but at least it was clear: the reception of baptism was a criminal act.

There ensued a persecution of the catechumens and the newly baptized, who were sought out by the police. Concerning the execution of the decree we have information in regard to Alexandria and Carthage alone, so that we do not know whether it extended to the whole Empire. Among the numerous martyrs at Alexandria was the father of the great Origen. The sixteen-year-old son wrote to his father in prison that he should not be seduced into apostasy through regard for his children. From Carthage we have the collection of records dealing with the martyrdom of the distinguished Vibia Per-

75

petua, twenty-two years of age, and of several companions. These acts belong to the most moving passages in all early Christian literature. Their chief element is a brief diary, written in prison by Perpetua after her baptism. Because she therein reports several visions, some have suspected that this group of martyrs belonged to the ecstatic Montanist sect, as though all saints who have had visions must have been Montanists. With her childlike disposition and her deep seriousness, Perpetua hardly fits into the life of this swarm, which incidentally had not yet been excluded from the Christian community.

It is noteworthy that the rescript of Trajan was not abrogated by the decree of Septimius Severus. The newly baptized were again given the possibility of redeeming themselves by offering sacrifice to the gods.

Why the persecution of the catechumens was soon brought to an end we do not know. There now followed a long period of relative peace, though individual martyrdoms still occurred from time to time. Thus, the martyrdom of Pope Callistus I in 222 is certain, despite the fact that no general persecution was raging. Such happenings were very likely cases of popular rioting. A full-scale persecution was undertaken by Emperor Maximinus the Thracian in 235. Little is known of it, and it seems to have been aimed especially at the clergy. Of the martyrs we know only Pope Pontian and the Roman priest, Hippolytus. In 217 Hippolytus had broken with Pope Callistus and had come forward as anti-pope. The government condemned both claimants, the legitimate successor of Callistus and the anti-pope, to forced labor in the mines of Sardinia. Since both were old and could not hope for release, Pontian laid down his office and let a new pope be elected in Rome. Hippolytus, whose return to the Church he thereby evidently intended to facilitate, called upon his schismatic followers to acknowledge the new pope. Damasus's epigram, which tells of this, was, it is true, composed more than a century later, but the fact that from the beginning Hippolytus was honored by the Roman Church as a martyr proves that he died in the Catholic communion. Heretical or schismatic martyrs, of whom there were not a few, were on principle debarred from liturgical cult. The abdication of Pope Pontian is the first of its kind in papal history.

DECIUS

In 250 Emperor Decius inaugurated a persecution on a vast scale. We know almost nothing of this emperor. Even the dates of his reign can be determined only approximately by means of coins. He was one of the many so-called Soldier Emperors who in the third century fought endlessly over the throne; he governed the entire Empire for a few months. For the others in this group we at least have the inferior imperial biographies of the so-called *Historia Augusta,* but for Decius not even this. Hence, it is all the more astonishing that some recent historians cannot do enough to extol his broad political views, his early Roman *virtus,* and his plan to renew and strengthen the whole Empire by means of religious unity.

Of all these fine things we know nothing, but we are well-acquainted with the technique of his persecution of Christians. It was decreed that on a fixed day all inhabitants of the Empire had to perform an act of worship of the gods. For this purpose inspectors were appointed in every locality, even in the least important villages. Everyone who had carried out the rite received from the inspectors a certificate to this effect. Everyone who, after a definite lapse of time, was not in possession of such a certificate of sacrifice was prosecuted as a criminal. Apparently, the Christians were not even mentioned in the decree, but it was clear that they alone were envisaged. Who else would have created any difficulty? In no other sort of religious practice in antiquity did the adherent of any cult encounter the slightest hindrance to performing an act of another cult. Besides the Christians, only the Jews would have no part of this, but the Jews had their special privileges and seem not to have been affected by the decree.

To carry out the policy demanded a huge organization. We possess vivid accounts of contemporaries as to how it took place in the large cities. In cities such as Rome and Carthage several groups of inspectors operated simultaneously. The inhabitants had to stand in line for hours, and often at evening were sent away till the next day. Thus it went on for weeks, until all had their certificates of sacrifice and were safe from the police. An unusually good fortune has preserved several originals of these certificates. In the Egyptian papyrus-finds more than forty certificates of this kind have so far come to light, all according to the same pattern, with nationality, personal description, and several signatures—real identification cards.

Many Christians succumbed to the first assault and offered sacrifice, amid the scornful amusement of watching heathens. This is made clear from the indignant letters of the bishops, though Cyprian of Carthage and Dionysius of Alexandria perhaps paint too dark a picture. Other Christians, as appears from the same accounts, bided their time and soon noticed that among the members of the board of inspectors some privately listened to reason. These officials were obliging enough to issue certificates not only for individual persons, but for entire households, without requiring the personal appearance of the individuals. Some issued certificates—for a small consideration, of course—without any sacrifice having been performed at all. One could even procure a certificate of sacrifice outside office hours from a friendly agent. Thus, eventually, a countless number of Christians who had never

78

sacrificed were in possession of certificates. The bishops were shocked and subjected such cheaters to strict ecclesiastical penance. The final result was that in the imperial chancery lay triumphant reports from the provinces in regard to the total extermination of Christianity, while the Christians, as numerout as before, but many of them with very anxious consciences, stood before their indignant bishops. If the whole matter is interpreted as a struggle between the imperial government and the Church, then in any case the government was not the victor. And for the Church it was not a victory which she could take pride in.

Why did not the Christians make a better showing? Because they were taken by surprise. The bishops had expected a persecution and had warned their flocks, but they had not counted on this new technique, and panic was the result. The reason, however, why the persecution finally ended in failure on the part of the government lay less in the inadequacy of the administrative apparatus than in the mistaken belief of the government that the Church could be destroyed if the individual faithful could be forced into sin.

After all, it seems that the greater number of Christians came through without sacrifice or certificate. And there were also not a few martyrs. In Rome Pope Fabian died on January 20, 250, one of the first victims of the persecution. Later, we hear of a group of Roman clerics who languished in prison for more than a year and were several times put to the torture. The priest Musaeus died in prison. In Carthage, too, where the traffic in certificates was especially flourishing, there were martyrs and steadfast confessors. We have the acts of the trial of the priest Pionius at Smyrna. The bishops of Antioch and Jerusalem likewise died as martyrs. The aging Origen was so severely tortured that he soon died as a result.

After the cessation of actual persecution, the situation remained insecure for Christians. Emperor Gallus, successor of Decius, who had perished in war against the barbarian invaders, banished Pope Cornelius and, when the latter died soon after, also his successor, Lucius I. Cyprian notes in a letter which he wrote about this time that, while dictating, he could hear the crowds gathered in the circus roaring their demands for his death. He urged that sinners who, as a result of the Decian persecution, had been doing penance for two years, be admitted to the sacraments, since, as he said, they would have need of strength from the Eucharist for the new persecution. Thus matters stood until 257, when once again a great persecution began.

VALERIAN

Emperor Valerian is described as being personally favorable to Christians. What influenced him to take action against them shortly before his own calamity in the Persian war is unknown. Probably the persecution was the work of his associates. This time it was much more capably organized. Obviously, the government had profited by what had happened under Decius. A first edict ordered the closing and confiscation of the Christian places of assembly and cemeteries, and at the same time the bishops, so far as they could be discovered, were sent into exile. The intention was clearly to wreck the ecclesiastical organization. Only in the following year did the real edict appear, once again as a penal law, with exact instructions in regard to the individual classes of persons and their degree of punishment.

The persecution was more cleverly carried out than that of Decius, but the Christians were better prepared than seven years previously. The tone of Cyprian's last letters is especially serious. In August, 258, he wrote that his Roman agents had sent him the text of the edict together with the news that on

August 6 the Roman bishop, Xystus, had been executed with four of his deacons. On September 14 his own head fell under the sword. The great bishop of Carthage died as he had lived. At his trial, the acts of which are extant, he showed once again his surpassing calmness. Having arrived at the place of execution, he ordered twenty-five gold pieces to be given to the executioner for his trouble.

Cyprian is one of the outstanding personages of primitive Christianity. His letters are a rich source for the knowledge of Christian life in the period of persecution. He was wholeheartedly devoted to the care of souls, and at the same time a refined and amiable personality. In particular questions he made serious mistakes, but at the height of his quarrel with Pope Stephen I it was love of the Church and of souls and not personal feelings that inspired his bitter words against the Roman See.

The pope whose execution Cyprian reported in what was almost the last letter he wrote was Xystus II, who had reigned only a year. With him were put to death four of his deacons, while before long other clerics suffered the same fate, among them, probably, the three remaining deacons. However, we are not certain that the celebrated martyr Lawrence was one of these. Lawrence is an historical figure and his martyrdom is established, but it may have occurred in the next persecution. To the Valerian persecution belong the martyrdoms of Fructuosus, bishop of Tarragona in Spain, with two deacons, concerning whom a brief court record is extant; of the bishops, Agapius and Secundus, the deacon Marianus, and the lector James at Lambesis in Africa; of a whole group of clerics, headed by Montanus and Lucius, at Carthage. Here was a systematic persecution of clerics, and this time we hear of no apostasies. Under Decius, even in the ranks of the clergy, apostasy had occurred frequently.

81

Emperor Valerian was taken captive in war by the Persians and disappeared. His son and co-emperor Gallienus had not favored the persecution, though the edict bore his name in addition to that of his father. Having become sole ruler, he put an end to the persecution and had the confiscated ecclesiastical property given back. The text of this decree of restitution survives.

ECCLESIASTICAL PROPERTY

How was it possible for the Church or particular Christian communities to possess immovable property while all the persecuting laws were in force or at least while there could be no recognition of the Church as a juridical person? This question has often been discussed, but there is no doubt about the fact. In the third century the Church possessed cemeteries and sacred edifices and in some regions productive real estate. The buildings were still quite modest, but by the third century they were definitely churches and not merely adapted private houses. The excavated basilica at Dura-Europos in Mesopotamia belongs to the early years of the third century. At Edessa in 202 the Christian basilica was badly damaged by a flood. Under Emperor Alexander Severus (222–235) the Roman Christian community instituted a suit against the association of tavern-keepers over a piece of property in the city. The emperor decided in favor of the Christians.

In the earliest period, of course, individual Christians were considered private owners. It has been supposed that the ecclesiastical communities of the third century had organized themselves into associations, somewhat like burial corporations, *vis-à-vis* the state. However, such an association would be possible only with the license of the government. Any form of subterfuge whereby the bishop would pose as the mere director of a corporation was excluded. The explanation is rather that in antiquity the state did not include under its jurisdiction all possible legal relations among men. Nowadays the individual needs a document, officially stamped by the state, in order to exist legally, whereas in antiquity one could not only exist, but possess, buy, sell, give, and inherit, without the issuance of a legal title by the state. In this way collective ownership was possible. Gallienus had such common property returned to the ecclesiastical communities, without conferring on them any legal recognition as corporations.

DIOCLETIAN

From the close of the Valerian persecution the Christians enjoyed over forty years of almost complete quiet. New and larger church buildings were erected, and conversions multiplied so that the number of Christians in the Empire may have doubled. It is noteworthy that in the entire history of the Church only periods of peace, and not persecutions, are favorable to the expansion of Christianity. The famous saying of Tertullian, that the blood of martyrs is the seed of new Christians, contains a depth of meaning, but is not to be understood in the sense that persecutions, and especially those of long duration, help the spread of the Church.

Emperor Diocletian, who revamped the entire imperial administration and above all vastly enlarged the bureaucracy, not only left the Christians in peace for almost twenty years, but even admitted them into the higher positions close to his own person. Not until near the end of his reign did he give his ear to the persuasions of the Caesar Galerius to undertake an extensive persecution. Diocletian listened reluctantly, for he was far too experienced an administrator not to see that a persecution would now assume much greater proportions than hitherto. And that is just what happened.

The persecution began in February, 303, with the destruc-

tion of the great Christian basilica in Nicomedia, the imperial
residence. The bishop, Anthimus, and several prominent Christians at the imperial court were put to death. At the same time
an edict was issued for the entire Empire, and at brief intervals
others followed. In these laws, which we know in great part
through summaries, were included all the decrees against
Christians issued by preceding emperors. The test of sacrifice,
introduced by Decius, was employed for discovering Christians, and Valerian's confiscation of ecclesiastical property
was renewed. This, however, was extended to include movable goods too—church furnishings, things collected for the
poor, and especially books and writings of every sort. The
zeal of the officials was concentrated on this last point during
the first two years of the persecution. Christians who surrendered writings or books were exempted from punishment,
just as though they had sacrificed. This manner of acting prepared for the Christians grounds for new conflicts of conscience and, after the persecution, for ugly disputes, in which
persons mutually reproached one another for having given up
such writings or for not having sufficiently defended them.[5]
There was no end to the searching of houses, destruction, and
other vexations. We still have police records from Africa, in
which everything, even the oil-containers and boots from the
wardrobe of the poor, is scrupulously noted.

Bloody martyrdoms were very numerous. From Palestine
and Egypt Eusebius gives an eyewitness account of horrifying

5 The resulting tense atmosphere provided the background for Donatism, which Father
Hertling does not treat. The reader is referred to J.-R. Palanque, P. de Labriolle, and G.
Bardy, De la paix constantinienne à la mort de Théodose, Vol. III of the Fliche-Martin
Histoire de l'église (Paris: 1945), pp. 41-52, 205-216, 458-461 [English translation: The
Church in the Christian Roman Empire, trans. Ernest C. Messenger, I (London: 1949),
34-50, 257-272, 630-634]; P. de Labriolle, G. Bardy, Louis Bréhier, and G. de Plinval,
De la mort de Théodose à l'élection de Grégoire le Grand, Vol. IV of the Fliche-
Martin Histoire de l'église (Paris: 1945), pp. 69-78; Philip Hughes, A History of the
Church, II (London: 1948), 2-13. (Translator's Note.)

details. Most of the martyrs who were later honored in the liturgy belong to this persecution, notably the famous Roman martyrs, Sebastian, Pancratius, Agnes, Soteris, Protus and Hyacinth, Peter and Marcellinus, and many others. We also have the acts of a group in Africa, Saturninus and his companions, who were surprised at Mass on Sunday; Agape, Irene, and other women at Thessalonica; Irenaeus, bishop of Sirmium; in Africa a bishop, Felix, who refused to surrender his books; Euplius, a deacon of Catania; Phileas, bishop of Tmuis in Egypt; Claudius, Asterius, and their companions in Cilicia; Julius of Dorostorus in Mysia; Dasius in Moesia; and Crispina in Africa.

Though there were executions in all parts of the Empire, the persecuting laws were not at this time everywhere enforced with equal rigor. Much depended on the attitude of the particular emperor in his own section of the Empire. Galerius continued the persecution till his death in 311, as did Maximinus Daia in the East. Maxentius, who governed Rome from 306, without having obtained recognition from the other emperors, seems not to have caused any martyrdoms. Lactantius reports that Constantius, who ruled the Gallic and British provinces, carried on the persecution only in appearance; nevertheless, we know of a fairly large number of martyrs from Gaul.

The worst years were those from 303 to 305. After that the situation became more calm in many places, although in the East executions occurred again and again. In 311 Peter, bishop of Alexandria, died a martyr. In the same year Galerius, a few days before his death, issued an edict which, while expressed in a tone very unfriendly to the Christians, contained the command to cease the persecution and to give back the property, even the churches, of the Christians. We know that in Rome Maxentius began at once to restore goods to Pope Melchiades. Thus, it cannot be said without qualification that

85

Constantine stopped the persecution. The persecution was practically at an end when he ascended the throne. But Constantine did give to imperial policy an orientation which was friendly to Christianity, and to the Church he gave that privileged position in the Empire which rendered impossible a revival of the old persecuting laws. To this extent the Christians are correct when they glorify Constantine as the real liberator of the Church.

THE PERSECUTIONS IN RETROSPECT

If one were to compile the names of individual martyrs from the contempory writers—from Eusebius, Lactantius, Cyprian, and the surviving court records and other reports of eyewitnesses—one would obtain merely a few hundred. It is clear that this number is too low. Contemporaries leave us in no doubt that the total was much greater. We have also a second way to establish the genuineness of a martyrdom, even when the name in question does not appear in any ancient writer. If a very old liturgical cult can be demonstrated, the martyr concerned may be regarded as historically established. The reason lies in the fact that in antiquity the cult of a martyr was very closely bound up with his tomb. Archaeological information about the method by which tombs were dealt with assures us that error and intentional deception could scarcely occur. It could happen that a martyr's tomb might fall into oblivion, but only with difficulty could one at a later time invent a tomb for that martyr. In this way the better known Roman martyrs, for example, can almost all be shown as historical, even though we may possess no information about them in contemporary writers. This archaeological or hagiographical method requires laborious study in each case, but today the task has, on the whole, been accomplished. It is scarcely to be expected that further important archaeological discoveries of this sort will still occur and, even less, that considerable changes will have to be made in the established results.

Of course, by this method only the fact of martyrdom, the name of the martyr, and the day of his death can be established; the day of death was included in the liturgical cult. The year of death may remain uncertain, even though most of the martyrs authenticated in this way must be placed in the Diocletian persecution, since, in many places, Rome for example, the cult of martyrs came into practice only in the second half of the third century. The martyrs of the earlier persecutions remained for the most part without a cult. The Roman martyr Justin, of the second century, was never honored as a saint in antiquity. His feast was not introduced in the Church until recent times.

The martyrs who can be proved by their cult are counted by the thousands. But we know no details about them—the manner of their deaths, their civic occupation, whether they were old or young, clerics or lay persons. This defect was noticed even in later antiquity and gave rise to the numerous legends of martyrs. People wished to have details concerning the martyrs, and, since none were known, writers compiled platitudes, crude descriptions of situations, possible and impossible tortures, and sometimes combined elements from genuine old reports of other martyrs. The result was a sort of barbarous world of romance. In it the martyr is represented as boastful and loquacious; he performs countless miracles and causes mass conversions, while the judge is regularly stupid and bloodthirsty. Very often the emperor appears in person as judge, a thing that very rarely occurred in actuality, and among such emperor-judges are named some who, like Alexander Severus and Numerian, were definitely not persecutors, or, in the accounts of Roman martyrs, Diocletian, who was almost never in Rome.

This literature of legend was much read in the Middle Ages and even into our day. It is to be regretted that through these stories the historically correct picture of the persecutions has been falsified. On the other hand, it would be a serious mistake to suppose that the martyrs concerning whom we possess such legendary accounts did not for this reason exist at all. The instances in which clearly fictitious names have slipped into the catalogue of the saints are very few. The case is different with regard to numbers. When in some legends there is mention of thousands of unnamed martyrs, no credence is to be placed in such figures.

THE NUMBER OF THE MARTYRS

It is not possible to estimate the total number of martyrs produced by the persecutions into the fourth century. At most the extreme limits can be fixed. Certainly there were not millions of them. Such numbers are excluded by the relatively small total of Christians. We would be obliged to hold that everywhere the Christians were almost entirely exterminated, whereas we actually find the individual communities very much alive after even the most severe storms of persecution. Besides, no particular writer of antiquity has reported such gigantic figures.

On the other hand, the number is not to be lowered excessively. All ancient writers who lived through a period of persecution give the impression that it was an extremely bloody affair. A few thousand martyrs, distributed over two and one-half centuries and the entire Empire, would not do justice to this general impression. One must assume a number in six figures.

At the same time it must be remembered that the number

of martyrs forms only a part of those who had to suffer for their Catholic Faith. The number of those who, for the sake of the Faith, had to endure prison and torture, exile, flight, confiscation, breakup of family, social ostracism, and every sort of vexation on the part of the police, exceeds by twenty times the number of those put to death. That there were also many who did not persevere under trial and thereby defiled their honor proves only how difficult the trial was.

THE IMPORTANCE OF THE PERSECUTIONS

The fact of the persecutions cannot be turned to account apologetically—though at times preachers do so—in the sense that the truth of the Catholic Faith can be demonstrated from the mere constancy of the martyrs, for almost every form of religion or religious association has had a number of martyrs in the course of history. Nevertheless, the question put by Tertullian around 200 is justified: "Is it to be said that all the many martyrs died for nothing?" [6]

The persecutions exerted a tremendous influence on the life of the primitive Church. This was partly negative. They prevented a more rapid expansion and hindered a richer development of Christian community life in many directions. The continuous disappearance of outstanding personalities meant constant losses, even if we seek in vain in the ancient authors for a word of regret, when such important men as Justin or Cyprian or Cornelius were snatched away in the very midst of their activity.

It was of benefit to the Church that in the persecutions she received a practical lesson in being independent of the authority of the state. The Christians, of course, were not urged into an attitude of hostility to the state; not a trace of this can be discovered in the worst persecutions. On the contrary, they

---

6 *De Praescriptionibus,* xxix (Migne, Patrologia Latina, II, col. 41).

experienced in their own bodies how desirable would be a just state which protected the rights of its citizens. Later, when the emperors became Christians, the Church would have been stifled by Caesaropapism had she not already learned in the persecutions to be independent and self-sufficient.

More than anything else, the example of heroism influenced the religious life of the Christians of later ages, and still does so today. In the persecutions the model of the Christian saint came into existence, not merely in the liturgical sense—for the liturgical veneration of saints actually proceeded from the cult of martyrs—but also in the sense of an ideal. The heroism of the martyr has in it nothing of fanaticism, nothing of jingoism and striking at random. On the other hand, it is far removed from the fatalistic endurance of whatever may come. It consists rather in perfect constancy in the service of God, undismayed by anything.

the age of the great church fathers and of the origins of monasticism

ALMOST every textbook treatment of Church History begins an entirely new age with Emperor Constantine, or, more exactly, with his Edict of Milan in favor of Christianity. This must not be taken to mean that the life of the Church changed essentially in 313, that she suddenly cast aside the cloak of secrecy and stepped out of darkness into a previously undreamed-of brightness. Throughout the third century and especially in its second half there was scarcely any darkness and secrecy. Yet, even after Constantine, the Christians continued for a long time to be a minority in the Empire.

CONSTANTINE

Constantine's personality impressed contemporaries, both Christians and heathens, tremendously. The praise which Eusebius and others lavish on him may be extravagant, but no one can doubt their sincere admiration. Constantine was a statesman of lofty stature. Admittedly, Diocletian had facilitated the task of administration, but Diocletian's constitution, with its multiplication of emperors, nearly split the Empire. Con-

91

stantine held it together. The founding of the new imperial capital, Constantinople, was, to use a present-day expression, a geopolitical event of first-rank importance. Through Constantine the Roman emperors first became monarchs or kings. Up to the time of his reign they had been dictators, often mere military dictators. The Byzantine emperors, as well as Charles the Great and the German emperors, would be successors of Constantine rather than of Caesar, Augustus, and Trajan.

In general, historians today have no love for Constantine. One often gets the impression that they would prefer to deny him any historical importance, and that, unable to do so, they emphasize his cruelty. Actually, Constantine did have several political opponents executed, including his brother-in-law, Licinius, and his own son, Crispus, but he by no means shed as much blood as that pattern of humaneness, Augustus. Special effort is made to disparage Constantine's religious attitude.

On this point it is really not easy to form a correct judgment. At the beginning of his reign he was definitely not a Christian, and he only decided to receive baptism on his deathbed. But it is just as certain that he was sincerely devoted to the Church and the bishops. He delighted to confer benefits on the Church. Political calculations played at most a secondary role in all this. In his day the Christians were still a minority in the Empire. In antiquity there was no such thing as a political party which supported the government, and even if there had been, the Christians were not a political party. Without doubt, a ruler's position is strengthened if he provides justice for a considerable part of his subjects who have hitherto been treated unjustly, but the effort to govern justly can hardly be termed political calculation.

To what extent Constantine embraced the Christian Faith

as the Truth is difficult to say. It is certain that, when he was preparing for his decisive struggle against Maxentius, he was personally convinced he had received a revelation or vision. Contemporary reports concerning this event do not agree in details of place, time, and manner, and since ultimately they must all go back to Constantine, one gets the impression that the emperor told the story later in different ways.

In the history of the Church Constantine's name is inseparably bound up with the Council of Nicaea, the first ecumenical council, which he summoned and to whose success he contributed greatly. Its occasion was Arianism, the first of the three great heresies which shook the Church in antiquity.

ARIANISM

THE BEGINNINGS OF THEOLOGY

By "theology" we understand the science of God and of all things insofar as they are related to God. Theology in the strict sense, or speculative theology, is the rational penetration of the revealed truths of Faith, the systematic knowledge of their relations to one another. Already in the second century we find the beginnings of theology. At that time it was the complex of problems which today we call the doctrines of the Trinity of God and the Incarnation of Christ that brought about the first attempts at speculative penetration. The term which summarized these questions was "the divine economy." In Tertullian we find that the simple faithful often displayed a definite distrust of these initial theological attempts.[1] Fresh from polytheism, they were happy to have embraced belief in the one and only God and wanted to hear of nothing else. "They were startled by the word 'economy,'" says Tertullian. This attitude was termed "Monarchianism." Monarchianism is

1 *Adversus Praxeam,* iii (Migne, Patrologia Latina, II, cols. 157 f.).

not a doctrinal system; rather, it signifies only the effort to maintain the truth of the unity and oneness of God in every respect, even if, in the process, other revealed truths, the Trinity and the divinity of Christ, are sacrificed.

At the turn of the second and third centuries there were two opposing tendencies in Monarchianism, the modalist and the dynamic. Modalistic Monarchianism is usually known as Sabellianism after its chief proponent, Sabellius. Sabellius, a Libyan, who taught in Rome and was condemned by Pope Callistus I (217–222), enunciated the formula: one God in three Persons. Following the classical usage, "Person" meant for him the role or "mask" of an actor. The one God is called Father, insofar as He acts as Creator and Ruler of the world; when He appears in the role of Saviour-made-Man, He is called Son; in the role of Dispenser of grace He is termed Holy Spirit. This formula had the advantage of allowing one to call Christ true God, but at the same time it abolished the real distinction of Father, Son, and Holy Spirit. According to it, God manifests Himself in a threefold manner (modus; hence, Modalism) and is thus described by three names. This teaching does not do justice to Holy Scripture, wherein the real distinction of at least the Father and the Son is clearly expressed. Hence, Sabellianism was very soon challenged. In Rome it was especially the learned priest Hippolytus who took upon himself the task of fighting it.

The other tendency in Monarchianism held to the real distinction between Father and Son, but, in order not to endanger the unity of God, made the Son subordinate to the Father; hence it is termed Subordinationism. The individual systems of this tendency differed one from the other in explaining in what sense Christ can still be called God—whether God dwelt in the Man Christ or bestowed on the Man Christ divine energy (dynamis; hence Dynamism). Pope Zephyrinus

(199–217), the predecessor of Callistus, had already con-demned these systems, but they continued to appear. In the second half of the third century, Paul of Samosata, bishop of Antioch, was deposed by a synod because of this sort of teaching, but it seems that similar doctrines were still being taught later at Antioch, especially by the learned Lucian, who died a martyr in 312. In the doctrinal controversies of that period Pope Dionysius (260–268) is already found making use of the expression, "the consubstantiality" (*consubstantialis* in Latin, *homoousios* in Greek) of the Father with the Son, by which the solution of the problem was later to be pro-vided.

ARIUS

For the moment, the great persecution of Diocletian dis-tracted attention from the sphere of theology, but soon after its close the dogmatic quarrels appeared again. Alexander, bishop of Alexandria, successor of the martyred Peter, called one of his priests, Arius, to task for his teaching. Arius, a skilful dialectician, had been a pupil of Lucian of Antioch. His thesis was this: if the Son is begotten of the Father, there was a time when the Son did not yet exist; it follows, then, that He is not from eternity and hence He is not God. Arius had friends not only among the clergy of Alexandria but also outside Egypt, notably Eusebius, bishop of Nicomedia, who likewise had studied under Lucian of Antioch. The affair seemed to the bishop of Alexandria sufficiently important to warrant a synod of almost one hundred Egyptian and Libyan bishops; here Arius and his adherents were excommunicated. Following cus-tom, Alexander made known this sentence to all the bishops of the Church. His circular, in which Eusebius of Nicomedia was also blamed, perhaps more severely than was necessary, caused tremendous excitement. Although unable to appreciate adequately the importance of the doctrine in question, Emperor Constantine felt concern for peace within the Church and decided to summon a gathering of all bishops to Nicaea.

THE COUNCIL OF NICAEA

Hosius, bishop of Córdoba in Spain, who was staying at the imperial court, presided. Pope Silvester I sent two Roman priests as his delegates, and they were the first to sign the acts after the president. Otherwise, only a few Westerners were present. Some three hundred bishops appeared; at most this was one-fourth of the episcopate, but this did not prevent the council's being later regarded as the legitimate representative of the universal Church. The emperor participated personally in the sessions and adroitly intervened whenever the discussions threatened to founder.

The learned historian of the Church, Eusebius, bishop of Caesarea in Palestine, submitted the baptismal creed of his church as the basis for the definition of the Faith. Like the so-called Apostles' Creed, this was one of the formularies then used in the baptismal liturgy. The assembly adopted the formula but inserted in the article on the procession of the Son from the Father the expression used in Rome, "consubstantial with the Father," as a clear condemnation of the theory of Arius. Eusebius of Caesarea did not agree to this addition, not because he adhered to Arius, but because he wanted to leave the matter undecided and did not fully grasp its theological importance. However, he and others yielded to the majority and to the imperial desire. Even Eusebius of Nicomedia signed. Arius and two Libyan bishops who upheld him were excommunicated.

The council then issued several canons concerning ecclesiastical discipline. The possibility of returning to the Church was made easy for the followers of the Meletian

Schism [2] in Egypt, which had originated during the Diocletian persecution, and also for the Novatians, who, like the Meletians, had not departed from Catholic doctrine. It was decided that returning clerics, even bishops, could retain their rank. The old controversy over the date of Easter was settled by the council's request that the emperor decree a uniform calendar by imperial law. To the church of Alexandria, which possessed the best astronomical facilities, Constantine committed the annual calculation of the Easter date.

The Council of Nicaea produced a profound impression on the whole Church. There had been great gatherings of bishops before, and heresies had been condemned. But to have the emperor himself convoke the synod and place at the disposal of the bishops the imperial post for their journey; to learn that the emperor had appeared in person at the sessions, had shown the utmost respect for the Fathers, and had personally guaranteed the purity of the Faith—all this could scarcely be comprehended by the Christians, who so recently had lived through the bloodiest of all persecutions. Among the bishops at the council were many who still bore the scars of torture. The change was too great not to have also produced less favorable consequences for the Church. The bishops, especially in the East, where they were more a part of the environment, cherished henceforth a devotion to the emperor and a confidence in him with regard to ecclesiastical matters that in time grew boundless. Constantine did not want to govern the Church. He had far too high an opinion of the Church for this and desired merely to be her benefactor. Nevertheless, he became the author of that peculiar relationship which is known as Caesaropapism and which, under his

2 See Jules Lebreton and Jacques Zeiller, *De la fin du 2e siècle à la paix constantinienne*, Vol. II of the Fliche-Martin *Histoire de l'église* (Paris: 1938), pp. 342 f., 472 f. [English translation: *The History of the Primitive Church*, trans. Ernest C. Messenger, II (New York: 1949), 1047 ff., 1204 f.] (Translator's note.)

successors, was to harm the Church almost more than the most brutal persecutions of the earlier emperors.

THE SEQUEL TO NICAEA

Some bishops, like Eusebius of Caesarea, had left Nicaea disappointed. Almost all of them, indeed, were against Arius and his denial of the divinity of Christ, but many were displeased with the expression *homoousios*, "consubstantial," for they feared it could be interpreted in the Sabellian sense. To many of the bishops the notion of the Church's teaching office was not as yet so clear that a doctrinal definition of the Church, when once made, would have been considered absolutely final and unalterable.

Of course, so long as Constantine was alive, no one would venture to come forward against the Council of Nicaea and its definition. In place of an open attack there quickly began intrigues against those bishops who made the proclamation of the Nicene Creed and the *homoousios* their special task. The spiritual director of these intrigues was Eusebius of Nicomedia. On account of his equivocal attitude at Nicaea, he had fallen into Constantine's disfavor. Through the intercession of Constantine's sister he was reinstated and eventually realized his dream of becoming bishop of the imperial capital, Constantinople.

Eusebius of Nicomedia is the first of that unpleasant type of pliant theologian and bishop who later was almost never absent from the courts of rulers eager to exert an influence on the destiny of the Church.

In the East the most active champions of *homoousios* were the bishops of the two pre-eminent sees, Eustathius of Antioch and Athanasius of Alexandria. Their opponents contrived to have both of them deposed—Eustathius at a synod in Antioch in 330, Athanasius at a similar meeting in Tyre in 335. They wanted the emperor to banish the two bishops and to pardon Arius, but Arius suddenly died before being reinstated in the Church, and the Catholics, who were observing the whole course of intrigue with mounting anger, saw in his passing the divine judgment.

CONSTANTIUS

Constantine died in 337, baptized on his deathbed by Eusebius of Nicomedia. His son and successor, Constantius, was of an entirely different character. He lacked his father's personal charm and vanity, and wanted to be, not the benefactor of the Church, but her master. His concern was not to maintain peace in the Church, but to impose his own Arian convictions. To him Arianism was more important than Christianity. Like his father he had himself baptized only shortly before his death. At the outset of his reign he had to reckon with his younger brother, Constans, who ruled the West and was a staunch upholder of Nicaea, but after Constans's death he became progressively more severe on Catholics.

Few of the bishops were really Arians at heart. Fundamentally, most of them would have preferred to confess the Faith of Nicaea, but they pampered the imperial desire and held synod after synod, incessantly elaborating new creeds which referred to Christ as Son of God in the strictest sense. All the while they avoided the crucial term *homoousios*. Before the Council of Nicaea most of these creeds could have been understood in an orthodox sense, but, once the Church had defined the matter, an intentional avoidance of the definitive formula was, to say the least, somewhat suspect. The emperor spared no harshness to force the stubborn adherents of Nicaea to sign one or another of these allegedly neutral formulae. Pope Liberius was carried off from Rome and deprived of all advisers—a trick used much later by Napoleon against Pius VII. Liberius was detained forcibly until he finally signed. Athanasius and Hilary, and later Jerome, blamed him for this weakness. To what degree this censure is justified we cannot say, for we do not know what document Liberius signed. Perhaps it was merely a declaration that he recognized Athanasius's deposition.

Though he had to go into banishment a total of five times, Athanasius of Alexandria remained the pillar of Nicene orthodoxy. Often the controversy was more over the person of Athanasius than the theology of the Trinity. Not inferior to him, either in firmness or in the vexations they had to endure, were the Western bishops, Hilary of Poitiers, the keenest theologian of the age, and Eusebius of Vercelli.

The Church at the middle of the fourth century is often represented as a composition of three parties: the real Arians, the staunch Nicenes, and, in the middle as the largest party, the undecided, whom persons like to term Semi-Arians. This is not wholly correct. The genuine Arians were not a party but a sect; they were regarded by all the others as cut off from the Church and were very few in number. By and large the colorless middle party was not a group with a uniform goal. The only thing its members had in common was their wish not to be Arians, and an injustice is done them when they are called Semi-Arians. If they avoided the expression *homoousios*, they often did so simply for the sake of peace. To their number belongs, among others, the outstanding shepherd of souls, Cyril, bishop of Jerusalem, who today is officially honored by the Church as one of her Doctors.

Many replaced the controversial *homoousios* with *homoios:* the Son is like the Father. This was a challenge to the Arians, who were thus known as Anomoians (*anomoios,* unlike), and it could be understood in the Nicene sense, especially if one added "like in all things," a formula popularized by Basil, bishop of Ancyra.

JULIAN THE APOSTATE

Constantius died in 361. The heir to the throne was Julian, son of a stepbrother of Constantine. He had been raised a Christian and may have been baptized. Throughout the reign of his cousin, Constantius, who condoned no trifling in matters of religion, Julian acted as a Christian. Having succeeded to the throne, however, he chose to be only a philosopher, and gave free scope to his hatred of Christianity. He was a capable general and an inferior administrator, unsteady, sensitive, vain, a dreamer. Today he might be called a neurotic. Modern historians are in the habit of praising him enthusiastically because of the great things he would have accomplished had a longer life been granted him. To judge by the evidence which he actually gave, it may rather be supposed that a longer reign would have made him a complete failure.

Julian at once issued a mass of anti-Christian decrees, not bloody edicts, but legal vexations—exclusion from office in the government and from the higher schools, and the revocation of the subsidies to the Church's poor-fund, granted by the state since Constantine. At the same time he tried to organize heathen religious communities. An immense fear obsessed Christianity, the dread of finding a new Decius or Diocletian. But Julian perished in the war against the Persians after a reign of less than two years.

Julian, who with all his deep hostility made a display of impartial justice, had from the very beginning allowed all the exiled bishops to return, with the petty objective of thereby further setting Catholics and Arians in opposition to one another. This measure actually contributed to the victory of the Catholics. The Arians had never been numerous and the death

101

of Constantius had deprived them of support. The difficulty consisted merely in reconciling the many Catholic bishops casting suspicion of heresy on one another in the dispute over *homoousios* and *homoios*. The dread of Julian's neo-paganism inclined them to peace.

Hilary returned from banishment to Gaul and succeeded in a synod at Paris in getting all the Gallic bishops to rally to *homoousios*. However, the use of *homoios* was also permitted, in order to express that the Son is true God like the Father. Around the same time Athanasius and Eusebius of Vercelli, likewise returning from exile, met in Alexandria. At a conference in which several other bishops took part, the principles for a general amnesty were agreed upon. Hitherto the chief difficulty had been that many bishops felt obliged to refuse communion not only with the Arians, but also with all who were in communion with Arians or with those suspected of Arianism, even though this contact had often occurred only under pressure from the government. It was now decided that, no matter with whom they had been in communion in the period of confusion and pressure, all bishops were to be regarded as belonging to the Catholic communion if they had signed no really Arian creed. They had only to manifest a clear adherence to the Faith of Nicaea. Furthermore, the use of particular technical terms in theology, especially "nature" and "person," which kept recurring in the debates over the Faith, was clarified. Because these expressions had in Latin another significance than they had in Greek, continual misunderstandings had arisen.

The conference commissioned Asterius, bishop of Petra, to make known these principles throughout the East and Eusebius of Vercelli to do the same in the West. Pope Liberius immediately agreed to them; Gaul was won over by Hilary; and together with Spain, Macedonia, and Greece, other lands followed.

This happy turn was due primarily to the aging Athanasius, whose conduct proved that he was by no means the fanatic he has been represented as. He was concerned only for the Faith and the Church, and not for the humiliation of his opponents. Throughout the West peace henceforth prevailed and there was scarcely any mention of Arianism. In the East, however, matters did not proceed so smoothly. Macedonius, bishop of Constantinople, propounded still another novel teaching, and Emperor Valens tended to favor the Arians. But Valens fell in battle against the Goths at Adrianople. His nephew, the young Gratian, who was under the influence of Saint Ambrose of Milan, named as his associate on the throne Theodosius, a fine ruler who stood firmly for the Catholic Faith and the Council of Nicaea. Theodosius convoked a great synod at Constantinople in 381. The most important bishops of the Greek-speaking provinces assembled there: Meletius of Antioch, Timothy of Alexandria, Cyril of Jerusalem, Gregory Nazianzen, Gregory of Nyssa and his brother, Peter of Sebaste, Amphilochius of Iconium, Diodorus of Tarsus. The discussions were stormy, not because of doctrine, for all present stood by the Nicene Creed, but because of personalities. Unable to effect peace, Saint Gregory Nazianzen resigned his dignity as bishop of Constantinople and withdrew from the council. The Council of Constantinople meant the end of Arianism. It maintained itself only outside the imperial frontier among the Goths and was destined later to play a role once more in the German tribes.

THE ECUMENICAL COUNCILS

The acts of the Council of Constantinople, like those of Nicaea, have not come down to us. Hence, it cannot be de-

103

termined whether the Creed which is now used in the Latin Mass was given its definitive formulation at this council. It is certain that the council defined the divinity of the Holy Spirit, thereby bringing the Trinitarian problems to a final settlement. Thus, it is likely that the expansion of the Nicene Creed by means of the article on the Holy Spirit was accomplished at this council. However, this enlarged Creed first appears at the Council of Chalcedon in 451 and it was there too that the council of 381 was first designated as ecumenical. In the West the Council of Constantinople was reckoned among the ecumenical councils only from the sixth century, and its dogmatic decrees alone, not its disciplinary canons, were recognized.

The notion of the general or ecumenical council as the most solemn expression of the Church's teaching office was only gradually conceived. How a council obtained its ecumenical character was not clear at first. It is certainly not due to the number of bishops present or to the representation of specific episcopal sees, such as all metropolitans or patriarchs. At the council of 381 the pope was not even represented by legates. Nor is it of essential importance how the council happened to meet or who summoned it. The ecumenical councils of antiquity were, as a matter of fact, convoked by the emperor. The only decisive element is that the decrees of a council be accepted by the pope, either at the council itself or at least through subsequent confirmation. But there are also instances of the decrees of a council having been approved by a pope without the council's being regarded as ecumenical, as, for example, the Council of Orange of 529 with its important decisions in regard to Semi-Pelagianism.

Up to the present, twenty councils have been accepted as ecumenical, but the historical importance of the individual councils varies. Councils are in complete accord with the constitution of the Church but are in no way essential. In the Church there are no matters which are the exclusive concern of a general council.

THE IMPORTANCE OF THE STRUGGLE AGAINST ARIANISM

Some modern profane historians write as though the doctrinal controversies of the fourth century had no intrinsic importance and apply to them such derogatory epithets as "priestly wrangling" and "subtleties." Only one who has no grasp of Christianity can talk like that. It is not entirely correct to label the whole affair a struggle. It was a defensive battle, in which the Church was warding off a heresy, a very dangerous heresy. At its best, Arianism, whose basic doctrine was the denial of the divinity of Christ, made of the Christian religion a philosophical monotheism, in which the revealed truths of salvation—the Incarnation, Redemption, grace, the sacraments—found no place or were admitted only in a distorted form. The struggle was not about mere words—*homoousios* or *homoios*, "consubstantial," "like," or "unlike." It was about fundamental teachings of Christianity. The Christian religion is so constituted that a single error in a fundamental point of doctrine destroys not only the doctrinal system but Christian life too.

On the other hand, one must not suppose that in the fourth century Christian life was shaken to its very foundations. The danger was great, so far as it went, but the danger was overcome. The overwhelming majority of the Catholic people remained untouched by heresy, even when some or many bishops signed questionable creeds or when individuals embraced heresy wholeheartedly. Saint Hilary describes the situation cleverly and with a certain humor: Even the Arian bishops dare not fail to call Christ God in the presence of the people. They take the expression "God" in a figurative sense, but the people understand it literally. They speak of Christ as God's Son in the sense in which all Christians become God's children by baptism, but the people understand the real divine Sonship. They say that the Son of God was before all times, and mean that He was created before all other creatures, but the people understand that He is from eternity. "Thus are the ears of the faithful holier than the hearts of the bishops." [3]

Of course, in the long run the heresy would penetrate the ranks of the faithful to some extent. Farseeing Catholic bishops took care that the liturgy was kept free of prayer formulae which could be interpreted in an Arian sense. Even old customary formulae which could be explained by the Arians in accord with their views were eliminated. The old doxology, "Glory be to the Father through the Son in the Holy Spirit," had hitherto been harmless, but since the Arians found in it a subordination of the Second and Third Divine Persons to the First Person, Athanasius, Basil, and others took pains to have it replaced by a formula that could not mislead: "Glory be to the Father and to the Son and to the Holy Spirit."

By vigilance of this type the defense against dangerous, erroneous teaching met with timely success all along the line of battle. Victory was won before the heresy could acquire deep roots. The defense as always brought a great gain: a whole generation of theologians got its training in the fight against the heresy and that training extended far beyond the subjects of dispute. With the decline of Arianism there begins in the Church a period of rich intellectual life, a period which, to be sure, lasted only a few decades, but on whose fruits we are still nourished—the age of the great Fathers of the Church.

---

[3] *Contra Auxentium*, 6 (Migne, Patrologia Latina, X [Paris: 1845], cols. 612 f.).

THE GREAT FATHERS OF THE CHURCH

THE BEGINNINGS OF CHRISTIAN LITERATURE

In the general history of literature the question has occasionally been raised whether one should speak of a special Christian literature in antiquity or whether the great Christian writers do not belong merely to their respective national literatures. Now there is no doubt that in a history of Greek literature Athanasius and John Chrysostom ought to have a place alongside Thucydides, Demosthenes, Plato, and Plutarch, just as in Latin literature Jerome and Augustine must stand beside Cicero and Livy. On the other hand, there is also justification for combining the Christian writers of antiquity in a particular literary group, for the linguistic or national point of view is not the only norm of judgment in the history of world literature.

Christian literature begins with the New Testament, a group of writings which stand by themselves in depth of content, nearness to life, and lasting influence among the written products of all mankind. In the generations following the apostles, literary production was so meager that in the second century we can hardly speak of a Christian literature. It is certain that some of it has been lost; what has survived—the letter of Pope Clement I, the letters of Ignatius, the writings of Justin and of the other Apologists—is of the utmost interest to history and theology. But these were only beginnings. At the turn of the second and third centuries we have the important works of four Christian authors, Clement and his pupil Origen in Alexandria; Irenaeus in Gaul, who, like them, wrote in Greek; and the Latin Tertullian in Africa. Clement and Origen introduced Greek philosophy, Plato's world of ideas, into Christian theology. This first effort did not start without clumsy errors, but both were professional writers and their stimulating influence on the later theologians was great. Neither Clement nor Origen produced a work that merits a place among the great productions of human literature. Tertullian would have possessed the qualities for this, with his extremely personal style, his wit, his familiarity with life; but his works are for the most part only brief occasional pieces, and he is ever the publicist, the controversialist, lacking the monumental, constructive trait. To an even greater extent the same observation would be true of Cyprian and his collected letters, so striking in individual passages of great beauty. After Cyprian's death, however, there was an interval of close to a century before Christian pens of any importance were again taken up; the single exception is Eusebius of Caesarea, the historian of the Church.

After the middle of the fourth century there began in the Church a great literary activity, the first real flowering of Christian literature. In mere volume it surpassed by far the comparatively modest output of the earlier period. It even came close to surpassing the classical literature in both Greek and Latin, at least insofar as such works have been preserved.

ATHANASIUS AND THE CAPPADOCIANS

The age of the great Fathers of the Church begins with Athanasius, bishop of Alexandria from 328 till his death in 373. His books are occasional writings, in defense of the teaching of the Council of Nicaea and against the Arians, but they have a theological value beyond their immediate purpose. Athanasius's biography of Saint Antony the Hermit had a triumphal literary progress throughout antiquity and more than any other book awakened an enthusiastic interest in monasticism.

When Athanasius died in 373, the intellectual leadership of the Catholics of the East was assumed by the Cappadocian

Basil, bishop of Caesarea in Pontus since 370 and already styled "the Great" by contemporaries. Basil sprang from a very wealthy family that had been Christian for generations and had endured much in the Diocletian persecution. He studied at the schools of higher learning in Caesarea in Palestine, Constantinople, and Athens in order to prepare himself for an official career. But, having returned home, he devoted himself to the complete service of God under the influence of his deeply pious older sister, Macrina. He became a monk and was soon chosen bishop. In this last capacity he had to endure the full assault of the Arians and died in 379, when scarcely fifty years old, just before the final victory over Arianism. His death was deeply bewailed by the whole Church. In his great doctrinal writings Basil, together with his friend Gregory Nazianzen, established the main features of Catholic speculation on the Trinity by means of clear definitions. For our knowledge of the fourth century, Basil's collection of letters is of the same importance as is Cyprian's for the third. In general, he bears a great similarity to Cyprian, whom, however, he far surpasses as a speculative theologian. We discover in him the same practical sense, the same care for the unity of the Church, the same princely charity. Like Cyprian, Basil was above all a shepherd of souls. They resemble each other in this too, that in their concern for the Church and for souls they at times voiced complaints against the Roman See. Through his monastic Rules Basil became the legislator of Greek monasticism and influenced that of the West.

A younger brother of Basil and Macrina was Gregory, bishop of Nyssa in Cappadocia. Superior to his brother in speculative ability, he was basically a philosopher rather than a theologian, and his Platonic train of thought removes him at times from the realism of the Christian revelation. Very moving is his biography of his sister, Macrina, a book filled with the Christian concept of the family and with a genuinely human emotion, something one scarcely expects to find in these Greek saints, who exteriorly liked to pose as Stoics.

The third great Cappadocian is Gregory Nazianzen, called by the Greeks simply "the Theologian." The son of a bishop, he studied together with Basil at Athens, where he was very highly esteemed by the other students. A fellow student at this time was the future emperor, Julian, whose nervous restlessness repelled Gregory. Basil consecrated his friend bishop of Sasima, a small see, but in 379 Gregory was called to Constantinople, where all the churches were still in the hands of the Arians. In a short time Gregory brought about a change in favor of the Catholics, and Emperor Theodosius I turned the cathedral over to him. As bishop of the imperial capital, he presided for a brief period over the council of 381. When his efforts to heal the schism then distracting the church of Antioch were unsuccessful, he was deeply hurt, resigned his episcopal office, and withdrew, first to the little diocese of Nazianzum, and then into complete retirement. Throughout his life Gregory was rather a poet and an ascetic than a pastor. A man of frail health and sensitive disposition, he was one of those who can never be happy on earth. But he was a powerful preacher, and his important place in Catholic theology is due to his numerous sermons of a dogmatic and panegyric character.

JOHN CHRYSOSTOM

Saint John Chrysostom, Gregory Nazianzen's second successor in the see of Constantinople, is the greatest of the Greek Fathers. He was a native of Antioch, where from 381 he labored as priest and preacher until 397, when, against his will, he was summoned to be bishop of the imperial capital. His frankness very soon incurred for him the animosity of the court. The bishops who sided with the court, among them Saint Epiphanius of Cyprus, renowned as a theological writer, contrived in 404 his deposition and exile. Chrysostom appealed to Pope Innocent I, and, because of popular pressure— for the people were devoted to him—was soon recalled, only to be banished once again. In exile he died of fatigue and vexation. His theological and literary importance rests on his more than 300 sermons, which not only form an extremely precious exegetical commentary on Holy Scripture, but also abound in dogmatic and moral content and in vivid particular features from Christian life. He has especially warm passages dealing with the Eucharist, the dignity of the priest, and the education of children. One of the greatest orators of all antiquity, Chrysostom was also a farsighted shepherd of souls.

AMBROSE

The first in time of the great Latin Fathers is Saint Ambrose. Born at Trier of a prominent Roman family, he dedicated himself to the service of the state. In 374 he was sent by the emperor as agent of the government to Milan, where the bishop, Auxentius, a staunch Arian, had died and it was feared that the new election might produce disorderly scenes. Ambrose behaved so admirably that the Milanese quickly elected him as their bishop, though he had not yet been even baptized. He at once received baptism and episcopal consecration and thenceforth was wholly a churchman, though he was never able or willing to belie the loyal imperial statesman. He placed at the service of souls his influence over the emperors and his classical eloquence, formed in the school of Cicero. To us his oratory appears at times cold and far too rhetorical, but in his own day it accomplished wonders. Through his preaching he won for Christianity the *rhetor* Augustine.

JEROME

Saint Jerome was a man of pronounced personal character-istics and a genuine scholar. He came from Stridon in Dal-matia—a place no longer known—studied in Rome, was bap-tized by Pope Liberius, and then went to the East, where for a time he lived among the monks and acquired a knowl-edge of Hebrew. Furthermore, he spoke and wrote fluent Greek. Paulinus, bishop of Antioch, ordained him priest, but the disturbances in the church of Antioch disgusted him and he went to Constantinople to hear Gregory Nazianzen. He formed a close friendship with Gregory of Nyssa. In 382 Pope Damasus I, with whom he had earlier corresponded, called him to Rome and entrusted him with the task of prepar-ing a new Latin text of Holy Scripture to replace the many inadequate translations used in the West. Jerome labored at this till the end of his days. His translation is a scholarly achievement, but at first it found little favor among the bishops. Only in the seventh century did it begin to make its way and obtain the name "Vulgate," that is, "commonly used." Even today it is the Scriptural text used by the Church in the liturgy and in theological studies in the schools, even though, with our modern methods, it is possible to improve on its particular shortcomings. In his grasp of textual criticism, Jerome was far ahead of his age. Many of his critical observa-tions have the genuine ring of modern scholarship. His knowl-edge of languages and of the topography of Palestine enabled him to include valuable information in his commentaries. Likewise, we owe to him many facts of the early history of the Church, especially in regard to literary matters.

While Jerome was applying himself at Rome to his scholarly work and at the same time was serving Pope Da-masus in caring for the already heavy correspondence of the Roman See, he formed around himself a circle of pious ladies whom he was able to fill with enthusiasm for the ideals of monasticism. At the same time he found powerful opponents among the Roman clergy, a situation brought on to a great extent by his own inconsiderate ways. When, on the death of his patron Damasus, he was not elected pope, he left Rome in great bitterness and went back to Bethlehem, where he again lived as a monk, ceaselessly occupied until advanced age with his learned works and gradually held in honor by all Christendom as its scholarly oracle. Of course, he tarnished his own reputation to some extent by his violence in literary controversy. Intolerant scholarly arrogance mingled in Jerome with humble asceticism and deep piety.

Jerome kept up an active exchange of letters with his ascetic friends. These letters, which are still among the most-read writings of the Fathers, have exercised a great influence on Catholic asceticism.

AUGUSTINE

Though he brightly blazed the trail for scholarship in the Church, especially through his biblical studies, Jerome was nevertheless outshone in general importance by the third of the great Latin Fathers, Augustine. Born at Thagaste in Numidia in 354, he was raised by a holy mother, Monica, but, in accord with the pernicious custom of the time, was not baptized. As a student at Carthage, he joined the Manichaean sect. This was a bizarre religion, more Persian than Christian, that had arisen in the third century. It is difficult to understand how one of such depth as Augustine could find satisfaction in it. He did not become a convinced adherent, but continued to speculate and to search for truth, unable either to find interior peace or to free himself from the shackles of sensuality. Even less was he contented in his position as professor of eloquence, first at Carthage, then for a short time at

Rome, and finally at Milan. In the last named city he heard the formally perfect pulpit discourses of the bishop, Ambrose. At first he listened with mere professional interest, but was gradually attracted by their content. After hard internal struggles, he had himself baptized by Ambrose in 387 and returned to his native Africa in order to devote himself entirely to God's service.

Augustine has described his interior transformation in the book which he called *Confessiones*. The title is not to be translated as "Confessions," but rather as "Praise," the glorification of the divine providence, which finally led him to salvation, despite all his opposition. The *Confessiones*, a book which is still read by all educated persons, is unique in ancient literature. In its pages the most delicate psychology and sublime flights of thought counterbalance each other.

Augustine was unable to remain in his ascetical retirement for long. In 391 the bishop of Hippo ordained him priest and designated him as his successor. From 395 till his death in 430 he was bishop of this little seaport, the modern Bona in Algeria. His pastoral activity was somewhat like that of a modern parish priest, but in his writings he embraced the whole Church. In addition to hundreds of sermons and letters, he published profound dogmatic treatises, especially in regard to the very difficult questions of grace and the divine means of salvation. In his later years he wrote *De Civitate Dei*, a Christian philosophy of history of great originality and genius.

Augustine was not so learned as Jerome and was not ashamed to ask the irritable hermit of Bethlehem for enlightenment on biblical questions in extremely courteous letters. Again, his Latin is not formally perfect and classical as is Jerome's. Augustine, who wanted always to give utterance to what was profound, struggled unceasingly with the expressing of his thought. He admitted to a friend: I am almost always dissatisfied with my own expression. Neither Ambrose nor John Chrysostom would have said that. But Augustine surpassed them all in speculative depths. His formulae were later more and more drawn upon by the Church for her definitions of Faith.

Augustine died on August 28, 430, while the Vandals were besieging Hippo. Some have found this circumstance symbolic, as though with his death ancient civilization expired, foundering in the flood of barbarism. Such a view would be misleading. The great Fathers and the greatest among them, Augustine, are not an end, a sunset glow, a final dying out of the millennial Graeco-Roman civilization. Rather, they are a beginning. They created a new civilization, or more correctly, they organically remoulded the thousand-year-old classical culture into a Christian one.

THE BEGINNINGS OF MONASTICISM

Some years ago there appeared a book on Protestant communities that resemble monasticism. A non-Catholic reviewer wrote the thoughtful warning that persons should not be deluded: "Where serious monastic beginnings are present, the path leads without fail to Rome." This, of course, is not to be understood as a dogma. The idea of cutting oneself off from the world in order to devote oneself to the service of God is found in religions which have nothing to do with the Catholic Church, for example, in Buddhism among the Lamas of Tibet. But the critic's observation is perceptive, since the monastic life, as it has developed in the Church, is inseparably bound up with her nature. It forms the very heart of the interior life in the Church. The Church has always fostered the monastic life with special care, not just because of its usefulness for culture and society, but because she sees in it the most perfect fulfillment of her pastoral work.

115

In the history of the Church the monastic life affords a sure criterion of the level of the interior life. Where monasteries flourish, the interior life flourishes, and, on the contrary, where they decay, it decays. Every opponent of the Church has thoroughly understood this. A chief feature on the program of all recent heresies and movements hostile to the Church has been opposition to the monasteries. Anti-monastic currents within the Church have always gone astray, when they have not actually ended in apostasy.

THE BEGINNINGS OF MONASTICISM

Like so many other great things in the Church, the monastic life arose, not through the initiative of the highest authorities, but from humble beginnings, almost of itself. We know the place and time of its origin: Egypt in the second half of the third century. It has often been asserted that the persecutions were its occasion—Christians who had fled into the desert undertook to live there as hermits. In reality, we encounter the first hermits in inhabited districts, very close to cities and villages; only gradually did they transfer their settlements to the uninhabited desert. The climate and soil of Egypt were propitious. In no other section of the then known world could one renounce the "world" and get along with a minimum of care for his daily bread, clothing, and habitation as there.

Yet, however favorable was its setting, Egyptian monasticism did not really originate spontaneously. It was inaugurated by men who with full awareness impressed upon it their personal individuality. At their head stand two personages, Antony and Pachomius.

Antony was the son of prosperous peasants of the middle Nile valley. Born soon after 250, he entered upon the eremitical life in the usual manner in the neighborhood of his native

116

village. It was only about the turn of the century that he withdrew into the desert between the Nile and the Red Sea; in an
oasis he built himself a cell and at once attracted some disciples. Saint Jerome and others visited the spot and described
it, and even today a monastery of Coptic monks continues to
exist there. Here Antony lived, occupying himself with prayer
and gardening, and here he died, a centenarian, around 356.
At times he visited his former disciples, who had built cells for
themselves among the rocks along the edge of the Nile valley.
Once, on the invitation of Athanasius, he journeyed even to
Alexandria to give testimony against the Arians. He was not a
cleric, but he always treated priests with great respect. He
knew only the Coptic vernacular and could neither read nor
write. But persons of all sorts turned to him for advice: Emperor Constantine and his sons wrote to him, Athanasius and
other bishops visited him. He gladly gave spiritual counsel,
though occasionally somewhat bluntly, for he was happiest
when alone. "He was a man of unique pattern," says Athanasius. And the same writer observes, "Not through writings,
not through worldly wisdom, not through any sort of ability,
but only through his piety did Antony become renowned."

The other great founder was Pachomius. He was an
organizer, and established a great monastery of monks living
a common life on the island of Tabennisi in Upper Egypt.
Later he made other foundations. For them he composed a
Rule, the oldest monastic Rule, which affords us an exact
insight into the life and activity of these monks. The principal
part of the day was taken up with handicrafts and agricultural
work. Each work group had its overseer; each overseer gave
to the abbot an account of the work accomplished. Real
Egyptians they were, as in the days of the Pharaohs and their
taskmasters, except that now everything was done voluntarily.

Pachomius died in 346, but his organization continued to

expand. Jerome reports that at Easter, when the monks of all the Pachomian monasteries traveled to Tabennisi, about 50,000 assembled. There are those who have unfairly sought to cast doubts on this number. Pachomian monasticism was a sort of social movement, and it was not piety alone that drew some to the monastery. There a person could labor under a regime worthy of his human dignity, rather than do compulsory work on the domains of the state. As early as 370 an imperial decree was concerned with the loss in service to the state that could arise.[4]

Besides the Pachomian monasteries there were numerous colonies of hermits along the edge of the desert on both sides of the Nile valley, and an especially large one in the Wadi Natrun, south of Alexandria. Some of them were begun by disciples of the great Antony, but they did not form an Order. The hermits lived in twos or threes in primitive cells or even in caves. They attended the liturgy in the nearest city, though the larger colonies had their own church and priests. At harvest time, when in Egypt every hand is needed, these hermits proceeded into the fertile Nile valley, and on the few bushels of grain that they earned were able to live out the year.

On the whole, Egyptian monasticism bore little similarity to the later monastic life. Even the Pachomian establishments resembled labor camps rather than monasteries. Much of it seems to us quite dependent on self-will and unregulated. And, above all, stability was lacking. It was even considered advantageous to wander from one colony to others and to study under various ascetics. Furthermore, there prevailed a definite striving after record achievements. The individual ascetics sought to outdo one another in fasting, penitential practices, and separation from the world, and in these endeavors idiosyncrasies were not absent. However, true piety cannot be

4 *Cod. Theod.*, XII, 1, 63.

118

denied these crude hermits. They received the sacraments faithfully, prayed much, and practiced virtues heroically—love of neighbor, meekness, patience, industry. Many sayings of these ancient Fathers, which were collected by contemporaries and have come down to us in extensive writings, testify to great warmth, ideal striving for perfection, and keen observation of the height and the depth of the human heart. It was to an extent a barbaric sort of striving for perfection, or rather a childlike one, but it was genuine.

SPREAD OF MONASTICISM IN THE EAST

From the middle of the fourth century the Catholics of other countries began to become more and more interested in Egyptian monasticism. In Rome people saw the first monks in 341, when Athanasius, persecuted by the Arians, visited Pope Julius I. The *Life of Saint Antony*, published by Athanasius soon after 360, made a deep impression. Augustine has very graphically described this impression in his *Confessiones*. Toward the end of the fourth century interest in monasticism became fashionable. Books were written about it, and many who went on pilgrimages to the Holy Land made a side-trip to Egypt, just to see the monks. The best men of the age— Basil, Gregory Nazianzen, Chrysostom, Jerome—prepared for their careers by protracted visits with the monks.

In the early fourth century there were settlements of monks in nearby Palestine, and before long in Syria and Asia Minor. Generally, the model was Egyptian monasticism, particularly in the form given by Antony and his disciples, that is, eremitical colonies or *"lauras,"* as they were called in Palestine. The strictly organized Pachomian type was too much related to the Egyptian national temperament to expand farther. The great legislator for Asia Minor, and eventually for all of Greek monasticism, was the Doctor of the Church and opponent of

119

the Arians, Basil, whose detailed monastic Rules are rather an ascetical manual than a constitution for monasteries.

The *laura* of Saint Sabas (✝532), still in existence in the wild rocky desert between Jerusalem and the Dead Sea, became very famous. Here in the sixth century lived Saint John Hesychastes (the Silent), a former bishop, and in the eighth century the Doctor of the Church, Saint John Damascene.

A special kind of monks were the *Akoimetoi*, or Sleepless, founded at the beginning of the fifth century by Saint Alexander and so called because, divided into several choirs, they took turns at the psalmody day and night. At Constantinople in 463 the ex-consul Flavius Studius founded for the *Akoimetoi* the monastery of Studion, named for him; it later went into decline until Saint Theodore the Studite (✝826) produced there a new flowering of the monastic life according to the Rule of Saint Basil. Theodore the Studite was an important theologian. As a fighter for Catholic orthodoxy and for the papal primacy he had to endure much persecution.

In Syria monasticism put forth some very unusual flowers. In the fifth century the Church historian Theodoret, bishop of Cyrrhus, tells in a very vivid manner of hermits who had themselves immured in their cells. However, this immurement was often only symbolic and did not prevent the hermits from taking part in the liturgy. The constant efforts of the Egyptian monks to seek ever stricter forms of asceticism impelled Saint Simeon to this extreme, that, instead of inclosing himself in his cell, he lived under the sky on a high pillar, protected only by a railing. Such a thing would be regarded as incredible or even insane, were it not carefully described by Theodoret and other eyewitnesses. Nevertheless, Simeon the Stylite (the pillar-stander) was a great spiritual leader; he preached from his pillar to thousands and brought about acts of expiation and conversions. After his death in 459 a basilica was built around his pillar, and its huge ruins still stand. Simeon found many imitators.

In general, it can be said that in the East monasticism was more self-willed, rougher, and in a sense more uncultured than it was in the West. History is able to recount several examples of crass ignorance in addition to many of genuine piety and virtue. These monks, who for the most part paid little heed to secular or spiritual authority, succumbed only too often to the danger of schism and heresy; but on the other hand, their very independence made them, in the face of emperors who favored heresy, more capable of resistance than were the courtier bishops. In the later struggle over holy images, Greek monasticism presented a united front against the emperor and held loyally to the Catholic Faith.

Eastern monasticism was a national monasticism in the good meaning as well as in the unfavorable sense. It took root in the people and in the soil and survived the separation of the Oriental peoples from the Church, which began in the fifth century. What good things the separated churches have preserved of a religious nature are for the most part to be ascribed to the credit of their monks.

MONASTICISM IN THE WEST

In the West too there were individual monasteries even in the fourth century. The oldest foundations were due to Martin, bishop of Tours, in Gaul and to Ambrose in Milan. Eusebius of Vercelli brought his clerics together in a common life on the model of the monks. Augustine did the same at Hippo. After 400, monastic establishments were numerous, especially in the south of Gaul. John Cassian, who seems to have been born in the East, founded several monasteries in and around Marseille and compiled for them his *Collationes*,

121

or conferences with the Egyptian monks, whom he had talked to during his sojourns of several years' duration in Egypt. The *Collationes* remained one of the most popular books of edification in the monasteries of the Middle Ages and into modern times.

LERINS

Not far from Marseille, on the island of Lérins near Cannes, Honoratus founded a monastery from which rolled forth a great monastic wave. Many of its monks became bishops in Gaul—Honoratus himself and Hilary were bishops of Arles, Eucherius of Lyon, Lupus of Troyes, Salonius of Geneva, Faustus of Riez, and in the sixth century the most celebrated of them all, Caesarius of Arles. These bishops propagated the monastic ideal in their churches. The flourishing condition of the church in Gaul under the first Merovingians is in great part to be ascribed to the influence of Lérins. Monks of this abbey were also prominent theological writers, particularly Vincent of Lérins, Salvian of Marseille, and Faustus of Riez.

From the first, the monks of Lérins were more cultured than those of the East. Except for this circle of influence, however, Western monasticism in the fifth and sixth centuries lagged behind its Greek counterpart. At the end of the sixth century there arose, again in Gaul, a new monastic center— Luxeuil.

THE IRISH MONKS

Saint Patrick, the Apostle of Ireland, had spent some time at Lérins, whence he transplanted the monastic institute to the Emerald Isle. When he died in 461, Ireland was not only a Christian land; its Church had received a monastic organization. Ireland had never belonged to the Roman Empire and it possessed no cities. The first centers of culture were the monasteries. The heroic legends, which among other peoples told of kings and battles, told among the Irish of monks and their wonderful deeds and their journeys to fabulous lands. The Church was monastic. The bishops were either themselves abbots or they were subject to the abbot of the monastery.

The real flowering of Irish monasticism occurred in the sixth century, when Clonard, Maghbile, Clonfert, and other monasteries arose. In 563 the elder Columba founded the monastery of Iona or Hy on an island off the western coast of what is now Scotland. The Anglo-Saxon historian, Bede, in the eighth century, calls the monks of Iona "Columbans," [5] the first example of referring to a monastic group by the name of its founder.

From the monastery of Bangor, situated on the Irish coast near Belfast, there went forth toward the end of the sixth century the younger Columba, or Columban, with twelve companions, among them Saint Gall, to labor on the continent for the Kingdom of God. This missionary urge was peculiar to the Irish monks. They gave to the Church on the mainland many valuable stimuli, and at the same time, through their hardheaded independence, caused a number of difficulties.

Columban proceeded to Burgundy, where he founded the great monastery of Luxeuil. In 610 he was expelled by Queen Brunhild, but Luxeuil remained standing. He preached in the region around Lake Constance and finally went to Italy, where in the Lombard Kingdom he founded the monastery of Bobbio, south of Piacenza. Gall, who had fallen out with Columban, remained in what is now Switzerland, where the name of the former monastery of Sankt Gallen still recalls his memory.

Columban was a forceful personality. It is incorrect to say,

---

5 *Historia Ecclesiastica Gentis Anglorum*, V, xxi (Migne, Patrologia Latina, XCV [Paris: 1861], col. 279).

as some historians do, that a new epoch in the history of the sacrament of penance began with him, but the influence of his penitential preaching was great. Monasteries following his Rule arose in regions where the monastic life had scarcely been known till then: Corbie, Rebais, Saint-Omer, and Remiremont in the northern part of the Frankish kingdom, and from Remiremont the several establishments between the Meuse and the Rhine—Echternach, Stavelot, Malmédy, Disibodenberg, Prüm, and Saint Goar. There were also monasteries of women following his Rule.

Scarcely anything survives of buildings from the time of Columban. The monasteries founded by him and his disciples all eventually accepted the Benedictine Rule. The Rule which Columban gave to his monasteries was brief and harsh. The abbot of Luxeuil exercised a sort of supreme authority over all the white-cowled monks. In the history of Canon Law Columban's name is sometimes connected with the origins of monastic exemption, that is, independence of the bishop's jurisdiction. This is correct insofar as Columban was accustomed to the circumstances of his native land and had no intention of placing himself under the diocesan bishop. His monasteries lay for the most part in isolated districts, and the bishops were not concerned with them, but one can hardly speak of a canonical privilege at this period.

BENEDICT

Columban and his sons were the forerunners and trailblazers of the most important of all the Orders, that of Saint Benedict. It is true that Benedict lived before Columban, but his institute did not spread until the seventh century and to a great extent on soil prepared by Columban.

For the life of Saint Benedict we possess a single source, the second book of the *Dialogues* of Saint Gregory the Great.

124

Gregory's hagiographical production has been subjected to rigorous criticism, and his biography of Saint Benedict offers little in the way of content, since for the most part it consists of a succession of marvelous happenings. Just the same, the main data can be regarded as certain.

Benedict was from Nursia in Umbria. He studied in Rome and, as a youth, withdrew to the mountain solitude of Subiaco, east of Tivoli, some time before 500. There he lived as a hermit and gathered about him his first disciples. Difficulties with the local clergy caused him to seek a new solitude. He found it on a mountain situated farther to the south, near San Germano, where he built his great monastery, Montecassino, and composed his world-famous *Rule for Monasteries*. The top of a mountain was later selected by many Benedictine houses as a suitable monastic site. Benedict died at Montecassino in or after 547.[6] The monastery was destroyed by the Lombards in 581 and rebuilt only much later. Its monks found refuge in Rome at the Lateran, where Gregory the Great became acquainted with them. After he had become pope, he made Saint Benedict famous throughout Christendom by his biography in the *Dialogues,* and he sent Benedictine monks to England.

As early as 610, only six years after Gregory's death, Pope Boniface IV referred to Benedict as the "sublime Lawgiver of monks." One after another, all the monasteries of Saint Columban adopted the Benedictine Rule and new monasteries based on the Rule were founded, the first known being one established in 630 in the diocese of Albi in the southern part of the Frankish kingdom. In the Carolingian age monk and Benedictine were synonyms.

---

6 The traditional date of Saint Benedict's death is 543, which Father Hertling gives, but recent scholarship places it in 547 at the earliest. See Philibert Schmitz, *Histoire de l'ordre de Saint-Benoît* (2d ed. rev.), I (Maredsous: 1948), 381-386. (Translator's note.)

Saint Benedict is thus not the founder of an Order in the sense that all Benedictine monasteries stemmed from Montecassino. Likewise, the monasteries following his Rule—and before long that included all monasteries in the West—did not constitute any juridical association among themselves. Nevertheless, Benedict belongs to the company of those great personages in the Church who have enriched Christian life with things of enduring value.

Benedict's Rule is not only an exhortation toward individual perfection, but is at the same time a monastic constitution. It created the type of Western monastery, the abbey. Its foundation is stability, to which the monk binds himself at his entry. No longer does he wander about from ascetic to ascetic, as in Egypt. The monastery offers him everything; it is his world, he has no yearning for the outside. The monastery is not a prison. It is comfortable and beautiful; it produces everything, better than outside. The abbot is the father of the monastic family. He does not rule by means of penal code and disciplinary measures, but by paternal authority. The liturgy, the monk's chief work, is rich and elevating, and does not crush by excessive lengthening of the time for prayer. The monk loves his monastery: it is his home, where reigns the Benedictine Peace that the world cannot give.

Is the Benedictine Rule strict or gentle? If by strict we mean order, discipline, and striving for a goal, then it is strict; but if by strict we mean harshness and stern demands on bodily strength, it is gentle.

Historians of all tendencies cannot do enough to show their high esteem of the Benedictine Order because of its services to European civilization. It is true that few of the intellectual treasures of classical antiquity would have come down to us had not the industrious monks of the early Middle Ages unceasingly collected, copied, and made use of the ancient manuscripts. The monks were often the only educated persons with time and tranquillity for such study. It is due to them that our present European civilization is closely bound up with the ancient Greeks and Romans rather than with the civilizations of the ancient Egyptians and Babylonians, worlds that for us have perished. But one must not suppose that Saint Benedict, or any other religious founder, wrote his Rule for the sake of cultural progress. Benedict wanted to point out the way to heaven. He wanted to establish on earth homes that would prepare for the heavenly home. He sought exactly what the Church seeks in her care of souls. The satisfying consequences for human cultural advance came, as it were, automatically.

the transformation of the primitive church into the european church of the middle ages

THE age of the great Fathers of the Church was followed by several centuries of far less brilliance. The Church, and with her the history of Europe, having just traveled through a smiling countryside, enters a dark tunnel which seems endless. Perhaps it would be more correct to say that an autumn of mature fruit and harvest is now succeeded by a winter of several centuries. And, just as in nature winter is not an absolutely dead season, but one in which energies and vital sap are made ready for the coming spring, so was this the situation in the Church. Externally, she comes forth from this winter sleep in a new garb, full of new vital forces.

Many causes conspired to reduce the ancient world to this state of weakness or paralysis, which for a time appears to be actual death. One of these causes is the occurrence of what is usually known collectively as the "European migration of nations."

THE MIGRATION OF NATIONS

In regard to the so-called migration of nations there has long prevailed a decidedly incorrect picture. In Italy, where significantly this phenomenon is termed, not the migration of nations, but the "invasion of the barbarians," there is a preference for supposing that wild Germanic hordes overwhelmed the country with fire and sword and reduced to a few ruins the flourishing culture of the ancient Roman Empire. In Germany, people like to think of powerful and noble warlords, who, hurrying through the world in an unprecedented victorious advance, established everywhere new and vigorous living states in place of the aged and rotting Empire. Today, because of painstaking research into details, especially in regard to economic history, we are in a position to present this entire period more soberly and hence more correctly.

First of all, we must understand that the "migration of nations" does not signify a sudden inundation, but rather a prolonged process of displacement and penetration which began long before the third century and came to an end only in the eleventh century. Wars were sometimes the occasion for the displacement of whole peoples and at other times they were its consequence, but frequently the emigration and the immigration were accomplished peaceably.

The political structure of the old Roman Empire never completely collapsed. From early in the fourth century the imperial capital was Constantinople, where the emperor resided. The state-like creations that came into existence in Gaul, Spain, and Italy were always regarded as parts of the Empire. Though their rulers might call themselves kings, they likewise bore military or civil titles as imperial officials. When in the sixth century the Emperor Justinian had the Vandal state in Africa conquered and transformed into a Roman province, his act was not interpreted as a new conquest, as an extension of the imperial frontiers. It was nothing more than what earlier emperors had done against refractory governors or usurpers.

Theodosius the Great's division of the Empire between his

129

two sons, Arcadius and Honorius, in 395 was nothing new. Already in the second century there had been co-rulers with the imperial title, and since the third century it had been customary for the co-emperors to govern separate regions. Imperial laws were always issued conjointly. There had never been such a thing as a Western Roman Empire in contra-distinction to an Eastern Roman Empire. The deposition in 476 of the "Western Roman" Emperor Romulus by a Germanic military commander signifies neither an end nor a beginning in history. It was only one of those little *coups d'état* which often occurred. Odoacer regarded himself, both before and after his *coup*, as commander or official of the emperor residing at Constantinople. Until the seventh century, when the advance of Islam began to change the whole political map of the Mediterranean basin, there is no question of a decisive political reorganization that ushered in the end of the old Roman Empire.

Of far greater significance than the new political structures which were undertaken by the Germanic kings in the frame-work of the Empire was the general decay of civilization, to which the Germanic immigration of course contributed, but of which it was by no means the sole or chief cause. This cultural decline can easily be detected in several fields. Roman inscriptions of the age of Augustus or of Hadrian should be compared with those of the fourth, fifth, and sixth centuries. Taste, symmetry, and execution are definitely inferior in the later ones; the ability to write correctly has disappeared. Literary production decreases, content becomes jejune, the horizon is narrow. In the fine arts the same phenomenon is to be observed.

However, there occurred no real break. It is not as though on one day civilization disappeared and barbarism took its place. Civilization and culture continued to exist, as did

130

economic and political institutions, but there took place a dilution, an impoverishment of them. The key to the whole phenomenon is supplied by the universal decline in population.

DEPOPULATION

When the Roman Empire had attained its full extent under Augustus and his first successors, embracing the Mediterranean lands and beyond, it must have counted some 60,000,000 inhabitants—far less than at present, when the same area contains almost 300,000,000. People did not jostle one another the way they now do, but there was nevertheless a sufficient population for economic and cultural exchange, and here and there even a dense population in the modern meaning, especially in Asia Minor, Egypt, North Africa, and southern Gaul. There were very few large cities, as this term is now understood, but many average-sized and small ones. Until the middle of the second century the population steadily increased, and under Marcus Aurelius it must have reached about 80,000,000. Then began an uninterrupted drop, which went on for centuries until Europe and the Near East were almost depopulated. We have abundant evidence of this situation. From the third century we hear of uncultivated land in fertile regions, the cities become smaller, Rome shrinks from perhaps 1,000,000 under the first emperors to 50,000 in the sixth century. Many cities disappear entirely; only Constantinople grows, and it does not become so large as was Old Rome in its prime.

The Germanic migration from northern Europe was able at most to retard the decline in population, not to stop it. The individual Germanic tribes did not comprise very large numbers. Though at times there are references to hundreds of thousands of warriors in the wars of conquest, these alarming

131

reports lack any statistical value. To the invaders was ceded a great part of the soil, usually two-thirds, and often this was done voluntarily, without there being any necessity for the Roman provincials to move elsewhere. Since the provinces were almost empty, the invaders were, so to speak, swallowed up. In the seventh century, when no further reinforcements came, Italy, the Alpine and Danubian provinces, Gaul, Britain, and Spain had perhaps 10,000,000 inhabitants among them.

The causes of this phenomenon, unique in the history of Europe if not in the history of the entire world, are difficult to determine. The beginning is known—the plague which the troops of Marcus Aurelius brought back from the Parthian war and which raged for years throughout the Empire. But pestilence alone is not a sufficient explanation. Europe recovered rather quickly from the best-known plague, the Black Death of the fourteenth century, and the Renaissance period, so grievously afflicted with infectious diseases, even shows a marked increase of population. Nor do war casualties provide the answer. In the regions affected by depopulation no more and no bloodier wars took place between the third century and the Carolingian epoch than in other centuries. Instead, still other factors, of a social and perhaps of a moral nature, must have conspired, but to determine them we have to depend on conjectures.

The consequence of this depopulation was the disappearance of culture. The ancient culture was not overwhelmed by wild barbarian hordes, but vanished for want of agents of transmission. The cities with their old monuments from the period of brilliance decayed, not because they were destroyed but because there was no longer anyone to maintain them. Gregory the Great tells that a bishop once visited Saint Benedict at Montecassino and expressed the fear that Totila, the new king of the Goths, would destroy Rome. Benedict

132

replied that Rome would not be destroyed by heathens but would slowly die through the ravages of storms, weather, and earthquakes. Gregory adds that the accuracy of this prophecy can be daily attested, since now here, now there, an ancient house or church collapses and vanishes. The last one who had seen to an extensive maintenance of the buildings in Rome had been the Gothic King Theodoric. After him no one bothered about the preservation of the now desolate magnificence of the past in the vast city that had become almost empty of human beings. The situation was similar everywhere else. Aqueducts destroyed in war were not repaired because of want of men to do the work. Harbors silted up, but they were no longer necessary, for no ships came any more. What was true of buildings was just as true of the intellectual sphere. The schools disappeared because there were no teachers or students. The book trade, so flourishing in antiquity, ceased because it had no public to patronize it, and with it disappeared also the inducement to literary production. This last withdrew into monasteries, where the monks were writing their chronicles.

However, the ancient culture never completely disappeared. There were always individuals who carried on the old traditions. Scanty as literature had become, there could always be found scattered individuals who not only wrote an elegant Latin but could even produce respectable verses, such as Venantius Fortunatus at the end of the sixth century, the author of the older *Pange Lingua*. In the fine arts every century had its isolated but not insignificant accomplishments. Characteristically, the fine arts were wholly dominated by Byzantium, which was least affected by the universal depopulation.

THE EXPANSION OF THE CHURCH

In this general decline the Catholic Church first made important progress in regard to numbers. In the age of

Constantine the Christians were still a minority in the Empire, at first certainly no more than one-fifth of the total population. Toward the close of the fourth century they had well exceeded one-half. Of course, the changed attitude of the government contributed to this growth, but this influence must not be overrated. Laws, such as those issued from 341 by Emperor Constantius against heathen worship, did not of themselves provide a stimulus for embracing Christianity. In the fourth century we everywhere find non-Christians in the highest offices. The tempo of the Church's growth in the fourth century was no faster than it had been in the third. Nevertheless, if we estimate the total number of Christians at from six to ten millions in 313, we may at least double this figure for 400.

Geographically, the entire territory of the Empire had long been occupied by Christian communities. Beyond the European frontier to the northeast, the line of the Rhine and the Danube, an advance was for the moment impossible, for there the pressure of population went in the opposite direction. But the ways lay open to the southeast, from Syria to Mesopotamia and Persia and from Egypt along the Red Sea. Here in the fourth century Christianity moved across the imperial frontiers. Christians had gone to Persia already in the third century, and in the fourth there were numerous communities which had to endure bloody persecutions. In South Arabia the Homerite or Sabaean peoples became entirely Christian. Abyssinia too accepted Christianity in the fourth century, and Athanasius consecrated a bishop for Axum. In the sixth century Cosmas Indicopleustes mentions a Greek-speaking Christian community on the island of Socotra and knows also, though only from hearsay, of Christians in South India. When and how these old communities originated is a matter of dispute. Likewise in the fourth century, Christianity reached the Caucasian districts, Georgia and Albania, which had never actually belonged to the Roman Empire. We must suppose that numerically all these distant outposts were still quite small. They were little points of further growth, buds full of hope. But all these hopes were to be stifled by the great heresies of the fifth century, long before Islam everywhere obstructed the road to the southeast.

THE BEGINNING OF THE REVOLT OF THE EAST
THE HERESIES OF THE FIFTH CENTURY

Although it had begun with the denial of the divinity of Christ, basically Arianism was not so much a Christological as an anti-Trinitarian heresy. Its defeat involved the definition of the dogma of the Trinity, the doctrine of One God in Three Persons. Not until then did theological speculation address itself to the question of the manner in which the Second Divine Person can be true Man.

NESTORIANISM

Antioch, the great West Syrian metropolis, had always produced outstanding theologians. In the history of theology one hears of an Antiochene school in opposition to the Alexandrian, but this must not be interpreted in the sense that in Antioch there was something in the nature of a faculty or university. However, the Antiochene theologians did have in common a decided bent toward rationalism. Especially in biblical exegesis they rejected the allegorical tendency which had been developed in Alexandria by Origen. The great John Chrysostom was an Antiochene. One of his teachers had been Diodorus, who died as bishop of Tarsus in 392, and one of his fellow students was Theodore, later bishop of Mopsuestia in Cilicia (✝428). While Chrysostom never departed from the traditional dogma, Diodorus and Theodore tried new paths in

135

Christological speculation. Both sought, though not in the same way, so to solve the Christological problem that the Second Divine Person, the Logos, would have taken up residence in the Man Christ, so that in Christ two Persons, a divine and a human, would have to be distinguished.

For the moment all this was mere academic theorizing. Diodorus of Tarsus and then Theodore of Mopsuestia died as esteemed bishops, in peace with the Church. But another Antiochene, the monk Nestorius, having become bishop of Constantinople in 428, brought the new theology to the attention of the people when he taught that Mary must not be termed Mother of God, since she is only the Mother of the Man Christ, not the Mother of the Divine Logos dwelling in the Man Christ.

The Catholic sense of the Faith had now been touched at a delicate spot. Intense excitement was the immediate result. Cyril, bishop of Alexandria, called attention to the new heresy in the pastoral letter which the bishops of Alexandria were accustomed to issue each year at Easter, and informed Pope Celestine I (422–433). Energetic intervention was all the more necessary since the matter concerned the bishop of the imperial capital. Neither Pope Celestine nor Cyril of Alexandria lost any time in making it.

On August 11, 430, the pope wrote to the bishop of Constantinople that, within ten days of receiving the papal letter, he must retract his teaching in writing; otherwise, he would be excluded from the communion of the Catholic Church. He sent this document to Alexandria and commissioned Cyril to execute it; if Nestorius should refuse to sign it, Cyril was to arrange a new election to the see of Constantinople. The pope also told him that he was sending copies of this mandate to the bishops of Antioch and Jerusalem and to the primate of Macedonia "in order that our judgment on Nestorius, or rather the divine judgment of Christ on him, may be known." One can hardly deny that the popes of antiquity felt themselves to be Christ's vicars for the whole Church.

Cyril of Alexandria accepted the pope's commission and drew up twelve theses, the celebrated Twelve Anathemas, which he submitted to Nestorius for his signature. Nestorius rejected them, and, in order to prevent the threatened deposition, induced Emperor Theodosius II to summon a general council. He counted on the lack of unity among the bishops and especially on John of Antioch, who was by no means in agreement with Cyril's Twelve Anathemas.

THE COUNCIL OF EPHESUS

At Pentecost of 431 the council met in the cathedral of Our Lady at Ephesus. Cyril was there, but John of Antioch and his Syrian bishops had not arrived. Cyril, who knew that the pope was behind him, at once opened the council, against the wish of the emperor and over the protests of the imperial commissioner. With 198 bishops, in the very first session he condemned the teaching of Nestorius and pronounced his deposition. Some days later John of Antioch arrived; with forty-three bishops and the imperial commissioner, he convoked a rival synod, which in turn deposed Cyril. Cyril, at whose synod the papal legates had meanwhile appeared, thereupon excommunicated John and his adherents. Such was the situation when the two councils came to an end.

Embarrassed, the emperor at first ratified both synods, which had excommunicated each other. Soon, however, under the influence of his pious and capable sister, Saint Pulcheria, he dropped Nestorius, had him replaced by a Catholic successor, and annulled the sentence of deposition against Cyril. Before long, Cyril was reconciled with John of Antioch. He

137

accepted the profession of Faith of the rival synod, with which no fault could be found, and John consented to the judgment on Nestorius. On this occasion Cyril showed that he was concerned only for the point at issue and that he was no mere violent fighter, as many recent historians paint him. And, through his quick and courageous action, he had demonstrated that the pope had entrusted to the right person the affairs of the Church in the East. His energetic intervention prevented the occurrence of a schism within the Empire. Only later, through a special coincidence of circumstances, would Nestorianism revive beyond the frontiers in Persia.

MONOPHYSITISM

The constant dread of witnessing a revival of the long condemned Sabellianism had earlier seduced many into challenging the definition of the Council of Nicaea. Similarly, after the condemnation of Nestorianism by the Council of Ephesus, the endeavor to give the *coup de grâce* to the already dead heresy caused some to fall into new errors. According to Catholic doctrine, Christ is a single Person who possesses both the divine and a human nature; but the monk Eutyches at Constantinople considered it improper to speak of two natures in Christ, since to him this approximated Nestorianism. Hence, his formula was: One nature (in Greek *mone physis*, thus, Monophysitism) in Christ, and this the divine nature. Christ is true God, but not at the same time man as we are. In Him the human nature has, as it were, been absorbed into the divine nature. For his teaching Eutyches could appeal to Cyril of Alexandria, who, in his anathemas against Nestorius, had indeed used the expression *mone physis*. By this Cyril had only meant what modern theologians term the *unio hypostatica*, the union of the two natures in one Person. The formula of Eutyches, on the other hand, touched the very foundations of the Catholic Faith. For if Christ was not true man, He did not really die on the Cross, and thus the entire work of Redemption was placed in doubt.

Flavian, bishop of Constantinople, grasped the significance of the matter and condemned Eutyches. In keeping with custom, he informed Rome of the sentence. Pope Leo I (440–461) not only approved it, but sent his famous *Tomus ad Flavianum*, an extraordinarily clear and profound exposition of the Catholic teaching on the points denied by Eutyches. The affair would have ended there had not the emperor interfered. This was still Theodosius II, who had once protected Nestorius and now came forward in behalf of Nestorius's opponent, Eutyches. Once again a council was summoned to Ephesus, once again the bishop of Alexandria was appointed to preside, but this time by the emperor and not by the pope. The bishop of Alexandria was no longer Saint Cyril, but his successor, Dioscorus, who wanted to ape the vigor of his predecessor without possessing his spirit. The council was a scandal. Eutyches was absolved, Flavian of Constantinople and other bishops were declared deposed, and Flavian was so grossly mistreated that he died a few days later. The indignant pope, to whom the deposed at once turned, coined the expression "Robber Synod" by which the council of 449 is still known in history. Naturally, it was not recognized as a general council.

CHALCEDON

In the midst of the prevailing confusion Theodosius II died. Marcian, husband of Saint Pulcheria, who had earlier proved herself the Church's guardian angel, became emperor. In 451 he was able to convoke to his residence at Chalcedon, opposite Constantinople, a genuine council which was attended by 630 bishops. This was the largest gathering of bishops in antiquity; only the Vatican Council of 1869–1870 has surpassed it in numbers. At Chalcedon, naturally, almost all those present were from the East, but the legates of the pope presided. Leo's dogmatic definition against Eutyches, the *Tomus ad Flavianum*, was read and accepted by the Fathers with the cry, "Peter has spoken through Leo." The Councils of Nicaea (325), Constantinople (381), and Ephesus (431) were again recognized as ecumenical, and the Robber Synod of Ephesus (449) was condemned. Dioscorus of Alexandria, author of the mischief, was deposed.

Once more everything seemed restored to the right track. And yet the decades following Chalcedon were among the saddest which the Church has had to endure. Inspired by various causes, the great revolts began in the East. Many bishops were subsequently not in agreement with Chalcedon, since they more and more feared that the condemnation of Monophysitism could finally lead once again to Nestorianism. Worse still was the fact that many lacked an awareness of the absolute unity of the Church. Since the days of Constantine they had become used to seeing in the emperor the real head of the Church. To them loyalty to the Church and loyalty to the emperor were one, and hence, when the idea of the Empire began gradually to disappear, the unity of the Church grew weaker. As yet there was no such thing as nationalism in the modern sense. Syria and Egypt did not dream of becoming independent national states, but they were no longer willing to be dictated to in regard to their religious convictions by the government at Byzantium.

Egypt was the first to separate from the Church. More correctly, it split in two—into a larger section, Coptic in nationality, with a Monophysite creed, and a smaller section which adhered to the Council of Chalcedon. Characteristically, those belonging to the second group were later termed

"Melchites," that is, imperialists, those loyal to the government. Around 460 the separation was complete; along with the dissident Coptic Church went also the Abyssinian Church, which was just coming into existence.

The far larger Syrian Church, the patriarchate of Antioch, comprising over 200 dioceses, also split into a Monophysite and a Melchite group. Furthermore, the Christians living beyond the imperial frontier in Mesopotamia and Persia, who likewise belonged to the patriarchate of Antioch, separated from it and in 486 established their own patriarchate of Ctesiphon-Seleucia on the lower Tigris. In 498, in order to emphasize its opposition to Monophysite Antioch, this new Church adopted a Nestorian creed.

THE HENOTICON

In an effort to halt the general defection, Emperor Zeno had the Alexandrian patriarch, Peter Mongus, and the Byzantine patriarch, Acacius, draw up a profession of Faith, which in 482 he published as an imperial edict under the title *Henoticon*, or creed of unity. In it Nestorius, Eutyches, and the Council of Chalcedon were rejected, and only Nicaea and Cyril's anathemas against Nestorius were to be regarded as norms of Faith. Instead of bringing about peace, this new act of imperial regulation of the Faith made the confusion worse. To the Catholics the *Henoticon* was unacceptable, because in it the Council of Chalcedon was rejected. Pope Felix II (483–492) thus excommunicated its author, Acacius of Constantinople, so that now for the first time [1] there was a schism between Rome and Byzantium which did not end until 519. For their part the Monophysites of Egypt and Syria had no intention of

---

[1] Actually Old Rome and New Rome had been separated by schism on previous occasions—over Arianism throughout most of the second half of the fourth century and from 404 to 415 in regard to the deposition of Saint John Chrysostom. (Translator's note.)

141

accepting the *Henoticon*, in which Eutyches was condemned. On the other hand, the Armenians accepted the *Henoticon*; they broke with Rome and remained in schism even after Byzantium had finally given up the *Henoticon*.

Thus, in a few decades, the Catholic Church had lost vast regions and precious centers of early Christian culture: Egypt, which had given her Origen and Athanasius and was the cradle of the monastic life; Syria, with its traditions reaching back to the time of the apostles, where in the fourth century, through Aphraates and the great Ephrem, the beginnings of an important Catholic national literature had been laid; Persia, Armenia, and other promising outposts of missionary expansion. The end had come for the conquest of Asia and East Africa, which had seemed so full of prospect since the fourth century. It was of no advantage to the Church that in the Middle Ages Nestorianism advanced from Persia into central Asia and China.

How great the loss was numerically is difficult to estimate. The lands concerned in the revolt were in the fifth century already greatly depopulated, and the revolt was not complete: in West Syria, Palestine, and Egypt there were still Catholic minorities. But the revolt must have affected from four to five millions, perhaps one-fourth of the total number of Catholics at that time.

THE SEPARATED EASTERN CHURCHES

Later, when the Byzantines finally separated from the Church, they took with them the minorities that had remained Catholic in the fifth century in Egypt and Syria, with the single exception of the Maronites of the Lebanon, who still today constitute a Catholic block of from three to four hundred thousand souls. In addition, of the old patriarchate of Antioch there still remain 184,000 Christians of Monophysite sects, a Catholic group of some 70,000 souls under the patriarch of Mardin on the upper Tigris, and more than 100,000 Catholic Greek Melchites. Of the East Syrian Church, which became Nestorian in the fifth century, there are today 48,000 Catholics, the so-called Chaldaeans, and 12,000 separated Nestorians. In the sixteenth century the Nestorians of South India changed to the Monophysite creed and today number 655,000, in addition to 537,000 Catholics. The schismatic Georgians and Armenians, who did not belong to Antioch, must be reckoned at about 2,000,000. There are perhaps from 50,000 to 100,000 Catholic Armenians, who are scattered over the entire East; but in regard to this nation, which even till the present day has endured ceaseless persecution, it is impossible to obtain exact numbers.

Of the old patriarchate of Alexandria there are still in Egypt almost 1,000,000 Monophysite Copts in addition to 45,000 Catholics. Of the Egyptian Melchites, who only separated from the Church at the time of the Byzantine schism, there are still 55,000, in addition to 25,000 who are again Catholics. The Monophysite Abyssinians count some 3,000,-000, in addition to perhaps 30,000 Catholics.

The remnants of the two great Oriental patriarchates thus comprise today around 6,000,000 Christians, of whom more than 1,000,000 again belong to the Catholic Church. All told, there are apparently more now than the old patriarchates possessed at the time of the separation; but they are almost swallowed up in the vastly increased population of those wide regions.

The Catholic Church cherishes with a sort of reverential love these small groups which have preserved their Christianity from antiquity, often in the face of the most difficult circumstances, and protects their venerable rites and customs. The fact that today a new ecclesiastical life is stirring among them everywhere is not to be underestimated. Still, this should not deceive us in regard to the fact that the great revolts of the fifth century were for the Church an irreparable loss. Thereby the Church was for almost a thousand years pushed off the soil of Asia and confined to Europe. The conquest of Asia, and in part that of Africa, which in antiquity seemed on the point of realization, had to start in modern times along an entirely different route and today is, so to speak, only in its beginnings.

For the Church in Europe, too, the revolt of the East was not without its repercussions. So long as the old patriarchates of Alexandria, Antioch, and Jerusalem retained their importance, they acted as a counterpoise to the preponderant position of the bishop of Constantinople. Alexandria especially had always been loyal to Rome. But after the Oriental patriarchates, through the loss of the greatest part of their flocks, sank to a status of slight importance, there grew up in the Church a sort of dualism—Old Rome and New Rome, the pope and the bishop of Constantinople. In theory the preeminence of the pope was not denied, but in practice the bishop of Byzantium considered himself almost as the pope of the East. Only when the glory of Alexandria, Antioch, and Jerusalem had disappeared did the bishop of the imperial capital begin to style himself the "ecumenical patriarch."

THE GROWTH IN EUROPE

In the West we see the contrary process in the fifth and sixth centuries; the Church gains instead of losing, but of course not all at once and not without setbacks. And such a reverse seemed to come first of all in the Germanic migrations, for many of the recently arrived peoples were Arians.

ARIANISM AMONG THE GERMANS

How Arianism, which since 381 was practically extinct in

the Empire, again revived among the Germans is not entirely clear. Among the Goths, who at the beginning of the fourth century lived south of the lower Danube, there were already Christians at that time. A bishop of the Goths, Theophilus, was present at the Council of Nicaea in 325. These were Catholics. Later too there were Catholic Goths, such as the martyr Sabas (✝372) and the colony in Constantinople, for which Chrysostom organized pastoral life in the Gothic language. But Arian missionaries were also busy among them, especially Ulfilas, who had been consecrated a bishop by Eusebius of Nicomedia in 341. Through his Gothic version of the Bible he became the creator of the oldest Germanic literary tongue. Very likely the Goths, who after the middle of the fourth century passed to Christianity in greater numbers, did not notice the difference. They wanted to embrace the religion of the Romans and obtained it from Constantinople, where the Arian Emperor Valens was reigning. When in 378 they came to war with the emperor and met their own tribesmen who were fighting on his side, they were surprised, as Isidore relates, that these professed another Faith and rejected communion with them.

This does not, of course, explain how the Gepids, Burgundians, Sueves, Vandals, Heruls, Lombards, and other peoples happened also to become Arians. Neither is it at all certain to what extent this was the situation. The ruling families, related to one another, were for the most part Arians, though not all individual members of these families were. The Frankish King Clovis, hitherto a heathen, became a Catholic in 496,[2] but one of his sisters was an Arian. The Arian Ostrogothic King Theodoric (✝526) had a Catholic mother. The

---

[2] The traditional date of Clovis's conversion is 496, but recent scholarship prefers 498 or 499. See P. de Labriolle in *De la mort de Théodose à l'élection de Grégoire le Grand*, Vol. IV of the Fliche-Martin *Histoire de l'église*, p. 395, footnote 5. (Translator's note.)

first duke of the Bavarians who is known by name, Garibald, and who is mentioned by Gregory of Tours, was a Catholic. His daughter, Theodelinda, married the Arian Lombard King Authari. The Arian Visigothic dynasty in Spain accepted Catholicism in 586. To what extent the retinues of these families were Arian is unknown. In part they were still heathen; at least the individual Germanic tribes were not infrequently termed simply heathens by the early writers. Of the Visigoths in Spain many were already Catholics before Recared's conversion. The Burgundians are called Arians by Gregory of Tours, Catholics by Orosius. Furthermore, we are not to imagine that these peoples were very numerous. They formed only a small ruling class in regions that were already only sparsely populated.

A religious census taken around 500 would, then, have shown scarcely a few hundred thousand, perhaps only several tens of thousands, of Arians among from five to seven million Catholics in the sphere of the Latin Church, Western Europe and Africa. In the course of the sixth century Arianism disappeared almost entirely, in any case earlier than the remnant of paganism. In the seventh century Western Europe can, for all practical purposes, be regarded as Catholic. At the same time this was the period of the lowest level of the general census of the population.

AFRICA

In Africa the Donatist schism did much damage to the Church in the fourth century. Nevertheless, at the time of Augustine (✝430) Catholic life was flourishing. Then came the conquest at the hands of the Arian Vandals, who staged several bloody persecutions of Catholics. The reconquest by Belisarius in 534 brought improvement. Several of the existing ruins of churches date from this period. But the population was in an uninterrupted decline. The fortified cities which Emperor Justinian founded were much smaller than the old ones. The artistically laid out aqueducts decayed from lack of skilled labor; the desert moved forward and buried in its sands the once fertile, arable land and the abandoned cities. When in 698 the Arabs took Carthage, Christianity vanished along with the last remains of Roman culture.

SPAIN

The Church in Spain was not seriously disturbed by the invasion of the Arian Visigoths from the beginning of the fifth century. The territory ruled by the Visigothic dynasty was for a long time not extensive, and it was only King Leovigild (568–586) who first governed the entire peninsula. With his son, Recared, the dynasty became Catholic. Now began a flourishing period for the Church, initiated by the two brothers, Leander and Isidore, who, one after the other, were bishops of Sevilla. In Toledo, which was the capital from the reign of Leovigild, eighteen councils were held between 400 and 701, and their *acta* are the primary sources for the condition of the Church. When the Arabs seized almost all of Spain from 711, the Church encountered various difficulties but no deterioration, and more than thirty sees continued in existence. Not until the ninth century were there spasmodic, bloody persecutions of Christians. More than from the Arabs, the Church in Spain suffered from the general decline of population and culture.

GAUL

In the great days of the Roman Empire Gaul, like Spain, contained some eight or nine million inhabitants, and in the sixth century, under the first Merovingians, it still possessed an important culture and economy. Even at the beginning of

147

the fourth century it had more than thirty sees. The influence of Lérins from the south, and later that of Luxeuil from Burgundy, made itself felt in a salutary way in the spiritual life. In the sixth century there were still such outstanding bishops as Avitus of Vienne (✝518) and Caesarius of Arles (✝542), who distinguished themselves as theological writers, and Gregory of Tours (✝594), whose *History of the Franks* and other works are the chief source for this period. Still, it is characteristic that Gregory of Tours was unable to write grammatically correct Latin. The many lives of saints from the Merovingian age, lives of bishops, monks, and nuns, not only strongly influenced mediaeval hagiography but contributed very much to determine the mediaeval type of saint. The numerous synods, which in Gaul were held, not in one capital as in Spain, but in various places, testify to an active ecclesiastical life. Under the later Merovingians, together with the political decay went also the ruin of culture and economy and the decline of ecclesiastical life. Here too the uninterrupted falling off of the population was a basic cause of the phenomenon of decline. Just the same, Gaul and the Frankish kingdom remained the nucleus around which the later European families of nations would be formed, and the center of gravity of ecclesiastical life more and more moved in that direction.

BRITAIN

Whereas on the continent the connection with Roman culture was never entirely broken, a real interruption took place in Britain. At the beginning of the fifth century the Roman garrisons and government officials withdrew. The Britons, far too weak numerically and harassed by the Scots pressing from the north, against whom the Romans had shielded them only with difficulty, were able to defend themselves in no other way than by appealing to Germanic peoples from the continent. These heathen Angles, Saxons, and Jutes in their turn pushed the Christian Britons into the mountainous districts of Wales and Cornwall, except for those who emigrated across the water to the peninsula named Brittany because of the new settlers. Thus, in the fifth century Christianity had almost wilted in Britain, while at the same time it was being brought to flower by Patrick and his successors in Ireland, which had never been Roman. From Ireland the related Scots were evangelized, and then Irish and Scottish monks began their activity in England. In 596 Pope Gregory the Great sent Benedictine monks to England, who quickly gave impetus to the work of conversion, though not without friction in regard to the Irish, who had preceded them and whose ecclesiastical usages differed greatly from the Roman. Bede's account of the new accession to the see of Canterbury in 669 throws light on the difficulties in this land, which was then so remote, and on the unfavorable situation. The only bishop had died and the English princes had sent an embassy to the pope to ask for a new one. The envoys, unaccustomed to the climate, all died in Rome. The pope now consecrated a Greek monk, Theodore, but it took him two years to reach England. Here he displayed great activity. A cultured Greek, he spread scholarship and personally instructed his clergy, even in the Greek language. Bede the Venerable (✝735), a Benedictine monk, shows a scholarship that is comprehensive for the age. His *Ecclesiastical History of the English Nation* is as fundamental as is the work of Gregory of Tours. Bede also translated the New Testament into Anglo-Saxon.

The English Church especially distinguished itself by its attachment to the Holy See. Pilgrimages to Rome and the sending of money to the popes were frequent. In the eighth

149

century England was able to dispatch numerous missionary priests to the continent.

CHRISTIANITY IN GERMANY

Germany, as a geographical expression, was in Roman times the land between the lower Rhine and the Elbe, which never belonged permanently to the Empire. The two Roman provinces along the entire left bank of the Rhine were known as Upper and Lower Germany, but were reckoned with Gaul. The land to the south of the Danube and the Alpine region made up the two provinces of Raetia and Noricum. The triangle between the Rhine and the upper Danube, between the provinces of Upper Germany and Raetia, was protected by a fortified military frontier, the *limes*, but was only sparsely inhabited and had no provincial government.

In all these districts ruled by the Romans there were individual Christians and Christian communities probably in the third century and certainly in the fourth. This is proved not only by the historical martyrdoms in the Diocletian persecution—Victor at Xanten, Afra at Augsburg, Florian at Lorch near Linz—but also by numerous early Christian discoveries. At the Synod of Arles in 314 Bishops Maternus of Cologne and Agroetius of Trier were present. Trier belonged to the province of Gallia Belgica. In Upper Germany were the bishoprics of Strasbourg, Augusta Rauracorum (Augst, near Basel), and Vindonissa (Windisch, northwest of Zürich); in Raetia, those of Augsburg and Chur; in Noricum, those of Lorch and Teurnia (near Spittal on the Drave). Probably there were also others.

In the third century began the moving of the Alemanni over the *limes* into the regions of the Neckar and of the Schwarzwald as well as into modern Alsace and northern Switzerland. The old bishoprics continued to exist, except that in the sixth century Vindonissa was replaced by Constance. From the beginning of the seventh century Irish monks labored in these lands as missionaries: for a short time Columban himself evangelized between Lake Constance and Lake Zürich, and his disciple Gall remained there. At this time the dukes of the Alemanni were already Catholic. In the eighth century came the Benedictines. Pirmin (✝753) in 724 founded the monastery of Reichenau on an island near Constance and other monasteries. From Sankt Gallen the monasteries of Füssen and Kempten were established at the beginning of the eighth century.

The old provinces of Raetia and Noricum were resettled by Bavarian immigrants. Here too the connection with the early Roman Christianity was never entirely broken. The Bavarian ducal family, the Agilulfings, were Catholic as early as the sixth century. In the seventh century the Irish-Burgundian monks came to Bavaria, among them Eustasius, Columban's successor as abbot of Luxeuil. It was only in the eighth century that episcopal sees were established. In 696 Duke Theodo called the Frankish Bishop Rupert to Regensburg. Rupert was one of the so-called wandering bishops, that is, missionary priests with episcopal consecration, whom we so often meet at this time. Theodo gave him the ruins of the Roman fortress of Juvavum, where Rupert built the monastery of Saint Peter, the origin of the later city of Salzburg. He preached in the Salzkammergut and in the Pongau, where he founded bishoprics. In Regensburg another wandering bishop, Emmeram, from Poitiers, erected the monastery since known by his name. Bishop Corbinian, sent to Bavaria by Pope Gregory II (715–731), became the first abbot of the monastery of Freising, which he had founded. In 716 Duke Theodo journeyed to Rome to come to an agreement with Gregory II in regard to the ecclesiastical organization, but it was carried out only after his death by Duke Otilo and Saint Boniface.

SAINT BONIFACE

The Anglo-Saxon Benedictine Winfrid, or Boniface, journeyed to Rome in 718 to see Pope Gregory II. The pontiff, who shortly before had sent Corbinian to Bavaria, appointed Boniface to the mission in Germany. He went first to Frisia, where his fellow countryman Willibrord had been laboring since 690 as a missionary and since 695 as bishop of Utrecht. Boniface then preached in Upper Hesse until Gregory II again called him to Rome and gave him episcopal consecration. Boniface visited Charles Martel to assure himself of his protection, and then worked in Lower Hesse and Thuringia, aided by Anglo-Saxon monks, who flocked to him from the English monasteries. Many monasteries arose on the newly-won soil—Amöneburg, Fulda, and Fritzlar in Hesse, Ohrdruf in Thuringia, Tauberbischofsheim, Kitzingen, Ochsenfurt, and Heidenheim in Franconia. Named by the pope archbishop and papal vicar for the entire German mission field, Boniface went to Rome for the third time in 738 in order to discuss with Gregory III the organization of the German Church. He then went first to Bavaria and in conjunction with Duke Otilo established four bishoprics—Passau, Regensburg, Salzburg, and Freising—to which were later added Eichstätt and Neuburg. Neuburg on the Danube was detached from Augsburg for the part of Bavaria east of the Lech, but in the ninth century it was given back.

In central Germany Boniface erected the bishoprics of Erfurt and Würzburg as well as that of Buraburg, which however was soon transferred to Fritzlar and later was united to the see of Paderborn, founded by Charles the Great. Boniface arranged several Frankish national synods and on behalf of

Pope Zachary consecrated Pepin as king. He took for himself the old see of Mainz, still existing from Roman times, but in 752 he consecrated his disciple Lullus as his successor and, as a venerable old man of seventy who had finished his life's work, went back to his first missionary field, Frisia, where paganism was still vigorous. There on June 5, 754, he suffered the much desired death of a martyr.

From time immemorial Boniface deservedly ranks as the Apostle of Germany, and his tomb in Fulda is one of the most revered religious sites on German soil. He was not the first to introduce Christianity into Germany, but it can be said that he made the German nation as such Catholic. From then on, in addition to Italy, Spain, Frankland, England, and Ireland, there was also a Catholic Germany, which was to play a great role in the history of the Church. Naturally, we must not exaggerate conditions in the Germany of Boniface's day. If the German Empire under the Saxon and Salian emperors in the tenth and eleventh centuries, when it had expanded considerably in the east and the north, contained hardly more than 3,000,000 inhabitants, we must for the eighth century assume a much smaller population. If we think of the entire region from Frisia to the Vosges and the Swiss Alps, from the Drave to the Bohemian Forest and the Harz, as comprising from one to two million persons, we will obtain a correct picture. Settlements lay as if lost in cleared areas within vast forests. Nowhere were there cities in the modern sense. The spots on which cities would later rise were forts, monasteries, and little market places. The writings of those in charge of the care of souls, such as Pirmin and Boniface, testify that in addition to genuine Christianity there were also much ignorance, crudeness, and remnants of paganism. And yet this nation was a little later to assume, even if only for a short time, the role of a sort of chosen people in the Church.

153

ITALY AND THE POPES

Of all the European countries perhaps Italy had to suffer most in the vicissitudes of the invasion period. However, the expedition of the Visigoth Alaric, who in 410 sacked Rome, was impressive rather than damaging. Amid the dread created by the news, Augustine in Africa began his philosophy of history, the *De Civitate Dei*. More injurious was the second sack of Rome at the hands of the Vandal Gaiseric, who crossed from Africa. Still, Rome at that time had enough vigor left to recover from such blows. The *coup d'état* of the imperial commander Odoacer, who in 476 deposed Emperor Romulus and styled himself king of Italy, produced scarcely a ripple, and the reign of the Ostrogoth Theodoric (489–526), who followed Odoacer, was a period of peace. Theodoric was an Arian, but he dealt fairly with the Catholics and maintained cordial relations with the popes. A contributing cause of this situation was the fact that since 484 there had been schism between the papacy and Constantinople due to the popes' rejection of Emperor Zeno's *Henoticon*. Of course, Theodoric wanted to be regarded as a prince of the Empire, but just the same he took a dim view of any leaning of the Italians in the direction of Byzantium. Thus, when in 519 Pope Hormisdas (514–523) succeeded in having Emperor Justin I and the patriarch of Constantinople abandon the *Henoticon* and sign a profession of Faith submitted by him, the aged king began to become suspicious of the Catholics. He had the senators Boethius and Symmachus executed and Pope John I, successor of Hormisdas, brought to Ravenna, where he died in prison.

EMPEROR JUSTINIAN I

Theodoric died in 526. The next year the great Justinian ascended the imperial throne. Before very long the influence of the imperial government was again felt in Italy. Justinian

154

had his general, Belisarius, who in 534 had recovered Africa, sail to Italy in order to put an end to Ostrogothic rule. In the long war which ensued Italy was again laid waste. Rome had to endure several sieges, and on one occasion all its inhabitants, who naturally could not have been very numerous, were sent away together with the pope.

Belisarius, even though he was a Catholic, acted in Rome in a decidedly autocratic fashion. He deposed Pope Silverius, whom he suspected of conspiring with the Goths, and in his place named Vigilius. The latter had his predecessor conveyed to the island of Palmaria, where he died. Vigilius was universally recognized as pope, but, whereas he had been ambitious for high position, he now had to do bitter penance, for he soon came into serious conflict with Emperor Justinian.

Justinian, the outstanding man of the sixth century, the restorer of direct Roman rule in the Mediterranean lands, the creator of the *Codex Juris*, the builder of Hagia Sophia, is to us a personality very difficult to comprehend. The air of mystery with which the Byzantine court delighted to surround itself renders almost impossible a judgment on his moral character as well as on his true political and religious intentions. It is certain that he was a tireless worker. As in all the spheres of politics and administration, so too in the field of religion he was indefatigably active as an ecclesiastical legislator and even as a theological writer. That his never-forgotten goal was the unity of the Catholic religion in the whole Empire admits of no doubt. But it is equally true that most of his measures, often accomplished in a violent manner, were either entirely bungled or were impossible of working in a convincing way. Justinian is one of those great men who have performed the superhuman, yet have created nothing really lasting.

In ecclesiastical policy his chief concern was to bring back the Monophysites to unity. Zeno's failure with the *Henoticon* had demonstrated that nothing could be gained from middle-of-the-road creeds, which satisfied neither friend nor foe. Justinian decided to give the death blow to the Monophysites, whose creed was kept alive on anti-Nestorianism, by condemning Nestorianism on a much broader basis than had previously been done. Not only Nestorius, but all writings which could be regarded as favorable to his doctrine, and especially the theology of Theodore of Mopsuestia, were to be included in the condemnation. These writings, summarized in three sections, acquired the epithet of "The Three Chapters." Vigilius, who had been made pope by the Byzantine court, was summoned to Constantinople, where he was kept for eight years. The condemnation of the Three Chapters provoked the deepest suspicion, not only in Vigilius but in most of the other bishops. It was regarded as unnecessary and as a veiled attack on the Council of Chalcedon. As such, it would strengthen rather than weaken the position of the Monophysites. On the other hand, no one could deny that the Three Chapters deserved theological censure. The pope did not attend the council of 553, which condemned the Three Chapters, but he subsequently ratified it, so that it took rank as the fifth ecumenical council. His action called forth a determined opposition in the West. All of Africa and the ecclesiastical provinces of Milan and Aquileia even withdrew from communion with him, but it was only in Aquileia that there ensued a real schism, which lasted for more than a century. The desired effect of the condemnation of the Three Chapters—a *rapprochement* between the Monophysites and the Catholic Church—was not realized.

The same sixth century in which Italy had suffered from the Gothic War witnessed in 568 the invasion of the Lombards. To be sure, they did not succeed in taking Rome, but they established themselves to the north of it in Spoleto and to the south in Benevento, and remained a continual threat. At first they persecuted Catholics, but under the double influence of the monastery of Bobbio, founded near their capital, Pavia, by Columban, and of their Queen Theodelinda, daughter of the Bavarian Duke Garibald, they began to become Catholics. The last Arian bishop was converted around the middle of the seventh century when the royal family was already Catholic. The Lombards too were not numerous, but the native population had by then become so sparse that they were assimilated to Roman culture much more slowly than had been the case with the Goths before them, and actually the process was never completed.

THE POPES AS RULERS OF ROME

Since the fifth century Italy had disappeared from the list of leading nations, but Rome had not. Though it now had far fewer inhabitants and lay almost in a desert, Rome was still definitely the center of the world. Constantinople was about ten times larger, could send out armies and fleets, and had the imperial court, the high government officials, the great merchants, scholars, and artists. Rome had none of these. Rome lived by the pope, belonged to the pope. The Holy See had become very wealthy through unending gifts; it possessed domains not only in the neighborhood of Rome, but in South Italy, Sicily, and outside Italy. Whereas formerly the emperors had had grain sent to Rome for distribution there, now that largess was made by the pope. The papal court was in many respects similar to the imperial, rather because of court ceremonial than the scandals, intrigues, struggles over the succession, and murders which occurred endlessly at Byzantium. The pope had his chancery and archives with specially trained officials, just as the old Roman emperors

157

had. He had his representatives, the *apocrisiarii*, at Byzantium and at the exarch's court in Ravenna. In several countries individual metropolitans were entrusted with special powers as papal vicars—the bishops of Arles for southern Gaul, of Thessalonica for Eastern Illyricum, of Salona for Western Illyricum.

But the pope was not a real sovereign or ruler of a state. Together with all other princes and rulers, no matter how independently they might act, the pope belonged in some way to the Empire. The actual sovereign was the emperor. But in fact the pope as early as the sixth century was really the lord of Rome, just as Lombard dukes were lords of Benevento or Spoleto. However, the pope was at the same time the spiritual ruler of the universal Church, a fact that gave him a fundamental distinction from other princes and lords.

GREGORY THE GREAT

How the pope at this period acted as ruler of the Church is best learned from the letters of Gregory the Great (590-604). Much of this pope's activity in government and administration, at least insofar as it could be carried on in writing, is contained in his 814 extant letters. Here are found letters to the contemporary emperors, Maurice and Phocas, as well as to the empresses; to the Merovingian kings and to Queen Brunhild of Burgundy; to the Anglo-Saxon kings and to King Recared of Spain; to particular provincial governors; to the stewards of the papal patrimonies in Sicily, Africa, Sardinia, and Gaul; and, most of all, to bishops. The letters to bishops fall into three classes. To the bishops of central and southern Italy and to those of Sicily the pope writes as to his immediate subordinates. With the rest of the bishops of the West he treats through the intermediary of the metropolitans of Carthage, Numidia, Thessalonica, Salona,

Ravenna, Milan, Arles, Vienne, Lyon, Autun. He had little correspondence with Spain, but among other things he bestowed upon Leander, bishop of Sevilla, the pallium, the mark of the archiepiscopal dignity. The third class consisted of the Oriental patriarchs of Alexandria, Antioch, and Jerusalem. Because of the defection of the Monophysites, they had, of course, lost the greatest part of their faithful, yet Gregory writes to them, not as a superior, but rather as to friends on a footing of equality. He delights to represent these patriarchs, so reduced in grandeur, as successors of Peter: Antioch was the Apostle's first see, Alexandria was established a see by his disciple, Mark; thus they form one single see, so to speak, with that of Rome.[3] But this did not prevent Gregory from sending quite earnest admonitions to these patriarchs now and then.

THE PATRIARCH OF CONSTANTINOPLE

Most difficult for the pope were his relations with the patriarch of Constantinople, and it is just as difficult for us to pass judgment on them. The bishops of Byzantium had at this time begun to style themselves "ecumenical patriarchs." Their privileged status in the Church has a long history.

The Council of Nicaea in 325 had prescribed that the customary precedence of the metropolitans in the individual provinces be maintained. In addition, the council had conferred on the bishop of Jerusalem a special position of honor without removing him from the jurisdiction of the metropolitan of Caesarea in Palestine. The Council of Constantinople in 381 divided the East into five ecclesiastical regions—Egypt (Alexandria), Syria (Antioch), Pontus (Caesarea in Cappadocia), Asia (Ephesus), and Thrace (Heraclea)—in imitation

---

3 *Epistolarum Liber VII, Epistola XL* (Migne, Patrologia Latina, LXXVII [Paris: 1849], cols. 898 ff.).

159

of the civil administration existing since Diocletian. This emperor had divided the Empire into four prefectures, in each of which there were several civil dioceses, and in each diocese several provinces. The prefecture of the East, as established by Diocletian, comprised five civil dioceses, which in 381 were made areas of ecclesiastical jurisdiction. In the rest of the Empire the old arrangement of one intermediate authority, the metropolitan, between the pope and the local bishops continued. In the East, however, another one was created, the "super-metropolitan." Furthermore, it was decreed that the bishop of Constantinople, though belonging to the "super-metropolitan" territory of Heraclea, should, as bishop of the imperial capital, have a primacy of honor before all other bishops with the sole exception of the bishop of Rome.

In 451 the Council of Chalcedon in its twenty-eighth canon went a step farther and bestowed on the bishop of Constantinople the right of consecrating the "super-metropolitans" of Ephesus, Caesarea in Cappadocia, and Heraclea, which was equivalent to combining these three "super-metropolitian" jurisdictions once again into a single unit. Pope Leo the Great at once protested against this canon. In 452 he told the emperor he could not allow the rights guaranteed to the bishops of the East by earlier councils to be curtailed. The see of Constantinople had not even been founded by the apostles, and its bishop should be content that, "with the aid of your piety and through my friendly consent," he had become bishop of the imperial capital.

The absence of historical grounds for its pretensions was felt in Constantinople itself. Hence, appeal was later made to the relics of the Apostle Andrew, which the city claimed to possess. Andrew was not only the brother of Saint Peter; he was called to be an apostle before Peter. Further, it was even discovered that Andrew had consecrated the first bishop of Byzantium.

Rome stubbornly refused to accept the twenty-eighth canon of Chalcedon, but had to reconcile itself to the fact that the bishop of Constantinople had stepped into the list of Eastern patriarchs and even occupied the first place among them. The title of "ecumenical patriarch," which the bishops of Byzantium assumed at the time of Gregory the Great, meant nothing else than this at first. They did not claim a real jurisdiction over the other patriarchs of Alexandria, Antioch, and Jerusalem, and still less did they thereby deny the primacy of the pope. But it was evident that the bishops of Byzantium had their own particular idea of the Church, that of a graduated hierarchy of officials on the model of the Byzantine state. Against this view was directed Gregory's attack on the title of "ecumenical patriarch." And he refused it for himself when the patriarch of Alexandria designated him as "universal pope." Gregory did not desire to be the top of a pyramid of officials in the Byzantine sense. The authority of the pope is based on entirely different foundations.

Gregory the Great had not long been dead when there occurred events that would give the entire political history of the ancient world a new direction, and would exert the greatest influence on the destinies of the Church. Islam appeared.

ISLAM

If by religion one understands a revealed Faith, then there are in the world today really only two great religions, Christianity and Islam. The third one, Buddhism, which on account of the number of its adherents persons like to equate with these two, makes no claim to be based on a divine revelation; hence, it is to be termed a *Weltanschauung* rather than a religion. Since in Christianity none of the bodies which have

161

separated from the Catholic Church, so far as they still hold the concept of revelation, can be termed world religions with regard to their numbers and expansion, we must say more exactly that there are today only two world religions, the Catholic Church and Islam.

Sociologically, the two do not admit of comparison. Islam is not a hierarchical unity, it has neither priesthood nor ritual sacrifice, and religiously it is split into two unequal halves, the Sunna and the Shi'a, not to mention smaller sects. What unites Moslems from Dakar and Zanzibar to those from Borneo, China, central Asia, and southeast Europe are two things: the Koran and Mecca. It is noteworthy that the veneration of Mecca is a pre-Mohammedan and properly heathen element, adapted unorganically, so to speak, to Islam. Still, despite its structure, so different from that of the Catholic Church, the unity of Islam is not to be underrated. It is far stronger than that existing among the Christian bodies which have separated from the Catholic Church.

The Church and Islam are, then, the two great rivals in the religious history of mankind. In the Mediterranean basin where they meet geographically the long history of these two has been one of enduring friction, sometimes open, sometimes latent. But thus far there has been no decisive struggle. One is to be expected in the near or remote future and it will decide the religion of Asia. In the political arena too, the possession of Asia has been at stake from the very beginning and will continue to be for centuries.

Consequently, the entry of Islam into world history in the seventh century is an event of the utmost significance for the history of the Church. Its influence on the destiny of the Church was of the strongest sort right from the start.

When Mohammed died in 632, his authority did not yet extend over all of Arabia. Only after his death did the adherents of the new religion break out of the North Arabian desert into civilized lands. In 635 Damascus fell into their hands; it would soon become the capital of the new empire. In 637 they took Lower Mesopotamia, in 638 Jerusalem, and shortly thereafter Upper Mesopotamia, where Edessa fell in 641. The Arabs then invaded Persia. In 646 the districts of Fars and Khorassan were conquered, and by 656 all of Persia to the Oxus and Armenia to the Caucasus were in their possession. Simultaneously, the conquest proceeded westward. Alexandria, and with it all of Egypt, fell in 642, and by 644 the coast as far as Tripolis had been conquered. Cyprus was occupied in 650. Then there was a standstill in the westward advance. Carthage was not taken till 698, but from then on the Arabs moved irresistibly along the northern coast of Africa. In 710 they were in Ceuta, in 711 they crossed the straits into Spain, in 712 they took Zaragoza, in 720 they were in Narbonne. In the East, Samarkand in Transoxiana had been conquered in 709, and in 712 the Indus had been reached. In India the conquests later extended still farther, but in Europe they came to an end. A prematurely undertaken siege of Constantinople in 717–718 failed and a limit was set to the advance into Frankland by the victory of Charles Martel at Poitiers in 732. Just the same, in less than a century the Arabs had conquered an empire which far surpassed the old Roman Empire, if not in population, surely in extent. And the Arabs now ruled the Mediterranean. In the ninth century they conquered Sicily and established their own bases on the European coast, at Fraxinetum, southwest of Cannes, from 889 to 975, and on the Garigliano, a three-days' march to the south of Rome, from 880 to 916.

The immediate losses of the Catholic Church through the Arab conquests were at first not so great as they might seem. The goal of the Arabs was to subject the world to the rule of

Allah, but they did not compel individuals to embrace Islam. Idolatry was, of course, an abomination to them, and where they encountered heathens they forced conversion. But the Christians and the Jews were not regarded as idolaters. They had their revelation, their *Kitab*, the Bible, which was esteemed in Islam. Hence, the Christians in the subjugated provinces were treated as citizens of the second class; they had to pay special taxes and were debarred from holding office in the state, but they were not molested in their Faith and worship.

In the eastern regions, Mesopotamia, Syria, and Egypt, there were now only a few Catholics. The far more numerous Monophysites often greeted the Arabs as their liberators from the Byzantine yoke. The only Catholic lands which came permanently under Arab rule were North Africa and Spain. In Spain the Church maintained herself; on the other hand, in Africa she entirely disappeared, though remarkably enough we learn of no forced conversions on a large scale. The explanation is that a Catholic population worthy of mention no longer existed there. The native Berber tribes of the interior had been neither Romanized nor Christianized, and now they accepted Islam. That Carthage held out for a time was due to its being a strong fortress with a Byzantine garrison. But there was scarcely a Latin Catholic population. In Africa the Church was not destroyed; she died out.

Thus, the immediate numerical loss to the Church through the Arab conquest was not too severe. Far more serious were the indirect effects. Missionary progress in the regions dominated by Islam was ended. This was due partly to the religious peculiarity of Islam, from which even today conversions to other religions are extremely rare. Partly too, it was because the Islamic world belongs to an entirely different culture in total isolation from Western culture.

Till now the Church had known no territorial limits. Suddenly a southern boundary which extended throughout the entire length of the Mediterranean and definitely barricaded the Near East was imposed upon her. This boundary, furthermore, ran dangerously close to Rome and shifted the geographical center of gravity of the Church northward into Gaul. Nor was this all. The alienation of the West from Byzantium was greatly strengthened by the Arabs. The Byzantine state, made smaller and poorer through the loss of its most valuable lands, now had to stop the Arab advance into Asia Minor, and so turned its back on the West. And the West, having nothing more to gain in the Mediterranean, turned its back on Byzantium. Between the two there existed a sort of no-man's land, the Balkan peninsula, where Slavic invaders were establishing their kingdoms, which sought company now with the West, now with the East, and thereby widened the breach still further.

The great *volte-face* in European politics, the alliance of the papacy and the Carolingian dynasty, which led to the formation of the European family of nations and gave to the Middle Ages their political and ecclesiastical aspect, was consequently a direct result of the Arab conquest. Modern historians are justified, then, when they say the Middle Ages began with the coming of Islam.

THE PAPACY AND THE FRANKS

In Italy a rather tolerable situation had been worked out in the seventh century in regard to the Lombards, who ruled the greatest part of the peninsula. Ravenna in the north, Naples, Apulia, and Calabria in the south, and Sicily still belonged to the emperor. Nominally still a part of the Empire, Rome was actually ruled by the pope. However, the Lombards had never entirely abandoned their designs on Rome, and in the eighth century their attitude again became warlike.

Pope Zachary (741–752) succeeded in arranging a twenty-years' peace with King Liutprand, but the latter's second successor, Aistulf, broke the treaty. He took Ravenna in 751 and prepared to conquer Rome. The result was the beginning of that tremendously important *volte-face* which turned the papacy politically from Byzantium to the Franks.

THE CORONATION OF PEPIN

In the Frankish kingdom a complete political change had occurred. The reins of government had been lost now for generations to the kings of the Merovingian dynasty, descendants of Clovis, and in their stead ruled various Mayors of the Palace, until the Carolingian family, originating in the Meuse region, seized the office of Mayor and made it hereditary. Charles Martel, who in 732 defeated the Arabs near Poitiers, belonged to this dynasty. His son Pepin, since 747 sole Mayor of the entire Frankish kingdom, extending from the Pyrenees to the Scheldt, the Weser, and the Lech, determined to transform the long existing situation of fact into one of law. He proposed to replace the powerless Merovingians by taking for himself the royal title. He sent Burchard, bishop of Würzburg, and Fulrad, abbot of Saint-Denis, to Rome as envoys to inquire of the pope whether he would approve such a step. Pope Zachary consented, whereupon Pepin was proclaimed king by the Frankish magnates. In 751 Saint Boniface anointed him by papal order. The last Merovingian, Childeric III, was sent to a monastery.

Thus had the die been cast. Between the pope and the Frankish kingdom there now existed more than an alliance. The pope had directly assumed responsibility for the legitimacy of the new Frankish dynasty. And partial motivation for the pope's action was the political estrangement of the

166

Holy See from Byzantium, which had long ago ceased to be concerned for the pope and his difficulties in Italy.

The workings of the new alliance were soon apparent. Pepin proceeded to Italy, defeated Aistulf, took over the former Byzantine territory of Ravenna, and gave it and a part of Umbria to the pope. This so-called Donation of Pepin is usually regarded as the origin of the States of the Church, or, more correctly, the Papal State. Such a view is, however, only partially true. If by the States of the Church one understands a territorial state in the modern sense, there were really no States of the Church throughout the entire mediaeval period. It was Alexander VI and Julius II who first laid the ground for them at the beginning of the sixteenth century. And if one means that as ruler of these states the pope exercised sovereign rights in and outside Rome, that was something he had been doing long before the Donation of Pepin.

THE DONATION OF CONSTANTINE

Hence it is of secondary importance whether or not the so-called Donation of Constantine, a forgery which is encountered in the ninth century and which from then until the fifteenth century was regarded as genuine, influenced the Donation of Pepin. According to the Donation of Constantine, that emperor handed over to Pope Silvester I dominion over Italy and the western provinces, thereby making him, so to speak, the emperor of the West. This is one of the numerous forgeries of the early Middle Ages whereby secular and ecclesiastical princes, families, and proprietors strove to give historical or juridical foundation to real or alleged legal claims, a procedure that to us seems quite barbarous or childish, but whose influence on the actual course of affairs must not be overrated. Just as no kingdom owes its origin to some courtly historian's claim for the dynasty's descent from an old hero, neither the sovereignty of the pope nor his other prerogatives owe their origin to some officious cleric's attempt to give a pseudo-historical basis to them.

Not the Donation of Pepin but the fact that he was anointed king by the Church is the outstanding historical event of this period, for it logically led a half-century later to the crowning by the pope of his son, Charles the Great, as emperor.

CHARLES THE GREAT

Charles greatly enlarged the kingdom of his father through conquest. In the south, it is true, he was compelled to yield again a part of the Spanish March that he had wrested from the Arabs, so that only Barcelona remained in Frankish hands. But he was successful in acquiring most of Italy. In 774 he became king of the Lombards, and as such was overlord of the Lombard principalities which were still in existence. The pope's domain was not touched but was instead extended by an amplification of the Donation of Pepin. Charles deposed the Agilulfings in Bavaria and incorporated the duchy and Carinthia into the Frankish kingdom. In the north he subjugated in several bloody campaigns the still mostly heathen Saxons between the Ems, the Weser, and the Elbe. And the Slavic tribes beyond the Elbe as far as the Oder and the Carpathians—Obotrites, Serbs, Czechs, Moravians—were reduced to partial dependence, as were the Avars to the Theiss and the Croats in the south.

The Empire of Charles the Great was by no means a unitary state. It was held together most of all by the overwhelming personality of its ruler. His character was not spotless and in many things it recalls certain semi-barbarous kinds of despots. But at the same time Charles the Great possessed a profound sense of responsibility. He aimed to be a Christian

168

ruler and understood his position as demanding a stern sense of duty. That he proceeded violently in the extirpation of heathenism, as among the Saxons, is repugnant to modern sentiment. But it cannot be denied that the Saxons embraced with special ardor the Catholic religion that was in the beginning forced upon them. Charles felt that he was the protector of the Church, and he often interfered in a very high-handed manner in ecclesiastical affairs, but one can hardly speak of a real Caesaropapism in his regard. For him the Church was something to be cared for, not a means to an end, not an instrument of government. A genuine Caesaropapism could not arise in the peculiar relationship created by the royal anointing of Pepin and the later imperial coronation of Charles. The pope quite definitely belonged to the Empire; he appealed to the emperor's protection and justice, he kept fealty to him as did any vassal. At the same time, as the highest authority on earth and not as a functionary performing a rite, the pope had given to the reigning dynasty the royal and the imperial dignity. Whoever desired later to possess the imperial status of Charles the Great could obtain it only from the pope, and he to whom the pope denied it was not an emperor. This wholly unique entwining of the two powers, involving the mutual subordination and superiority of each, dominated the great policies of the Middle Ages into the thirteenth century and beyond.

THE SCHISM OF THE BYZANTINE CHURCH

Without doubt, the establishing of the Western Empire by Pope Leo III and Charles the Great hastened the alienation of the Byzantine Church to its complete and final separation from Rome. Yet, it would be false to maintain that the loss of the Greek Church was, as it were, the price which the popes paid for their alliance with the new European family of nations.

The schism was long in preparation, and on the other hand it was not so inevitable that, even after Charles's imperial coronation, it could not have been prevented. It endured several centuries until the breach became really irreparable.

MONOTHELITISM

The quarrel over the Three Chapters in the sixth century had not really been an opposition between West and East, between the Latin and the Greek worlds. In fact, the pope finally even took the side of the Greeks against a part of the Latin Church. Likewise, the great theological dispute of the seventh century, that over Monothelitism, was not a struggle between Greeks and Latins, although it too originated in Byzantium.

Monothelitism was a new effort to meet the Monophysites halfway. The new formula declared: in Christ there are two natures, the divine and the human, but only one will (*thelema*). With this the Monophysites would, it was felt, be satisfied, for according to the new formula not the whole human nature, it is true, but nevertheless a part of it, and that the most important part, was blended with the divine nature, or rather was absorbed by it. On the other hand, the formula would be acceptable to the Catholics, for they could not maintain that in Christ there were two volitional principles in conflict with each other.

In all this there was no question of a mere subtlety, as those unacquainted with theology like to assert, for any dilution of the dogma of the hypostatic union immediately touches the foundations of the Catholic Faith. It is as though a mathematician would busy himself with a slight change in the Pythagorean theorem. There would at once result an entirely perverted mathematics in its entire field. Hence, the new theological formula immediately encountered sharp opposition from the Greek theologians, especially from Sophronius, soon to become patriarch of Jerusalem, and the monk Maximus Confessor, the outstanding Byzantine theologian of the seventh century, who was at the same time a zealous champion of the infallibility and primacy of the Roman bishop. On the Monothelite side were Sergius, patriarch of Constantinople from 610 to 638, and Emperor Heraclius (610–641). Sergius turned to Pope Honorius I (625–638), from whom he obtained a letter couched in general terms, which shows at the same time that the pope had no intention of allowing any alteration of Catholic dogma and that he failed to grasp the dangerous character of the real sense of the new formula.

Emperor Heraclius issued in 638 an imperial edict, the *Ecthesis,* in which the Monothelite formula was prescribed as the rule of Faith. Since the *Ecthesis* met with strong opposition, especially from the successors of Honorius, the next emperor, Constans II (641–668), withdrew it and published a new edict, the *Typos,* in which future dispute about one or two wills in Christ was forbidden. But since the question had now been raised, the teaching authority of the Church could not simply ignore it. Pope Martin I (649–653) expounded in a Roman synod the Catholic doctrine of the two wills as a dogma of Faith and excommunicated those who denied it. For this reason the emperor had him sent into exile at Cherson on the Black Sea, where he quickly died. He is honored as a martyr.

THE SIXTH ECUMENICAL COUNCIL

Peace was finally brought about by Emperor Constantine IV (668–685). At the sixth ecumenical council, held in Constantinople in 680, the proceeding at Chalcedon was repeated. As at that time the dogmatic constitution of Pope Leo the Great had been adopted, unchanged, by the council, so now the constitution of Pope Agatho (678–681) was accepted. At the same time the long dead authors of the Monothelite heresy, including the Patriarch Sergius and Pope Honorius, were visited with anathema.

The Roman See's approval of the anathema against Honorius is surprising at first sight. It was unjustified to the extent that Honorius had expounded no false teaching. Maximus Confessor had already made this quite clear. But apart from this, did there not lie in the confirmation of the anathema against Honorius an indirect denial of papal infallibility? When the succeeding popes at their accession made their profession of Faith, in which, as the formulae of the *Liber Diurnus* prove, they reckoned Honorius with the other heretics, were they not thereby expressing at least the possibility that a pope can err in matters of Faith?

On closer examination of the documents issued by Rome, however, it is seen that the popes were always careful not to mention Honorius as an actual heretic. In each instance Honorius is condemned only because, as Pope Leo II wrote in 682 to the Spanish bishops, he "did not immediately at the very start repress the heresy, as his apostolic office required, but promoted it by his negligence," or, as the formula in the *Liber Diurnus* puts it, because he "abetted (*fomentum impendit*) the wicked assertions." The Roman See constantly intended, during and after the Monothelite dispute, to uphold its claim never to have erred in matters of Faith. When at the Vatican Council, almost twelve hundred years later, there was discussion of the defining of papal infallibility and the opponents of the definition brought up the so-called "question of Honorius," all the source material was carefully investigated and the objections were refuted as untenable.

The next emperor, Justinian II (685–695 and 705–711), in 692 summoned to Constantinople a council which was to issue disciplinary canons as a supplement to the two preceding ecumenical councils of 553 and 680, since these had concerned themselves only with dogmatic questions. Hence, this council is known to history as the Quinisext, *i.e.*, the supplement to the fifth and sixth general councils, or as the Council *in Trullo*, because it was held in the same domed hall (*trullum*) of the imperial palace as the sixth general council. Among other things, the Quinisext renewed the twenty-eighth canon of Chalcedon concerning the jurisdiction of the Byzantine patriarch over the East, which had already at that time been rejected by the pope. Now too Pope Sergius I (687–701) declined to ratify it. An imperial embassy, which intended to force him by violence to give his signature, was, likewise by violence, sent home. This time no schism occurred, but, what was perhaps worse, persons gradually became accustomed to the situation that ecclesiastical questions relating to Rome and Constantinople should remain unsettled, that open disobedience should no longer be challenged.

THE QUARREL OVER IMAGES

Further confusion, greater than hitherto, was produced in the Byzantine Church in the eighth century by the quarrel over sacred images. Once again it was an emperor who began the controversy. In 726 Leo III the Isaurian decreed the removal of all pictorial representations of angels and saints from the churches, and four years later the order was extended also to images of Christ and of our Lady. What determined the emperor to this unusual proceeding, which recalls the ritual laws of Joseph II that were ridiculed by Frederick the Great, is hard to say. A consciousness of inferiority had a share in it, the anxiety of the cultivated *vis-à-vis* the piety of the common people, the desire for an aesthetic, purified, undemonstrative practice of religion without any condescension to the

173

mob—things which even today occasionally plague cultured Catholics. In addition, there may have been in Leo III special anxieties of inferiority with regard to the new neighbors, the Moslems, who despised every pictorial representation of sacred things as idolatry. The Greeks must not expose themselves to the charge of standing on a lower rung in religious matters than the Arabs.

The imperial decrees concerning images were at once enforced with the greatest harshness, but they produced a violent reaction throughout the Greek Church. It was especially the monks who led the opposition. Bloody martyrdoms ensued, and Saint Germanus, patriarch of Constantinople, was deposed. In the quarrel over images the Greek Church was at its best. The opposition was at the same time a demonstration against Caesaropapism. The theologians wrote ardently in favor of the veneration of images, particularly Saint John Damascene (✝749), a Doctor of the Church, who, to be sure, was safe from the clutches of the police, since the monastery of Saint Sabas near Jerusalem, where he lived, lay in the Moslem caliphate. The patriarchs of Alexandria, Antioch, and Jerusalem condemned iconoclasm, as did Pope Gregory III (731–741), after his predecessor, Gregory II, had admonished the emperor in vain. The emperor replied with reprisals against the Holy See. He withdrew the bishops of Illyricum, Sicily, and South Italy from the immediate jurisdiction of the pope, subjecting them to the patriarch of Constantinople, and at the same time confiscated the papal patrimonies in these lands.

Thus, the struggle was a war of the emperor against the pope, but not of the Greek Church against the Latin. Many Greek monks fled to Rome, where at this time a whole series of Greek monasteries came into existence.

The next emperor, Constantine V Copronymos (741–

775), continued the war against images. He even succeeded in convoking in 754 a great synod at Constantinople, which condemned the veneration of images. This passed itself off as the seventh ecumenical council, but of course it was not acknowledged by the rest of the Church. After the deaths of Constantine V and his successor, Leo IV (775–780), the latter's widow,[4] Irene, acting as regent, repealed the iconoclastic laws. The Patriarch Tarasius, with legates of Pope Hadrian I, held in Nicaea a new council in 787, the legitimate seventh general council, at which the Catholic teaching on the veneration of images was expounded.

In the ninth century Emperor Leo V the Armenian revived iconoclasm. He renewed the decrees of the pseudo-synod of 754 and deposed the Patriarch Nicephorus, who had opposed them. Once more there were deeds of violence and martyrdoms; once more the Greek theologians defended the Catholic teaching against the emperor, especially Theodore, the holy abbot of the monastery of Studion in Constantinople, who was exiled for his pains. Once more too it was an imperial widow and regent, Theodora, who in 843 ended the strife. As a memorial there was instituted on the first Sunday of Lent the "Great Feast of Orthodoxy," which is still celebrated in the Greek Church.

The struggle over images, in which the popes together with the largest part of the Greek Church had fought against the Caesaropapistic desires of the emperor, strengthened the unity of the Greeks with Rome on ecclesiastical grounds, even if the political differences between emperor and pope contributed to the popes' seeking an alliance with the Frankish kings. The fact that, nevertheless, soon after the final settlement of the quarrel over images there occurred the schism of

4 Irene was not the widow of Constantine V, as the German text states (p. 123), but of his son and successor, Leo IV. (Translator's note.)

the Greek Church from Rome had other and mostly personal causes. Indeed, this break had been prepared by much that had occurred in the preceding centuries, but it cannot be said that the breach followed of necessity. The history of the Byzantine Church displays no uniform line of a growing alienation from Rome. It is all the more tragic in that the one who brought about the break—Photius—was one of the most outstanding figures in the Byzantine Church, a man to whom patristic scholarship is especially indebted.

PHOTIUS [5]

In 858 Ignatius, patriarch of Constantinople, was deposed in consequence of court intrigues, and in his place the government appointed the scholarly and highly cultured Photius, a layman. Ignatius turned to Pope Nicholas I (858–867), who declared the election of Photius unlawful. Photius assembled a synod in 867 and in turn declared the pope deposed. He even asked the Frankish king-emperor, Louis II, to execute this sentence, not because he really hoped to induce the Western emperor to act against the pope, but in order to emphasize that he by no means acknowledged the primacy of the Roman bishop.

In 867 the Emperor Michael III, who had upheld Photius, was overthrown. His successor, Basil I, deposed Photius, restored Ignatius to the patriarchal see, and made peace with Rome. A council at Constantinople, the eighth ecumenical council of 869–870, condemned Photius and recognized Ignatius. Ignatius, however, proved himself not very grateful to the papacy when he incorporated into the Byzantine patri-

[5] The reader is referred to Francis Dvornik, *The Photian Schism: History and Legend* (Cambridge University Press: 1948); Emile Amann, *L'époque carolingienne*, Vol. VI of the Fliche-Martin *Histoire de l'église* (Paris: 1947), pp. 465-501; Philip Hughes *op. cit.*, II, 169-178. (Translator's note.)

archate the newly converted Bulgars, who had placed themselves directly under the pope.

When Ignatius died in 877, Photius was again named patriarch by the same Emperor Basil who had previously deposed him. He seems now to have been recognized by the pope. Once again he held a council, in which the eighth general council of 869 was rejected and all papal jurisdiction over the East was denied.[6] Pope John VIII (872–882) naturally declined to ratify this synod, but among the Greeks it was thenceforward regarded as the real eighth general council in place of the council of 869, which the Latins acknowledged. The later fortunes of Photius are veiled in obscurity. Whether he was formally excommunicated by the pope has not been established, but in 886 he was deposed by Emperor Leo VI and seems to have died soon after.

Superficially, the quarrel over Photius had not substantially changed the relations of the Byzantine Church to the universal Church, though to the other unsolved questions was now added that concerning the eighth general council. But in a sense people had become accustomed to these open wounds in the unity of the Church. On this side and on that, persons did not yet regard themselves as being in a state of schism. Nevertheless it can be said that from Photius the schism was in existence, if not formally, at least materially. The idea of the Church as held by the Byzantines had changed. Their doctrine of the five patriarchates—Rome, Constantinople, Alexandria, Antioch, and Jerusalem—as the integral com-

---

[6] Having received word of the favorable dispositions of Photius and of Emperor Basil I, Pope John VIII decided in the spring of 879 to recognize Photius and canceled all sentences of the council of 869; at the council of 879 Photius made the promises required by the Holy See and was solemnly recognized by the legates. John VIII accepted all that the council of 879 had done, and peace reigned between Old and New Rome. See Dvornik, *op. cit.*, pp. 159-201; Amann, *op. cit.*, pp. 493-497; Hughes, *op. cit.*, pp. 177 f. (Translator's note.)

ponents of the Church had moved so gradually into the foreground that no place remained any longer for the original constitution of the Church. If the Byzantine theologians until now had never denied in theory the jurisdictional primacy of the successor of Peter, if some, like Maximus Confessor and Theodore the Studite, had energetically defended it, they had grown increasingly more accustomed to consider the pope merely as the patriarch of the West. The real incongruity—that the three Oriental patriarchates existed in little more than name and that the patriarch of Constantinople now ruled over a comparatively small territory, while the so-called Roman patriarchate embraced all the rest of Christendom—did not concern them.

These ideas had already been disseminated before Photius. The really new element that he added to them, whereby he became, if not the actual, at least the spiritual author of the final schism, was an aversion, coupled with scorn, for Rome and all that was Latin, on which all later efforts for a *rapprochement* were to founder. The Church historian and later cardinal, Hergenröther, in his book on Photius that appeared a century ago and has influenced all present-day history, has endeavored to show in a fine chapter how this antipathy, gradually increasing to hatred, goes far back and really begins with the transfer of the imperial capital from Rome to Constantinople. On the other hand, however, it must be emphasized that in the rich theological literature of the Byzantine Church before Photius there is no trace of hatred or contempt of Rome. Persons had come into conflict with the pope; they had been dissatisfied with many of his procedures (in the fourth century the great champion of Church unity, Saint Basil, had sighed at times at the exaggerated bluntness of the Roman "coryphaeus"). But persons had not found it humiliating to submit again and again to the pope, to accept his doctrinal decisions, and to condemn their own heretical patriarchs from Macedonius to Sergius and Pyrrhus. With Photius the situation changed. He, the very learned layman, the greatest scholar of his time, introduced Greek national vanity into the ecclesiastical sphere. From now on the pope was no longer appealed to for help, as just recently in the quarrel over images; no longer did they say, "Peter has spoken through Leo," as once at Chalcedon. At most one could conclude agreements with the Roman patriarch as with a party to a contract.

CONSEQUENCES OF THE GREEK SCHISM

The loss of Byzantium was for the Catholic Church an extraordinarily momentous event, scarcely less important than the appearance of Islam. At the time of Photius, and all the more in the eleventh century when the schism formally became a permanent situation, this loss might have seemed relatively small, for the Byzantine Empire had greatly shrunk. Especially after it had lost its very heart, Asia Minor, to the Seljuks in the eleventh century, the emperor ruled only the depopulated Balkan peninsula and, of course, the great cosmopolitan capital, Constantinople. The number of the faithful who separated from Rome with the Greek patriarch was small in comparison with the wide European lands which remained loyal to Rome and were then beginning slowly to grow in population. But for the future the consequences were serious. In addition to the southern boundary created by Islam, the Church had now acquired also an eastern boundary, which extended northward more and more until finally it reached the Baltic and severed the entire Eurasian continent. The settling of the eastern plains on the other side of this frontier by the Russian peoples belongs, of course, to a much later time, and the fact that even today the Church has continued to be

179

excluded from this region has still other causes than the Byzantine schism. Nevertheless, the ground was then laid for it. The Islamic southern boundary has long ago been partly broken, partly outflanked, by the Church; she has a firm foothold in all of Africa and South Asia. But northeast Europe and all of northern Asia are still closed to her.

Islam and the Byzantine schism kept the Church confined to western and central Europe throughout the entire Middle Ages. From the standpoint of her universality this was a great defect. On the other hand, this centuries-long confinement contributed much to strengthen the Church inwardly. Upon the withdrawal of Byzantium the pope was, so to speak, the sole master of the house. Though inside this house there might still be as much quarreling and friction as before, there was no longer any center of agitation within the Church, as Byzantium had unquestionably been since the days of Arianism.

Without any doubt Byzantium, through its separation from the universal Church, lost incomparably more than did the Church herself. The imperishable values which Greek Christianity had created since the days of the apostles and which lay stored in the writings of the great Fathers were faithfully guarded by the Catholic Church as her property, from which she still draws. Even without Byzantium the Catholic Church has more and more become a world Church, developing consistently to her present flowering.

the RETURN fROM BARBARISM

T HE barbarism which had spread over Europe in the wake of the "migration of nations," or, more correctly, the dying out of nations, reached its lowest point at different periods in different regions. Whereas in Frankland, England, and Germany the climb upward had begun as early as the eighth century, though very slowly and with interruptions, Italy and Rome did not sink into the depths of barbarism until the tenth century.

Italy, so completely dependent on the Mediterranean, was the most affected in this area by the political and economic changes. Previously situated in the center of the world, where all cultural roads crossed, it now lay on the extreme border. Had not the popes been in Rome, constantly focusing upon themselves the eyes of all Christianity, Italy would hardly have played more of a role in the early Middle Ages than did Scandinavia. Just the same, the Holy See itself did not escape the effects of this cultural decay. Actually, the tenth century was the darkest in the entire history of the papacy. The popes no longer influenced European politics and exercised but little influence on the Church.

THE POPES AFTER CHARLES THE GREAT

In the epoch immediately following Charles the Great this decline of papal authority was not yet perceptible, partly because in the ninth century several unusually outstanding personalities occupied the See of Peter: Leo IV, Nicholas I, Hadrian II, and John VIII.

Leo IV (847–855) had before all else to arrange a defense against the Saracens. In 849 he won an important naval victory over the Arabs off Ostia. He was then able to build for Rome at Città Vecchia a new fortified harbor, which he called Leopolis. In 846 the Saracens had extended their raids to Rome and had even plundered the basilicas of the apostles. Leo surrounded the area of the Vatican with a wall, so that it was included within the circuit of Rome as the Leonine City.

Nicholas I (858–867), hailed by admiring contemporaries as another Elias, brought several unruly bishops to obedience, among them the archbishop of Ravenna and the proud but very capable Hincmar of Reims. He excommunicated the Frankish King Lothar II for refusing to dismiss his concubine, Waldrada. He intervened in the disorders of the Byzantine Church when he entered the lists against Photius in favor of the banished patriarch, Ignatius. To the Bulgars, who had established themselves south of the lower Danube and had accepted Christianity, he sent missionaries and doctrinal instructions which are valuable for the history of theology.

Hadrian II (867–872) arranged for the eighth ecumenical council at Constantinople in 869 at which Ignatius was reinstated, but he could not prevent Ignatius from alienating the Bulgars from Rome and drawing them toward Constantinople. On the other hand, he named Saint Methodius, who had labored originally by order of the Byzantine emperor as missionary among the Slavs, his legate and made him archbishop of Sirmium (Mitrovitza on the Save). Methodius and his brother Cyril were from Thessalonica. After some temporary activity among the Turkish Khazars of the Crimea, they went in 863 to Moravia. They celebrated the liturgy in the Slavonic tongue, for which they invented a special script, the Glagolithic. Nicholas I summoned them to Rome for a report, and there Cyril died. Hadrian II sent Methodius back to Moravia, approved the Slavonic liturgy, and protected him against the hostility of the Bavarian bishops of Regensburg and Passau, who had already undertaken missionary work in Bohemia and Moravia and hence claimed previous rights to those regions. The Slavonic liturgy later disappeared in Bohemia and Moravia, whereas it took root among the Bulgars and the Serbs, and then among the Russians.

John VIII (872–882) recognized Photius as patriarch after the death of Ignatius, but rejected [1] the council of 879 with its anti-Roman decrees of Photian inspiration. He too had Saint Methodius come to Rome and defended him against persecution on the part of the Bavarians. John VIII was the last great pope of this period. After him began for the papacy that dark epoch, the *saeculum obscurum*, the dark century, or the iron century, as the Italian historians call it; but "iron" does not mean that we are here concerned with an age of warlike deeds or of heroism. It was a time of trivial circumstances, in which only dwarfs produced their mischief.

THE DARK CENTURY OF THE PAPACY

To the great misfortune of the popes of this age, the Empire, which according to its very inspiration was supposed to protect and aid the papacy in case of need, collapsed. The Empire of Charles the Great was divided among his numerous descendants and thereby lost its vigor. The imperial crown passed from one to another of these princes. With Charles the Fat, who in 887 was deposed by the magnates, Charlemagne's great political structure broke up into several weak kingdoms.[2]

[1] See *supra*, p. 177, footnote 6. (Translator's note.)

[2] The year 887 marks the total collapse of the already tottering Carolingian Empire,

Pope Formosus (891–896) crowned as emperor Guido, duke of Spoleto, who on his mother's side was a great-grandson of Louis the Pious. Against him and his son, Lambert of Spoleto, the crown was claimed by Arnulf, king of Germany, also a great-grandson of Louis the Pious but of illegitimate birth. Formosus gave the imperial crown to Arnulf too in 896.[3] From then on there prevailed in Rome ceaseless civil war between Spoletans and anti-Spoletans, between opponents and adherents of Pope Formosus, long after Formosus had died. In all this the imperial idea completely disappeared. Now there remained only the feuds of the Roman families, who sought to impose their own members as popes and to overthrow the popes set up by other families. The anarchy was so great that we know only the names of some of these popes, who often were in office for only a few weeks or days, and we cannot always be sure whether they were legitimate popes.

One reason for this is, of course, the paucity of sources. There were no orderly records kept; there was no historical writing. One can safely doubt whether all these popes could read and write. The sole narrative source is Liutprand of Cremona, who resided away from Rome; he was a dreary gossip, who related only a *chronique scandaleuse* and nothing of real importance.

A rather credibly attested tale, which illustrates the barbarism of the time, relates that Pope Stephen VII disinterred

but the Carolingian dynasty did not come to an end, even in the legitimate line. The dynasty continued to reign in East Frankland until 911, in the person of the illegitimate Arnulf and of his son, Louis the Child. For the moment it lost the West Frankish throne to Eudes, count of Paris, but the legitimate branch of the Carolingians again held it from 898 to 922 and from 936 to 987. (Translator's note.)

[3] Formosus was not forced to crown Arnulf, as the German text declares (p. 129); he invited the king to Rome, in the hope of thereby shaking off the oppressive control exercised by Guy of Spoleto and his son, Lambert. See Emile Amann and Auguste Dumas, *L'église au pouvoir des laïques (888-1057)*, Vol. VII of the Fliche-Martin *Histoire de l'église* (Paris: 1943), pp. 18-24. (Translator's note.)

the corpse of Formosus, held a trial over it, and then had it cast into the Tiber. He was himself soon after strangled in prison.

THE COUNTS OF TUSCULUM

Among the Roman families that were quarreling over the papacy, that of the counts of Tusculum (Frascati) acquired a particular importance. They were the ancestors of the still existing princely family of Colonna. Alberic II, count of Tusculum, was Prince of Rome, under the title *Princeps et Senator*, from 932 till his death in 954. His brother was Pope John XI (931–936). Though a child of his barbarous age, Alberic ruled well. After his brother's death he appointed an excellent Benedictine pope as Leo VII (936–939), who summoned the great Abbot Odo of Cluny to Rome and with him undertook a reform of the monasteries. Alberic presented Odo with the monastery of Saints Alexius and Boniface on the Aventine, whence missionaries were soon dispatched to the northern Slavs. The pope appointed the archbishop of Mainz his vicar for Germany. The relations of the papacy with the churches abroad, almost extinct since the time of Formosus, were now resumed. Pope Agapitus II (946–955) arranged with the German King Otto I for the ecclesiastical organization of Saxony.

Before his death Alberic recommended that his son Octavian be elected pope, for in the existing circumstances it was better that the spiritual and the temporal power in Rome be united in one hand. It was unfortunate, however, that Octavian, who styled himself John XII (955–964), was only eighteen at his election and soon showed himself to be utterly devoid of seriousness. He took a momentous step when he called the German King Otto I to his aid against his oppressor, Berengar of Ivrea, who had set himself up as king of Italy. Otto came to Rome in 962, and John XII crowned him

185

emperor. Otto's last predecessors had been emperors only in name, and since 915 no imperial coronation had taken place. Now the papacy again had a real protector, and Otto and his successors of the Saxon and Salian dynasties were not only extraordinarily capable, but likewise deeply religious men who were mindful of the welfare of the Church. The papacy's ability to work its slow way upward out of the abyss of the tenth century was in great part due to these rulers, whose particular activity was often, it is true, quite arbitrary.

At first, of course, the confusion became still worse. Scarcely had Otto turned his back, when the frivolous John XII began to conspire against him. Otto returned to Rome, the pope fled, and the emperor declared him deposed. Otto had a certain Leo VIII elected pope. Hardly had the emperor again departed before the Romans expelled his pope and called back John XII, who took bloody vengeance on his enemies, but soon died. He was one of the most unworthy of the popes, even in his private life. The Romans chose in his place Benedict V, who was nicknamed *Grammaticus*, "the educated," a rarity at that time. But the emperor once more returned, again installed his Leo VIII, and exiled Benedict to Hamburg, where he died in the reputation of sanctity.

THE CRESCENTII

On the death of Leo VIII, which occurred soon after, the Crescentii, who were then the leading family in Rome, set up John XIII (965–972) as pope. He supported Otto and crowned his son, Otto II, as emperor. Then occurred new scandals. The Crescentii had Benedict VI (973–974) murdered and named Boniface VII pope.[4] The usurper, who had

---

[4] Father Hertling calls the usurper Boniface VI and remarks, "Die Päpste mit der Ziffer VI haben fast stets Unheil angerichtet" (p. 130). But the real Boniface VI reigned for a few days in 896, according to the revised papal list of Monsignor Angelo Mercati

had a share in the death of his predecessor, fled with the papal treasure to Constantinople on the approach of Otto II. He returned as soon as the emperor had withdrawn, and had John XIV, a worthy man who had been elected in the meantime, shut up and starved in the Castel Sant' Angelo, and then suddenly died. His corpse was hung up by the furious Romans before the Lateran on the statue of Marcus Aurelius, which now stands on the square before the Capitol. His successor, John XV (985–996), was expelled by the Crescentii, but was brought back to Rome by the widow of Otto II, the Empress Theophano, a Byzantine princess. From then on a more peaceful period ensued for the papacy.

No present-day yardstick can be applied to these shocking scandals. Today any such tottering of the Holy See would lead to scarcely conceivable consequences for the universal Church. But at that time there were no enemies of the Church, no movements for revolt. On the other hand, one is not to suppose that the sad events in Rome left the rest of Christendom indifferent. At a synod at Reims in 991 a bishop criticized the Roman state of affairs, especially of course the crime of Boniface VII that had happened almost twenty years previously, and exclaimed:

> A pope who possesses no charity, but is merely swollen with knowledge, would be anti-Christ. But if he has neither charity nor knowledge, he stands as an idol in the temple of God. How are we to obtain guidance from a stone block?

GERMANY UNDER THE SAXON EMPERORS

The German dynasty that wore the imperial crown from 962 was a family of saints. Otto I's mother, Mathilda, his wife,

---

(*Annuario Pontificio*, 1947). The usurper of 974 called himself Boniface VII; he is now regarded as an anti-pope, both in 974 and again in 984-985. (Translator's note.)

Adelaide, and his brother, Bruno, archbishop of Cologne, are honored as saints. His great-nephew and third successor was the Emperor Saint Henry, husband of Saint Cunegunda. Henry's sister, Saint Gisela, married Saint Stephen, king of Hungary, and was the mother of Saint Emeric.

The condition of the Church in Germany reflected the example of the dynasty. Saint Bruno, brother of Otto I, was not only archbishop of Cologne but at the same time duke of Lorraine, and there he fostered the Benedictine monastic reform originating in Gorze near Metz. Friend and adviser of Otto I was Saint Ulric, bishop of Augsburg († 973). He aided Otto in defeating the Hungarians at the battle of the Lechfeld in 955, which put an end to their depredations in South Germany.

Ulric was educated in the monastery of Sankt Gallen, which was then a center of sacred and profane learning. For a time the prior at Sankt Gallen was Blessed Notker, later bishop of Liége (972–1008), a nephew of Otto I. Another Notker, the celebrated and saintly Labeo, spent his entire life as a teacher at Sankt Gallen (†1022). He translated Latin classics into German and played an important role in the formation of the German literary tongue.

A friend of Ulric of Augsburg was Saint Conrad, who is venerated as the patron of the diocese of Freiburg. He was bishop of Constance from 934 to 975 and, among other things, founded the Benedictine monastery of Weingarten. His second successor, Saint Gebhard of Constance (980–995), established the abbey of Petershausen.

A great personality, both as bishop and as statesman, was Willigis, archbishop of Mainz, chancellor and regent of the Empire following the deaths of Otto II and Otto III. He too is honored as a saint. From his circle came Burchard, bishop of Worms (✝1025), whose collection of decretals plays an important part in the history of Canon Law.

In Bavaria at this period there labored Saint Wolfgang, bishop of Regensburg (972–994), formerly a Benedictine of Einsiedeln. He unselfishly co-operated in the founding of the see of Prague in 973, which was carved from his territory. In Bohemia paganism had long maintained itself, and in 935 the anti-Christian faction had assassinated Duke Wenceslas. From the erection of the see of Prague by Duke Boleslas II, Bohemia was definitely Catholic. As second bishop of Prague, Willigis of Mainz, to whose province the diocese belonged, consecrated the Czech Vojtjech, or Adalbert, who however soon laid aside his rank and joined the Benedictines at Sant' Alessio in Rome. At the command of the pope he had to return to Prague in 992. He introduced the Benedictines into Bohemia and founded the abbey of Brevnow. Finally, he went as missionary to the heathen Prussians and died a martyr at Tenkitten near the later Königsberg. The same fate befell Bruno of Querfurt, like Adalbert a personal friend of Otto III. In 1004 Bruno had been consecrated a missionary bishop and in 1008 he and eighteen companions were murdered at Braunsberg.

In the East March, governed since 975 by the Babenberg ducal line, Pilgrim, bishop of Passau (971–991), displayed great activity. He held synods at Lorch near Linz and at Mautern and Mistelbach near Vienna, and in 984 founded a community of canons at Melk, which later adopted the Benedictine Rule.

In the early eleventh century lived two saintly bishops of Hildesheim, Bernward (✝1022) and Godehard (✝1038), and the friend of Emperor Henry II, Poppo, an ascetic of Flemish origin, who was abbot of Stavelot from 1020 and was entrusted with the supervision of the Benedictine monasteries, such as Echternach, Hersfeld, and Sankt Gallen, where he was active in the spirit of the Cluniac reform. To the north another friend of Henry II was laboring at the same time, Meginwerk or Meinwerk (✝1036), consecrated bishop of Paderborn by Willigis in 1009. He brought his hitherto poor and insignificant diocese to a flourishing state, built the cathedral, and in 1015 founded the monastery of Abdinghof, which he colonized with Benedictines from Cluny.

This was the epoch of the earliest Romanesque architecture in Germany, which, while heavy, is elegant and full of the joy of living and of piety, evocative of spring or childhood. Of the little that still remains today, the canonical church of Gernrode dates from the tenth century, as does the castle church of Quedlinburg, where Henry I, the father of Otto I, was buried. Of Meinwerk's constructions in Paderborn the charming Bartholomew chapel is preserved; of those of Bernward of Hildesheim, who himself was an artist, the splendid Saint Michael's church. In the south, too, there are extant church edifices from this time, such as the canonical church of Moosburg near Freising and the monastic church of Reichenau near Constance, which of course contains still older elements. Of the great cathedrals which were begun around 1000, in Worms, in Mainz by Willigis, in Bamberg by Henry II, nothing is left, for their proportions no longer satisfied the succeeding generation, which put gigantic imperial cathedrals in their place.

CLUNY

One might compare the history of the Church to a symphony which is constructed as a fugue: at specified moments new parts, new instruments, are added, which seem for an interval to have sole command until they blend with the constantly swelling general choir. Such an instrument, which at first resounded as in a desert and in time filled the whole contemporary world, was the monastery of Cluny.

Cluny lies—or lay, for now scarcely any remains are left of its gigantic Romanesque basilica, which was destroyed in the French Revolution—eighty kilometers north of Lyon, not very far from Luxeuil and from the spots where later Cîteaux and then Prémontré were founded. It is noteworthy that from this region proceeded the great monastic impulses; in the Middle Ages it lay, so to speak, in the heart of Europe. But the monks were certainly not interested in utilizing commercial routes. They were seeking solitude, and they established their monasteries away from the great highways of the world.

Cluny was founded in 910 by Duke William of Aquitaine. According to the foundation charter, the new monastery was to be subject to no secular or spiritual lord, but only to the Holy See, and in token of this it was to pay a truly mediaeval feudal tax of five gold pieces every fifth year for the maintenance of the lamps that burned before the tombs of the apostles in Rome. For a monastery to be placed immediately under the Holy See was nothing new, and yet in this circumstance lay one of the germs of Cluny's future greatness, one of the points of its later program. A glance at the prevailing political and social system will clarify the situation.

FEUDALISM

The old Roman Empire had been a state managed by officials. The power of the emperor rested on his uniting the authority of the highest officials in his own hands. He was commander-in-chief of the army—that is what was meant by *imperator*—supreme judge, head of the civil administration and of finances. The mediaeval ruler was not an official, but a landlord. The land, the soil, belonged to the king. He, however, did not exploit it, but conferred it as benefices, or fiefs, on his vassals, who in return had to give him service, primarily in war. The vassal could in turn confer parts of his benefice and thereby acquire his own vassals. These vassalage relationships could be extremely loose. Hence, we have in the Middle Ages a quite different idea of the state, or, more correctly, there were actually no states in the Middle Ages but rather a multiplicity of great and small landlords, who stood in the most varied, constantly changing, and often even non-existing juridical relationships to one another. For this reason the political maps of the Middle Ages are often misleading when they represent large territories with definite colors as though we could say at any given moment whether "Italy" or "Burgundy" or "Aquitaine" belonged to "Germany" or to "France." Feudal relationships constantly criss-crossed. A prince might be for a specified piece of land the vassal of another prince, who perhaps for his part held other estates from him in fief. Not only land but rights, tolls, and rents were conferred as fiefs.

In the ancient hierarchical state there lay for the Church the danger of being incorporated into the officialdom, so that the bishops would become state functionaries. The Byzantine Church succumbed to this danger. In the Western Middle Ages this danger did not exist, but there was another—that the Church would be sucked into the whirlpool of feudalism, that the bishops, abbots, and parish priests would become the vassals of great or lesser princes.

PROPRIETARY CHURCHES

The feudal lord who built a church on his land gave it as a benefice to a priest, who thereby became his vassal. The number of proprietary churches, as they were called, little by little greatly surpassed the number of churches which stood in no feudal relationship. The same thing happened to monasteries. The founder gave his proprietary monastery as a fief to the abbot, and of course to each succeeding abbot. But since he always remained the feudal lord, he could also give a part of the benefice to someone else who did not even belong to the monastery. Thus there were often richly endowed monasteries which had scarcely the means of livelihood, because a secular priest or even a lay person drew the greatest part of the revenues in the capacity of secular abbot.

Similarly, the princes regarded themselves as feudal lords of the bishops, especially in Germany, where most of the bishoprics had been founded by the kings and had been endowed with property.

So long as the feudal lord was conscientiously mindful of the interests of the Church and of the care of souls, no evil consequences of this system were apparent. On the contrary, the proprietary church and the proprietary monastery found in their feudal lord a protector against encroachments. But, all things considered, the system was decidedly risky. It could too easily happen that entirely unsuitable persons acquired possession of ecclesiastical jurisdiction, merely because they had rendered services to the prince or because the prince was expecting services of them. This danger threatened the monasteries especially. A monastery is an uncommonly sensitive instrument. An unsuitable abbot can in a short time ruin the most flourishing one. In fact, in the later Carolingian period all of Europe was full of monasteries, but under the pressure of the proprietary system, they attained to no real flowering.

THE RISE OF CLUNY

In these circumstances it was of especial importance that Cluny from the very beginning was explicitly founded not as a proprietary monastery but as a wholly ecclesiastical institution. The emancipation of the Church from the mediaeval

193

feudal system became in time one of the chief points in Cluny's program. The monastery became a symbol when it placed itself under the exclusive protection of the Holy See. To Cluny's ultramontanism, strong from the beginning, was logically added before long the struggle for the freedom of the papacy from the secular power. One must remember that the pope under whom Cluny placed itself in its foundation charter was Sergius III. For the Church it was the darkest period of the dark century, when the counts of Tusculum were ruling Rome and were treating the Holy See itself as a proprietary Church.

The first abbot of Cluny was Berno, who at once made it a model monastery. Already under the second abbot, Odo (926–942), its reputation spread far beyond the boundaries of France. There followed Aymard (942–954), who regulated the economic situation of the monastery, Majolus (954–994), and then two great men, who together ruled for more than a century, Odilo (994–1049) and Hugh (1049–1109); the last named definitively codified the rules and customs of Cluny. The unfortunate Abbot Pons (1109–1122), who was deposed and excommunicated, was succeeded, after the brief reign of Hugh II, by another great man, Peter the Venerable (1122–1156), whose abbacy marks the zenith of Cluny's power and external brilliance.

New monasteries were founded from Cluny and a number of already existing monasteries were given to it. In the time of Odo the abbot of Cluny ruled more than sixty-five monasteries. The annexed monasteries stood in dependence on Cluny, usually in the sense that they were governed by a prior named by the abbot of Cluny. Their novices were formed at Cluny. At the same time there were monasteries which, without entering into a real union with Cluny, accepted the Cluniac customs and introduced reform, partly with the aid of monks from Cluny. Some of these constituted, with the reformed monasteries dependent on them, unions which were scarcely less important than Cluny itself, such as Aurillac in the Auvergne, Gorze in Lorraine, Hirsau in the Schwarzwald of Württemberg, and Cava in South Italy. The Hirsau reform spread extensively in Germany as far as Thuringia. The ruins of the church of Paulinzella near Rudolstadt still bear witness to the Hirsau school of architecture, which created the purest works of German Romanesque in the twelfth century. Cava, near Salerno, which is still in existence, was founded in 1011 by the Lombard Alferius, who had become a monk at Cluny under Odilo. In the twelfth century there were subject to the abbot of Cava throughout South Italy, Sicily, and Palestine twenty-nine abbeys, ninety priories, and 340 churches, with a total of 5,000 monks. The Cluniac reform was introduced into Spain by King Alfonso VI [5] of Asturias and Castile, into England by William the Conqueror.

The reasons for the growth of Cluny and the tremendous influence which it exercised over the entire Church by virtue of its reforms are to be found especially in the personality and the unusually long reigns of the abbots. In the two and one-half centuries from its foundation till the death of Peter the Venerable Cluny had eight [6] abbots, whereas in the same space of time there were fifty-two popes. Seven of these eight abbots are honored as saints. Through them Cluny and its entire federation acquired continuity, solidity, and a definite goal. This orientation toward a fixed aim does not mean that

[5] The Cluniac observance was introduced into Catalonia in 962, into Aragón in 1025, into Castile and León in 1032; it was King Alfonso VI (1065-1109), however, who especially encouraged its spread in Spain. See Justo Pérez de Urbel, "The Benedictines in Spain," *The American Benedictine Review*, VI (1955), 191-195. (Translator's note.)

[6] In reality Cluny had nine abbots during this period of brilliance, but the tenure of Hugh II was so brief that he is frequently overlooked. (Translator's note.)

Cluny indulged in "power politics" or set out on a career of conquest. The Cluniacs wanted only to be monks, strict monks. But Cluny gradually embraced so large a part of the Church that it almost became the Church.

At Cluny there was an extraordinary amount of praying, almost too much, and no time was left for scholarly studies. The Cistercians later upbraided the Cluniacs with merely praying and not working. But they really prayed, and the people had confidence in their prayer. Prayer for the dead, which they especially fostered, and their generosity to the poor were the sources of their wealth. The faithful gave gladly and handsomely, because they knew that Cluny forgot neither their dead nor the poor. In 998 Odilo introduced the Commemoration of All Souls as a special feast, which in 1030 was fixed on November 2, when it is still observed by the entire Church.

THE HERMITS

Besides the Cluniacs, and in part under their influence, there arose early in the eleventh century still another monastic movement, likewise based on the Benedictine Rule—the congregations of hermits. Their center was North Italy.

The most complete possible separation from the world had always been the monastic ideal since the days of the Egyptian monks. However, experience had taught that this ideal was not realized by mere solitude, far from any community and independent of any obedience. The hermit of the popular legends, the forest dweller, was not a recognized monastic type. But it was readily admitted that one or even several could withdraw into a cell near the church of the monastery, where they would live under the obedience of the monastery and from where they would take part in divine worship, while for the rest they would live in voluntary confinement. Such

196

cells of retirement existed beside many monasteries, and they were usually inhabited.

Saint Wiborada was such a recluse near the monastery of Sankt Gallen. Through her cell window she instructed in the spiritual life the young Saint Ulric, the later great bishop of Augsburg. In 926 she was murdered in her cell by the Magyars. Another famous recluse was Simon, an Armenian Basilian monk, who, after long wanderings as a pilgrim, had himself inclosed at the monastery of Polirone near Mantua and died in 1016. Another Simon, a Greek from Syracuse, lived as a recluse in the Porta Nigra at Trier; he died in 1035.

In the ninth century the priest Grimlach at Reims had composed a Rule for recluses, who for the most part lived in their cells, not alone, but in groups of two or three. In it he described exactly how the cells were to be constructed, with a window into the church and a speaking grill toward the outside, as well as a small garden and even a bathroom.

The idea of establishing an entire monastery of recluses, or a hermit colony, stems from Saint Romuald. Romuald had constantly sought the most strenuous form of life, but only when, in a Cluniac monastery in the Pyrenees, he had learned to know the supreme value of order and discipline did he find his ideal. From 992 he founded his hermit colonies at Fonte Avellana, Pomposa, and Pereum near Ravenna. Emperor Otto III, who highly revered him and under his guidance undertook austere penitential works, induced him to accept the abbacy of Sant' Apollinare in Classe, but he laid down the dignity and in 1012 founded near Arrezo a colony called Camaldoli, from which the entire congregation later received the name of Camaldolese. Camaldoli consists of two inclosures: the monastery buildings for the administration and for the forming of the novices, and, some distance away, the hermit village, surrounded by high walls. Each monk has his hut with work-shop and garden. In the center stands the church.

After Romuald's death in 1027 other hermitages arose—Vallombrosa near Florence, Camaldoli near Naples. And the Carthusians, who originated toward the end of the eleventh century, are a continuation of the form of life introduced by Romuald, even though they do not have the Rule of Saint Benedict as their basis.

The Camaldolese monasteries formed only a loose federation, but all placed themselves under the special protection of the Holy See. Because of their extraordinarily austere manner of life they were never very numerous, but they contributed much to the religious revival of the eleventh century. From them proceeded Peter Damiani, one of the chief fighters for reform.

What the Camaldolese as well as the Cluniacs especially brought about was the example of deep religious earnestness. Earnestness and a consciousness of responsibility were sadly lacking in too many secular lords, who regarded their bishops, abbots, and priests almost as servants. Earnestness and a consciousness of responsibility were gravely lacking in the wild Rome of the tenth century, even in the popes themselves. Of course, salvation could not come from the silent example of the monks by itself. Especially in Rome there was need of a strong hand which would take vigorous action. To perform this the emperors were called upon.

THE NEW LINE OF POPES UNDER IMPERIAL INFLUENCE

Otto I and his son, Otto II, who died far too young, had interfered at Rome with the best of intentions but without achieving real success. Strangely enough, the third Otto, who personally did not possess the characteristics of a strong man, was more successful because of his youthfulness, since he was able to profit by the steadily mounting respect acquired for the imperial crown by his father and grandfather.

GREGORY V AND SILVESTER II

When John XV died in 996, Otto III was already on his way to Rome; the Romans asked him to appoint the new pope. Otto was then only sixteen. Deeply religious and educated by the best teachers of the day, he was also an enthusiastic idealist, who dreamed of the glory of the old Roman Empire. He named as pope his court chaplain and relative, Bruno, who was himself only twenty-four and as much an idealist as the emperor. Bruno was elected pope as Gregory V, but in 999 he died after a beginning full of great prospects. Thereupon Otto III appointed his former teacher, Gerbert, as pope. Gerbert was a Frenchman, archbishop of Reims and later of Ravenna, so highly regarded for his learning that popular legend made him a magician. Gerbert, who styled himself Silvester II, was also an idealist like Gregory V, but he was a mature man. For the first time in many years the Church again had a pope who watched over Christendom from a lofty tower. Silvester established the hierarchy for the Poles, who were now almost entirely Christian, with Gniezno as the metropolitan see, and for the Hungarians with Gran as the metropolitan. He conferred the royal title on Saint Stephen, hitherto only the duke of the Hungarians.

NEW DOMINATION OF THE TUSCULAN HOUSE

After the premature death of Otto III in 1002, strife again broke out in Rome between the counts of Tusculum and the Crescentii. The Crescentii had already caused disturbances under Gregory V. Now again they set up an anti-pope, but the new emperor, Henry II, secured the rights of the legitimate pope, Benedict VIII (1012–1024), of the Tusculan family.

Benedict VIII supported Pisa and Genoa in their naval victory over the Saracens off Luna, as a result of which Sardinia was taken from the Moslems. In 1020 the pope went to Germany and consecrated the cathedral of Bamberg, built by Henry II. Then he and the emperor together presided over a synod at Pavia, in which the celibacy of the clergy was insisted upon. Furthermore, decrees were also issued against simony, the giving of consecration for money or other payments. Under the term "simony" were gradually included all abuses which resulted from the system of proprietary churches and in general from the feudal dependence of the Church, abuses which finally led to the investiture quarrel.

The counts of Tusculum were again, as a century earlier, the masters of Rome. Alberic, brother of Benedict VIII, ruled the Papal State as consul. On Benedict's death a third brother became Pope John XIX.[7] He crowned Conrad II emperor in the presence of King Rudolf III of Burgundy and King Cnut of Denmark and England. For the rest, the pope cared most of all for money. The Byzantine Emperor Basil II offered him a bribe to acknowledge the patriarch of Constantinople's title of "ecumenical patriarch," which earlier popes had always denied. John XIX was only too willing, but could not withstand the indignation of the Cluniacs. After his death in 1033 the Tusculan house, which wanted at any cost to fill the Holy See with one of its own, made Alberic's thirteen-year-old son, Theophylact, pope. The Romans eventually expelled the worthless youth, who was known as Benedict IX, but Emperor Conrad II brought him back, for he was actually the legitimate pope. Once again he was driven out, and once again he returned. Finally, in an effort to put an end to the scandal, the wealthy archpriest of San Giovanni in Porta Latina, John

[7] Monsignor Mercati's papal list calls this pope John XIX, whereas Father Hertling calls him John XX (p. 139). (Translator's note.)

Gratian, promised him a considerable pension if he would retire. The condition was accepted by Benedict, against whom an anti-pope, Silvester III, had already been set up by another faction.

INTERFERENCE OF HENRY III

John Gratian had acted with the best of intentions, but it was very unwise that he now accepted election as pope. Gregory VI, as he called himself, possessed all the requisite qualifications. His accession was enthusiastically hailed by sincere churchmen, such as Peter Damiani. But since now the struggle against simony, the buying and selling of ecclesiastical office, formed a chief point in the reform program, it was at least extremely embarrassing and awkward that the pope had given his predecessor money to induce him to abdicate. Besides, Benedict IX soon regretted his retirement. He again came forth as pope, and the anti-pope, Silvester III, was also to be reckoned with. In this hopeless situation only the emperor could be of assistance, and hence Henry III, Conrad's successor, was called to Italy. He held a synod at Sutri, north of Rome. Benedict IX, who had already abdicated, and Silvester III, who had never been lawful pope, were deposed outright, and Gregory VI consented to his own deposition. In order that no new schism might result, the emperor took him to Germany. He was accompanied by a young Roman cleric, Hildebrand, who was soon to play a great role in the Church. Gregory VI died at Cologne in 1047.

The emperor stood forth as the sole authority from whom order could be expected, and all agreed that he should simply designate the next popes. His first two choices, Clement II, formerly bishop of Bamberg, and Damasus II, bishop of Brixen, both of them excellent men, died very soon after their accession. Henry III next named as pope the bishop of

Toul, an Alsatian. But Leo IX insisted on a regular election at Rome. On his way there he took with him the young Hildebrand, who after Gregory VI's death had become a monk. Hildebrand served him and the succeeding popes in various positions of responsibility until his own election as pope, and became so much the very soul of the reform that it is correct to refer to this period as the Age of Hildebrand. Leo IX held several synods, not only at Rome but at Pavia, Reims, Mainz, and elsewhere. In them the reform program received its complete formulation: the struggle against simony and against the conferring of ecclesiastical offices by laymen and the enforcing of clerical celibacy. In 1052 Leo IX turned his attention to the growing power of the Normans in South Italy.

THE NORTHMEN

The Northmen are the ancestors of the modern Danes and Norwegians. Their Viking expeditions, whereby they at first raided England and then, from the ninth century, France, were nothing else but piratical invasions. In 845 they destroyed Hamburg, so that the see was transferred to Bremen. Around 860 they appeared in the Mediterranean and plundered in the territory of Pisa. The cultural decline in France under the later Carolingians is closely connected with the continued damage wrought by the Northmen. In the same ninth century Northmen under Rurik established the Grand Principality of Novgorod on Lake Ilmen, the Varangian state, one of the nuclei of the later Russian Empire. They colonized the Faroes, Iceland, and Greenland. One group of this individualistic people accepted from the French king, Charles the Simple (893–923), territory in northern France early in the tenth century, and from them this district was called Normandy. There they became Catholics. The first duke of Normandy, Rollo or Robert, was baptized in 912, around the same time that Cluny was founded. Though from now on they were civilized Christians, they were still adventurers. From 1017 the Norman Rainulf was employed as a mercenary captain by various princes in South Italy and in 1030 he received from the Byzantines in Naples the little county of Aversa. Soon after, in 1035, the Hauteville brothers, William, Drogo, and Humphrey, entered the service of the Lombard prince of Salerno, Guaimar IV. For a time William also fought for the Byzantines, but fell out with them because he received no pay, and in 1042 made himself independent as duke of Apulia. In 1046 he was joined from Normandy by his younger brother, Robert, surnamed Guiscard, the Sly Fox, who from that time became the soul of the Norman enterprises. In 1047 they took Benevento.

Leo IX regarded the restless Normans with suspicion and finally decided to fight against them. With his tiny army he was taken prisoner by the Normans, who themselves numbered only a few hundred men. As good Christians the Normans treated their exalted captive so honorably that he accepted friendship with them. They even ceded to him Benevento, which henceforth belonged as an enclave to the Papal State.

THE BYZANTINE SCHISM

In the same year, 1053, the patriarch of Constantinople, Michael Caerularius, made an unexpected attack on the Latins. He had the Latin churches and monasteries in Constantinople closed and circulated bitter attacks against the whole Latin Church. Leo IX sent as legates to Byzantium Humbert, bishop of Silva Candida, and Frederick of Lorraine.[8] The

8 The German text reads: "Leo IX. schickte . . . nach Byzanz . . . den Abt von Montecassino, Stephan von Lothringen" (p. 141). Actually it was Frederick of Lorraine who formed part of the embassy to Constantinople in 1054; he did not become abbot of Montecassino and cardinal until 1057. See Amann and Dumas, op. cit., pp. 109 f. (Translator's note.)

emperor received them cordially, but the patriarch denied them his communion. Hence they laid a bull of excommunication on the altar of Hagia Sophia and departed. At the time this action produced only a slight impression, at least in the West. Persons had long been accustomed to such conflicts with the Byzantine patriarch. No one thought that this time more than two centuries would pass before another union would be achieved. And when it finally came, the union was but temporary.

Leo IX died in 1054. He was succeeded by Gebhard, bishop of Eichstätt, as Victor II. With the emperor attending, the new pope held a synod at Florence, once more against simony and the violators of celibacy. In France he had similar synods held by Hildebrand. During his pontificate the Emperor Henry III, not yet forty years old, died. On his deathbed he designated the pope as imperial vicar. At Aachen Victor II crowned Henry IV, who was still a minor, as king of Germany.

Henry III had been an unusually well-endowed prince of broad outlook, serious and devout in his personal life. The Church was deeply indebted to him. He restored to the papacy its world position. In him care for the Church was not synonymous with the mastery of Italy, as would be the case with his successors. His successors, especially the Hohenstaufen, destroyed the Empire by their policy of aggrandizement within Italy. Henry III was far removed from such a program. On the other hand, the way in which he disposed of the papacy, deposed and appointed popes, was endurable and even beneficent in an age of serious crisis, but it would not do for such a situation to continue indefinitely. From the time that the popes, through the emperor's efforts, were again what they ought to be, they no longer needed any guardian.

The great movement for the emancipation of the Church, which, proceeding from Cluny, had gradually taken hold of all Christendom, would necessarily turn at last against the excessive influence of the emperor in the papal election. Because of the frankly ecclesiastical bent of Henry III the problem would perhaps have been solved without conflict if he had lived longer.

THE PAPAL ELECTIONS UNDER HILDEBRAND'S INFLUENCE

On the death of Victor II there occurred for the first time in many years a purely ecclesiastical papal election. Under Hildebrand's influence the abbot of Montecassino, Frederick of Lorraine, was elected as Stephen X.[9] Wishing to avoid discord with the imperial court, Hildebrand later sought the approbation of the widowed empress, who was ruling for young Henry IV.

Stephen X was surrounded by outstanding cardinals—Humbert, bishop of Silva Candida, who had earlier undertaken with him the embassy to Constantinople to see Michael Caerularius; Anselm, bishop of Lucca; Stephen of San Crisogono, a Cluniac; the Lombard Dauferius or Desiderius, a Benedictine of Cava and Stephen's successor as abbot of Montecassino. Stephen X added to this group the prior of Fonte Avellana, Peter Damiani, whom he made bishop of Ostia. Surpassing all the others was Hildebrand, who in 1059 became archdeacon of the Roman Church.

---

9 There has long been confusion in the numerotation of the popes named Stephen. Its source is the fact that in 752 a Stephen survived his election only two days and was not consecrated bishop; several papal lists omit him, while others count him as Stephen II. Monsignor Mercati includes him in his catalogue. Following Monsignor Mercati, the present translator calls the pope who tried the dead Formosus Stephen VII (*supra.* pp. 184 f.), whereas Father Hertling calls him Stephen VI (p. 129); both the German original and this translation call Frederick of Lorraine Stephen X. (Translator's note.)

THE COLLEGE OF CARDINALS

At that time the College of Cardinals was constituted somewhat differently from its present form. "Cardinal" was a title originally applied to the priests of the Roman titular churches, later called pastors, and to the seven deacons. They signed synodal acts after the pope and the six suburbicarian bishops. Hence, in the early Middle Ages "cardinal" was not yet a title of honor, and it was also found outside Rome. In the eleventh century the popes began to call outstanding non-Roman priests to Rome, especially monks of the Cluniac reform, and make them cardinals, bestowing upon each a Roman church or a suburbicarian bishopric. The custom of conferring the title of cardinal on non-Roman bishops who did not reside in Rome began only in the twelfth century. The first known case is that of an archbishop of Mainz in 1153. The cardinalitial dignity acquired its essential importance from its exclusive right of electing the pope. Events followng the death of Stephen X provided the occasion for this.

For the last time the Tusculan house, now acting in cooperation with the Crescentii, tried to possess Saint Peter's See. The cardinals did not care to accept Benedict X, whom the nobles had appointed, and left Rome. In Siena, under the protection of the countess of Tuscany, the lawful pope was elected in the person of Gerard, bishop of Florence, who became Nicholas II (1059–1061). Beatrice, countess of Tuscany, had married as her second husband Godfrey the Bearded, duke of Lorraine, brother of Stephen X. She and, to a greater degree, her daughter Matilda became the most important supporters of the Holy See in its fight for independence. Hildebrand, by force of arms, brought the new pope to Rome and expelled Benedict X.

THE DECREE ON PAPAL ELECTIONS

Nicholas now held at the Lateran a synod whose decrees of unusual significance he made known to all Christendom in the encyclical *Vigilantiae Universali*. The already well-known demands were reiterated: no cleric might accept investiture, that is, the bestowal of any ecclesiastical position, from laymen; every simoniacal transaction in the granting of consecrations or the conferring of benefices was forbidden; if a priest did not observe celibacy, the people were not to attend his Mass. This strong directive, which was almost like excommunication, was new. Also new was the pope's express desire that all priests lead a common life like that of monks. This last was only an exhortation and not a law, but, as the sequel showed, it would effect a complete reform in the clergy. The most important decree, however, concerned the election of the pope. As experience had shown, a great part of the evil in the Church derived from a doubt about the law, whereby it was not clear who could lawfully take part in the papal election. Everyone could plead some sort of right, in accordance with the principle of *communio*, which held that every election was valid in which the common will of the Church found expression. Thus, circumstances could bring it about that the wish of the Roman people or of the Roman nobles or of the emperor as protector of the Church could be regarded as the wish of the Church. Papal elections up to this time, despite their variety of forms, had thus been valid. But a method of election based merely on custom did not prevent disputes, though it could prevent interference on the part of the irresponsible.

The Lateran Synod of 1059 decreed, therefore, that for the future only the cardinals were to have an active right of election. The rest of the clergy and the Roman people were to manifest their consent only after the election had been completed. The emperor's right was circumscribed by the very general formula *salvo debito honore et reverentia,* which, in the context, could mean only that, after the election had taken place, notification should be sent to the emperor out of respect for his office. At the same time it was emphasized that the imperial dignity was a privilege personally bestowed in each case by the pope.

Since it had been anticipated that the new regulation of papal elections, as well as the decrees regarding investiture, would sooner or later lead to difficulties with the imperial court, the pope had to look about for political allies. The tireless Hildebrand went to South Italy and contracted an alliance, the Treaty of Melfi, with Robert Guiscard. The rule of the Normans, hitherto based on the right of conquest, was legitimatized by the pope. Robert Guiscard received as fiefs from the pope Apulia and Calabria, and, if the projected conquest should succeed, also Sicily; for these lands he took the vassal's oath to the pope.

ALEXANDER II (1061–1073)

On the early death of Nicholas II, Anselm, bishop of Lucca, was chosen as Alexander II, according to the norms of the new decree on elections. The German regency for young Henry IV did not recognize the election and set up Cadalus, bishop of Parma, as anti-pope. Cadalus, who assumed the name of Honorius II, succeeded in seizing Rome with the aid of German troops. But the efforts of Peter Damiani kept Italy on the side of Alexander II, and when the powerful archbishop of Cologne, Anno, won Germany too for the legitimate pope, the anti-pope had to disappear. Times had changed. It was not yet twenty years since Emperor

Henry III had deposed three claimants to the papacy without fear of contradiction.

Alexander II was a staunch reformer. As a priest at Milan he had brought about a popular movement, the *Pataria*, against simoniacal and incontinent clerics. As pope he summoned to Rome the deacon Ariald and the knight Herlembald, leaders of the *Pataria*, which had also expanded to other Lombard cities. Alexander confirmed the *Pataria* in consistory, and conferred on Herlembald the Church's banner. A unique event: the pope summons the laity to rebellion against the hierarchy! But the reform movement had now sunk deep roots, and Alexander II and his friends, Hildebrand and Peter Damiani, were not inclined to stop it. Alexander II made extensive use of the papal authority without regard for persons. He threatened with excommunication the young King Henry IV, who had just married and already wanted a divorce. He brought before his tribunal the stubborn Anno of Cologne, to whom he was greatly indebted.

In 1071 Alexander consecrated the new basilica at Montecassino. Besides numerous bishops there were present Cardinals Peter Damiani and Hildebrand, Abbot Desiderius, and the Norman and Lombard princes of South Italy, Richard of Capua, Landulf of Benevento, and Gisulf of Salerno. It was like a review of the pope's *fideles*. Only in Rome was Alexander II unable to manage the barons. He had to look on while the Cenci deprived him of Sant' Angelo and collected tolls on the bridge. This too was symbolic. From now on the popes were again really popes, who ruled the whole Church, but they were not so much masters of Rome. Many subsequent popes resided outside Rome.

GREGORY VII (1073–1085)

Alexander II died on April 21, 1073. Hildebrand as archdeacon conducted the funeral on the following day, and the people there acclaimed him as the new pope. The cardinals at once went to San Pietro in Vincoli and canonically elected him. Hildebrand, always prudent, postponed his coronation until the consent of the German king, Henry IV, had arrived. In memory of the noble Gregory VI, whom he had once accompanied into exile, he called himself Gregory VII.

Gregory VII belongs to those men of world history whose mere names arouse the most contradictory emotions. Hence it is not easy to give an exact judgment in regard to his personality. Gregorovius (✝1891), filled as he was with a real hatred of all things Catholic and papal, finds that, when compared with Gregory VII, Napoleon was a hack barbarian. Gregorovius makes Gregory a magician who with invisible weapons struck terror into the whole world. The Church counts Gregory VII among her saints and annually celebrates his feast on May 25, but there are Catholics to whom he is the type of political, not religious, pope. It is clear that Gregory made a powerful impression on his contemporaries. Saint Peter Damiani jokingly referred to him as a holy Satan, by which he meant the restless, consuming thing that Gregory really was. Like the Apostle Paul, Gregory VII was an insignificant little man, quick, tireless, filled with personal courage, of incredible vitality. Zeal ate him up, but it was zeal for God's house. To him everything was business; he was never without a goal. In this he resembles Ignatius of Loyola.

His letters, almost all of which have been preserved, afford an insight into his activity as pope. He wrote to most of the archbishops and bishops of France, Germany, Italy, and to a lesser extent to those of Spain; to Abbots Hugh of Cluny, William of Hirsau, Desiderius of Montecassino; to Lanfranc, archbishop of Canterbury; to the bishops of Prague and Gran; to the Armenian archbishop of Synnada. He corresponded with all the European princes: with King Henry IV of Germany, King Philip I of France, King William the Conqueror of

England, King Alfonso VI of Castile, King Sancho of Aragón, Kings Solomon and Ladislas of Hungary, the kings of Denmark, Norway, and Sweden, King Demetrius of the Russians, King Michael of Slavonia, Duke Wratislas of Bohemia, Duke Boleslas of Poland, the counts of Flanders, the Byzantine Emperor Michael VII, despite the schism, and even with the emir of Morocco.

These were no mere letters of courtesy. They have much to say about the rights of the Church, simony, improvement of morals, and excommunication.

This universal activity of Gregory VII must be kept in view in order to grasp in a proper light his celebrated clash with Henry IV. The graphic emphasis which modern historical writing has given to the scene at Canossa could mislead one into seeing in this conflict the entire content of Gregory's pontificate. To humble Henry IV was not his lifework. On the contrary, he had always striven to avoid an encounter with the king.

Gregory VII did not begin his pontificate with a new program. He continued what the popes since Leo IX had worked for: moral reform in the clergy and the emancipation of the Church from lay power. The main point was attained before Gregory became pope. The ideas of the reform had become the common property of all. Christianity once more had respect for the hierarchy and for the Church's right to the care of souls. This result was in great part Gregory's work before he became pope. It can be said that he accomplished more as Hildebrand than as Gregory VII.

CONFLICT WITH HENRY IV

The reason why a break with the German king did come lay less in the nature of the affair than in the character of

Henry IV. He was twenty-three at the time of Gregory's accession. A faulty upbringing and, even more, unfortunate occurrences had not allowed him to acquire any moral maturity.
He had no real strength of character. Without regard for
circumstances, he was now haughty and arrogant, now despondent and despairing. What he lacked in strength he sought
to compensate by craftiness. Today such a man would be
termed hysteric. He was not manly; he was as unable to rule
as he was to bring order into his private morals. Contemporaries had no respect for him, and even modern historians
who like to represent him as unjustly persecuted have not
succeeded in making a great man out of him. Our human sympathy goes out to Henry IV only insofar as he was unlucky
in almost all his undertakings.

At the beginning of his reign Henry IV frequently asserted that he would observe the urgently repeated prohibition of lay investiture. In Germany there existed the difficulty
that the bishops were also imperial officials and princes. It
was clear that the king could confer no ecclesiastical jurisdiction, but it could not be expected that he would allow his
highest vassals to be named by the pope. That a solution was
possible was shown later by the Concordat of Worms. How
Gregory VII interpreted the solution we do not know. The
conflict arose not over the fundamental question but over a
practical case, when in 1075 Henry IV, without consulting
the pope, named a new archbishop for Milan. The archbishop
of Milan was not a prince of the Empire in the sense that the
archbishop of Mainz or of Cologne was. Here was a clear
encroachment into the ecclesiastical sphere that was regarded
by the king as a challenge and was accepted as such by the
pope. Gregory VII sent a sharp note and threatened excommunication.

212

Henry IV acted as though this were an unprecedented provocation from the pope. In January, 1076, he assembled twenty-six bishops at Worms and quickly declared the pope deposed. He wrote to the "pseudo-monk Hildebrand" a letter which can only be regarded as an outburst of childish rage. When this document reached Rome in February, Gregory VII pronounced Henry's excommunication and released his subjects from their oaths of loyalty.

For a pope to excommunicate a prince because of open contempt of divine or ecclesiastical law was not without precedent. Earlier Nicholas I had excommunicated King Lothar II of Lorraine because of his concubine, Waldrada, and no one had disputed his right to do so. In the present case, of course, it was to be anticipated that Henry IV would not submit and that he would perhaps proceed with force against the pope. In the event of war Gregory could count on few allies—the Lombard *Pataria*, Countess Matilda of Tuscany, and Robert Guiscard with his Normans.

War did not result immediately, however, for the German princes ranged themselves on the pope's side. At the Diet of Tribur, near Mainz, in October, 1076, they decided that the king must for the moment abstain from the government and, in the event that within a year he was not loosed from the ban, that he must give up the crown. At the same time they invited the pope to come to Germany.

CANOSSA

Gregory proceeded to North Italy, from where the German princes had promised to conduct him across the Alps. But before the expected escort arrived, Henry IV appeared with an armed force in North Italy. Gregory withdrew into the Apennines, to the strong castle of Canossa, south of Parma, which belonged to the loyal Countess Matilda. With him were Ma-

213

tilda, Countess Adelaide of Turin, and Abbot Hugh of Cluny. Henry made no attack but dispatched quite humble letters, in which he promised everything that the pope wanted, if only he were loosed from the ban of the Church. Finally he appeared in person, and in the garb of a penitent stationed himself before the castle gate.

Gregory VII was of sterner stuff than were the pious princesses in the castle; with tears they implored him to yield. But he was in serious dilemma. As a priest he could not refuse absolution to a sinner who asked pardon with all the marks of repentance. As one who knew men, he had to say to himself that no trust was to be placed in a man who yesterday had raged against him in an exaggerated fashion and today in just as exaggerated a fashion was offering submission. Finally, as a politician he knew that he was making a serious mistake. But the priest in him conquered. He granted absolution from the ban of the Church. Henry promised and swore to all that the pope demanded. The pope sent a detailed letter directly from Canossa to the German princes, and in it one can clearly see his embarrassment.

Such was the celebrated scene at Canossa. It is more famous than it deserves to be. "To go to Canossa" has become a familiar expression, especially since Bismarck at the time of the *Kulturkampf* exclaimed, "We are not going to Canossa!" It was only in the nineteenth century, through the efforts of German historians and publicists, that Canossa took on the character of a national disgrace. Even in Luther's day, when persons began to seek historical facts that would prove the hostility of the papacy toward the German Empire, incidents from the period of the Hohenstaufen played a role, but never Canossa. Only with the liberalist view of history did Canossa become the symbol of a grasping for domination on the part of the pope, who with cruel joy humbled a German king beneath his feet.

All this is a basic misunderstanding, not only of the spirit of the Middle Ages, but also of the very course of events. If anyone triumphed at Canossa, it was surely not Gregory VII. Until then the pope had been master of the situation. The German princes had acquiesced in his sentence and deposed the king. As soon as the pope had become reconciled with the king, the German princes became rebels. On all sides the pope had placed himself in an awkward position; he had let go the reins. Gregory VII would not have been Hildebrand had he not at once recognized that.

GREGORY'S END

The German princes paid no attention to Henry's absolution. At the Diet of Forchheim in March, 1077, they elected a new king, Duke Rudolf of Swabia. Civil war thereupon broke out between the two claimants. Gregory took Rudolf's side, and since there was no move to fulfill the promises sworn at Canossa, he again excommunicated Henry. But Henry still had adherents, and Rudolf fell in battle against him. The new anti-king, Hermann of Salm, was powerless. Henry, insolent because of the turn of events, gave vent to his anger at the pope. At a synod in Brixen Gregory VII was declared deposed and Guibert, archbishop of Ravenna, was named anti-pope as Clement III. Henry invaded Italy but did not take Rome till 1083, and it was only in the following year that he obtained control of Saint Peter's and the Leonine City. Gregory shut himself up in the Castel Sant' Angelo. The excommunicated king had himself crowned emperor by his pope. Finally, Robert Guiscard drew near with his Normans, expelled the Germans, and freed the pope. The liberators conducted themselves so outrageously in the city that popular fury turned

215

against Gregory VII. Hence, he went with the departing Normans to Salerno, where he died on May 25, 1085. According to his biographer, Paul of Bernried, he paraphrased, when dying, the words of the forty-fourth psalm, "I have loved justice and hated iniquity," but instead of continuing, "therefore God hath anointed me with the oil of gladness," he ended with the bitter sentence, "therefore I die in exile."

Without doubt Gregory VII took too grim a view of death. The great reform work was not interrupted by his apparent defeat. And the apparent defeat was not too dangerous. Henry IV, after his Roman adventure, was not more powerful than before, whereas the moral prestige of the papacy had incomparably risen. Scarcely forty years had elapsed since Henry III had driven the unworthy Benedict IX, the youth Theophylact, from the See of Peter. All Christendom felt that the embittered old man who now died at Salerno was the Vicar of Christ on earth.

GREGORY'S SUCCESSORS

After Gregory's death no one wanted to be pope. The cardinals twice elected Abbot Desiderius of Montecassino, but only after the third time did he accept.[10] Then he wanted to resign. Rome was half destroyed. The pope had no money. Not without reason had some of the recent popes retained their bishoprics: Clement II had retained Bamberg, Victor II Eichstätt, and Alexander II Lucca in order to have revenue and to be able to live. Desiderius, or Victor III, as he finally styled himself, was wealthy as abbot of Montecassino. He even promised to pay a salary to whoever would accept the tiara, an offer that smacked of an inverted form of simony.

[10] For another version of the circumstances surrounding Victor III's election and reign see Augustin Fliche, *La réforme grégorienne et la réconquête chrétienne* (1057-1123), Vol. VIII of the Fliche-Martin *Histoire de l'église* (Paris: 1944), pp. 163-177. (Translator's note.)

Never before had so reluctant a person been made pope. Nevertheless, Victor III, who had been a pillar of the reform under Gregory VII and his predecessors, made it clear that he intended to tread the path of Gregory VII. But he died in 1087.

Once again a Benedictine was chosen, the Frenchman, Urban II (1088–1099). He had been a novice at Cava and later prior of Cluny. Gregory VII had summoned him to Rome and made him a cardinal. If Gregorovius likens Urban II to Augustus and Gregory VII to Caesar, he is correct in this respect that Urban was the more fortunate heir of his greater predecessor. But in other respects the comparison is unsuitable, for the greatest mediaeval popes bore little resemblance to founders or rulers of empires. Urban II had to spend a very long time outside Rome, with the Normans and in France, because Rome was in the possession of the anti-pope Clement III. Urban II made the regulations against simony and lay investiture more severe. He excommunicated the French king, Philip I, who had put away his wife and had abducted another woman. The king submitted but later relapsed and was again excommunicated by Paschal II. In 1085 the Moslems were expelled from Toledo, the former capital of Spain. Urban II once more named the archbishop of Toledo primate of Spain. To Count Roger of Sicily he sent a bull which, misunderstood unintentionally or intentionally by the later Sicilian kings, formed the basis for their claims to a State-Church under the title of *Monarchia Sicula.* Urban II intervened in the great affairs of world history when he called the crusading movement into being.[11]

While Urban II was ruling the Church from his watch-

11 The translator has omitted Father Hertling's statement that a band of crusaders aided Urban II to expel the anti-pope from Rome in 1095 (p. 150). This was effected with the help of Matilda's troops in 1094, as is indicated in the following paragraph in the English text; Urban obtained complete possession of Rome in 1098. See Fliche, *op. cit.,* pp. 246, 309. (Translator's note.)

tower and by means of the crusade was placing himself at the head of the European princes, Henry IV stayed, almost forgotten, in North Italy, mostly at Verona, and fought against the troops of Countess Matilda. This loyal princess, who supported Urban II just as she had earlier supported Gregory VII, was not ashamed to marry Duke Welf of Bavaria, some twenty-seven years her junior, in order to win him to the pope's side. With the aid of Matilda's forces, Urban was finally able to expel the anti-pope from Rome in 1094, although it was only in 1097 that Henry IV returned ingloriously to Germany. He succeeded in putting down the rebellion of his oldest son, Conrad, but at last his second son, Henry, also revolted, took him prisoner, and compelled him to abdicate. Soon afterwards Henry IV died, without having been released from the ban of the Church.

After Urban II another Benedictine, Paschal II (1099–1118), was chosen pope. In his long and on the whole peaceful reign the city of Rome recovered from the devastations of the last decades and the neglect of the last two centuries. It was rebuilt. In place of the old ruined basilicas there arose new ones, which in part still stand—Santa Maria in Trastevere, San Crisogono, San Clemente, Santi Quattro Coronati. Likewise, the many very graceful Romanesque bell towers, which are so characteristic of Rome, belong to the twelfth century, as well as the pleasing ornamental design for pavements, ambos, and altars with rich application of variegated mosaic stones, which is known as the cosmatesque style.

THE END OF THE INVESTITURE QUARREL

The struggle with the German king over investiture was not yet at an end. With the other kingdoms a *modus vivendi* was found without too great difficulty. In 1098 Urban II had come to an agreement with France, whereby the king gave up the conferring of the ring and staff, that is, the naming of the bishops; in return, the pope granted him the right of confirming the canonically made election and of investing the elected prelate with the temporalities. The new German king, Henry V, was not inclined to relinquish his claims, though at the beginning, while he was still not sure of the crown and needed the pope's aid, he had made the most beautiful promises. Paschal II was determined to end the tiresome strife at any price. When in 1111 Henry V came to Rome to receive the imperial crown, the pope proposed that the German bishops simply renounce their feudal holdings in the Empire. Then they would no longer be vassals of the king, who would have thus no further reason to interfere in ecclesiastical elections. This was almost what is today termed "separation of Church and state." Such a thing was impractical in the Middle Ages. The proposal did honor to the idealism of this pope from the cloister, but it showed that he did not grasp the situation in Germany. The German bishops angrily rejected it, and stormy scenes occurred at the synod in Saint Peter's. Thereupon Henry V simply made the pope a prisoner and extorted from him the grant of unlimited investiture. When Henry had left Rome, the pope revoked the forcibly wrested concessions. The emperor came back and began to besiege the pope in Rome. During the war Paschal II died.

In his place was elected Gelasius II, a Benedictine of Montecassino, the fifth monk [12] to become pope since 1073. He

[12] In the German text (p. 142) it is said that "Stephan X. war der erste Cluniazenser auf dem Stuhl Petri," and further (p. 151) that Gelasius II was "seit Gregor VII. der fünfte Papst cluniazensischer Observanz." These statements have been omitted in the English translation. Stephen X, Victor III, and Gelasius II had all been monks of Montecassino, but the cradle of the Order did not belong to the Congregation of Cluny. Gregory VII seems to have been a monk of Santa Maria on the Aventine, which was Cluniac, and Urban II and Paschal II had been monks of Cluny. Throughout this chapter, Father Hertling perhaps overstresses Cluny's influence on the reform of the secular Church. (Translator's note.)

withdrew from Rome to Gaetà, and when Henry V besieged him there he excommunicated him and fled to Cluny.There he died, scarcely a year after his election.

THE CONCORDAT OF WORMS

According to custom, the election occurred at the place where the pope had died. No monk, however, was elected, but the archbishop of Vienne, a farseeing statesman of princely stock, Calixtus II. After long negotiations, he finally succeeded in arranging with Henry V that agreement which has become famous in history as the Concordat of Worms. The emperor first of all promised to make amends, as far as possible, for all the temporal losses which the Holy See had incurred, "since the beginning of this quarrel," under his father or himself. For the future he promised to give up investiture and to allow free canonical election of bishops and abbots in all churches pertaining to the Empire. For his part, the pope permitted that in the territory of the German crown the king should be present at elections and in the case of a disputed election he, together with the bishops of the ecclesiastical province, could decide the matter. In all territories of the Empire he could, after the completed canonical election, proceed to the investiture with the temporalities and the obligations attached to them.

With this the investiture quarrel, or simply the Quarrel, as contemporaries called it, came to an end. One might ask whether the pope had finally obtained much, whether the Concordat of Worms was a victory of the Church. The popes had for decades suffered the greatest wrongs, waged wars, issued excommunications. The settlement for all this was the German king's promise to perform the investiture of bishops after instead of before election. He still retained a great possibility of influencing the election according to his wishes. Was not the investiture quarrel one of those frequent conflicts between state and Church from which the Church must finally be content to escape without too serious a loss?

It would be incorrect to represent the investiture quarrel as a conflict between Church and state. To interpret Church and state as two societies independent of each other but to some extent overlapping is not valid for the Middle Ages. In the Middle Ages there were princes but not states. The Church needed the princes, she supported herself on them, she was grateful to them and granted them privileges. It was of no great advantage to the Church to humble princes or to exploit her rights to the utmost. What the Church desired, in the Middle Ages and after, was the right to be the healer of souls. As soon as rulers saw bishops as pastors of souls and not merely as imperial vassals, princely co-operation became very desirable to the Church. The princes were themselves members of the Church and in their own way responsible for the spiritual welfare of their subjects. The original program of the Cluniacs did not envisage the overthrowing or weakening of the princes or the transforming of the world into an ecclesiastical state; its plan, rather, was to remind the princes of their role in the work of saving souls. One of their chief responsibilities would be not to keep the Church in a dependence which would render impossible the exercise of her obligations toward souls. This necessary freedom was attained more through an idea pervading all Christendom than through individual agreements and treaties. The investiture quarrel led to a victory for the Church, a victory that became glorious once it was realized that an opponent need not be forced to his knees. Not Canossa, which was only an unimportant episode, but the Concordat of Worms, is the true symbol of this victory.

In a very definite way the investiture quarrel marks the

end of the barbarian Middle Ages. Princes and peoples had learned that more is accomplished through law than through crude force. This does not mean, of course, that an ideal age had begun. No such age has ever existed in human history. But with the twelfth century began a unique cultural community of Christian peoples thoroughly penetrated with the ecclesiastical spirit. Out of that cultural community, which today seems inseparably linked to the notion of the Middle Ages, would come imperishable values for the Church and for the world.

ecclesiastical life in the middle ages

EVEN in the high Middle Ages, the twelfth and thirteenth centuries, the Church, geographically, was still small. To the southern Mediterranean frontier facing Islam, which came into being in the seventh century, there was added at the time of the final separation of the Greeks an eastern frontier, which extended roughly from the Straits of Otranto to the Gulf of Riga. But all of Europe lying within these boundaries was now civilized and Catholic and constituted a single cultural community, a family of nations. The whole area was populated. In the thirteenth century the Church embraced more than 30,000,000 souls, more than she had ever before had. Since antiquity the Church's territory had become smaller, but she had increased noticeably in unity and inner strength.

THE DIOCESES

In the eleventh and twelfth centuries many new sees were established, so that in the thirteenth century the entire Church counted more than 500 dioceses. Of these a disproportionately large number lay in Italy, especially in South Italy, where, so to speak, there existed two strata of dioceses, the old ones of

223

Roman-Byzantine origin and the new ones founded by the Normans. To the old metropolitan sees of Naples, Bari, Brindisi, Capua, Amalfi, Salerno, and Benevento were added in the eleventh century the metropolitan sees of Otranto, Reggio, Sorrento, Taranto, Trani, Cosenza, Acerenza, Conza, and Manfredonia, and in the twelfth century the three Sicilian sees of Palermo, Messina, and Monreale. The many central Italian dioceses stood directly under Rome. In the north were the four great ancient provinces of Milan, Ravenna, Aquileia-Grado, and Old Aquileia, to which was added Pisa in the eleventh century. In Sardinia, which was wrested from the Arabs in the eleventh century, arose three provinces—Cagliari, Sassari, and Oristano.

In France the old ecclesiastical provinces of the fifth and sixth centuries remained almost unchanged—Arles, Vienne, Lyon, Besançon, Sens, Bordeaux, Tours, Reims, Rouen, Bourges, with Auch added in the ninth century.

Spain, which, except for Granada, was again under Christian rule from the decisive battle of Las Navas de Tolosa in 1212 and the subsequent conquests of Fernando III, had reconstituted its old metropolitan sees of Tarragona and Toledo, and likewise Sevilla, which was reconquered in 1248; in Sevilla the episcopal succession had been interrupted for the last several centuries. The metropolitan see of Mérida was transferred in 1120 to Santiago de Compostela. In Portugal Braga was established as a new metropolitan see in 1104.

In England there were two metropolitans—Canterbury in the south with more than twenty suffragans; York in the north. To York belonged also the nine Scottish dioceses until Clement III in 1188 withdrew them from the province and subjected them directly to Rome.

In Ireland the ancient province of Armagh was divided into four provinces, Armagh, Cashel, Dublin, and Tuam, in 1152.

Scandinavia had three archbishoprics. Lund, situated on Swedish soil, was from 1104 the metropolitan for the eight Danish dioceses. Trondhjem in Norway and Upsala in Sweden became metropolitan sees in 1152 and 1164 respectively.

The Baltic dioceses in the recently converted territory of the Teutonic Knights were all erected in the thirteenth century. Riga (1251) was the metropolitan, with Semgallen (Selburg), Kurland (Pilten), Samland (Fischhausen), Ermland (Frauenburg), Pomerania (Riesenburg), Kulm, and Marienwerder as its province.

The Polish province, established in 1000, embraced in the twelfth century the metropolitan see of Gniezno and seven dioceses, among them Breslau.

From the beginning of the eleventh century Hungary had two metropolitan sees, Gran and Kalocsa, with ten suffragans.

In Dalmatia the ancient metropolitan see of Salona had been transferred in the seventh century to Spalato. In the twelfth century Zara was established as a new province to which belonged the little sees on the Dalmatian islands under Venetian rule.

In Germany Mainz was by far the largest province. To it belonged the sees of Worms, Speyer, Strasbourg, Constance, Chur, Augsburg, Eichstätt, Würzburg, Halberstadt, and Hildesheim, as well as all of Bohemia and Moravia with the dioceses of Prague and Olmütz. Among them, cutting the province of Mainz into two unequal halves, lay the diocese of Bamberg, founded by Emperor Henry II and immediately subject to the Holy See. To the province of Cologne belonged Münster, Osnabrück, and Minden, as well as Utrecht and Liége, and, from 1169, Cambrai too. Trier had as suffragans Metz, Toul, and Verdun.

The archbishopric of Magdeburg, founded by Otto I in 968, had as suffragans Havelberg, Brandenburg, Meissen, and

Merseburg, all erected in the tenth century. To the archbishopric of Bremen were subject the dioceses of Lübeck,
Ratzeburg, and Schwerin, founded in the twelfth century.

Since 798 Salzburg had been the metropolitan for the
German southeast. To it belonged the old Bavarian dioceses of
Regensburg, Passau, Freising, and Brixen in the Tyrol. Gurk
in Carinthia was added in the eleventh century, Seckau and
Lavant in Styria in the thirteenth. The see of Chiemsee was
erected in 1215.

All told, Germany in the thirteenth century comprised six
provinces with forty-three dioceses.

THE PARISHES

The mediaeval dioceses were on the average much larger
than those of antiquity, but smaller than those of today,
especially in regard to population. The parishes, however, were
much more extensive. In Christian antiquity there had been
no parishes. Each Christian community had its bishop. If a
new community was formed in another place, it too received a
bishop. From the fifth and sixth centuries no more episcopal
sees were erected in small villages, but the lesser communities
were administered by priests, who were subject to the bishop of
the principal place. This was the beginning of parishes. These
priests were known as *plebani, curati,* or *rectores ecclesiae*.
The title *parochus* first appears in the sixteenth century. The
earlier system endured to this extent, that throughout the
entire Middle Ages every city had only a single pastor, who of
course could be aided by several assistant priests. Many of
the famous mediaeval cathedrals were erected as urban parish
churches or as collegiate churches, such as Sankt Stephan in
Vienna, the Frauenkirche in Munich, the Freiburg Münster,
and Sainte-Gudule in Brussels. Rural pastors were few and
sparse into the thirteenth century. It was something special for

a village to possess a parish church. Evidence of this is seen in such place-names as Pfarrkirchen, Kirchdorf, and in Italy Pieve (from *plebania,* parish), as appears in Pieve di Cadore, Città della Pieve. Beginning in the thirteenth century excessively large parishes in numerous districts were divided. The many small Gothic rural parish churches which are encountered everywhere on German soil come from this period. At such divisions the mother parish retained definite rights. Baptism was administered only in the old parish, and on solemnities the faithful had to go there for divine worship.

THE CLERGY

In the Middle Ages there were too many clerics rather than too few. Selection and training were usually faulty, as nothing similar to modern seminaries existed. When in the thirteenth century the universities came into being, theological lectures were, it is true, given at some but by no means at all of them; however, no university studies were required for ordination to the priesthood. It is estimated that about one percent of the mediaeval clerics went through the universities, a statistic that is less astounding when we realize that not all priests were by any means active in the care of souls. A large number lived as chaplains in the retinues of the feudal lords, as benefice-holders in the proprietary churches, or as canons in the collegiate churches, and had no other duty than to celebrate Mass on specified days, and, if they were canons, to attend choir. Hence, the situation with regard to the care of souls was not at all ideal. There was nothing in the way of systematic catechetical instruction of the young. Laments over the religious ignorance of the rural folk especially were only too justified. The uneducated clerics were held in little esteem, especially if they also lived in a dissolute fashion, which was often enough the case. Hence the monks, especially the austere Cluniacs and later the Cistercians, enjoyed great respect.

The improvement of the clergy assigned to the care of souls was a principal point in the reform efforts of the eleventh century. Since the influential personalities in the Church either were Cluniacs or were sympathetic toward Cluny, this reform was carried through along monastic lines. The reformers considered as one of their chief means the enforcing of the common life of the clergy in the manner of monks.

The idea itself was not new. Since, at the end of the fourth century, Eusebius at Vercelli and Augustine at Hippo had bound their clerics to a monastic common life, the notion had existed as an ideal and was often repeated at councils, even though it was seldom enforced in actual practice. Chrodegang, bishop of Metz in the eighth century, wrote a Rule for his canons after the style of a monastic Rule. The Frankish imperial synod of 817 issued a Rule for clerics, which was gathered from Jerome, Augustine, and conciliar canons. Its author was probably the Benedictine, Benedict of Aniane, who also, at the command of Emperor Louis the Pious, enforced a reform of monasteries. In the face of the actual difficulties, especially the system of proprietary churches, all these attempts to bind the clergy to the *vita communis* failed.

THE CANONS REGULAR

The Lateran Synod of 1059 gave a new impulse to the movement, and this time it became a reality. In the future, real clerical monasteries were established at many cathedrals and other churches, and in them the common life was enforced, with prohibition of private property. Thus there arose, without the ecclesiastical legislator's having at first so intended, a new Order, the Canons Regular, or, as they were later called, the Augustinian Canons.

"Canons" was a title originally denoting all clerics who were inscribed in the *matricula* (in Greek, *canon*) of a church. Later the title was usually interpreted to mean a cleric who was obliged to live a life in accord with the canons. In both cases all clerics were envisaged. Legally there was no such thing as an uncanonical cleric. The eleventh-century reform was thus aimed at the entire clergy. All were to live canonically, but now "canonically" signified "in the manner of monks." The earlier canonical Rules had required the common life, but private property was still allowed. Nicholas II's Lateran Synod, whose decrees were repeated by Alexander II in 1063, desired that all clerics observe evangelical poverty. This corresponded entirely to the monastic trend of the age. Saint Peter Damiani maintained in all seriousness that the apostles and their first successors had really been monks.[1] It is quite characteristic of the Cluniac-Gregorian reform that it laid down almost impossible ideals in the hope of attaining at least a part of them.

So it was in this matter. Not all clerics became monks, but a large number dedicated themselves to what was really a monastic life. Since the Rule of Saint Benedict was unsuitable for priests laboring in the constant care of souls, they selected the much broader Rule of Saint Augustine, which had been written originally for consecrated virgins living in common. At the beginning of the twelfth century it was introduced into most of the new chapters, which before long united into congregations, just as the Benedictines had their congregations of Cluny, Cava, Hirsau, and Camaldoli. Of the Augustinian congregations of canons special importance is attached to those of Saint-Victor at Paris in the twelfth century and Windesheim in Holland and northern Germany in the fifteenth century, and above all to the renowned Premonstratensian

---

[1] *Opusculum XXVIII* (Migne, Patrologia Latina, CXLV [Paris: 1853], cols. 511 ff.).

Order, founded by Saint Norbert. The bull of confirmation in 1126 enumerates nine Premonstratensian abbeys, among them Kappenberg in Westphalia. To these were added the still existing abbeys of Wilten near Innsbruck and Tongerloo in Belgium in 1128, and Strahov-Prague in 1140; by 1160 there were about one hundred, by 1230 more than a thousand. Norbert died as archbishop of Magdeburg in 1134. In many dioceses the Premonstratensians provided the bishop and cathedral chapter, especially in the German northeast at Brandenburg, Havelberg, Ratzeburg, and Riga. This was quite in keeping with the idea of Canons Regular, who wanted only to be the reformed diocesan clergy. Hence, they were not exempt from the episcopal jurisdiction, as were the Benedictines.

Today there are fewer institutes of Canons Regular. But in their day they carried out an important mission. From the close of the eleventh century there was again an esteemed class of priests in the care of souls, priests living up to the ideals of their vocation.

THE CISTERCIANS

The history of monasticism is not like the peaceful flowing of a stream. Rather, it moves along by fits and starts, like the periodic inundations of the Nile in Egypt, its home. The reason lies in the fact that in monasticism personality plays a role such as perhaps it plays in no other facet of the Church's life. The history of monasticism is the history of the great founders and of the great reformers. But this is not to be understood as though each new wave displaces the earlier ones. Almost every great Order retains its enduring task in the Church, even after its first brilliance has faded.

Cluny, Camaldoli, and the Canons Regular had been such new waves or new voices in the choir. From then on, wave followed wave, some almost simultaneously, in the twelfth and thirteenth centuries. The first were the Cistercians.

At the close of the eleventh century Cluny stood at the zenith of its power, though not, of course, of power in the sense of domination or of imperialism. However, Cluny had, so to speak, a religious monopoly in the Church. Monasteries which followed customs other than those of Cluny hardly existed any longer. A reaction could scarcely fail to manifest itself. Cluny was not degenerate, but it was one-sided. It was *an* ideal form of monastic life, but not *the* ideal form. Hence, at the turn of the eleventh and twelfth centuries there arose almost at the same time monasteries which traveled another road than that of Cluny—in France Fontevrault near Poitiers and Savigny in Normandy, in Italy Montevergine and Pulsano. A new monastery of this sort was that which was founded in 1098 not far from Dijon, that of Cistertium or Cîteaux.

The beginnings were modest. When in 1111 a part of the monks fell victims to an epidemic, Abbot Stephen Harding, an Englishman, considered closing the monastery. But in the following year a young Burgundian noble, Bernard, entered as a novice, along with thirty companions. From then on the crowds never ceased. In 1113 the first daughter monastery, La Ferté, was founded; it was followed by Pontigny in 1114, and in 1115 by Morimond and Clairvaux, the last named having as its abbot the then twenty-five-year-old Bernard. At the General Chapter of 1119 Bernard and Stephen Harding drew up the statutes of the new Order, which they called the *Carta Caritatis,* the "Constitutions of Love." Calixtus II gave an oral approval immediately, which was definitely and solemnly confirmed by Eugene III, himself a Cistercian.

The characteristics of the Cistercian Order were the austere manner of life and the poverty of the individual monk; even the churches had to be simple. The old Cistercian churches can still be recognized by the rectangular choir instead of a crown of chapels and by the absence of steeples. They were not even allowed to have stained glass windows. The monastery had landed property, which the monks themselves worked. The Cistercians became leaders in mediaeval agriculture, and many districts in central and eastern Europe were opened up for farming by them. Place-names, such as Zisterdorf, still recall them. The organization of the Order was based, in true Benedictine fashion, on the permanently established autonomous abbey. Novel features, however, were the requirement that the abbots had to meet annually in General Chapter and the provision that the abbot of Cîteaux named annual visitators who then reported to the Chapter. This arrangement turned out to be so salutary that in 1215 the Lateran Council prescribed it for the other Orders. In piety the Cistercians were especially distinguished for their devotion to our Lady, to whom all their churches were dedicated.

The expansion of the Cistercians proceeded with extraordinary rapidity. By 1350 more than 600 abbeys had arisen, over and above the older ones which joined the Order. In addition to France and Germany, Ireland was one of the lands where they spread most quickly. They were introduced into Ireland by Saint Malachy, archbishop of Armagh and friend of Saint Bernard; he died at Clairvaux in 1148. It was the boast of the Cistercians that they could journey through all of Germany without having to put up at a strange hospice. Apart from the excellence of their constitution, the surpassing personality of Saint Bernard was one of the chief reasons for the esteem and rapid spread of the Order.

Bernard personified, in their best characteristics, the Middle Ages and the French national spirit. From his writings resound deep piety, heroic devotion to the highest ideals, sagacity, and broad outlook. His Latin is no dead tongue. It is not the language of Cicero, but just the same it is a profoundly vivid medium of expression, flashing with spirit and even with wit, and always marked by a melodious quality.

THE MILITARY ORDERS

At the very time of the founding of the Cistercians and partly with their co-operation there proceeded from the ranks of the crusaders in Palestine a new wave of Orders, the Military Orders, which, after having been transplanted to Europe, enjoyed a period of the greatest popularity.

In 1119 the French crusading knight Hugh de Payns, with seven others, made a vow of obedience to the patriarch of Jerusalem together with the promise of assuming the protection of the pilgrims from the infidel. They led a common life like that of the Canons Regular. King Baldwin II made over to them a part of his palace, not far from the Temple, and thus they received the name of Templars. Hugh de Payns went to Europe and in 1128 obtained approval of his foundation from papal legates at the Synod of Troyes. Saint Bernard composed for him a monastic Rule and wrote a treatise, *On the Praise of the New Knighthood*, which made the Order known in Europe. The Templars adopted the white habit of the Cistercians. Eugene III added a red cross, to be worn on their cloak. The definitive organization was confirmed by Innocent II in 1139. The Order consisted of three classes: the knights, celibate but not priests, from whose numbers the Master General was elected; the chaplains; and the brothers, who served in arms and cared for the sick. The great popularity of the Templars, especially in France, brought them much wealth and thereby contributed to their tragic fall in 1312.

Even more famous than the Templars was another Military Order, which originated at the same time and also in Jerusalem, at the hospice for pilgrims; for this reason its members were called the Hospitalers and also the Order of Saint John the Baptist, and, from their later sites, the Knights of Rhodes and the Maltese Knights. Raymond du Puy drew up their original Rule in 1125. Their organization was similar to that of the Templars. Even in the sixteenth century this Order attracted the notice of all Christendom because of its heroic defense of the island of Malta.

Somewhat later the Teutonic Order arose from the hospice established in Acre by crusaders from Bremen and Lübeck. The real founder was Duke Frederick of Swabia, who adopted the Rule of the Templars for them. In 1191 Clement III gave his approval, and in 1197 Emperor Henry VI presented the knights with their first monastery on European soil at Palermo. The knights soon sought a new field of activity in the European northeast. In 1226 the duke of Masovia gave the Kulm district to the Grand Master, Hermann of Salza. The Teutonic Knights united with the Knights of Christ, or Brothers of the Sword, founded in 1202 by the bishop of Riga, and in time conquered and Christianized an entire state. The first local master in Prussia, Hermann Balk (✝1239), founded Thorn, Kulm, Marienwerder, Rheden, and Elbing; in 1255 Königsberg was founded, in 1276 Marienburg. The seat of the Grand Master was at first Acre, then Venice, and from 1309 the Marienburg. At the present time the castles and churches built by the Teutonic Knights in the elegant late Gothic style, the so-called Brick Gothic, still give to those regions a picturesque landscape. Through their defeat at Tannenberg in 1410 the Teutonic Knights came under Polish suzerainty.

Similar Military Orders were founded in Spain for the war against the Moslems, such as the Order of Calatrava (1180).

Several of the Military Orders of this period continue in some form to the present day, in spite of many vicissitudes. The Maltese Knights are a company of nobles with a social and charitable purpose, as is also their Protestant branch, the Johannites in northern Germany. Of the Teutonic Knights a remnant survives as a simple Order of priests. Others have become purely honorary Orders, in which only the old titles, such as Grand Cross, Commander Cross, Knight Cross, recall the former Military Orders. A few, which today wear some sort of Merit Cross or Honor Cross, are still aware of their connection with the crusading movement.

The Military Orders were too much a product of the circumstances of the time and of the mediaeval feudal system to acquire enduring importance in the Church. But in their day they accomplished much good. In the Christian people they aroused an interest in the spread of the Faith and they organized charitable activity. As regards the monastic life in the Church, they were of significance to this extent, that they were the first to select a definite external activity as their task over and above the striving for personal sanctification. In this way they prepared the ground for the later active Orders.

Especially was this the case with the Trinitarians, who set for themselves as a task the care of Christian slaves. They were somewhat like the Military Orders, but were established as Canons Regular. Their founders were the Provençal, John of Matha (✝1213), and the French prince, Félix de Valois (✝1212). In 1198 Innocent III gave his approbation. The first expedition to Africa, led by two English Trinitarians, brought back to Europe 186 freed Christian slaves. Soon more followed. With success came rich resources. The Order spread especially in England and Ireland, where it possessed close to one hundred monasteries.

Of almost equal popularity were the Mercedarians, originating in an association of Catalonian knights who assumed as their task the protection of the coasts against pirates. The transformation to a Military Order was effected by Peter

Nolasco and the great Dominican, Raymond of Peñafort (1223). Peter Nolasco brought back 400 freed slaves from his first expedition into the Moslem south of Spain. On the whole, the number of slaves freed by the Order of Our Lady of Mercy is estimated at 70,000. In 1318 John XXII decreed that the Prior General was to be chosen from the class of priests. Thereupon, the knights left the Order and founded the Military Order of Montesa. From that time the Mercedarians were reckoned among the Mendicant Orders. Later they found a wide field of activity in the Spanish colonies in America.

THE MENDICANT ORDERS

THE RELIGIOUS SITUATION AT THE BEGINNING OF THE THIRTEENTH CENTURY

The entire eleventh century had been an age of religious recovery. Capable popes had, despite continued political powerlessness, raised the religious prestige of the papacy to a height scarcely reached before. Nascent Scholasticism brought not only progress in ecclesiastical scholarship but also a hitherto unknown deepening and enriching of religious fervor. Religious Orders came into existence one after another. The crusading movement enkindled an unprecedented religious ardor. As always in such periods of deep religious feeling, crises were not wanting. There was much that was unhealthy, much shade in addition to light, just as later in the Reformation period. The high-strung ideas of Joachim of Flora (✝1202) spread like an esoteric doctrine among the pious. Almost for the first time in the history of the Church there appeared unhealthy mass phenomena, spiritualist movements, which, more or less unconsciously, sought to withdraw from ecclesiastical authority. The sad Children's Crusade of 1212 and later the demonstrations of the flagellants are only especially outstanding individual examples of morbid mass suggestion.

This was connected with the first symptoms of change in the social condition of Europe. The population of Christian Europe in the thirteenth century exceeded 30,000,000. In the preceding centuries the common folk had scarcely made themselves felt in history, but now we hear of popular movements, of the masses. Before the twelfth century there were hardly any cities deserving of the name, but now they arose, first in Italy, then in Germany and France, and with them came a new lay culture. The old feudal system lost its absolute value. The prince, the landed proprietor, saw himself facing not just followers and vassals but a people. There began also a sort of class struggle, in which underground movements, which today we would label socialistic, were not lacking.

Still, the whole of life was penetrated with a religious spirit, so that even these underground movements presented themselves in religious dress, as sects or heresies. But they were no longer the heresies of theologians, who denied individual points of doctrine or were at variance with ecclesiastical authority; they were popular currents, without much dogmatic content, with much obscure religious enthusiasm.

Typical in this respect were the "Poor Men of Lyon," originally a sort of Order, founded by the Lyonese merchant Waldo, and hence later known as Waldensians. In a famine in 1176 Waldo gave his money to the poor, came forward as a wandering preacher with companions, and called for a return to primitive Christianity. The "perfect" among the Waldensians made the three vows of poverty, chastity, and obedience. Laymen celebrated the Eucharist.

More dangerous, because more widespread and farther removed from the Catholic Faith, were the group called Albigenses, from the city of Albi in the south of France, or

Cathari. The Novatians of the third century had first termed themselves the Cathari, or "the pure." The Albigenses, however, did not spring from them but rather from the Manichaeans, even though it is difficult to prove a relationship, since frequently the same phenomena occur among secret sects in general. The Albigenses rejected any visible Church, every spiritual and secular authority, war, and the death penalty. They had only one sacrament, the "Baptism of the Spirit" or *Consolamentum,* which, however, only the "perfect" received, and these were then obliged to a strict asceticism. The rest received the *Consolamentum* only on their deathbed. At the beginning of the thirteenth century the Albigenses were a serious danger to Church and state. Innocent III summoned the French king to a crusade against them. This precipitated a real war which was conducted with great cruelty on both sides.

Since at that time similar currents were noticeable also in many places outside France, a general crisis seemed to be brewing. In a sense, they resembled an earthquake, the violent rumblings that customarily precede a volcanic eruption. That no explosion, with incalculable results, did occur was due to individual men who steered the new spirit which had seized upon the people into healthy and thoroughly ecclesiastical paths—the founders of the Mendicant Orders and, at their head, Saint Francis of Assisi.

SAINT FRANCIS

We are better informed in regard to the life of Saint Francis than we are in the case of most other mediaeval saints. He was born at Assisi in 1182, the son of a wealthy merchant, and received a good education. Only gradually did he turn to a life of piety; in 1206 he renounced his inheritance and began a sort of eremitical life. From 1208 he came forth as a preacher of penance, though still a layman. His first companions joined him. Until that time his life outwardly resembled that of Waldo and of other contemporary idealists. But Francis was no anti-clerical enthusiast. He went to Rome and was presented to Innocent III by the Benedictine Cardinal John Colonna. The great pope gave him oral permission to continue his preaching of penance, accepted his vow of obedience, and granted him the tonsure as a sign of his clerical status. From all sides companions now flocked to him. At Pentecost of 1219 there was held in Assisi a Chapter which gave a kind of organization to the nascent Order. Ministers Provincial were appointed and the first groups were sent into foreign lands. The expedition to Morocco ended with the martyrdom of the first five missionaries; their remains were carried to Portugal. This incident made such an impression on the young canon, Fernando of Coimbra, that he hurried to Italy and joined Saint Francis. He took the name of Anthony, and as Anthony of Padua became one of the most lastingly revered saints of the Church.

Present at the Pentecost Chapter of 1220 was Cardinal Ugolino, the later Pope Gregory IX, who henceforth was the great protector of Saint Francis and his Order. Differences of opinion arose with regard to the organization. The Ministers Provincial wanted stern legislation. Francis had long been sickly and in particular his eyes became ever worse. He laid aside the direction of his Order and had a vicar elected. However, at the request of the Chapter, he composed the Rule for the Order. The next year, 1221, some 3,000 brethren came to the Chapter. Since they had to camp in the open, it is termed in the history of the Order the "Chapter of Mats." On Monte La Verna near Arezzo, where Francis had withdrawn into solitude, he received the stigmata on September 14, 1224. His sickness grew worse and on October 3, 1226, he died, aged forty-four, in the Portiuncula monastery near Assisi.

239

Some draw a wholly false picture of Saint Francis's personality. He was neither an enthusiastic fanatic nor a daydreaming child, playing with blossoms and the rays of the sun. He was in every respect a man, simple, natural, sensible. He was not a theologian, but he had the thoroughly healthy Faith of the Catholic people. He was a man of few words and very unassuming. He admitted the work of others in his foundation. In some of the anecdotes that have been handed down he actually appears as an unpractical dreamer, but in reality he was intelligent, prudent, realistic. He co-operated well with the ecclesiastical authorities. In asceticism he was quite austere, as he was in his demands on his disciples, especially with regard to poverty. But he was not gloomy; on the contrary, he was of a radiant gentleness and goodness, even if he did not sparkle wittily and cleverly as later Philip Neri or Don Bosco did. He was not a jurist or organizer; yet the popular movement which he called into being—and it really was a popular movement—possessed in itself nothing of unregulated mass enthusiasm, as with some non-Christian religious founders. Surely this modest, physically insignificant little man belongs to the greatest personalities of world history. He personifies a degree of closeness to God and of union with God such as has been attained by very few others.

Most saints have their opponents, in their lifetime and later. Today Francis still has no opponents. Not all understand him, but all, even non-Catholics, love him.

THE DOMINICANS

Quite different from Francis was the second of the great religious founders of the thirteenth century, Saint Dominic. He has by no means attained the popularity of the Poverello of Assisi, but his work was of no less importance in the history of the Church.

Dominic was born in 1170 at Caleruega in Old Castile. He studied theology at the school of Palencia, which soon afterward attained university status, and in 1195 became a canon at Osma. In 1201, in co-operation with the bishop, he effected the transformation of the cathedral chapter into Canons Regular following the Rule of Saint Augustine. He accompanied the bishop on a journey to southern France, where the Albigensian War was raging. Dominic remained there, began to preach, and became convinced that little was accomplished by the defeat of the rebellious heretics. He resolved to found a teaching and preaching Order. He acquired a patron in Archbishop Fulco of Toulouse, a Cistercian, with whom he went in 1215 to the Lateran Council at Rome. Innocent III approved his plan, but asked him to adopt one of the already sanctioned Rules. Dominic selected the Rule he had himself been observing, that of Saint Augustine, and drew up the constitutions, in which he took much from the Premonstratensians and the Canons Regular. In 1216 he received the definitive approval of Honorius III. The first monastery was at the church of Saint Romanus in Toulouse, handed over to him by Fulco. Soon more were founded. Dominic died at Bologna in 1221. The work of organization was completed by his successor, Jordan of Saxony.

The constitutions of the Dominican Order are still admired and have served as models for all later ones, especially those of Ignatius of Loyola. The Dominicans were the first centralized Order. The legislative power belongs to the General Chapter, the full executive authority to the Master General. Especially stressed is obedience, which is vowed to the Master General as the single vow, embracing in itself all the religious obligations of the other vows.

In poverty and austerity of life the Dominicans were not so radical as the Franciscans. With them everything is oriented to the pastoral goal of teaching and preaching. From the beginning they were an Order of priests and before all else fostered studies as the foundation for preaching to the people. Already in Saint Dominic's own lifetime, in 1218, the Dominicans began to lecture at the University of Paris, where, with Albert the Great and Thomas Aquinas, they attained the height of their fame. Because of their deep theological training, they seemed to Gregory IX especially qualified for the Tribunal of the Faith, the Inquisition, which at that time was a necessity in regions infected by insidious heresies, such as the south of France and North Italy. The Dominicans from then on made themselves many enemies by their activity as inquisitors, but they also accomplished much for the purity of the Faith.

CANON 13 OF THE FOURTH LATERAN COUNCIL

In its thirteenth canon the Fourth Lateran Council of 1215 had decreed:

> In order that the too great variety of Orders may not cause confusion in the Church of God, new forms of the religious life are for the future strictly forbidden. Whoever wishes to go to the cloister is to enter one of the approved Orders, and whoever wishes to found a new monastery is to choose for it one of the approved Rules.

This decree had certainly been issued with reference to the many quasi-religious movements of the day, among which anti-clerical and heretical tendencies lay concealed, as in the case of the Waldensians. It is possible that some of the Fathers of the council had in view the Mendicant Orders, then just coming into existence, and that they did not yet trust them. However, the decree must be understood in the terms of Canon Law, which regards a prohibition as a matter that must be made dependent on a special permission. In other words, the entire monastic system was definitely subjected by the council of 1215 to the supervision of the Holy See. The eremitical congregations of the eleventh century had already sought papal confirmation of their foundations. Beginning with the Cistercians, it had become customary also to obtain papal approval of the text of the Rule or of the constitutions, as the Trinitarians had done shortly before the council. Out of this custom grew a law, and thereby the monastic life obtained a great extension of its possibilities.

Until this time tradition prevailed as a norm for the religious life. He was a monk who lived like the ancient monks. From now on, he was a religious whom the Church acknowledged as such, even though his manner of life was quite different from that of the ancient monks. Thus, far from throttling religious life, the Lateran Council signified rather an expansion of its scope. As a matter of fact, new foundations and approbations multiplied in the succeeding years.

THE OTHER MENDICANTS

The Dominicans obtained confirmation in 1216, the Franciscans in 1223. The next were the Carmelites. Originating in the Holy Land, not as a Military Order but as a community of hermits, they received approval of their first Rule from Honorius III in 1226. When conditions in Palestine became intolerable, they moved in 1238 to Cyprus and from there to Europe. The organizer of the Order in Europe was an Englishman, Simon Stock. His transformation of the Carmelites from hermits to Mendicants was sanctioned by Innocent IV in 1247. They did not achieve any great importance until the sixteenth century.

In 1235 Gregory IX confirmed the Mercedarians and in 1239 the Second Order of Saint Francis, or Poor Clares. The change from a congregation of hermits to the Mendicants was made by still another Order with a great future, the Augustinian Hermits. In 1243 Innocent IV united into a congregation several unions of hermits in Tuscany. In 1256 Alexander IV added still others, so that a great Order came into being, which, like the Dominicans with whom it had in common the Rule of Saint Augustine, zealously devoted itself to study.

The Mendicant Orders founded or approved after the Lateran Council were marked by a rapid growth. The Dominicans, scarcely a century after their founding, counted twenty-one provinces and 562 houses. Although the Franciscans were checked by the quarrel over poverty and the resulting internal schism, their strongest branch, the Observants, numbered over 20,000 members in 1,400 cloisters at the middle of the fifteenth century. Most numerous toward the close of the fifteenth century seem to have been the Augustinian Hermits, with some 30,000 members. This Order, to which, as is known, Luther belonged, was the hardest hit by the Reformation.

THE INFLUENCE OF THE MENDICANTS ON THE CARE OF SOULS

What was essentially new about the Mendicants was not really the personal poverty of the individual religious. An austere manner of life and the renunciation of private property had been practiced by all earlier Orders, most recently by the Cistercians in a special degree. The new element was that even the monastery was not to possess anything. The monastery of the Mendicants was not an abbey with forests, fishponds, arable land, tenants, and dependent peasants, but a minimum of accommodations such as a man required only for life—a few rooms near a church, perhaps a small garden, and nothing else. For the Mendicants, their home was no longer the monastery, but the society of the Order. Stability and permanent location, the basis of the monastic life since Benedict, was relinquished. Such a thing is, of course, possible only when compensated by the greatest personal frugality.

Thus a type of Order was created which met the challenge of the growing social change. The Mendicants lived among the people, no longer as spiritual lords, feudal lords, but as brethren among those like them. They exercised the care of souls, not on the basis of rights, but of mutual trust. The people did not have to go to them; they went to the people. For this reason preaching occupied so important a position among them from the beginning; they desired not to compel, but to convince, to instruct. Hence, there was much versatility in their methods of caring for souls. The Mendicants went to the rural folk, to the children, to soldiers, into prisons, to heretics and pagans. With them begins an entirely new epoch in the history of the care of souls. Hitherto the care of souls had been esteemed, perhaps even feared, but now it was loved.

Chiefly through the so-called Third Orders for the laity did the Mendicants perform their pastoral work. With these groups begins the history of confraternities within the Church, without which even today we could not imagine the successful care of souls. The Third Orders were for the laity a school of sanctity. Among the earliest Franciscan tertiaries were Saint Elizabeth of Thuringia and Saint Louis of France. Today the lay tertiaries number more than one million.

SCHOLASTICISM

The barbarian centuries had brought no progress in scientific theology. The writings of the great Fathers of the fourth and fifth centuries, especially of Augustine, were read, copied, and admired, but in the West this study was restricted almost entirely to the Latin Fathers. The start of an independent investigation of problems was provided by a teacher at the Palace School of Charles the Bald, John the Irishman, known as Scotus or Eriugena (✝after 870). But he remained unique. New efforts, the dialectic method, the application to theological questions of strict rules of reasoning, arose in the circle of Gerbert of Aurillac (✝1003 as Pope Silvester II). His pupil, Fulbert (✝1029 as bishop of Chartres), the latter's pupil Berengar of Tours, and Berengar's opponent, the Benedictine Lanfranc of Pavia (✝1089 as archbishop of Canterbury), are reckoned among the prescholastics.

The real scholastic method arose in the twelfth century. In addition to the general progress of culture, special causes were also at work: a new acquaintance with the writings of the Greek philosophers, especially Aristotle, partly direct but even more by means of Arabic translations and adaptations, which found entrance through Spain; and at the same time the creation of a systematic higher education, at first in cathedral and monastic schools, later in *Studia Generalia* or universities. From the activity of the schools Scholasticism took its name.

The real founder of Scholasticism was Saint Anselm of Aosta, pupil of Lanfranc, abbot of Bec in Normandy, and later archbishop of Canterbury (✝1109).[2] Among the more celebrated schools, that of the canons of Saint-Victor de Paris, founded by William of Champeaux (✝1121 as bishop of Châlons), was of special importance; it produced several great theologians, among them Hugh of Saint-Victor (✝1141). To this age of early Scholasticism, as the period before the rise of the universities is called, belong also Gilbert de la Porrée (Porretanus, ✝1142 as bishop of Poitiers), Roscelin of Com-

[2] The German text (p. 169) calls Anselm Lanfranc's successor as abbot of Bec. Lanfranc was never abbot of Bec. While prior of Bec, he was named abbot of Saint-Etienne de Caen in 1063 and became archbishop of Canterbury in 1070. Anselm succeeded him as prior of Bec; in 1078, on the death of Herluin, Anselm became Bec's second abbot; in 1093 he succeeded Lanfranc as archbishop of Canterbury. (Translator's note.)

piègne (✝1121), the latter's pupil, Abélard (✝1142), a keen student, who, however, was led into some errors by his over-emphasis on dialectics, and finally Peter of Novara, famous as Peter Lombard (✝1160 as bishop of Paris), or the "Master of the Sentences," who wrote the classic theological text, which the later scholastics, including Thomas Aquinas, commented on.

THE UNIVERSITIES

Toward the end of the twelfth century arose the first real universities, not out of cathedral or monastic schools, but through the voluntary union of teachers and students, who obtained from the temporal prince and especially from the pope extensive privileges, including their own peculiar jurisdiction. They also acquired ecclesiastical benefices as their allotted foundation. The first such *Studia Generalia*, as they were termed, originated at Paris, Bologna, and Oxford. The later universities were for the most part founded by the temporal prince, but always with the papal privilege. Among the oldest of this kind are those at Naples, founded in 1224 by Frederick II, Toulouse by Gregory IX in 1229, Rome [3] by Innocent IV in 1244, and in Spain those of Palencia and Salamanca, founded respectively in 1212 and 1243. In the territories of the German Empire the first universities were founded in the fourteenth century: Prague by Charles IV in 1348, Vienna in 1365, Heidelberg in 1385, Cologne in 1388, Erfurt in 1392.

The studies at the universities were organized in four faculties—theology, law, medicine, and the liberal arts, this

[3] The University of the Roman Court, founded by Innocent IV, was migratory, following the pope; it is distinct from the University of Rome, founded in 1303 by Boniface VIII and refounded in 1431. These two different *studia* merged early in the sixteenth century. (Translator's note.)

247

last corresponding to our faculty of philosophy. All universities had an arts faculty, but those universities without a theological faculty of their own still bore a wholly ecclesiastical character. Colleges, or the so-called "burses," were instituted for the students in university cities. From such a burse, founded by Robert de Sorbon, a court chaplain of Saint Louis, the entire University of Paris later was referred to as the Sorbonne. The University of Paris always ranked as the first in Christendom and as the model for the rest.

With the establishment of universities and in particular with the coming of the Mendicant Orders to them begins the springtime of mediaeval theology, the age of Scholasticism.

The thirteenth century can be compared in the wealth of its theological production and intellectual attainment only with the period around 400, the age of the great Fathers. The greatest names in the golden age of Scholasticism are as follows. From the Franciscan Order came the Englishman, Alexander of Hales (✝1245), lector at Paris; John Fidanza of Bagnorea in Tuscany, surnamed Bonaventura (✝1274), General of the Order and likewise lector at Paris; John Peter Olivi (✝1298); Roger Bacon (✝1294); John Duns Scotus, lector at Oxford, Paris, and Cologne, where he died in 1308. To the Dominican Order belonged the greatest of the great, the Neapolitan Thomas Aquinas (✝1274), who must be reckoned among the most important thinkers of mankind and whose influence on theology endures undiminished to the present day; his teacher, the Swabian Albert the Great (✝1280); the polyhistor, Vincent of Beauvais (✝1264); Peter of Tarantaise (✝1276 as Pope Innocent V). Among the secular clergy were Henry of Ghent (✝1293), lector at Paris; Raymond Lull of Mallorca (✝1316); Robert Grosseteste (✝1253), lector at Oxford.

Perhaps nowhere else is the perfect cultural unity of the

Middle Ages so well shown as here, where no national barriers existed. However, one cannot properly speak of a cultural primacy of the Church; the Church did not assume a leading position within the intellectual culture, but rather the whole intellectual culture was ecclesiastical from the ground up. There was no other.

SCHOLASTICISM'S IMPACT ON THE SPIRITUAL LIFE

Scholasticism as a method is nothing else than the application of the reasoning process to the data of the Christian revelation. Such an application occurs in every science, and thereby scientific knowledge is distinguished from a mere mass of facts. The material of theology is contained in the occurrences and teachings given in Holy Scripture and likewise in the Church's living understanding of the Faith, whether this has been established in the authoritative writings of the early Fathers or is expressed in the decrees and institutions of the Church. This material is now systematically organized into correlated fields of inquiry or tractates: What is God? Who is Christ? What is the Church? How is man's salvation effected? In this way are defined the notions out of which the system of Faith is put together: nature and supernature, grace, sacraments, justification, sin, law, redemption, Faith. The mysteries, the secrets of Faith, do not thereby cease to remain mysteries, but by means of the definition of notions the frontiers distinguishing the super-rational from the irrational are determined. Hence, no new hitherto unbelieved truths of revelation are discovered, but those constantly believed are perceived in their context. That Mary had been specially chosen by God and endowed in a unique manner with privileges whereby she was distinguished from all other human beings was always believed. But in order that the essence of these privileges could be defined as the "Immaculate Conception," it was first necessary that the nature of original sin be clearly worked out and likewise the connection between original sin and the work of redemption. Incidentally, this example shows that mediaeval Scholasticism by no means solved all questions, and it is not to be supposed that nothing further was left, so to speak, for later theologians to do. With regard to the Immaculate Conception, the state of the question was clearly grasped in the thirteenth century, and the road for solving the difficulties was indicated by Duns Scotus. But it was not for several centuries that the final solution was reached.

At its best, mediaeval Scholasticism lacked the possibility of critical theological investigation. It lacked the systematic, historical and especially the philosophical knowledge of meaning and changes of meaning in human speech. Furthermore, theological knowledge was retarded in many points by the absence of a scientific observation of nature. In a later age great progress could still be made here.

Nevertheless, the enrichment through Scholasticism of religious life within the Church was extraordinarily great. The ancients had known that man should not sin; they had also understood that not all sins are of equal gravity. But they had no clear grasp of the soul's supernatural life, of the state of sanctifying grace, and hence they did not know how to distinguish which are the sins that destroy the life of grace and which do not. The grace-giving acts of the Church were familiar to the ancients, and their use of them can be traced back to the earliest period. But only Scholasticism set aside for them the common idea of "sacrament," clarifying the manner of operation and the conditions for the effecting of the sacraments. One should recall with what theological helplessness the bishops of the third century faced the question as to whether baptism administered by non-Catholics is valid. The ancients knew that the faithful can and must submit their personal sins to the Church's power of the keys and that the Church has the power of forgiving these sins; but when and how this forgiveness occurs and under what circumstances it is perhaps not effected they were unable to say.

The ancients knew that in the Mass Christ's Sacrifice is renewed and that the faithful in Communion receive the true Body and the true Blood of Christ. But it was Scholasticism that was first able to define the notion of transubstantiation, thereby giving to Catholic piety a new impulse of the utmost importance.

THE BLESSED SACRAMENT

The theological discussions relating to the nature of the Sacrament of the Altar had begun in the prescholastic period. In the eleventh century Berengar of Tours had sought to explain Christ's presence as not real but dynamic. Condemned by several synods, he submitted in 1079 in the presence of Gregory VII. The final definition by means of the notion of transubstantiation was made in 1215 at the Fourth Lateran Council, which also made into ecclesiastical law the duty of annual Confession and of Easter Communion.

The effect of this theological clarification did not at once manifest itself in more frequent reception of the sacrament, and even Thomas Aquinas discussed the question of whether it is advisable to communicate daily. Saint Louis, we know, received the sacrament six times a year. The primitive Rule of the Poor Clares allowed the nuns seven days of Communion a year. But soon there grew devotion to Christ in the sacrament, in the tabernacle, that devotion which antiquity did not know in this way and without which we could not today imagine Catholic piety.

In the twelfth century the desire of the faithful to see the consecrated Species led to the rite of the Elevation in the Mass, at first only that of the Host, later of the Chalice too. The devotion was crowned by the introduction of the feast of Corpus Christi in the thirteenth century. The first stimulus to this came from a simple nun, Saint Juliana of Liége (✝1258). The cardinal-legate, Hugh de Saint-Cher, O.P., and the archdeacon of Liége, Jacques Pantaléon of Troyes, were entrusted with the investigation of her visions pertaining to this matter. The decision was favorable. Thereupon the bishop of Liége in 1246 introduced the feast in his diocese, as did Cardinal Hugh in his West German legatine territory. In 1261 Pantaléon of Troyes ascended the papal throne as Urban IV, and in 1264 he established the feast in the entire Church. By papal commission no less a person than Saint Thomas Aquinas composed the liturgical Office, including the beautiful hymns *Lauda Sion* and *Pange Lingua*. At first there was no procession; there is evidence for it at Cologne in 1279, Hildesheim in 1301, and Augsburg in 1305.

DEVOTIONS

Just as the Commemoration of All Souls is the liturgical monument of the Cluniacs, so the feast of Corpus Christi is the monument of the scholastic theology of the thirteenth century. In general, Scholasticism in part directly created the great devotions of Catholic piety, in part made possible their development. A "devotion" originates when a single thing in the deposit of Faith, be it a mystery or a person, is made the object of special honor. Thus we do not speak of a "devotion to God," but of a devotion to the divine providence or to the mystery of the Most Holy Trinity; not of a "devotion to Jesus," but to His Name, His Childhood, His Passion, His Heart, His Kingship. Through the growth of devotions Catholic prayer has received a special depth and warmth, and only a total misunderstanding of the individuality of the Catholic religion can see in this a weakening or perversion or destruction of the essence. In devotions the simple Christian learns in prayer the deepest truths of Faith. The Church has always promoted devotions and not merely tolerated them as "private devotions." The official liturgy is wholly saturated with them, and to remove them from the liturgy would mean to disavow the entire past of the Church and to wish to lead the liturgy back to a primitive, undeveloped stage.

However, devotions could arise only on the soil of a sound theology, and here Scholasticism created the broadest possibilities with its analytical method and its keen definition of ideas. Hence, simultaneously with Scholasticism, we find arising the great devotions and the great men and women of prayer. The devotion to the Childhood of Jesus, to which the Franciscans, with their representation of the crib, gave a very popular expression, stimulated the devotion to the Mother of God and led to the honoring of the Holy Family and of Saint Joseph. The cult of Saint Joseph grew strong only in the fourteenth and fifteenth centuries, with Gerson, Pierre d'Ailly, and Bernardine of Siena, though its beginnings, like those of many other devotions, reach back to Saint Bernard. Meditation on the Passion of Christ, also popularized by the Franciscans especially, became the favorite devotion of all interior souls in the Middle Ages. Out of the veneration of the Five Wounds grew the devotion to the Sacred Heart, which is already found in Saint Gertrude of Helfta, O.S.B. (†1302), and other German mystics. In Italy evidence of this devotion is found in the piety of Margaret of Cortona (†1297) and, in the fourteenth century, of Angela of Foligno and Ubertino of Casale. The Servites especially fostered devotion to the Sorrowful Mother. A monument of this devotion is the hymn

Stabat Mater, written in the thirteenth century, for in general devotions contributed a rich stimulus to creative art.

CANON LAW

The twelfth century brought important progress for the entire Church through the creation of an ecclesiastical jurisprudence. There had been law in the Church from the beginning, ever since the apostles had appointed administrators and issued conciliar decrees and the earliest popes and bishops had imposed excommunication and had again restored to communion. At least in the third century, if not earlier, there were collections of customs and traditions, at first still interspersed with practical instructions or edifying admonitions. From the fourth century these collections became more specific; henceforth there were admitted into them only conciliar canons almost exclusively, and, from the end of the fourth century, also papal decrees, the so-called decretals. These collections were made by particular churches or even by private individuals, but just the same they all had a definite common basis. A collection originating in Gaul in the ninth century has an evil reputation because of the many clumsy forgeries contained in it. The unknown compiler claims to be Saint Isidore of Sevilla (✝636), or at least he was taken for him. In the Middle Ages occasional doubts as to its genuineness were expressed; these became stronger in the fifteenth century, especially with Cardinal Nicholas of Cusa and Cardinal Torquemada and then with the Protestants, until finally all its defenders were silenced. Pseudo-Isidore caused much embarrassment and, like all falsifiers, did a disservice to the Church, which he no doubt intended to serve.

From the tenth century the canonical collections multiplied: Regino, abbot of Prüm in the Eifel (✝915); Burchard, bishop of Worms (✝1025); the younger Anselm of Lucca (✝1086);

254

Cardinal Deusdedit (1087), and Yves, bishop of Chartres (1095). The real founder of Canon Law as a science was the Camaldolese Gratian, who around 1140 in his *Concordia Discordantium Canonum* ("Agreement of [apparently] Disagreeing Canons") created not only a collection of decrees but a systematic study. This *Decretum Gratiani*, as it was later called, was still just a private undertaking. Gregory IX was the first to issue an official codification of Canon Law. By his authority the Dominican Raymond of Peñafort in 1234 published five books of decretals. In 1298 Boniface VIII added a sixth book, and in 1314 Clement V added two books of constitutions.[4]

These canonical books were supplemented in the fourteenth and fifteenth centuries by two private collections: the *Extravagantes* (hitherto uncodified decretals) of John XXII and the *Extravagantes Communes*. All these canonical collections from the *Decretum Gratiani* were, after the invention of printing, printed together as the *Corpus Juris Canonici* and formed the basis of the study of ecclesiastical law till they were superseded in 1917 by the *Codex Juris Canonici*.

4 Clement V died before he had formally promulgated his collection; it was revised and promulgated by John XXII in 1317. (Translator's note.)

the external fortunes of the church in the twelfth and thirteenth centuries

THE CRUSADES

A CONSIDERATION of the crusading movement makes us keenly aware of the distance which separates the modern world from the spirit of the Middle Ages. It is almost easier for us to penetrate into the psychology of the age of the Christian persecutions than into that of the crusades, though the latter is almost a thousand years closer to us. Because of this difficulty we must be reserved in our judgment, in our praise and blame.

The capture of Jerusalem by the Seljuks in 1070 provided the external occasion for the crusades. The pilgrimages to the holy places of Palestine, which had flourished especially in the fourth and fifth centuries, had not been interrupted by the Arab conquest of the country in 637. The Seljuk Turks, who put an end to the temporal authority of the caliph in the eleventh century, were barbarians in comparison with the earlier Arabs, and from the beginning were much more anti-Christian than these had been. In 1055 they took Bagdad and Mosul, quickly extended their dominion to Armenia and Syria, and from 1071 brought almost all of Asia Minor under their rule, so that the remnant of the Roman Empire and Constantinople itself were directly threatened.

In 1074 Gregory VII had planned to summon all of Christendom, including the Byzantines, to the war against this dangerous enemy, but the investiture quarrel prevented his carrying this out. Urban II, urged by Emperor Alexius Comnenus (1081–1118), again took up the plan and, at the synods of Piacenza and Clermont in 1095, succeeded in fanning a mighty enthusiasm for the undertaking, whose difficulty was apparent to no one. All who promised participation adorned their garments, usually on the right shoulder, with a cross, and hence they were termed *cruciati* or crusaders.

For the knights from the several kingdoms Constantinople was designated as meeting-place. Before they assembled there, Peter of Amiens, a questionable figure who posed as a pilgrim from Jerusalem without having been there, gathered a crusading army of French peasants. They moved into the Rhineland, where they were strengthened by reinforcements, and indulged their crusading zeal by persecuting the Jews, thus bringing discredit on the whole movement. A part of this wild throng reached Constantinople but was slaughtered as soon as it touched the soil of Asia Minor.

THE CAPTURE OF JERUSALEM

When the knights had assembled in Constantinople, the emperor demanded, to their great amazement, that they take an oath of fealty to him. In several victories they forced their way slowly through Asia Minor, following approximately the route of the modern Anatolian railway. In 1098, while they were in Antioch, Jerusalem, which had belonged to the Caliphate of Cairo before the Seljuk invasion, was reconquered by the Egyptians. But the crusaders were not stopped by this. Under the leadership of the Walloon knight, Godfrey de Bouillon, they took Jerusalem by storm on July 15, 1099. The first goal of the crusaders was attained.

In the territory they had conquered the knights now organized feudal states in the mediaeval pattern. A principality of Antioch, under the Norman Bohémond, son of Robert Guiscard, and a county of Edessa, under Godfrey's brother, Baldwin de Bouillon, were erected. Godfrey himself received the kingdom of Jerusalem, but he refused the royal title and died a few months after the conquest. Hence, the first actual king of Jerusalem was his brother Baldwin. Likewise, a Latin hierarchy was set up, with patriarchs at Jerusalem and Antioch and several suffragans. More of the old Christian population was then surviving in Syria and Palestine than is the case today.

The crusades were always regarded by the Islamic historians as an unjust offensive war of conquest. But the Moslems hardly have a right to such an opinion, when one considers that neither the Arabs nor the Egyptians nor the Seljuks possessed any other claim on these lands than that of violent conquest. Whatever one may think of it, the pope and the Christian princes and knights of that time had not the slightest doubt as to the fairness of the matter. Not only the possession of the holy places, but the righteousness of every war against the infidel was to them self-evident, exactly as it was to the Moslems on their part.

In the following years a continual supply of reinforcements came from the West. In 1101 a fourth principality, the county of Tripolis in Syria, was established. The crusaders who remained in the country built churches and castles, of which many grand remains still exist. The first reverse occurred when in 1144 the Turkish emir of Mosul took Edessa.

The alarm of the West was great and Saint Bernard, who was then at the height of his reputation, succeeded in launching a new crusade, in which the German Emperor Conrad III and the French King Louis VII participated. Some of the crusaders, coming by sea from northern Europe, paused to aid King Afonso I of Portugal take Lisbon from the Moors in 1147. But this was their sole success. The Germans were seriously defeated near Dorylaeum in Asia Minor. An attack on Damascus failed. Saint Bernard had to listen to bitter reproaches.

SALADIN

The remaining Christian states were able to maintain themselves for a time only because they were attacked by no powerful opponent. But such a one was found in the great Saladin, who had been vizier of Egypt since 1171. In 1174 he became sultan of Egypt and extended his rule over Syria and then over Mesopotamia in 1183. Saladin was not only a powerful warrior but a man of noble character, one of the best that Islam has produced. In comparison with him, the ceaselessly quarreling crusading knights, who had completely lost sight of their original goal, make a painful impression. Saladin defeated the Christians overwhelmingly in the battle of Hattin close by the Lake of Genesareth. The king of Jerusalem, Guy of Lusignan, was taken prisoner. The whole country, including Jerusalem, surrendered to the victor, and the Christians retained only the strongholds of Tyre, Tripolis, and Antioch.

Once again the Christians bestirred themselves to a third crusade at the call of Gregory VIII (1187) and of his successor, Clement III (1187–1191). The land route was followed by the Germans, led by the aged Emperor Frederick Barbarossa. They gained a victory at Iconium and were approaching Antioch when the emperor drowned in a river. Thereupon, most of the Germans turned back. Philip II of France and Richard Lionheart of England went by sea, and on the way

259

the latter conquered Cyprus. Guy of Lusignan had been set free by Saladin and was besieging the port city of Acre, which had been lost with the rest of Palestine after the battle of Hattin. Acre was taken with the aid of the newly arrived crusaders. Richard Lionheart agreed to an armistice with Saladin: the Christians were granted the coastal strip from Jaffa to Tyre, with Acre as the principal port. They could go unarmed to Jerusalem as pilgrims.

Thus the outcome of this greatest crusade was slight. The unending dissensions of the princes and knights, not the least those of Richard Lionheart, as quarrelsome as he was brave, ruined everything. Leopold VI, duke of Austria, who was seriously vexed with him, avenged himself by taking him by surprise on the return journey. He handed Richard over to the German Emperor Henry VI, as prisoner, until the English paid a ransom. This crime against the inviolable person of a crusading king was a European scandal and only contributed to lessen still more the reputation of the movement.

One happy result was that in 1197 Henry VI sent an expedition from Apulia to the East, which took Beirut, so that the Palestinian coastal strip was united with Antioch.

THE CRUSADE AGAINST CONSTANTINOPLE

The great Pope Innocent III contrived a new crusade. The republic of Venice was willing to furnish the ships. While the knights, almost all of whom came this time from France, were gathering in Venice, there appeared in the city in 1201 the young prince, Alexius, a fugitive from Constantinople, who asked help from the crusaders. With this the crusade and the entire European policy with regard to the East received a new orientation.

Since the eleventh century Venice, Byzantium, and the Normans had fought for control of the Adriatic. The Venetians were especially concerned that exit from the Adriatic be not denied them. So long as Robert Guiscard and his son Bohémond sought to establish themselves in Epirus and Albania, the Venetians co-operated with the Byzantines against the Normans. But when the Byzantines occupied Corfù in 1149 and even Ancona in 1151, Venice allied with the Normans against them. From that time the dislike of the Greeks for the Venetians increased. Emperor Manuel I, of the Comneni dynasty, had all Venetians in Constantinople imprisoned in 1171. When, after his death in 1180, his widow, Mary of Antioch, a westerner who ruled for young Alexius II, introduced a policy favorable to Venice, another Comneni prince, Andronicus, stirred up a revolution. The young Emperor Alexius and all Venetians were murdered and Andronicus took the throne in 1183. However, he was killed in 1185 by his son-in-law, Isaac Angelus. Isaac reigned until 1195, when he was overthrown, blinded and imprisoned by his brother, Alexius III. Isaac's son, Alexius IV, succeeded in escaping from his uncle's prison in 1201 and thus reached Venice, where the crusaders were gathering.

The doge, Enrico Dandalo, exploited this unique opportunity. The crusaders were in his hands. He directed the fleet to Constantinople. On the way the crusaders had to conquer Zara for the Venetians. Constantinople was taken in 1203 and Alexius IV was placed on the throne. The Greeks quickly rebelled and killed him. For the second time the crusaders conquered Constantinople and now they gave no further thought to the crusade. The Byzantine Empire was changed into a feudal state on the western model. Count Baldwin of Flanders became emperor, but his immediate rule was limited to Constantinople and a few islands. In addition, there were a kingdom of Thessalonica, duchies of Philippopolis and Athens, and a principality of the Morea. The Venetians took much for themselves. A new hierarchy was created with a Latin patriarch at Constantinople, to whom were subject twenty-two metropolitans and fifty-eight bishops. Innocent III was by no means pleased that the Venetians had given such a turn to his crusade, but in the face of the *fait accompli* he confirmed the new ecclesiastical organization.

From the viewpoint of the overall policy, the whole affair would not have been adverse to the crusading movement. There could scarcely be any question of justice or injustice in regard to the hopeless situation in the Byzantine Empire, particularly in what concerns the frightful Comneni. And a principal reason why the crusaders could not hold Palestine had been their lack of a base. Had the Latin Empire in the Balkan peninsula been full of vitality, it would have provided such a base. But this was not realized for the reason that the conquest was not complete. The Comneni maintained themselves in Epirus and Trebizond, where they continued to bear the imperial title, and opposite Constantinople arose a Greek state of Nicaea under Theodore Lascaris, who likewise assumed the imperial title. Hence there was no question of a connection with Palestine, and, besides, the Latin Empire suffered from the feudal organization and from minor and incompetent rulers.

Innocent III now sought to bring about a real crusade; he died, however, before King Andrew II of Hungary and Duke Leopold VII of Austria set out for Acre in 1217. They accomplished nothing. In the following year the titular king of Jerusalem, John of Brienne, with the papal legate Pelagius, attacked Egypt and then seized the important port of Damietta. This was a wise policy, for history has learned that Palestine cannot long be held without Egypt. Even Saladin had come from Egypt. But the expedition ended miserably when the Egyptians cut the dikes of the Nile and put the country around Damietta under water.

THE LAST CRUSADES

Emperor Frederick II, Barbarossa's grandson, had several times vowed a crusade. Urged on by Pope Gregory IX, he finally assembled an army at Brindisi in 1227; however, a pestilence soon broke out and many knights died, among them Louis, landgrave of Thuringia, the husband of Saint Elizabeth. Frederick II finally sailed, but fell sick and returned. Gregory IX, long provoked at Frederick, excommunicated him. Frederick nevertheless actually went to Palestine with a small band and obtained from the sultan a quite favorable treaty: the Christians gave up the rest of Syria, but retained Jerusalem, Bethlehem, Nazareth, and a strip of territory connecting the holy places with the port of Acre. The excommunicated emperor crowned himself king of Jerusalem in the basilica of the Holy Sepulcher, while the patriarch laid an interdict. Then Frederick returned to Apulia. The situation which he had created did not long endure; in 1244 Jerusalem was finally taken from the Christians, who retained only Jaffa, Acre, and, to the north, Antioch.

In 1245 the Council of Lyon voted a new crusade, but since the quarrel between Emperor Frederick II and the pope continued and the crusading enthusiasm had to a great extent disappeared, only the French king, Saint Louis IX (1226–1270), undertook the journey to the East. In 1249 he captured Damietta, but was taken prisoner and had to pay ransom. He remained in a private capacity in Palestine, where he purchased the freedom of many Christian slaves, and then returned home in 1254.

The year 1261 saw the end of the Latin Empire. Supported by the Genoese, who were jealous of the Venetians, the emperor of Nicaea, Michael Palaeologus, took Constantinople. Emperor Baldwin II, the Latin patriarch, and the Venetians fled. However, many islands continued under Venetian rule. In the Peloponnesus the principality of the Morea under the capable dynasty of Villehardouin maintained itself till 1446; the duchy of Athens, where the Florentine merchant family of Acciajuoli ruled from 1333, existed till 1456. In 1268 the Christians lost Jaffa and Antioch. Only Acre remained. Louis IX set out once more, but got only as far as Carthage, where he died of pestilence. Acre too fell in 1291.

WHY THE CRUSADES FAILED

The mighty efforts of two centuries were in vain. The popes are often reproached with having thrown Christendom into this unfortunate policy of war, while forgetting their real office. It is correct to say that without the popes the crusades would neither have begun nor long endured. Like the Christian princes, Urban II and his successors can truthfully be blamed for grossly underrating the difficulties of the undertaking. The popes presupposed in men an idealism which only a few possessed, an idealism never found in the masses. Had all the crusaders been like the first and the last, Godfrey de Bouillon and Saint Louis, success would not have been absent. And yet, though failure always produces a bad impression in history, no one can attribute to the popes any moral reproach or challenge the purity of their purpose.

One can, however, inquire into the reasons for this failure. The main cause is found in the insufficiency of mediaeval methods of warfare. The crusading knights were not by any means lacking in personal bravery; they were, however, in need of strategy and, above all, co-operation. One need only compare the really strategic military expeditions of the ancient Romans—Lucullus, Sulla, Pompey, Vespasian—in the

264

same regions. The crusaders did not know their opponents, and their numbers were far too meager. The size of the crusading armies, and accordingly the total losses, is greatly exaggerated by earlier historians. It cannot be denied that the leading statesmen regarded the attacks on Constantinople and Egypt as politically wise. But the more the goals moved from the religious to the political sphere, so much the more did the understanding and sympathy of the masses disappear.

Despite their eventual failure, the crusades were of the greatest influence on the destiny of Europe and of the Church. In the cultural realm they perhaps exerted less influence than is claimed by profane historians. For in Asia Minor, North Syria, and Palestine the crusaders scarcely came into contact with the real Islamic culture. The undeniable cultural influence of Islam of the thirteenth century came rather through Spain. But by means of the crusades was created the concept of the Western family of peoples, Christendom, which replaced the old idea of emperor and Empire. The emperor had been the protector of the Church; in the new view of Christendom was contained the notion of expansion, which expressed itself in a missionary movement. The Teutonic Order, founded at the siege of Acre, transferred its activity, with logical consistency, to the Christianization of the heathens of northern Europe. Spain, which had its own crusades and its own military Orders, passed as a matter of course from reconquest to conquest. In the very epoch of the crusades, people learned that conquest for the Kingdom of Christ cannot occur merely by means of the sword. In 1219 Francis sent his first missionaries to Morocco. The Spaniard Dominic founded his teaching and preaching Order in the atmosphere of the Albigensian Crusade. Ignatius of Loyola, who extended the missionary idea to a movement embracing the whole Church, cannot be understood unless one knows how very vital the old crusading ideal was to him.

THE POPES OF THE TWELFTH CENTURY

The twelfth and thirteenth centuries, the period from Gregory VII and Urban II to Boniface VIII, the age of the crusades, of the Cistercians, of the Mendicant Orders, and of Scholasticism, was in many respects a time of flowering for the Church. Nevertheless, the frequent claim that the papal power reached its zenith in these years is scarcely correct in any respect. The high Middle Ages had genuinely worthy, and in some cases even extremely capable, popes, but so far were they from being "powerful" that they often could just barely defend themselves against their political opponents.

THE SCHISM OF 1130

After the death of Calixtus II, who by means of the Concordat of Worms had brought the investiture quarrel to an end, the papacy almost experienced a relapse into the dark times of the tenth century. In Rome two family factions, the Frangipani and the Pierleoni, again confronted each other. The Pierleoni were of Jewish descent but had been Christians for three generations. In 1124 matters came to a schism, but the Frangipani established their pope, Honorius II. On his death in 1130 the cardinals favoring the Frangipani hastily elected Innocent II with sixteen votes, while a few hours later the others, with twenty-four votes, elected Cardinal Pierleone as Anacletus II. The Romans declared for the popular Pierleone. Innocent II went to France, where Saint Bernard acknowledged him on the ground that he had been elected by the smaller but "sounder" party. This principle of the *senior pars* was not entirely safe, but the authority of Saint Bernard was then so great in Christendom that France, Germany, and England ranged themselves on the side of Innocent II. Anacletus II had his chief supporter in the Norman Duke Roger II,

266

husband of his sister, Alberia. Anacletus bestowed upon this outstanding prince the title of king of Sicily.

Anacletus II died in 1138, and Innocent II, thenceforth undoubtedly the legitimate pope, took the field against Roger of Sicily, but, like Leo IX, was taken prisoner by him and made peace, confirming Roger's royal title. In his last years the Romans rose against Innocent and set up a republic, with Jordan Pierleone, Anacletus's brother, as *patricius*. The next two popes, Celestine II and Lucius II, reigned only briefly and vainly endeavored to become masters of the Roman Republic. Lucius II was killed on the Capitol by a stone hurled by an opponent.

The cardinals now elected the saintly Cistercian, Bernardo Pignatelli of Pisa, abbot of Sant' Anastasio near Rome (Tre Fontane), who called himself Eugene III. He was a disciple of Saint Bernard, who composed for him the famous *De Consideratione Sui*, a sort of spiritual mirror. Eugene III left Rome immediately after his election and spent most of his time in France. In the last year of his pontificate (1153) he made a treaty with the young German king, Frederick Barbarossa, at Constance: Frederick was to help the pope against the hostile Romans and Normans and in return receive the imperial crown. Once again an opportunity arrived for the German emperor to come forward as protector of the Church, an opportunity which could have been advantageous for both parties. Instead there arose a protracted conflict between emperor and pope, whereby the German Empire suffered the gravest harm and finally European politics were entirely altered.

BARBAROSSA

History has enveloped the Hohenstaufen dynasty in a poetic brilliance which, viewed from the German standpoint, it certainly does not merit. Instead of dedicating themselves to the great cultural projects and potentialities which then existed to the east for the German people, these emperors devoted all their efforts to becoming territorial lords of Italy, a goal which, in the circumstances, could never have been entirely attained. The conflict between Barbarossa and his most powerful vassal, the Guelf Duke Henry the Lion, was essentially a conflict between German policies to the east and to the south. Barbarossa won. Without any doubt he was a knightly character. But even in him was manifest that wavering of character and excessive self-confidence which later operated so disastrously in his grandson, Frederick II. The popes had no intention of weakening emperor and Empire; on the contrary, they expected protection and help from the emperor. On the other hand, they were unwilling simply to be subordinate. Finally, almost all of the popes with whom the Hohenstaufen had to deal were uncommonly able men.

In keeping with the Treaty of Constance, Barbarossa went to Italy in 1155, put an end to the Roman Republic, and received the imperial crown. The pope was Hadrian IV (1154–1159), the only Englishman to sit on Saint Peter's throne. Since 1147 the head of the Roman Republic had been the priest, Arnold of Brescia. He was executed as a rebel. When Gregorovius puts Arnold at the head of his list of martyrs for liberty, men who have perished at the stake while their spirit nevertheless rises from the flames like the phoenix, what he says is not only inexact—Arnold was not burned, but hanged —but also betrays a serious misunderstanding of Italian history. Arnold of Brescia was rather one of those many Italian pulpit politicians, who were everywhere organizing revolt with inadequate means and thereby hindered for centuries Italy's attaining a salutary political life.

Even at his first meeting with the pope Barbarossa showed

his touchiness when he declined to hold the pope's stirrup in welcoming him. He did so only when his attendants remonstrated that this was merely in keeping with the traditional ceremonial and implied no humiliation. Such trivialities have often exercised great influence in history, since history is made not by abstract principles but by living human beings. Frederick became all the more irritated when the pope in a letter used the expression that he had conferred on him the imperial crown and many other *beneficia*. By "benefice" the emperor understood "fief," but the pope at once explained that he wished only to remind him of his "benefits," or good services. Frederick's sensitivity was nourished by his chancellor, Rainald of Dassel, who in 1159 became archbishop of Cologne.

A conflict with the city of Milan once more brought the emperor to Italy in 1158. Milan was destroyed. In a diet at Roncaglia near Piacenza Frederick exacted the feudal oath from the Italian bishops and issued decrees of a Caesaropapist tone. Hadrian IV, who had already protected himself by an alliance with King William I of Sicily, intended to excommunicate the emperor, but died at Anagni in 1159.

ALEXANDER III (1159–1181)

On the death of the English pope a schism occurred. Most of the cardinals elected the capable Rolando Bandinelli as Alexander III; as chancellor of his predecessor he had been *persona non grata* with the Germans. A small minority of the cardinals set up Octavian Colonna as Victor IV, whom Barbarossa, on the advice of Rainald of Dassel, recognized. On Alexander's side were the kings of France and England and many German bishops. Still more important, even after the death of Saint Bernard (1153), was the support of the Cistercian Order. In Italy, where, earlier than in Germany, the cities were beginning to establish themselves as independent communes with political importance, there arose a league of cities opposed to the emperor. At first there were four— Verona, Vicenza, Padua, and Venice. Finally they numbered twenty-two, most of them being in Lombardy, where the destruction of Milan had not been forgotten. Because the predominant membership was from this region, the association was known as the Lombard League. South of the Po it built a league fortress, called Alessandria after the pope.

On the death of Victor IV, Barbarossa set up a new anti-pope, Paschal III, came to Rome, and in 1167 had himself once more crowned emperor. It was Paschal III who canonized Charles the Great. The deed was invalid, but later popes tolerated the celebration of his feast, at least in Aachen. Barbarossa's army, encamped outside Rome, was for the most part wiped out by a pestilence, to which Rainald of Dassel also succumbed. The emperor, as if in flight, returned to Germany. Not till 1174 did he return to Italy with a new army; he besieged Alessandria in vain, and finally in 1176 was decisively defeated by the troops of the Lombard League at Legnano. He concluded an armistice and made peace first with the pope, whom he met at Venice in 1177. The emperor forsook the anti-pope Calixtus III, successor of Paschal III, and gave up the usurped goods and rights of the Church; the pope lifted the excommunication and confirmed the German bishops whom the emperor had appointed. Peace with the Lombard League was arrived at only in 1183 at Constance.

Alexander III, who up to now had lived mostly in France, was conducted back to Rome by imperial troops. There in 1179 he held a synod at the Lateran which is counted as the eleventh ecumenical council. In order to prevent a repetition of the circumstances of his own election, he issued a decree, still in force,[1] that for the papal election a two-thirds majority is required.

The next popes, Lucius III (1181–1185), Urban III (1185–1187), and Gregory VIII (1187), lived in a sort of peace with the emperor, but not with the Romans. Urban and Gregory did not go to Rome at all. Only with Clement III (1187–1191) was the papacy able to return to the Eternal City. The aged Barbarossa complied with Clement's call to a crusade, with the intention of making amends for his previous injustice. In Asia Minor he met a tragic end.

BEGINNING OF THE QUARREL OVER SICILY

Barbarossa's successor was his twenty-five-year-old son, Henry VI. At the same time Celestine III, aged eighty-five, became pope. In 1191 he crowned Henry emperor. Henry's wife was Constance, daughter of King Roger II of Sicily and of Alberia Pierleone. When Constance's nephew, King William II, died without issue in 1189, Henry claimed the succession. However, the Sicilian and Neapolitan magnates wanted as king Tancred of Lecce, an illegitimate son of Constance's brother, Duke Roger. The rights in the situation were in doubt, and the decision belonged to the pope as overlord of Sicily.

For the pope it was of the utmost concern that the same great power not be established in North Italy and in Naples and Sicily. The Holy See, which was unarmed and hence politically powerless, could preserve its independence only if a political balance prevailed in Italy. Celestine III, therefore, decided for Tancred. As so often happened in the political history of the papacy, he had thereby come out for the faction

<hr/>

[1] On December 8, 1945, by the Apostolic Constitution "Vacantis Apostolicae Sedis," Pope Pius XII decreed that for the future a two-thirds majority plus one is required for a valid election (*Acta Apostolicae Sedis*, XXXVIII, No. 3 [February 4, 1946], 87). (Translator's note.)

that was destined by fate to suffer defeat. Tancred died in 1194 and Henry now acquired possession of the whole kingdom without further thought of the pope's feudal suzerainty. Since he took bloody vengeance on his enemies, the situation seemed ripe for his excommunication, but the pope, now ninety-two years old, was unwilling to take this extreme step. Then Henry died at Messina on September 28, 1197, and the pope followed him three months later.

INNOCENT III

While Hadrian IV, Alexander III, and even the aged Celestine III had been uncommonly energetic popes, there now mounted the Throne of Saint Peter a man whom contemporaries and, to an even greater degree, later historians gazed at in awe: Lothario, of the house of the counts of Segni, who styled himself Innocent III. At his election he was only thirty-seven.

In the political sphere two principal tasks confronted Innocent III. The one was to bring order at last to Rome and the Papal State; the other was to solve the Sicilian question. In Rome there were at that time two authorities, with not always clearly defined competence: one was the prefect of the city, originally an official named by the emperor, whose dignity had, however, been for some time hereditary in the family of the lords of Vico; the other was the senator, or even several senators, elected by the people. Innocent changed both functions into papal magistracies. Just the same, Rome did not cease to be an autonomous commune. During the pontificate of Innocent III Rome waged war against another papal city, Viterbo. Anything was possible to mediaeval sovereignty. The rest of the Papal State hardly existed even in name. The former fiefs of Countess Matilda of Tuscany, the duchy of Spoleto, and the district of Ancona, the so-called Pentapolis, where imperial vassals had everywhere established themselves, were again to some extent brought under papal rule by Innocent.

In the kingdom of Sicily and Naples the situation had been completely altered by the premature death of Henry VI. The heir to the throne was a three-year-old child, the future Emperor Frederick II. On this side no danger for the pope existed. Henry VI had himself, when dying, asked the pope to preserve the crown for his son, and his widow, Constance, who also died in 1198, made the pope Frederick's guardian. Thus Innocent III administered the kingdom until his ward attained his majority in 1208.

THE STRUGGLE OVER THE GERMAN THRONE

In Germany the death of Henry VI had led to a disputed royal election. A part of the princes chose Henry's brother, Philip of Swabia, while a smaller faction elected the Guelf Otto, son of Henry the Lion and nephew of King Richard Lionheart. Both kings requested the imperial crown. Innocent III, therefore, had to give a decision, but he was in no hurry. Not until 1202 did he lay down the legal principle, in the celebrated decretal *Venerabilem*. According to ancient German law it pertained to the princes to elect the king. Since, however, the German royal dignity included the expectation of the imperial crown, and the imperial crown was bestowed by the pope, it pertained to the pope to approve the person whom he was to crown emperor. The pope could not be required to anoint and crown "a tyrant or fool, heretic or heathen." The same principle now came into play in the case of a contested election. Here too the pope had the right to decide for one of the two competitors. In the present case there was the added fact that both parties had repeatedly asked him for such a decision.

Innocent III decided as the interests of the Church seemed to demand: Rome should not again be encircled, as was the case under Henry VI. The Hohenstaufen Frederick II was the lawful heir of Sicily, and Innocent had no intention of diminishing his ward's inheritance. However, a Hohenstaufen should not, for that very reason, again wear the imperial crown, but the Guelf Otto, who had no claim to Sicily and who recognized the re-establishment of the Papal State in central Italy. Innocent III was later reproached with desiring to weaken Germany and extend his own power. This is incorrect. The pope was on the defensive. He fought for his own independence and at the same time for the freedom of the Church.

It may, of course, be said that it was a question of more than immediate political tactics. It was at the same time a war over ideas. The imperial office, as the Hohenstaufen conceived it, was no longer that of Charles the Great, the Ottos, and the Salians. The Hohenstaufen no longer wished to be protectors of the Church. They already approximated a more modern, profane idea of the state. They wanted a territorial empire, in which the pope would occupy the position of first imperial bishop, somewhat as, for his part, was the patriarch of Constantinople. Innocent III still fought for the old religious concept of the imperial crown.

The pope had not the means of aiding the Guelf to victory by force of arms. Philip kept the upper hand in the field, but he and his supporters realized that they must tone down their earlier claims in order to come to peace with the pope. An agreement was reached in May, 1208. Envoys were already *en route* to proclaim the peace, when in June, 1208, Philip was murdered in Bamberg by the Count Palatine Otto of Wittelsbach out of private revenge. The princes, weary of the long struggle, recognized the Guelf as king. For his part, Otto IV once again acknowledged the re-establishment of the pope in the Papal State and the pope's feudal lordship over Sicily. He was crowned emperor in the fall of 1209.

But now it was Otto the Guelf who took up the old Hohenstaufen ideas. Without regard for his earlier promises he prepared to conquer Sicily. Innocent III saw that he had been cruelly deceived. Hence, he turned from Otto, excommunicated him, and favored the election of Frederick II, his former ward, who had meanwhile attained his majority. Otto lost all support and withdrew to his duchy, where he died in 1218. But Frederick had had to promise on oath not to unite the two crowns of Germany and Sicily. Frederick's year-old son Henry was named heir of Sicily, which was not elective like Germany.

THE POPE AS FEUDAL LORD OF ENGLAND

Innocent came into sharp conflict with the English King John, because the latter refused to accept the archbishop of Canterbury named by the pope, Stephen Langton. Langton was a professor at Paris and is well-known to biblical scholars as the originator of the chapter divisions of Holy Scripture. When the king did not yield, the pope laid an interdict on England. By the mediaeval interdict is meant a sort of strike on the part of the clergy. All ecclesiastical rites, including every public divine service and even the administration of the sacraments of the dying, ceased. The king tried to compel the clergy to ignore the interdict. Thereupon, the pope declared him excommunicated and deposed, and entrusted the French king, who was the English king's overlord for his continental possessions, with the carrying out of the sentence (1212). Since his magnates abandoned him, John submitted to the pope and, in order not to lose the crown, accepted his kingdom from him as a fief. This is the origin of his nickname,

"John Lackland." [2] Hereafter the pope supported him against the barons. When in 1215 these forced from the king the Magna Carta, the basis of the later English constitution, Innocent proceeded against them with ecclesiastical penalties, even against Stephen Langton, who made common cause with the barons.

Thus, Innocent III had intervened in the struggle over the German throne; he was feudal overlord of Sicily and England, and, since Aragón, Portugal, Hungary, and Bulgaria stood in a kind of feudal relationship to the Holy See, he could for a moment almost be regarded as the emperor of Europe. Later historians, especially the German historians of the nineteenth century, have given ecstatic expression to their amazement at this situation. Everywhere in the historical presentations one can read of Innocent as the zenith of the development of the papacy's power. Curiously enough, this is even copied by Catholic Church historians, from whom one should expect a more correct judgment of the papacy and of mediaeval conditions.

As a matter of fact, Innocent III was not "more powerful" than the popes before and after him, such as Gregory VII, Urban II, Alexander III, and Boniface VIII. His financial and military means were modest, as has been the case with all the popes. It was only a most unusual set of circumstances that brought him on several occasions into a position to exercise simultaneously functions as ruler and as the highest moral authority. But this was more or less the situation of all the popes of the Middle Ages.

One might ask whether such a position is altogether desirable for the pope and the Church. It is desirable and necessary

[2] Father Hertling's explanation of John's nickname is unusual. Most writers claim that he received it as a child from his father, Henry II, who had already, before John's birth, divided his domains among his older sons and had nothing left for his favorite. (Translator's note.)

that the pope have the possibility of defending the rights of the Church and of addressing when necessary the consciences of rulers; it would also seem desirable that he should, through peaceful arbitration, settle difficulties that otherwise would be decided only by violent means. On the other hand, however, the role of permanent arbiter would bring to the papacy an enormous amount of hatred, from which the entire Church would have to suffer. Likewise, the pope does not possess the material means to enforce this authority where it is not voluntarily recognized. This was exactly the situation even at the time of Innocent III.

The popes of the Middle Ages, as also the later ones, were always careful to enforce their moral authority amid constantly changing circumstances, though not always with the same skill and not always with the same result. It would be wrong to make these successes or failures, often dependent on chance, into enduring concepts of history and to construct a graph of papal power, showing its rise, zenith, and decline. Of course, the presentation of history would in this way become more dramatic; the important thing, however, is not drama, but fact.

INNOCENT III'S SIGNIFICANCE IN THE
INTERNAL AFFAIRS OF THE CHURCH

The importance of the pontificate of Innocent III lies far more in the sphere of the internal affairs of the Church than in politics, where he could neither prevent the crusade against Constantinople nor steer the German crises to his own purposes. Under Innocent III, who was himself an indefatigable worker, the organization of the papal curia made important progress toward extensive centralization. Under him and with his express encouragement there arose the great Mendicant Orders, which gave a new orientation not only to monastic life but to the entire care of souls. In 1215 Innocent held at the

Lateran the twelfth ecumenical council, the most brilliant of all mediaeval ecclesiastical assemblies. More than 1,200 prelates and envoys of almost all the princes of Christendom were present. With regard to accomplishments, no council from Nicaea to Trent issued weightier decrees. The erroneous doctrines of the Albigenses and Waldensians and the bewildering ideas of Abbot Joachim of Flora were condemned. Against the Albigenses the doctrine of the Blessed Sacrament, Transubstantiation, was defined. Easter Communion was made a law binding on all. The founding of new Orders or new forms of monastic life was made dependent on the approval of the Holy See, a decision that turned out to be of the greatest importance for the further development of religious life.

THE CONNECTION WITH FRANCE

THE WAR WITH FREDERICK II

Innocent III's successors, Honorius III (1216–1227) and Gregory IX (1227–1241), continued his work in the internal government of the Church. Gregory IX, Innocent's nephew, had, as Cardinal Ugolino, protected and encouraged Saint Francis and his Order in every way. As pope he has perpetuated his name in the first codification of Canon Law in 1234. In politics both Honorius and Gregory were constantly at odds with Frederick II (1212–1250).

The personality of this prince has from his own day been judged in very different ways. Like all the Hohenstaufen, he was brilliantly endowed, haughty like his grandfather, Barbarossa, but without the latter's chivalrous nature, dissolute and treacherous, and in regard to religion was of an indifference that is quite foreign to the Middle Ages. Some see in him a forerunner of the Renaissance or even of the Enlightenment. He governed Sicily well, but he was the gravedigger of the

German Empire. As is usual in so prolonged a conflict, perhaps not every undertaking of the popes against him can be approved, but the blame lay to a far greater extent on Frederick's side.

Frederick II had no intention of loosing the connection of the Sicilian with the German crown, as he had earlier sworn to do when he still needed the pope. It was made clear how correctly Celestine III and Innocent III had viewed the situation when they had sought to hinder this union in the interests of the Church. The chief sufferer was Italy, which was torn by the factional strife of Ghibellines and Guelfs, of the Hohenstaufen and anti-Hohenstaufen parties.

Gregory IX's second [3] successor, Innocent IV (1243–1254), fled from Frederick to Lyon, where he resided from 1244 to 1251. At the thirteenth ecumenical council at Lyon in 1245 he renewed the Church's ban on Frederick. When the latter was dying in 1250 at Fiorentino in Apulia, the archbishop of Palermo absolved him, and Frederick's will shows that at the end he repented and wanted to make amends. In Germany there was no further concern for an emperor who almost never came there, and other kings, who lacked all importance, were elected.

Frederick's son, Conrad IV, who could not maintain himself in Germany, hastened to Italy after his father's death in order to save at least the Sicilian inheritance, but in 1254 he died at Lavello. The German kingship survived only as a title, and the period till the election of Rudolf of Habsburg in 1273 is known as the Interregnum. In Sicily reigned the excommunicated Manfred, an illegitimate son of Frederick II.

Innocent IV was succeeded by Alexander IV (1254–1261), of the same family, the counts of Segni, to which

[3] Father Hertling calls Innocent IV Gregory's successor. In reality Gregory was immediately followed by Celestine IV, who died two weeks after his election. (Translator's note.)

Clement III, Innocent III, and Gregory IX had belonged. When he died at Viterbo in 1261, there was elected a Frenchman, Urban IV (1261–1264), whose short pontificate marks a turning point in the history of the papacy and in European politics. Because of the continuing insecure situation in Rome he never went there, but resided at Viterbo, where he was elected, and at Orvieto and Perugia. To put an end to the unhealthy situation in Italy, he invited the brother of Saint Louis IX of France, the unsaintly Charles of Anjou, to come there and promised to invest him with the kingdom of Naples and Sicily. Urban did not live to carry out his promise, but the decisive step had been taken: the definite turning away from the German kings, who from protectors of the papacy had become its enemies, and the veering toward France, which was at that time the rising, in fact the unique, great power in Europe.

FRANCE

The preponderance of France finds expression even in regard to population. In the thirteenth century Italy had from five to six million inhabitants, of whom scarcely 1,000,000 lived in the kingdom of Naples and Sicily; Germany had about 8,000,000, England 2,000,000, Spain, now for the most part freed from the Moors, from five to six million, France 14,000,000. The University of Paris was the intellectual center of Christendom. The Gothic style in art originated in France and spread elsewhere. Before the rise of mercantilism France was also the economic center of Europe. Furthermore, in the thirteenth century France had an ideal ruler, Louis IX (1226–1270), who, it is true, was not always lucky in his individual political undertakings, but who, through his personal character, conferred on the French crown and nation a religious aura which, in comparison with the contemporary German ruler, Frederick II, could not but win the prize.

Urban IV consciously promoted the *volte-face* toward France. He appointed many French cardinals and thus it came about that among his successors there were several Frenchmen. The first of these, Clement IV (1265–1268), Foulquois le Gros, who earlier as a layman had sat in Louis IX's council, crowned Charles of Anjou king of Naples and Sicily. Manfred fell in battle against Charles at Benevento in 1266.

THE LAST POPES OF THE THIRTEENTH CENTURY

With Urban IV and Clement IV begins a series of quite short pontificates, which for the most part alternated with long vacancies of the Holy See. After the death of Clement IV the vacancy lasted for thirty-three months. In the fifty-two years from the death of Urban IV to the election of John XXII the Holy See was unoccupied for eleven years. These popes were almost never in Rome, and since at that time the conclave always took place where the pope had died, almost all of them were elected outside Rome, usually in Perugia or Viterbo. The city of Rome fell prey to utter neglect. At the beginning of the twelfth century it had been much rebuilt and decorated, but since then it had decayed. The Romans continued to shake off the yokes of tyrants and to set up consuls and tribunes of the people. The city had only a few thousand inhabitants and in this regard was greatly surpassed by Angevin Naples.

All these popes were highly respected men, and some of them are honored as saints. The Dominican Peter of Tarentaise, who died as Innocent V in 1276 after a pontificate of five months, was an outstanding theologian. In 1274, after the disappearance of the Latin Empire of Constantinople, Gregory X arranged with the Greeks a union, which, however, was not lasting. Nevertheless, in these papal elections the spirit of the waning thirteenth century made itself felt. It was a time of political weariness and religious overexcitement, the age of the agitation of the "Spirituals" in the Franciscan Order, of the ideas of Joachim of Flora, of the apocalyptic expectation of a *"papa angelicus."* Hence, even in the conclaves there was a seeking after unusual candidates. Gregory X, otherwise an admirable pope, was elected while he was lingering in the Holy Land as a crusader. He was not a cardinal or even a priest. The Portuguese John XXI (1276–1277), a physician and philosopher, had been, previous to his election, the personal physician of Gregory X. The princes, too, especially the king of Naples, desired an "angel pope," that is, an elderly man with as little knowledge of politics as possible, with whom they could accomplish what they wanted.

Exaggerated religiosity triumphed when in 1294, after a vacancy of twenty-seven months, the hermit Peter was fetched from his cell in the Abruzzi and made pope as Celestine V.

NAPLES UNDER THE ANGEVINS

Even after Manfred's defeat a Hohenstaufen party continued to exist in the kingdom of Naples. It induced the last heir of the Hohenstaufen, the fifteen-year-old son of Conrad IV, Conradin, who was being brought up in Germany, to undertake a romantic expedition to Italy. Charles of Anjou easily defeated the youth at the battle of Tagliacozzo. Conradin fled, was taken prisoner and brought to Naples, where he was beheaded. Because of the then close connection between the king of Naples and the popes this deed did not aid in raising the reputation of the papacy. Even worse was the fact that Charles persuaded Pope Martin IV (1281–1285) to excommunicate the Byzantine Emperor Michael VIII, who in 1274 had established the union with Gregory X at Lyon. In

1282 the Sicilians rose against Charles of Anjou in the bloody "Sicilian Vespers." The king of Aragón, Peter III, a son-in-law of Manfred, seized the island as heir of the Hohenstaufen, and from then on it was separated from the kingdom of Naples. Martin IV, entirely dependent on Naples, had a crusade preached against Sicily and Aragón.

This dependence continued also under the next king, Charles II (1285–1309). It was he who in 1294 contrived the election of the hermit Peter as pope and induced him to reside in Naples. But Celestine V was a genuine saint who realized his own unfitness for the papacy. After six months he abdicated. In the mighty Angevin fortress at Naples, still standing, Cardinal Benedict Gaetano was elected in his place as Boniface VIII. With this there again entered the political arena a powerful pope, who was, however, one of the unluckiest ever to have ruled the Church.

BONIFACE VIII (1294–1303)

In order to escape the unworthy dependence on the king of Naples, Boniface VIII at once transferred his residence to Rome, contrary to Charles' wish. To prevent the exploitation of the person of the ingenuous Celestine V in the interests of a schism, he kept his predecessor in a sort of honorable custody in a castle at Anagni till the saint's death in 1296. He did not realize that thereby he incurred from the first the enmity of the many adherents of the "angel pope." This was a character trait of Boniface VIII; excellent jurist that he was, he relied unwaveringly on abstract right, on his own right, and confronted with an almost childish lightheartedness the possible consequence of his action.

BEGINNING OF THE CONFLICT WITH FRANCE

In 1285 the ancient royal house of Scotland became extinct. This event produced not only internal confusion, but also an endless struggle between the kings of France and England, both of whom claimed the inheritance.[4] Thus there began almost two centuries of war, which weakened both England and France and prepared the decline of the mediaeval Christian family of peoples. Boniface VIII perceived from the start the pernicious character of this war. For him it also meant the disappearance of any hope of reviving the crusades. His diplomatic endeavors were wrecked, however, not so much by the opposition of the English King Edward I (1272–1307) as by that of Philip the Fair (1285–1314) of France. This grandson of Saint Louis was a capable and conscientious ruler and far superior to the pope as a politician. Boniface's proceedings against him were often quite naïve. When his exhortations to peace were not heeded, he decided to employ sanctions after the manner of an Innocent III. By the bull *Clericis Laicos* he forbade the French prelates to pay taxes to the king. He intended thereby to rally the prelates, who were always complaining of the pressure of taxation, and at the same time to close to the king the sources of money for his warlike undertakings against England. Philip the Fair replied by forbidding any export of money from France to Italy. At the time the *Camera Apostolica* received most of its revenue through this channel, and thus Boniface VIII revoked his

---

[4] The Scottish dynasty ended in the male line with the death of King Alexander III in 1286; his successor was his granddaughter, Margaret of Norway, who died in 1290 *en route* to Scotland. A host of pretenders thereupon advanced more or less tenuous claims to the vacant throne, but among them was *not* Edward I of England or Philip IV of France. However, as feudal overlord, Edward upheld his right to dispose of the crown, which he awarded in 1292 to John Baliol. The war between England and France erupted in 1293, and its source was the friction existing between the two kings in regard to Edward's position as Philip's vassal for Aquitaine. In 1295 John Baliol, resenting Edward's stern requirements in his capacity as Scotland's overlord, allied with France. See Maurice Powicke, *The Thirteenth Century: 1216-1307* (Oxford: 1953), pp. 597-606, 612 f., 644 f. (Translator's note.)

prohibition. In token of the reconciliation he canonized Louis IX, Philip's grandfather.

THE JUBILEE

Boniface proclaimed a jubilee for 1300. The term was borrowed from the Old Testament Jobel Year. All debts and other obligations were supposed to cease for the occasion, and the faithful were to have the opportunity of an especially comprehensive and solemn absolution from the guilt and, so far as this was within the Church's power, from the punishments of sin. The notion of a life-long penance or general penance, which earlier in the fifth and sixth centuries had led to the origin of the penitential vow, had always remained alive. The crusading vow was thus interpreted. The jubilee included another consideration too. The penitential discipline of the Middle Ages, with all its censures and reserved cases, had become extremely complicated, and hence this kind of single alleviation of the difficulties of absolution must have been looked upon as a benefaction. The idea met with an enthusiastic response. From all Christendom pilgrims streamed to Rome to visit the tombs of the apostles and gain the jubilee indulgence. For a moment the city of Rome was again the center of Christendom.

The jubilee was a great success. But immediately afterwards the conflict with Philip again erupted. When the king had a papal legate imprisoned, the pope, in the bull *Ausculta Fili,* cited him before his tribunal in Rome. Philip published a quite different and far more violent text of the bull and a coarse reply to it; though he did not dispatch the answer, he nevertheless obtained his end. The whole nation ranged itself on the side of the allegedly gravely insulted king against the pope.

285

THE BULL UNAM SANCTAM

Boniface VIII now issued the bull *Unam Sanctam*, in which he explained the idea of the two swords, the spiritual and the temporal. The spiritual sword is to be wielded by the Church, the temporal for the Church. The bull comes to a climax in the sentence: "We declare and define that it is necessary for the salvation of every human being that he be subject to the Roman Pontiff." This sentence can, of course, be correctly understood, and it then contains the traditional doctrine still held by the Church that the pope is the Vicar of Christ and that hence all Christians, even princes, are subordinate to him. Uttered, however, at this moment and so sharply, it could give the impression that the pope was claiming a direct power of ruling France.

Philip exploited the pope's awkward procedure to pose as the one unjustly attacked. He decided on the pope's deposition and appealed to a general council and to the future pope. To intensify still further the prevailing mood, Philip had the wildest accusations against Boniface brought before the States General at Paris: he was a simoniac and a heretic; he denied that the French had immortal souls, for he had stated that he would rather be a dog than a Frenchman; he had murdered Celestine V; he occupied himself with magic and maintained a termagant. Naturally, such nonsense was not believed by everyone, not even in France. But Boniface had known how to make himself all sorts of enemies, and thus this agitation was extremely serious.

In 1296 Boniface had excommunicated King Frederick II, son and successor of Peter of Aragón and Sicily, thereby arousing against himself the Ghibellines of Italy, who regarded the Aragonese as heirs of the Hohenstaufen. From the beginning he had been at odds with the "Spiritual" faction of the Franciscans. To this faction belonged the powerful Colonna family, which then had two cardinals, James and Peter. Cardinal James Colonna was a pious man of mystical tendencies; his sister, Blessed Margaret Colonna, had died as a Poor Clare in 1280. In 1297 Stephen Colonna in a clever *coup de main* plundered the papal treasury. Boniface summoned the entire family, including the two cardinals, before his tribunal, and had a crusade preached against them. This abuse illustrates the low level to which the crusading idea had sunk. Palestrina, the chief fortress of the Colonna, was taken and destroyed, and their property in Latium was confiscated. Acting imprudently once more, Boniface apportioned it among his nephews, the Gaetani. The Colonnas fled to France and made common cause with Philip the Fair.

ANAGNI

Philip was preparing his *coup d'état*. For this purpose he sent to Italy his chancellor, Guillaume de Nogaret. The pope was staying at Anagni, his usual residence. Suspecting nothing, he was preparing a new bull in which the excommunication and deposition of Philip were to be declared. But his plans were frustrated, for on September 7, 1303, Nogaret, together with Sciarra Colonna and 600 armed men, fell upon the defenseless city. The septuagenarian pope awaited them in full pontificals, a cross in his hand, and to their abuse merely replied, "Here is my neck, here is my head." The *coup d'état*, however, had been poorly arranged. Nogaret did not know what to do with the pope, and he had too few helpers. On September 9 the citizens of Anagni rose and expelled Nogaret and Sciarra Colonna. The liberated pope was honorably conducted back to Rome by 400 Roman knights, and there on October 11 he died of shock.

The attack on Anagni was, to be sure, a crime, a sacrilege. Before and after it there were other and greater outrages, but the attack on Anagni belongs to those occurrences which become symbols in history. This was the case with the Edict

287

of Milan. There were edicts favorable to the Christians before Constantine and persecutions after him; yet the Edict of 313 closed one period and inaugurated another.

However, it would be an error so to interpret the symbol of Anagni, as has often been done, as if from that point the mediaeval power of the popes, their political overlordship of Christianity, had ended. In the sense in which some historians delight to present it, there was no papal "power" in the entire Middle Ages. To attack and imprison a pope with 600 determined men would have been possible throughout the Middle Ages, even under Innocent III. What suffered a shock in Anagni was not the political or even the military power of the pope, which was always almost non-existent, but his moral prestige. That such an outrage could be undertaken, and even more that it remained unpunished, shows that on the part of rulers the attitude to religion was on the point of changing fundamentally. From a common duty, which they, like all the faithful, had to comply with, religion was becoming for rulers a mere activity, which they arranged like other activities, according to political calculations. To this extent Anagni means in Church History the end of the Middle Ages.

It could be asked who bears the guilt, not for the attack, because only Philip and Nogaret were guilty of that, but for the moral defeat of the papacy. Boniface VIII is certainly not blameless. In spite of his strict application of the law he did not understand how to give his dealings that power of conviction which all the activities of a pope must have. Gregory VII appeared before Christendom as the defender of the rights of the Church, and so did the popes who resisted the Hohenstaufen. But Boniface VIII appeared only too much as an aggressor. He could not have said with Gregory, "I have loved justice, therefore I die in exile," nor later with Pius IX, *"Non possumus."*

the exile at avignon and the great schism

BENEDICT XI, who occupied the See of Peter for a few months after Boniface VIII, died in Perugia, where, according to the prevailing custom, the cardinals then assembled for the conclave. They were entirely overshadowed by the opposition which the unfortunate pontificate of Boniface VIII had created: on the one side stood the supporters of Philip the Fair and of the Colonna family, deeply offended by Boniface VIII; and on the other side the friends of the ill-starred pope. For eleven months no agreement could be reached, but then a middle way was proposed. The supporters of Boniface VIII designated three French cardinals, who as such could be acceptable to Philip the Fair and who, likewise, were not conspicuous as enemies of Boniface VIII. The French for their part showed their willingness to oblige by electing from the three the archbishop of Bordeaux, Bertrand de Got, who had received the cardinalitial dignity from Boniface VIII and furthermore was not at the moment a subject of the French king, since the English had taken Bordeaux in 1303.

THE TRANSFER OF THE PAPAL RESIDENCE TO FRANCE

Bertrand de Got, who styled himself Clement V, was not present at the conclave. He did not go to Italy, but summoned the cardinals to Lyon for the coronation; however, the seat of the papal curia was not yet transferred to France. The treasure remained in a safe place at Assisi. Although Clement really intended to go to Rome eventually, he stayed in various French cities. From 1309 he settled in Avignon.

The position of the pope, confronted with pressure from the French king, was difficult. To remove a stumbling block, he annulled the bull *Unam Sanctam* for France, thereby making clear that he had no desire to challenge the king's power in the temporal sphere. Philip the Fair, however, was not overly interested in this material concession; rather he demanded a formal trial which would declare Boniface VIII to have been an unlawful pope, a request to which no pope could agree. To this was now added a second demand of a very dangerous character. The king required of the pope the abolition of the Order of Templars.

THE DESTRUCTION OF THE TEMPLARS

The Order of Knights Templars had been in existence for almost two centuries. Founded in Palestine by crusaders, it later spread to Europe, especially in France, and had not yet lost its original purpose, which was partly charitable and partly military. Only a short time previously Acre, the last base in Palestine, had fallen. But even if there were to be no more crusades, which no one at that time believed, the Templars could still seek for themselves a new field of knightly activity, as had the Hospitalers, who continued in the Mediterranean the war against the Turks, or the Teutonic Knights, who colonized and Christianized the northeast, or the Spanish Military Orders, which warred against the Moors and liberated Christian slaves.

Philip the Fair claimed to have acquired knowledge of secret atrocities among the Templars—idolatry, the most shameful immorality, and other crimes. In 1307 he had all the French Templars, about 2,000 in number, imprisoned. The extravagant charges, which recall the enormities alleged by the same king against Boniface VIII, merit no credence whatsoever. Individual lapses were to be found among the Templars, just as in any other religious community; but neither then nor later was any proof of real crimes produced. However, they had to be guilty because they were wealthy, and the king coveted their possessions. Since the property of the Templars had the character of ecclesiastical charitable institutes, the king needed the pope's co-operation in dissolving the Order. To intimidate the pope, he submitted to him confessions wrung by torture, which confirmed the accusations. The weak Clement V let himself be imposed upon. He was in constant fear that, if he antagonized the king, he would be forced to start proceedings against Boniface VIII. Finally, he summoned a general council to Vienne in 1311 in order to transfer to it the responsibility. However, the Fathers of the council were not convinced of the guilt of the Templars by the documents laid before them. Meanwhile, many Templars had already been executed. The pope, under unrelenting pressure from the king, who was present at the council, at last found a way out. Without a judicial sentence, he suppressed the Order by an executive decree, a right which every pope has in regard to any Order. The property, in order not to be diverted from its original purpose, was awarded to the Knights of Rhodes and other Military Orders, who, however, actually acquired little of it. The executions, which can with difficulty be termed administrative measures, continued. Finally, in 1314 the Grand Master, Jacques de Molay, maintaining to the end the innocence of his subjects, was burned.

The destruction of the Templars is one of the greatest scandals which Church History has to record. The memory of

Clement V, who played Pilate's role in it, is grievously burdened.

JOHN XXII (1316–1334)

On the death of Clement V the Holy See remained vacant for more than two years. Finally, in 1316, Cardinal Jacques d'Euse, bishop of Avignon, was elected at Lyon. He called himself John XXII.

John XXII is the most important pope of the fourteenth century. Excelling both as a jurist and as an administrator, above all else a tireless worker, in politics firmer than Clement V and cleverer and luckier than Boniface VIII, he would have belonged among the greatest popes of all centuries, if he had possessed a broader vision and if his thinking had been more related to the salvation of souls and to the papal office. Just as he obstinately defended his own peculiar opinions in his capacity of theologian, so too in politics he was shortsighted and thus caused much harm, especially in Germany.

In the German Empire the death of Henry VII of the Luxemburg dynasty (1314) was followed by a contested election. Both claimants, Duke Louis of Bavaria and Duke Frederick of Austria, appealed to the pope as arbiter. John XXII accepted the appeal but issued no decision, not even after Louis of Bavaria had defeated his opponent in 1322 and had been accepted as king throughout Germany. Instead, on the basis of a long obsolete right, he named an imperial vicar for Italy for the period of the vacancy of the imperial throne; he selected for this post the old enemy of the German Empire, King Robert of Naples. Louis the Bavarian, who was no statesman and even less a theologian, could only consider himself attacked without reason. He too appointed an imperial vicar for Italy, whereupon the pope threatened him with the ban of the Church. Louis appealed to a general council, and since he had thereby formally placed himself in the wrong, John XXII actually excommunicated him in 1324. To Louis's court there now flocked all the opponents of the pope and the papacy: Michele of Cesena, the Minister General of the Franciscans, who was at variance with his own Order because of the dispute over poverty; the Englishman William of Ockam, likewise a Franciscan and famous as a philosopher; the Parisian professors Marsiglio of Padua and John of Jandun. In the literary propaganda which stemmed from these circles the whole doctrine of the primacy was practically denied. This was the first anti-papal agitation on a grand scale in the theological and juridical fields. Louis the Bavarian stood apart personally from this activity and would gladly have made peace with the pope. But at Sachsenhausen in 1324 the German princes protested the excommunication of their king and declared John XXII a heretic. The pope could no longer remain indifferent. He placed all Germany under interdict. Louis the Bavarian went to Rome, allowed himself to receive there the imperial crown from Sciarra Colonna, the old enemy of the pope, and set up an anti-pope. After Louis's inglorious departure from Italy, the anti-pope hurried to Avignon and begged pardon from John XXII.

Thus at his death John XXII left the situation in Germany in a hopelessly bungled condition. Though formally he was almost always in the right, he cannot escape blame. For in conflicts, the pope, to a greater extent than a secular ruler, must be careful that his measures be not only juridically well-founded but that they also be effective.

THE PAPAL FINANCES

On the other hand, John XXII's pontificate was of great importance in the field of ecclesiastical administration. Considered in a merely superficial aspect, far more was done at

Avignon in the way of writing than had previously been the case at Rome. Now for the first time the papal curia assumed the character of a central administration. It still retains this, and in an ever increasing manner. John XXII devoted particular attention to finances. The financial basis of the Holy See was the *census*, that is, the revenues from the papal territories and the feudal payments from princes invested by the pope with fiefs, notably the king of Naples. To the *census* pertained likewise the chancery fees which were paid for the expediting of decrees of every sort, from the conferring of the pallium on archbishops to the customary privileges and dispensations. All this existed before the Avignon period. Furthermore, the collecting of taxes on ecclesiastical benefices was not new. But it was systematically extended and perfected by the Avignon popes and especially by John XXII. It comprised now the *fructus medii temporis,* which meant that the revenues of an ecclesiastical benefice from the death or resignation of the incumbent till the investiture of his successor flowed into the *Camera Apostolica.* Even after he had taken possession, the new incumbent of the benefice turned over to the *Camera* a part of his first year's income; this was known as the *annates,* or revenues of the first year. By virtue of the *exspectatio* a candidate could have a benefice that was not yet vacant reserved for himself, but for it he had to make a sort of down payment.

These and similar sources of money, which were newly introduced in the Avignon period or were collected more efficiently than earlier, had, of course, their somber side. Where it was a question merely of corporate bodies with no obligation in regard to the care of souls, as in the case of many chapters, no objection could be made to the fact that, for a payment, there was acquired a title to a pension; but the

situation was quite different when it concerned offices connected with the care of souls.

On the other hand, if in many presentations of history
there occur worn-out references to the financial adroitness and
to the traffic in benefices of the Avignon curia, that is, to say
the least, a very superficial view of the situation. The curia,
like every great central administration, had to have a financial
basis. The revenues from the Papal State were at that time
almost non-existent. Besides, it was not reasonable for a small
Italian territory to have to bear the whole burden of the ecclesiastical government. The Avignon "financial skill" was nothing more than a taxation of ecclesiastical property in all lands.
This taxation did not affect the people but the prelates and
other users of ecclesiastical goods and, to an extent, the
princes, at least indirectly.

The total of the revenues in question is often grossly exaggerated in history books. The note of the Florentine chronicler,
Villani, that John XXII left behind a treasury of 25,000,000
gold *scudi*, has been cited again and again in amazement and
indignation. We know today that it was actually 750,000. The
judgment of posterity has been influenced even more by Petrarch, who painted in darkest colors the avarice of the Avignon curia. But Petrarch was himself a keen benefice-hunter,
and the abundance that was made possible for him in Avignon
was far from satisfying to him; hence his bitterness.

These benefice-seekers who haunted Avignon and later
Rome and who did not disappear until the period of the Council of Trent were an unpleasant by-product of the curia's administrative system. There were clerics who at times lingered
for years at the curia and did nothing but wait for the vacancy
of benefices. Incidentally, it appears that conditions were not
in too bad a state, even with the financial demands of the

curia: despite all the various taxes, fees, and other payments, it was still worthwhile to apply to it for benefices.

THE LATER POPES AT AVIGNON

John XXII's successor was Benedict XII (1334–1342), a serious, pious Cistercian. He would have been glad to end the unfortunate quarrel with Louis the Bavarian, but the French king and the Neapolitan king knew how to thwart his efforts, for they feared that the pope would become too independent politically through a reconciliation with Germany and hence would be able to restore the curia to Rome. Benedict XII, for his part, hardly contemplated a return to Rome, for he began to build in Avignon the mighty palace which even today dominates the city, one of the greatest monuments of late Gothic. The unending quarrel with Germany brought it about that in 1338, at Rhens on the Rhine, the electoral princes declared by law that the election of the German king and emperor was independent of the pope. Thereby the pope lost one of his most important political prerogatives.

The next pope, Clement VI (1342–1352), purchased for the Papal State the city of Avignon and its territory, which hitherto had belonged to the kingdom of Naples and where the pope had lived, so to speak, as a guest. The stay of the pope in the city on the Rhone seemed on the point of becoming permanent. In the quarrel with the emperor, Clement VI took a more drastic step: he renewed the excommunication of Louis the Bavarian and called upon the electoral princes to choose a new king. Since Louis was himself constantly losing adherents in Germany, the electors, who only recently had rejected any intervention of the pope, agreed and selected as German king Henry VII's grandson, Charles of Luxemburg, king of Bohemia. Before war could break out between the Luxemburger and the Bavarian, Louis died and Charles IV was accepted by all. Thus the miserable quarrel ended of itself. But immense harm had been done to ecclesiastical life in Germany, which had lain under interdict for twenty years, and to the papacy itself, for it was difficult to convince the Germans that they had been justly dealt with by the French popes.

At the election of the next pope, Innocent VI (1352–1362), the cardinals laid down an election capitulation, the first in history. By this is meant a sworn agreement in which all the cardinals obliged themselves, in the event of their own election to the papacy, to definite restrictions on their spiritual and sovereign authority. Such agreements had already played a role in episcopal elections, and from 1519 a capitulation was regularly an element in the imperial election. Later, such arrangements were strictly forbidden in ecclesiastical elections; in papal elections they are in any case invalid, because the pope always possesses the fullness of authority and cannot limit himself. Nevertheless, the capitulations represented a moral pressure and at least indicated the growing power of the cardinals, who began to consider the pope as one of their number—another unpleasant phenomenon of the Avignon period.

Innocent VI had to occupy himself with the affairs of the city of Rome, where complete anarchy reigned. The ceaseless feuds of Colonna and Orsini led to popular risings. Twice the Roman notary, Cola di Rienzo, was able, as "tribune of the people," to seize power in the city; the second time (1354) he was recognized by the pope, but he met his death in a new popular tumult. The pope sent as legate to Italy the Spanish Cardinal Aegidius Albornoz to establish order. He could not have made a better choice than this outstanding statesman. As just as he was energetic, Albornoz regulated the situation in the Papal State as well as could be done in a mediaeval principality. Henceforth there was no obstacle to the pope's returning to Rome.

Even in Avignon no one could close his eyes to the necessity that, sooner or later, the papacy must again transfer its seat to Rome. Innocent VI's successor, the saintly Urban V (1362–1370), was urged from all sides, not only by Petrarch, in whom the national rather than the ecclesiastical viewpoint seems to have predominated, but also by Saint Birgitta of Sweden, who, after numerous pilgrimages, had settled near the holy shrines of Rome, and by the German Emperor Charles IV. Hence, Urban V decided on at least a visit to Rome. He was, of course, everywhere welcomed with joy by the Italians, who had not seen a pope for sixty-three years; but Urban found conditions in Rome far worse than he had expected and soon returned to Avignon. Nevertheless, with this journey the stone was put in motion; the spell was broken. The exile at Avignon was at an end.

JUDGMENT ON AVIGNON

The stay of the popes at Avignon was generally regarded by the older Church historians as a disastrous period. The expressions "exile," "banishment," "Babylonian Captivity," which were already used by contemporaries, are still met in historical writings. However, a calmer and more objective judgment has long prevailed.

First of all, the expressions "exile" or even "captivity" are entirely misleading. In Avignon the popes were sheltered more securely and more decently than in Rome. In Avignon there were no Orsini and Colonna, no Guelfs and Ghibellines, no street rioting and tribunes of the people. The popes of the thirteenth century, in fact from Gregory VII, had had real reason to seek asylum outside Rome. Some had never been able to enter the Eternal City during their entire pontificate. And it cannot be denied that Avignon was a very favorable site for the papal curia. For a long time Rome had not lain at the geographical center of Christendom. Since the crusades had failed and little hope remained of cracking the Islamic wall to the south and the southeast, the center of gravity of Christendom had again moved to the northwest. In every respect, including the intellectual, the leading power was France; the lands then affected by France's leadership—England, Scotland, Flanders, Aragón, and Castile—lay nearer to Avignon than to Rome; rising Bohemia and economically important North Italy were not much more distant. Avignon could be reached from almost everywhere without having to cross mountains; it was not cut off from the north like Rome by the Alps and the Apennines. Considered merely from the standpoint of administrative technique, Avignon was still more favored. Of course, and herein lay Avignon's weakness, the Church is not merely an administrative machine, the pope is not a mere supreme official. Avignon had no Apostle Peter, no tombs of the martyrs, no millennial tradition. The pope is the head of the Church because he is the successor of Saint Peter as first bishop of Rome, and he is bishop of Rome because he is the head of the Church.

That in Avignon seven successive popes were Frenchmen cannot be termed a grievance; for one would have to prove that Frenchmen were less suited for the highest dignity in the Church than were others. The real evil lay not in the persons of the popes but in the circumstance that the papacy itself had become a national institution or at least seemed to be. Just as the papacy is not an Italian institution or must not appear to be such, so also it must not be French. But when the popes and almost all the cardinals and curial officials were French and their seat was entirely surrounded by France and France was the single European great power, it could not but result that to other nations and to the French themselves the papacy appeared to be a national institution and that all the actions of the popes were judged from this viewpoint.

All in all, it cannot be said that the Avignon popes governed the Church badly. As a matter of fact, they considerably raised the prestige of the papacy, which had suffered the most severe shocks from the election of Celestine V and the affair at Anagni. When the curia returned to Rome, there were many reasons to hope for a new period of brilliance. That it did not take place is due to the Great Schism, which at once broke out and which itself was caused, at least indirectly, by the prolonged absence from Rome.

THE GREAT SCHISM

THE RETURN TO ROME

Urban V died not long after his return to Avignon. Immediately after his departure from Rome disturbances broke out all over Italy; their center was the republic of Florence. The Italians have never understood what is self-evident to Catholics of other lands, that the pope is still the supreme head of the Church even when he does not advance their local interests. The new pope, Gregory XI, sent to Italy some Breton mercenaries, who incurred general hatred by their excesses. Their leader was Cardinal Robert of Geneva, the later anti-pope Clement VII. Interdict was laid on Florence in 1376.

At this time there lived in Siena a pious virgin, Catherine Benincasa, a divinely favored mystic, who was likewise highly intelligent and farsighted. She was very little concerned with nations, but only with the Church and souls. Catherine was not a nun, but a Dominican tertiary. She exerted herself in person and through letters to reconcile the republic of

300

Florence with the pope and thereby to make possible the return of the pope to Rome. Although she was not yet thirty years old, her prestige was so great that the pope, the Florentines, and others accepted her advice with reverence and in a sense recognized her as their diplomatic intermediary. In 1376 she went to Avignon.

Of course, it was not only the admonitions of Saint Catherine that moved Gregory XI to the final return to Rome. But even contemporaries attributed the chief merit to her. On September 13, 1376, Gregory XI left Avignon forever. In Genoa he was met by Catherine, who had in the meantime been to Florence. The cardinals continually pressed the pope to go back to France. Catherine used all her influence and candidly told the pope that he must conquer his timidity and irresolution. On December 5 the pope landed at Corneto in the Papal State. From here he had to negotiate with the city of Rome and not until January 17, 1377, was he able to enter the Eternal City.

The return had occurred almost too soon. All Italy was still in ferment, and at that very moment Robert of Geneva with his mercenaries was staging a blood bath at Cesena, so that everything was stirred up anew. By his prudent behavior the pope succeeded in calming spirits and even in preparing an agreement with Florence. However, before the peace became a reality, he died at Rome on March 27, 1378.

THE ELECTION OF URBAN VI

Sixteen cardinals entered the conclave at the Vatican— four Italians, one Spaniard, and eleven Frenchmen. Several had remained behind in Avignon. The Romans demonstrated in the square before Saint Peter's, rang the bells uninterruptedly, and shouted for a Roman pope. In all haste the cardinals elected the archbishop of Bari, Bartholomeo Prignano. He was not a cardinal, but he was a native Italian, a subject of the Neapolitan Angevins; he had long lived in Avignon, and thus he was regarded as a compromise candidate. While the pope-elect, who was present in Rome, was on his way to the Vatican, the mob, unaware that the election had taken place, invaded the palace. The cardinals and conclavists, believing their lives to be in danger, hastily dressed the aged Cardinal Tibaldeschi, a Roman, in the papal garments, seated him on the throne, and fled. The old man long endeavored in vain to explain to the excited crowd that another had been elected. At length the people became calm. The next day the city magistrate apologized in the presence of the cardinals and asserted that all now knew that not Tibaldeschi but Prignano had been elected. Hence, with the traditional ceremonies, Prignano was crowned as Urban VI. The cardinals informed the princes of the result of the election. The cardinals still at Avignon sent written congratulations.

All would have turned out well had not Urban VI from the beginning exhibited an imprudence and obstinacy that almost leave doubts as to whether his mind was entirely normal. He treated the cardinals, who in any case were sighing for Avignon, as crudely as possible, yet neglected to appoint other cardinals on whom he could rely. Furthermore, he immediately quarreled with Queen Joanna I of Naples. The cardinals regretted their choice. On the plea of the summer's heat they disappeared from Rome and met in Anagni. Even the Italians were there; the aged Tibaldeschi was already dead. From Anagni on August 9, 1378, they issued a manifesto in which they declared that the election of four months ago had been made under force and was therefore invalid. The queen of Naples and the French King Charles V promised their assistance. The cardinals went to Fondi under the protection of Count Gaetano, with whom Urban VI had also quarreled, and as soon as the letter of the French king arrived they elected Cardinal Robert of Geneva as Clement VII. With this began the Great Western Schism, destined to last thirty-nine years.

THE SCHISM

It was extremely difficult for Christendom to decide on which side lay right. The election of Urban VI had occurred under unusual circumstances. Qualified witnesses, the electors themselves, had declared that they had acted under violence and compulsion. Clement VII, unanimously elected by the cardinals, established himself at Avignon, where for more than two generations Christendom had been accustomed to seek the pope. It is no wonder, then, that even the best men were not in agreement. Careful investigations have so cleared up the incidents of the election of Urban VI that we can now safely say it was valid. Fear of the rioting mob only hastened the election; it did not dictate the choice. The comedy of Tibaldeschi clearly proves that the cardinals feared they had elected a candidate unacceptable to the people. That they afterwards did homage to Urban, received Communion from him, and asked favors for themselves, is of less importance; it can indeed be explained not so much by fear of the people as by fear of Urban.

At the time, however, all this was by no means clear. Even saints, such as the Dominican Vincent Ferrer, were on the side of the anti-pope. Catherine of Siena, on the other hand, adhered to Urban. She sent the cardinals a letter full of glowing indignation, yet at the same time did not spare the obstinate pope candid admonitions.

Urban was recognized from the beginning by Emperor Charles IV, who, however, died in 1378; by his successor Wenceslas (1378–1400); by Italy except for the kingdom of

Naples; and by England, Hungary, and Scandinavia. To the obedience of the Avignon pope belonged France, Spain, Sicily, Naples, Savoy, Scotland, Portugal, and part of Germany. But the obediences varied. Often dioceses and Orders were split. Naturally, political opposition came into play, such as the hostility between France and England. After some first hesitation the University of Paris acknowledged Clement VII, but eventually it adopted a strict neutrality.

Of course, this was an extremely sad and, in the long run, pernicious state of affairs for the Church. One should not, however, imagine that the immediate harm to the care of souls was too great. Among the faithful there was no falling away from the faith, no heretical doctrine, no rebellion against ecclesiastical authority. No one doubted that the unity of the Church continued in the communion of the successor of Peter, but no one knew which of the two claimants was this successor. At least in the regions where the dioceses themselves were not split, the care of souls continued in the customary way. On the whole, of course, harm could not fail to appear. The schism did not beget religious indifference, but on the contrary religious overexcitement. The whole Church became, so to speak, nervous. Fantastic plans of reform made their appearance.

THE RIVAL LINES OF POPES

The unfortunate Urban VI, instead of devoting himself to the ending of the schism, warred against Naples in a sort of monomania. He excommunicated Queen Joanna, proclaimed a "crusade" against her, called upon her cousin, Charles of Durazzo, to overthrow her, and, when Charles had conquered Naples, broke with him too and excommunicated him. His own cardinals rebelled, and Urban had some of them executed. He died at Rome in 1389, unregretted. His successor, Boniface IX (1389–1404), made peace with King Ladislas of Naples, son of Charles of Durazzo, and was then recognized throughout Italy. But since Ladislas laid claim to Hungary, in opposition to King Sigismund of Bohemia, the latter passed to the side of the anti-pope. After the short reign of Innocent VII (1404–1406), the Venetian Gregory XII (1406–1415) was elected.

At Avignon Clement VII was succeeded by the Spaniard Pedro de Luna, who became Benedict XIII (1394–1423).

Meanwhile, on all sides, especially at the University of Paris, plans were proposed for remedying the schism. One possibility would have been for one or both of the two claimants to abdicate voluntarily. Or both could select a court of arbitration and bind themselves to submit to its decision. Most popular was the idea of summoning a general council which could depose one or both claimants, even against their will. Benedict XIII and Gregory XII negotiated through envoys at Marseille in 1407 in regard to bringing about a personal interview. But the negotiations aborted and injured the prestige of both, because people began to question the good will of the two popes. Finally, the two colleges of cardinals and most princes withdrew their obedience and summoned a general council to meet at Pisa in 1409.

THE COUNCIL OF PISA

The Council of Pisa was very well attended and would have been an authentic ecumenical council if the pope had been represented. It took the stand that both claimants, as disturbers of the unity of the Church, were under suspicion of heresy and hence were to be regarded as deposed. As yet there was no talk of a power of the council over the pope. Proceeding from the fiction that the papal throne was unoccupied, both colleges of cardinals elected the archbishop of

305

Milan, a Greek from Crete, as Pope Alexander V. He took up residence in Bologna and was acknowledged by most countries. Spain, Portugal, and Scotland upheld Benedict XIII, while Gregory XII had the obedience of the German King Rupert of the Palatinate, King Ladislas of Naples, and a part of Italy. When Alexander V died after a year, he received as his successor John XXIII. Thus there were now three popes instead of two and it had become still harder to decide which was the real one. Even later no one in Rome presumed to regard the two Pisan popes simply as anti-popes. The next pope who assumed the name of Clement called himself Clement VII (1523–1534), but the next Alexander styled himself Alexander VI (1492–1503). Even among the portraits of the popes at San Paolo, Alexander V and John XXIII are still found in the series. It was only in 1947 that they were stricken from the *Annuario Pontificio*.

THE COUNCIL OF CONSTANCE

A new general council now seemed all the more the only hope. The German King Sigismund (1410–1437) induced John XXIII to convoke the council as pope in the usual way. It met at Constance in 1414.

John XXIII had agreed to this because he felt certain of the majority of the prelates at the council. Scarcely had he arrived in Constance, however, when he became convinced that the atmosphere was unfavorable to him. An entirely new form of organization was decided upon: voting would not be by heads, but, following the model of the universities, by nations. Five nations were recognized—the German, French, English, Italian, and the college of cardinals. Thus the preponderance of the many Italian prelates who adhered to John XXIII was wrecked. At the same time it was decided that for this once not only the bishops but also the theologians, canonists, and ambassadors of princes should have a seat and a vote in the individual nations.

When John XXIII saw the waning of his hopes of being confirmed by the council as pope, he secretly left Constance, hoping thereby to disrupt the gathering. As a matter of fact, many regarded the council as shipwrecked. But it was unthinkable to elect a fourth pope. At this juncture Jean Gerson, the celebrated chancellor of the University of Paris, and Cardinal Pierre d'Ailly, called the council together. They declared that the council was superior to the pope and hence did not need his authorization and could not be dissolved by him. This principle was theologically impossible, but in their desperation the Fathers did not know what else to try. John XXIII was captured in flight, brought back to Constance, and deposed. He recognized his situation as lost and submitted. One of the three popes was removed.

Gregory XII, who was now ninety years old, let the council know that he was prepared to abdicate if, for the sake of form, it would allow itself to be summoned by him as a council. The council agreed to this, and he abdicated. He received the title of Cardinal of Porto and died in 1417, a month before the election of Martin V. Many saw in this a sign that he had been the legitimate pope.

Now only Benedict XIII was left. The tireless Emperor Sigismund journeyed to Perpignan to induce him to resign. But Benedict was firmly convinced of the justice of his position and did not yield. The Spaniards, who alone constituted his obedience, repudiated him, and since he no longer had any adherents the council could depose him without risk. The Spaniards took their places in the council as the sixth nation. The cardinals entered the conclave and on November 11, 1417, elected as Pope Martin V Otto Colonna, who had been made a cardinal by Innocent VII of the Roman line. With this the Great Schism was at an end.

John XXIII was freed from custody by Martin V and received the title of Cardinal of Frascati, but he died soon after. Cosimo de' Medici had a tomb built for him by Donatello in the baptistery of Florence, and on it can be read the cautious inscription: "Baldassare Cossa, John XXIII, who once was pope." Benedict XIII resided in the castle of Peñiscola and continued to dress as pope. The king of Aragón, Alfonso V, permitted this in order to be able, if necessary, to exercise some slight pressure on the real pope. He took care that, after his death in 1423, Benedict XIII received a successor, a canon of Barcelona, who styled himself Clement VIII.

THE EPOCH OF THE CONCILIAR THEORY
AFTER THE COUNCIL OF CONSTANCE

PASTOR'S HISTORY OF THE POPES

It is with the election of Martin V in 1417 that Ludwig von Pastor (1854–1928) begins his *Geschichte der Päpste seit dem Ausgang des Mittelalters*.[1] This work comprises twenty-two volumes, the first of which appeared in 1886; the last ones, extending to 1799, were issued posthumously in 1933, but they had been substantially completed by him. Pastor's presentation, based on comprehensive study in archives and libraries and at times displaying brilliance of style, has so moulded the history of the Church for the four centuries he covers that it is neither possible nor desirable to ignore it. It will always be possible further to clarify single points, but there are very few prospects of uncovering anything sub-

---

[1] In the German original, Pastor's work consists of sixteen volumes, several of which are in more than one part. The English translation comprises forty volumes. Pastor actually begins with a brief account (more than 200 pages) of the Renaissance, the Avignon sojourn, and the Great Western Schism. (Translator's note.)

stantially new. Naturally, Pastor is taken to task by different groups. To non-Catholics his presentation is too Catholic, to some Catholics it is not sufficiently apologetic. Individual nations are in general dissatisfied with him in those sections where, in their opinion, he ought to bring them into bolder relief. But basically this merely shows how unpartisan he was. This does not mean that we need to follow him in all his judgments of value. In general he overemphasizes the cultural primacy of the popes. Likewise, he may have been too easy on some popes, such as Pius V and Clement VIII, and too severe on others, such as Eugene IV, Clement VII, and Innocent X. He does not do full justice to the political importance of Alexander VI.

MARTIN V (1417–1431)

After the stress of the schism and of the Council of Constance, the new pope had as his principal concern to calm the Church, as it were, and lead it back to a normal life; at the same time there was some question of again making Rome, neglected for centuries, the real center of Christendom. For both tasks Martin V, a serious, sensible Roman of a great family, was the right man.

First of all, he disappointed, while still in Constance, the expectations of the overheated members of the council by not accepting in their entirety the many reform decrees issued by that assembly. To many reform then meant especially that the Holy See should no longer receive money. Instead of allowing his conduct to be dictated by the excited council, Martin V negotiated concordats with individual nations.

In Italy he recognized Queen Joanna II (1414–1435), who had succeeded her brother Ladislas in the government of Naples and had hitherto opposed the Roman See. The Papal

State had almost wholly fallen into the hands of one of the so numerous contemporary *condottieri*, Braccio of Montone, known as Fortebraccio. Martin V took him into the papal service and had him subject Bologna. The Papal State was still, in true mediaeval fashion, a mixture of more or less autonomous feudal lordships, communes, and provinces, with extremely complicated systems of rights and privileges. On the whole, Martin V restored the order which Cardinal Albornoz had earlier established. Just the same, it was still far from being a state in the modern sense, but from then on the pope was to some extent its ruler. This was a blessing for the city of Rome, where Martin returned in 1420, which was in an unbelievably decayed condition. It was still a century before Rome again numbered 50,000 inhabitants. The jubilee of 1425 for the first time in years brought many pilgrims to Rome.

Martin V appointed few cardinals, but they were good ones: Domenico Capranica, Cesarini, Ardicino della Porta, Niccolò Albergati, and some non-Italians. In 1429, through negotiations with Alfonso V of Aragón, he liquidated the remnant of the schism. The "pope" at Peñiscola, Clement VIII, abdicated, and his "cardinals," to save face, elected Martin V. The canonist Alfonso Borgia of Valencia, who had performed good services on this occasion, was named by Martin bishop of Valencia. He later became Pope Calixtus III.

The Council of Constance had decreed that a new general council should meet in five years and thereafter every ten years. Martin V wished rightly to have nothing to do with such a permanent ecclesiastical parliament. But since at that time Christendom looked to a general council for its welfare, he decided in the last year of his pontificate to summon a council to Basel, naming as its president Cardinal Cesarini. The pope died before the council met.

EUGENE IV (1431–1447)

His successor was the Venetian, Eugene IV, an Augustinian Hermit of ascetic life and nephew of Gregory XII. His pontificate began under bad omens. The first was the crushing defeat of the crusading army fighting against the Hussites at Taus in 1431. The second was a serious conflict with the family of his predecessor, the powerful Colonnas, and the third was the disastrous decision to dissolve the Council of Basel, which had just begun. The pope's distrust was justified, but in this way he drove the council into the schism that he wanted to avoid. The loyal Cesarini, whom Martin V had appointed his legate at the council, vainly urged prudence. The Fathers of the council did not submit, but renewed the declaration of Constance that the council was superior to the pope. As the political situation in Italy became ever more threatening for the pope through the hostility of the Colonnas, of Duke Filippo Visconti of Milan, and of Fortebraccio, he withdrew the bull of dissolution without thereby accepting the decrees already issued.

The duke of Milan contrived at Rome a revolution against the pope. Once again the republic was proclaimed. The pope, pursued with stones, fled to a Tiber skiff. He went to Florence and settled at the Dominican monastery at Santa Maria Novella. The Fathers at Basel grew increasingly bolder because of the pope's political powerlessness. They issued radical reform decrees for the pope, abolishing all the taxes and other revenues of the curia. But they deceived themselves in regarding the pope as already beaten. The capable, if harsh, Cardinal Vitelleschi restored order in Rome and the Papal State. The pope's prestige rose mightily when an embassy of the Greek emperor asked him to inaugurate negotiations for reunion. Since Basel was inconvenient for the Greeks, Eugene IV ordered the transfer of the council to Ferrara. This was for the

311

Fathers at Basel a powerful blow. The elements loyal to the pope—Cesarini, Nicholas of Cusa, and others—went to Ferrara. The rest remained behind in Basel to prevent a moral victory for the pope, but they could not be regarded as a legitimate council.

THE UNION WITH THE GREEKS

To Ferrara in 1437 came 700 Greeks, all that the Greek Church could exhibit of worthiness and learning, headed by Emperor John VIII Palaeologus, the Patriarch Joseph of Constantinople, Archbishops Mark of Ephesus, Bessarion of Nicaea, Isidore of Kiev, and the scholarly Gemistos Plethon. Among the Latins the most outstanding names were those of Cardinal Niccolò Albergati, who presided, the humanist Thomas Parentucelli, later Pope Nicholas V, and Ambrose Traversari, general of the Camaldolese. The negotiations were exceedingly difficult and frequently threatened to collapse. Chiefly on financial grounds the council was transferred in 1439 to Florence, where on July 6 the union was solemnly proclaimed. There quickly followed unions with the lesser Oriental Churches—with the Armenians in 1439, the Monophysite Jacobites of Egypt and Ethiopia in 1441, the East Syrian Jacobites in 1444, and the Nestorian Chaldees in 1445.

The union of Florence, like the earlier ones, was of slight duration. However, it would be unjust to doubt the good will of the Greeks, even if there were some among them who accepted it only exteriorly and, scarcely back home, again fell away, like Gemistos Plethon, who was more a Platonist than a Christian and despised the Latins as barbarians. To be sure, political reasons swayed the Greeks—the need of support from the West in view of the growing danger from the Turks. Emperor John VIII did little to carry out the union, but his brother and successor, Constantine XI, renewed it in 1452 and remained faithful until the end. It would have required a longer period to eradicate the schism, deeply rooted as it was in clergy and people. But in 1453 the Turks took Constantinople and forcibly restored the old situation.

One need not doubt the good will of the Greeks, but it may be wondered whether all of them had a correct notion of the union, whether they did not conceive it rather as a sort of treaty among equals than as a real submission to the Church and her head. Only recently they had seen the Latin Church split into several obediences under several popes. They themselves were now such an obedience, negotiating with the others. As a matter of fact Greek envoys had been present at Pisa and Constance. The essential difference, however, lay in this, that in the Latin schism there was never a doubt of law as to whether the Roman bishop was the head of the Church, but only a doubt of fact as to what person was at the moment the legitimate Roman bishop. Hence, the Latin schism could be settled by an agreement or arrangement, whereas the Byzantine schism could be healed only by a one-sided submission.

However, the work of union at Florence was not in vain. The Latins, who had lost almost all contact with the Greek Church, knew now what were the real points of controversy. Above all, at Florence once and for all it was made clear that the question of rite had nothing to do with the union—in other words, a Greek converted to the Catholic Church did not have to adopt the Latin rite. In the discussions at Constance this had been still doubtful. Since all the Orientals clung passionately to their beautiful, ancient, and revered liturgical usages, this was an important point. The Florentine decrees, then, remained the basis for all later unions.

313

THE SCHISM OF BASEL

The success of the Council of Ferrara-Florence was so obvious that the Fathers at Basel were faced with the alternative of submitting or of going into open schism. They chose the latter and set up an anti-pope. Since they needed a brilliant name, their gaze fell on a widower, Amadeus VIII, count and, since 1416, duke of Savoy, who had partially handed over the government to his son and was living a sort of hermit existence on the Lake of Geneva. Curiously enough, this otherwise not unintelligent prince accepted the election and had himself consecrated a bishop. He called himself Felix V. The Great Western Schism was still so vivid in the memory of all that no one found joy in this little schism. The princes, however, did not neglect the opportunity to extort concessions from the Church. Charles VII of France had already in 1438, before the election of Felix V, on the basis of the decrees of Basel, issued the Pragmatic Sanction of Bourges, whereby the Church of France became almost independent of the pope—the foundation of the later "Gallican Liberties." The German electoral princes declared a sort of neutrality *vis-à-vis* both popes. Alfonso V of Aragón recognized Felix V, not because he seriously regarded him as legitimate, but because he wished, in regard to the pope, to have at hand a pledge that he could exchange for Naples. Joanna II, the last of the Angevin house, had adopted Alfonso of Aragón, who was already king of Sicily, and had named him heir of Naples. He needed only the consent of the papal suzerain. But Eugene IV would have preferred Duke René, of the younger line of Anjou, who likewise regarded himself as heir. Alfonso defeated René in battle and proposed a compromise to the pope: he would drop Felix V, and the pope would in exchange invest him with Naples and allow his illegitimate son Ferrante to succeed him in Naples, though not in Aragón. The agreement was realized in 1444.

Once more the bishop of Valencia, Alfonso Borgia, performed good services, for which he became a cardinal.

Now too the city of Rome was safe on all sides, and Eugene IV could return there after an absence of nine years. Ever since the popes have only rarely left the Eternal City for any length of time.

The negotiations with the German princes and with the new Emperor Frederick III likewise developed favorably. The pope was represented by Parentucelli and Nicholas of Cusa, the emperor by his secretary, Enea Silvio Piccolomini. Eugene IV did not live to see the final settlement, but on his deathbed he knew that the schism was at an end.

NICHOLAS V (1447–1455)

His successor was Thomas Parentucelli, a refined humanist, who had worked himself up from poor circumstances. Nicholas V assumed the papacy under much more auspicious omens than had his predecessor. The Concordat of Vienna with the emperor was signed in 1448 and at the same time that of Aschaffenburg with the electors; thus did the Council of Basel come to an end. It had to leave imperial territory, and hence Basel, and went to its pope at Lausanne. Felix V laid aside his dignity, and the Fathers elected Nicholas V, who absolved them from censure and made Felix a cardinal. Since then no one has shown any desire to set up an anti-pope.

During the peaceful pontificate of Nicholas V humanism and Renaissance art entered the papal court. Nicholas V founded the Vatican Library, commissioned Fra Angelico da Fiesole, and planned a splendid new construction in place of the much dilapidated Saint Peter's of the fourth century. However, fifty years were to elapse before Julius II began the work.

CALIXTUS III (1455–1458)

During the pontificate of Nicholas V the gaze of Christendom had been directed eastward. Following the heavy defeats of the Hungarians at Varna in 1444 and at Kossovo in 1448 occurred the capture of Constantinople by the Turks in 1453. In the conclave the cardinals almost elected the Greek Cardinal Bessarion, who surely would have been a worthy choice. Finally they decided for the politically farsighted Spaniard, Alfonso Borgia. Calixtus III sent the excellent Cardinal Carvajal with assistance to the Hungarians. He was joined by the fiery Franciscan, Juan de Capistrano. With their help the Hungarians under John Hunyady won a striking victory at Belgrade over the Turks, which could not, however, put a permanent halt to their advance. Unfortunately, Calixtus III bequeathed to the Church a sad inheritance when he elevated to the cardinalate his careless nephew, Rodrigo Borgia, the later Alexander VI.

PIUS II (1458–1464)

There now mounted the Throne of Saint Peter a most extraordinary man, Enea Silvio Piccolomini, as Pius II. Behind him lay a stirring past. He had taken part in the Council of Basel, had then entered the service of the anti-pope Felix V, and finally had become secretary of Emperor Frederick III. Already a humanist of European renown, he played a prominent role in effecting the Concordat of Vienna. Eugene IV absolved him from the censures he had incurred as a schismatic and made him bishop, first of Trieste, then of Siena.

Pius II was a humanist and romanticist of great versatility. Even as pope he was an author, always in the most elegant Latin, on many subjects, such as the geography of Asia. He loved nature and at times held consistories in the open under shady trees. This was no longer the Middle Ages. Since, by

316

the frivolous writings of his youth, he had given much scandal, he issued a bull containing the celebrated sentence: "Forget Aeneas and hear Pius."

In politics he had some successes. He induced King Louis XI of France to abolish the virtually schismatic Pragmatic Sanction of Bourges. From the half-Hussite Bohemian King George of Podiebrad he obtained at least an embassy of obedience. He subdued the dangerous tyrant of Rimini, Sigismondo Malatesta. But he did not achieve his main goal, a European coalition against the Turks. Despite their defeat at Belgrade, the Turks had occupied Serbia, Bosnia, and Epirus. All the heroism of the Hungarians and of the Albanian national hero, Skanderbeg, was unable to stop them. And the remnants of the Byzantine Empire—Trebizond, the Morea, the Aegean islands—fell, one after the other. Pius II invited all Christian princes to a congress at Mantua and went there in person, but obtained only promises. Above all, the pope lacked money. This situation was somewhat rectified by the discovery in 1462 of rich alum deposits at Città Vecchia in the Papal State. This mineral, then necessary as a dye, had had to be brought from the East till now. The yearly income from it is estimated at 300,000 ducats. Pius II destined the revenue from the new alum mines for the war against the Turks. He now decided to undertake a crusade in person, without awaiting the princes, hoping to influence them by his example. He was being thoroughly mediaeval in so thinking. All, including the princes, tried to dissuade him. Already seriously ill, he left Rome with a motley army and reluctant prelates. A dying man, he reached Ancona, where the Venetian ships were to assemble. What would have come of this strange expedition against the Turks no one can say, but very likely it would have been a complete failure. It did not get that far. When the Venetian fleet, which had allowed itself all the time possible, finally arrived on August 12, 1464, the pope could only have himself carried to a window to see the vessels. The following day he died and all quickly returned home.

The next pope, the Venetian Paul II, a nephew of Eugene IV, has immortalized his name at Rome through the erection of the splendid palace still known as the Palazzo Venezia. He was a good man, but in comparison with his five predecessors since the Council of Constance he was merely mediocre. Under him a definite secularization of the papal court was in progress, and under his successors this tendency would bring the papacy and the entire Church to the brink of ruin.

THE HUSSITES IN BOHEMIA

One of the most unpleasant legacies of the Council of Constance was the Hussite affair, whereby Bohemia, situated in the very heart of Europe, rich and aspiring, was almost separated from the Church for a long period. John Hus, professor of theology at Prague, was not only a priest of un-blemished life but an ardent Czech patriot. For the Czech literary tongue he performed a service similar to that of Luther for the German language. At the University of Prague he obtained in 1409 an alteration of the statutes to confer a pre-ponderant influence on the Czechs, with the result that several thousand German students and their professors migrated to Leipzig. He soon came into conflict with his archbishop and was excommunicated. Since, influenced by the English heretic Wyclif, he also taught definite errors in theology, he was sum-moned before the Council of Constance. He went there, provided with a safe-conduct by Emperor Sigismund. The council would have done well to wait until a pope was elected, for popes are accustomed to dealing more calmly and more moderately with such matters than are stormy assemblies. But the council, whose legitimacy was subject to well-founded doubts, needed to prove itself a genuine council by so clearly conciliar an activity as the condemnation of a heresy. Since Hus refused to make any retraction, he was handed over to the "secular tribunal" as an obstinate heretic, which he certainly was, and in spite of the imperial safe-conduct was burned at the stake on July 6, 1415.

The surrender to the secular tribunal was then little more than a ceremony. Just the same, throughout the Middle Ages and later, so long as heresy was universally regarded as a capital crime by the state, the Church held to this formality in order to show that a spiritual judge may not inflict the death penalty.[2]

The execution of Hus was naturally regarded by Bohemian patriots as a serious injustice. The national movement now assumed an expressly anti-ecclesiastical and violent character. Thus, the theological opinions held by Hus played a less prominent role. The distinctive religious note was the receiving of Communion under both species, *sub utraque specie;* hence, the later epithet "Utraquists." The name "Hussites" dates from 1420, when Martin V called for a crusade in response to ever-increasing acts of violence. However, the Hussites won battle after battle—Deutschbrod in 1421, Aussig in 1426, Mies in 1427, Taus in 1431. The Council of Basel, in the so-called Compacts of Prague, ranged itself on the side of the Hussites.

From 1419 to 1437 Emperor Sigismund, of the Luxemburg dynasty, was king of Bohemia; his successors in Bohemia were his son-in-law, Albert II of Austria, who ruled until 1439, and then Albert's minor son, Ladislas Postumus, until 1457. After the death of Ladislas, the Bohemian estates elected as king George of Podiebrad, the head of the moderate Utraquist

2 In regard to this question see Alaphridus Ottaviani, *Institutiones Juris Publici Ecclesiastici,* I (3d ed.; Città del Vaticano: 1947), 324 ff. (Translator's note.)

faction. Podiebrad (1458–1471) promised Pius II he would abandon the Compacts of Prague and restore ecclesiastical unity. But he did not do so; on the contrary, he supported the strongly Hussite archbishop of Prague, Rokyzana, whom the pope did not recognize. The pope could not endure this double game for long. At the urging of Cardinal Carvajal, who was well-acquainted with the Bohemian situation, Paul II decided in 1466 to excommunicate Podiebrad. Nevertheless, the other princes, including Emperor Frederick III, did nothing against him. Podiebrad and Rokyzana died in 1471. The Catholic Ladislas II, of the Jagiellon dynasty, became king of Bohemia and also, in 1490, king of Hungary. The tension now slackened. There was no formal schism; Utraquist communities existed side by side with those of the Catholics and were distinguished from them almost solely by receiving Communion under both species and honoring Hus as a martyr. Nevertheless, ecclesiastical life in Bohemia was long obstructed.

A SURVEY OF RELIGIOUS LIFE FROM 1300 TO 1450

The frequently unfavorable circumstances of ecclesiastical politics in the period of the Avignon residence, during the Great Western Schism, and in the decades immediately following could give rise to the impression that this was an epoch of religious decline. In this general sense, such was definitely not the case. If artistic production is a reliable indication of the spirit of an age, then a glance at late Gothic art, especially sculpture, suffices to make clear the deep religious values which at this time were alive in extensive strata of the population. It is true that much in the details of the care of souls was not ideal. The religious formation of clergy and people had, of course, unquestionably progressed since the twelfth and thirteenth centuries, but it still left much to be desired. The ceaseless quarrels between the secular clergy, who for their part upheld the parochial rights, and the regulars, especially the Mendicants, who to a great extent did the actual pastoral work, were deplorable. There were failings on both sides. Secular and regular clergy of all ranks were still far removed from that complete sense of responsibility which was at stake.

The interior religious life of this epoch gives the impression, not of decline, but rather of restraint. The fourteenth and fifteenth centuries were turned strongly inward. They were a time of religious thinkers and seekers, of mystics, of interior prayer. The saints, of whom there were then many, stood for the most part aside from the great events in the world and the Church. But it is not to be thought that they held aloof from the Church. As yet there was no non-ecclesiastical piety. The saints did not withdraw from the Church, but into the Church. Many suffered severely amid exterior circumstances, especially at the time of the schism, as, for example, Blessed Peter of Luxemburg, a Saint Aloysius at the schismatic curia of Avignon. Peter was a Luxemburg prince, a pious and precocious boy, made cardinal at the age of fifteen by the anti-pope Clement VII and brought to Avignon, where he exhausted himself in prayer, penance, and plans for the settlement of the schism until his death at the age of eighteen.

The predominance of holy women among the saints of this age is striking. Until the thirteenth century there were very few canonized women. But now we find Saint Birgitta of Sweden (✝1373), foundress of the Bridgettine Order, and her daughter, Saint Catherine (✝1381); Saint Juliana Falconieri (✝1341), foundress of the Servite nuns; the Augustinian hermitesses, Clara of Montefalco (✝1368) in Umbria, her sister, Blessed Joanna, and Saint Rita of Cascia (✝1457); Saint Frances of Rome (✝1440), foundress of the Olivetan Oblates. Among the Franciscan nuns the outstanding ones were Blessed Angela of Foligno (✝1309), widow, foundress of the Regular Tertiaries; the Poor Clares, Saint Nicoletta (or Coleta) Boilet of Corbie (✝1447) and Saint Catherine of Bologna (✝1463); Blessed Luitgard of Wittichen (✝1348) in the Schwarzwald; Blessed Elizabeth Achler of Waldsee (✝1420) in Württemberg, called the "Good Beth." There were still more highly favored souls among the Dominican nuns: in addition to the famous Saint Catherine of Siena (✝1380), Saint Agnes of Montepulciano (✝1317), and Blessed Clara Gambacorta of Pisa (✝1419), the "Teresa" of the Dominicans, there were the numerous mystics in the German monasteries of Unterlinden at Kolmar, Töss at Wintherthur, Engeltal at Nürnberg (Blessed Christina Ebner, ✝1356), and Medingen at Dillingen (Blessed Margareta Ebner, ✝1351).

DEVOTIO MODERNA

A special current in the spiritual life, which in time embraced wide circles, was the *devotio moderna,* as contemporaries termed it. The canon Gerhard Groot of Deventer (✝1384) and his pupil and successor Florentius Radewijns (✝1400) are regarded as its founders. The quasi-monastic communities of priests which they established were known as the "Brothers of the Common Life" or *"Fraterherren."* The *devotio moderna* was not an exclusive spirituality as falsely imagined by some today, a spirituality separated and almost opposed to other currents of piety.[3] The *devotio moderna* consisted rather in emphasizing a simple and sensible method in the striving after perfection and especially in the effort to develop the interior life. It presupposes, not highly favored

---

[3] Cf. Hughes, *op. cit.,* III (New York: 1947), 216-228, for a less favorable viewpoint. (Translator's note.)

souls, but average persons who desire to foster the inner life while following the path of serious ordinary tasks.

Jean Gerson (✝1429), chancellor of the Sorbonne and celebrated for his role at the Council of Constance, and the Belgian Carthusian, Dionysius Ryckel (✝1471), an extraordinarily prolific author, were close to the *devotio moderna*. But the real centers of the spread of the *devotio moderna* were the old Orders, which were then establishing reform congregations everywhere. In 1386 the Augustinian canonicate of Windesheim at Zwolle was founded by disciples of Gerhard Groot; a century later it was the head of a congregation of eighty-six monasteries of men and several of women. In Italy Luigi Barbo, a relative of Paul II, founded at Santa Justina of Padua in 1412 a reformed Benedictine congregation; this became the model for the Congregation of Valladolid (1450), which in time comprised all the Spanish Benedictine monasteries. In Germany arose the similar monastic congregations of Kastl in the Upper Palatinate (1404), Melk (1418), and Bursfeld near Göttingen (1439).

In general, Germany occupied a leading place in religious life in the fourteenth and fifteenth centuries, and this was especially the case with the Low Countries, which were then a part of the Empire. The three great mystical authors of the fourteenth century—the Thuringian Meister Eckhard (✝1326), John Tauler (✝1361) of Strasbourg, and the Swabian Henry Suso (✝1366), all of them Dominicans—were Germans. From Kempen on the lower Rhine came Thomas Hemerken (✝1471), a pupil of Radewijns, later of the monastery of Agnetenberg at Zwolle. Whether he was the author or only the popularizer of the *Imitation of Christ*, the most widely read Christian devotional book to this day, is a question not yet satisfactorily settled.

323

the age of humanism and the renaissance

H UMAN activity, which forms the subject of history, goes forward unceasingly, year by year, from generation to generation, century by century. Much changes, much remains; but there never comes a halting point, a year or a decade when one can say that precisely here an old age ends and a new one begins. One can divide the course of history into whatever epochs one desires, but there are always transitional periods in which old and new intermingle. Hence, it is not possible to fix definitely when the Middle Ages ceased and the modern age began. There were typically mediaeval ideas and institutions which continued into the eighteenth century and beyond, while on the other hand many things which have contributed to the formation of the modern period have their roots in the thirteenth century.

Just the same, it cannot be denied that there are certain periods in which the transition occurs more rapidly than in others, when more of the old disappears and more of the new arises than is usual. Unquestionably, from the middle of the fifteenth to the middle of the sixteenth century is such a period.

324

SOCIAL AND ECONOMIC CHANGES

In the thirteenth century, which we are accustomed to regard as the zenith of the Middle Ages, the population of Europe, apart from the then sparsely inhabited regions comprising modern Russia and the Balkan countries, must have amounted to 30,000,000. This number steadily mounted; even the worst pestilence in history, the Black Death at the middle of the fourteenth century, only delayed the growth temporarily. By 1500 the population exceeded 50,000,000. Europe was, of course, still far from being overpopulated and there were as yet no masses crowding one another for room, but the panorama of historical occurrence became more sweeping. Wars grew bloodier, social revolution more violent, government and administration more complicated and more difficult.

In the fourteenth and fifteenth centuries began the great age of commerce, when cities dedicated to trade became cosmopolitan centers. Through Genoa and Venice passed goods from the Near and the Far East. Chinese silk and Indian spices came to Europe via central Asia and the Genoese colonies on the Black Sea. In the north the world port was Bruges, whose place was taken by Antwerp after the middle of the fifteenth century. The Mediterranean and eastern commerce converged on Venice and Genoa. But from the Hansa cities of the north and northeast, the merchant business of the Baltic flowed into Bruges and Antwerp. On the land route between Venice and Bruges arose the continental reshipment centers, Ulm, Augsburg, Nürnberg. Finance lay so completely in the hands of Italians that "Lombard" came to be synonymous with money lender, banker. However, "Lombard" did not really refer to natives of Lombardy, but rather to the great banking houses of Siena and Florence—the Bardi, the Peruzzi, the Accaiuoli, the Alberti, and finally, that house whose operations were the most successful, the Medici. These banking houses, with branches and agencies in London, Paris, Bruges, and Avignon, undertook financial transactions for cities, kings, and popes. Thus in the fifteenth century Italy replaced France as the richest country of Europe. While Italy was the economic center of Europe, it remained divided and powerless politically. Politics did not yet travel the roads of economics and commerce; states were still wholly dynastic and feudal. Even the Hansa cities of the north and the rich Flemish centers did not constitute independent political entities.

With the increasing circulation of money, the standard of living rose everywhere. People became more civilized, more wealthy. In the early Middle Ages the "people" scarcely made themselves noticed, but in the twelfth and thirteenth centuries we perceive, for the first time, popular tendencies, almost of a socialistic character. From the end of the fourteenth century there was a *bourgeoisie*. The *bourgeois* became richer than princes. The duke of Burgundy borrowed money from his Flemish townsmen, Charles V from the Fuggers of Augsburg, Leo X from Agostino Chigi and the Florentines.

TECHNICAL INVENTIONS

The fifteenth century witnessed technical inventions, not indeed in such abundance or of so sensational a character as those of the nineteenth century, but inventions hardly less decisive for history. One of them was the compass. Invented in the fourteenth century, apparently by sailors from Amalfi, it led in the fifteenth century to a complete transformation of navigation. Ships were no longer restricted to coastal sailings; the great voyages of discovery became possible. Geographical maps took more correct form, or, rather, for the first time real maps were drawn. The new geographical concept of the world worked an influence upon intellectual culture which can scarcely be overestimated. The same is true of the study of the laws of nature, begun by the great scholastics of the thirteenth century, Albertus Magnus and Roger Bacon, and brought to culmination in Copernicus's (1473–1543) discovery of the heliocentric system. The new and more realistic aspect of the world led to a religious crisis. Hitherto, mankind had moved, so to speak, in a mythical world of marvels, accepting the unreal, the real, and the apparent without astonishment. The new realistic men believed that, by standing with both feet on reality, they would remove all veils, and religion now appeared to them as something unreal, a mythology.

The invention of gunpowder, used for the first time at the battle of Crécy in 1346, gradually transformed the whole system of warfare and, with it, politics. Knights and squires were replaced by soldiers and armies. Gonsalvo de Córdova, commander-in-chief of Ferdinand the Catholic, became the founder of modern military science. But perhaps most momentous of all for the intellectual culture of mankind was an invention of the mid-fifteenth century—the art of printing.

THE NEW TYPE OF MAN

The intellectual and artistic movements which we term "humanism" and "the Renaissance" did not create the new type of man as an original. Rather the opposite is true: awakening mankind felt itself drawn to a preoccupation with classical antiquity and loved to adorn itself in classical dress, but in reality Renaissance men of all countries, including Italy, were as different as possible from the ancient Romans and Greeks. The principal characteristic of the new humanists was a vast arrogance: conceit, pride, consciousness of strength, cult of personality, even Titanism. Everywhere they endeavored to break bonds; the laws of the Church and of the state, traditional rules, appeared as chains, and every society as an unjustified restriction on the individual. The new ideals did

327

not come into being by means of historical investigation of antiquity; these men possessed no genuine historical sense. What drove them was opposition, protest.

The conduct of the Renaissance men was not so humanistic as one would expect from their enthusiasm for Plato and the Stoics, Cicero and the ancient Roman *virtus*. They imagined themselves heroes and supermen, but were often very weak characters: thoughtless and extravagant, malicious, mendacious, and cruel, flagrantly immoral, without a sense of shame or self-control. They boasted of their vices, thereby betraying their attitude of protest. But, above all, the humanists were marked by boundless vanity. They unceasingly burned incense to one another, they talked about immortal fame. Perhaps in no other age have there lived so many "immortal" poets and literary men, princes and statesmen, who created nothing immortal.

Only in one field did this curious epoch produce anything genuinely immortal: in the fine arts. This is almost the sole aspect which the historian can consider with unmixed joy.

Mankind at this time exhibited a definite likeness to a youngster at the age of puberty: it suddenly recognized the reality of life, became conscious of its own strength, rebelled against its own childhood, against rules and teachers; obedience appeared as compulsion, as injustice; it wanted greatness, in good as well as in evil, and staggered hither and thither between a hazy idealism and a clumsy brutality. There were not, as is sometimes said, two currents, a Christian and a pagan Renaissance, good and bad men, who opposed one another. The whole spirit was in the same men, often curiously unbalanced and in confusion.

The Church's task in this general ferment of spirits was that of the teacher *vis-à-vis* the growing youth: to lead him out of rules that have been only customary or imposed into

328

rules that are consciously accepted. Mere force or mere severity accomplishes nothing for the teacher in this case; he is not to suppress the obscure idealism of his pupil, but must set him high goals worth striving for. In any teaching that is the most difficult thing, and here it was especially difficult, since the Church is not a teacher who stands outside mankind. The pillars of the Church were themselves more or less seized by this fermentation, were themselves in the same state of puberty.

However, the Church has overcome even the greatest crises which have confronted her. At the end of the Renaissance she stood incomparably more spiritual, more glorious, purer than at the beginning, but she had lost a great many of her adherents. Throughout the Middle Ages, the Church had, so to speak, covered with her wings all of European humanity, good and bad. After the Renaissance, she stood as a well-disciplined army that faced another hostile army.

THE RENAISSANCE POPES

It was a misfortune for the Church that, right at the beginning of the new age, she was given a series of popes who were among the most calamitous in the whole long papal succession. They were brilliant men after the fashion of the age, genuine Renaissance characters, but they were lacking in a high moral earnestness and sense of responsibility. Some of them were deeply immersed in the vices of their time.

From the close of the Great Western Schism capable popes, watching from their high tower, had ruled. With Paul II a definite deterioration set in, and under his successors calamity befell the Church.

SIXTUS IV (1471–1484)

Pope Sixtus IV came from Liguria. A Franciscan, he had

risen to Minister General of his Order before becoming a cardinal. Personally an irreproachable and pious priest, on the papal throne he revealed not only outstanding ability as a ruler but also serious weaknesses in his character.

Sixtus, sprung from quite modest conditions, was a man of culture, a high-minded patron of art and learning. Under him the humanists, whom Paul II had shoved aside, were again held in esteem at the papal court. He built the splendid hospital of the Holy Spirit, which still stands, the church of Santa Maria del Popolo, famed for its wonderful sepulchral monuments in the purest Quattrocento, Santa Maria della Pace, and at the Vatican Palace the Sistine Chapel. He brought to Rome and commissioned the greatest painters of the day—Ghirlandaio, Botticelli, Perugino, Pinturicchio, Melozzo da Forlì. In Renaissance art one can correctly speak of an epoch of Sixtus IV.

In the history of theology Sixtus IV will always be mentioned for his two dogmatic constitutions on the Immaculate Conception. As he was an ardent client of the Mother of God, he dedicated the Sistine Chapel to this mystery of Faith.

Sixtus IV was one of those princely characters who prefer above all to give, to dispense, to show favor, but in all this he knew no moderation, so that he finally gave everything to everybody. He endowed his own Order of Conventual Franciscans with such excessive privileges that even by contemporaries they were mockingly termed the *Mare Magnum*. In the same way he conferred indulgences on all sides; but since, according to the prevailing custom, indulgences were connected with alms, this lavish grant could easily appear as a money transaction, especially since the money that poured in was not applied solely to purely ecclesiastical ends, as it should have been. In this respect a sense of responsibility was more and more lacking in the popes and the Roman Curia. Furthermore, Sixtus made dangerously liberal concessions to the princes. Extensive privileges in the appointment of bishops, for example, were the more risky because at this period State-Church tendencies were noticeable in many governments. He allowed the Spanish Inquisition to become so much an instrument of the government that later popes had to put up with the greatest annoyances in order to reassert to some extent their authority over this institution, which was purely ecclesiastical in its essence.

It was also unfortunate that Sixtus allowed himself to wander too far along the political labyrinth of the small Italian states. The chief players on this political chessboard were, besides the Roman factions of Colonna and Orsini, King Ferrante of Naples, the Sforzas of Milan, Lorenzo the Magnificent of Florence, and the republic of Venice. The grounds of conflict varied—Siena, Urbino, Ferrara—and so did the political alignments. Most of the time Sixtus stood with Ferrante of Naples against the Medici. But he also fell out with Ferrante and even defeated him in battle at Campo Morto in the Pomptine Marshes, one of the rare victories of papal troops. The wars of the period, carried on by mercenary captains, the *condottieri*, who were always changing employers, were not too bloody, but the fact that a pope took part in all these complications of politics damaged his prestige. Rather than considering the pope as the common father of Christendom, the people saw him as one of the ordinary Italian princes, and not even one of the most powerful princes.

In 1478 the wealthy Florentine family of the Pazzi made an attempt to overturn by a *coup d'état* the rule of the Medici. The plot failed, but there was much bloodshed; Lorenzo's brother, Giuliano de' Medici, was assassinated, and the Medici took a cruel vengeance. The pope was only too much involved in the affair. One of the conspirators, a nephew of the pope,

Girolamo Riario, had deceived his uncle by insisting that no deaths would follow. Sixtus let himself be won over and, under this condition, gave consent.

That the pope figured so prominently in the unsavory political events of the age was due in great part to his nephews, but Sixtus was himself culpable in allowing them to hold such influential positions. The very fact that in the thirteen years of his pontificate he made six nephews cardinals was unusual. Worse was the fact that scarcely one of them deserved the purple. The most capable of them, Giuliano della Rovere, later Pope Julius II, did not live a chaste life. The grandson of his sister Bianca Riario, Raffael, who became a cardinal at the age of sixteen, is famous as the builder of the magnificent Cancelleria palace, but later, under Leo X, he played an evil role. Totally unfit was Pietro Riario, who became a cardinal at twenty-five and died three years later as a result of his shameless debauchery. Another nephew, Giovanni della Rovere, received as his wife the heiress of the duchy of Urbino, and through this union the Rovere entered the sovereign houses of Italy.

During this pontificate quite a number of outstanding older cardinals died—Torquemada, Carvajal, Bessarion, Forteguerri, Latino Orsini, Angelo Capranica, Ammanati. In place of these excellent princes of the Church Sixtus, with incredible weakness, appointed insignificant, young, and, in part, vicious persons—Giovanni d'Aragona, a son of the evil Ferrante of Naples; Giambattista Cibò, a weak character who became Pope Innocent VIII; the highly born but unworthy Ascanio Sforza, Battista Orsini, Giovanni Battista Savelli, Giovanni Colonna, and the twenty-three-year-old, totally worthless Sclafenati. It was these last who in 1492 brought about the election of Alexander VI.

It is only with sadness that one can behold the splendid

tomb of Sixtus IV with his wonderfully strong face—one of the best creations of Renaissance sculpture.

INNOCENT VIII (1484–1492)

The new and evil spirit in the College of Cardinals was manifest in the conclave. Rodrigo Borgia, nephew of Calixtus III, felt that his time had come and promised rewards to the electors. He won over Ascanio Sforza, Raffael Riario, Giovanni of Naples, and others, but his mortal enemy, Giuliano della Rovere, thwarted his efforts. Giuliano did not expect the tiara for himself this time; he was only forty-one years old. But he wanted a pope who would be dependent on him. He too resorted to corruption and his candidate was victorious: Giambattista Cibò, who became Innocent VIII.

Innocent, a Genoese, was a kind but extraordinarily weak man. Before his entry into the clerical state he had two illegitimate children, Teodorina and Franceschetto. The pope married Franceschetto to Magdalena, daughter of Lorenzo the Magnificent. This was supposed to be a political move, for it meant reconciliation with Florence and the Medici, who had been so hostile toward Sixtus IV. But it was an unprecedented scandal. The noble Cardinal Aegidius of Viterbo later wrote the bitter sentence: "Innocent VIII was the first among the popes publicly to display his children, publicly to officiate at their marriages; would that this matter, lacking a precedent, had later remained unimitated!" The marriage took place at the Vatican. The illustrious Medici demanded a favor in return. He did not rest until he had extorted from the weak pope the cardinalate for his thirteen-year-old son, Giovanni de' Medici, who later became Pope Leo X.

Innocent VIII was likewise unable to keep aloof from Italian wars and politics. He was involved in the terrible so-called Barons' War, a revolt of the Neapolitan magnates against Ferrante. The pope supported the barons, who had many grievances, and excommunicated Ferrante, but thereby fell out with Milan and Florence and even with Ferdinand of Aragón and Matthias Corvinus of Hungary. In 1485 Ferrante's son, Alfonso of Calabria, besieged the city of Rome.

Innocent VIII has often been taken to task by the later German historians for his bull of 1484 regarding witches. The bull was addressed to the inquisitors of the diocese of Constance and declared that witchcraft and magic pertain to the court of the Inquisition. The two inquisitors of Constance, Henry Institoris and Jakob Sprenger, thereupon published the unfortunate treatise, *The Hammer of Witches,* which first appeared in 1487 and which had many reprints. Thus there began in Germany the sad witchcraft delusion. But it would be unjust to name Innocent VIII as its author. He could not foresee the evil effects of his bull. Very few witchcraft trials were held in Rome then or later. Innocent VIII belongs to that list of popes who have disgraced the See of Peter not because of his bull, but because of his weakness of character and the scandal he caused. The chief blame falls on Cardinal Giuliano della Rovere, who for personal reasons raised to the papacy a man of mediocre gifts and dominated him during his entire pontificate. Innocent VIII received a magnificent bronze tomb in Saint Peter's which is still admired by Roman pilgrims.

ALEXANDER VI (1492–1503)

As he had done in the preceding conclave, so now again the vice-chancellor, Cardinal Rodrigo Borgia, offered bribes to the electors, and this time he acquired two-thirds of the votes. He styled himself Alexander VI. The election was valid, but revealed in the electors an unprecedented lack of a sense of responsibility.

The profligacy of Cardinal Borgia had long been generally known. Pius II had had to reprove him earnestly for his shameful conduct. He lived in a sort of wedlock with a married Roman lady, Vanozza de Cataneis, and at the same time maintained still other illicit relationships. Even as pope he had a son. By Vanozza he had four children, all of whom lived at their father's court. The oldest, Juan, duke of Gandia, a libertine like his father, was assassinated in 1500 by an unknown hand. Alexander, who had especially loved this son, was deeply grieved and saw in the murder a divine punishment. In letters to the Christian princes he expressed his desire to better his life; but not much change was to be observed. The second son, the famous and notorious Cesare, was made a cardinal at the age of seventeen, but after six years he resigned the dignity. He was not a priest, but a subdeacon, and by means of a dispensation granted by his father he married the French princess, Charlotte d'Albret. The king of France bestowed upon him the title of duke of Valentinois. Alexander married his third son, Jofré, to an illegitimate daughter of Alfonso of Naples, son and successor of Ferrante; he became prince of Squillace. By this marriage policy Alexander sought not only to provide for his children, but to secure himself politically on all sides.

Lucrezia, the youngest of Vanozza's children, was married in 1493 to a Sforza. However, this marriage was annulled on the ground of non-consummation, and Lucrezia obtained as her new husband an illegitimate son of Alfonso of Naples, Alfonso of Bisceglie. This husband, whom Lucrezia loved deeply, was murdered in 1500 by her brother, Cesare. Alexander VI did not dare call his son to account for the crime. Lucrezia, who was not vicious but very frivolous, was at once married to the heir of Ferrara. As duchess of Ferrara she was universally beloved, pious and virtuous, but, like all of Alexander's children, she died at an early age.

In politics Alexander VI faced two principal tasks. One of these was to preserve from total disintegration the Papal State, where the numerous local princes were hardly papal vassals even in name and were becoming ever more independent; the other was the always vital relationship of the Papal State with the kingdom of Naples.

THE STRUGGLE FOR NAPLES

Directly beyond Tivoli and Terracina lay the Neapolitan frontier. From the northeast and the southeast Neapolitan troops could stand before Rome after a two-days' march. A too powerful Naples was always a danger for Rome, and *a fortiori* a foreign power could not be allowed to establish itself in Naples.

In 1494 the old sinner, King Ferrante, died; his son, Alfonso, and his grandson, Ferrante II, quickly followed him, one after the other, into the grave. Of the illegitimate line of the dynasty of Aragón only the childless Federigo, Ferrante's younger son, survived. The Spanish King Ferdinand, of the legitimate dynasty of Aragón, resolved to seize the inheritance, but the same idea was entertained by the French King Charles VIII, who regarded himself as heir of the house of Aragón. He entered Italy with an army that was unusually large for those days and, without meeting opposition, reached Rome by way of Florence. Alexander VI found himself in a very difficult position. Charles VIII had as his guest Alexander's mortal enemy, Cardinal Giuliano della Rovere, who had fled to France soon after Alexander's election and was loudly calling for the deposition of the simoniacally elected pope. Charles VIII demanded of the pope the investiture of Naples. If he complied with this demand the pope would avoid deposition, it is true, but he would fall into complete dependence on France and, furthermore, incur the anger of the Spaniards, his own countrymen. Alexander negotiated so skilfully in Rome with the French king that the latter accorded him the customary obedience, whereby the danger of deposition was eliminated; yet at the same time the pope avoided formally investing the king with Naples. Charles VIII moved on and had himself crowned king at Naples. Behind his back, however, Alexander contrived a league with Spain, the emperor, Venice, and Milan. Ferdinand of Aragón sent to the Neapolitan theater of war the best commander of the age, Gonsalvo de Córdova. Charles VIII hastily returned to France, where he soon died. Alexander made peace with his successor, Louis XII, and Cesare was married to a French princess. Thus far the policy of the militarily powerless pope had been completely successful.

Ferdinand of Aragón and Louis XII of France agreed to partition the Neapolitan inheritance. Ferdinand, who already possessed Sicily, would receive Apulia and Calabria; Louis XII, Naples and the Abruzzi; both would be vassals of the Holy See. Alexander consented, but almost immediately war broke out between the two rivals, and the French were totally defeated by Gonsalvo de Córdova. The entire kingdom of Naples was now definitively united with the crown of Aragón. The thing Alexander and his predecessors had constantly sought to prevent now came to pass: a European great power was at the gates of Rome. The popes were to feel the consequences throughout the sixteenth century. Of course, it was to prove fortunate that this power was Spain.

THE PAPAL STATE

At the end of the Middle Ages all the states of Europe experienced the change from the feudal system to the modern territorial state. In the place of more or less independent barons and other landed proprietors, who often left the crown little authority, there appeared a centralized hierarchy of officials under a strict central administration. First in France, then in Spain and England, this transformation was perfected in the fifteenth century. The modern concept of the state was conceived. In Germany the same process led to the opposite result: in place of the old imperial vassals there appeared many small and petty territorial principalities as sovereign states in the modern sense. The German king was henceforth only as important as his own hereditary domain.

The Papal State too threatened to disintegrate into nothing but individual sovereign states. That this process was checked at the eleventh hour is due most of all to Alexander VI. At his command Cesare subjected in lightning-like campaigns Imola, Forlì, Faenza, Urbino, Camerino, Sinigaglia, and other small cities and lordships, expelled their dynasts or brought them under control, and everywhere placed his garrisons in the citadels. The atrocities which Cesare perpetrated in this connection can be as little excused as can the means which he and his father employed in obtaining funds for these military expeditions. Cesare had a nephew of Paul II, the aged and very wealthy Cardinal Michiel, who was not dying quickly enough, assassinated in order that his fortune might be confiscated, and it appears that Alexander knew of this. Many historians defend the view that Cesare did not want to restore the Papal State but to create for himself a Borgia kingdom in central Italy. This is hardly correct. Even though Cesare can be credited with all sorts of adventurous schemes, still it must be remembered that his father would not live forever and that no succeeding pope would ever accept such a creation. That Alexander conferred on him for his accomplishments the title of duke of the Romagna and of Urbino proves nothing in this regard. Be that as it may, nothing came of all this, for, when Cesare stood at the height of his power, Alexander died at the age of seventy-three, of malaria and not of poison as is so often asserted. In his case it is necessary to make the ordinarily obvious observation that the pope died fortified with the sacraments of the Church. It was only much later that Alexander VI received an exceptionally modest sepulchral monument in the small Spanish national church of Santa Maria in Monserrato, where he was buried along with his uncle, Calixtus III.

From time immemorial Alexander VI and his family have stimulated the imagination of writers of every sort. A real "Age of the Borgias" has been created, in which only the dagger and poison and adultery play a role. In these circles Alexander and even more Cesare and Lucrezia have become true "dime novel" characters and cinema monsters. Even the serious Pastor, though he worked only with strictly genuine documents in studying the facts, was unable to refrain from giving to his brilliantly written account of Alexander VI a melodramatic air which is otherwise foreign to his history.

There have also been apologists who have sought to white-wash Alexander VI. This is hopeless. But it is also a mistake when, on principle, opponents of the Catholic Faith set out, with their fervent declamations of righteous anger, to strike at the Church or the papacy. By their indignation, however, they show that they have a much higher opinion of the Church than they wish to admit. For, if Alexander VI had not been a pope, but a king or emperor or president, he would undoubtedly be regarded as one of the great and successful statesmen and rulers of his age, and the stains on his private life and the unscrupulosity of his political means would be overlooked. Of a pope, however, more is rightly demanded.

339

SAVONAROLA

In a certain sense Savonarola can be called the antagonist of Alexander VI. More than anything else, Savonarola's struggle and tragic end illuminate this age, when good and evil mingled so curiously.

Girolamo Savonarola, born at Ferrara in 1452, was a Dominican and since 1491 had been prior of the convent of San Marco at Florence. He not only introduced a strict reform in his monastery but with the ardor of a prophet preached publicly against the corruption in the Church, especially among the clergy. Because of him the city of Florence divided into two factions, the Piagnoni (the weepers; devotees and adherents of Savonarola) and the Arrabiati (the enraged; opponents of Savonarola and supporters of the Medici). When Charles VIII, *en route* to Naples, entered Florence in 1494, Savonarola hailed this enemy of Alexander VI as an envoy of God, who would set in motion the longed-for reform of the Church. But this was a strange delusion, for Charles VIII bore little resemblance to a reformer. With Charles's aid Savonarola did succeed in expelling the Medici from Florence. Relying on the Piagnoni, he introduced at Florence a sort of theocratic republic and actually effected a great moral improvement. But when, with increasing violence, he thundered from the pulpit against Alexander VI, his person and his policies, the pope summoned him to Rome to answer for his bold words. Since Savonarola did not obey, the pope forbade him to preach. At first Savonarola complied, but had the agitation continued by his confreres in the Order. The pope thereupon withdrew the convent of San Marco from the province to which it had hitherto belonged and placed it under the Roman provincial. Savonarola no longer submitted and was excommunicated by the pope in 1497 for continued disobedience. He declared the excommunication invalid, resumed his preaching, and called for a council to depose the pope.

Savonarola was firmly convinced that he had a special commission from God. He frequently asserted that, in case of need, God would confirm this mission by miracles. He himself was ready to go through the test of fire. Finally, one of the Franciscans of Santa Croce, who had held themselves aloof from the ferment, proclaimed that he was ready to go with Savonarola into the fire: they would both be burned to death and thus the scandal would end. The whole population passionately demanded the ordeal—the adherents of Savonarola, because they expected a miracle; his opponents, because they hoped to get rid of him. The *signoria* of Florence approved the experiment and decreed that the Dominicans must leave the city if the Dominican or both men perished in the fire; otherwise, the Franciscans would have to leave. Alexander VI learned of the plan and issued a strict prohibition, but the people of Florence were far too excited to listen to reason from any source.

On the appointed day two pyres were erected in the public square of the city. Amid the utmost popular tension the two religious communities approached in procession. It caused much dissatisfaction that, in place of Savonarola, another Dominican wanted to undertake the proof, and still more that the latter wanted to carry along the Blessed Sacrament into the fire as a sort of protection. The Franciscans and the people protested, the Dominicans insisted, and the *signoria* sent both parties home. Now the fury of the people, who regarded themselves as deceived, turned on Savonarola. The Arrabiati contrived his arrest. A process defying all justice was initiated against him. Alexander VI vainly tried to bring the affair to Rome. Savonarola and two other Dominicans were condemned to the gallows in Florence and their corpses were publicly burned.

Saint Philip Neri, a native of Florence, later honored Savonarola as a saint. Even today opinions are divided in regard to him. However, only one verdict is possible. A blameless life and ascetic conduct do not suffice to make a saint; otherwise, Novatian, Hus, and many other heretics were saints. Furthermore, it is not enough that a person wish to be a Catholic and not attack any dogmas. In addition, the saint must possess that deep humility which at the critical moment makes him submit to the authority established by God. It is characteristic that Newman, who displayed this genuine Catholic humility under the most difficult circumstances, held Savonarola in slight esteem, despite his own deep veneration for Philip Neri. To reach a verdict on Savonarola, one need only compare him with Catherine of Siena, who, against universal public opinion, clung loyally and bravely to a pope who caused the Church hardly less harm than Alexander VI. Incidentally, in the entire affair of Savonarola, Alexander VI, though provoked personally to a very high degree, conducted himself with moderation and according to law.

PIUS III (SEPTEMBER TO OCTOBER, 1503)

After the death of Alexander VI the conclave elected Cardinal Piccolomini, a quiet, pious man, who had kept aloof from political matters under the last popes. However, he was ill and weak and he died after a month. Hence, it was all the more remarkable that in this brief period the power of Cesare Borgia, of whom all expected the worst, collapsed like a house of cards. Cesare had taken part with his father in that garden party at which Alexander contracted deadly malaria, and at the time of the conclave he himself lay prostrate with a serious fever. He later admitted to his friend Machiavelli that he had made provisions for all possibilities that could occur at the death of his father except for the one possibility that at that crisis he might himself be fighting for his life. Thus, at the decisive moment he lost the reins and almost all his supporters. Unarmed and despondent, he fled to Naples, though still convalescent, and from there he went to his wife's relatives in Navarre. Here, scarcely thirty-one years old, he perished in a feud.

JULIUS II (1503–1513)

As by a miracle the Borgias had been removed and the hour of their great opponent, Giuliano della Rovere, now struck. He had openly aspired to the tiara and was actually by far the most outstanding of the cardinals. The conclave lasted only a few hours. As Julius II he at once issued a bull in which all simoniacal machinations in the papal election were strictly forbidden. In this way he struck a blow at his own previous behavior.

Julius II was sixty years old at the time of his election. In his youth he had entered his uncle's Order of Conventual Franciscans, and that uncle, at the time of his own election as Sixtus IV, had soon made him a cardinal. Giuliano lived no better than many others. He had three daughters. Above all he was a warrior and a politician. Under Sixtus IV he had conducted military expeditions like a *condottiero*; he completely dominated the weak Innocent VIII, whose election he had arranged. He conspired with Charles VIII of France and with Savonarola against Alexander VI. Julius II had much to atone for.

Having become pope, he wanted to be nothing other than pope. He desired to lift the papacy once again to an independent, powerful, and glorious position. One should not, for that reason, say that he was rather a prince than a priest. The

343

papal position as he imagined it appeared to him to be necessary for the exercise of the spiritual government, and so it was at that time. Julius II was a sincere believer. The inspiration which he gave to the greatest artists of the day—Bramante, Raffael, Michelangelo—was deeply religious.

Julius II was indeed no saint, but he was a great character. There was nothing petty, nothing despicable in this forceful man. His wrath engendered fear in all, but not hate. He was a Lear, every inch a king; a Titan, such as Michelangelo painted and chiseled. Michelangelo, himself a Titan, was the intimate friend of Julius II; yet the two constantly quarreled. Savonarola, Alexander VI, and Cesare had also been giants, though of course the last two lacked the idealism of the Rovere pope. Of the Titans of this amazing age Julius II was undoubtedly the greatest. Contemporaries called him *"Il Terribile."* One must study his portraits, not the famous one by Raffael, in which he is represented with a long beard, which he grew in his last years after a serious illness, but the woodcut by Burgkmair or the medallion by Caradosso, in which he is beardless, with the powerful chin and the firmly closed mouth —a dread-inspiring countenance, but not one of a tyrant.

The Papal State, which Alexander VI had brought under control, was well-governed by Julius II. He established a uniform silver currency, the *giuli*, later called *paoli*. Because of his capable financial administration some regarded him as miserly, but he was not. He had money for great undertakings, including art. But first of all, he had to complete the work of Alexander VI. While Cesare was subjugating the Romagna, the Venetians had seized important papal cities in the north, and Bologna had made itself almost independent under the Bentivogli. Julius II resolved personally to subject Bologna. With only 2,000 soldiers, but accompanied by the cardinals and the entire curia, he moved on Bologna by forced marches, in order to arrive there before the French troops whom Louis XII was sending to help him. The refractory tyrant, Bentivoglio, fled, the city submitted to the pope and received a new constitution. The classically inspired Romans insisted on receiving the returning pope as an ancient *triumphator*.

As Venice still declined to give up the cities taken from the Papal State, Julius II brought into being the League of Cambrai, whereby the emperor, France, and Spain joined with him against the republic. The league's army defeated the Venetians at the battle of Agnadello. However, Julius had no desire to destroy the republic of Venice, and still less did he wish French expansion in North Italy. Hence, he made a separate peace with Venice, received back his cities, and then joined Venice, Spain, and the Swiss against France. Such about-faces were then customary. France took up the war, the pope went again to camp and participated in person at the siege of the fortress of Mirandola. But all his courage could not prevent the French from gaining ground and taking Bologna.

Louis XII wished to attack the pope on the spiritual plane and summoned a general council to Pisa in order to effect a schism. Julius acted with the speed of lightning. He deposed and excommunicated two cardinals who had allowed themselves to be won over. Then he himself summoned a general council to Rome. It was attended by only a few prelates and issued no decrees of importance, but it is enumerated in the series of ecumenical councils as the Fifth Lateran Council and it accomplished its purpose of preventing a schism. The gathering at Pisa ended miserably. The canons of the cathedral kept their church locked and in the city no notary could be found to draw up the acts.

In the field, on the other hand, the French achieved success, defeating the league army in the great battle of Ravenna. The papal legate, the young Cardinal Giovanni de'

Medici, was made prisoner. But the best French commander, the chivalrous Gaston de Foix, fell in the engagement and from then on the tide turned. Milan, Genoa, and other cities revolted against France, and soon after the victory at Ravenna the French had to evacuate all of North Italy. Thus in the end the policy of Julius II was victorious. The entire Papal State was recovered, Venice was humbled, and no great foreign power remained in North Italy. In the south, however, the Spaniards were firmly entrenched. When Italian historians glorify Julius II as the national liberator, they are exaggerating. Julius II was not fighting for any Italian national state. What he aimed at was only the political independence of the Holy See, and this he attained.

Julius II's sepulchral monument is the statue of Moses by Michelangelo, a symbolic figure which is equaled by no plastic work of antiquity nor by any modern heroic monument. His personal monument, however, is Saint Peter's basilica, the gigantic domed construction which he planned with Bramante and of which he laid the cornerstone in 1506.

LEO X (1513–1521)

Leo X was the lucky heir of his mighty predecessor. Indeed, he has robbed him of a part of his fame: in the Roman Renaissance one ought to speak of a Julian Age rather than of a Medicean Age.

Giovanni de' Medici had always been fortune's child. The son of Lorenzo the Magnificent, he enjoyed the best education the period could offer. One of his teachers was the celebrated Platonist, Marsilio Ficino. At the age of thirteen he became a cardinal, when his sister married the son of the weak Innocent VIII. The Medici were expelled from Florence by Charles VIII and Savonarola, but Giovanni, who at the death of his brother Piero had become head of the family, did not give up hope of a return. Taken captive at the battle of Ravenna as papal legate, he soon succeeded in escaping, and a year later recovered, through a simple *coup d'état*, the rule of Florence. Another year later, at the age of thirty-eight, he was elected pope.

At his elevation to the papacy, the son of Lorenzo was enthusiastically greeted by humanists, poets, and artists. A famous epigram stated that, after the rule of Venus (Alexander VI) and of Mars (Julius II), the kingdom of Minerva had now come. That the pope personified the Kingdom of Christ seems to have escaped these strange Christians.

Leo X was not a great genius like his predecessor. He was kind, gay, and pleasant. Delighted at having become pope, he wanted others also to be happy. He gave prodigally on all sides, to the poor and the not-so-poor. He loved art, but preferred music, poetry, and the theater to the monumental arts. He himself took delight in the capers of his court jesters. Never, not even in his youth, had he been guilty of moral lapses. He performed, piously and with edification, the liturgical functions of his high office. But the conduct at his court was decidedly not of a spiritual character. Every autumn he went off on a magnificent court hunt, usually in the district between Rome and Città Vecchia; in this the peasants gained more than they would have received from the best harvest. But Leo's royal generosity degenerated into extravagance. People said mockingly that he had used up three pontificates: the public treasury that his thrifty predecessor had left, the revenues of his own government, and the income of his successor, who would have to pay his debts. Leo X's worldly ways appear all the more embarrassing when it is recalled that under him began the great revolt in the north. While Luther was posting his theses at Wittenberg, comedies were being produced at the Vatican. Under Julius II the situation of the

Church had become serious, but not yet desperate; now it was desperate, but it was not taken seriously. Amid laughter and dancing it was reeling closer to the abyss.

In politics Leo X was on the whole successful. Trained, as a real Medici, in all the contemporary arts of diplomacy, he constantly changed his attitude, conspired now with the French against the emperor, now with the emperor against the French, then with both at the same time, but he always remained master of the situation. Since, in addition to the Papal State, he also ruled Florence, the papacy was at that time a politically great power.

THE CONSPIRACY OF THE CARDINALS

The extent to which matters had progressed in Rome is illustrated by the conspiracy of the cardinals in 1517, the year of Luther's theses. Leo X was beloved, but among the younger cardinals were several discontented spirits. The chief of the conspiracy, Cardinal Petrucci, was spurred on by political jealousy, for until recently his family had occupied in Siena a position similar to that of the Medici in Florence. Petrucci plotted to murder the pope with the aid of his physician. He won to himself Cardinals Sauli, Soderini, Accolti, Castellesi, and even the old camerlengo, Raffael Riario, nephew of Sixtus IV. How far all of these were implicated in the attempted murder is uncertain, but they did not try to stop Petrucci. Riario was hoping to become pope in this way. The affair was discovered, and Leo X acted vigorously. Petrucci was executed, the rest escaped with heavy fines. Leo X at once took the correct step of naming on one day thirty-one new cardinals; thereby not only did the entire College of Cardinals acquire a new aspect, but the pope once more became sole master in his house, after the long period, stretching back almost to Avignon, when the cardinals had dealt with the pope virtually as independent princes. Among the newcomers were several excellent men: De Cupis, Campeggio, Adrian of Utrecht, soon to be Pope Adrian VI, and three generals of Orders—Cristofero Numai of the Franciscans, the noble Aegidius of Viterbo of the Augustinians, and Thomas de Vio of Gaetà, usually known as Cajetanus, of the Dominicans, the most important theologian of the age.

Through these promotions to the Sacred College Leo X made some amends and even sowed the seeds of a better development in the future. However, on the whole, he cannot be numbered among the popes who have honored the Throne of Saint Peter.

ADRIAN VI (1522–1523)

The death of Leo was completely unexpected, and it made clear how much he had dominated policy. His cousin, Cardinal Giulio de' Medici, who as vice-chancellor and secretary of state had been his principal collaborator, inherited his prestige. Politically, Giulio de' Medici stood entirely on the side of the rising monarchy of Charles V. But in the College of Cardinals there was also a strong anti-Medici faction in opposition to the autocratic government of Leo X. The opposition did not abate until Cardinal de' Medici had proposed the absent Cardinal Adrian of Utrecht, bishop of Tortosa, and the famed Cardinal Cajetan had thrown his influence into the scales on behalf of this candidate.

Eventually, neither the Romans nor the cardinals themselves were happy over this election. Adrian was a Dutchman, and hence, according to Roman ideas, a barbarian. He had been the tutor of Charles V and had later conducted the government of Spain for Charles, at first with Cardinal Cisneros, and, after the latter's death, by himself. He appeared so much the emperor's creature that many felt it would have

349

been just as well to have elected the emperor as pope. When after eight months he finally came to Rome, where up to now no one had known him, the chagrin was even greater. Adrian was an exemplary priest, pious, ascetic, learned, but for Medicean Rome he was much too serious, dull, pedantic, and commonplace. He was rather a professor than a statesman, rather a monk than a prince. He was too old to change, and he was unable to tear himself away from his former associates. The Dutchmen whom he brought with him—Enkevoirt, Ingen-winkel, Dirk van Heeze, highly respectable men—excited the scorn of the Romans by their very names. Perhaps with time he might have succeeded, but he died after a year. On his tomb in the German national church of Santa Maria dell' Anima are the words: "Unfortunately, even for the best man, much depends upon the age in which he lives." In the intervening centuries the cardinals have never again chosen a Dutchman. Nevertheless, the mere fact of Adrian's election demonstrates that even in this evil period an awareness of clerical responsibility had not yet died out at the Roman Curia.

CLEMENT VII (1523–1534)

The new conclave lasted fifty days. It was a question of only two real candidates: Cardinals Giulio de' Medici and Alessandro Farnese. Extraordinary ability was Farnese's recommendation, but outstanding political prestige won the election for de' Medici. The choice was not in the best interests of the Church.

Clement VII was very unlike his cousin, Leo X. He was a tireless worker, thrifty, serious, not with the professorial gravity of his Dutch predecessor but with the quiet dignity of the *grand seigneur* of a princely house. Leo X had been unusually ugly, but amiable, charming, and sociable; Clement VII was a handsome man, but cold and reserved. Only in one respect did he surpass his cousin: if Leo X had been cunning, wary, and clever in politics, Clement was all this and more. This oversubtlety was to be his ruin.

At the beginning of his pontificate occurred the famous battle of Pavia, in which Charles V defeated and captured the French King Francis I. Francis did not intend to fulfill the intolerable terms with which he purchased his freedom, and he immediately formed with Venice, Milan, and Florence the League of Cognac against Charles. Clement VII, who had hitherto been generally amicable to the emperor, felt that the hour had come to shake off the increasingly uncomfortable imperial pressure. He joined the league. Charles V did not delay in accepting the challenge. When the situation became serious, all withdrew from the league, including Francis, and the pope stood by himself facing the gravely provoked emperor. Charles V, who always wanted to be a loyal son of the Church, asked his theologians and canonists whether he might proceed in arms against the pope. Most of them replied in the affirmative, because the pope was in a sense the aggressor. And now occurred what the popes had always dreaded since the days of the Hohenstaufen and had sought to prevent: Charles attacked simultaneously from his Neapolitan kingdom and from the north. The northern army consisted of Spanish, Italian, and German mercenaries, mostly Protestants, under Frundsberg. There were 22,000 soldiers, a large army for that day, and Charles V, who never had any money, left this mob to its own devices, so that it soon began to mutiny and advanced against Rome, plundering on its own responsibility. The wild rabble by-passed Florence, which paid blackmail, and stormed Rome on May 6, 1527. The pope, who had missed the opportune moments for surrender, for resistance, and for escape, fled to Sant' Angelo and was besieged there, while the soldiers perpetrated the most savage outrages in the city.

Such was the *Sacco di Roma*, which recalled the days of

Alaric and Gaiseric and put to a horrible end the luxurious and frivolous Rome of the Renaissance. The impression created in Europe was enormous. Charles V, who bore the responsibility, was bitterly blamed by his own Spaniards. The Franciscan Cardinal Quiñones, who had great influence with Charles, told him to his face that he should no longer call himself emperor but Luther's field marshal.

Clement VII ransomed himself after seven months of a long siege, when the effort was already under way to blow up Sant' Angelo by mines, and fled in disguise to Orvieto. Only after a year did he return to the almost deserted city. When there was nothing else to loot in Rome, the imperial troops, decimated by pestilence and hunger, had finally moved on to Naples.

Peace between emperor and pope was signed at Barcelona in 1529. The two heads of Christendom met in Bologna, where Clement crowned Charles emperor. The dependence of the Holy See on the Spanish and imperial world power was greater than ever, and all the subtleties of papal policy and all sacrifices had been in vain. But this was not the essential misfortune; worse was the fact that the heads of Christendom had engaged in conflict at the moment when the revolt from the Church in the north was beginning to assume very threatening proportions. Clement VII was not a bad pope; he did not dishonor the See of Peter as some of his recent predecessors. More, perhaps, than is usually considered, he even encouraged several hopeful signs of ecclesiastical life in Italy. But he was a weak pope, one who did not understand how to rise above the petty demands of the political working-day and to devote himself with all his strength in the Church's difficult hour to the great tasks which Providence had then allotted to the papacy.

the protestant revolt

MARTIN LUTHER AND THE REVOLT IN GERMANY

MARTIN LUTHER was born at Eisleben in 1483, the son of a miner. At the age of twenty-two he joined the Augustinian Hermits at Erfurt and in 1507 was ordained a priest. In 1510 he visited Rome on business for his Order. From 1512 until his death he was professor of theology at the University of Wittenberg. As a religious he was pious and conscientious, in fact scrupulous, filled with a sincere aspiration for sanctity, but insufficiently formed in scholastic theology and too self-willed to accept advice from others. He tended to brooding. The fundamental problem of his whole life became the question whether and in what way he could be absolutely certain about his eternal salvation. This did not seem possible through definite works availing to salvation and the fulfillment of definite laws: man can never know whether he has really fulfilled them. He believed rather that he would find the solution in unconditional Faith in divine grace. He confused the basic Catholic teaching on Christian hope with the personal conviction of the fulfillment of this hope. Consequently, salutary works, the observance of the positive as well as of the negative commandments, appeared to him, if not superfluous, at least not necessary. Man could not gain a claim to salvation by means of definite deeds or omissions; he obtained this salvation by believing firmly.

These ideas occur already in his early lectures. He first came into conflict with ecclesiastical authority on the occasion of the preaching of an indulgence by the Dominican Tetzel. Since Julius II had in 1506 begun the building of the new Saint Peter's basilica at Rome, the faithful of all countries had been called upon to contribute to it. Indulgences were granted to those who, in addition to other good works, made a contribution according to their discretion. Preachers were appointed to urge this and to transmit the money received to the bishops and to Rome. Tetzel did this in Thuringia. The situation was neither new nor obnoxious to mediaeval men. The faithful cared little whether the indulgence money was used with that conscientiousness to which the ecclesiastical authorities were obliged; they were concerned with the good work. Even Luther's protest was not directed against mismanagement of funds, although much could have been said in regard to the irresponsible financial activity at the papal court of the time. Rather, Luther made use of the occasion of the preaching of the indulgence to come forward openly with his new doctrine of justification by Faith alone and without good works. He did so when he posted his ninety-five theses, wherein, in accordance with academic custom, he issued a challenge to a disputation on various theological matters, especially on indulgences and on the value of good works in general.

Luther's theses, though in form only a traditional university affair, spread at once throughout all Germany and produced a tremendous sensation. Even at Rome notice was quickly taken of them. As early as 1518 Leo X cited Luther to Rome, but the pope acceded to his request that he be allowed to justify himself before the papal legate, Cardinal Cajetan, who was then staying at Augsburg. Luther did not accept the disavowal required of him by Cajetan and instead appealed to a general council, thereby entering upon the path of rebellion. In 1520 Leo X issued the bull *Exsurge*, in which Luther's unorthodox doctrines were condemned and he himself was threatened with excommunication. Since even now Luther did not submit, but publicly burned the bull at Wittenberg, he was solemnly excommunicated in 1521. Leo X cannot be reproached with having taken the affair too lightly from the start.

LUTHER'S PERSONALITY

It is not easy to form a true picture of Luther's personality, not because he was an especially complex character, difficult to understand, but for the reason that in the imagination of many he has become a sort of mythical figure, a symbol of all possible good and evil. The real Luther was neither a monster nor a saint. Humanly attractive in him are his great vitality and originality, but they often degenerated into lack of restraint. He was sometimes incredibly coarse and filthy, and when hatred overpowered him he could talk like a person out of his mind. Some of this can be dismissed as crude honesty, but at times there appears something which causes amazement, something almost demoniacal. On the other hand it would be unjust to judge him solely by these passionate utterances in his writings, which, of course, when taken out of context, have a frantic ring about them. Luther often expressed openly what he thought at the moment, and frequently very imprudently. He was not a hypocrite nor a cunning diplomat, yet he lied incredibly much, with a blunt simplicity that almost atones for his distortion of the truth. Luther was pious. He firmly believed in the divinity of Christ and loved the Saviour. It is almost pathetic how in the midst of the most violent abuse of holy things his love of God breaks through. Everything was personal with him. Every theological opponent was to him a personal enemy to whom he credited all baseness. In some of his propositions one has the impression that he drew them up chiefly in order to irritate his opponents. On the whole he was not a systematic thinker. That he involved himself in contradictions did not disturb him. Against the Catholics he argued for free investigation of the Bible, but among his own adherents he countenanced no difference of opinion.

Without any doubt Luther has exercised a formative influence on the German character, and this influence was on the whole unfortunate rather than favorable. In recent times traits which have so constantly prejudiced other peoples against the Germans—arrogance, braggadoccio, tendency to confuse pounding the table with energy, attributes for which one seeks in vain in the German of the Middle Ages—go back in some way to Luther, and above all to that dilettantism in the supreme questions, on the basis of which each believes he can prepare his own *Weltanschauung* according to his own discretion.

BEGINNING OF THE REVOLT

After the excommunication of 1521 matters were not favorable for Luther. The emperor outlawed him; many universities, including that of Paris, which was still at that time a European power, declared against him; and the English King Henry VIII wrote a book against him. But now the German princes intervened, notably the elector of Saxony, Luther's territorial lord. He rescued him from outlawry by having him brought to the Wartburg, where Luther began his precious translation of the Bible. The elector allowed Luther's friends in Wittenberg to abandon Catholic worship and permitted priests to marry. Luther himself did not marry until 1525. Since the emperor had gone to Spain, the Catholic princes took matters into their own hands and formed a league for the protection of the Catholic religion. These were especially Archduke Ferdinand, brother of Charles V, the duke of Bavaria, and the South German prince-bishops. The princes who stood with Luther and the elector of Saxony countered with the League of Torgau. To prevent civil war, the Diet of Speyer in 1526 decreed that for the present each prince could in his own territory introduce or retain the form of religion which he preferred till the general council which was expected to meet soon should solve the questions in dispute. At the moment people regarded the whole affair as a quarrel among Catholics and saw in a gathering of all Catholic bishops the court to which all would submit. In the same fateful year, 1526, in which the Lutheran princes formed their league and the diet awarded them the right to a change of religion, Clement VII joined the ill-starred League of Cognac against the emperor, thereby playing into the hands of the Lutheran princes.

In addition to Electoral Saxony, the princes of Hesse, Mecklenburg, and Braunschweig and several imperial cities made use of their right of changing religion. East Prussia, the land of the Teutonic Order, had become Lutheran the previous year, when the Grand Master, Albert of Brandenburg, transformed it into a secular duchy and placed it under the suzerainty of the Polish king. The rapid progress of the Reformation alarmed the remaining princes and at a new Diet of Speyer in 1529 it was decided that no further changes were to be made until a council could meet. Six imperial princes and fourteen cities protested against this decree and hence were labeled "Protestants."

After Charles V had made peace with the pope and had received the imperial crown, he returned to Germany and summoned a diet to meet at Augsburg in 1530. Here the

Protestants submitted a detailed profession of Faith, the celebrated *Confessio Augustana*. Its author was Melanchthon, Luther's loyal collaborator and, though a layman, a better theologian. Charles V engaged in no negotiations and simply commanded all to return to Catholic doctrine.

THE LEAGUE OF SCHMALKALD

The Protestant princes, whose number was growing, formed a new league at Schmalkald against the emperor. A fresh circumstance came to their aid. The Turks, who had besieged Vienna in 1529, were advancing ever more threateningly, and the emperor needed the support of all the German princes to protect the Empire from this peril. The Protestants utilized this pressure to extort favorable terms from him. In return for their aid against the Turks, he had to allow, in the religious Peace of Nürnberg in 1532, that everything remain in the *status quo* till the council. However, by now they were no longer in earnest in regard to a council. When in 1536 Pope Paul III finally summoned the frequently demanded gathering, the Protestant princes and Luther himself declined to participate. During the new absence of the emperor they admitted additional members into the League of Schmalkald, in violation of the Peace of Nürnberg.

Now the emperor decided upon armed intervention. He returned to Germany and in 1547 defeated the League of Schmalkald at the battle of Mühlberg. Of the defeated he demanded only that they submit to the council, which had meanwhile met at Trent. Luther had died the year previous. Once again the Protestant cause seemed lost.

But now a new turn occurred. While Charles V was preparing for the battle of Mühlberg, Paul III transferred the council from Trent to Bologna. Not only was the emperor personally offended by this step, which was taken against his

358

wish, but he also felt that, in the eyes of the Protestants, a council held in the territory of the Papal State would not have the necessary independence. Hence, he disregarded the council and resolved, on his own responsibility, to effect a reconciliation with the Protestants by means of a compromise. This was a very risky path, the path which the Byzantine emperors had tried again and again, and always fruitlessly, with the heretics of antiquity. But Charles V was not a theologian and looked at everything from the ruler's standpoint. Accordingly, at the Diet of Augsburg he published the so-called *Interim*, a sort of neutral formula of Faith, containing concessions in regard to the chalice for the laity, the marriage of priests, and the secularization of ecclesiastical goods. He did not understand that the already deep differences of belief could no longer be settled by this method. Nevertheless, he had brought the Protestant princes so far that they promised to attend the council after Paul III's successor had transferred it back to Trent, when a new blow completely destroyed the work of peace that embodied such dim prospects.

THE PEACE OF AUGSBURG

The elector of Saxony had secretly concluded an alliance with France and was preparing a *coup d'état*. He planned to surprise the emperor at Innsbruck and seize his person. Charles V succeeded in escaping at the last moment, but, since he was in no position to conduct a simultaneous war against the Turks, France, and the Protestant princes, he concluded with the princes a kind of armistice, the Treaty of Passau, in 1552. Then, long weary of ruling, he turned over the further conduct of the affair to his brother Ferdinand, whom he had had elected German king in 1531. The latter in 1555 made at Augsburg a definitive peace with the Protestant princes on the following basis:

1. The new religion, according to the *Confessio Augustana* of 1530, was recognized as of equal rank in the Empire with the Catholic religion.

2. It pertained to the princes, and not to their subjects, to determine which religion was to prevail in the individual territories, though the subjects could depart in the event that they were unwilling to accept the Faith of their prince.

3. Spiritual princes (bishops and abbots) who desired to embrace the new religion could do so only personally and, in the event that they did, lost their territory, since it was not their inherited property.

In this way peace was established, at least superficially, in Germany. The principle that the territorial lord could determine the Faith of his subjects seems to us today quite wrong, but at least it put a definite limit to the revolt from the Church. From then on, Germany was split into large, small, and petty territories belonging to two different religions. For there could no longer be any doubt that there were really two different religions. The Protestants rejected the authority of pope and council, the Church's teaching office, the ordination of bishops and priests, the Sacrifice of the Mass, the veneration of Our Lady and the saints, the doctrine of justification by the sacraments and good works, the sacrament of penance, the inspiration of part of the Bible, and much else, so that of the Catholic catechism little remained other than Faith in the Trinity and in the divinity of Christ. They no longer belonged to the Catholic Church and no longer wished to belong to it.

CHARLES V

The life of Charles V was filled with tragedy, like the life of his son, Philip II, and the lives of almost all great rulers. He was noble in every sense of the word, a gentleman of that outstanding and manly type which is rarely found today. Of a

360

sickly body and troubled from an early age by the gout, he was still proficient in all knightly skills, a splendid horseman and successful general. He was of a melancholic temperament. He never laughed. His grandfather, the always cheerful Emperor Maximilian, was displeased at the excessive seriousness of the youth. In the mature man this seriousness often became depression, perhaps a legacy from his mentally deranged mother, and it weakened his resolution. His seriousness was further accentuated by a highly developed sense of responsibility. He was free of vanity and ambition, but for him the position of ruler implied that he was God's vicar. He felt responsible for the destiny of the Church and the salvation of souls in the Empire confided to him. He sought to fulfill this obligation with or without the pope, and, if necessary, against him. This can the more readily be understood if one considers the popes with whom he had chiefly to deal—the frivolous Leo X and the incompetent Clement VII. Charles V was not a theologian and, despite his many spiritual and secular advisers, he was a solitary. In ecclesiastical questions he was often seriously wrong, but when he was wrong, he believed he was merely doing his duty. Charles V stood above nationality. In equal measure his most trusted advisers were the Belgian Granvel, the Piedmontese Gattinara, and the Spaniard Loaysa. At first he was more Netherlandish—he was born in Ghent— though French was his mother tongue; later he inclined more toward the Spanish, but, unlike his son, Philip II, he never became a complete Spaniard. He was deeply pious, prayed much, performed penitential exercises, but he likewise paid his toll to human weakness. Before his marriage to Isabella of Portugal he had a daughter, Margaret, and when he was a widower, a son, Don Juan of Austria, who would become famous as the victor of Lepanto. Charles' end showed how little he loved power. Already in 1521 he had given the hereditary Austrian lands to his brother Ferdinand and in 1531 the German royal crown likewise; in 1555 he gave the Netherlands and Burgundy to his son Philip, and in the following year the Spanish and Neapolitan royal crowns. Finally, he gave up the imperial crown and took up residence at Yuste in Spain, near a Hieronymite monastery, not as a friar but as a pious private individual. There he died in 1558 at the age of fifty-eight.

THE REVOLT IN SWITZERLAND

ZWINGLI

In Switzerland a movement of revolt was begun in 1519 by the secular priest, Ulric Zwingli, independently of the movement then in progress in Electoral Saxony, but strongly influenced by Luther in doctrine. Of course, Zwingli differed from him in essential points, especially in his teaching on the Eucharist. Luther held firmly and absolutely the presence of Christ in Communion, though he denied the substantial change of the bread and wine, rejected the sacrificial character of the Mass, and declared it to be idolatry. Zwingli denied any presence of Christ. Violent arguments took place on this point between Lutherans and the adherents of Zwingli, and even later the Confession of Augsburg and the Swiss Confession remained different.

In Switzerland there soon resulted a civil war between the Zwinglian cantons and those that remained Catholic. The Catholics were victorious in the battle of Kappel and Zwingli himself fell, but in the treaty of peace the two religions, the Swiss and the Catholic, were recognized as equal, so that in Switzerland there was a condition of separate religious territories similar to that resulting in Germany from the religious peace of Augsburg.

CALVIN

A much greater significance than Zwingli's, and one extending far beyond Switzerland, was acquired by John Calvin, a native of Noyon in France, who in his *Institutio Christianae Religionis*, published in 1536, proposed the doctrine of the irrevocable predestination of man, either to salvation or to damnation. Luther had in places come dangerously close to this teaching, necessarily so once he had abandoned the freedom of the will; but Luther had hesitated to draw the extreme consequences. Calvin now did so with strict logic.

Since in the France of Francis I non-Catholic doctrines were not allowed, Calvin settled in Geneva. Geneva belonged to the German Empire; in name the territorial lord was the bishop, who from 1535 resided at Annecy, and the overlord was the duke of Savoy as imperial vicar. In reality the city was independent. Calvin set up a sort of theocratic republic and till his death in 1564 conducted a stern government. In 1556 he founded the theological academy, in which teachers of the new Faith were educated; in time they spread it afar—in France, England, Scotland, parts of the Netherlands and Germany, and even in Hungary. Calvinism was more of a theology than was Lutheranism, which could rather be termed a method. Hence, Calvinism was spread more by individual theological teachers and, unlike Lutheranism, did not comprise entire territories but particular persons and groups in whom it sank deep roots.

ENGLAND

In the fifteenth century England had endured violent shocks. The so-called Hundred Years' War, in reality protracted over an even longer span of time, in which England temporarily conquered half of France, had ended with the loss of all continental holdings and in the complete exhaustion of the kingdom. The subsequent Wars of the Roses, a struggle between two branches of the royal house, Lancaster and York, whose vicissitudes have become through Shakespeare's dramas the common possession of all educated persons, led finally to the ruin of both lines. When at length the unusually capable Henry VII of the house of Tudor held all authority in his own hands, he was able, since the old feudal nobility had been almost wiped out in the dynastic struggle, to introduce absolute monarchy with a centralized administration and officialdom, the same result that was then taking place in France and Spain. The country recovered with surprising rapidity. The many constructions from this age, in the late Gothic or so-called Tudor style, still convey that impression.

In 1509 Henry VII was succeeded by his eighteen-year-old son, Henry VIII, who was as capable as his father but still more despotic and, in character, inconstant and immoral. His chancellor was Cardinal Wolsey.[1] Wolsey aspired to be pope and in fact governed the Church in England like a pope, especially when Adrian VI made him legate for his lifetime with very extensive authority. Wolsey's supervision, to which the still famed Christ Church College at Oxford bears witness, could have been salutary for the English Church, had he been a character like Cisneros, who at the same time occupied a quite similar position in Spain.

Soon after Luther's appearance Henry VIII had composed a polemic against him, and for this Leo X had bestowed upon him the title of "Defender of the Faith," still borne by the British monarch. It was not theological considerations but a matrimonial matter that impelled Henry VIII to break with the Church.

---

[1] The German text (p. 247) refers to Wolsey as archbishop of Canterbury. But the ill-starred cardinal was archbishop of York. (Translator's note.)

HENRY VIII'S DIVORCE

Henry's wife was Catherine, daughter of Ferdinand and Isabella of Spain and youngest sister of Charles V's mother, the unbalanced Juana. At first the marriage was happy, but Henry became unfaithful and finally determined to marry his mistress of the moment, Anne Boleyn, and make her queen. An ecclesiastical trial for a divorce was conducted with great sophistry. Wolsey gave his aid. At first he thought it was only a question of a separation from Catherine, and later he lacked the courage to withdraw. With the utmost importunity Henry implored from Clement VII, who was then living as a poor refugee in Orvieto after the sack of Rome, a sort of dispensation whereby his marriage with Catherine would be declared invalid. Clement VII knew that this was impossible, but by various delaying moves he tried to gain time, and hence he created the impression that the king's affair had some prospects of success.

Several years elapsed in these fruitless negotiations. Wolsey died in complete disgrace. Henry named as archbishop of Canterbury the pliant and unscrupulous Thomas Cranmer, who now without any ado declared the nullity of the marriage with Catherine. Henry VIII had not even waited for this before the public coronation of Anne Boleyn took place.

Clement VII could no longer hope to gain by delay and did his duty by declaring invalid the new marriage with Anne during Catherine's lifetime and excommunicating the king. Thereupon, in the parliament of 1534 Henry VIII proclaimed the separation of the English Church from that of Rome and set up the royal supremacy in place of papal jurisdiction in England.

In this separation there was no question of a new doctrine or a new worship. To many the whole affair must have seemed

365

one of those conflicts between king and pope which were so frequent in the Middle Ages; in fact, Charles V, who was always loyal to the Church, had only recently been in conflict with Clement VII. Thus, in the English Church, so used to servility because of Wolsey's supervision, little opposition arose. Individual resistance, such as that of the bishop of Rochester, John Fisher, who had fearlessly defended the rights of Queen Catherine, and that of the jurist and statesman, Thomas More, was punished by execution.

THOMAS MORE

Thomas More is one of the noblest characters in English history. Precocious and highly cultured, a humanist of European renown, especially through his book *Utopia*, a sort of ideal state or mirror of states, whose title is still proverbial, and in addition an ideal father and an always cheerful and witty companion, he had a brilliant public career as Speaker of parliament and in various offices of government until Henry VIII named him Wolsey's successor as Lord Chancellor. He had hoped to be able to bring back the king, who always esteemed him highly, to the right path, and when this was seen to be impossible he withdrew into private life. He refused the oath demanded of him in regard to the king's ecclesiastical supremacy, and this caused his death. In 1886, along with fifty-three other English martyrs, he was beatified by Leo XIII, and he and John Fisher were canonized by Pius XI.

SCANDINAVIA AND THE BALTIC LANDS

The three northern kingdoms of Sweden, Norway, and Denmark had been united since the Union of Kalmar in 1397 in the person of the king of Denmark, but since 1448 Sweden was almost independent. The occasion of the separation of Sweden from the Church was afforded by the quarrel of the archbishop of Upsala, Gustav Trolle (1515–1535), with the administrator, Sture. Sture imprisoned the archbishop and compelled him to abdicate, whereupon the pope excommunicated him and laid an interdict on Sweden. At this, King Christian II of Denmark marched into Sweden and had himself crowned king of Sweden in 1520 by Archbishop Trolle. Christian at once executed two bishops, opponents of Trolle, and other magnates in the so-called "Blood Bath of Stockholm." A revolution now occurred in Sweden. The union with Denmark was dissolved, the Lutheran Gustavus Vasa was proclaimed king, and Protestantism was introduced. This was, however, hardly a religious war, for Christian II too was inclined toward Lutheranism.

Nevertheless, Denmark remained Catholic for a few more years. Christian II was expelled in 1523, and it was not until the reign of Christian III (1534–1559) that the Reformation was introduced into Denmark and also into Norway and Iceland. He had an ecclesiastical constitution drawn up by Bugenhagen, a friend and pupil of Luther, just as had been done in the German Protestant states. In Scandinavia the work of introducing the new religion was gone about in a clever way: profiting by the experiences in Germany, the innovators simply retained the external form of Catholic worship so that the people hardly realized the change of religion.

In the Baltic states, which were ruled by the Teutonic Order, the revolt began in 1525 when the Grand Master, Albert of Brandenburg, transformed East Prussia into a secular duchy. His brother William, archbishop of Riga since 1539, introduced the Reformation into Livonia. The other states of the Order, Kurland and Esthonia, remained Catholic till 1562. In that year the Commander Gotthard von Ketteler changed Kurland into a secular duchy with the *Confessio Augustana* and, in imitation of Albert of Brandenburg, placed it under

367

Polish suzerainty. He ceded Esthonia to already Protestant Sweden. Finland too, which belonged to Sweden, had become Protestant with that kingdom.

REASONS FOR THE REVOLT

By the middle of the sixteenth century a great part of Europe had revolted from the Church—England, all the countries around the Baltic Sea, many states in central Germany. Soon the northern Netherlands followed suit. These countries formed, so to speak, a compact block, so that now the Church had suddenly received a northern geographical frontier, extending from the mouth of the Rhine eastward, just as in the seventh century she had acquired a southern boundary because of Islam. But even below this northern frontier her stability was in many places in jeopardy. In South Germany and Switzerland whole territories had revolted, and in those parts of Germany that remained Catholic, as well as in Austria, Hungary, Transylvania, Poland, France, and Scotland, Lutheran or Calvinist islands and centers had everywhere been established. Only Italy and Spain had remained entirely Catholic.

By a mere counting of heads the greater part of Europe was still Catholic. Around the middle of the sixteenth century the population of Europe, exclusive of Russia and the Balkan lands, can be estimated at about 60,000,000 souls, of whom about fifteen to twenty millions, or almost one-third, had separated from the Church. Still, never before had the Church suffered so numerous a defection, not even in the fifth century when the Nestorians and Monophysites, scarcely more than three to four millions altogether, had withdrawn, nor in the Byzantine Schism, for, when Byzantium separated, the Christians in the Greek lands had already greatly decreased in numbers and the Russian lands were still almost unoccupied in comparison with their later population.

How could so great a defection have occurred in so few decades and without any hostile external conquest? This question has from time immemorial intrigued historians of all schools.

One cannot say—though at times it is said—that for a long time, since the Great Western Schism, if not since Avignon, centrifugal forces had been at work in the Church. On the contrary, during the Great Western Schism the desire of the people for the unity of the Church displayed itself with almost violent force. The very fact that no one wanted to hear of any more splits in the Church caused the failure and death of the Council of Basel. From that time until Luther almost a century elapsed.

The most widespread view is that the abuses in the Church in the fifteenth and early sixteenth century led necessarily to the revolt. In this connection people think first of all of the secularization of the papal court and like to feel that, in a sense, Luther led the reaction against Alexander VI. But this is incorrect. Such brief formulae are of little use in the presentation of history. There have always been abuses in the Church, sometimes greater, sometimes smaller. The parable of the cockle in the wheat holds for all time. Abuses in ecclesiastical government have often led to controversies, to insubordination, but not to a change of religion, to heresy. The numerous heresies which are encountered in the course of Church history, from those of the Gnostics and Arians to those of the Jansenists, Old Catholics, and Modernists, were never reactions against abuses and never arose in periods and places of special decline in religious life, but rather in a religious atmosphere of high tension.

If corruption in the Church had been the reason for the

separation, the lines of separation would have had to run in quite a different way. In that case it would have been the best elements, who no longer found in the ancient Church the satisfaction of their ideal aspirations, that turned their backs and established a new, purer, and more ideal Church. But it cannot be maintained that such was the case. To be sure, there were also idealists among the reformers who revolted at this time, but it is by no means true that the world had split into two camps, the good and the bad. The line of separation ran rather right through the masses, in all directions; good and bad were on both sides.

Neither can it be said that nationality and national character caused the separation, somewhat as though Catholicism corresponded rather with Romance individuality and Protestantism with Germanic. That England revolted was certainly not due to Germanic national character; that France, having almost revolted, found its way back to the Church was not in the slightest way connected with the Romance spirit. In Germany after the separation there were Germans on both sides. Incidentally, if one wants to label Lutheranism typically Germanic, Calvinism must be called a Latin growth.

Furthermore, it is entirely untrue that Catholicism hardly corresponded to the German national spirit. The entire German Middle Ages prove the contrary. A German who would hold this view must disavow the entire past of his nation, its Catholic emperors, knights and crusaders, thinkers and mystics, the German cathedrals, the German saints. The most Catholic of all devotions—devotion to the Blessed Sacrament and the veneration of the Mother of God—took root in Germany as everywhere else. Corpus Christi is almost a German feast; it originated at Liége, which then belonged to the Empire, and spread first in Lower Germany, before the pope granted it to the universal Church.

370

Catchword explanations such as the above bring one nowhere near historical truth. History is made by individual men. In it there is no place for fate, for necessity, for blind evolution. If Luther had not appeared, or had appeared in a different manner, German history would have taken a different course, and if Henry VIII had been able to control his passions, England would not have revolted. The real responsibility falls upon the individual princes—the electors of Saxony and Brandenburg, the landgrave of Hesse, the Teutonic Grand Master, the kings of Sweden, Denmark, and England.

If the abuses in the Church had necessarily led to the separation, the result would have had to be the same everywhere. But the much-blamed abuses also existed in countries and states which finally remained Catholic. Fidelity in these places also depended on individuals. Where the prince remained Catholic, as in Bavaria, or where the prince revolted but experienced resistance, as in the electorate of Cologne, the country remained Catholic.

As regards Germany, there is surely no German today who does not regret the cleavage in Faith. The Catholic must regret that a revolt occurred, the Protestant that it was not entirely successful. But each bemoans the split, because it was for Germany worse than two lost world wars. Now there are among the Catholics some who, out of an ardent desire for a reconciliation, would like to say: Let us assume the whole blame; let us say calmly that Luther erred in individual points of doctrine but on the whole was right; the popes, bishops, and ecclesiastical institutions of the age were to blame; the Catholic Church has a broad back, hence let us saddle her with the whole affair and bury the hatchet! Such a viewpoint does all honor to the good heart of its champion. But history cannot go along with it. In the sight of history the fact remains that the reformers of the sixteenth century revolted from the

Church, not that the Church revolted from them. That no blame for this attaches to their present-day descendants is clear. But the division can only be eliminated by their finding the way back to the Church from which their forefathers withdrew.

the catholic Restoration

I N THE history of the Church the great nations alternate in the leading role in Europe. In the tenth and eleventh centuries the part fell to Germany; in the thirteenth century it was played by France. At the end of the fifteenth and throughout the sixteenth century leadership was assumed by a nation which hitherto had stood almost entirely apart—Spain. It had long been preparing for this role.

SPAIN UNDER FERDINAND AND ISABELLA

Since the repulse of the Moors in the twelfth and at the beginning of the thirteenth century, four kingdoms existed in the Iberian peninsula: Portugal, a kingdom since 1139; Castile; Aragón; and, in the northeast, little Navarre. In Castile and Aragón two lines of the same dynasty reigned throughout the fifteenth century. Henry III (✝1406) was king of Castile, while his brother, Ferdinand I (✝1416), was king of Aragón and Sicily. Henry's granddaughter, Isabella, married Ferdinand's grandson, Ferdinand II, in 1469, and thenceforth the two crowns remained united. Granada, the last remnant of Moorish rule, was conquered in 1492, and in 1512 Navarre was united with Castile, so that from then on the entire peninsula, except for Portugal, constituted a single kingdom.

Contemporary with the dynastic unification was the change

373

from a mediaeval feudal state to a territorial state with government by officials. This was the work of the unusually capable ruling pair, Ferdinand and Isabella, who thereby lifted Spain to the status of a European great power and, through their general, Gonsalvo de Córdova, to that of the leading military power. Ferdinand was as unscrupulous as the other Renaissance princes, whom he excelled only in his gifts as a ruler; Isabella was an ideal character, the *mulier fortis* of Scripture, well-educated along humanist lines, deeply pious, chaste, and virtuous. To her is due the chief merit that, along with the political progress in Spain, religious advances went hand in hand.

Two successive great princes of the Church were the ecclesiastical leaders in Spain at this time. The first of these was Pedro González de Mendoza, son of the knightly poet, the marqués de Santillana. In 1473 he became a cardinal and chancellor of Ferdinand and Isabella, in 1482 archbishop of Toledo and primate of Spain. He was especially great in his zeal for souls, composed a catechism, and founded many pious institutes and splendid church buildings. This was the age of the early Spanish Renaissance, whose rich decorative sculpture, suggestive of the silversmith's art, bears the name of plateresque style. At his death in 1495 Mendoza was succeeded by the Franciscan, Ximenes de Cisneros, Isabella's confessor, who is regarded as even more outstanding. Above all, Cisneros favored studies. In 1500 he founded the University of Alcalá. To biblical scholars he is familiar as the editor in 1514 of the first polyglot Bible.

The effort to maintain the unity and purity of the Faith led to rigorous measures. In 1492 all Jews were expelled from Spain. Some of them went to the Netherlands, others to the East, where Spanish-speaking Jews are still found. Jews and

Moslems who had themselves baptized were observed with distrust by the Inquisition.

Successful as was the long reign of Ferdinand and Isabella, their family affairs were beset by misfortune. Family tragedy has remained the inheritance of the Spanish royal house. Of their children only two daughters survived. The younger, Catherine, married Henry VIII of England, to her own personal tragedy; the elder, heiress of the Spanish crowns, lapsed into incurable insanity soon after her marriage to Philip of Habsburg, son of Emperor Maximilian. Philip died in 1506 and thus, at the death of Ferdinand II in 1516, the crowns of Castile, Navarre, Aragón, Sicily, and Naples were inherited by the son of mad Juana and grandson of the emperor, the then sixteen-year-old Charles V. Three years later Maximilian died and Charles fell heir to the Austrian lands, the Netherlands, and the German imperial crown. Spain, which since 1492 also possessed extensive territories in America, had become a world empire. Spanish culture and customs were imprinted on the entire sixteenth century, from military science to fashions in dress and the so-called Spanish court ceremonial, which, however, was of Burgundian origin and only came to Spain with Charles V.

SPAIN IN THE SIXTEENTH CENTURY

At the beginning of the sixteenth century the population of Spain mounted to well over 10,000,000 souls and seems, despite the emigration to America, to have kept increasing for a time, even though the recently estimated figure of 17,000,000 for the end of the sixteenth century may be an exaggeration. The religious flowering, which had begun under Ferdinand and Isabella, endured throughout the whole sixteenth century. Spanish theology occupied the position which that at Paris had held in the Middle Ages. Above all it was the Dominican

375

Order which produced great theologians—Francisco de Vitoria (✝1546) and his pupil, Melchior Cano (✝1560), the founder of that branch of the theological science which is now termed Fundamental Theology; Domenico de Soto (✝1560); Bartolomeo de Medina (✝1581), the founder of the system of moral probabilism; finally, the pugnacious Domenico Báñez (✝1604). Toward the end of the century the Jesuits too produced important representatives—the very controversial Luis Molina (✝1600); the keen Gabriel Vásquez (✝1604); and the most celebrated of them all, Francisco Suárez (✝1617). Among the ascetical authors should be mentioned the Dominican Luis of Granada (✝1588) and the Jesuit Alfonso Rodríguez (✝1616).

Most of all, Spain was then a land of saints. Of the first importance, besides Ignatius Loyola (✝1556) and Francis Xavier (✝1552), were the two reformers of the Carmelite Order, Teresa of Avila (✝1582) and the Doctor of the Church, John of the Cross (✝1591). Along with them stood the Franciscans, Peter of Alcántara (✝1562) and Paschal Baylón (✝1592), the Augustinian Hermit Thomas of Villanova, who died as archbishop of Valencia in 1555, Francis Borgia (✝1572), duke of Gandia before his entry into the Society of Jesus, and Blessed John Avila (✝1569), the Apostle of Andalusía.

PHILIP II

The ruler of Spain in the second half of the sixteenth century was Philip II (1556–1598), one of the greatest and at the same time one of the most misunderstood figures of modern history. In Germany, through Schiller's wholly unhistorical drama, Don Carlos, Philip II has become a phantom; in England he has become the incarnation of the darkness, cruelty, and backwardness which were attributed to the

376

Catholic Church. The historical Philip II was entirely different. In character he was very much like his father, Charles V—serious, taciturn, lonely—but even more than Charles V he lived wholly for duty and lay stifled under responsibility; in addition, he possessed a gigantic capacity for work and, in contradistinction to his warlike father, was completely unmilitary. Philip II was deeply religious. In his monastery-palace of the Escorial, which he built for himself in a lonely spot, he passed many days in prayer and silent meditation. He could be harsh and unbending; he drove several popes who had to deal with him almost to despair; he made many mistakes in politics. But all this was not the consequence of love of power or of vanity, of which he was completely free, but of his sense of responsibility. He trembled before God, but he felt himself to be God's deputy and responsible to God alone. That Philip II, who in his family was pursued by the severest misfortunes, left no capable successor, so that, as a consequence, Spain rapidly declined in the seventeenth century from the pinnacle to which he had lifted it is not his fault. The claim of foreign writers that he drained Spain to exhaustion is one of the many unproved generalities in which the historical criticism of Spain has been so rich for ages.

It is not true that the entire ecclesiastical renewal in the period of the Renaissance proceeded from Spain. But it was of the utmost importance for the Church that in the sixteenth century there was at least one country, one great power, which remained wholly untouched by the religious revolt and that this country was able at the moment of crisis to supply the Church with rich regenerating forces.

PAUL III

Although no causal relationship existed between the secularization of papal government since Sixtus IV and the revolt in northern Europe, just the same any intelligent and sincere Catholic could easily foresee an impending connection that would have mutual effects. There was a need for enlightened action. There were not lacking such sensible persons from the beginning of the sixteenth century, and as a matter of fact the Church experienced, from the middle of the century, a powerful upsurge in all fields. This revival has been termed the "Counter-Reformation," and the expression has become so natural that it can be disregarded only with difficulty. Throughout his *History of the Popes* Pastor has used the expression "Catholic Restoration," which is more correct. However one may prefer to call this period, in any case it must be made clear that the recovery in ecclesiastical life was not a reaction to the revolt of the north. In fact, it began in the lands which were on the whole not affected by the Protestant Revolt—Spain and Italy.

Clement VII was succeeded by a pope whose pontificate, more than most others, forms a landmark in the history of the Church, Paul III (1534–1549). We do not mean, of course, that, alone or even principally, he caused the revival, something that could not be the work of one pope only. But Paul III determined the new course in Church administration. He was the helmsman who took control of the barque, which till now had let itself be driven by the wind, and altered the sail at the right moment.

Alessandro Farnese derived wholly from the unspiritual Rome of the Renaissance. His family was prominent: his mother was a Gaetani; his sister Julia, called "La Bella" because of her beauty, married an Orsini. Alexander VI made the twenty-five-year-old Alessandro a cardinal, not because of his merits but because he was the brother of the beautiful Julia, who enjoyed the pope's favor. At that time Farnese lived no better than many others at the Roman court. He had a mistress and by her a son, Pier Luigi, who was later to play a role in history. In time he became more serious, especially from his ordination to the priesthood in 1519. Because of his intelligence, business ability, and experience, he occupied under Leo X a prominent position in the College of Cardinals. In the conclave of 1523 he was almost elected pope. The dying Clement VII recommended him as his only possible successor. The election lasted but a few hours.

Paul III was one of the most intelligent men who have ever occupied the Throne of Peter. Exteriorly an old man—he was sixty-six at his election, eighty-one at his death—of small stature, weary and bent, with a long white beard, but with flashing, eager eyes—thus did Titian often paint him. Paul III was passionate, but always master of himself. Outstanding in his knowledge and handling of men, he was an expert in the art of discovering worthwhile men and in placing them in the right positions. As pope he had a great fault—his excessive concern for his family. In this respect he completely followed in the path of the Rovere and the Borgias. On his son, Pier Luigi, he bestowed the duchy of Parma, which had belonged to the Papal State since Julius II, and thus he implicated himself in dangerous political strife. The Farnese remained dukes of Parma till the extinction of the family in 1731. The last Farnese died as widow of Philip V of Spain. Of the three sons of Pier Luigi, grandsons of the pope, Ottavio was destined to inherit the duchy of Parma; he was married to Charles V's illegitimate daughter, Margaret. The other two, Alessandro and Ranuccio, were made cardinals while very young. Ranuccio died early, but in time Alessandro became an unusually capable and worthy prince of the Church.

REFORM OF THE COLLEGE OF CARDINALS

Paul III first undertook reform in that place from which corruption had proceeded—the College of Cardinals. His nominations of cardinals were events. In 1535 he elevated Saint

John Fisher, who was awaiting in prison his impending execution. He could no longer serve the Church, but his nomination had symbolic significance. With him were elevated Simonetta, Caracciolo, the Benedictine Cortese, wholesomely strict churchmen, and, towering above them all, the noble Gasparo Contarini, a layman and senator of Venice. In the following year the red hat was bestowed upon the founder of the Theatines, the stern Gian Pietro Carafa, whose name, like Contarini's, signified a program; the pious and refined humanist, Sadoleto; Reginald Pole, related to the English royal house, friend and companion of Contarini; Giovanni del Monte, later Pope Julius III. In 1538 the important Spanish theologian, Juan Alvárez de Toledo, a Dominican, became a cardinal; in 1539 Pietro Bembo, a celebrated humanist, who had earlier been frivolous, but now led a serious religious life, and the industrious, scholarly, and saintly Marcello Cervini, who was to be the second successor of Paul III; in 1542 the admirable Dominican, Tommaso Badia, like Contarini a patron of Saint Ignatius Loyola and his institute, and Giovanni Morone, one of the best political brains the Church then had; in 1544 the bishop of Augsburg, Otto Truchsess von Waldburg, one of the first German bishops to oppose the religious revolt with all his might.

Paul III raised to the cardinalate a whole series of scarcely less important men, and thus within a few years he had restored the college to what it should be—a body of talent and merit, of scholarship and sanctity of life, of pastoral and political foresight.

Of his best cardinals Paul III formed a commission to draw up proposals of reform. The soul of this commission till his far too early death in 1542 was Cardinal Contarini. Its work formed the basis for the reform decrees of the Council of Trent.

PREPARATIONS FOR THE COUNCIL

As long as the German Protestants believed that they belonged to the universal Church, they had been the loudest in calling for a council. Later, Catholics of all countries joined in this desire. The conviction that a council, and it alone, could cure all evils stemmed from the conciliar epoch of the fifteenth century. The pope, however, had to see to it that the precedents of Pisa, Constance, and Basel be not repeated, and that a council not again claim supreme authority in the Church.

Soon after his accession Paul III summoned to Rome Vergerio, the nuncio at Vienna, for a report on the situation in Germany. In order not to be disturbed, the pope retired with him to the Villa Magliana. Vergerio was amazed at how little the curia was abreast of the German situation. After the pope had been thoroughly informed, he sent Vergerio on a tour of the German princes to invite them to the council; Mantua was designated as the place of meeting. Vergerio went to Berlin, where he conferred with the Hohenzollern elector, Joachim II, who was not yet openly a Lutheran; then he went to Wittenberg, where he met Luther. The nuncio found him arrogant, almost demoniacal, but Luther promised to go to Mantua. Vergerio did not then guess that thirteen years later he himself would embrace Protestantism.

Luther's promise to attend the council was perhaps seriously given; he was never lacking in personal courage. But the princes of the League of Schmalkald decided not to send representatives or even to recognize the council. In this they were supported by Henry VIII, who had already fallen out with the Church, and by Francis I, who, though a Catholic, wished to thwart the council, since he dreaded from it an increase in the power of his old opponent, Charles V.

To the earlier grounds for opposition between Charles V and Francis I had been added, since the death of the last

381

Sforza in 1535, the question of Milan. Both laid claim to the duchy. Paul III wanted neither of them to acquire it, but would have settled for a French prince. The rivalry resulted in war. Under the circumstances a council was unthinkable. Paul III finally journeyed personally to Nizza and negotiated there separately with the two monarchs. He at least obtained an ending of the war.

Now came new difficulties, this time from the duke of Mantua. To hold the council in his city he laid down such impossible conditions that the pope had to look elsewhere. The place ought to be conveniently located for the Germans but lying neither in imperial nor in papal territory. Paul resolved on Vicenza, which belonged to Venice. The papal legates solemnly entered Vicenza, but no one else appeared, so that the pope suspended the council which had not even been opened. The emperor and his brother, Ferdinand, had at the time no interest in the council. They were concerned only for union with the Protestants and expected to attain the goal by religious discussions and agreements.

In 1542 Paul III, who wanted in any case to bring the council into being, moved a step closer to the Germans. He summoned the council to Trent in imperial territory. He sent as legates his best diplomat, Morone, and the English Cardinal Pole, whose peaceful dispositions were well-known. Only a few prelates appeared. The emperor's representative, Granvella, did nothing but cause difficulty. There was no hope of any participation by France so long as the quarrel with the emperor was not settled. Once again, then, the pope suspended the council.

OPENING OF THE COUNCIL

Finally in 1544 Charles V and Francis I came to an agreement over Milan in the Treaty of Crespy. Both were now for the council. Thus, on December 13, 1545, more than ten years after the first announcement, it could be solemnly opened at Trent. The presidents were the cardinal-legates, Monte, Cervini, and Pole. At first only twenty-five bishops were present, along with five generals of Orders, among them the excellent Seripando, general of the Augustinian Hermits to whom Luther had belonged.

Difficulties immediately arose in regard to the order of business. The pope wanted before all else doctrinal definitions as clarification of the doctrinal disputes. Charles V wanted the theological questions deferred in order not to irritate the Protestants and instead desired reform decrees, whereby the Church's good will would be proved to the Protestants. It was decided that in each session doctrinal decrees and reform decrees would be issued simultaneously.

In 1546 two sessions were held. In the one which ranks as the fourth session of the council the decree on the canon of Holy Scripture was published; in the fifth, the doctrine of original sin. The time between was taken up with theological conferences. The number of bishops, many of whom brought their theological advisers, grew. In the following year the envoys of the king of France arrived. In the sixth session the decree on justification was published, the central point of the whole theological quarrel. This doctrinal decree is a theological masterpiece, careful and lucid. The Catholic teaching on the sacraments in general and on baptism in particular was defined in the seventh session. Then occurred an interruption.

The unfortunate question of Milan had again led to strained relations, this time between emperor and pope. Paul III would have liked to see as duke of Milan his son, Pier Luigi, who already held Parma and Piacenza. The imperial governor of Milan, Gonzaga, believed he was serving the emperor by having Pier Luigi Farnese murdered. Paul III, deeply affected and understandably suspicious that the crime had not been perpetrated without the emperor's knowledge, and furthermore long dissatisfied with the excessive pressure that Charles V was exerting at Trent, now transferred the council to Bologna in papal territory. For his part the emperor was highly incensed and withdrew from the council at the very moment when he had decisively defeated the League of Schmalkald at Mühlberg. Paul III died before an agreement could be reached between emperor and pope.

The attitude of Paul III in the Milanese question and the transfer of the council, which was equivalent to a blast, were undoubtedly mistakes. Nevertheless, to Paul III belongs the merit of having brought the council into existence after endless difficulties and of having indicated to it the correct procedure. Under more favorable circumstances his successors would be able to reap where he had sown.

NEW ORDERS

Paul III's name is linked with the new wave of Orders of Clerics Regular, just as is that of Innocent III with the Mendicant movement. Already in the time of Leo X there had arisen in Rome a community of pious priests and lay persons, the "Oratory of Divine Love," whose center was the little church of San Girolamo della Carità, still standing. A chief concern of these men was the spread of frequent Communion, which was then almost unknown. Similar circles were established in North Italy at Verona, Vicenza, Brescia, and Venice. Some of the men proceeding from these centers became leaders of the movement of restoration in Italy: Gian Matteo Giberti, who as bishop of Verona had zealously carried out reforms long before the Council of Trent and whom Charles Borromeo later took for his model; Lippomano, much read popular author and likewise bishop of Verona and later of Bergamo;

the pious humanist, Giovenale Manetti; Cardinals Sadoleto and Carafa; and finally Saint Cajetan of Tiene.

The Oratory of Divine Love was not an Order and in general had no strict organization. But Cajetan and Carafa founded a real Order of an entirely new sort: priests who devoted themselves to the care of souls, without monastic customs and austerities, and externally scarcely to be distinguished from secular priests living in common. They called themselves simply "reformed clerics" or "clerics regular." Later, when Carafa had become bishop of Chieti, the ancient Theate Marucinorum, people began to call the priests of the Order of the *Episcopus Theatinus* "Theatines." The new Order was confirmed by Clement VII in 1525 and was already influential by the example of a strictly clerical mode of life. The name "Theatines" became synonymous with a program or slogan and, in the mouths of the worldly-minded, with bigotry.

In consultation with Carafa, Saint Jerome Miani founded in North Italy a similar Order of Clerics Regular, which, from a small town near Bergamo, received the name of Somasco. Paul III confirmed it in 1540. Greater importance was acquired by another clerical Order, founded at Milan by Saint Antonio Zaccaria and called, after his first church, the Barnabites, which was confirmed by Paul III in 1535.

THE SOCIETY OF JESUS

The greatest expansion of all fell to the lot of the Order of Clerics Regular of the Society of Jesus, or Jesuit Order, approved by Paul III in 1540. Its founder was Ignatius of Loyola, a Spanish knight of the Basque region. Ignatius, or Iñigo, as he was originally called, grievously wounded at the siege of Pamplona in 1521, was converted by reading the lives of the saints during a long convalescence and resolved upon a life

385

dedicated entirely to the service of God. Introduced by the Catalan Benedictines of Montserrat into the rudiments of the spiritual life, he went by himself as pilgrim to Palestine in 1523 to devote himself, in the spirit of the Spanish crusading movement, to the conversion of the Moslems. The Franciscans, appointed by the Church as custodians of the Holy Land, wanted no unauthorized preachers and sent him back home. Ignatius realized that he must become a priest and began his studies, first at Barcelona, then at the universities of Alcalá and Salamanca, and finally at Paris, where he won valuable companions among the students—the pious Savoyard Le Fèbre, the clever Spaniard Laynez, who was to play a great role at the Council of Trent, and a young man who was to become one of the most famous saints of modern times, the Navarrese Francis Xavier. With these and other companions Ignatius in 1534 pronounced the religious vows on Montmartre. At the same time they obliged themselves to a journey to the Holy Land, probably not to remain there but merely as pilgrims. When the carrying out of this plan was prevented by the war between Venice and the Turks, they went to Rome, having meanwhile been ordained priests, in order to place themselves at the pope's disposal. Paul III, advised by Contarini, approved the new Order and began at once to make use of its members. At the request of the king of Portugal, he sent Francis Xavier to the Indies in 1540. In 1543 the first German Jesuit, Saint Peter Canisius, joined the Society, and in 1548 followed the duke of Gandia, Francis Borgia, great-grandson of Alexander VI and personal friend of Charles V; Francis Borgia's entry produced a deep impression throughout Europe.

IGNATIUS LOYOLA

Ignatius Loyola is one of the great men in the Church's history, in a class with Benedict, Romuald, Bernard, Francis of

Assisi, and Dominic, not only as the founder of a great Order but as an individual. His was, however, no brilliant personality. He had neither Bernard's enchanting eloquence nor Francis's attractive simplicity. In him everything was business, a part of a plan, a program. His goal was to lead himself and others as near to God as possible. His formula, "All for God's greater glory," signified not any seeking after ecclesiastical political power, but the effort to fulfill God's will in all things, for God wills only His own greater glory. Ignatius is best understood from his *Book of Spiritual Exercises*, which, according to a well-known expression of Saint Francis de Sales, has produced more saints than it contains letters. Through the *Book of Spiritual Exercises* Ignatius has become one of the classical masters of the spiritual life. But this does not mean that he created a new spirituality. His book raises no weighty new problems. It is simply a textbook of Christianity, of simple Christian heroism.

In a certain sense Ignatius was overshadowed by his own creation, the Jesuit Order. Around this Order friend and foe have, in the course of time, heaped such a mountain of legend that it is often difficult even for Catholics to form a correct picture of it. The Jesuits neither were nor are a secret society or Catholic Masonic Lodge or General Staff or spiritual tendency within the Church. They are simply a religious Order. There is in them nothing more secret than in the Capuchins or Benedictines or the Missionaries of Steyl. There is nothing military about them, at least if by "military" is meant drill, pluck, and aggressiveness. That at their head stands a General, just as at the head of many other Orders, is nothing more than the Latin *praepositus generalis*, the general head. The significance of the Jesuits in the history of the Church consists in this, that from the beginning they have accomplished much that is excellent in many fields through many of their members; but just as there is in the history of art no "Jesuit style," so too in the Church there was and is no Jesuit spiritual direction.

IMPORTANCE OF THE CLERICS REGULAR

In the newly instituted Clerics Regular the circle of possibilities in the religious life was once again expanded. By virtue of the fact that the new Orders in their manner of life gave up much of monastic austerity, they became more mobile, more adaptable, and by substituting the monarchical for the capitular method of government they economized time and energy in many respects. Much that in the older Orders had to go through legal channels is in the newer Orders settled by simple administrative methods. This, of course, presupposes a definite renunciation on the part of the individual members; they have little share in the government, almost no place and voice. The introduction of the so-called "simple vows," which in most of the newer Orders take the place of "solemn vows," facilitates the administration of discipline, since according to Canon Law the simple vows can more easily be dispensed from and thus the superiors can with less difficulty remove unsuitable elements. It can well be said that since the sixteenth century the whole of religious life in the Church has experienced a profound transformation. However, this transformation stands in no causal connection with the revolt in Germany. The new type of Order and the individual new Orders were not founded with regard to the Protestants, as a sort of defense— not even the Jesuits.

THE CAPUCHINS

Still another Order arose at this time, one that quickly attained to great popularity—the Capuchins. They are not Clerics Regular, but a branch of the Franciscan Order. The desire for a return to the primitive poverty and austerity of Saint Francis had quite frequently led to the rise of reformed convents and reformed congregations within the Order. In 1525 Matthew of Bassi (Basci) instituted such a reform of an almost eremitical character. In 1528 Clement VII confirmed the union of the new convents, freed them from their connection with the Observants, and placed them, with their own Vicar General, under the Minister General of the Conventuals. Matthew became the first Vicar General, but he soon left his foundation and returned to the Observants. His successor, Luigi of Fossombrone, was expelled from the Order in 1536. The third Vicar General, the saintly Bernardine of Asti, consolidated the tottering institute, but his successor, Bernardine Occhino of Siena, fled from the Order in 1542 and became a Calvinist. It was as if Providence desired to show that it could call an Order into existence with wholly unsuitable means. The defection of Occhino led, moreover, to a salutary crisis, not only in the Capuchin Order but throughout Italy.

CRISIS OF THE FAITH IN ITALY

Occhino had been the spiritual disciple of the Spaniard Juan Valdés, a pious layman living in Naples, who with his obscure emotional spiritual doctrine had attracted many desirous of an interior life, particularly women, among them even the noble poetess, Vittoria Colonna. The strongly Church-minded Theatines were the first to whom the new piety became suspect. Valdés, however, died at peace with the Church in 1541. Occhino was at that time the most celebrated preacher in Italy; Giberti and other friends of reform esteemed him highly, as did even Paul III. Occhino's friend and follower was the Augustinian canon Peter Vermigli, likewise an outstanding preacher, who disseminated his new ideas especially at Lucca. When finally in 1542 Occhino and Vermigli were denounced at Rome for heresy, they realized that their game was over and fled to Calvin in Geneva. The scandal was great but beneficial. All eyes turned to the idealists who for a time had been influenced by Valdés's ideas, such as Vittoria Colonna, the friend of Michelangelo, and Contarini and Pole.

Paul III acted energetically. At Carafa's instigation he organized the Inquisition for all Italy, where, without the harshness of its Spanish counterpart but no less effectively, it broke up the heretical circles that had been formed by the activity of Occhino and Vermigli. Thus was Italy preserved for the Catholic Faith before any revolt on a greater scale could occur. The Capuchin Order, from which the crisis had arisen, flourished from then on and became one of the chief means of furthering the general religious advance.

RETROSPECT

In many ways the pontificate of Paul III marks a turning point in Church history. Much was yet lacking, and Paul III himself was no saint, but a great beginning had been made. From now on there was a strong reform party in the Church, no longer secretly and underground, as in the days of Leo X and Clement VII, but open and including bishops and cardinals; indeed, it was no longer a party, for the pope had consciously placed himself at its head. The road lay open for a general renewal of the Church.

THE CLOSE OF THE COUNCIL OF TRENT

JULIUS III (1550–1555)

The conclave following the death of Paul III was a disappointment for the reform party. Cardinal Monte, elected as a compromise candidate after violent strife on the part of the political factions, the imperial and the French, was not an ideal figure, unspiritual and pleasure-loving as he was. Right from the start he provoked great scandal when he elevated to the cardinalate Innocenzo del Monte, a dissolute seventeen-year-old boy of his household—an event that occasioned the worst rumors. The reform party—Carafa, Pole, and others—protested vigorously but in vain.

Nevertheless, Julius III understood that he must continue along the path taken by Paul III. His other nominations to the cardinalate were good, he encouraged the Jesuits, and after numerous difficulties brought about the resumption of the Council of Trent. In two sessions the important decrees on the Eucharist and the sacrament of penance were published. When, because of the rebellion of the elector of Saxony, a new dissension resulted between the emperor and the king of France, the council had to be interrupted once again.

MARCELLUS II (1555)

On the death of Julius III the strongly ecclesiastical-minded cardinals determined not to tolerate another compromise. They wanted to elect only the best. Cardinal Pole, who had almost been elected in the last conclave, was in England as legate and hence it was deemed proper not to elect him. Thus there remained Carafa and Cervini as the best. But Carafa was so dreaded that all preferred Cervini, and Carafa himself used all his own influence in behalf of his much younger colleague. Thus, after a short conclave, the better of the best was chosen as Marcellus II. The reform seemed in sight, when the new pope died after three weeks. The impression was shattering. Seripando believed this was God's way of showing that the salvation of the Church would not be effected through human means.

PAUL IV (1555–1559)

Once again the absent Pole was passed over. Carafa was

feared, even by the strict churchmen, because of his harshness. Moreover, Charles V had given him the veto; that is, he had made use of the right which Catholic sovereigns had, or claimed to have, of excluding undesirable candidates from the papacy. Just the same, Carafa was elected, thanks especially to the dexterity of the young Cardinal Alessandro Farnese, grandson of Paul III.

At the time of his election Paul IV was seventy-nine years old. That he, who had never sought the papacy, whom no one liked, and before whom all, even the most passionate, quailed, had become pope contrary to the veto of Charles V—all this seemed to him a miracle. This intensified his consciousness of ruling. Besides, he had always entertained the highest opinion of the dignity and power of the pope. He believed he could manage princes and people after the manner of Innocent III, without noticing that the times had changed. Though he had grown grey in the business of the Church, he had always remained fundamentally a religious, foreign to this world.

As secretary of state he named his nephew, Carlo Carafa, a cunning and unscrupulous man, who had it at heart to procure for his family a principality—if not Naples, then at least Siena.

Paul IV was a fiery Italian patriot. He hated Charles V, whom he could pardon neither for the sack of Rome nor for his alleged encouragement of the Protestants; above all, he hated the Spaniards, who ruled his Neapolitan homeland and whom he regarded as a mixture of Jews and Moslems. For a trivial reason he declared war on Spain, at the instigation of Carlo Carafa. Paul IV certainly expected the aid of France, but France displayed no eagerness to become again involved in Italian adventures. Thus, with his tiny army, the pope faced the Spanish world power as the aggressor. Philip II, who had meanwhile received the government from his father, had the duke of Alba proceed to Rome with superior forces. The pope quickly had to make peace and he could be glad that his opponent was Philip II, who demanded nothing from him but peace. This almost ridiculous war, which was really only a military demonstration, had a profound effect. From now on it was clear that the Papal State was not a European great power, as it might have appeared at the time of Julius II and Leo X. It was a blessing for the Church that among the means whereby the papacy endeavored to accomplish its pastoral duty warlike world politics would no longer play a role.

In the ecclesiastical sphere Paul IV remained the strict reformer that he had always been. He named his cardinals in this vein: the Theatine Scotti, the Franciscan Dolera, and a saint, the Dominican Ghislieri, later Pope Pius V. He managed the Inquisition, like everything else, in an exaggerated fashion. Even Cardinal Morone, wholly dedicated to the Church, was put in prison on a suspicion of heresy. Finally, he banished his nephews, including Cardinal Carlo Carafa, suddenly and dramatically.

Paul IV was one of those men for whom it is a misfortune to be placed at the top. As a religious founder and a cardinal he had accomplished the extraordinary and would perhaps have been venerated as a saint; as pope, he disappointed almost all expectations.

PIUS IV (1559–1566)

Even though there was no further question of the Papal State as a military power, still the Catholic princes were as interested as before in papal elections. In particular, Philip II must have desired that another Paul IV not be elected. Under pressure from him and because of the decisive influence of Cardinals Carlo Carafa [1] and Alessandro Farnese, Gianangelo de' Medici was elected as Pius IV.

[1] On the death of Paul IV, his banished nephew, Cardinal Carlo Carafa, was

Both contemporaries and later historians have complained about the pressure which Philip II exerted on papal elections. But it must be kept in mind that Philip II's position in the world and in the Church at that period demanded that the cardinals take his wishes into consideration. At the same time it cannot be denied that the popes chosen under this pressure were among the best who have ever governed the Church.

Pius IV, a Milanese and not connected with the Florentine Medici, had not been a striking figure as a cardinal. Personally rather worldly-minded, clever and moderate, he was the opposite of his predecessor. Following the evil custom of the Renaissance popes, he at once gathered a crowd of relatives at his court and loaded them with revenues, functions, and titles. But among them was one who was to become Pius IV's good angel—Charles Borromeo. Pius IV made the twenty-one-year-old youth a cardinal and secretary of state and did not have to regret this choice. It was due to Borromeo that his uncle's pontificate was so universally beneficial for the Church. But it is no less a credit to Pius IV that he gave his nephew a free hand in everything and upheld him, even if he occasionally sighed at the young man's "Theatine-like ardor."

Charles Borromeo, of perhaps no more than mediocre endowment, but a tireless, extremely conscientious worker and always devoted to the highest religious ideals, was then not yet the stern ascetic who later, as archbishop of Milan, engraved his portrait in Church History with indelible lines. Nevertheless, his example was already working wonders at the papal court. From him the curia received that thoroughly spiritual and priestly stamp which had been so lacking under the

---

restored to his rights in the Sacred College by the cardinals who had assembled for the new election. See L. Cristiani, *L'église à l'époque du concile de Trente*, Vol. XVII of the Fliche-Martin *Histoire de l'église* (Paris: 1948), pp. 173 f. In regard to the career, disgrace, reinstatement, and final fall of this unworthy Prince of the Church, see *ibid.*, pp. 150-171, 173-175, 184-188. (Translator's note.)

Renaissance popes and which the brief pontificates of Marcellus II and Paul IV had been unable to restore.

Less praise is due to Pius IV for the trial to which he subjected the nephews of his predecessor. The Carafas had merited stern punishment; Cardinal Carlo Carafa had shamefully abused the confidence of his aged uncle and had urged him into the unfortunate war with Spain. Among his closest relatives murders had occurred and Carlo had known of them. But the trial was unjustly conducted. The fiscal procurator or state's advocate, Pallantieri, was a notorious enemy of the Carafas. Cardinal Carlo Carafa and his brother, the duke of Paliano, were condemned to death and executed and the family property was confiscated. Pius IV's successor, Saint Pius V, later restored to the Carafas their goods and in turn condemned to death the unjust fiscal procurator, who was guilty of much else besides. The trial of the Carafas, scandalous in itself, had, nevertheless, a fortunate effect: the nephews of later popes no longer aspired after sovereign states of their own, as had the Rovere, the Borgias, the Medici, the Farnese, but were satisfied with wealth and aristocratic titles. In this diminished form nepotism was still far from praiseworthy, but it was at least less dangerous for the Church.

CLOSE OF THE COUNCIL OF TRENT

Pius IV's glory consists in his continuing the Council of Trent and bringing it to a successful conclusion. Once again the tireless Borromeo had to overcome the greatest diplomatic difficulties till in 1562 the sessions could again be resumed. The number of Fathers of the Council was now larger than before. More than 200 prelates took part in the twenty-first session. In this was promulgated the decree on Communion under both species, that had formed a chief point of contention with the innovators. It was stated that the laity are not obliged to communicate under both species, that under each of the two species the entire sacrament is received, and that the Church can prescribe a definite form of receiving the sacrament which the individual may not alter to suit his pleasure. Pius IV, by the way, had already conceded the chalice to the laity in the ecclesiastical provinces of Mainz, Trier, and Salzburg, and in Bohemia and Hungary, since the Catholic princes had asked for it in the hope of thereby removing a stumbling block for the Protestants. But the desired effect failed to appear. The Catholic population derived little pleasure from this concession; the Protestants interpreted it as weakness. Finally, the same princes who had urged it asked for its revocation.

The twenty-second session brought the doctrinal decree on the Sacrifice of the Mass and reform decrees on the worthy celebration of worship. The twenty-third session dealt with priestly ordination and issued decrees on the training of aspirants to the priesthood, especially through the establishing of seminaries. In the twenty-fourth session the doctrine of the sacrament of matrimony was defined, the canonical impediments were reduced, and the legislation on marriage was simplified. In the twenty-fifth session the doctrines of Purgatory, the veneration of the saints, and indulgences were proclaimed. Then the Fathers themselves called for the end of the council, in the conviction that the chief work had been accomplished and that the rest could be done by the pope in the usual way. Since Borromeo and the pope himself also desired the close, the president, Cardinal Morone, declared the council at an end in solemn session on December 4, 1563. In the following year Pius IV confirmed all the decrees of the entire council by one bull. The decrees were printed, and a special congregation of cardinals was established for their authentic interpretation.

396

IMPORTANCE OF THE COUNCIL OF TRENT

The Council of Trent surpasses, not merely in length of duration, but in importance for the inner life of the Church all other ecumenical councils. It did not attain to its primary goal, the winning back of the Protestants, but it extended far beyond this goal of the moment. Above all, it brought clarity to many doctrinal questions. From now on everyone was faced with the simple question whether or not he would be a Catholic. There could no longer be any wavering neutrality, any personal temporizing with conviction. In this the decrees and discussions of Trent displayed a religious depth and theological force making clear to all that there could be no question of spiritual decay in the Church. Since the height of Scholasticism, since the time of Thomas and Bonaventure, the course had been down rather than up. The Council of Trent strengthened the confidence of the Church in her teaching function, in her hierarchy.

The reform decrees also effected a confidence in the hierarchical and sacramental organization of the Church. The council required the residence of pastors, especially of the bishops, and at the same time the unhindered exercise of their function. It recommended frequent diocesan and provincial synods, prescribed careful selection and training of the clergy, and occupied itself thoroughly with the dignity of the divine worship. Throughout, its attitude had to do with the care of souls. The Council of Trent could be termed the "council of the sacramental care of souls." It was decidedly friendly toward the Orders. High estimation of the religious state has always been a characteristic of truly Catholic thinking. Many of the most outstanding theologians at Trent were themselves religious, especially of the Dominican Order, to which also many of the bishops at the council belonged.

For the system of benefices the Council of Trent intro-

duced decisive innovations. The old "financial skills," expec-
tancies, regressions, accessions, that had done so much harm
since Avignon, were entirely abolished, much was energetically
reformed, the accumulation of several benefices in one hand
was forbidden and rendered impossible by the duty of residence. The pope wholeheartedly agreed that thereby he and
the curia should lose a great part of their income.

On the other hand it would be incorrect to think, as sometimes happens, that the Council of Trent brought into ecclesiastical life a new course, another spirit. It brought clarity and
neatness; it strengthened courage and sense of responsibility;
but it did not create any new type of saint. Such was unnecessary. Trent is a landmark in the Church's road of life,
not a detour.

THE GREAT POPES AFTER TRENT

PIUS V (1566–1572)

After Pius IV had died in Borromeo's arms, a saint, the
Dominican Michael Ghislieri, was elected as Pius V, through
the co-operation of Cardinals Farnese and Borromeo. The Romans were not particularly pleased; they feared a return of
the days of Paul IV, whose friend Ghislieri had been. Pius V
realized this and said jokingly, "If God helps me, they will be
more distressed over my death than over my election." And so
it happened.

Pius V was elected at the right time. The laws had been
issued, reform had been introduced in all fields; now good
example must do the rest. Pius V was wholly absorbed in his
spiritual function. No longer was there a trace of the princely
allure of the Renaissance period. In him everything was piety,
zeal, churchmanship. If in his zeal, especially for public morality, he sometimes went perhaps too far and could be almost

petty, he was still far removed from the inconsiderate harshness of Paul IV.

Even the holiest pope cannot hold himself aloof from politics, since he must care for the Catholics of the whole world. Pius V's solemn excommunication of Queen Elizabeth I of England can be judged from various standpoints. The step was formally justified, for Elizabeth had definitively led her country into the arms of Protestantism. But actually the sentence could change nothing and it now aggravated the situation of the still loyal Catholics of England. On the other hand, the Turkish policy of this originally most unwarlike pope was a brilliant success.

The threat to the Christian West from the Turks had become increasingly more serious since the beginning of the sixteenth century. After the battle of Mohacs in 1526 they had occupied most of Hungary; in 1529 they besieged Vienna and as a result compelled the emperor more and more to make concessions to the Protestants as the price of their aid against the Moslems. From the middle of the century they also gained ground in the Mediterranean. The siege of Malta was, it is true, frustrated by the Maltese Knights, but in the next year (1566) the Venetians lost their Aegean islands, Chios, Andros, and Naxos, and Turkish vessels appeared in the Adriatic. Finally in 1569 the Turks demanded Cyprus from the Venetians and threatened war.

Pius V worked for a league of all Christian states. He sent envoys even to Russia. In the end only Philip II was ready, but the Spaniards were not desired by the Venetians as allies. At length it was possible to assemble a great fleet—111 Venetian ships, eighty-one Spanish, and the twelve papal vessels, which served, so to speak, as the connecting link. At Lepanto, at the entrance to the Gulf of Corinth, this fleet met the Turks, and here on October 7, 1571, took place the greatest naval

399

engagement from the days of Augustus until Trafalgar. The Christians lost 7,000 dead, but the Turkish fleet was almost entirely wiped out. The rejoicing in Europe was enormous, and everywhere a principal merit for the victory was attributed to the pope.

The victory at Lepanto could not be exploited tactically because discord immediately broke out again among the victors. Just the same, its effect was great. The Turks had lost their reputation for invincibility, the Turkish Empire fell into difficult internal crises because of the defeat, and Turkish dominance in the Mediterranean was forever ended.

Scarcely six months after the victory Pius V died, as holy in death as in life, in the habit of Saint Dominic. The prayer of his last illness was: "Lord, multiply my sufferings, and also my patience." In 1712 Clement XI canonized him. His relics repose in Santa Maria Maggiore.

GREGORY XIII (1572–1585)

Once again the leaders in the conclave were Cardinals Farnese and Borromeo. Many would have liked Farnese as pope, but Philip II vetoed him, for he wanted no pope from one of the Italian princely families. Hence, in a very brief time Farnese and Borromeo agreed on Cardinal Boncompagni.

Gregory XIII remained throughout his life the objective, sober jurist that he was when he was lecturing at the University of Bologna, where, among others, Morone, Pole, Otto Truchsess, and Stanislas Hosius had been his pupils. In addition, he had acquired through many years of service at the curia and on diplomatic missions political foresight and great experience of affairs. Friendship with Charles Borromeo had further deepened this serious man religiously.

As pope too Gregory XIII remained sincerely attached to the holy archbishop of Milan and gladly took advice from the thirty-six years younger man, though the latter, who consistently demanded the utmost from himself and others, was not always a suitable counselor. It was with deep grief that the pope received in 1584 the news of the saint's death.

Gregory XIII governed entirely in the spirit of the Council of Trent, of his holy predecessor, and of Borromeo. He encouraged the Orders, though he did not care to raise any religious to the cardinalate. For the Jesuits, whom he especially esteemed, he built the spacious Collegio Romano. This institution, no longer housed in the original buildings, is one of the papal universities at Rome; the first University of Rome, founded by Boniface VIII in 1303 and known from the sixteenth century as the "Sapienza," has been a state institution since 1870. Gregory XIII, himself a former university professor, was very much interested in his foundation, which became known as the "Gregorianum." When the celebrated Spanish theologian, Francisco Suárez, was called to Rome, the pope personally attended his inaugural lecture.

Gregory XIII furthered the studies and the formation of the clergy. He founded a series of seminaries for countries where the revolt from the Faith had spread and helped others by means of rich endowments, such as the German College, the Germanicum at Rome, and the English College at Douai.

As an expert in law and administration, he enlarged and reorganized the channels of the Church's central government, the congregations of cardinals, a work which his successor, Sixtus V, completed. These two popes gave to the Roman Curia the form which it still retains. Gregory XIII likewise revamped the system of nunciatures. At that time four permanent nunciatures existed in Italy—in the kingdom of Naples, in the duchy of Savoy at Turin, in the grand duchy of Florence, and in the republic of Venice; in addition there was one each in Vienna and in the kingdoms of France, Spain,

Portugal, and Poland. Gregory XIII erected two more, one for West Germany at Cologne and one for Switzerland.

Finally, Gregory XIII's name is linked with the reform of the calendar. The one then in use, that introduced by Julius Caesar, was already ten days behind the solar year. Through a new arrangement of the leap year, Gregory XIII brought the calendar to the correct form. In the Protestant countries this reform, whose qualifications no one denied, was not accepted for a long time out of aversion for the papacy; in some instances it was not adopted until the eighteenth century. The Russians have only very recently submitted to it.

SAINTS AT ROME

During the entire second half of the sixteenth century there labored at Rome as the tireless confessor, friend, and adviser of high and low, Saint Philip Neri, always gay and original, yet ever wise and sensible. The Congregation of the Oratory, founded by him, was not a real Order, but a society of priests without vows. Philip Neri was no scholar, but he gave much intellectual stimulation. His pupil, Cesare Baronius, published in 1588 the first volume of his *Annals*, the first history of the Church to be based on original sources in the modern sense, and Gregory XIII took a lively interest in it. Philip Neri was also the first to redirect attention to the Roman catacombs.

Philip Neri was united in intimate friendship with Ignatius Loyola until the latter's death in 1556. Later he became acquainted with other canonized saints, with the Capuchin lay brother, Felix of Cantalice, who, as a simple collector of alms, edified all Rome for forty years, and with Saint Camillo de Lellis, who founded his own Order of Clerics Regular for the spiritual care of the sick and the dying. The red cross which Camillo and his religious wore on their breasts and which they made familiar in all hospitals and camps became in time the universal symbol of the service of the sick, especially in war.

SIXTUS V (1585–1590)

After the death of Gregory XIII a quite extraordinary man was elected pope, the Franciscan Felice, known as Montalto from his home or as Peretti from his father. He was of the most humble origin. Saint Pius V had made him a cardinal. A whole wreath of legends has been woven around Sixtus V; the material for this was provided by his stern measures against bandits, among other things. Against this scourge, which was found not only in the Papal State but in Naples and elsewhere, he proceeded with firmness and skill; he did not, however, eradicate it. Some say his attempt did great harm to the entire country by having the forests of the Roman Campagna cut down to deprive the robbers of their hiding places. This, too, belongs to legend. There were no real forests in the Roman Campagna. On the other hand, the great building activity of Sixtus V is no legend. Under him the cupola of Saint Peter's was finished. That part of the Vatican where the popes reside today and the new Lateran palace were constructed. Even more than by particular buildings Sixtus V transformed the panorama of Rome by installing aqueducts whereby the new quarters became inhabitable and by fashioning great rows of streets according to the city-building principles of the new Baroque. It is not too much to maintain that Sixtus V gave to the city in great part that monumental character which the numerous disfigurements of modern and recent times have not been able entirely to efface.

In these undertakings Sixtus V was inspired by the wholly pastoral idea already manifested by Nicholas V and Julius II: that the capital of Christendom must, even externally, leave a dignified and elevating impression on the pilgrims constantly streaming there from all parts of the world.

For the government of the Church the pontificate of Sixtus V is important because of his completing the organization of the congregations of cardinals. Besides the six for the administration of the Papal State, there were nine for the government of the Church. Of these he created that of the consistory for the appointment of bishops, that of regulars for the religious Orders, and that of rites for divine worship and canonizations. Through the congregations of cardinals, which correspond somewhat to the cabinet of a secular government, the routine of Papal affairs was handled more quickly and more uniformly. Individual matters came into the hands of experts. It was also Sixtus V who fixed the total number of cardinals at seventy.

CLEMENT VIII (1592–1605)

The three popes who immediately followed Sixtus V— Urban VII, Gregory XIV, and Innocent IX—died so quickly after their election that their pontificates have left no very significant traces. Not until 1592 was an important pope again elected: Ippolito Aldobrandini as Clement VIII.

Before the election an exciting incident occurred in the conclave. The majority of the cardinals wanted to elect the excellent Cardinal Santori and for this purpose met in the Capella Paolina at the very start of the conclave. Since, according to the law of the Church, the expression of the wills of two-thirds of the cardinals sufficed to make a pope, no matter how this will was expressed, Santori could believe that he was already elected. Many cardinals were of the same opinion and began to request favors of the new pope. The dean, however, maintained that a mere being together for the purpose of election did not signify an expression of wills and insisted on a regular balloting. It turned out that Santori did not acquire the necessary two-thirds. This was clear evidence how very much times had changed. In the Middle Ages a schism would certainly have resulted; but Santori immediately submitted, even though he was grievously disappointed, and took part in the rest of the balloting just as if nothing had happened.

Clement VIII was a serious man, industrious and filled with a sense of responsibility, scrupulous and therefore slow and ponderous. He was deeply pious. The fact that he celebrated Mass daily was at that time nothing unusual, but he also confessed daily to the learned Baronius. Often he took his place in the confessional at Saint Peter's, like a simple priest. On Fridays he fasted on bread and water. On other days several poor persons were always entertained at meals in his own dining room. Often he himself served them. In his room were placed several skulls to remind him constantly of the transitoriness of earthly things.

Such ascetical practices may appear to us somewhat theatrical, but they reveal the piety of the early Baroque Age. Even the art of the Baroque, sculpture more so than architecture, has in it something of the theatrical. One need only compare the pathetic statues of saints which were made in the seventeenth century, perhaps of Ignatius Loyola or of Philip Neri, with the unassuming appearance of these saints as reported by contemporaries. From this it does not follow, however, that the piety and asceticism of the Baroque Age were not genuine. At the time all this was meant in deep earnestness. If a bishop like Charles Borromeo led a penitential procession, barefoot and with a rope around his neck, this was no bizarre hankering after praise but sprang from an exalted consciousness of responsibility and made a corresponding impression on contemporaries. In any case, a pope like Clement VIII showed clearly how much the times had changed, not only since

405

Alexander VI and Leo X, but even since Paul III, whose pontificate had ended scarcely a half-century earlier.

In curious contrast to the seriousness and conscientiousness of Clement VIII is the fact that he too enriched his nephews, the Aldobrandini, excessively. These nephews, like the succeeding Borghese, Ludovisi, Barberini, and Pamfili, built for themselves in Rome and the vicinity elegant palaces and villas with splendid gardens, art collections, and precious libraries. Their names are celebrated in the history of art, but it must be said that the great services which many of them undoubtedly rendered in high positions in the Church bear no relation to the huge incomes which the popes conferred upon them and which ultimately derived from the goods of the Church. Contemporary kings and princes may have used state revenues to shower on their favorites, but one expects a greater sense of responsibility in popes than in kings.

THE QUESTION OF GRACE

Under Clement VIII there broke out among Catholic theologians a learned controversy which for years was to divide ecclesiastical circles and, quite characteristic of the time, European cabinets—the so-called question of grace. It was concerned with the exceptionally difficult complex of problems in regard to the necessity of grace, divine predestination, and the freedom of the human will. Luther as well as Calvin had gone shipwreck on these very questions. The Council of Trent had laid down the essential lines: on the one hand, divine grace is necessary for the attaining of salvation in general and for each salutary act of man; on the other hand, the human will is so completely free that man bears the full responsibility of his deeds and no man succumbs to eternal damnation without personal guilt. This knowledge is sufficient for the faithful. The wider theological question was: If God knows in advance the favorable or unfavorable result of His distribution of grace, why does He not give to each man that measure of grace of which He foreknows he stands in need? Is not that decree of God whereby He imparts to a man grace whose unfavorable result He foreknows synonymous with Calvin's idea of absolute predestination to hell? And, on the other hand, if it is not the divine decree of predestination but the free will of man that decides, does not then the very necessity of grace fall into danger, as with the old Pelagians?

The dispute erupted because of a book of the Spanish professor of theology, Luis Molina (✝1600), of the Society of Jesus. The solution sought for in it seemed too Pelagian to the Dominicans, whereas on the contrary the Jesuits found that the Dominicans, in their refutation of Molina, came far too close to Calvinism. Clement VIII brought the dispute to Rome and appointed a special congregation of cardinals to examine Molina's book. In vain Jesuit theologians declared that to them it was not a matter of choosing to defend a book, since some regarded individual formulae as questionable; they simply had to undertake its defense. With infinite pains in seventeen sessions of the congregation passages from the Fathers and other authorities were discussed without any progress being made. Clement VIII, though personally little versed in speculative theology, desired to examine every point himself. To no purpose the distinguished Jesuit Bellarmine, whom he highly esteemed and whom he had made a cardinal, advised him not to step down into the theological arena. The pope's task was not to go into a professional study of the problem, but, by questioning the bishops and other competent teachers, to ascertain the Church's belief and then to issue his judicial decision or, if that was unnecessary, to enjoin silence on the disputing factions. Clement VIII sent Bellarmine to Capua as archbishop and continued the fruitless discussions.

Only his second successor, Paul V, acted according to Bellarmine's advice. He dissolved the congregation of cardinals and decreed that the two parties were not to cast suspicion of heresy on each other. In other respects the differing systems of interpretation could be taught in the schools, until an official decision was given. The entire affair, though seemingly sterile, was not without great importance, even apart from its very stimulating effect on scientific theology. It had shown by an impressive example that through divergent systems of interpretation dogma itself must not be brought into jeopardy. Such differences are, to be sure, not desirable in themselves; we should prefer the full truth to the most discerning working hypotheses. But since all human knowledge, theological knowledge included, is only imperfect, it is good to know the limits which separate the certain possession of Faith from human speculation. Thereby theology gains the freedom of investigation which it needs as a science.

If Clement VIII wasted much time and energy in this controversy, out of pure scrupulosity, without reaching his goal, there was granted to him in the field of ecclesiastical politics, again thanks to his conscientiousness, one of the greatest successes which have ever fallen to the lot of a pope in modern times: the definitive preservation of France in the Catholic Faith through the conversion of Henry IV.

408

the baroque age in europe

Just as the decline of ecclesiastical life in various regions was not the actual cause of the revolt from the Faith, so too the general religious revival in the countries that remained loyal did not at once bring the revolt to a standstill, and much less could it recover what had been lost.

ENGLAND

Since 1534 England had been separated from the Church by the Act of Supremacy, without for the moment having introduced any contrary teachings. Henry VIII contented himself with suppressing all monasteries and canonical institutes, some 950 of them, and annexing them to the royal fisc. The picturesque ruins of many a monastery in England still bear witness to this spoliation. Under the minor-aged son of Henry's third marriage, Edward VI (1547–1553), began the defection of the kingdom from Catholic dogma. For divine worship a new ritual, the *Book of Common Prayer*, was introduced in 1549, and in 1552 a new creed, of a Calvinist slant, was imposed. After Edward's early death, Henry VIII's daughter by his first marriage, Mary I, a Catholic, became queen in accord with the English law of succession. Against the advice of her kinsman, the gentle Cardinal Pole, she carried through with great rigor the restoration of the country to Catholicism. She had 280 sentences of death carried out, for which reason the English have given her the nickname of "Bloody Mary," though the epithet "bloody" was equally deserved by her father, Henry VIII, and her successor, Elizabeth I. Even Thomas Cranmer, who had dissolved her mother's marriage with Henry VIII, was executed. She lost popular sympathy especially when she married her cousin, Philip II of Spain, a step which Cardinal Pole had sought in vain to prevent. Furthermore, her reign of five years was too brief to consolidate the country in Catholicism, and thus after her death occurred a natural reaction in favor of Protestantism.

Mary's successor was her half sister, Elizabeth I. The intransigent Catholics denied Elizabeth's right of succession, since she was born of the invalid marriage of Henry VIII with Anne Boleyn, and regarded as queen of England Mary, queen of Scotland, of the house of Stuart, granddaughter of Henry VIII's sister Margaret. For this reason Elizabeth, even though under her predecessor she had publicly professed the Catholic Faith, was forced to the side of the Protestants, who recognized her mother's marriage and hence her own right of succession. Elizabeth, also with great rigor, definitely transformed the country into a Protestant one under the guise of Anglicanism. During her reign 124 priests and sixty-one lay persons were put to death for their Catholic Faith. The sixteen Catholic bishops were deposed, but the episcopal organization remained and the archbishop of Canterbury, Matthew Parker, consecrated Anglican bishops.

ANGLICAN ORDERS

It was long debated whether the Orders then conferred by Parker and all the succeeding Orders of the Anglican hierarchy up to the present were valid, and consequently whether the Anglicans possess the Eucharist, as is the undoubted case in regard to the Orientals, who, though separated from the

410

Church, are validly ordained. The question was only settled in 1896 by Pope Leo XIII. Painstaking historical investigation of the Anglican sources has demonstrated that Parker possessed no real episcopal consecration, since his consecrator, Barlow, though himself a bishop, used an entirely unsatisfactory formula of consecration and, furthermore, had absolutely no intention of conferring a sacrament according to the mind of the Church. Whether historical facts of this sort, the so-called *facta dogmatica*, which as such are not contained in revelation but stand in close relation to the Faith, are embraced by papal infallibility is a question affirmatively answered by all theologians.

Elizabeth's long reign was one of the most successful in history. It not only brought the kingdom peace and prosperity, but laid the groundwork for England's position as a world power. Hence, all is forgiven her—the execution of her rival, Mary Stuart of Scotland, the killing of many noble Englishmen, and her disedifying private life. In her reign patriotism, dynastic loyalty, and hatred of Rome so coalesced that it became ever more difficult, even without the persecuting laws, for faithful Catholics to be both Englishmen and Catholics. Care of souls was extremely dangerous. English priests were educated on the continent in seminaries at Rome, Valladolid, and Douai, and could carry out their ministry at home only in secret. The number of Catholics decreased. Around 1800 they were scarcely more than 40,000.

SCOTLAND

When in 1561 the nineteen-year-old Mary Stuart assumed the government,[1] the Scottish nobility was already Protestant

[1] Mary Stuart was born in 1542 and became queen of Scotland a week later on the death of her father, James V. Her mother, Mary of Guise, acted as regent in the most difficult circumstances. The child queen was sent for safety to France in 1548, and in

to a great extent. Mary fought courageously for her throne and her Catholic Faith, but made one mistake after another and finally fled to England, where she was kept in prison for nineteen years and was at length put to death. Her son James, who had been taken from her and raised a Protestant, became king of Scotland. When, on the death of Elizabeth of England in 1603, the posterity of Henry VIII came to an end, James, as nearest heir, became king of England too. Since then both countries have been united under a Protestant dynasty. In Scotland, however, there were proportionately more Catholics than in England. Even today there are islands with an old Catholic population.

IRELAND

During the Middle Ages Ireland, amid varying fortunes, had been more or less dependent on England. In 1541 Henry VIII assumed the title of king of Ireland. But all efforts to lead the Irish population into Anglicanism failed. Only in the north of the island, in Ulster, did this policy succeed, and then more through the emigration of Protestant colonists from England and Scotland. That the Irish preserved their Catholicism despite the worst oppression was later to be of the greatest importance for the rebirth of the Church in England and still more in the United States.

THE LOW COUNTRIES

To his son, Philip II, Charles V had turned over the Low Countries, comprising not only modern Holland and Belgium but Artois, with Lille and Cambrai, and likewise Luxemburg and Franche Comté. Philip endeavored to oppose the anti-

---

1558 she married the dauphin, Francis. With him she ascended the French throne in 1559, but he died the next year. In 1561 Mary returned to Scotland to assume the government. (Translator's note.)

Spanish and Protestant movement in the country by means of harsh, perhaps too harsh, measures. He introduced the Inquisition and obtained from the pope an increase in the number of bishoprics from four to eighteen. This, too, was popularly viewed as an act of pressure on Philip's part. In 1566 open rebellion resulted. Philip sent as governor his best general, the duke of Alba, who, however, could not gain any lasting victory. His successor, Alessandro Farnese, great-grandson of Paul III and grandson of Charles V, preserved the provinces south of the Meuse and the Scheldt, at least, as Spanish and Catholic. The north, as the United Netherlands, formed henceforth a sovereign state, nominally a part of the German Empire until this bond was dissolved by the Peace of West-phalia in 1648. Calvinism was the state religion, but there continued to be a Catholic minority, for whom in 1602 the Vicariate Apostolic of Utrecht was established.

GERMANY AFTER THE PEACE OF AUGSBURG

Since most of the Protestant princes had already made use of the right to determine the religion of their subjects, the religious peace of 1555 did not change the general situation to a very great extent. Nevertheless, Protestantism still won new territories—the Palatinate in 1556, Baden-Durlach in 1556, Braunschweig-Wolfenbüttel in 1568. Each change of government could mean a change of religion. Thus, in 1569 Baden-Baden again became Catholic, and the Palatinate changed four times between the Lutheran and the Calvinist Confessions until the end of the sixteenth century.

Although it had been specified in the Peace of Augsburg by the so-called *reservatum ecclesiasticum* that the right of reformation did not include the ecclesiastical principalities, the lands composing the former provinces of Magdeburg and Bremen remained definitely lost to the Church. In Cologne

413

Archbishop Hermann von Wied (1515–1546) had already tried to reform his electorate but failed because of opposition on the part of the Catholics and of the emperor. Once again Archbishop Gebhard von Waldburg (1577–1583) tried it, but was forcibly expelled by Ernst of Bavaria, whom the chapter had elected in his place. This so-called War of Cologne, trivial in itself, marks the turning point of the advance of Protestantism in West Germany.

Protestantism was never introduced into the Austrian hereditary lands, but Emperor Maximilian II (1564–1576), son of Ferdinand I, and Maximilian's brother, Charles, archduke of Inner Austria (Styria, Carinthia, Carniola, Görz), allowed Protestants so much freedom that not only almost all the lower nobility but also a great part of the population turned to the new doctrine. Still greater privileges were bestowed upon the innovators in Bohemia and Saxony by the next emperor, Maximilian's son, Rudolf II (1576–1612). No change took place until the son of Charles of Inner Austria, Ferdinand II, emperor from 1619 to 1637, who had inherited from his Bavarian mother a staunchly Catholic attitude, reunited the Austrian hereditary lands.

In South Germany, meanwhile, the princes who remained Catholic had begun for their part to make use of the right of reformation to re-establish the Catholic religion in their territories. This had been first done by Otto Truchsess von Waldburg, as prince-bishop of Augsburg. He was followed in 1573 by Julius Echter von Mespelbrunn for Würzburg, in 1574 by Daniel Brendel von Homburg for the electorate of Mainz, and in 1564 by one of the secular princes, Duke Albert V of Bavaria. Alarmed by this counter-reformation, the Protestant princes joined together in 1608 in the "Union" under the leadership of the Elector Palatine, whereupon the Catholic princes, under the leadership of the duke of Bavaria, replied with the formation of the "League." Events were leading to war.

THE THIRTY YEARS' WAR

The war broke out in 1618 in Bohemia, where the Protestant estates rose in defense of the privileges granted them by Emperor Rudolf. They chose the Elector Palatine as king of Bohemia. Emperor Ferdinand II and the Catholic League defeated the Bohemians in the battle of the White Mountain at Prague. The Protestant Union continued the war in Germany, but the generals of the League and of the emperor, Tilly and Wallenstein, won battle after battle and brought the greater part of Germany under control. In 1629 the emperor issued the Edict of Restitution: all ecclesiastical principalities and all ecclesiastical goods, dioceses, parishes, and monasteries which had been confiscated since 1552 contrary to the stipulated *reservatum ecclesiasticum* were to be restored. Since the emperor now had the power to enforce this decree, the future of Protestantism in Germany seemed everywhere in jeopardy, as it had after the battle of Mühlberg. Once again the religious union of Germany seemed at hand.

GUSTAVUS ADOLPHUS OF SWEDEN

The intervention of the Swedish king, Gustavus II Adolphus, brought a complete reversal. Sweden, which had already sought to force the Poles from the Baltic Sea, could not permit the imperial power to be established there. How far Gustavus Adolphus's political plans extended we do not know, for a premature death prevented his carrying them to completion. But he certainly entertained the desire of helping his Protestant co-religionists in Germany. Gustavus Adolphus, a brilliant soldier, equaled only by Wallenstein among the great generals of the age, defeated Tilly at Leipzig and drove him

415

back to the Danube, where Tilly found his death in a new defeat. But Gustavus Adolphus too fell in battle against Wallenstein, at Lützen near Leipzig in 1632. Wallenstein himself, whose political attitude had always been suspect, was murdered at Eger by his officers in 1634.

From then on the war dissolved into the individual campaigns of Swedish, imperial, Bavarian, and other generals, with the result that Germany was devastated on all sides. France too, which had already passively supported Gustavus Adolphus, interfered actively now. The French were later to regret seriously their radically wrong policy, pursued since the days of Luther, of always supporting the Protestant princes against the emperors.

Finally, in 1648 a general peace was brought about, called the Peace of Westphalia after the Westphalian cities where the negotiations took place, Münster and Osnabrück. The Calvinist Confession was recognized for the Empire along with that of Augsburg. In the individual territories the *status quo* was to be maintained, but this *status quo*, which had been so often advanced, was now fixed at the year 1624. For their pains Sweden and France received important lands on the Baltic and the upper Rhine. Pope Innocent X protested this peace, which not only seriously weakened Germany but once again infringed on the rights of the Church. Nevertheless there now began for Germany, which in places had lost as much as two-thirds of its inhabitants, a real period of peace, even in regard to religion.

BOHEMIA

The old Utraquists, united since 1475 with one of the half-schismatic "brotherhoods," had at first resisted invading Protestant doctrines. The "Bohemian Confession," drawn up by them in 1575, was, however, similar to Protestantism, and the

Bohemian Brethren took for themselves the privileges granted to the Protestants by the royal decree of Rudolf II. A powerful Catholic reaction was soon under way, especially when the capable Brus of Müglitz mounted the archiepiscopal throne of Prague, vacant for 120 years. How serious the danger was that all Bohemia would become Protestant appears in the fact that in 1596 only 336 of the 1,366 parishes in the country had a Catholic pastor. The battle of the White Mountain in 1620 was a defeat for the Protestants as well as for the Bohemian Brethren. Special merit for the re-Catholicizing of Bohemia after the battle of the White Mountain belongs to Carlo Carafa, nuncio at Vienna from 1621 to 1628, and even more to the archbishop of Prague, Cardinal Harrach (1624–1667), together with the important Capuchin, Valerian Magni. Naturally, the Thirty Years' War caused a drop in the population of Bohemia, from 2,500,000 to 800,000. But the country was able to recover and from then on remained almost wholly Catholic.

POLAND AND SWEDEN

Under the last Jagiellon, the weak King Sigismund II (1548–1572), Protestantism—Lutherans, Calvinists, Bohemian Brethren, and others—penetrated throughout Poland. Before the election of the new king, the Protestants at Warsaw entered into a league to secure their liberty under the future government. But in Poland too there occurred a Catholic restoration, due especially to the activity of the outstanding bishop of Ermland, Stanislas Hosius, whom Paul III made a cardinal, and later of the Jesuit, Peter Skarga (✝1612), to whom the Polish language is so much indebted and who was known as the Polish Chrysostom. Hosius brought the Jesuits to Poland, where they soon opened higher schools in all the larger cities. King Stephen Báthory (1575–1586), who had been prince of Transylvania, and King Sigismund III (1587–1632), of the Swedish house of Vasa, were staunch Catholics. Thus, for the most part Poland was preserved for the Catholic religion.

Through Poland it seemed for a time that there was still hope for Sweden's return to the Faith. John III of Sweden (1568–1592), son of Gustavus I Vasa, had as his wife a Catholic Jagiellon princess. He undertook negotiations with Rome, and Gregory XIII sent to Stockholm the Jesuit Possevino. In 1578 the king embraced Catholicism, but it proved impossible to effect a conversion of the country. When his son Sigismund, also a Catholic, who was already king of Poland, mounted the Swedish throne, he had to promise to leave Protestantism untouched. Several years later he lost the crown of Sweden because of his Catholic profession and was deposed by his father's brother, Charles IX, who, like his son and successor, Gustavus II Adolphus, was a strong Protestant. That Christina, the daughter of Gustavus Adolphus, became a Catholic after her abdication in 1654 had no influence on Sweden's history.

THE UKRAINE

Since 1386 the Lithuanian Jagiellons had also been kings of Poland, but the two kingdoms of Lithuania and Poland were not united until 1569, when the Jagiellon dynasty was on the point of becoming extinct. At that time Lithuania extended southward beyond the Dnieper and included the Ruthenians of the Ukraine, who, since the dissolution of the Union of Florence, had again become schismatics. Chiefly through the efforts of the Jesuits Skarga and Possevino at the Synod of Brest-Litovsk in 1596 the metropolitan of Kiev and seven eparchies, or suffragan dioceses, were restored to Catholicism. Despite numerous vicissitudes and the very difficult situation of the unfortunate Ukrainian people, this union has persisted to the present [2] and still forms the numerically largest group following an Oriental rite within the Catholic Church.

HUNGARY

Protestantism penetrated Hungary very early. Through the battle of Mohacs in 1526, in which King Louis II, of the Jagiellon dynasty, met his death, most of Hungary passed under Turkish rule. The Turkish district extended as far as Lake Balaton and embraced the entire plain of the Danube and the Theiss, including Budapest and the metropolitan see of Gran. The succession to the throne of Hungary was claimed by the German king, Ferdinand I, whose wife was a sister of Louis II, and by John Zapolya, prince of Transylvania. The struggle between them ended in 1538, when Zapolya became king of Transylvania with a part of Slovakia as far as Kassa, while Ferdinand kept western Slovakia, unoccupied Hungary, and Croatia. In the confused political situation the Church's position grew even worse, until a change was effected by the activity of Pàzmany. Peter Pàzmany, born a Calvinist, became a Jesuit after his conversion and from 1616 to 1637 was cardinal-archbishop of Gran. He was one of the most important men in the history of Hungary. Nevertheless, Protestantism was encouraged from Transylvania, and in 1645 by the Treaty of Linz the Protestants obtained the free exercise of religion for all of Hungary. Only the expulsion of the Turks by Emperor Leopold I (1658–1705) and the union of all the lands of the Crown of Saint Stephen under the Habsburgs secured for the Catholic Church predominance in these polyglot lands. By the efforts of the archbishop of Gran,

---

[2] On March 8, 1946, a Soviet-dominated synod, in which the Catholic Ukrainian hierarchy did not participate, declared the Union of Brest-Litovsk abrogated. (Translator's note.)

419

Cardinal Kollonitsch, a union of the schismatic Wallachians living in Hungary was effected in 1697, and for them several sees of the Rumanian rite were erected.

FRANCE

By far the most important struggle which the Church had to wage in the sixteenth century was that for France. Had all France then revolted from the Church, as it long seemed would happen, the Church would not indeed have foundered, but her development would have been retarded for centuries.

Though the claim of France to be the eldest daughter of the Church, though the *"Gesta Dei per Francos"* be disputed or ridiculed by other peoples, still it can hardly be denied that France, almost from the days of Clovis, was the geographical core of the Church as well as her spiritual center. Almost all the great religious movements of the Middle Ages proceeded from France—Cluny and Clairvaux, the crusades, Gothic art, Scholasticism. It is noteworthy that the great foreign monastic founders, the Irish Columban in the sixth century, the Germans Bruno and Norbert in the eleventh and twelfth, the Spaniards Dominic and Ignatius in the thirteenth and the sixteenth, began their work in France; that the princes of Scholasticism, the Lombard Peter, the English Alexander of Hales, the German Albert the Great, and the Neapolitan Thomas Aquinas, taught at Paris. To be sure, France had also sinned much against the Church and the papacy. But the deeds of Philip the Fair, the Avignon exile, the Great Western Schism, and the conciliar theory had all been in some way the expression of France's physical and spiritual superiority. If the revolt of England and of half of Germany was a heavy blow for the Church, a revolt on the part of France would have had incalculable consequences.

The French Kings Francis I (1515–1547) and Henry II

420

(1547–1559) more or less openly supported the German Protestant princes in their struggle against the emperor, because they expected from the religious split in Germany a weakening of Charles V's political power. At the same time and for the same political reason they wanted no doctrinal division in their own country. While they kept Lutheranism beyond their frontiers, they could not prevent the formation of a Calvinist party under the political leadership of the house of Bourbon.

The dukes of Bourbon were a younger branch of the French royal house, descended from Robert, a son of Saint Louis. The head of the house was Duke Anthony, who bore the title of king of Navarre. The greatest part of this ancient Basque kingdom had come under Spanish rule since 1512–1515. In the final struggles for the capital, Pamplona, young Iñigo of Loyola had in 1521 received his serious wound. It was not, however, this royal title that gave the house of Bourbon its importance, but rather the possible extinction of the reigning Valois dynasty in France. Should this happen, the Bourbons would become kings of France.

The political leader of the Catholic party was Francis of Guise, duke of Lorraine, a cousin of Anthony of Bourbon-Navarre. In the event of the extinction of the house of Valois, his plan was to exclude from the succession the Calvinist house of Bourbon and make the Catholic Guises kings of France.

THE HUGUENOT WARS

On the death of Henry II, his widow, Catherine de' Medici, a great-niece of Leo X, conducted the government for her young sons. A true Medici, unprincipled and extremely crafty, she wanted to be on bad terms with no one and ended by falling out with all. She took Anthony of Navarre as co-regent and in union with him granted to the Calvinists the free exercise of their religion in 1562. At the time, free practice of religion in France as elsewhere meant for the most part that everything was permissible against the Catholic Church. Civil war was the result—the eight so-called Huguenot Wars, which lasted from 1562 to 1588. The name "Huguenot" for the French Calvinists presumably derives from the Swiss "confederates."

Almost immediately Anthony of Navarre and Francis of Guise died, and leadership fell to their sons, Henry of Navarre and Henry of Guise. Queen Catherine betrothed her daughter, Margaret, to Henry of Navarre in order to win the Calvinists, but then conspired with the Guises to prevent the Calvinists' becoming too powerful. The marriage of Henry of Navarre was to be the occasion she would use to rid herself of the Calvinist leaders, who had to come to Paris for the wedding. The *coup* failed. The queen and her supporters, frightened by the failure and dreading the vengeance of the Calvinists, prepared for them a more terrible blood bath than had been originally planned. This was the notorious "Saint Bartholomew's Night" or the "Bloody Wedding of Paris."

Naturally, by this crime the queen did the Catholics a bad service. The civil war was resumed with new intensity. Meanwhile, Catherine's last son, Henry III, had become king, and since he, like his already dead brothers, was childless, the extinction of the Valois dynasty was near at hand. Henry of Navarre, the heir to the throne, had quickly become a Catholic in the terror of Saint Bartholomew's Night, but in 1576 he returned to Calvinism. The Catholic party, determined at all costs not to have a Protestant king, formed the "Holy League" and allied with Philip II of Spain. The League wanted most of all to bring the pope to its side in order that, by ecclesiastical censures, he could separate from Henry of Navarre his numerous Catholic adherents. But Sixtus V was too astute a politician not to foresee the final victory of Henry of Navarre. Of course, he desired a Catholic king for France, but he hoped this could be effected otherwise than by having Philip II place the duke of Guise on the throne. Philip II and the Catholic League severely blamed this attitude of the pope. This was one of those cases, not uncommon in history, when Catholic hotspurs want to be more Catholic than the pope.

THE CONVERSION OF HENRY IV

The situation developed into the decisive "War of the Three Henries": King Henry III, Henry of Navarre, and Henry of Guise. The king had Henry of Guise assassinated in 1588 and was himself murdered the next year. The throne was vacant. Since there was no Guise alive, the League thought of giving the crown to the aged Cardinal Bourbon, brother of Anthony of Navarre. But he was in Henry of Navarre's prison and died in 1590. All realized that Henry of Navarre, as a Bourbon and as husband of the last Valois, must become king. And Henry realized that he must become a Catholic in order really to be king. In his mouth has been placed the famous saying, *"Paris vaut bien une messe"*—Paris is well worth a Mass. In 1593 he became a Catholic for the "forum of conscience," as ecclesiastical law expresses it; only the pope could effect his public reception. Henry IV sent agents to Rome and asked the lifting of the Church's censures.

It is easy to understand that the extremely conscientious Clement VIII hesitated. As a politician he had to welcome Henry's return, but at the same time he could only mistrust a man who had already changed his religion twice. As a priest he could not refuse the request for admission to the Church, if the required guarantees were given. Henry IV gave these guarantees through his envoy, Duperron, the later cardinal, who, himself a convert and a priest, had instructed Henry IV in the Catholic Faith. Thus in 1595 occurred the memorable absolution of Henry IV by the pope, whereby France definitely again became a Catholic power.

In the sequel Henry IV justified the pope's confidence. He especially furthered internal peace in his country, desolated by decades of civil war, and for this end granted to the Huguenots toleration and by the Edict of Nantes of 1598 even more extensive privileges; only a fanatic could blame him for this policy. Though his private life left much to be desired, he remained a faithful Catholic, and in his reign began the reflowering of the Catholic Church in France. In the seventeenth century France could again assume the role which Spain had occupied in the sixteenth century: the spiritual leader among the nations of the world.

THE NUMBER OF CATHOLICS AFTER THE REFORMATION

After the religious chaos of the sixteenth century, peace returned in the first half of the seventeenth. As on the third day of Creation land and water separated, so now there were Catholic countries and Protestant countries. The Protestant countries, of course, differed greatly among themselves in regard to doctrine and religious organization, but they had this one thing in common: they no longer belonged to the Catholic Church.

The separation was according to territories. For the seventeenth and eighteenth centuries one can draw an exact map of the confessions, whereas today everything is so confused that a visual representation of religions upon a geographical map is scarcely possible. State, dynasty, and religion were then almost identical ideas. Even in Germany, where the religious map of the seventeenth and eighteenth centuries apparently shows a mixture, there were in actuality individual territories which were entirely Catholic or entirely Protestant, and the same is true of the Swiss cantons. To be sure, there was in some Catholic countries a Protestant *diaspora*, especially in France, Hungary, and Poland, and on the other hand a Catholic *diaspora* existed in Protestant England, Holland, and in the Protestant parts of Germany; but these were numerically so slight that they hardly counted. The only Catholic land of any size that was under non-Catholic rule was Ireland.

On the map the northern boundary of the Church in the seventeenth and eighteenth centuries can be taken as a line running from the southern coast of England through the middle of Europe to the northwest corner of Bohemia. Catholic Ireland lay to the north of this line. In West Germany Westphalia extended beyond the boundary to the north as a wide Catholic bay, and in central Germany the Protestant district in Thuringia and central Franconia extended southward as a patchwork. From the northern side of Bohemia the Catholic frontier then bent far to the north to Lithuania, to end finally at the north-south wall erected by the Russian-Byzantine schism.

As regards population, until the end of the eighteenth century we still have no real numbers and statistics. The estimates of contemporaries and of modern historians are often at variance, especially for France, Germany, and Spain. According to a quite recent study,[3] all of Europe around 1700 must have contained some 90,000,000 inhabitants. Of these, fifteen to eighteen millions belonged to European Russia and the then Turkish Balkan peninsula, and were for the most part Orthodox; Protestants of all denominations amounted to about 22,000,000; the remaining 50,000,000 were Catholics.

3 Jos. Grisar, *Studi e Testi*, 125 (Città del Vaticano: 1946). This reference is reproduced, without verification, from the German original.

Accordingly, in the two centuries since the Reformation the Catholic population had grown through natural increase to the number it counted in the period before the revolt. Moreover, at this time one may assume from five to ten millions in the colonies, especially the American colonies, so that the total number of Catholics rises to about 60,000,000, somewhat double the probable figure for the thirteenth century.

France had by far the largest Catholic population, some nineteen or twenty millions, one-third of the entire Church. In the second place stood Spain. The population of the mother country had declined in the seventeenth century, but nevertheless it still amounted to over 10,000,000, while that of the colonies had grown. Germany had almost as many inhabitants as France, but of these only eight to ten millions were Catholics, so that Germany had about as many Catholics as Italy. Poland and Lithuania can be estimated at 5,000,000 Catholics, the Low Countries at 2,000,000. Portugal had no more than 2,000,000. Ireland, the Catholic Swiss cantons, the English *diaspora*, and other fragments comprised altogether little more than 1,000,000.

In Catholic countries the people continued to live in the harmony of a common religion. But there was still a great difference from the Middle Ages. Then there had been in Europe, apart from the schismatic East with which there was little connection, only the one Christian family of nations. Europe was the Catholic Church, and outside was the world of unbelievers. Now in Europe itself there was everywhere a non-Catholic foreign land. In the Middle Ages there had been dissensions between princes and popes, but no one had denied the Church as such. In the Middle Ages there was, so to speak, no particular merit in being a Catholic, but now it had become more difficult. Now in Europe itself there was a broad front which opposed the Church and reproached her with all the sins of the past and present.

On the other hand, the Church had begun to expand beyond Europe. She was still far from being the world Church of today, but she was likewise no longer the territorially confined Church of the Middle Ages. Already there were reserves for the future.

In the countries that remained Catholic matters went well —almost too well—for the Church. Most of them once again experienced a flowering in the seventeenth century and the early years of the eighteenth. No one guessed that a new and difficult crisis was developing for the end of the eighteenth century.

POLITICAL CHANGES IN EUROPE AFTER THE THIRTY YEARS' WAR

In 1683 the Turks besieged Vienna for the second time, but suffered so serious a defeat that in the following years they could be driven far to the east by the troops of Emperor Leopold I (1658–1705). At the end of the seventeenth century all of Hungary and Transylvania as far as the Carpathians were again under Catholic rule. On the other hand, a danger for the Church lay in the growth of Prussia into a Protestant great power, bringing more and more Catholic districts under its rule. The duchy of Cleve and the county of Mark became Prussian in 1666, Guelders in 1715, and finally Silesia in 1763. Frederick the Great (1740–1768) took pains, of course, to leave unchanged the legal position of the Catholics. Nevertheless, until 1788 the popes could not bring themselves formally to recognize the royal title that had been assumed by the elector of Brandenburg in 1701. The partitions of Poland, which began in 1772 and finally brought the greatest part of this old Catholic kingdom under Russian rule, were detrimental to ecclesiastical life. However, there was definite

427

progress since the days of the Reformation in that the political vicissitudes of territories were no longer regarded, without more ado, as synonymous with changes in religion.

The political changes in Western Europe involved only Catholic dynasties. On the extinction of the Spanish Habsburgs in 1700, the Bourbons acquired the crown. By the Peace of Rastatt in 1714 Austria received the Spanish Netherlands and, temporarily, till 1735, Naples too. Even the advance of France toward the Rhine—Strasbourg was acquired in 1681 —was without direct consequences for the Church.

FRANCE AS THE LEADING CATHOLIC POWER

Since the conversion of Henry IV France had again, as in the Middle Ages, assumed the leading position in the Catholic Church. It is noteworthy that among the kings who ruled France in the so-called Age of Absolutism there was no Saint Louis and no Philip II. But the religious life of the nation was strong, despite the example of the princes. Louis XIII (1610–1643), son of Henry IV, was good but insignificant and helpless. His son, Louis XIV (1643–1715), in whose long reign falls the real maturity of the French Church, was indeed one of the greatest monarchs in history, but far removed from the ideal of a Christian ruler, not only because of his alliance with the Turks against the emperor and his unfeeling conduct in regard to the popes, especially Innocent XI, but still more because of his immoral private life. His great-grandson and successor, Louis XV (1715–1774), was immoral and at the same time incompetent. Furthermore, the ministers, who in the Age of Absolutism often had more to say than the kings, were by no means always Church-minded men.

A curious phenomenon of the period were the ministers of state adorned with the cardinalitial purple. There were some of them also outside France, such as Cardinal Klesl, chancellor of Emperor Matthias till his downfall in 1618; Cardinal Nidhard (✝1681) at the court of Philip IV of Spain; and Cardinal Alberoni at that of Philip V of Spain from 1714 until his fall in 1719. But the most famous were in France: Cardinal Richelieu, sole manager of policies under Louis XIII from 1624 till his death in 1642, and his successor, Cardinal Mazarin, an Italian, who conducted the government during the minority of Louis XIV till 1661. Under Louis XV a similar position was held for a time by Cardinal Fleury (✝1743) and Cardinal Bernis, who became foreign minister in 1757 and ambassador to Rome in 1769. These statesmen in the purple were often of little use to the Church. Ordinarily, this service to the Church was accomplished rather by the court confessors, who were also characteristic figures of the time. These were usually Jesuits or other religious, who in their difficult position could do much good or at least could prevent some evil. Especially well-known are William Lamormaini, confessor of Emperor Ferdinand II from 1624 till 1637, and Francis Lachaise, to whose lot fell from 1675 the thorny task of being spiritual adviser of Louis XIV.

BISHOPS, SPIRITUAL DIRECTORS, SAINTS

At this epoch the French episcopate possessed an unusually large number of important shepherds of souls, many of whom were also prominent literary men. At their head stands the Doctor of the Church, Saint Francis de Sales (✝1622), bishop of Geneva-Annecy, one of the most read ascetical writers of modern times. Others were Cardinal Duperron, who played a prominent role in the conversion of Henry IV and died in 1618 as archbishop of Sens, and the famed pulpit orators, Bossuet, bishop of Meaux (✝1704), Fléchier, bishop of Nîmes (✝1710), and Fénelon, bishop of Cambrai (✝1715). Other excellent pastors were Godeau, bishop of Vence

429

(✝1672), one of the first members of the French Academy, and Huet, bishop of Avranches (✝1721), who in his philosophical writings inclined strongly toward skepticism. Some were infected with Jansenism, but this did not prevent their being good pastors in their own way, such as Gilbert Choisseul du Plessis, bishop of Comminges and afterwards of Tournai (✝1689), and Etienne Le Camus, cardinal-archbishop of Grenoble (✝1707).

Outside the episcopate also the epoch was rich in spiritual directors and saints. The greatest of these was Vincent de Paul (✝1660), who, as the founder of modern charity, has become one of the most popular of saints. Other great figures were Cardinal Bérulle (✝1629), almoner of Henry IV and finally president of the Council of State, founder of the French Oratory, and important ascetical writer; the saintly pastor of Saint-Sulpice in Paris, Olier (✝1657), founder of the Sulpicians; Saint John Eudes (✝1680), like Olier and Vincent de Paul one of the great educators of the clergy; Saint Jean-Baptiste de la Salle (✝1719), founder of the Christian Brothers; Saint Peter Fourier (✝1640), Augustinian canon and founder of a congregation of teaching Sisters; Saint John Francis Regis (✝1640), Jesuit and missionary among the people in Languedoc; and the celebrated preacher at Notre Dame, Bourdaloue (✝1704).

Among the holy women the most outstanding were Louise Le Gras de Marillac, a widow who, with Vincent de Paul, founded the Sisters of Charity; and Saint Jane Frances de Chantal, foundress, with Francis de Sales, of the Order of the Visitation. From this order came Saint Margaret Mary Alacoque, who, by means of a new stimulus to the devotion to the Sacred Heart of Jesus, gave a very strong impulse to all of Catholic piety.

Without any doubt France in this period enriched the

Church with enduring values, no less than in the thirteenth century, the age of Scholasticism and of the Mendicants. This does not prevent some elements in the spirituality of the time from appearing strange to us today, because they were too much connected with the age. First of all was the strongly courtly and elegant character of ecclesiastical life. Piety was the fashion. Bishops and saints moved in the salons and around the royal court. Bossuet, Huet, and Fénelon were tutors of princes. Bérulle and Vincent de Paul sat in the royal council. Even the most zealous diocesan bishops had to be constantly at Paris. Another peculiarity was the raising of the individual direction of souls to an art. Of spiritual conferences and letters of direction there was no end. Not that success did not follow —there were much genuine virtue and sanctity, but at times it was sanctity in a powdered wig.

JANSENISM

The learned Netherlander, Cornelius Jansen, Latinized as Jansenius, bishop of Ypres, left at his death in 1638 a work on the theology of Saint Augustine, in which he taught the complete depravity of human nature by virtue of original sin and the irresistibility of divine grace, thereby coming dangerously close to Calvinism. The book was condemned by Urban VIII in 1642, but it found many defenders. There have always been many persons who in theology regard what is lofty as correct and in morality what is stricter as better. This could especially be the case in an age of high-strung religiosity, such as certainly existed in France in the seventeenth century. The Jansenists had no thought of separating themselves from the Church. They overflowed with "churchliness." They wanted to reform the Church. Their center was Port-Royal, a monastery of Cistercian nuns under the rule of the virtuous Abbess Angélique Arnault (✝1661). Her brother, Antoine Arnault

431

(✝1694), a doctor of the Sorbonne, was the spiritual leader of the movement. In 1643 he published a book that quickly became famous, *On Frequent Communion*, in which he so exaggerated the requirements for the reception of Communion that among the Jansenists it was regarded as more perfect to abstain from the Eucharist out of reverence.

Between the fundamental theological doctrine of Jansenius that man cannot resist divine grace and the extreme rigorism in asceticism and morality required by the Jansenists, there exists no necessary logical connection but rather a psychological one, especially insofar as both, the Jansenist doctrine on grace and their moral doctrine, were directed against the Jesuits. On the side of the Jansenists gathered all to whom the Jesuits were distasteful. The gifted Blaise Pascal, in his *Lettres à un provincial*, which despite all censures were read throughout Europe, coined the catchword of the "lax Jesuit system of morality," whereby he seriously obstructed the Order's activity.

To come forward against overzealous extremists is always a thankless task, and thus the combating of Jansenism turned out to be very difficult. Saint Vincent de Paul, who as an experienced shepherd of souls had an exact knowledge of the unfavorable effects of Jansenism, succeeded in inducing eighty-eight French bishops to protest to Innocent X. In 1653 the pope condemned five dogmatic propositions in which the doctrine of Jansenius was summarized. The Jansenists declared that the propositions were in fact heretical, but that Jansenius had not taught them. It was only under Innocent's second successor, Clement IX, that the Jansenists made a sort of submission. However, this so-called Clementine Peace was interpreted by the Jansenists in the sense rather of a papal recognition. Once again excitement grew when, by the bull *Unigenitus* in 1713, Clement XI condemned the doctrines of the French Jansenist Quesnel, who had emigrated to the Netherlands. Acceptance or rejection of the bull *Unigenitus* became from then on the point separating Catholics and Jansenists. But now Jansenism went into an unceasing decline. The last bishop who still publicly favored the Jansenists, Cardinal de Noailles of Paris, submitted before his death in 1729. The nuns of Port-Royal, who had already incurred interdict in 1669, were finally excommunicated in 1707, and their monastery was torn down by the government. In Holland there still exists a Jansenist community of a few thousand souls. They long ago separated from the Catholic Church, but have validly ordained bishops and priests.

As a dogmatic heresy Jansenism never had many adherents and caused still fewer defections from the Church. But in piety and asceticism its influence extended very widely. Some of its demands, pushed to extremes, in regard to worthiness for the priestly vocation and for the reception of the sacraments, absolute obedience to one's private spiritual director, and the separating of pure love of God from the motive of hope, had their effects for a long time afterwards and it was only in the course of the nineteenth century that such ideas could be brought back to proper moderation.

GALLICANISM

By "Gallicanism" is understood principally the summing up of the so-called "Gallican Liberties," that is, the rights and privileges which the French king and his government had long possessed or had believed they possessed, especially in regard to the filling of ecclesiastical positions and the taxing of ecclesiastical property, as well as the prerogatives of the French clergy, such as the "appeal against abuse" from the spiritual to the secular court. These privileges, already summed up in the Pragmatic Sanction of Bourges in 1438, but never recognized *in toto* by the popes, frequently gave occasion to quarrels between the French government and Rome over ecclesiastical rights. In the Age of Absolutism these liberties, which originally concerned only the canonical sphere, received a theological basis too and thereby acquired importance even beyond the frontiers of France. To the pope, so it was explained, belonged no power in temporal affairs, not even indirectly; in purely ecclesiastical matters his primacy was limited by the power of a general council; his definitions of Faith were dependent on the consent of the universal Church. In this sense Gallicanism received, under Louis XIV, its classical formulation at the hands of Bossuet in the Four Gallican Articles of 1682, which were made into law by the king and were prescribed for teaching in theological schools. Innocent XI protested the Four Gallican Articles, it is true, but thereafter the popes avoided an express condemnation of them in order not to provoke a schism. There resulted a curious alignment of fronts: the Jansenists, who were for the most part combated by the government, were at first against Gallicanism, though they were of an anti-papal mind; their opponents, in part even the Jesuits, ranged themselves on the side of Gallicanism, because of their extreme trust in the efficacy of the government, though they were for the papacy. Later, it is true, Gallicanism and Jansenism frequently coalesced into a single anti-papal tendency.

Even after the middle of the eighteenth century Gallicanism influenced the State-Church and anti-papal theories of Hontheim, auxiliary bishop of Trier, who in his work that appeared in 1763 under the pseudonym of Febronius attacked the papal primacy with a vast amount of learning; the State-Church ideas of Emperor Joseph II; and in Italy the decrees of the Jansenist-Febronian diocesan synod of Pistoia in 1786.

434

GERMANY IN THE BAROQUE AGE

The parts of Germany that remained Catholic recovered with surprising rapidity from the harm of the Thirty Years' War. A new life spirit appeared, a healthy joy at being alive, expressed in the countless ecclesiastical and profane buildings and sculptures in the Baroque style, which still imprint their stamp on the scenery of South Germany and Austria. Almost all of them originated in the decades before and after 1700. There are churches and monasteries of vast size, such as the incomparable Melk on the Danube, Sankt Florian at Linz, Ottobeuren in the Bavarian Allgäu, Weingarten in Württemberg, Einsiedeln in Switzerland, Fourteen Holy Helpers at Bamberg, as well as small pilgrimage and village churches, often in remote mountain valleys, and columns in honor of the Trinity and of Our Lady, which adorn the city squares, as well as wayside shrines on lonely country roads. Before this rich art, which at its best had a counterpart in contemporary Italy, later generations stood unappreciative. Today we again not only know the high artistic value of the German Baroque but can also appreciate its religious content.

Of course, these religious values must not be overrated. There was no flaming spirituality, no ardent mysticism. The Catholics of the German Baroque Age did not wrestle with problems. They were in secure possession of the truth, they were at peace with God and the world, they looked forward to heaven. Theirs was a thoroughly localized religion, deeply rooted, pervading all of life. It produced no great saints, but neither was it a breeding ground of Jansenism and Illuminism.

Among the spiritual directors of the age were some splendid local figures, who were, however, hardly of such importance that they would have become well-known beyond the frontiers of Germany. Such were the venerable Bartholomew Holzhauser (✝1658), canon at Tittmoning on the Inn, then dean at Saint John in the Tyrol, and finally pastor at Bingen, who gathered the parochial clergy into communities and exercised a healthy influence on the training of priests; the saintly missionary, Philip Jeningen, Jesuit of Eichstätt, who died at Ellwangen in 1704; Ulric Megerle (✝1709), from Baden, who, having become famous at Vienna as an Augustinian Hermit under the name of Abraham of Saint Clare, was a clever and blunt popular preacher and writer and dared to declare the most unpalatable truths to the Viennese court; and the elegant poet, Frederick von Spee (✝1635), a Jesuit, who was one of the first to oppose the dreadful evils connected with witch trials. Very widely read popular authors were the pious Capuchin, Martin Cochem (✝1712), and the Cologne Premonstratensian, Leonard Goffine (✝1719), whose *Handpostille*, an explanation of the Sunday Gospels, first appearing in 1687, was one of the most treasured family books till far into the nineteenth century. One need only compare Bartholomew Holzhauser with Olier, the founder of the Sulpicians, or Martin of Cochem with his equally deeply pious confrere, Joseph of Paris (✝1638), the inspired political collaborator of Richelieu, or Blessed Crescentia of Kaufbeuren (✝1744) with Saint Margaret Mary Alacoque, to understand the entire difference then existing between religious life in Germany and in France. Both were thoroughly Catholic, but German piety, with all its genuineness and frankness, was lacking in the urge toward great things, which was certainly a characteristic of the contemporary French spirituality.

The religious influence of Catholic Germany then extended far eastward, to Bohemia, Silesia, Poland, Hungary, and the South Slavs. However, with regard to religion the Baroque Age definitely had its dark side. Things went too well for the clergy, the bishops, and the monasteries. They were not wicked, they did not live riotously, but they did live too much like great lords, too unspiritually. They erected castles and palaces from the pure joy of building. Each prince-bishop and each prince-abbot wanted to be a little Louis XIV, to have a little Versailles, as did also the temporal princes of the age. This was not because, as is often stated, most of the contemporary German bishops came from noble families. A noble can be as good a bishop as anyone else, and the abbots, who often came from very humble circumstances, were every bit as ostentatious as the spiritual lords in the feudal cathedral chapters. Nor is it true that the spiritual rulers oppressed the people and forgot the needy. The old saying, that it is good to dwell under the crosier, was true until the end of the eighteenth century. Charity and social relief were still for the most part in the hands of the clergy, and the poor were thereby benefited. The evil was rather that people felt too secure. The sense of responsibility for the near future was lost. No one felt that people were living on a volcano, that the Church always lives on a volcano.

ITALY

In Italy too the religious spirit of the seventeenth and eighteenth centuries was reflected in the ecclesiastical Baroque art. Apart from the great Roman constructions of Bernini and Borromini and to an extent those of the Venetian Longhena, the Baroque style produced perhaps fewer monumental works than it did in South Germany, but on the other hand it accomplished more in the interior decoration of churches and chapels in gold stucco, colored marble, statues, and altarpieces, ordered by monasteries, communities, and families, and in the imaginative madonnas in the houses, which still, in Rome and Naples and even in the smallest villages, bear testimony to the deeply rooted spirit of Faith of the age.

Italy too was at this time a land of saints. A special type,

437

particularly in the south, were the preachers and missionaries who tirelessly wandered through cities and mountain villages. Among the earliest of this sort were the Capuchins, Saint Joseph of Leonissa (✝1612) and Saint Lawrence of Brindisi (✝1619); later the Franciscans, Saint Pacificus of Sanseverino (✝1721), Saint John Joseph of the Cross (✝1734), and Saint Leonard of Port Maurice (✝1751); and the Jesuits, Saint Francis of Geronimo (✝1716), the Apostle of Naples, and Blessed Anthony Baldinucci (✝1717) in Latium. Outshining all these was Saint Alphonsus de Liguori (✝1787), a Neapolitan and bishop of Santa Agata dei Goti, who founded his own Order of missionaries, the Redemptorists. The effort to train capable confessors led him to the field of moral theology, in which he became one of the first authorities. In 1871 Pius IX declared him a Doctor of the Church. The Passionists, founded by Saint Paul of the Cross (✝1775), were another Order with an unusually austere mode of life, devoted to missions among the people. In Rome Saint John Baptist de Rossi (✝1764) labored as a diligent shepherd of souls in the unassuming position of a canon at Santa Maria in Cosmedin. Mystical gifts of a high order distinguished Saint Joseph of Cupertino (✝1663), a Franciscan Conventual, and a whole series of holy women, such as the Franciscan tertiary, Hyacintha Mariscotti (✝1640), the Capuchins, Veronica Giuliani (✝1727) and Magdalena Martinengo (✝1737), and the Carmelites, Mary of the Angels (Countess Baldissero, ✝1661) and Margaret Redi (✝1770). Saint Lucia Filippini (✝1732) founded a society of teaching Sisters.

Among the Italian bishops of the seventeenth century the outstanding ones, in addition to Saint Robert Bellarmine (✝1621), were the nephew of Saint Charles, Federigo Borromeo (✝1631), cardinal-archbishop of Milan, founder of the Ambrosiana, of whom Manzoni has sketched an ideal

438

portrait in *J Promessi Sposi*, and Blessed Gregory Barbarigo (✝1697), cardinal and bishop of Padua.

In the second half of the eighteenth century Italy, like the other Catholic countries, had its intellectual class of "the enlightened," even in high ecclesiastical circles. On the whole, however, it can be said that hardly another people was religiously so well-prepared to survive the crisis that occurred at the end of the century.

ECCLESIASTICAL SCHOLARSHIP

In the bustle of ecclesiastical scholarship in the seventeenth and eighteenth centuries history stands in the foreground. Church History, patristics, archaeology, and liturgy were developed into independent disciplines. Here too France took the lead. The Benedictine congregation of Saint-Maur created model editions of the Fathers, which still form the basis of all scholarly theological libraries. The names of the important scholars among the Maurists—d'Achéry (✝1685), Ruinart (✝1709), Martène (✝1739), Montfaucon (✝1741), and the greatest of them, Mabillon (✝1707)—are familiar to every researcher. Likewise deserving of mention as textual critics were the Jesuit Sirmond (✝1651) and the layman, Henri de Valois (✝1676), known as Valesius. The works of Tillemont (✝1698) are of lasting value for the study of Christian antiquity. Denis Petau (Petavius, ✝1652), a Jesuit, is regarded as the founder of the history of dogma.

A special institute for the investigation of hagiographical texts arose in Belgium, founded by the Jesuit Bollandus (✝1665). The most outstanding of the later "Bollandists" was Daniel Papebroch (✝1714), who together with Mabillon can be considered the real founder of modern historical criticism.

Of the Italian ecclesiastical historians mention should be made of the Cistercian Ughelli (✝1670), the Dominican

439

Mamachi (✝1792), who came out against Febronius, the Theatine Cardinal Thomasius (✝1713), important for his liturgical studies, and the tireless Muratori (✝1750). The investigation of the catacombs was raised by Bosio (✝1629) to the rank of a real science. In Rome worked the historian of the Franciscan Order, the Irishman Luke Wadding (✝1657), the convert Lukas Holstenius, from Hamburg, who died in 1661 as librarian of the Vatican, and the brothers Assemani (✝1768 and 1782), from the Lebanon, who as outstanding orientalists were also active at the Vatican. To the portrait of contemporary scholarly Rome belongs also the polyhistor, Athanasius Kircher (✝1680) of Fulda, a Jesuit, who cannot be placed in any one category.

Together with Church History blossomed the historical investigation of law. The voluminous collections of texts of Labbé (✝1670), Hardouin (✝1729), and Mansi (✝1769) still form the basis for the study of the councils. Other legal historians were the French Oratorian Thomassin (✝1695) and the Bolognese Prospero Lambertini, who died in 1758 as Pope Benedict XIV.

To the ecclesiastical as well as the profane scholarship of the Baroque Age pertained a polygraphic impulse to place its joy in finding and sifting rather than the need of presenting new pioneering ideas. In this collecting and investigating of even remote fields of knowledge appears the age's optimism in regard to truth: all truth can only be of use to religion, and the Church does not need to fear even the most acute criticism of her foundations.

THE POPES FROM 1605 TO 1740

The popes of the sixteenth century, from Paul III on, had for the most part been distinguished men, of sharply cut and expressive faces, very different from one another, yet almost all of them men of action who did much that was important in mostly brief reigns. In the sixteenth century the voice of the pope was again heard in the Church and in the world. In the seventeenth and eighteenth centuries everything was different. The age of giants was followed by an age, not of dwarfs, it is true, but of *epigoni*. They were not lacking in good will. They were all splendid priests, and there was no Alexander VI among them. They were not blind to the evils and perils of the age. But the Catholic governments had gradually spun so tight a net around them that they could no longer stir. There was no longer a Philip II, who with his chivalrous obstinacy made the popes of his day accomplish so much but fundamentally aspired to the same things as they did. The Catholic princes of the later Baroque Age no longer wanted the pope to join with them to fight for the Kingdom of God, but they desired to humiliate him, to make him feel his powerlessness. Catholic feeling was revolted by these kings and their ministers, who deliberately acted toward the pope as wicked sons, who at every opportunity remind their aged father that he merely enjoys the bread of charity and should be glad that he is tolerated in the house.

Paul V (1605–1621) was a pious man and a capable ruler of the Papal State. Under him the population of Rome mounted to more than 100,000, a number which had not been reached since antiquity. He completed the basilica of Saint Peter, whose façade displays his name in gigantic letters. Following the prevailing abuse, he so enriched his family, the Borghese, that henceforth they were among Rome's wealthiest. He is familiar to historians as the founder of the Vatican archives.

With the republic of Venice Paul V came into sharp conflict over ecclesiastical rights. It formed a prelude to the intentional insults and infringements of rights in which in the seventeenth and eighteenth centuries governments, claiming to be Catholic, took such delight in regard to the pope. The occasion was trivial, but the *signoria* was determined to prosecute the quarrel to extremes. It staged an effective literary agitation through its official theologian, Paolo Sarpi, an evil hypocrite, who to the end passed himself off as a regular priest, though interiorly he had long ago broken with the Church. The pope laid an interdict on all the territory of the republic, which finally yielded sufficiently to allow the pope to make at least an honorable settlement. But this was the last time that a pope in mediaeval fashion covered an entire country with interdict. Sarpi's attempt to make Venice Protestant failed.

Gregory XV (1621–1623), Alessandro Ludovisi, regulated the method of voting in papal elections that is still followed.[4] He founded the Congregation *De Propaganda Fide* as the supreme governing authority for the missions; its name became familiar throughout the world. Through the canonization of Ignatius Loyola, Francis Xavier, Teresa, and Philip Neri he impressed the seal, so to speak, on the great century of the Catholic Restoration.

Urban VIII (1623–1644) enriched his family, the Barberini, in an improper fashion also. Roman Baroque art reached its zenith during his pontificate. It was the age of Bernini and Borromini. Under Urban VIII occurred the first condemnation of Jansenius and the unfortunate process against Galileo. The Copernican system, advocated by Galileo, had hitherto hardly been challenged by theologians. It was only when Holy Scripture was brought into the discussion, partly by Galileo himself, that the ecclesiastical authorities felt the need of

---

[4] For the most recent regulations in regard to the conclave, see the Apostolic Constitution "Vacantis Apostolicae Sedis," of December 8, 1945 (*Acta Apostolicae Sedis*, XXXVIII, No. 3 [February 4, 1946]). (Translator's note.)

intervening. The process was conducted by the Roman judges in good faith and in proper forms, and Galileo made a disavowal. But the whole affair was a serious mistake which furnished the future with matter for scornful comments, though at the same time it served as a warning to ecclesiastical authorities of the future.

Innocent X (1644–1655) was already seventy years old when elected, difficult to deal with, suspicious, unsociable, but clever. His features are familiar to every art lover through Velásquez's incomparable portrait in the Galleria Doria. He too unduly enriched his family, the Pamfili, and allowed to his sister-in-law, Olimpia Maidalchini, excessive influence at court. But he was the first pope in a long time not to make a nephew secretary of state, a post he conferred on the excellent Fabio Chigi, hitherto nuncio in Germany. From then on there existed in the College of Cardinals, which had up to now been regularly split into political factions under the leadership of the nephews of the last popes, a neutral and purely ecclesiastical party, the so-called Squadrone Volante, which in the next elections exercised a salutary influence. Only a bigot could blame Innocent X for protesting the Treaty of Westphalia, which did such serious harm to the Church. The flowering of the Roman Baroque continued. On the best buildings of the Eternal City the visitor still encounters the heraldic dove of the Pamfili. Bernini then created one of his best works, the colonnades of Saint Peter's.

Alexander VII (1655–1667), Fabio Chigi, had been secretary of state under his predecessor. In his pontificate began the friction with Louis XIV, who seized Avignon and sent troops to Rome. The Treaty of Pisa (1664) brought a tolerable settlement. The arrival of Queen Christina of Sweden, daughter of Gustavus Adolphus, caused a great stir in Roman society. She had become a Catholic after her abdication in

1654 and settled permanently in Rome. Alexander VII and his successors treated her with the utmost courtesy, though she was not always an easy guest. She died in 1689.

After Alexander VII another secretary of state, Rospigliosi, was elected as Clement IX, but he died after two years. His successor, Clement X (1670–1676), Emilio Altieri, was eighty years old at the time of his election. In this circumstance is revealed the unwholesome influence of the Catholic governments, who preferred a frail old man on the Throne of Peter.

Innocent XI (1676–1689) was an important pope, less for his gifts and erudition than for his character. He was an ascetic, somewhat foreign to the world, conscientious to the point of scrupulosity, often strange in his views, but wholly devoted to duty.[5] To his family, the Odescalchi, he gave nothing, and even when governments loaded them with titles and revenues in order to win the pope's favor, he allowed them no influence. To the exertions and support of this pope is due a great share in the freeing of Vienna from the Turkish siege in 1683. The Turkish standards in Santa Maria della Vittoria, sent to Rome by the grateful victors, still recall this. With Louis XIV, who to the great grief of the pope supported the Turks, Innocent XI came into sharp collision because of an incident, trifling in itself, which developed, however, into a test of strength between king and pope. The many embassies in Rome had in the course of time extended their extraterritoriality to the entire district around their palaces, so that half the city consisted of asylums into which the Roman police were not permitted to penetrate. In agreement with the governments, Innocent XI abolished this nuisance, but, on grounds of prestige, Louis XIV refused to comply. The pope declined to receive his new ambassador, and when the latter, in accord with his instructions, adopted a most challenging attitude, the

5 Innocent XI was beatified on October 7, 1956. (Translator's note.)

pope excommunicated him and laid an interdict on the French national church. Louis XIV imprisoned the nuncio to Paris, but the pope was unmoved. The king finally had to recall his ambassador and renounce the right of asylum.

The next pope, Alexander VIII (1689–1691), was almost eighty years old at his election and quickly died. And his successor, Innocent XII (1691–1700), was seventy-two. He obtained from Louis XIV the repeal of the Four Gallican Articles and issued a decree against nepotism, whereby this abuse, which had so often seriously injured the moral prestige of the Holy See, was ended, at least in principle. During the next conclave the War of the Spanish Succession (1700–1713) broke out. The new pope, Clement XI (1700–1721), accepted the office only with reluctance, because he felt that he was incapable of it. Actually, the political reins slipped from his grasp entirely, and in the treaty of peace not the slightest consideration was taken of the pope and the Church. The pontificates of Innocent XIII (1721–1724) and Benedict XIII (1724–1730) left few traces in history. Benedict XIII was a saintly man and had been an excellent archbishop of Benevento, but at the time of his election to the papacy he was seventy-five years old and let himself be managed by favorites. Clement XII (1730–1740) was already seventy-eight, blind, and bedridden. The papacy was on the point of falling into oblivion.

the Beginnings of the church in america

IN ANTIQUITY the geographical location of the Church was the Mediterranean world. The Mediterranean lands, politically united in the Roman Empire before the beginning of Christianity, were the furthest advanced and at the time the most densely populated of the three great cultural areas of mankind. With the other two, India and China, the Mediterranean region was seldom in contact, even if there were individual threads here and there.

From the seventh century there existed a fourth cultural world, that of Islam, which, like a rank growth, spread in all directions out of Arabia, taking an entirely irregular course but following intrinsic geographical laws. The centrally located ancient culture area, the Indian, while not absorbed, was to a great extent overlaid by Islam, and the Western Christian culture was pushed from the southern shore of the Mediterranean and out of its entire eastern basin. Western culture and with it the Church were confined within the essentially European peninsula, where they expanded during the Middle Ages into the far north and to the east, regions where the Roman Empire had never penetrated.

In its great outlines human history has been concerned from time immemorial with the possession of Asia, or, more correctly, with the possession of monsoon Asia. For Asia essentially consists of two worlds—the densely populated and culturally rich monsoon lands of the south and southeast, and the almost uninhabited deserts, steppes, and forest lands of the center and north. At least since Alexander the Great Europe has aspired after Asia. And Islam had its chief expansion in this direction. The crusades had been a frontal attack of Europe on Asia. They were wrecked on the Near Eastern bulwark of Islam. Their only result was that the natural route from Europe to monsoon Asia, the route through the Red Sea, closed more tightly than before. The route through central Asia, which Islam had not yet barricaded, still lay open. Europe took this route in the late Middle Ages. Merchants and missionaries moved along it even to the Far East, and for a time in the fourteenth century there was a Catholic see of Peking. Finally, this thread also broke, after the Mongols, at the end of the fourteenth century and the beginning of the fifteenth, had transformed the entire world of inner Asia, and especially when the Turks in 1475 destroyed the last Genoese colonies on the Black Sea. Europe was completely cut off from monsoon Asia by the Islamic wall.

But the impulse toward Asia did not come to rest. From 1415 the Portuguese had been groping along the west coast of Africa southward, and in 1486 they reached Africa's southern tip. They had outflanked the Islamic block and now the sea route to monsoon Asia lay open to them.

The Spaniards believed they could reach the goal directly by sailing from Europe in a straight line westward toward Asia, without the arduous circumnavigation of Africa. The spherical shape of the world had been familiar to geographers since antiquity, though the sphere was regarded as much smaller than it is. This was Columbus's good fortune. The distance from Lisbon to Zipangu, as people still called Japan, was reckoned at 104 equatorial degrees [1] by the Venetian geographer, Toscanelli. In reality the distance is more than twice as great. Columbus would never have considered the voyage if he had not relied on Toscanelli. No one suspected that in the near neighborhood of Europe a gigantic double continent extended across the entire breadth of the earth's sphere and that just behind it began the greatest of all oceans. Thus Columbus, who was by no means looking for new lands, but only for a new sea route, made the greatest of all geographical discoveries and gave human history an incomparable impetus.

In all world history there is scarcely anything more sublime than the voyages of these Portuguese, Spaniards, and Italians —geographically half-blind, technically quite unsatisfactorily equipped—who themselves hardly knew how bold they were.

Although the great voyages of discovery were intended first of all to be of use for acquiring wealth and political power, nevertheless, from the beginning, the expansion of Christianity was also their goal. Spaniards and Portuguese could not think otherwise. Struggle against unbelievers, conquest, and the spread of Christendom were for them one and the same idea. This fusion of conquest and evangelization was no assurance that everything would be done in the spirit of the Gospel, any more than had been the case in the Middle Ages when central and northern Europe were Christianized. But the final result was that wide regions with great future possibilities were opened up to the Church. To the Spaniards and Portuguese belongs the credit for beginning the transforming of European culture into a world culture, the European

[1] According to Friedrich Streicher ("Toscanelli," *The Catholic Encyclopedia*, XIV [New York: 1912], 786 f.), Toscanelli was convinced "that the transverse extent of Europe and Asia covered nearly two-thirds of the earth, that is 230° of latitude, so that the western route across the ocean could only cover 130°." (Translator's note.)

Church into a world Church. In this sense it is doubly deplorable that, just at the moment when the Church prepared to burst her existing geographical bonds and spread herself over the whole earth, in Europe itself so many precious lands separated from her.

THE POLITICAL OCCUPATION OF AMERICA

In the course of time four European powers acquired possessions in America and impressed their stamp on the new continents—Spain, Portugal, France, and England. For a time Sweden, Denmark, and Holland also sought a share of territory. Sweden and Denmark never achieved any sizable occupation and eventually withdrew. Around the middle of the seventeenth century Holland was on the verge of founding a colonial empire, but its possessions lay too far from one another. The Dutch could not long hold either New Amsterdam, the modern New York, or Pernambuco, which they took from the Portuguese. In the end, they retained only a small remnant in the Antilles and in Guiana.

Portugal remained in uninterrupted possession of Brazil, apart from the short-lived Dutch occupation of Pernambuco (1630–1654). Portugal did not aspire to an expansion of its American possessions. There were no boundary disputes, because between the Portuguese possessions and their only neighbors, the Spanish colonies, lay a wide no man's land. Only in the south, in the La Plata region, did the two colonial empires jostle each other, so that there frontier regulations had to be drawn up.

The real struggle over America, therefore, was fought between Spain, England, and France. It was long doubtful which of the three would secure final predominance. In the end, none of them obtained it.

Spain was on the scene before the other powers. In the

Andean lands and as far as the La Plata its domination was from the beginning undisputed, and the same is true for Mexico. But Spain advanced its rule beyond present-day Mexico on the North American continent into Texas and California and very early also into Florida. In these regions there was bound to occur in time an argument with the power which would acquire predominance in the north, whether it was England or France.

It was not until more than a century had passed that England and France began to follow Spain in establishing political rule in America. At first this occurred as a result of commercial undertakings and almost simultaneously in three localities: the French at Quebec and the English at Boston and in Virginia and Maryland. From the start occasions of friction were not lacking, especially at the mouth of the Saint Lawrence, where the English and the French territories touched. They became aggravated when the English sought to establish themselves also to the north of the French on Hudson Bay. The English Hudson's Bay Company had been founded by Prince Rupert of the Palatinate, the adventurous son of the "winter-king." The tension became intolerable when the French pushed deep into their hinterland, the region of the Great Lakes, reached the Mississippi in 1673, and sailed down the river to the gulf, where they founded New Orleans. Thereby the English colonies were surrounded from the rear, and the French advanced from the middle Mississippi up the Ohio toward the east. Here, on the upper Ohio, the definitive struggle broke out, in which neither of the parties suspected they were fighting on the inexhaustible coal fields which in days to come were to support North America's heavy industry.

The great English-French colonial war lasted from 1754 to 1760, when the French army at Montreal surrendered. In the Peace of Paris of 1763 France ceded all of Canada and the territory east of the Mississippi to England. The remainder of the French colonies, the whole country west of the Mississippi, a vast tract but hardly settled and almost unexplored, held no further interest for France and was voluntarily yielded to the Spanish, who in 1769 took possession.

Thus there were now left only two powers, England and Spain, on the North American continent, and of these Spain held the larger, but England the more valuable part. However, before a conflict could arise between them, the colonies made themselves independent, first the English, then the Spanish, and America ceased to be European colonial territory.

THE COLONIZATION OF AMERICA

THE NATIVE POPULATION

An estimate of the native population of "Indians," who apparently came originally from Asia, is scarcely possible for the time of the discovery of America. Real censuses do not exist, and therefore we are dependent on the impressions of the discoverers or conquerors. To the inability of earlier ages to estimate populations special sources of error are added: *e.g.*, the estimates among the Spanish conquerors of the greatly superior forces which they withstood, as when Córtez with scarcely 3,000 men undertook to attack the entire Aztec empire. The passion for the glory of having conquered such masses caused the numbers to grow; similarly, great enthusiasm for mass conversions prevailed among the missionaries. According to one report, the Spaniards in Mexico alone must have baptized over 9,000,000 from 1526 to 1540—almost as many as the total number of inhabitants of Spain. In addition, there are the atrocity accounts of Las Casas, according to which the Indians of Haiti until 1514 declined from 3,000,000 to 14,000 because of the cruelty of the Spaniards. The flat

451

estimates in regard to Latin America are therefore apparently far too high. Historians' concept of the ancient cultures of the Aztecs, Mayas, and Incas too easily leads them to apply present-day standards and to imagine a cultured state with a population of millions. On the other hand, North American historians, eager to refute the accusation of genocide, are perhaps prone to reduce the number of red men killed by the whites.

We can therefore at most make our estimates only in vague terms. In Mexico and Peru, the only regions with a somewhat concentrated native population, there may have been a few million inhabitants. North America, apart from Mexico, had less than 1,000,000; South America, outside Peru, did not have much more. Thus, at the time of the discovery the entire double continent was relatively uninhabited. Thus, too, it is hardly correct to speak, as is often done, of the Indians as the ancient legitimate owners of the country. This is true for Mexico and Peru, but not for the greatest part of the rest of the continents. A handful of men is in no position to possess millions of square kilometers of land for the improvement of which they lack every means. However, this is not to say that the Indians were not in places sufficiently numerous to cause serious difficulties for the new settlers, as in the case of the Iroquois in Canada and the Guarani in Paraná. Furthermore, the small number of Indians cannot serve to palliate the many injustices and atrocities which almost everywhere they endured as a result of the colonization.

EUROPEAN COLONIZATION

The first enumeration in New France, or Canada, in 1660 amounted to 3,418 colonists. From then on the number mounted steadily, and a century later, when Canada was ceded to England (1763), the population had reached 70,000.

In this figure are, of course, included the colonists in Louisiana, which meant the entire Mississippi region. However, in this territory, then so remote, the colonists were less numerous than in Canada, even though today a whole series of place names along the Mississippi—Prairie du Chien, Dubuque, Saint Louis, Florissant, Cape Girardeau, New Orleans—recall the French colonization. After 1763 French immigration, and with it Catholic immigration, ceased. Instead, settlers from the English colonies now moved to Canada, whose population in 1784 is given as 130,000.

The first English colonists were brought to Newfoundland in 1583. In 1765 the island counted 15,000 settlers. The immigration to the continent began with Virginia in 1607 when Jamestown was founded after two previous attempts at colonization, in 1585 and 1587, had come to nothing. A little later, in 1620, the famed *Mayflower* expedition reached New England. In 1630 Boston was founded; it became the principal port of English North America and upheld its supremacy during the entire colonial period, until it was overshadowed by Philadelphia at the beginning of the nineteenth century.

The English colonies expanded from these two centers, Boston in the north and Virginia in the south, which were in the beginning separated by New Netherlands (New York). Around 1640 New England counted 18,000 settlers; in 1688 the number had risen to 56,000. The southern colonies grew more rapidly. In 1688 Virginia had 50,000 settlers, Maryland 25,000, and the middle section, New York and Connecticut, which had meanwhile become English, had together some 40,000. At the close of the eighteenth century the combined English colonies had already exceeded 200,000.

In the eighteenth century the immigration from England was very slight, and in the northern section it almost entirely ceased. But the population grew quickly through natural increase. By the middle of the eighteenth century it had passed the million mark, and at the time of the Declaration of Independence the United States counted some 2,200,000 inhabitants.

The Spanish territories exhibit quite a different picture in regard to colonization. The Spaniards came to America not so much as rural settlers, but rather as officials, soldiers, and merchants, usually without wives. The chief Spanish territories, Mexico and Peru, were not uninhabited, but possessed an indigenous population standing at a certain height of culture. Accordingly, from the beginning a strong intermixture of populations was bound to occur.

Immigration from the Spanish mother country was never very strong. Spain had no surplus population. At the end of the sixteenth century it had probably not much more than 10,000,000 inhabitants. The assertion, often heard, that Spain exhausted itself through continued emigration, is not correct when stated in this general way. It is true that in the seventeenth century the population of Castile decreased, but that of Aragón and Catalonia grew. For the year 1723 an estimate of 7,600,000—possibly too low—is made for Spain. The first real census, in 1787, yielded 10,268,150 for Spain.

Even England, at the end of the seventeenth century, had only 5,000,000 inhabitants, and if Scotland and Ireland are counted in, a good 7,000,000; hence, the figures are somewhat less than for Spain. But whereas the English colonial territory in America scarcely embraced 500,000 square kilometers, the Spanish colonies in the sixteenth century covered about 5,000,000 square kilometers, and thus were ten times larger. More striking is the fact that France, which with 19,000,000 stood by far at the top of the European states at the close of the seventeenth century, sent relatively few settlers to America.

In 1574 the Spanish population in America is reckoned at

152,000. Figures for the total population, inclusive of *mestizos* and Indians, insofar as they were obtainable, are first available from the end of the eighteenth century. The first enumeration in the viceroyalty of New Spain (Mexico) in 1793 yielded 4,483,569 inhabitants, and 1,076,997 for the viceroyalty of Peru in 1794. In the viceroyalty of New Granada (Colombia and Venezuela) the census gave around the same time some 2,000,000. For the La Plata we have no figures, but less than 1,000,000 is probably correct, for at the time of their declarations of independence Argentina counted less than 700,000 and Uruguay only 70,000. If we include also the comparatively densely populated Spanish Antilles and the very sparsely settled territories of Florida, Texas, and California, we obtain for the Spanish regions at the end of the eighteenth century a total population of far more than 10,000,000, whereas contemporary English North America had still by no means reached a figure of 3,000,000.

Furthermore, the method of colonization in Spanish territory was totally different from what it was in the English and French north. The Spaniards settled in cities. They formed the intellectual upper class. The Indians continued to be or became farmers. Whereas in the north till the middle of the eighteenth century there were few cities of importance besides Boston and Quebec, there arose in the Spanish lands in the sixteenth century many urban centers of commerce, industry, and culture.

THE CITIES

Some cities were already in existence before the arrival of the Spaniards. Mexico City, the capital of the Aztecs, going back to the fourteenth century, is said to have contained a half-million inhabitants at the time of its conquest by Córtez in 1521. Though this is surely an exaggeration, Mexico City, as the capital of New Spain, remained one of the most important centers in America. The university was opened as early as 1553, and in 1573 the cornerstone of the famed cathedral was laid.

Of the old Inca cities, Quito, taken by Pizarro in 1533, became an important center, while the capital, Cuzco, whose beginnings reach back to the eleventh century, lost importance, even though it too received a university in 1692.

The new Spanish foundations indicate the direction in which colonization advanced. La Habana in Cuba was founded in 1511, Panamá in 1519. Then followed the Caribbean coastal cities—Cumaná in Venezuela in 1521, Santa Marta in 1525, and Cartagena in 1533—and before long the cities in the interior of modern Colombia—Popayán and Bogotá in 1538, Antioquia in 1541; Medellín was not founded until 1674.

On the Pacific coast Benalcazar established the port of Guayaquil in 1531, and in 1535 Pizarro founded Ciudad de los Reyes, or Lima, which thereafter long remained the capital of all of Spanish South America. The University of Lima was opened in 1551, even before that of Mexico, and hence it is the oldest in all America. From Peru were then founded the cities in the west of what is now Argentina: Santiago del Estero in 1553, Tucumán in 1565, Córdoba in 1573, Salta in 1582. Argentina was settled not from the La Plata mouth but from the west. Buenos Aires arose in 1580, but long remained insignificant. In 1664 it contained only 4,000 inhabitants; in 1744 it had 10,000. This is connected with the fact that all the commerce had to go by the Caribbean Sea and even to Argentina over the route Portobello, Panamá, Lake Titicaca, Tucumán. Not until 1748 was the route around Cape Horn in general use, and not until 1778 was the harbor of Buenos Aires opened to commerce.

456

Santiago de Chile was founded from Peru in 1541.

In what is now the United States the Spaniards founded Saint Augustine in Florida in 1565 and Santa Fe in present-day New Mexico in 1609, the two oldest cities in the North American Union. Tucson in Arizona was laid out by Jesuit missionaries in 1692.

Many of these Spanish foundations of the sixteenth and seventeenth centuries are large cities today. However, the number of inhabitants in the colonial period should not be imagined as very great. The most populous city in the new world must for a long time have been Potosí in Bolivia, whose silver mines, exploited even in pre-Spanish days, provided more than half of the world's production. At the height of its mining Potosí is said to have had 150,000 inhabitants, or, according to others, even 200,000; today it has 35,000. La Paz in Bolivia, founded in 1548, had 12,000 in 1675, 21,000 in 1769; today it has 152,000. Even Lima at the beginning of the eighteenth century must have had not much over 30,000 inhabitants; today, with its suburbs, it has 400,000.

Even in Europe the vast growth of cities did not occur before the nineteenth century. Before the Revolution, Paris is estimated at from 640,000 to 670,000 inhabitants, whereas around 1600 it had had not many more than 200,000. The other European capitals were all considerably smaller— Vienna, 175,000 in 1754; Berlin, from 13,000 to 15,000 in 1625 and 104,525 in 1769; Copenhagen, 20,000 in 1635 and 90,000 in 1787. The same is true of the great commercial cities —Amsterdam, 105,000 in 1622; Rotterdam, 53,000 in 1795; Lyon, 135,000 in 1787; Marseille, 89,000 in 1787; Zürich, 10,000 in 1671; Geneva, 16,000 in 1693. Even Venice at the period of the greatest flourishing of the republic never had more than 150,000 inhabitants.

Hence, it would be just as incorrect to imagine the Spanish

colonial period as an epoch of a flowering never again attained, as, on the contrary, to hold that the new republics created everything out of nothing from the time of their independence. The growth of the population and of the cities of Latin America seems on the whole to have progressed far more continuously than some recent historical presentations indicate.

Brazil is estimated at 2,850,000 inhabitants in 1798. Portugal, which in 1732 possessed 2,000,000 inhabitants, had a much smaller population to send overseas than Spain, and, besides, in the colonial period its chief expansion was toward Africa and Asia. Hence, to a great degree the native population accounts for the relatively high number of inhabitants of Brazil.

Of course, all these population figures are more or less uncertain. Humboldt for his part estimates the total population of Spanish America, including the Antilles, at more than 18,000,000, a figure which is still quoted occasionally, whereas from 12,000,000 to 15,000,000 is really nearer to the truth. All the more is a division according to races entirely impossible. Even today an official census is gathered from a viewpoint other than the merely biological. Such a division also has little significance, at least for Church History. Today there are in both Americas perhaps 25,000,000 negroes, of whom more than 10,000,000 live in the United States, 8,000,000 in tropical South America, and 5,000,000 in the Antilles. Humboldt estimates the number of negroes in the Spanish colonies outside the Antilles at the end of the eighteenth century at 776,000, and in the Antilles at 600,000. In these estimates are included mulattoes, but it is difficult to draw a line. In any case, the negroes increased less through reinforcements from Africa than through natural growth on the spot, and this in great measure not until the nineteenth century. In regard to the importation of slaves in colonial times there has been a

458

wise reluctance to apply statistics. On the other hand, the atrocity reports are useless for statistical purposes.

THE CHURCH IN SPANISH AMERICA

BEGINNINGS

On his first voyage in 1492 Columbus was accompanied by a ship's chaplain, Pedro de Arenas, who thus was the first priest to tread the soil of America. On the other hand, the Catalan, Bernardo Boil,[2] a Minim and disciple of Saint Francis of Paola, made the second voyage and is usually considered the first missionary. The number of missionaries soon increased.

In 1516 Cardinal Cisneros prescribed that every Spanish vessel must take along a priest; in 1526 Charles V decreed that every Spanish fleet was to bring religious as missionaries to America. Thus, from the very beginning, the throng of religious sent as missionaries to America was not insignificant, especially Franciscans, Dominicans, Augustinian Hermits, and Mercedarians.

By 1509 the Franciscans had three convents with fifteen clerics on Haiti. In 1510 the Dominicans settled on the island. Twenty-four Franciscans came to Puerto Rico in 1511.

As early as 1504, before the Spaniards had obtained a

2 There has long been much confusion in regard to the identity of Bernardo Boil. According to Stephen M. Donovan, "Buil," *The Catholic Encyclopedia*, III (New York: 1908), 40, there were two religious, a Franciscan and a Benedictine, named Bernardo Buil or Boil or Boyl, contemporaries in Spain. Pope Alexander VI seems to have named the Franciscan, Bernardo Boil, first vicar apostolic of the New World in 1493; but King Ferdinand wanted the post for his trusted agent, Bernardo Boyl, the Benedictine, and falsified the papal bull in favor of the latter, who thus actually became the first vicar apostolic, accompanying Columbus on his second voyage in 1493. According to Philibert Schmitz, *Histoire de l'ordre de Saint Benoît*, IV (Maredsous: 1948), 210, Boil may have been a Benedictine, but when leaving for America with Columbus he wore the habit of the recently founded Minims. See also *The Encyclopedia Americana*, IV (New York: 1948), 164 f. (Translator's note.)

foothold on the continent, it was decided to establish a hierarchy for the Antilles. The first sees actually to be established came into existence only in 1511—Santo Domingo and Concepción de la Vega in Haiti, San Juan in Puerto Rico, and soon afterward Baracoa and Santiago in Cuba.

MEXICO

Even before the conquest by Córtez, when as yet there was little information about the country, a bishopric had been planned for the Yucatán peninsula. The first bishop, Julián Garcés, a Dominican, did not arrive in his diocese until 1521, and in the meantime the see had been transferred to Tlaxcala in Mexico proper. This see, later moved to Puebla, is thus the oldest on the American continent. The real founder of the Mexican Church is the Franciscan Juan de Zumarraga, an outstanding man who in 1527 was named first bishop of Mexico City and who died in 1548. He established missions, schools, charitable institutes, and a printing press, from which came forth in 1535, as the first book printed in America, the *Scala Spiritualis* of the Greek Father, John Climacus, much read in monasteries; in 1546 the first catechism in an Indian tongue appeared. Of importance were the conferences in which Juan de Zumarraga called upon ecclesiastical dignitaries and religious superiors to consider missionary and social questions.

Even in the lifetime of Juan de Zumarraga three new bishoprics were erected—Oaxaca (today Antequera) in 1535, Michoacan (today Morelia) in 1536, and in 1546 Chiapa, whose bishop for a time was the famed Bartolomé de las Casas. The bishopric of Chiapa later declined, as did that of Vera Paz, founded in 1561. In addition, the sixteenth century also witnessed the founding of Guadalajara in 1548 and Veracruz in 1561. All these sees lay close together in a comparatively small district. It was only later that three sees were established

460

in the less populated north of Mexico—Nueva Vizcaya (Durango) in 1620, Linares (Monterey) in 1777, and Sonora in 1779.

Until 1545 the Mexican dioceses belonged to the ecclesiastical province of Sevilla. In that year Mexico City was made an archbishopric and remained the metropolitan see for New Spain until the nineteenth century.

The Mexican dioceses were not lacking in external splendor. All had their cathedral chapter, with numerous dignitaries and canons, well-endowed benefices, higher and lower schools, pious foundations, charitable institutes, and numerous monasteries. The ecclesiastical buildings of the period, especially those of the seventeenth century, monasteries and cathedrals that still give to the Mexican landscape that character of an ancient and deeply planted Catholic culture, stand in magnificence and artistic value not far behind the ecclesiastical buildings of Spain's best epoch. A few decades after the original conquest Mexico proper was no longer a mission land. At the close of the sixteenth century it counted 470 parishes. The country parishes, mostly administered by religious, had, if they expanded, several stations which were regularly visited by priests. The population, Spaniards, Indians, and *mestizos,* was practically all Catholic. Only the north was mission territory.

It was a disadvantage that almost all the bishops had to come from Spain, even after Mexico had long possessed a sufficient native clergy. It has been estimated that in the seventeenth century out of ninety-two bishops, four-fifths came from Europe. They were all worthy prelates, but they remained somewhat foreign to the country, learned none of the very vivid Indian tongues, and were happy at the thought of a return home. In addition, new appointments, all of which had to go through the royal council for Indian affairs at Sevilla, were often long delayed by the exceedingly slow routine of

461

business. In the seventeenth century Oaxaca was without a bishop for twenty-nine years, Guadalajara for thirty-two, Michoacan for thirty-five, and the archiepiscopal see of Mexico City for forty-six.

A further disadvantage lay in the ceaseless quarrels and processes of the bishops with their chapters, the monasteries, the viceroy, and the royal court over territorial boundaries, jurisdiction, authority, and even ceremonial matters. This was an evil of the time, not only in Latin America but in Spain and other European countries. A recent Mexican historian of the Church wonders how the bishops, always engaged in litigation, found time to govern their dioceses.

From the beginning, the actual pastoral work lay to a great extent in the hands of the religious. At the middle of the sixteenth century the Franciscans already had 300 of their number in Mexico, and at the beginning of the seventeenth century there were 174 Franciscan monasteries there. The Dominicans were less numerous, but just the same they had at the beginning of the seventeenth century 600 members in three provinces. The Augustinian Hermits numbered 800 around the same time. Their principal monastery in Mexico City was founded by Doña Isabel Montezuma, daughter of the last Aztec ruler. The first Jesuits arrived in 1572. In the lifetime of Saint Ignatius the Franciscans had written to Philip II that he should send Jesuits, "for success derives more from virtue than from the religious habit." The Jesuits in Mexico, about 350 of them continuously, were less numerous than the older Orders, but they had colleges for the education of youth in all the larger cities, three of them in Mexico City alone.

PERU

Whereas in Mexico the real colonial territory formed a compact, thickly populated area, smaller than the Spanish motherland, the viceroyalty of Peru extended over a vast area in which the individual colonized sections were separated like islands by broad, almost uninhabited tracts. There were four chief centers of culture: one on the Caribbean coast around Cartagena and three in the high Andean basins, Bogotá in modern Colombia, Quito in modern Ecuador, and the region around Lake Titicaca, now belonging partly to Peru and partly to Bolivia. Lima, lying lonely on the coast, formed a sort of suburb to this last. Still farther to the south were two centers, one on each side of the Andean chain: Santiago de Chile to the west and Tucumán to the east.

The first episcopal sees arose in central America—Panamá in 1520, Nicaragua in 1521. The next were the dioceses along the Caribbean—Santiago de Venezuela (Caracas) in 1530, Santa Marta in 1531, Cartagena in 1534. The diocese of Lima was established in 1543, and two years later it was elevated to archiepiscopal rank. In 1564 a second archbishopric, Bogotá, was created, to which the northern dioceses on the Atlantic side were subjected; the Pacific side, from Panamá to Chile, belonged to Lima. Charcas in what was then Upper Peru became the third metropolitan see in 1609; Charcas is the modern Sucre, the capital of Bolivia. To Charcas belonged the Andean dioceses of Santa Cruz de la Sierra, La Paz, Ayacucho, and also Tucumán, Buenos Aires, and Asunción. This ecclesiastical organization persisted until the end of the colonial period; even the establishment of the two new viceroyalties of New Granada (Colombia) in 1710 and La Plata in 1776 occasioned no changes.

Throughout the entire colonial period the chief ecclesiastical center was Lima. At the close of the sixteenth century its university had twenty chairs, 180 doctors and masters, and 1,200 students. The cathedral chapter counted five dignitaries, twenty-two canons, and thirty chaplains. The greatest brilliance was bestowed upon the archiepiscopal see of Lima by its second archbishop, Saint Toribio Alfonso Mogrobejo (1581–1606), the Charles Borromeo of America. He held three provincial councils and thirteen diocesan synods. At his first council in 1582 a larger and a smaller catechism were composed, as well as a manual for confessors and a handbook of sermons, all of which were printed in Spanish and in two Indian tongues. Toribio was able to carry out three visitations of his diocese, which embraced approximately the whole of modern Peru; on the fourth visitation he died. He is said to have administered confirmation 1,000,000 times.

In the time of Toribio the city of Lima had five parishes, ten hospitals and other institutes of charity, eight convents of women, and sixteen of men. Of these, three each belonged to the Franciscans, Dominicans, Augustinians, and Mercedarians. The Jesuits had four, among them a higher school for young Indians. The English geographer, W. Burck, at the beginning of the eighteenth century was struck by the unusually large number of ecclesiastical institutions in Lima. He counted fifty-four churches, twenty monasteries of men, twelve of women, and many charitable institutes.

Just as in Mexico, so too in South America there still exist splendid church buildings from the colonial period, at Lima, Cuzco, and, above all, Quito.

CONVERSION OF THE NATIVES

Missionary methods in South America were at first quite primitive. For the most part it was enough for the natives to destroy their cult images, or let them be destroyed, in order to receive baptism *en masse*. In this was seen a willingness to accept Christianity; doctrinal and moral instruction was left to later organized pastoral work. It is to be supposed that many of the natives at first understood the reception of baptism as a

464

sign of submission to their new masters, against whom their former rulers and their ancient gods had shown themselves powerless.

In Mexico, Peru, and in general in regions of intensive colonization, baptism was quickly followed by an orderly and effective care of souls. Everywhere, even in the smallest villages, arose schools or at least *doctrinas*, or catechetical centers. There were enough priests engaged in pastoral work. The Inquisition saw to it—and, according to the many extant records, without excessive severity—that the rest of the heathen customs and institutions disappeared. Furthermore, since in these regions there occurred a strong mixture of population as a result of marriages between Spanish born Christians and Indian converts, a fully Christian indigenous population came into existence in a few decades.

In the regions isolated from civilization—really the whole territory outside the relatively small islands of culture—many missionary expeditions were arranged by religious in order to reach the most thinly scattered native population. The missionaries spared themselves no labor and sacrifice; they achieved successes, but usually only temporarily. It was in the isolated districts that contact with the few Europeans did extraordinary damage, because there the Indians came to look upon the European as merely a hostile exploiter and not also as a peaceful harbinger of civilization, as was the case in the regions of organized colonization. Hence, the missionaries inaugurated as early as the sixteenth century a special method, the so-called Reductions.

THE REDUCTIONS

The Reductions were villages in which the Indians wandering in the vicinity were gathered and, under the patriarchal government of the missionaries, with the exclusion of all other

Europeans, were educated with great success in Christian and civilized life. Most celebrated of all were the so-called Jesuit Reductions of Paraguay, which, however, lay partly in the territory of modern Argentina and Brazil. The Jesuits were neither the first nor the only missionaries to employ the method of Reductions. The Reductions had their beginning in Paraguay in 1610, in agreement with the Spanish government, which approved the exclusion of Europeans. At first they had much to endure from the so-called Paulistas, hordes of *mestizos* from the Brazilian colony of São Paulo, who conducted slave hunts on a vast scale. The missionaries termed them "Mamelukes." They finally armed their Indians and in 1641 inflicted on the Paulistas a decisive defeat. Thenceforth the Reductions had peace, but the wildest rumors gained circulation among the Europeans in regard to this inaccessible Jesuit state, which, incidentally, never comprised more than from thirty to thirty-two adjoining Reductions with at most 150,000 Indians. With the expulsion of the Jesuits after the middle of the eighteenth century, the Jesuit Reductions collapsed, and today their ruins are still encountered in the primeval forest. Those of the Franciscans in other districts continued to exist.

Today the Reductions are variously judged by theorists of the missions and by historians. No one denies that in their day they accomplished much that was great; the reports of the morally pure and sincerely pious lives of the Indians on the Reductions are too well-attested. But it is asked whether the Reductions might not have been too artificial and especially why the missionaries obtained no native priesthood to take their places in time. It may perhaps be said that the missionaries acted rather as shepherds of souls, on whom at the moment the salvation of individuals depended, rather than as farseeing politicians. They could hardly foresee that the power

466

of the state, with which they were in complete understanding, would suddenly destroy their work.

If one considers the care of souls as a whole in the colonial period, one can only say that the successes were uncommonly great, however one may judge individual points. If today far more than 100,000,000 Catholics live in Latin America, almost one-third of the universal Church, among whom the heterodox constitute a disappearing minority, the credit is due to the care of souls in the colonial period.

SAINTS AND OTHER OUTSTANDING PERSONALITIES

Among the well-known martyrs of Nagasaki, who in 1597 were the first to suffer death in Japan and were canonized in 1862, was a native Mexican, the Franciscan Philip de las Casas. Also a Franciscan was Sebastián de Aparicio, beatified in 1768. Born in Spain, he came early to Mexico, was for a long time a shipper between the capital and Veracruz, became wealthy and founded a convent of Poor Clares in Mexico, became a friar as a widower at the age of seventy-two, lived in Puebla as a collecting brother, distinguished for his sense of humor and the gift of miracles, like the Capuchin brother, Felix of Cantalice, in Rome, and died almost a centenarian in 1600.

The apparition of the Mother of God at Guadalupe on December 9, 1531, exercised a powerful influence over popular piety in Mexico. The person favored with the apparition was a simple Indian, and the devotion spread first of all among the Indians until it became Mexico's national devotion. In many old Mexican churches are still seen magnificent Guadalupe altars of the Baroque Age, abundantly decorated with sculpture and gold.

New Granada was the scene of the brief but very success-

467

ful missionary activity of Saint Louis Bertrand, a Dominican, who between 1562 and 1569 is said to have baptized 25,000 natives. Another born Spaniard, Saint Peter Claver, was active from 1616 in the port city of Cartagena as apostle of the whites and especially of the negro slaves, who were landed here and then distributed in the interior. With touching devotion, Peter Claver took care of them till his death in 1654. He is one of the heroes of Christian charity, along with Vincent de Paul, Cottolengo, and Damian de Veuster. Hardly inferior to him was another Jesuit, Alonso Sandoval, who, somewhat later than Claver, also worked in behalf of the negroes at Cartagena and in the interior.

Lima had still other saints contemporary with Archbishop Toribio. In 1610 occurred the death of Saint Francis Solano, a Franciscan, who labored long in Peru as an itinerant preacher; in 1617, that of Saint Rose of Lima, a Dominican tertiary. Similar to her was Saint Mariana de Paredes, who died at the age of twenty-seven and is honored beside the "Rose of Lima" as the "Lily of Quito." Among the numerous saintly religious of the period can be mentioned Blessed John Messias (✝1675), a Dominican lay brother; the Jesuit, James Alvárez de Paz, well-known as an ascetical author, who died at Potosí in 1620; and the Oratorian, Miguel de Rivera, who died at Lima in 1680.

A noble, if very controversial, personality was the famous Bartolomé de las Casas. Born at Sevilla in 1474, he came to Haiti in 1502 and became a priest there in 1510. His life's aim was to protect the Indians from exploitation and violence at the hands of the colonists. Seven times during his stormy life he traveled to Spain for this purpose. Cardinal Cisneros conferred special authority upon him. In 1523 he became a Dominican and in 1543 bishop of Chiapa, where, however, he resided only briefly. Las Casas would have been able, with his matchless idealism, to accomplish great things had he not created opposition everywhere because of his vehemence, lack of docility, and extravagances. He expected all salvation from laws and decrees of the Spanish government, which from the beginning was entirely favorable to the Indians. The real difficulties lay in local enforcement, which involved situations the restlessly wandering man was unable to grasp. The complaints and tales of atrocity with which he filled Spain and finally Europe brought upon the Spanish colonizers a partly undeserved evil reputation and were of little service to the Indians. He is still extolled by some historians, particularly non-Catholics, as the "Apostle of humanity," and on the other hand he is often severely taken to task by Spanish and American researchers as one of the chief authors of the "Black Legend."

A zealot of another sort was the Navarrese, Juan de Palafox, bishop of Puebla in Mexico from 1639 to 1654 and later of Osma in Spain, where, well-known as a writer, he died in the reputation of sanctity in 1659. Palafox was an efficient organizer and for a brief time held the position of viceroy, but he had a peculiarity—a passionate antipathy toward all religious and especially toward the Jesuits. There was no end to the conflicts between him and the regular clergy. Around the middle of the seventeenth century such a basic hostility toward the Orders was rather rare. When it became the fashion a century later, people again remembered Palafox and eagerly pushed the cause of his beatification. In the entire activity for the suppression of the Society of Jesus the Palafox cause played quite a role. When, however, the Society had been done away with, interest in Palafox waned, and his canonization has never advanced beyond the introductory stage.

THE ROYAL PATRONAGE

The reconquest of Spain from the Moslems had been interpreted by the entire nation from time immemorial as a religious affair, a crusade. The Spanish kings' struggle to spread God's Kingdom was, even to the popes, something worthy of special consideration. Ferdinand and Isabella had obtained from Innocent VIII the patronage of all ecclesiastical benefices in the yet to be conquered territory of Granada and with it the right to present all holders of ecclesiastical posts, even bishops. The conquest of Granada occurred in 1492 and in the same year Columbus reached the West Indies. The conquest in the New World appeared as the continuation of the reconquest in Spain. In 1508 Julius II extended the right of patronage from Granada to the new conquests; at the time, of course, no one could guess to what dimension they would grow.

Patronage was understood by the Spanish kings, especially Charles V and Philip II, not only as a right but as a heavy responsibility. Philip II regarded himself as the pope's vicar, having the duty of spreading the Faith in the new lands. This idea of the royal vicariate was reduced to theological form at the beginning of the seventeenth century by the canonist Solórzano. The administration of the patronage was connected with the inexorable bureaucratic methods of the Spanish government. All ecclesiastical positions in America, from that of archbishop of Mexico City or of Lima to the lowliest sacristan, were filled by the government. Nuncios and apostolic legates were not admitted, and the Congregation of Propaganda was completely eliminated, even from the missions to the heathens. All protests of Propaganda, even the placing of Solórzano on the Index, were fruitless.

A royal decree of 1629 required of the bishops an oath "at no time and in no way to oppose Our royal patronage."

470

Among other things this meant that the relations of the bishops with Rome could go only through the hands of the Indian council. A particular abuse was the institution of bishops by the government alone, without any canonical confirmation by the pope. They were, to be sure, only "bishops-elect" then, but were nevertheless in full possession of their authority.

On the other hand, it cannot be denied that the crown was always serious about the duties connected with patronage. The external condition of the Church, well-organized and even illustrious, was a result of patronage. So long as a monarch as interested in the salvation of souls as was Philip II stood at the head of affairs, the excessive attachment of the Church to the state machinery was not too harmful. It did not become dangerous until, in the eighteenth century, the government itself became more and more influenced by rationalistic and non-ecclesiastical ideas. The urgent separation of the Church from the tutelage of the state could be effected only amid the most serious crises.

BRAZIL

COLONIZATION

When, by the Treaty of Tordesillas in 1494, the line of demarcation between the Spanish and the Portuguese worlds was established, the existence of Brazil was not yet known; in other words, it was not known that the lands discovered in the Far West, which people took for parts of Asia, pushed a continental flank so far eastward toward Europe that it had to fall within the Portuguese zone. This became clear only as a result of Cabral's expedition in 1500. For the present Portugal was satisfied with indicating its sovereign rights over the newly discovered territory. The establishment of particular cities goes far back—in the north Recife (Pernambuco) in 1525, Bahia

471

in 1549; in the center, Rio, founded by the Portuguese in 1556 and re-established by the French in 1565; and in the south São Vincente in 1532 and São Paulo in 1554. Stronger immigration did not take place until the middle of the seventeenth century, after the Dutch and the French had been finally expelled. Then too, the mother country, counting hardly 2,000,000, had no surplus population to send.

Brazil's center of gravity in the colonial period lay in the north. Here was the capital, São Salvador da Bahia de todos os Santos, residence of the governor, later of the viceroy, till 1763, and seat of the archbishop. At the beginning of the nineteenth century the city of Bahia had 45,000 inhabitants; today it has 300,000. At the end of the sixteenth century the Capitania Bahia counted only 16,000, but by the end of the colonial period it had grown to 200,000. It and the Capitania Pernambuco, comprising 300,000 inhabitants, were around 1800 by far the most populous districts of Brazil. On the other hand, Pará (Belem), founded in 1616, acquired greater importance only in the nineteenth century, after the opening of navigation on the Amazon to all nations in 1867; today it has a population of 236,000.

To the south Rio de Janeiro was always an important harbor. Its importance grew when in 1763 it became the seat of government. But Rio never became a real center of colonization, for it is without a coastal plain and is cut off from the interior by mountains extremely difficult to cross, a circumstance that is not so disadvantageous today. Nevertheless, at the end of the colonial period Rio, with 50,000 inhabitants, was Brazil's largest city and has grown into the modern city of millions.

It was São Paulo that was the real center of colonization in the south. The city of São Paulo, which today has a population of millions, had only 15,000 inhabitants at the beginning of the nineteenth century, and the former port of São Vincente is today of little importance, having been overshadowed by Santos. But it was there that the *mestizo* population of Paulistas, or "Mamelukes," as they were termed by the missionaries, originated. They were wild freebooters who extended their expeditions for hunting slaves far into the interior and into the Paraná region. In the seventeenth century they were the terror of both the Indians and the missionaries, although, especially since in time they spread all over Brazil, they had a prominent share in the colonization of the country. The present large cities of the south, Porto Alegre and Rio Grande do Sul, founded in 1743 and 1747 respectively, did not arise till toward the end of the colonial period.

Until the nineteenth century Brazil was essentially only a long and by no means compact coastal strip, a line of moderately large islands. In the interior there was nowhere a political frontier until in 1750 the Treaty of Madrid marked out a western boundary, at least on the map.

THE CHURCH IN BRAZIL

The Brazilian colony belonged at first to the diocese of Funchal. Only in 1551 was the first see, that of Bahia, established in the country; it was separated from Funchal and subjected to the metropolitan of Lisbon. For more than a century Bahia remained the only bishopric in the colony. In 1676 it was elevated to archiepiscopal rank and at the same time Olinda in the north and Rio in the south were erected as suffragan sees. Once again, almost a century later, in 1745 the two new dioceses of Mariana and São Paulo were established in the vast territory of Rio, which embraced the entire center and south, and in addition the two prelacies of Matto Grosso and Goyaz for the interior. The two northernmost dioceses, São Luiz do Maranhão (1677) and Belem-Pará (1719), were

473

erected as suffragans of Lisbon; they were not united to the then single province of Bahia until 1827.

Pastoral activity and especially the care of the Indians lay for the most part, in Brazil just as in Spanish America, in the hands of religious. The first Franciscans arrived in Brazil as early as 1503, but were soon murdered by natives. Later there were two provinces of Franciscans, Bahia and Rio. At the end of the colonial period, when the number of religious everywhere declined, they still counted 160 members. The Calced Carmelites, with 300 members in three provinces—Bahia, Rio, Pernambuco—were then the strongest Order. The Capuchins, chiefly Italians, who from the beginning of the seventeenth century had displayed great activity, had at the beginning of the eighteenth century dropped to thirty. The Benedictines possessed five abbeys—Bahia, Pernambuco, Rio, São Paulo, Parahyba.

The Jesuits came in 1549. The superior of the mission, Manuel Nobrega, especially promoted the establishment of a local bishopric (Bahia). The Brazilian province of the Order was erected in 1553, and at the death of Saint Ignatius in 1556 comprised only twenty-eight members. Bahia and São Vincente became the chief stations. The visitator, Ignatius de Azevedo, when he was bringing a supply of forty young religious to Brazil in 1570, was captured *en route* by Calvinist pirates and, with all his companions, was murdered; they were beatified in 1854. A group of twelve religious met a similar fate the next year (1571). In 1622 the Jesuit province included 180 members. The most outstanding of the Jesuit missionaries was José de Anchieta, whose name lives on as one of the apostles of Brazil. He was from the Canary Islands and came to Brazil in 1553 at the age of twenty. He was provincial of the Order and missionary, renowned for his knowledge of languages and the gift of miracles; he composed catechisms, songs, dictionaries, and grammars. He died at Retirygba in 1597; the process of his beatification was introduced in 1736.

On the whole, in Brazil the Church grew more slowly than in the Spanish lands, where she had attained her shining hour at the end of the sixteenth and the beginning of the seventeenth century. Portugal's chief interest was directed toward Africa and Asia, and Brazil remained a second-rate colony. However, in Brazil today many ecclesiastical buildings, especially at Bahia and Olinda, recall the colonial period, even if in splendor they are not to be compared with Goa. The difficulties for ecclesiastical life were the same as in the Spanish parts of America. There were officials who supported the missionaries in every way, such as Governor Men de Sa (1537); but in general the complaints in regard to the conduct of the Europeans, such as those sent to the mother country by Nobrega, were as bad as those of Bartolomé de las Casas. In Brazil too, therefore, recourse was had to the system of Reductions (*aldeas*). The first bishop, Pedro Fernandez Sardinha, who came to Bahia in 1552, was good, but the clergy whom he brought along from the homeland spoiled everything. In 1556 the bishop fell into the hands of the Indians, who ate him. Just as in the Spanish territories, so too in Brazil patronage operated unfavorably by providing almost all the bishops from Portugal. At the beginning of the nineteenth century, of all the prelates of Brazil only the occupant of Goyaz was native-born.

NORTH AMERICA

In comparison with the Spanish colonies, where as early as the sixteenth century we find a Catholic population counted by the millions with a pastoral organization in the European style, the origins of the Church in North America were exceedingly humble.

CANADA

In French Canada, which, by virtue of the almost exclusively Catholic immigration, gave promise of becoming a Catholic country, the lack was neither in priests nor in missionary ardor, but in inhabitants. Around the middle of the seventeenth century there were still not 4,000 colonists. The Indian tribes were small, great as was the trouble they caused the colonists. The famous Hurons are mentioned in 1639 as amounting to 12,000 in thirty-two villages, but at that time almost all of them were heathens.

The first Jesuits came to Canada in 1611, followed by quite a large number of Franciscans, the Capuchins in 1630, and the Sulpicians in 1640. Quebec, founded in 1608, received a vicar apostolic in 1658 and became a bishopric in 1674. It remained until the end of the eighteenth century the only see in North America.

In 1639 the Ursulines came to Quebec from Tours, under the leadership of the Venerable Marie de l'Incarnation. This outstanding woman, one of the great mystics of modern times, merits a place of honor among the pioneers of the Faith in the new world. No less famous are the Jesuit missionaries, Isaac Jogues, Brébeuf, Lallemand, and others, who died for the Faith in the mission field between 1646 and 1649 and were canonized in 1930. They are known as the Canadian martyrs, though the localities of their activity lie today in the territory of the United States for the most part. The number of Indians converted by these and other heralds of the Faith was quite small in this very sparsely populated country.

THE ENGLISH COLONIES

The first group of Catholic immigrants came to the newly founded colony of Maryland in 1634, accompanied by two

Jesuits. The Catholic[3] founder of the colony, Cecil Calvert, son of the convert Lord Baltimore, sent his brother Leonard at the head of the band. The governor erected chapels for Catholics and Protestants and practiced toleration. Later laws of the colony forbade Catholic edifices of worship in Maryland. The Jesuits had to furnish chapels in their private dwellings. Liturgical books could not be printed. The Fathers prepared manuscript missals, examplars of which still exist.

The Catholics in Maryland belonged to the jurisdiction of the vicar apostolic of London. He reported to Propaganda in 1756 that in Maryland there were some 4,000 communicants and in Pennsylvania 2,000, who were cared for by sixteen Jesuits. Some years later he estimated the Catholics in the two colonies at more than 20,000. In the other colonies there were at most isolated bands of Catholics. Catholic priests could not stop even temporarily in New York.

When in 1760 the French army at Montreal capitulated, the governor of Canada, the marquis de Vandreuil, made religious toleration of the Catholics who were to come under English rule a condition of surrender. The English government gave this promise likewise in the peace of 1763, whereby all of Canada and Louisiana to the Mississippi fell to England. Hence, the English colonies obtained an increase of almost 100,000 Catholics, distributed over Canada and the present states of Ohio, Indiana, Illinois, Michigan, and Wisconsin.

The English government not only kept its agreement in regard to toleration but in 1774 in the Quebec Act gave to the Catholic communities in the newly acquired lands the right of juridical personality. This did not, however, prevent the expropriation and dispersal of the small Catholic communities

[3] In the German text (p. 319) it is stated that Cecil Calvert was not a Catholic. This is an error. The English translation has added the reference to Leonard Calvert. (Translator's note.)

founded earlier in the south by the Spaniards at Natchez, Mobile, Saint Augustine, and Pensacola.

Among the intransigent Protestants in the older colonies the Quebec Act stirred up a storm of indignation and became a chief occasion for the outbreak in 1775 of the War for Independence.[4] From the American viewpoint it was a misfortune that the movement for independence had an anti-Catholic note of this sort, for Canada was thereby alienated from the American cause. Canada, mostly Catholic, only recently English, and hence bound to that country by no tradition, would doubtless have joined in the movement for independence, had it not been repelled by the coarse baiting of Catholics as this was staged especially at New York by John Jay and his associates.

The leaders of the independence movement, the Congress and Washington himself, realized this. Washington had hardly assumed the command before Boston when he abolished Pope Day, a malicious anti-Catholic celebration in memory of the Gunpowder Plot. When Benjamin Franklin went to Quebec in 1776 to obtain at least the neutrality of Canada, he took with him a priest, John Carroll, a native American descended from a distinguished English family, who later became first bishop of Baltimore. Carroll, in conversations with the bishop of Quebec and the Canadian clergy, was given to understand that it was too late.

The War of Independence was waged with varying success until finally in 1781 Washington succeeded in inclosing the English supreme commander, Lord Cornwallis, in Yorktown and in forcing his capitulation. After difficult negotiations peace was concluded at Paris in 1783. Canada remained English; the United States acquired the country as far as the Mis-

---

[4] Though it is true that the Quebec Act did cause great indignation among the American Protestant colonists, Father Hertling overemphasizes its influence on the origin of the Revolutionary War; it was only one of several contributing factors. (Translator's note.)

sissippi; Florida, the southern coast, and the territory beyond the Mississippi remained Spanish.

The constitutions of the individual states of the Union were at first still quite intolerant. In New Hampshire no Catholic could be governor, senator, or member of the assembly. In New Jersey and the two Carolinas Catholics were excluded from all state offices. In New York they could not even possess civic rights. At first only Pennsylvania, Delaware, Maryland, and Virginia granted to Catholics full equality before the law.

Even though the anti-Catholic mood did not disappear, such laws could not be maintained after the war for the freedom and full equality of all Americans had been fought. Catholics were helped by the fact that the first European powers to recognize the new Union were Catholic France in 1778 and Catholic Spain in 1779. Their envoys and the chaplains of their forces publicly celebrated Catholic worship in places where it had hitherto been unknown. The constitution of 1787 prescribed in Article VI that civic rights were not to be made dependent on religion. The Congress of 1789 decreed separation of Church and state, which in this case was not, as was mostly true elsewhere, synonymous with confiscation of ecclesiastical property, but rather meant real freedom for Catholics. In addition, the Congress of 1791 granted full freedom of press, speech, and assembly.

For the Catholics of the United States, then numbering about 18,000 and hitherto belonging to the Vicariate Apostolic of London, the Holy See established a special vicariate apostolic, which as early as 1789 was transformed into the see of Baltimore. The first bishop was the Jesuit, John Carroll.

RETROSPECT

The establishment and spread of the Church in America

meant not only the achieving of an instantaneous missionary success but the beginning of a complete transformation of the geography of the Church. The European circle had been broken and the way was open to the world Church; furthermore, a greater equilibrium of peoples within the Church was prepared for. Since the early Middle Ages almost always one nation or state had played a leading role in the Church—Germany, France, Spain, and again France. From the time that there were Catholic multitudes also on the other side of the Atlantic, the preponderance of particular European nations ceased, and in its place appeared a certain equal interchange and competition of all. Today a good third of all Catholics reside in the two American continents, and yet it cannot be said that the Church's center of gravity has shifted to America. Today the Church is no longer attached to a geographical center, as was true of the Middle Ages.

Contemporaneous with the rise of Catholic populations in America began the missionary advance toward South Asia, chiefly under Portuguese leadership. But here the circumstances were quite different, so that almost nowhere was it possible to build up Catholic populations as in America. Even today South Asia, though no longer a pioneering land, is still a *diaspora*. Only a small fragment of the total Catholic population lives in Asia. Whereas America today sends out missionaries in all directions, Asia is still dependent on reinforcements from outside. In one respect, of course, the Asiatic missions have exercised since the sixteenth century a strong influence on European Church History: they have kindled in Europe enthusiasm for the missions and have kept it alive. The increase of religious vocations among the Catholic youth in the sixteenth and seventeenth centuries and still more in the nineteenth is connected with this missionary enthusiasm.

480

the french revolution

THE spiritual currents which pervaded wide circles in the eighteenth century, especially its second half, were basically nothing other than a continuation of humanism. Whatever they were called—*Aufklärung* in Germany, rationalism in England, *lumières* in France, *illuminismo* in Italy—the psychological root was the same. The realistic conception of the world, only suspected by the humanists of the fifteenth century and sketched with wholly inadequate means, was constructed into a real *Weltanschauung* by the rationalists of the eighteenth century on the foundation of the study of nature, which had meanwhile made great progress. To humanism religion had appeared as unreal, as a myth. The *Aufklärung* not only separated knowledge derived from reason and knowledge derived from Faith, but rejected knowledge derived from Faith as utterly unreasonable.

THE FATHERS OF THE AUFKLÄRUNG

It might be asked why the *Aufklärung* came so late and not as a direct connection with humanism. In part the reason is that the religious struggles of the sixteenth century distracted men's minds from the basic problems of philosophy. Here as elsewhere in history one must beware of assuming necessary, inevitable developments. The *Aufklärung* was brought about,

481

like all spiritual movements, by individual men. Prepared by the English natural philosophers and epistemologists, Lord Herbert (✝1648), Thomas Hobbes (✝1679), and John Locke (✝1704), it simultaneously acquired an intellectual and an anti-religious form in France. Here the Protestant Pierre Bayle (✝1706), whose much-published *Dictionnaire historique et critique* first appeared in 1697, can be regarded as its founder. The polygraphic trend which is peculiar to the French *Aufklärung* is still more prominent in the great *Encyclopédie* (1751–1780) of d'Alembert (✝1783) and Diderot (✝1784). Independent thinkers were Montesquieu (✝1755), who by virtue of his *De l'esprit des lois* (1748) can be looked upon as the founder of the idea of the liberal state, and Rousseau (✝1778), the philosophical forerunner of the great Revolution. Voltaire (✝1778), in whom rejection of religion became a wild hatred, was rather a poet and publicist than a philosopher. In addition to French wit, a definite superficiality and shallowness characterized almost all the philosophers of the *Aufklärung*. Instead of solutions to the ultimate problems of life, they frequently offered only banalities in an ingenious form. Philosophical thought was hardly enriched by them. Only Kant (✝1804), who was at first influenced by rationalism but eventually went his own way, made a real contribution to speculative thought.

Among the cultured public, even in Catholic circles, the *Aufklärung* became a system of catchwords, a fashion. Everything dripped with reason, universal love of mankind, and religious toleration. Disbelief was called reason and the immoral was termed natural. In practice there was little to be seen of universal love of mankind, and religious toleration expressed itself in a real hatred of the Church and her institutions, especially the monasteries. The change was astonishing. In the seventeenth century it had been fashionable to have an austere religious as spiritual director and to converse in the salons on the efficacy of grace; in the eighteenth it was the correct thing to be Voltairian and to poke fun at priests and monks. Only the cultured arrogance remained the same.

THE STRUGGLE AGAINST THE JESUITS

The spirit of the new age sought a field of activity and found it in the fight against the Jesuit Order, which was looked upon as the incarnation of ecclesiastical Catholicism. In this lay a strange delusion, for the Jesuit Order was far from having the power and influence ascribed to it. Around the middle of the eighteenth century the Society of Jesus counted 22,000 members, half of whom were novices, clerics pursuing studies, and lay brothers. Of the priests a considerable number lived as missionaries in countries beyond the sea. The struggle against the Turks in its most perilous period had not so occupied ministers and diplomats as did now the suppressing of this Order, which was only one of many. With amazement one learns that even in Rome, at regularly held meetings attended by high-ranking prelates, plans were elaborated against the Order.

The occasions and pretexts for the suppression of the Order differed from state to state. In Portugal the opportunity came from the fact that the Indians of South Brazil had taken up arms to prevent the razing of the Reductions; in Spain, it was a conspiracy against the king, which no one really believed in; in France, the bankruptcy of the procurator of the Jesuit Mission on Martinique, for which the whole Order was held responsible without its being allowed to cover the deficit. Portugal had the Jesuits loaded onto ships, when they were not imprisoned, and conveyed to the Papal State (1759). The Spanish Jesuits were put ashore on Corsica, because the pope

483

refused a second such disembarkation in the Papal State. In France the Order was suppressed in 1762 by a state decree, but the individuals were allowed to remain in the country as secular priests.

The Society of Jesus still existed in Germany, Austria, parts of Eastern Europe, and Italy. Empress Maria Theresa loved the Order and opposed its expulsion from the state. Hence, the governments pressed for a general suppression of the Order by the pope. Maria Theresa, who in 1770 had married her daughter, Marie Antoinette, to the heir to the French throne, did not wish to incur the displeasure of the allied Western powers and gave her consent. Thereupon Clement XIV decreed the ecclesiastical dissolution of the entire Order in 1773. The general of the Order, Ricci, was imprisoned in the Castel Sant' Angelo, where he died in 1775. The goods of the Order, which were far less valuable than had been expected, were for the most part squandered.

The suppression was a moral defeat for the papacy and resulted in great gaps in missionary countries and in Europe in regard to the care of souls, particularly in the education of youth. Both then and later Clement XIV was severely blamed. However, it is difficult to see what else he could have done. The allied governments of Portugal, Spain, Naples, and France were definitely determined to go to the extreme limit. Clement XIV was no prophet and thus could not know that within a few years the great Revolution would overthrow all these governments. Incidentally, as was later to appear, the suppression was a fortunate thing for the Society of Jesus. In the nineteenth century it could rise again, surrounded with the halo of martyrdom. The other Orders, which suffered scarcely less severely during the general upheaval, had to start over again without this aura.

484

THE LAST POPES BEFORE THE REVOLUTION

The blind Clement XII was succeeded by Benedict XIV (1740–1758), Prospero Lambertini. He was an outstanding scholar, canonist, and historian, and his works on the canonization of saints and on the diocesan synod are still highly esteemed. Benedict XIV had an extremely amiable and gay nature, not entirely free from that harmless vanity which is not rarely found in highly cultured Italians. He strove by his willingness to oblige, his personal prestige, and friendly gestures to halt the assaults of the increasingly hostile governments and of the rationalists standing behind them. He went so far as to exchange courtesies with Voltaire. He at least achieved this, that he was himself extolled by rationalists and non-Catholics—not exactly the highest honor for a pope—but actually he obtained little of value. Nevertheless, Benedict XIV surrendered no essential points and by his skill considerably raised the moral esteem of the Holy See, which had been at a very low ebb for a century.

Under Benedict XIV the fight against the Society of Jesus came more and more into the foreground. Benedict, who regarded the Order highly, considered it expedient not to defend it publicly and even made a few anti-Jesuit gestures. His successor, the Venetian Rezzonico, Clement XIII (1758–1769), went the opposite way. He issued a bull in which he praised the Order before the whole world and renewed its confirmation. His entire pontificate was filled with the struggle against the Jesuits. But all his firmness could not prevent the suppression of the Order in Portugal, Spain, Naples, and France. In the conclave following his death the question of the Jesuits played the decisive role. The pressure of the governments on the cardinals was scandalous. Finally, the Conventual Franciscan Lorenzo Ganganelli was elected as Clement XIV (1769–1774); to him the governments looked for the

485

suppression of the Jesuits, although he had refused to give an express promise as a condition of his election, as had been expected of him. In fact, for over three years he withstood the violent pressure of the governments, especially that of the Spanish ambassador, Monino. When in 1773 he finally signed the brief of suppression, he was already broken in body and soul. His successor was Gian Angelo Braschi, who became Pius VI.

PIUS VI (1775–1799)

With the suppression of the Jesuit Order a political relaxation actually occurred, and the new pope could enjoy a few peaceful years. But it was like a dull sunset after a brief thunderstorm, which was to be followed by a far greater storm during the night. The city of Rome again experienced a sort of glittering age. Visits to Italy had become fashionable and enthusiasm for antiquity reawakened. As never before the pope could receive in Rome princes and other prominent guests without distinction of religion. The pope himself was a devotee of antiquity. He is the real creator of the Vatican Museum of Antiquities. In 1763 he summoned the famed Winckelman, who had become a Catholic in 1754, to be superintendent of all antiquities.

In 1782 the pope decided to travel to Vienna in order, by a personal interview, to dissuade Emperor Joseph II from his ever more arbitrary ecclesiastical reforms. The journey, the stay in Vienna, and the return trip by way of Munich had the appearance of a triumphal tour. People flocked from everywhere to see the pope and receive his blessing. But the trip did not achieve its goal. The emperor did not fail in attentiveness and the next year returned the visit at Rome. Once again it was shown that the Catholic governments were always ready to overwhelm the pope with honors, but for the rest they intended to act in the Church as though he did not exist.

Still, Pius VI endeavored to carry out his pastoral functions so far as he could. After the outbreak of the French Revolution he condemned in 1791 the Civil Constitution of the Clergy and in 1794 the strongly Jansenist Synod of Pistoia. Then came the end. The troops of the Revolution overran the Papal State. In 1797 Pius VI had to conclude the humiliating peace of Tolentino, which bankrupted him. In the following year he was dragged from Rome; at first he was taken here and there in Italy and finally was carried to France, where, already an old man of eighty-two, he succumbed at Valence to the sufferings of his journey. It seemed as though the waves of the Revolution had swallowed up the papacy.

THE FRENCH REVOLUTION

The social revolution with which the eighteenth century ended and the nineteenth began was one of the most decisive events that had hitherto occurred in the world. It is to be expected that the historical writing of later centuries will extend the Middle Ages to the French Revolution and only then have the modern period begin. This is the more to be expected because, contemporaneously with the social revolution in Europe, the American countries freed themselves politically from Europe, and thus history, which hitherto had been almost exclusively European, became world history.

Neither the political nor the social revolution was aimed directly and chiefly at the Catholic Church. But the Church so stood in the very midst of general occurrences that, like the states, she had to endure the most violent shocks. Her position was so grievously damaged that in many fields she had, in a sense, to begin over. At the same time, however, she became free of several bonds which had hitherto checked her development.

THE EVENTS IN FRANCE

The state of the French public finances, already seriously thrown into confusion under Louis XIV (1643–1715), had been even more intolerable under the long misgovernment of Louis XV (1715–1774). In order to introduce a reorganization, Louis XVI in 1789 decided to convoke the States General, which had not met since 1614. A few years earlier, in 1783, peace between England and the new American Union had been concluded at Versailles, with the general recognition by the European powers of a state based entirely on democratic foundations. The French States General declared itself the Constituent National Assembly after this model. In August, 1789, the Declaration of the Rights of Man was proclaimed and a frenzy of democratic enthusiasm seized the whole nation. On the motion of the bishop of Autun, Talleyrand, all ecclesiastical goods were declared state property (November, 1789), which was equivalent to a wholesale robbery at the Church's expense. Almost all social explosions follow the law of least resistance and hence at the beginning take a course hostile to the Church. If it had been hoped by voluntary renunciation of the property to bring the National Assembly into a channel less unfriendly to the Church, this proved to be a delusion. In February, 1790, the Orders were abolished; in July, fifty-one of the 134 bishoprics; and it was decreed that priests and bishops were to be elected by their congregations. The anti-ecclesiastical laws were united in the Civil Constitution of the Clergy and an oath in regard to them was required of the clergy. Of the bishops, five took the oath; out of some 100,000 priests, about one-third complied, but of these many later disavowed the act, when in April, 1791, the pope declared the oath unlawful. The National Assembly proceeded against the non-juring priests with force. By April, 1793, more than 3,600 of them had been imprisoned and exiled, mostly to Cayenne. Some 40,000 left the country. In many places they gave edification by their religious behavior and were received very cordially not only in Catholic lands, but even in England, where about 4,000 found refuge. This was not without importance for the revival of the Catholic Church in England. In September, 1792, over and above other prisoners, 191 non-juring priests, among them three bishops, were murdered. They were beatified as martyrs in 1926.

The worst period was under the National Convention (1792–1795). Christianity, even its calendar with Sundays and feasts, was abolished by law. In the desecrated churches a ridiculous cult of reason was introduced with disgusting ceremonies. The rule of the Directory (1795–1799) brought some improvement. The oath of priests to the Civil Constitution was no longer demanded. Many priests who had hitherto hid themselves could again begin publicly to hold divine worship. But in 1797 there were new deportations of priests to Cayenne. Meanwhile the political rule of revolutionary France had expanded ever farther by means of the victorious "Coalition Wars" (1792–1797 and 1799–1802). Holland, Belgium, the entire left bank of the Rhine, Switzerland, North Italy, and Naples were, one after another, either incorporated into France or transformed into dependent republics. By the Treaty of Tolentino (February, 1797) the pope had to cede Ferrara, Bologna, and the Romagna, and pay the sum of 35,000,000 francs, which was impossible at the time for a small state. Nevertheless, the next year Rome was occupied, a republic proclaimed, and the octogenarian pope, Pius VI, was first carried around as a prisoner in North Italy and finally, a dying man, was brought over the Alps to Valence, where he succumbed on August 22, 1799.

PIUS VII (1800–1823)

The new pope, Pius VII, a Benedictine, was elected at Venice under Austrian protection. Rarely has a pontificate begun under such hopeless auspices. The pope had nothing— no money, no capital, scarcely even a connection with the churches. But he had an extraordinarily capable secretary of state, Ercole Consalvi. At first some hope appeared. Napoleon, First Consul since 1799, exhibited a desire for a concordat. It came into being in July, 1801, with quite unusual conditions. France received a new arrangement of dioceses, which numbered sixty. All previous bishops had to resign. Some of them could, however, be again appointed. The right of nomination belonged to the consul, as formerly to the king. The Church renounced the goods secularized in 1789, and the state undertook to pay the salaries of the clergy. A series of points, which the pope did not and could not concede, were added by Napoleon unilaterally to the concordat as the "Organic Articles"; among them were the *placet* of the government for ecclesiastical decrees, the obliging of teachers in the higher schools to the Gallican Articles of 1682, and the recourse from the spiritual to the temporal court. A like concordat, arranged in 1803 with the Italian Republic, was marred by similar unilateral additions. The pope protested, but in 1804 he went to Paris for the imperial coronation on which Napoleon set great value, for thereby his emperorship acquired the appearance of legitimacy. When he no longer needed the pope, he dispensed with all further regard for him. In 1806 he compelled him to dismiss Consalvi. In February, 1806, Rome had been occupied by French troops, and in May, 1809, Rome and the Papal State were annexed to the French Empire. There-

490

upon Pius VII excommunicated Napoleon. The emperor had him arrested at the Quirinal and brought to Savona; the cardinals were taken to Paris. In Savona Pius VII was treated as a prisoner. During the Russian campaign he was interned at Fontainebleau near Paris. There, after his return from the army in January, 1813, Napoleon negotiated for a new concordat, which involved a renunciation of the Papal State by the pope. Pius VII, without advisers and under the most inconsiderate pressure from Napoleon, consented. When later the cardinals were allowed to advise him, he realized that he had gone too far and withdrew his consent. Napoleon had him brought back to Savona. When, in March, 1814, the allies were nearing Paris, he was set free and could return to Rome.

THE SECULARIZATION IN GERMANY

In the peace of Lunéville in 1801 the entire left bank of the Rhine was ceded to France. With this the three spiritual electorates of Mainz, Cologne, and Trier ceased to exist. In exchange for their surrendered territories the temporal princes were presented with the prospects of compensation from the Church's possessions and the imperial cities. The negotiations on this subject led in February, 1803, to the decree of the imperial Diet of Regensburg, which went much farther than had been agreed upon at Lunéville. All spiritual principalities and lordships in the Empire, including more than 200 monasteries, were distributed among the temporal princes. Thereby the individual states received much more than they had lost on the left bank of the Rhine—Prussia five times more, Bavaria seven times more. The revenues of which the Church in Germany was thus deprived are estimated at 21,000,000 florins annually, and the monastic goods are not included in this figure. Much of value, even works of art and, especially, monastic libraries, was in this way dissipated. Resistance was hardly noticed.

The secularization of 1803 was as momentous an event as the expropriation of ecclesiastical goods in France in 1789. The damage to the German Church was great. It is, indeed, true that the sovereignty of the spiritual princes and the really vast wealth of the Church were not an ideal situation. In the German clergy, particularly the higher ranks, there was much that was unspiritual. But one may not hold that the clergy were trained into pious shepherds of souls through the spoliation of their goods. The secularization caused a host of charitable institutes to perish, especially Catholic schools, including eighteen of university rank. The consequence was that among the German Catholics a strong lack of education was noticeable until after the middle of the nineteenth century. Through the secularization the Protestants acquired a political preponderance that did not correspond to their actual numbers. Of the princes who formed the German Confederation and later the new German Empire only two were Catholics, the kings of Bavaria and Saxony. Millions of Catholics who until now had lived under Catholic governments came, as a result of the secularization, under Protestant sovereignty; the reverse was much less common. Furthermore, for the moment the ecclesiastical organization was to a great extent destroyed. Until 1814 only five of the German sees were occupied.

The worst thing, however, not only for the Church, was the dreadful example of a complete disregard of rights by the states. It was not in the era of princely absolutism but in the succeeding age of the Revolution that the state learned to stretch out its hand for the property of its subjects. To this extent, the Revolution begins the epoch of the ever growing omnipotence of the state, from the results of which mankind is still suffering. The struggle against this omnipotence of the state and for the rights of the individual became from then on one of the weightiest tasks of the Church.

the nineteenth century

THE external course of Church history in the nineteenth century was in great measure determined by the entirely altered concept of the state. The Church, of course, is not dependent on the state in her inner life. In every country she can develop under any reasonable form of state and any proper method of government. But since she operates in the same geographical space as the state, and since the same men are the object of her care as of the state's, and since she furthermore possesses no physical means of power for making her way—or, in comparison with the state, only dwindling and slight means—the actual attitude of the state is for her, not indeed of decisive, but of great significance.

This was at least the fourth time that the Church encountered a new idea of the state. The ancient Roman Empire had been a bureaucratic and military state, a single state embracing the entire known world. At bottom, however, it had been only an administrative machinery which was comparatively involved. It had been replaced in the Middle Ages by the princely feudal system, into which ecclesiastical functions had been incorporated to a degree that was not, perhaps, ideal. The fifteenth and sixteenth centuries introduced the territorial states, countries with only one prince at their head, who through his officials ruled his territory, his property, in a fully independent manner.

THE NEW CONCEPT OF THE STATE

An entirely new concept of the state resulted from the French Revolution and the formation of the American republics. No longer did the dynasty constitute the state, but the country and its population became the formative elements. The population gives itself its constitution and thus creates the state, monarchical or republican, and this state now comes forth, *vis-à-vis* the population, as a creation endowed with a life of its own. It is in reality an abstraction rather than a physical person, as was the mediaeval prince; but life and activity are attributed to it, as to a physical person. The inhabitants of the country are the state, but the individual is the subject of the state, exactly as, or even more than, he was previously the subject of the prince.

In this new concept of the state lay the roots of state omnipotence and nationalism, the two dominant factors governing most recent history. Quite some time elapsed, of course, before all the consequences of this notion were realized. In Europe it does not really confront us in its full development until after the revolution of 1848.

THE WILL OF THE PEOPLE

Every sovereign power consists of three elements: the legislative, the judiciary, and the administrative or executive authority. None of these three functions can actually be exercised by the totality of the population, but only by individuals in accordance with the will of the whole. The fundamental problem of every kind of democracy consists, therefore, in the manner of expressing the will of the people, or rather in the manner of determining this. First of all, the mass of people has as many wills as there are individuals constituting it. If one takes as his criterion the majority, that is, if one regards as the will of the people that on which an absolute or a relative majority agrees, this already implies a limitation of the concept "democracy," because then not the will of the whole people dominates, but a greater or lesser number of individual persons, more or less opposed by others, who are of another will.

The entire nineteenth century was dominated by the impulse to establish the mere number of votes as a determining principle. Rights of voting were developed partially according to this tendency in the individual countries. In the constitutions originating or modified immediately after 1848 parliamentary elections were still for the most part indirect; that is, the primary electors chose the so-called delegates, who in turn elected the legislators. There were also rights of voting according to classes, in which the votes of the electors who had to bear more responsibility and a heavier burden of taxation had more weight. Likewise, elections were generally based on the regional principle—each legislator came from a local voting center. In such a way it was hoped that the real will of the population could be ascertained and that thereby the momentary mood of the irresponsible masses could be prevented from deciding the issue. The same end was envisaged by the bicameral system of government that was established in almost all states. In time these limitations disappeared and made way for voting methods that were based even more on arithmetical sums.

At first, individual personages well-known to the voters were elected to the legislative bodies; these did not unite into groups or parties until they had entered the chamber. Only toward the end of the nineteenth century did the parties become permanent organizations, no longer of legislators but of the voters. Finally, it was not the legislators but the party lists that were elected. In this way the original democratic idea was transformed into its opposite. No longer was it the people who ruled through men sent to Parliament by confident electors, but rather the party leadership, to which the voters as well as the individual legislators had to submit.

From this to the exercise of power by the party leadership was only a step. In states originally governed by democratic methods, it now became possible to take the further step to party terror and party dictatorship, in which ultimately the decision no longer depended on the number of party members but on the maneuvering powers of the organization in question. Minority party dictatorships were not unusual in both South America and Europe.

STATE OMNIPOTENCE

If, through the parliamentary system, the Church was confronted with entirely new problems, the development of the state's omnipotence, likewise a nineteenth-century phenomenon, complicated them even more.

The two were related. It is an irony of history that those who imagined they were fighting for the liberty of mankind, and for this reason called themselves liberals, actually forged the chains of the state from which mankind was to endure so much suffering. And today it is just as ironical when we hear how the liberals of a century ago unceasingly accused the Church of enslaving peoples and individuals and conscience. As a matter of fact, Catholics in general were very hard pressed to maintain, in the presence of the liberal state, their right "to be saved in their own way" and not to be dictated to in all the details of their patriotic convictions by governments which, one after another, were constantly altering such patriotic notions.

The modern states brought more and more tasks within the sphere of their legislation and administration. In this way the Church was indirectly concerned in many areas, especially when there was a question of marriage, the family, the school and education, and welfare work. The Church was directly touched when the states proceeded to regulate ecclesiastical property, ecclesiastical organization, and the care of souls in the strict sense.

Some of this was not new to the nineteenth century. In the epoch of princely absolutism the Church had had to fight continuously for her freedom to fill pastoral offices. In this regard the new circumstances even brought an alleviation. But on the whole the Church was more and more compelled to fight against governments that were drawing everything into their own sphere. It was not alone a struggle to preserve and protect rights pertaining to the care of souls. Often the bare possibility of performing any parochial work at all was at stake.

This situation was aggravated by a far-reaching change in the notion of right and justice. The nineteenth century was quite plainly a juristic century. Perhaps in no other age did juridical scholarship so flourish, was there so much attention devoted to the administration of justice, was there such a profusion of legislative activity displayed. But the nineteenth century was all too prone to mistake legality for justice. People got into the habit of not asking whether governments possessed a right to their measures so long as these measures took place within the frame of the constitution and were voted by a majority of the chamber. Hence, in the most juristic of all centuries acts of injustice and even of violence could appear, such as not even the barbaric times of the early Middle Ages had known: unilateral cancellations of concordats and treaties that had recently been solemnly entered into, violent expropriation of the goods of the Church, suppression of religious

497

communities, expulsion of clerics, punitive measures because of pastoral activities—all in the name of law.

The result of all this was that in most countries during the nineteenth century the Church found herself in a struggle, sometimes open, sometimes latent, with the constantly changing parties and the governments set up or supported by them. This does not mean that the Church pursued a definite political program of her own. At most it can be said that the Church inclined in politics toward a more conservative tendency and in general desired the preservation of the existing situation. Usually, even a hostile government becomes in time more accessible to peaceful considerations, and the Church can arrive at a *modus vivendi* with it. In violent revolutions, on the contrary, experience teaches that the stability of the Church is usually injured.

POLITICAL CHARACTER OF THE CATHOLICS

Although the Church has no political program, except that she wants to be able to maintain her rights, nevertheless, as ever wider circles of the population were authorized and compelled to participate in political life in the nineteenth century, there developed in the Catholics of the individual countries an attitude of agreement on many issues, in a sense a definite political character. Originally, the Catholics were usually on the side of authority. Only when state governments adopted an attitude of hostility to the Church did the Catholics see themselves forced, entirely against their will, into an attitude of opposition, which expressed itself more by annoyance and aloofness than in an active or violent resistance. In political life the Catholic often has something of the narrow-minded, the coxcomb, the timid about him. He loves his religion and its customs, his family, his home, his country, but he would prefer to be left in peace. He avoids conflicts. In the countries in which political parties representing the interests of the Church were formed, it was for the most part less difficult to convince the Catholics of the correctness and necessity of such a program than to bring them to the ballot boxes on the specified day. The Catholic is prone to trust fine words and promises. If an anti-clerical government makes little friendly gestures, he believes everything is again all right. But his endurance has limits too. State omnipotence, the endeavor of governments to regulate everything, is repugnant to him. When aroused he can give proof of the most tenacious opposition. It was characteristic that in the United States during the long struggle concerning the state's prohibition of alcohol the Catholics were usually against prohibition, not from ethical considerations and even more not from dipsomania, but from instinct. They did not want their private affairs dictated by the state.

In many countries, if not in most of them, state governments gave Catholics a fundamentally wrong treatment, though there was scarcely a part of the population which would have been easier to govern. This was connected with the extreme notion of the state and of nationalism, proper to the nineteenth century. National pride and megalomania replaced love of home and country. In politics it was often not the country's advantage but its prestige that was decisive—in colonial policy, commercial policy, and often even within individual branches of the economic system. Hence also the effort of states to control as far as possible the education of youth. In the textbooks prescribed by governments the ideas of national unity and freedom, of power and fame and glory, were hammered into the children, often with ridiculously untrue statements. Because of this mentality, the Catholic Church appeared to many governments as a foreign and therefore hostile power. The activity of the Church seemed to them an interference from without, which offended national vanity. The Catholics of the country seemed like a national minority, an *Irredenta*, which gravitated around a foreign political center. Some regarded as a national humiliation the need of concluding, or even of negotiating, treaties with "Rome."

All this was, of course, a false view, and accordingly the treatment of Catholics as nationally unreliable or suspicious elements was thoroughly wrong and not only unjust but also contrary to the interest of the state. There were, it is true, in all countries individual Catholics, weak souls, who reacted to this pressure of mind with excessive allegiance and sought at every opportunity to conduct themselves as one-hundred percent nationalists. The majority did not allow themselves to become confused in their patriotism and loyalty, but they did become anxious and angry.

POLITICAL HAPPENINGS IN PARTICULAR COUNTRIES

On the whole, almost always the same performance was repeated in the several countries in the nineteenth century: as soon as an extreme liberal government came into power, ecclesiastical property was confiscated, religious Orders were expelled, bishops were annoyed, freedom of instruction was restricted. When a more moderate ministry was again in control, the Holy See, usually on the surrender of some advantages, concluded a concordat, which was then violated by the next liberal government.

PORTUGAL

In Portugal it was at first a struggle for the throne which let loose a regular persecution. When in 1826 King João VI, a product of the age of Pombal, died, his oldest son, Pedro, emperor of Brazil since 1822, renounced his right to the Portuguese throne in favor of his seven-year-old daughter, Maria da

500

Gloria. By so doing he infringed on the right of succession of his brother, Miguel, who was friendly with the Church and whom the majority of the population supported. With foreign help Dom Pedro succeeded in expelling his brother in 1834. The regency for Maria da Gloria, regarding the Church as Miguel's ally, imprisoned priests, deposed bishops, confiscated Church property, and suppressed all monasteries of men. Maria, having assumed the government, restored relations with the Holy See in 1840, but died in 1853. The anti-clerical ministries lasted longer. A concordat concluded in 1857 was not even published. In 1862 Pius IX admonished the bishops on account of their weakness vis-à-vis the government. Only two of them appeared at the Vatican Council. Toward the end of the century the situation of the Church improved. But in 1908 King Carlos I was murdered; in 1910 his successor, Manuel II, was exiled, and the new republic immediately began with the expulsion of the Jesuits, the confiscation of ecclesiastical goods, the so-called separation of Church and state, and the excesses usual in such cases. In 1913 diplomatic relations with the Holy See were broken off.

SPAIN

The liberal and somewhat anti-clerical constitution of the Cortes of Cádiz (1812) had not been put into operation in the country, which was in the hands of the French. When in 1814 Fernando VII returned, he abolished it, but in 1820 he was compelled by a revolution to restore it. The constitutional government forced upon him expelled the Jesuits, whose Order had only recently been restored, confiscated Church property, and severely penalized priests who refused to take the oath of loyalty. The king, it is true, succeeded in once again restoring the absolute authority of the crown, but after his death in 1833 a new revolution broke out, aggravated by

501

civil war over the royal succession. The struggle was similar to the contemporary one in Portugal. Though Fernando had named as his successor his three-year-old daughter, Isabella, his brother, Don Carlos, claimed the crown as the nearest male heir. Don Carlos had many supporters, especially in the strongly Catholic Basque provinces. The regency for Isabella, in which for a time General Espartero played the dictator, was definitely anti-clerical. In 1837 it declared all Church property the possession of the state. By 1841 only six sees were occupied. Only when Espartero had been overthrown and Isabella had assumed the government did the situation improve. In the concordat of 1851 the Church renounced a great part of her property, while the state undertook the obligations connected with it. The exiling of Isabella in 1868 and the acceptance of the crown by Amadeo, son of Victor Emmanuel of Italy, did not give the Church reason for much hope; however, Amadeo soon had to yield (1873), and Isabella's son, Alfonso XII, issued a new constitution in 1876, in which the Catholic religion was again declared the religion of the state. But toward the end of the century the signs of a new storm increased. The well-meaning Alfonso XIII, who was quite friendly toward the Church, had to submit again and again to liberal ministries. The wild demonstrations which were organized throughout Spain in 1909 as a consequence of the execution of the anarchist and freethinker, Ferrer, were a dangerous symptom. The explosion, however, did not follow until after World War I.

FRANCE

After the restoration of the Bourbon monarchy in 1814 the internal policy of France was at first determined by reaction against the preceding age of revolution and war. The concordat of 1801 was substantially renewed by the treaty of

1822. But the reign of Charles X (1824–1830) brought a liberal parliamentary majority, which among other things carried out the expulsion of the Jesuits. From the July Revolution of 1830 the Catholic religion was no longer recognized as the religion of the state, but only as that of the majority of Frenchmen. The powerfully strengthened Catholic movement in the country made itself felt in politics. In a tough fight for freedom of education the Catholics, under the leadership of Montalembert, achieved important successes. Full freedom of education was granted in 1850. The empire of Napoleon III (1852–1870) had exteriorly the aspect of an age of splendor for the Church in France. Empress Eugénie, who was loyally devoted to the Church, exercised important influence, but the emperor was personally not religious. His attitude in the Roman Question, then disturbing all Catholics, was curious, for he protected the pope and at the same time furthered in every way the Italian national movement that was directed against the pope. In Napoleon III's reign anti-clericalism grew powerfully in France, and after his overthrow in 1870 it dominated politics. The national hero, Gambetta, uttered in 1877 the famous remark: "Clericalism is the enemy." In 1880 all teaching establishments of the Jesuits were closed, in 1881 the laicization of schools was decreed, in 1882 divorce was legally permitted, in 1886 the teaching of religion was abolished. From 1900 anti-clerical laws multiplied, until in 1904 all teaching Orders of men and women were suppressed, a step which led to the closing of 14,000 Catholic schools. In the same year diplomatic relations with the Holy See were broken off. The so-called separation of Church and state was completed in 1905 in such a way that the state kept the property taken from the Church, but discontinued all payments for the support of the clergy and of institutions for the care of souls. Incidentally, the state experienced little profit in the confiscation of

Church property. The anticipated superabundance of blessings did not materialize, for the monasteries were by no means so wealthy as had been thought, and most everything disappeared at the liquidation into the pockets of officials. The Catholics, chiefly because of their lack of political unity, were not in a position to hinder the anti-clerical laws in Parliament, but on the other hand their influence on public opinion was far too great to allow a government to proceed far along these extreme paths. Nevertheless, the Church's legal insecurity persisted.

THE NETHERLANDS

Calvinism was abolished as the state religion in the Netherlands in 1798. The union with Belgium (1815–1830) even brought to the country a Catholic majority. But the concordat of 1827 was not carried out, and in 1830 Belgium became independent. The Catholics were again in the minority, but they banded together and the government was generally peaceable and well-intentioned. The Catholic hierarchy, with an archbishopric and four bishoprics, was reestablished in 1853. The Catholics, well-organized and unhampered in their freedom of movement, could achieve important success in the care of souls, especially in the school system.

BELGIUM

The constitution of 1830 was favorable to the Church. It allowed the free nomination of bishops by the pope and full liberty of education and assembly. Here too, of course, there occurred liberal parliamentary majorities and ministries, and in 1879 an anti-clerical education law was passed. But in 1884 the Catholics again had the majority. From 1895 religious instruction was obligatory in public schools.

504

ENGLAND

In contrast with other countries, in England the ideas of the French Revolution in regard to equality and democracy were to the advantage of Catholics. Many exiled French priests found refuge in England. Before the end of the eighteenth century several of the old coercive and penal laws were revoked. The Irish lawyer and statesman, Daniel O'Connell, obtained full civil equality for Catholics in the Emancipation Bill of 1829. The number of Catholics, which around 1800 had been far below 100,000 in England, exclusive of Ireland, grew steadily. The so-called Oxford Movement from 1833 not only produced many conversions but also raised the prestige of the Catholic population. The obligations of the Irish Catholics toward the Anglican Church were abolished in 1838, and in 1845 the Church in Ireland received the right to possess property. Not without opposition was the Catholic hierarchy restored in England in 1850, with one archbishopric and twelve bishoprics, and in Scotland in 1878 with two archbishoprics and four suffragans. Since none of the former goods of the Church were in existence, and since the government permitted great freedom in regard to schools and assembly, the concluding of a concordat with England was never necessary. It is said that on his deathbed in 1910 King Edward VII became a Catholic. At the accession of his successor the anti-Catholic elements in the coronation oath were omitted.

CANADA

In Canada there prevailed for the Church the same favorable conditions as in the English mother country. An obstacle here was the extremely strong opposition between the Catholics of French speech and those of English speech, which, however, encouraged a beneficial competition.

505

THE UNITED STATES

The constitution of the United States, which ignored every religion and emphasized only the equality of the rights of the individual, was favorable for the Catholic minority. Less indifferent than the constitution, however, was the population in many places, and the Catholics, especially in the first half of the nineteenth century, had to complain of a lack of protection of their rights and even of acts of violence. Likewise, at first the Catholics were very poor. Until far beyond the middle of the century the Church was dependent on Europe, not only for supplies of priests but also to a great extent for funds. All the more astonishing was the activity of the Catholics, who, although they constituted scarcely one-fifth of the population, gradually obtained a highly respected position in the state and in society.[1]

When the hierarchy of the United States was established in 1789, the entire territory of the young republic constituted a single diocese with a Catholic population of 18,000. The zealous activity of the first bishop of Baltimore, John Carroll, and of the Sulpicians who came to his aid soon effected a gradual increase in the number of clergy and faithful. As early

[1] The remainder of this section, dealing with the Church in the United States, has been added by the translator as a supplement to Father Hertling's very brief treatment. The pertinent literature is already quite extensive; the following are suggested for fuller treatment and bibliography: John Gilmary Shea, *History of the Catholic Church within the Limits of the United States* (4 vols., New York: 1886-1892); John Tracy Ellis, *The Life of James Cardinal Gibbons* (2 vols., Milwaukee: 1952); Peter Guilday, *A History of the Councils of Baltimore* (New York: 1932), *The Life and Times of John Carroll* (2 vols., New York: 1922), *The Life and Times of John England* (2 vols., New York: 1927); Theodore Maynard, *The Story of American Catholicism* (New York: 1942); Annabelle M. Melville, *John Carroll of Baltimore: Founder of the American Catholic Hierarchy* (New York: 1955); *Catholicism in America: A Series of Articles from The Commonweal* (New York: 1953); the several studies emanating from the seminar in American Church History at the Catholic University of America, under the direction of Monsignor Guilday and of Monsignor Ellis; numerous articles in *The Catholic Encyclopedia* (17 vols., New York: 1907-1922) and in *The Catholic Historical Review, Mid-America, The Americas,* and other periodicals. (Translator's note.)

as 1791 two important educational institutions, Saint Mary's Seminary at Baltimore and Georgetown College near Washington, opened their doors. In 1808 Baltimore was elevated to metropolitan rank, with New York, Philadelphia, Boston, and Bardstown as its suffragans. The new Church had been directly organized by the papacy with no intervention on the part of the state. The Holy See left much autonomy to the bishops, whose numbers slowly grew; they were outstanding for their zeal and spirit of initiative.

The early bishops were faced with numerous difficulties in the first decades of the nineteenth century. The vast territory constantly expanded with the ever-advancing frontier. There were not enough priests, and not all of those that were available were suitable. Among the first generation of priests were a large number of French expatriates; an excessive number of them became bishops, a fact which was resented by the constantly growing Anglo-Saxon and Irish element. Since too often the French bishops knew English only imperfectly, the American Church risked the danger of being regarded as a foreign thing. By 1850, however, the episcopate had taken on that Irish coloring which it was to retain into the next century. A further source of difficulty derived from the independent spirit of many of the laity, who too often interfered in the parochial and diocesan administration. The laws of the several states required that a board of lay trustees control the temporal affairs of churches; many trustees were imbued with Protestant ideas in regard to temporal administration and, led by refractory priests, even tried to invade the spiritual sphere. Several small schisms were the unpleasant result. But the bishops resisted vigorously and eventually obtained changes in the civil law.

From 1840 Irish and German immigration led to a sudden increase of the Catholic population, and simultaneously the

United States spread to the Rio Grande and the Pacific. In the former Mexican territories reform and reorganization were urgent, in the Mid-West and the West mission conditions prevailed, and in the East there were far too few priests to care for the ever-increasing flocks. But the bishops met the several challenges courageously, and generous help came from Europe in the form of priests, religious, and money. The immigrants clung to their national customs and traditions, and there loomed the threat that the American Church would consist of distinct national groups. The problem of harmonious fusion and unification and of a uniform discipline led to the holding of the First Plenary Council of Baltimore in 1852; here the canonical legislation of the Provincial Council of Baltimore of 1849 was extended to the entire country.

By 1846 there were twenty-one dioceses in the United States. Six new provinces were established between 1846 and 1852. But the number of native vocations was still too meager and it was necessary to keep relying on Europe. Consequently, many Americans of Anglo-Saxon origin, suspicious of the immigrants, became very hostile to the Church. This feeling manifested itself in the Native American Movement and the No Popery agitation of the 1840's and in a far more serious and violent form in the Know-Nothing movement between 1853 and 1855. A non-violent revival of bigotry occurred with the founding in 1887 of the American Protective Association. Most of the Catholics, especially the immigrants, were rather timid about calling attention to their Faith, but several converts, notably Orestes Brownson and Isaac Hecker, urged boldness in resisting Protestant prejudice and the growing materialist mentality. In general, the Catholics sympathized with the South in the slavery question and hence were subjected to further criticism, but the charitable work of priests and sisters and the preservation of religious unity during the War Between the States enhanced the prestige of the Church.

The non-religious character of the American public schools alarmed the bishops and the Second Plenary Council of Baltimore in 1866 called for the establishing of parochial schools. The laity responded generously, especially from the last decades of the century, and the rapid growth of the religious Orders enabled these schools to be staffed. Throughout the nineteenth century several colleges for men were founded, and from the end of the century a few for women. The council of 1866 had broached the subject of a Catholic university, and the Third Plenary Council, meeting in Baltimore in 1884, called for the founding of such an institution at Washington. Despite numerous difficulties and much opposition, even from some of the bishops, the Catholic University of America was finally established in 1889. Numerous religious houses quickly sprang up around it. Elsewhere too Catholic graduate and professional schools were erected.

In the United States Catholicism was essentially urban. The immigrants sought the cities, and the bishops encouraged them to stay there for the sake of preserving their Faith. Most Catholics belonged to an economically inferior class of meager intellectual culture. This proletarian character of the American Catholics in the ports and industrial centers of the northeast partly explains the small number of conversions. The hierarchy was not in sympathy with labor organizations and movements for social relief, because it associated such ideas with the contemporary anti-clerical agitation in Europe. However, it was an outstanding American bishop, James Gibbons of Baltimore, who in 1887 prevailed upon the Holy See to reverse its earlier condemnation of the Knights of Labor.

American Catholics, very many of them of recent foreign origin, kept somewhat apart from the rest of their fellow citizens and exercised little real influence in the nation. With the second half of the nineteenth century, however, the social ostracism imposed upon them began to lessen and the American Church came of age when in 1875 Archbishop John McCloskey of New York became the first American cardinal. Earlier, Pope Pius IX had desired to send an apostolic delegate to the United States. In 1853 he commissioned Archbishop Gaetano Bedini to explore the possibilities, but the poor reception accorded the visitor caused the temporary abandonment of the idea. However, despite the objections of numerous bishops, Leo XIII in 1893 named Archbishop Francesco Satolli as first apostolic delegate, with residence in Washington.

Just the same, the real leader of American Catholics was James Gibbons. This eminent personage was vicar apostolic of North Carolina from 1868 to 1872, then bishop of Richmond till 1877, and archbishop of Baltimore from 1877 until his death in 1921. In 1886 he received the red hat. For Catholics and Protestants he became the living embodiment of the Church in the United States, and he used his great influence to foster good will, especially when the Ku Klux Klan stirred up a new wave of bigotry. He also led the opposition to the strong movement, Cahenslyism, for national churches and schools and for the naming of bishops according to national proportions. The loyal stand taken by the hierarchy during World War I helped to break down these national divisions and weld the Church into a unity.

The numerical growth of the American Church has been steady. The Catholics numbered 318,000 in 1830, 663,000 in 1840, 1,600,000 in 1850, 4,000,000 in 1866, 6,000,000 in 1878, and 20,000,000 in 1921. Even more important, most of them have actually practiced their Faith. The growing prestige of this young Church was recognized early in the twentieth century with the increase in the number of American cardinals. The purple was conferred upon Archbishops John Farley of

New York and William O'Connell of Boston in 1911; Archbishop Dennis Dougherty of Philadelphia in 1921; Archbishops Patrick Hayes of New York and George Mundelein of Chicago in 1924; Archbishops John Glennon of Saint Louis, Edward Mooney of Detroit, Samuel Stritch of Chicago, and Francis Spellman of New York in 1946; and Archbishop Francis McIntyre of Los Angeles in 1953. In the difficult years after World War II, several American prelates were entrusted by the Holy See with very delicate diplomatic missions— Bishop Joseph Hurley of Saint Augustine in Yugoslavia, Bishop Gerald O'Hara of Savannah-Atlanta in Rumania, Bishop Aloysius Muench of Fargo in Germany. In recognition of their services, all three of these prelates received the personal rank of archbishop. Expelled from Rumania, Archbishop O'Hara became successively nuncio to Ireland and apostolic delegate to Great Britain.

The Official Catholic Directory for 1956 gives the following figures for the now vigorous American Church: twenty-six archdioceses, 105 dioceses, two vicariates apostolic, and one abbey *nullius*. The hierarchy comprises four cardinals, thirty-seven archbishops, and 173 bishops. There are 48,349 priests, 16,193 parishes, 8,868 brothers, and 159,545 sisters. The educational system boasts ninety-eight diocesan seminaries, 407 religious seminaries and scholasticates, 254 colleges and universities, 2,383 high schools, and 9,568 elementary schools, with 6,805,129 youth under Catholic instruction. The total Catholic population is 33,574,017.

LATIN AMERICA

In contrast to England and the United States, in Latin America questions of ecclesiastical politics occupied the foreground. The new governments regarded themselves as the lawful successors of the Spanish government, even in regard to the ecclesiastical patronage. Spain, however, was unwilling to yield this right of the crown, even after it possessed no further political power in America. The Holy See, influenced by the Holy Alliance, at first considered the new states as rebels and stood on the side of the written law, including the Spanish patronage. Thus it happened that after the conclusion of the wars of independence, lasting almost twenty years, in all of Latin America there were hardly any bishops.

At first the Holy See sought to name vicars apostolic, as in missionary lands. But neither Spain nor the Catholics in America would agree to this. In 1828 Leo XII named two bishops for Colombia on the recommendation of President Bolívar, but at the same time he informed the Spanish government that he thereby intended no transfer of the patronage to the president. However, Fernando VII at once severed diplomatic relations with the Holy See. In the conclave of 1830 the Spanish government issued the veto against Cardinal Giustiniani, formerly nuncio at Madrid, because of his attitude in regard to the patronage. When, however, Fernando VII died in 1833 and Spain was paralyzed by civil war, Gregory XVI formally recognized the republic of Colombia and sent a nuncio. Soon a recognition by the papacy of the remaining states followed and thus the American "Investiture Quarrel" came to an end.

But in other respects the religious situation in the new republics began under unfavorable auspices. Most ecclesiastical institutes, especially the higher schools, were ruined. There was a lack of aspirants for the clergy and of an educated Catholic laity. Liberal anti-clericalism, that disastrous legacy of recent Spanish rule, could freely develop in America, whereas in Europe it was kept for a time within bounds by the reaction of the era of Metternich. In America the struggle against Church and clergy often appeared as a struggle against Spain and the European system.

512

Not until after the middle of the nineteenth century could the Holy See conclude concordats with some of the new republics—with Costa Rica and Guatemala in 1852, with Honduras and Nicaragua in 1861, with El Salvador in 1862. In Venezuela, immediately after the signing of the concordat in 1862, a persecution of the Church broke out, and it was only after 1875 that normal conditions returned. In Ecuador the important and staunchly Catholic President García Moreno made a concordat in 1862. After his assassination in 1877 it was broken, but in 1881 and 1890 it was restored in a different form. A concordat with Colombia was concluded in 1881 and was completed by supplementary provisions in 1890. In the other republics the so-called separation of Church and state prevailed. But even where there were concordats their value was lessened by the unending changes of government and policy.

Greatest of all, perhaps, was the legal insecurity from which the Church had to suffer in Mexico. It has been calculated that up to 1867 Mexico changed its constitution thirty-six times and had seventy-two heads of state. The empire of Maximilian of Austria (1864–1867), on which some Catholics placed their hopes, turned out to be a disappointment, for Maximilian was himself a liberal and was killed after three years. The new president, the Indian Benito Juárez, who had overthrown the emperor, acted against the Church as a persecutor of the worst sort. Only the long presidency of Porfirio Díaz from 1877 brought to the Church in Mexico greater peace, but even in the twentieth century severe persecutions erupted.

On the whole, the Church in Latin America made far greater progress, both internally and externally, than the unfavorable political conditions would have warranted. In the Latin nations one not rarely finds the phenomenon that people

513

and government go quite different ways. Reality does not always correspond to the text of existing laws. If, for instance, one constantly reads in the history of these states about the suppressing or expelling of the Orders, this does mean the customary damages in goods and chattels, but the religious generally either did not leave or they returned very soon. Thus the care of souls for the most part continued undisturbed, though subject to all kinds of vexations. The number of dioceses in Spanish America, which at the end of the colonial period amounted to forty-two, has more than tripled since then. The number of Catholics mounted from some 13,000,000 to more than five times that number.

In Brazil the transition from the colonial epoch was accomplished less violently than in Spanish America, because though Brazil separated from Portugal as an independent state in 1822, the Portuguese dynasty continued to rule there till 1889. Hence there was no "Investiture Quarrel." Of course, the independent government was quite full of Pombal's rationalistic and Caesaropapist ideas, and from 1830 there were many anti-clerical laws. In 1855 the Orders were forbidden to accept novices, in 1878 foreign Orders were entirely proscribed, and in the course of time much ecclesiastical property was expropriated. After the overthrow of the empire in 1889 the republic proclaimed full separation of Church and state. Hence the Orders could return openly and the missions among the natives could be resumed. The number of the Brazilian dioceses increased between 1800 and 1920 from seven to sixty-seven; the Catholics from 3,000,000 to 40,000,000.

CHURCH POLITICS IN ITALY. THE END OF THE PAPAL STATE

The Congress of Vienna had restored the kingdom of the Two Sicilies and the Papal State to their former status. A collateral line of the house of Austria reigned in the grand duchy of Tuscany. In the north lay the kingdom of Sardinia, to which Genoa as well as Piedmont belonged, and the small duchies of Parma and Modena. Lombardy and Venetia were Austrian provinces.

In the Papal State there occurred in 1831–1832 and again in 1843–1845 periods of serious unrest, which were calmed with Austrian and French military help. The cause was an easily understood dissatisfaction with the papal method of government, which among other things admitted no laymen to official posts. This meant that all state officials wore clerical garb and were counted among the clergy, though many of them had no higher Orders and could, if they had saved enough for themselves, quit the official career and marry. Such persons were often of service neither as officials nor in the care of souls, and it was an easy task for agitators to direct all the unrest among the people against the clergy as the ruling caste and hence against the Church herself. It is a fact that this unrest was artificially stirred up by all sorts of secret societies. The abuses in government were by no means so bad as they were painted by later historians. It is correct that Gregory XVI (1831–1846) was totally uninterested in the railroad, just coming into use. But that was hardly a reason for the people to take up arms.

Agitation against the papal administration gradually combined with the strivings for the political unification of all Italy. It was in keeping with the spirit of the nineteenth century to imagine the well-being of a people as possible only within the framework of a centralized power. Some, even prominent Catholics, thought of a confederation or federal state under the political and military leadership of the king of Sardinia, with the pope as a sort of honorary president. The Piedmontese patriots desired more: the elimination of all dynasties except that of Savoy, even the territorial dominion of the

515

pope, and a unified Piedmontese Italian state. Catholics in all parts of Italy fell thereby into the most difficult conflicts of conscience between loyalty to the pope and love for the nation.

In the beginning great hopes were placed on Pope Pius IX, elected in 1846, who seemed to manifest, by demonstrative political amnesties and democratic reforms, his sympathy even toward the movement for unification. The nationalistic secret societies sought, by false rejoicing, to push the politically inexperienced pope ever farther. But when, in the spring of 1848, he declined to join in Sardinia's national war of liberation against Austria, they felt their time had come and unleashed an open revolution in Rome. Pius IX fled to Gaetà in the kingdom of Naples, and in Rome a republic was proclaimed under Giuseppe Mazzini (February to July, 1849).

The Piedmontese were defeated in their war against Austria. French troops took Rome, and the pope came back. Externally, the former order was restored. But to Italian patriots it was now clear that the founding of a unified national state could come, no longer with the pope, but only against him. The secret and the open agitation became stronger. The kingdom of Sardinia under Victor Emmanuel II (1849–1878) and his prime minister, Cavour (1852–1861), one of the most outstanding statesmen of the century, now took an anti-clerical path in internal policy. Cavour's slogan, "A free Church in a free state," with which many became enraptured, was one of those numerous liberal phrases which mean essentially nothing. Cavour succeeded in winning Emperor Napoleon III for the Italian national cause. The war of 1859, in which the Austrians were defeated by the French, was decisive. Lombardy, Tuscany, Parma, and Modena were added to the new kingdom of Italy. The pope himself demanded that Austria withdraw its troops from the north of the Papal State. Thereupon, this province fell to Italy.

Giuseppe Garibaldi, acting as leader of a band of volunteers, but in reality working for Piedmont, conquered Sicily and Naples in 1860. In the same year Piedmontese troops overran Umbria and defeated the papal army at Castelfidardo.

The pope was now left with but Rome and Latium, and even here he was supported only by a French garrison. Napoleon III, in deference to the French Catholics, would not dare abandon the pope entirely. In the convention of September, 1864, Italy even had to oblige itself not to encroach upon the rest of the Papal State. However, in 1867 Garibaldi ventured to undertake an attack. He was, it is true, beaten at Mentana, quite near Rome, but when, on account of the war with Germany, the French troops were recalled in the summer of 1870, and on September 2 Napoleon was made prisoner at Sedan, the Italian troops crossed the frontier and moved on Rome. The pope knew that the end had come. He gave orders to return the cannonade, but at the first breach in the ancient city wall to raise the white flag. This occurred on September 20, 1870, and the Piedmontese occupied Rome. The heroic songs by which the "storming of the Porta Pia" was later celebrated do not entirely correspond to the real facts.

The pope shut himself up in the Vatican and rejected all negotiations, including the Law of Guarantees issued by Italy on May 13, 1871, whereby inviolability, rights of sovereignty, and an annual payment of 3,250,000 lire were offered him.

Thus was the dream of the Italian patriots realized, but in such a way that the best elements in the nation could not really be gladdened by it. It was a political mistake that the seat of government was transferred to Rome and the king took up residence in the papal palace on the Quirinal. In this way the anti-clerical character of the new state was, so to speak, perpetuated, and the royal court, which was shunned by the other Catholic princes and by the "black aristocracy" of

Rome, was put permanently in an awkward position. In the same way, looking back one must really label it a mistake that the pope in the *Non Expedit*, which was in force until 1905, forbade Italian Catholics to take part in parliamentary elections. The pope's desire to avoid every appearance of recognizing the new government and to keep constantly before the eyes of Catholics the illegality of the existing situation was justified; but the consequence was that the Italian Catholics were deprived of political training and Parliament was dominated by anti-clerical elements.

The attitude of the government thus remained permanently hostile. The monasteries, even venerable Montecassino, were declared national property and to some extent were turned into schools or barracks. The schools remained without religious instruction. Wild demonstrations, as at the unveiling of the monument to Giordano Bruno in Rome in 1889 or at the transfer of the corpse of Pius IX, were allowed by the government. On the other hand, the Italian statesmen were in a condition of continual anxiety because of the "Roman Question" and strove, at least outside Rome, to make a good impression by all sorts of obliging gestures. Even so anti-clerical a prime minister as Francesco Crispi undertook secret negotiations with the Vatican, but of course they came to nothing. This anxiety manifested itself even during World War I, when, in the secret Treaty of London of April 26, 1915, Italy had its allies promise to exclude the pope from any share in the peace negotiations.

The annexation of the Papal State by Italy was doubtless a serious violation of rights and it was interpreted as such by the Catholics of the entire world. The pope could not but protest against this spoliation of the Church, and continued to do so long after it had taken place. The pope is not, so to speak, the private owner of ecclesiastical property, but only its

518

administrator. If in the case of the Renaissance popes it is regarded as a violation of duty that they detached parts of the Papal State for their families, then all the more Pius IX could not present the whole to the kingdom of Italy. On the other hand, it cannot be denied that in many respects it was beneficial to the Church that the pope was no longer an Italian ruler. The Middle Ages and the period of princely absolutism were generally able to conceive of authority only in the form of sovereignty. At that time the pope had to be also a king in order to be able to exercise his spiritual authority; he had to stand in the ranks of the other territorial princes. In the modern age, with its completely changed notion of the state, matters were different. For his task as ruler of the world Church it was of no special advantage for the pope to be simultaneously president or constitutional monarch of a small Italian country; rather, it was a hindrance.

THE POLITICAL SITUATION OF THE CHURCH IN GERMANY

In 1817 Bavaria concluded a concordat in which the still existing circumscription of dioceses was determined—the archdiocese of Munich-Freising, with the bishoprics of Augsburg, Regensburg, and Passau, and the archdiocese of Bamberg, with the bishoprics of Würzburg, Eichstätt, and Speyer. The king nominated the bishops, while the pope gave them canonical institution. The bishops had free communication with Rome and surveillance over the state schools in matters of faith and morals. Bishoprics, cathedral chapters, and seminaries were endowed by the state. Nothing further was said of the secularized former goods of the Church. However, this concordat was at once supplemented and to an extent nullified by a state decree on religion, which was published with the new Bavarian constitution of 1818. Among other things this reintroduced the royal *placet*. A pedantic Caesaropapistic

519

trend remained henceforth characteristic of the Bavarian method of government. But because of the correct attitude of the monarchs and the strict integrity of the officials scarcely any serious conflicts arose, even when, as was usual from 1848, liberal ministries were in power.

With Prussia a sort of concordat came into existence in 1821, when Pius VII issued a bull and the king published it as a law of the state. The ecclesiastical province of Cologne was again established, with Trier, Münster, and Paderborn as suffragans; the province of Gniezno-Poznan was also established, with Kulm as suffragan, and in addition the two exempt sees of Breslau and Ermland. The bishops were to be elected by the cathedral chapters, but candidates unacceptable to the king were to be excluded. The state endowed the bishoprics. As in the Bavarian concordat, nothing was said of the former goods of the Church, which was equivalent to a renunciation by the Church.

A similar agreement with Hanover in 1824 established the sees of Hildesheim and Osnabrück. The king, who was at that time also king of Great Britain, obtained the right to exclude undesirable candidates in episcopal elections, that is, to strike out all except three.

For southwestern Germany the archbishopric of Freiburg (Baden) was established in 1821, with the suffragan sees of Rottenburg (Württemberg), Mainz (Hesse-Darmstadt), Fulda (Electoral Hesse), and Limburg (Nassau and Frankfurt). In regard to the filling of the sees, after long and difficult negotiations an agreement was reached similar to that of Prussia.

Throughout most of the nineteenth century the ecclesiastical situation in Germany remained satisfactory, even with regard to co-operation with the state authorities. There were really few countries which could enjoy an officialdom of such integrity and such ability as the German states in the nineteenth century, in which, of course, the German mania for regimenting even the slightest details was not absent. The Catholics had to complain of a definite neglect in public life, especially in regard to the higher school system. At the seventeen German universities there were hardly any Catholic professors. In this, however, it was not only the undoubted Protestant prejudice which existed in many places that was to blame, but also a definite lack of education on the part of the Catholics.

However, even in Germany the Church was not spared struggle. Not long after the regulation of the Church's legal position there arose in Prussia a sharp conflict in regard to mixed marriages. According to Prussian law children had to be raised in the religion of their father. When the archbishop of Cologne, Clement August von Droste-Vischering, insisted on the Church's standpoint, he was imprisoned in 1837. The same fate befell the archbishop of Gniezno-Poznan, Martin von Dunin, in 1839. The indignation of Catholics reached such a pitch that the government yielded, and an agreement in accord with Catholic canon law was realized.

Likewise in other German states, such as Baden, Württemberg, and Nassau, passing conflicts occurred before 1870 between the bishops and the governments, but these did little damage and kept alive among Catholics their dislike of a too far-reaching tutelage of the state.

THE KULTURKAMPF

The year 1871 brought the victory over France and the change, long desired by many, from a confederation to a federal state. The king of Prussia assumed the title of German emperor. Under the stimulation of the unprecedented success in arms and thanks to the political guidance of the first imperial chancellor and creator of the imperial constitution, Otto von Bismarck, the new German Empire at once occupied one of the first places among the great powers.

The German Catholics, especially in the south, were perhaps on the average less intoxicated by patriotic enthusiasm than other sections of the population. And it was not to their taste when some wanted to see in the victory over France a divine judgment in favor of Protestant arms and in the new imperial title an evangelical emperorship. However, no one could maintain that Catholics had not done their duty in the war, exactly like others, or that they were hostile toward the new imperial constitution. It is not easy really to say why Bismarck, his work of imperial unification scarcely created, picked his quarrel with the Church. In any case, rational political considerations alone do not explain it.

The term *"Kulturkampf,"* coined in 1873 by the free-thinking deputy Virchow, was supposed to mean that it was question of a struggle of modern progress against mediaeval stagnation. It was led by Bismarck as Prussian prime minister, but in particular points it shifted to imperial legislation.

In 1871 the Catholic department in the Prussian ministry of worship, which up till then had guarded the constitutional rights of the Church, was abolished. In the same year began the legislation, with an appendix to the penal code, on the abuse of the pulpit for discussion of state affairs in a manner endangering the public peace, a paragraph which allowed of a very elastic interpretation. An imperial law of 1872 caused the expulsion of the Jesuits, Redemptorists, Lazarists, and Madames of the Sacred Heart, as "related to the Jesuits." This was followed by a whole series of laws, among them one on the institution of a Prussian law court for ecclesiastical affairs which could depose clerics (1873), and one on expulsion, forfeiture of goods, and loss of citizenship because of the unauthorized exercise of ecclesiastical functions (1874). Since the new laws were contrary to the Prussian constitution of 1850, in which self-government was assured the Catholic Church, the articles concerned were stricken from the constitution in 1875. Joint use of Catholic churches and of ecclesiastical revenues was awarded to the Old Catholics.

The result was that by 1878 nine of the twelve Prussian sees and more than 1,000 parishes were vacant. More than 2,000 clergymen had received fines or imprisonment. Even the celebration of Mass and the administration of the sacraments of the dying were, in certain circumstances, punishable as unauthorized exercise of ecclesiastical functions.

THE CENTER

The Catholics displayed not only passive resistance by paying the fines of bishops and priests, boycotting "state priests," and, when they could do nothing else, holding lay worship, but also carried on an effective and energetic defensive activity in the Prussian chamber of deputies and the Reichstag. Since 1852 there had existed in the Prussian chamber of deputies a small "Catholic fraction," founded by the brothers Peter and August Reichensperger of Cologne, and since 1858 termed, because of its seats in the middle of the chamber, the "fraction of the center." During the Kulturkampf it grew rapidly and in time became the strongest party in the Reichstag. Chairman of the Reichstag was the Bavarian deputy, von Frankenstein (1875–1890); in both bodies the intellectual leader was the former Hanoverian minister, Ludwig Windthorst (✝1890). With him collaborated Hermann von Mallinkrodt (✝1874), the two Reichenspergers, Schorlemer-Alst, Heeringen, Huene, Galen, Hompesch, Hertling, Ernst Lieber, and Ballestrem, who was president of the Reichstag

523

from 1895 to 1906—all of them men to whom the Catholic people were attached with a special kind of enthusiasm.

The Center did not want to be a religious party, but a party for the protection of right. Its program included the preservation of the federal constitution of the Empire against tendencies toward unification into one state; protection of civil as well as of religious liberty against legislative encroachments; protection of the socially underprivileged. The social tasks were adopted into the program at the meeting in Soest in 1870. That Germany was the first country to introduce planned social legislation was in great part due to the Center.

In political questions the Center preserved its independence even in regard to the pope. During the negotiations for the ending of the *Kulturkampf* Leo XIII privately communicated to Windthorst his desire that the Center vote for a military bill of the government in order not to endanger these negotiations. Windthorst declined, but let the pope know, in case he interpreted this as disobedience, that the Center was prepared to disband. Leo XIII later approved this attitude.

As the great statesman that he undoubtedly was, Bismarck acknowledged after some time that his *Kulturkampf* was a failure. Even in 1878 and 1879 secret discussions took place between Bismarck and the nuncios to Munich and Vienna. Diplomatic relations between Prussia and Rome were resumed in 1882 after an interruption of ten years. The Prussian government had "discretionary power" given it by the Landtag in order to relax the enforcement of the religious laws. One after another the laws themselves disappeared: in 1883 the malicious "culture examination" of clerics, in 1886 the royal tribunal for ecclesiastical affairs, in 1890 the law of expatriation. The suspended salaries, which had swollen to 16,000-000 marks, were paid in 1891. The Jesuit law was in force

524

for the longest period of time; it was partially repealed in 1904 but not totally until 1917.

The moral effect of the resistance to the *Kulturkampf* was great in every respect. The German Center became the model for the formation of similar parties in other lands. In time, however, when the actual struggle abated, less satisfying aspects appeared. The Center became almost too powerful. The Catholic deputies themselves said jokingly, *"Das Zentrum ist auf der schiefen Ebene nach oben."* Among the Catholics of the country the defensive attitude gradually disappeared, though not nearly everything had been won. The ideal of equality was still far from realized. Many remembered the reproach constantly heard in the *Kulturkampf* that Catholics were enemies of the Empire, not good Germans. During the conflict people had put up with this reproach, but the next generation reacted in an extreme manner. The German Catholics became too excessively devoted to the state. At every opportunity they sought to prove their German sentiment, as if they had to make up for old failings. The Center's social policy approached dangerously close to State Socialism. The Catholics rejoiced if, among the hundred ministers that were then in Germany, even one was a Catholic, as though that was something special in a country which was one-third Catholic.

SWITZERLAND

The very complicated diocesan arrangement of Switzerland was regulated to some extent in 1823 and 1828. Soon, however, serious conflicts occurred between the Catholics and the liberal Protestants. In the canton of Aargau all monasteries were suppressed in 1841. Freebooting expeditions were undertaken against Catholic Lucerne. In 1845 seven Catholic cantons allied in defense of their rights, but in 1847 they were defeated in the so-called Sonderbund War. The federal constitution of 1848 was hostile to the Church. The bishop of Fribourg, Marilley, was imprisoned and then banished. The new federal constitution of 1874 was more moderate, but still quite Erastian. The Jesuits continued to be excluded from Swiss territory. The nuncio had to leave the country. In several cantons, such as Basel, Bern, and Zürich, violence was perpetrated against Catholics. Many churches were turned over to the Old Catholics. In time, however, just as in Germany, the *Kulturkampf* laws were partly repealed, partly evaded.

AUSTRIA

The ideas of the French Revolution did not have very much influence in the Austrian monarchy. During the long reign of Emperor Franz I (1792–1835) the Empire, though frequently defeated in the field by Napoleon, rose to the position of a leading power in Europe. This ascendancy was due especially to the imperial chancellor, Prince Clement Metternich (1809–1848), who, however, exercised far less influence in the internal policies of Austria than he did in the rest of Europe. Austria was governed by Josephist liberal officials. Emperor Franz, a nephew of Joseph II, was personally far removed from the *Aufklärung* and liberalism. The enemy of all revolution, with a strongly legalistic mind, he was uninterested in any change in the Josephist ecclesiastical legislation, with which he was personally not in sympathy, but he mitigated its harshness by prudent and well-intentioned government. For Metternich, who was personally a freethinker in religion, the Church was especially useful for keeping order in the country. The new constitution after the revolution of 1848 and the fall of Metternich brought greater freedom to the Church. Through the efforts of Archbishop Rauscher of Vienna and the kindness of the new emperor, Franz Josef I, a favorable concordat was concluded in 1855, which did away with the extensive remains of Josephism. It was, however, never entirely carried out; in 1868 it was violated by new laws regarding marriage and schools, and in 1874 it was denounced by the government. But a real *Kulturkampf* did not break out, primarily because Emperor Franz Josef I cultivated a most proper attitude in religious matters. Stubborn in regard to Rome, he tolerated no encroachments on the part of his officials, who were mostly liberals. When in 1868 Bishop Rudigier of Linz was arrested by the government, the emperor immediately set him at liberty. He allowed no attacks on the theological faculty of the University of Innsbruck, which was conducted by the Jesuits. In filling the bishoprics of his Empire he let himself be guided mostly by ecclesiastical and pastoral considerations, though he enjoyed a liberal right of nomination.

For all that, much was lacking to the Church in Austria. To the outside world Austria appeared as the stronghold of Catholicism, but this impression came chiefly from a sort of veneer which hid much internal hostility. The so-called *intelligentsia* was for the most part liberal and only nominally Catholic. The populations of the several lands were more and more seized by nationalistic passions, which diminished the Catholic sentiment of unity. From the so-called *Ausgleich* with Hungary in 1867, which actually meant the beginning of the end for the monarchy, it was no longer possible to withstand the wave of nationalism. The German Austrians for their part gravitated repeatedly toward the German Empire, which seemed to them an incarnation of Protestantism. The Austrian suffered continually from an inferiority complex and an admiration for the outside world. Nevertheless, the Catholics of the various nations united in political parties,

527

particularly the Germans in the Christian Social Party, founded by Karl Lueger, mayor of Vienna. These Catholic groups, separated by sharp nationalistic opposition, could not, and to an extent would not, delay the disintegration of the monarchy, but brought it about that in the successor states the interests of the Church would, to a degree, be protected from the beginning.

RUSSIA

Since the partition of Poland, staunchly Catholic populations belonged to the Russian Empire: Poles, Lithuanians, and the Catholic Ruthenians of the Ukraine. Under Czar Paul I (1796–1801) three Ruthenian sees were restored and the Latin archbishopric of Mohilew, with Saint Petersburg as its seat, was established. To these was added in 1818 the archbishopric of Warsaw, with seven suffragans. Under Nicholas I (1825–1855) a regular persecution began with all the weapons of Caesaropapism, "Russification," and force. Three Ruthenian bishops with 1,500,000 faithful were compelled to pass over to the schism. The Catholics had to pay for the abortive revolt of the Poles in 1830. When in 1845 the czar visited Rome, Gregory XVI remonstrated earnestly with him. Hence in 1847 a concordat was reached, but it was not carried out by Russia in a very loyal fashion and after the Polish revolt of 1863 it was entirely abrogated. In 1882 Alexander III concluded a new concordat, and in 1894 diplomatic relations with the pope, interrupted since 1860, were resumed. Still, oppression and especially the efforts for "Russification" continued. The revolution of 1905 brought some alleviation in the religious legislation, as a consequence of which more than 200,000 schismatics in the western provinces returned to the Catholic Church.

528

THE GREAT POPES OF THE NINETEENTH CENTURY

In the course of time the government of the Church has grown into such a mighty structure that it might seem that the personalities of the individual popes no longer played the role that was still somewhat theirs in the sixteenth and seventeenth centuries. The actual work of saving souls, of course, occurs not from the center, from Rome, but from the bishops, pastors, and religious in the various countries. This was always the case. It is also true that the central government, the Roman Curia, in all its many-sided ramifications has its firmly organized method of business, in which even a change of pontificate brings no upheaval.[2] However, the last hundred years show that the personality of the reigning head is still of the greatest influence on the destinies of the Church.

The series of popes of the nineteenth century begins with Pius VII (1800–1823), the noble sufferer who steered the Church out of the storms of the Napoleonic epoch into more peaceful waters. The next two, Leo XII (1823–1829) and Pius VIII (1829–1830), continued his work, but reigned so briefly as to leave no deep traces. Gregory XVI (1831–1846) seemed to many contemporaries a stranger to this world and reactionary: a stranger to this world because he came from the Camaldolese Order; reactionary, because he firmly opposed with all his might the swelling flood of liberalism and followed politically the system of the Holy Alliance. Today one will hardly be able to uphold this unfavorable judgment. His opposition to liberal theological ideas by a series of doctrinal condemnations redounds to his merit. As ruler of the small

[2] Interesting in this connection is the advance summary report of the American Institute of Management, published in January, 1956. The purpose of this Institute is to evaluate the efficiency of business corporations. In 1948 it received permission to extend its studies to the Holy See and the Church; it awards the Church a score of 88 percent for management excellence—an unusually high rating, according to the standards of the Institute. (Translator's note.)

Papal State, he was, to be sure, powerless in the face of the growing political ferment, but in the government of the Church he showed great foresight. Among other things, his name is closely linked with the rise of the Church in America and with the modern missionary system.

PIUS IX (1846–1878)

After Gregory's death a quite extraordinary man ascended Saint Peter's Throne: Giovanni Maria Mastai-Ferretti, Pius IX. Not only was the length of this pontificate extraordinary— thirty-one years—but also the effects which it left behind. It might be doubted whether Pius IX was by nature especially equipped for a role in world history. He was perhaps less brilliantly endowed than some of his predecessors. In politics he unquestionably made mistakes. He did not know men, like Paul III did, and often erred in his judgment of persons. He has been reproached with vanity. While it is true that he desired and caused his successes and triumphs, one should not forget that his personal successes were at the same time successes of the Church. This is true of any pope. The uniqueness of his position makes it impossible for the man to withdraw modestly behind his work. In any case, Pius IX was an enchanting personality and there has hardly been another pope so beloved by the Catholics of the whole world, so much respected by non-Catholics. To the unprecedented heavy blows of his pontificate, culminating in the seizure of the Papal State, he opposed a matchless dignity, and the last seven years, which he spent as a landless prince in the Vatican, were more like a lasting triumph than an imprisonment.

The territorial growth of the Church was reflected in his pontificate. Pius IX established the hierarchy in England in 1850 and in Holland in 1853, and erected a total of twenty-nine archbishoprics and 132 bishoprics. From the middle of

530

the century the steamship and the railroad made world-wide communication easier. Between the individual churches and the center, Rome, a closer union developed, so that the faithful thronged to the Eternal City in numbers never before seen. In 1854, at the definition of the Immaculate Conception, and in 1862, at the canonization of the first martyrs of the Japanese Church, Pius IX saw himself surrounded by a gathering of the princes of the Church which surpassed the most ecumenical of past councils. When in 1867 the pope celebrated the eighteenth centenary of the deaths of the Apostles Peter and Paul, about 500 bishops were in attendance.

THE VATICAN COUNCIL

These brilliant gatherings certainly nurtured in Pius IX the idea of summoning a real general council. There was not at stake, as so often was true on the occasions of previous councils, any acute question for whose settlement a great ecclesiastical assembly seemed necessary. The plan now was rather to oppose tendencies hostile to the Faith and to the Church with an impressive demonstration, somewhat like an army review. Quite soon after the announcing of the council in 1868, however, there were many who desired to define the doctrine of the pope's infallibility in matters of Faith and morals. This teaching had for centuries been presented as theological doctrine in most Catholic schools, and within the Church it had hardly ever been disputed. Even now it was a question not so much of the correctness or falseness of this teaching, but rather of whether it could claim the rank of a revealed truth of Faith. In theological language, the point at issue was not its *veritas* but its *definibilitas*.

The desire for the definition had hardly been expressed when waves of agitation mounted to the heights. Even the European governments were seized by it. The Bavarian liberal prime minister, Prince Hohenlohe, the later imperial German chancellor, sent a circular letter to the powers with the suggestion of common action against the council in the event that infallibility was to be defined. The powers did not interfere, but they closely followed the preparations for the council with suspicious attentiveness.

The pope appointed as president the former archbishop of Munich-Freising, Cardinal Reisach, and, when the latter became mortally ill before the council opened, Cardinal De Angelis. Bishop Fessler of Sankt Pölten became secretary. On hand were 770 prelates, more than three-fourths of those then entitled to a vote in the Church, which had not been the case in any earlier council. In view of the large number of participants and of the subjects submitted for discussion, the conduct of business was rendered very difficult. Even the variations in the pronunciation of Latin caused trouble. The sessions took place in Saint Peter's.

The council was opened on December 8, 1869. Not until March, 1870, did the chair decide to open for discussion the question of infallibility, which from the beginning had stood at the center of interest. The bishops were divided into two factions. The leaders of the "infallibilists" were Deschamps of Mechlin, Manning of Westminster, Pie of Poitiers, Martin of Paderborn, Senestrey of Regensburg, Gasser of Brixen. The chiefs of the "anti-infallibilists" included Darboy of Paris, Dupanloup of Orléans, Ketteler of Mainz, Hefele of Rottenburg, Dinkel of Augsburg, Schwarzenberg of Prague, Rauscher of Vienna, Strossmayer of Djakowo in Slavonia, Kenrick of Saint Louis. These were all Church-minded men, many of them outstanding shepherds. They feared the definition would aggravate the agitation of enemies, make conversions difficult, and produce defections. The friends of the definition, on the contrary, could plead that, once the question had been raised, it was no longer possible to evade a decision on grounds of opportunism, since this would be almost synonymous to a condemnation by the council of the Church's teaching.

Among the theologians and laity not represented at the council were of course many who in a journalistic war attacked the teaching itself. The intellectual leader of this circle was the celebrated Munich professor of Church History, Ignaz Döllinger, who for some time had entertained a bitter frame of mind in regard to the papacy and the curia.

In the decisive discussion of July 13, 1870, the vote was 451 in favor of the definition, sixty-two with reservations (*placet iuxta modum*), and eighty-eight opposed. Ketteler on his knees implored the pope not to proclaim the dogma. But after matters had developed to this extent, the pope could do nothing else. Thereupon, fifty-five bishops asked to be allowed to absent themselves from the solemn session and departed. Thus on July 18 the proclamation of the dogma of infallibility took place with 533 affirmative and 2 negative votes. When the Franco-Prussian War broke out on July 19, even more prelates departed. On September 20 the Piedmontese occupied Rome. The council was therewith adjourned for an unspecified time. Of the fifty-one topics prepared, only two were finished.

At first it seemed as if the apprehensions of the minority would materialize. The bishops who had voted in the negative submitted with exemplary correctness, last of all Hefele (1871) and Strossmayer (1872); but in Germany, Switzerland, and France there were defections from the Church. The deserters in Germany founded the "Old Catholic" Church, despite Döllinger's admonitions, and had a bishop consecrated for themselves by Dutch Jansenists. Döllinger himself was excommunicated by the archbishop of Munich but did not act as a schismatic. He died in 1890, unreconciled with the Church. In Switzerland a "Christian Catholic" Church was formed. During the *Kulturkampf* the Old Catholics were encouraged by the governments in Prussia, Baden, and even Bavaria. In 1879 they counted more than 50,000 adherents, mostly intellectuals—quite a loss for the Church in Germany. But from then on they declined constantly. When the *"Los-von-Rom"* movement took place in Austria in 1897, some 20,000 of the deserters joined the Old Catholics. Today they number only a few thousand.

SIGNIFICANCE OF THE VATICAN COUNCIL

Although the Vatican Council remained unfinished, its significance is very great. At the time all felt that it raised the moral prestige of the Church and of the papacy; hence the unusual displeasure of all the Church's opponents. Curiously, the storm was directed almost wholly against the dogma of papal infallibility. Many did not even notice that the simultaneously defined doctrine of the immediate jurisdiction of the pope over the entire Church (*in omnes et singulos pastores et fideles*) was almost more important. Through it a revival of the old ideas of Gallicanism, Febronianism, and related systems, as well as the Anglican notion of the three equal sister churches, the Roman, the Oriental, and the Anglican, became once and for all impossible. It was, of course, absurd for the Austrian government to denounce its concordat on the ground that one of the parties to the treaty, the pope, had, by means of the conciliar definition, become another party. Pope and Church had not been transformed by the council, but the council had brought clarity in fundamental teachings. Nor is it correct that, through the Vatican Council, centralization in the Church has risen to unlimited powers. The government of the Church has not become different since the council. There cannot be in the Church a centralization in the sense in which this catchword is usually understood, because the jurisdiction of the individual bishops over their churches has its origin in the same divine right as the pope's universal jurisdiction.

The many preliminaries for the questions not touched upon at the council were not in vain. The recent codification of Canon Law, begun by Pius X, goes back basically to the suggestions given by the Vatican Council.

THE LAST YEARS OF PIUS IX

The exciting events of 1870 helped intensify in a manner rarely experienced before a love and veneration for the pope among Catholics throughout the whole world. This did not appear merely in the celebrations in honor of the harassed old man on Saint Peter's Throne—for the golden jubilee of his priesthood in 1869, for the silver jubilee of his pontificate in 1871, for the thirtieth year of his pontificate in 1876, and for the golden jubilee of his episcopate in 1877. These celebrations were more like demonstrations. The pilgrimage to Rome became really a pilgrimage to the pope. To see the pope became the heart's desire of Catholics, the great event in their lives, to be told to their children and grandchildren. The pope's picture hung in their homes; his death was felt as a personal loss.

It is not easy, especially for non-Catholics, to form a correct notion of the love of the faithful for the pope as it has existed especially from the time of Pius IX. The Catholic loves the person of the pope because of his office, and the office because of the person. For the pope he entertains a religious respect, without regarding him as a higher sort of being or ascribing preternatural powers to him.

LEO XIII (1878–1903)

The Catholic world was equally enthusiastic about the great Pius's successor, Joachim Pecci, Leo XIII, different though he was from his predecessor. Curiously, the difference was even external: Pius IX, who came from a noble house, had almost coarse features; Leo XIII, of a bourgeois family, was of a distinguished appearance, thoroughly spiritual, like a being from another world.

In political affairs no changes occurred with regard to Italy. The pope remained in the Vatican as a "prisoner," but he displayed a world-wide activity. In his pontificate 248 new dioceses were erected. Special significance attaches to the many didactic encyclicals in which Leo XIII took a stand on the great questions moving the world: socialism (*Quod Apostolici Muneris*, 1878), the state (*Diuturnum Illud*, 1881, and *Immortale Dei*, 1885), the social problem (*Rerum Novarum*, 1891), and others. However, while some think they must hail Leo XIII as the "workingman's pope," this notion is, to say the least, misleading. Demagogic tendencies were alien to him. He stressed the Christian principles concerning right and justice in state and community in opposition to partial and erroneous notions. He provided a ground plan from which the activity of Christian social philosophers, statesmen, and politicians has taken its direction. For this purpose his encyclicals were frequently reprinted, translated, and commented upon. They won respectful attention from friend and foe.

In the second half of the nineteenth century great political value was attached to the visits of heads of states. Since Leo XIII held to the principle of not receiving guests of the king of Italy, Catholic princes remained away from Rome. Non-Catholic monarchs, like Emperor William II and King Edward VII, were, however, allowed to visit him in the Vatican. In 1885 Bismarck entrusted to him arbitration between Germany and Spain in regard to the Caroline Islands. Perhaps Leo XIII somewhat overrated the value of diplomatic relations, particularly of the representative sort, corresponding to the practice of the day. This would explain his strong veneration for Innocent III, to whom he erected a monument in the Vatican. However, it cannot be denied that the pope then enjoyed a world-wide prestige not before attained.

PIUS X (1903–1914)

When on July 20, 1903, Leo XIII died at the age of ninety-three, there took place a definite reaction, to the extent that, after the "political" pope, a more "pastoral" pope was desired. Epithets of this sort are, of course, of little meaning. Leo XIII had been a priest, through and through.

In the conclave the Austrian emperor, through the cardinal of Cracow, vetoed Cardinal Rampolla, who had been secretary of state. The reasons for this sensational move, especially to what extent the German government also took a hand in it, have never been satisfactorily explained. Incidentally, the veto exercised no decisive influence on the election; in the succeeding balloting Rampolla received one more vote. But the cardinals finally decided upon the patriarch of Venice, Cardinal Sarto. One of his first acts was to abolish the veto definitively. No opposition from the governments was encountered.

Pius X had risen from the ranks; he was not a scholar or esthete, like Leo XIII, who in his leisure hours composed fine Latin hymns, but he was a practical man. As early as 1904 he set up a commission which was to prepare the new code of the entire Canon Law. This great undertaking was completed only under his successor. Pius X began a reorganization of the congregations of cardinals, which was finished in 1908. In this, among other things, the dioceses of North America, which were still under the Congregation of the Propaganda, were placed on an administrative basis equal with the dioceses of other countries. In 1909 he created the *Acta Apostolicae Sedis* as the official organ of the curia. A sweeping reform of the breviary occurred in 1911. Of incalculable effect on the spiritual life in the Church were the decrees on frequent Communion in 1905 and the early admission of children to Communion in 1910.

One of the greatest successes of this pontificate was the warding off of the insidious heresy of Modernism. As might be expected in a delicate and complicated matter of this sort, some proceedings in this struggle were variously judged, even by loyal Catholics. There were not lacking those extreme ecclesiastics who felt they must suspect perfectly loyal Catholics of Modernism. Unfortunately, in his last years the nearly eighty-year-old pope put more faith in such denunciations than was good. On the whole, however, the speedy and radical triumph over Modernism was one of the most beneficent events of recent Church History. The encyclical *Pascendi* of 1907, in which the condemnation culminated, is in its way a theological masterpiece. It deservedly takes rank beside Leo the Great's *Tomus ad Flavianum* and the Tridentine decrees on justification.

Without making a display of piety in striking gestures, Pius X was a deeply pious man, plain and simple, entirely a priest and pastor. He died on August 20, 1914, a few days after the outbreak of World War I. He was beatified in 1951 and canonized in 1954.

THE CARE OF SOULS IN THE NINETEENTH CENTURY

THE PENETRATION OF THE MASSES

There is, even among Catholics, a common opinion that the Church to a great degree lost her influence over wide sections of the people in the nineteenth century. It is based on the observation that, from the middle of the nineteenth century at the latest, there were in almost all countries, even those that had earlier been wholly Catholic, broad strata of the population who were estranged from the Church inwardly and outwardly, who were perhaps baptized and let themselves be counted as Catholics in statistics—and often not even that— but who for the rest displayed toward the Church an indifference that changed, at times, into hostility. People speak with justification of a neo-paganism.

This impression is further strengthened by the consideration of political history. In almost all countries Catholics appear as a minority, often an oppressed and persecuted one. If in places they offered vigorous resistance and obtained important successes, they nevertheless remained a minority.

Before one undertakes an investigation to determine why the Church was pushed back all along the line and lost her influence over the masses, one must make sure that such a situation corresponds to the facts. If attention is directed merely to the purely numerical growth of the Church, it is seen that the number of her members has risen from 130,- 000,000 around 1800 to more than 350,000,000 today. As regards the interior life, it can hardly be denied that at the end of the nineteenth century it was far more intense and active in all fields than it had been at the beginning. Hence, it would be just as correct to say that in the nineteenth century the Church did not lose, but rather won the masses.

The Church possesses no human stock which endures over the centuries, no human capital, so to speak. She must win anew and hold each individual human being, each generation. In an epoch of extraordinary increase of population, such as the nineteenth century, it can happen that the Church may not adapt her pastoral program quickly enough to assure contact with the new generations. Untouched by the outmoded system, the new generations grow up outside the Church. In this sense the Church has no more lost the neo-pagans of Europe

539

and America than she has lost the Negroes of Africa or the 400,000,000 Chinese; for she has never possessed them. It must, then, be the task of history to investigate the growth of the Church spatially and numerically, a growth that was, in fact, extraordinarily rapid. Afterwards, one may ask why this growth was not more rapid.

GROWTH OF POPULATION

In all parts of the world the nineteenth century was an age of unprecedented increase of the human race. This increase extended even to Africa and especially to Asia, but there to a great degree it eludes our historical grasp, whereas for Europe and America we can utilize approximate estimates. Around 1800 Europe had from 180,000,000 to 190,000,000 inhabitants and today numbers about 500,000,000. America as a whole must have had slightly more than 20,000,000 inhabitants around 1800 and now has about 300,000,000, a great part of whom have come from Europe. Thus we have to take account not only of a growth in population, but at the same time of a displacement in population, a genuine migration of nations, such as history has never before known in the proportions involved. Of course, the 300,000,000 did not really emigrate from Europe. The real growth in America took place on the spot. From 1820 to 1920 immigration to the United States from Europe totaled 34,000,000, but at the same time the population increased to about 120,000,000.

The task of the Church was to create adequate institutions for the care of souls in the midst of these moving and newly rising masses of population. This had to be done not only in the American New World but also in Europe, in large cities, especially, but in other places as well, whenever the pastoral practices hitherto in use no longer availed.

Around 1800 there were as yet no cities of millions. The

largest cities then were London, with close to 1,000,000, and Paris, with 547,000 inhabitants. Today there are throughout the world some forty vast cities, among them a number with a predominantly Catholic population: in America, Buenos Aires, Rio, São Paulo, Mexico City, Habana, Montreal; in Europe, Barcelona, Madrid, Paris, Vienna, Warsaw, Budapest, Rome. In addition, there are several predominantly or wholly Catholic cities which approach the million mark, such as Brussels, Prague, Cologne, Munich, Milan, and Naples. Other centers have become cities of millions, cities in which there were only a few Catholics at the beginning of the nineteenth century but in which today there are Catholic communities counted by the hundreds of thousands, such as London, Berlin, and above all, New York, Philadelphia, and Chicago. Boston, once the stronghold of Puritanism, has grown to 800,000 inhabitants, two-thirds of whom are Catholics.

This growth was not entirely healthy. The cities grew at the expense of the rural population, which almost everywhere declined. Especially, however, the excessive increase occurred not on the basis of a corresponding increase in births but to a great extent because of fewer deaths. In the nineteenth century medical science celebrated genuine triumphs. Through the discovery and removal of all sorts of excitants of disease, it was able to make cities healthy and combat epidemics with preventive measures; it instructed people in healthy living habits, lessened infant mortality, found cures for sicknesses which had earlier always been fatal. At the same time life expectancy was almost doubled. This was, indeed, an event of the first importance for cultural history, but it also had its dark side. Many social conflicts, much unrest and economic stagnation stem less from the growing number of men than from the growing age of the population.

541

INCREASE OF PASTORAL CENTERS

In view of the persistent increase of population, the most urgent task was the creating of new pastoral centers. The Church did not fail to meet this need in the nineteenth century.

In Europe the increase of pastoral centers was less striking insofar as the number of dioceses remained almost unchanged. Only in England was the hierarchy newly created. To the thirteen dioceses erected there in 1850 seven more were added by 1924—Leeds and Middlesborough in 1878, Portsmouth in 1882, Menevia in 1898, Cardiff in 1916, Brentwood in 1917, Lancaster in 1924—and six in Scotland in 1878. On the European mainland only a few dioceses of importance were newly established: in Italy, Livorno in 1806, Cuneo in 1817, Foggia in 1855; in France, Laval in 1855, Lourdes in 1912, Lille in 1913. In Germany, by the reorganization at the beginning of the nineteenth century, Chiemsee, Constance, and Worms were suppressed and in their place Limburg and Rottenburg (1821) were erected. It was only in the twentieth century that there occurred an increase in the number of dioceses through the founding of Meissen (1921), Aachen, and Berlin (1929). After World War I several new dioceses were established in Poland: Lodz (1920), Czenstochowa, Kattowice, Lomza, and Pinsk (1925).

On the other hand, an uncommonly large number of new pastoral centers of lesser rank were created. Especially in the rapidly growing metropolitan and industrial areas hundreds of new parishes were erected. It can be said without exaggeration that in the nineteenth century more parish churches were built than in all earlier centuries taken together. These mostly neo-Gothic and to some extent really monumental church edifices constitute in many places a characteristic feature of the modern urban scene. From the artistic viewpoint it is often

542

a subject of regret that for this extraordinarily bustling building activity no original ecclesiastical style of construction was
available. But a time would come when the artistic value of
these creations in the Rhineland, Westphalia, northern France,
Vienna, and elsewhere would again be discovered.

The progress of the care of souls in North America was
extraordinarily impressive. The diocese of Boston may serve
as an example. In 1844 it embraced the states of Massachu-
setts, New Hampshire, Vermont, and Maine, that is, the
entire northeast corner of the United States. In this extensive
territory lived 30,000 Catholics, with thirty-two churches and
twenty-six priests at their service. A century later this district
had been divided into six dioceses, with 2,300,000 Catholics,
1,145 churches, 2,076 secular priests, and 808 religious priests.

In this we must not overlook the fact that the number of
priests did not keep step with the growth of the Catholic
population. If today the total number of priests in the entire
Church may be estimated at more than 300,000 in a total
population of 350,000,000, this means hardly one priest for
1,000 Catholics. In many dioceses the situation is more favorable. Thus, for example, Westminster has one priest for 420
Catholics, Baltimore has one for 320. On the other hand, there
are regions with a pronounced dearth of priests, like Brazil,
which has only 4,000 priests for more than 30,000,000 Catholics. In the seventeenth and eighteenth centuries there were
more priests proportionately in the whole Church. But in the
nineteenth and twentieth centuries the activity of the individual priests became much more intensive. Formerly, a considerable part of the secular and religious priests were seldom
or never active in the care of souls. Today, even in Europe, the
many merely beneficed or Mass-priests have almost entirely
disappeared. This has its cause not only in the fact that in
the whole body of the clergy zeal for souls and a sense of

responsibility have unquestionably become stronger, but also in the completely altered economic situation of the clergy.

THE ECONOMIC BASIS OF THE CHURCH IN THE NINETEENTH CENTURY

By virtue of the great secularizations at the end of the eighteenth century and the beginning of the nineteenth, the economic basis of the Church was completely altered in most European countries. Till then most ecclesiastical institutions had depended almost entirely on their endowments, usually on landed property. It is estimated that in France before the Revolution about one-tenth of all the soil belonged to ecclesiastical institutions. In most countries the state assumed, at least in the beginning, a part of the obligations connected with the confiscated Church property, the support of the clergy and the maintenance of church edifices being a minimum. These contributions were scantily apportioned from the start and became less in consequence of the inflation prevailing throughout the nineteenth century. Furthermore, they were dependent on the good will or arbitrariness of the ruling government. Hence, increasingly the Church depended on the freewill offerings of the faithful. This was all the more the case in lands where no former Church property was in existence, as in England and North America, or where the states shunned their obligations, as in the numerous countries of South America previously under the patronage of Spain. These freewill offerings took various forms, from the simple church collection to individual donations and bequests. In the United States the income of the churches at first depended mostly on pew rental. Even today it is still principally the collection basket that defrays in North America the vast outlay for the care of souls and for charity. Throughout the world Mass stipends furnish a definite share for the support of the clergy.

In the matter of property the Church had become unquestionably poorer. But under the new circumstances she had
more resources, more returns. Of course, she did not change
to a centralized economy in the nineteenth century. The individual ecclesiastical institutions—dioceses, parishes, schools,
charitable organizations, societies, monasteries—remained economically independent. However, the central authorities, as
well as the subordinate administrative units, were more productive, because they were no longer bound in the old way to
foundations and landowning. Besides, since they lived, so to
speak, from hand to mouth, they were less exposed to violent
seizures from without. The persistent local injuries in which
the history of the nineteenth century so abounds could be
compensated comparatively easily and rapidly.

THE RELIGIOUS ORDERS IN THE NINETEENTH CENTURY

Perhaps the most conspicuous feature of ecclesiastical life
in the nineteenth century is the extraordinary progress of the
religious life. In this the nineteenth century is to be compared
only with the thirteenth, the age of the Mendicant Orders,
though now, corresponding to the general growth of the
Church, everything took on far greater proportions.

The anti-religious spirit of the *Aufklärung,* the political
revolutions, and the secularizations had done such serious
damage to the religious state that not only the Society of Jesus,
officially suppressed in 1773, but almost all other Orders had,
so to speak, to begin over again. With some of them it was not
until far beyond the middle of the nineteenth century that
they again attained their former number of members. Some
were so badly hit that, despite great growth, they have not
even today reached their previous condition. In 1782 the
Capuchins numbered 26,826 members; in 1853 they still

amounted to 11,045, but then they declined to 7,500 by 1888, and only recently have they reached 12,000.

The Benedictines, almost wiped out by the great monastic suppressions, were re-established in Hungary in 1802, in Bavaria (Metten) in 1827, in France (Solesmes) in 1833; they were established in Australia in 1833 and 1845 and in North America in 1846. Around the middle of the century there were again between 1,500 and 1,600 Black Benedictines, and by 1900 they had grown to 5,244. Today there are more than 10,000 Benedictine monks. Their abbeys, scattered throughout the world, are not as elaborate and wealthy as formerly, but in far-reaching religious radiation they need not fear comparison with the best days of their Order.

Around the middle of the nineteenth century the Franciscans were the most numerous Order of men, with between 13,000 and 14,000 members, and since then they have doubled in size. Of great advantage was the amalgamation, carried out in 1897, of the congregations, hitherto almost independent, of Observants, Alcantarines, Recollects, and others, into a great administrative unity with common statutes. The Dominicans too have doubled their number in the past century. In the period of the Revolution the Lazarists declined to a few hundred and then they again increased to more than 4,000.

In 1803 there were only thirty Christian Brothers left. There were 570 in 1820, 1,420 in 1830, 6,609 in 1854, and 15,060 (not counting novices and candidates) in 1899. Then, of course, occurred a setback because of their expulsion from France.

In 1816, two years after its restoration, the Society of Jesus numbered 674 members; the figure was 4,652 in 1846, 12,070 in 1886, 15,160 in 1900, and today it is 28,000.

A persistent and at times even a very rapid growth characterizes the unusually numerous congregations founded only in the nineteenth century, such as the Oblates of the Immaculate Conception (1816), the Claretians, the White Fathers, the Fathers of the Holy Spirit, the Sacred Heart Missionaries, the Missionaries of Steyl (1875), and the Salvatorians (1881). The Redemptorists, whose founding goes back to the eighteenth century, numbered 3,580 in 1907 and 6,240 in 1933. Most astonishing is the spread of the Salesians of Saint John Bosco, established in 1859. In 1907 they numbered 4,137; there were 9,415 of them in 1933, and today they count more than 15,000. At present, less than a century after their founding, they rank in the third place among clerical orders in regard to numbers.

Even more striking than the increase in the Orders of men was the growth of the Orders of women in the nineteenth century. One could actually speak of a century of Orders of women.

There were 3,000 Ursulines in 1845; there are 13,000 today. In the same period the Visitandines grew from 3,000 to 8,000. The Daughters of Charity of Saint Vincent de Paul were estimated at 20,000 in 1877 and number about 60,000 today. The multiplication of communities of Sisters that were founded only in the nineteenth century is almost incalculable. The Madames of the Sacred Heart, established in 1800, include over 7,000 Sisters today; the Sisters of the Good Shepherd, founded at Angers in 1829, amount to 11,000; the Franciscan Missionaries of Mary, originating in Brittany only in 1877, numbered 6,500 in 1933.

German-speaking lands shared prominently in the new foundations. In Alsace in 1832 a branch of the Daughters of Charity was established, which today, divided among several independent motherhouses, embraces over 22,000 Sisters. Also in Alsace in 1849 Elizabeth Eppinger founded the Niederbronn Sisters, of whom there are 6,000 today. In Switzerland

547

the Capuchin, Theodosius Florentini, founded the Sisters of the Cross, whose two branches, of Menzingen and Ingenbohl, together number over 10,000 Sisters today. The Poor School Sisters, instituted by Caroline Gerhardinger of Regensburg in 1833, have more then 10,000 members today. A comparable growth is displayed by the Poor Sisters of the Infant Jesus (Aachen, 1843), the Sisters of Christian Love (founded at Paderborn in 1849 by Pauline von Mallinkrodt, sister of the prominent Centrist), the Handmaids of Christ (Dernbach), the Sisters of Providence (Münster), and others.

In particular, many of the German congregations of Sisters took root in North America. The United States proved to be an especially fruitful soil for female religious vocations. Today a total of more than 150,000 women religious labor in the Union. A great part of the American Catholics, men included, receives its education in the schools of Sisters.

The numerical growth whose ground was laid in the nineteenth century did not attain its full development until the twentieth. In the first third of the twentieth century the number of female religious more than doubled itself throughout the world.

In the religious life mere number of members is by no means the only decisive factor. A small community can carry out its purpose and lead its members to Christian perfection. However, strong external growth is generally always a sign of internal strength, and in any case the number of vocations is an almost sure indicator of the spiritual life of a period and of a country. In this respect France and Germany led the way for a great part of the nineteenth century, and were later joined by Belgium and the Netherlands. Today the United States and Spain provide the highest percentage of vocations.

Despite the apparent diversity of new institutes, one can still speak of a nineteenth century type. The new congregations continued the development which was introduced by the Clerics Regular of the sixteenth century: sanctification of the individuals by means of serious work in accord with their purpose rather than an austere manner of life, by strong emphasis on interior growth through contemplative prayer, strict organization, and easy mobility in the service of the work.

Already a group of founders of Orders in the nineteenth century has been canonized: Don Bosco (✝1888) in 1934; Jeanne Antide Thouret (✝1826) in 1934; Sophie Barat (✝1825), foundress of the Madames of the Sacred Heart, in 1925; Francesca Cabrini (✝1917), foundress of a congregation for the care of Italian emigrants, in 1946; Euphrasia Pelletier (✝1868), foundress of the Sisters of the Good Shepherd, in 1940.

THEOLOGY

The nineteenth century produced no theologians of first rank, no Thomas Aquinas or Augustine; but it did produce much serious work. On the whole, scholarly production increased considerably from the middle of the century, especially because of the rise of specialized theological periodicals in all the larger countries. In the course of the years many of these grew into real theological libraries. The oldest still in existence is the *Tübinger Quartalschrift*, founded in 1819. Furthermore, periodicals intended for wider circles appeared, which very often treated theological questions. One of the first of these was *Der Katholik* (Mainz, 1821); later ones were *La Civiltà Cattolica* (Rome, 1850), *Études* (Paris, 1856), *Stimmen aus Maria Laach* (1871; now *Stimmen der Zeit*), and the like in almost all countries. For the essential theological work definite centers were formed, usually in connection with universities: Tübingen, Munich, Mainz, Bonn, Münster, Innsbruck, Fri-

549

bourg in Switzerland, Louvain, Paris, Toulouse, Rome. In publication special significance attaches to the great Catholic publishing firms: Herder (Freiburg-im-Breisgau), Pustet (Regensburg), Bachem (Cologne), Benziger (chiefly in North America), Desclée (Mechlin), Burns and Oates (London), and the Parisian houses of Lethielleux, Beauchesne, and others.

To a great degree theological work in the nineteenth century concentrated on the field of apologetics in the broad sense, occupying itself with what is often called the "question of *Weltanschauung*." Catholic theology avoids this expression, which implies a definite relativity and subjectivity. It was the ancient problem of Faith and knowledge, of revelation and reason, which, in accord with the advances in knowledge in both fields, always assumes new forms. In Germany the Bonn professor of theology, Georg Hermes (✝1831), proceeding from Kant and rejecting Scholasticism, wanted to demonstrate the mysteries of Faith from reason. In France the so-called Traditionalists, De Bonald (✝1840), Bautain (✝1867), professor at Strasbourg, and Bonnetty (✝1879), sought a solution by the opposite extreme, when, also rejecting Scholasticism, they entirely separated knowledge derived from reason and knowledge derived from Faith and declared that philosophical proof of the suppositions of Faith is impossible. Both systems were condemned by the Church—Hermesianism in 1835, Traditionalism in 1855. The Italian priest Rosmini (✝1855), a saintly religious founder, took his own special path: to him the thinking subject somehow appears as a formative factor in both philosophical and theological knowledge. He too was anti-Scholastic or, more correctly, non-Scholastic, and through an arbitrary explanation of Scholastic terminology he made untenable assertions, which were likewise condemned after his death (1887).

Meanwhile, a powerful movement of revival in the in-

THE NINETEENTH CENTURY

terpretation of Scholasticism had begun. It proceeded chiefly
from the Roman educational institutions, where the Dominican Zigliara (✝1893, a cardinal) and the Jesuits, Perrone
(✝1876), Franzelin, a Tyrolese (✝1886, a cardinal), Libera-
tore (✝1892), and others, restored philosophical knowledge
to its proper place in the theological system. The Jesuit, Joseph
Kleutgen (✝1883) of Dortmund, who was likewise active at
Rome, became through his *Theologie der Vorzeit* (1853) and
his *Philosophie der Vorzeit* (1860) a pioneer in the revival of
Scholasticism in Germany. In his encyclical *Aeterni Patris* of
1879 Leo XIII pointed expressly to Saint Thomas Aquinas as
the master. In the basic question of apologetics the Vatican
Council brought clarification with its definition that "God can
be known with certainty by natural reason from the works of
creation."

However, toward the end of the century there arose a
current of broad ramifications among theologians, especially in
France, Germany, Italy, and England, who, under the influence
of non-Catholic biblical criticism and theories of the evolution
of dogma, began again to despair of reconciling Faith and
knowledge and sought new solutions in the sense of Kantian
Immanentism. The intellectual leaders of this movement were:
in France, the biblical critic Alfred Loisy; in England, the
apologetic journalist George Tyrrell, S.J.; in Italy Romolo
Murri and later Ernesto Buonaiuti. The many writings of this
group, of a dazzling erudition and an alarmingly triumphant
apologetic tone, were hardly perceived by most Catholics as
dangerous. The decree *Lamentabili* of the Holy Office in 1907
and the encyclical *Pascendi* that followed it were like an exposure. In these Pius X showed that all these seemingly hetero-
geneous tendencies sprang from a common root and had
already withdrawn far from the foundations of the Catholic
Faith. For the new heresy he coined the term "Modernism"

551

and proceeded firmly against its representatives. Only isolated defections took place. Tyrrell, dismissed from his Order, died unreconciled with the Church in 1909, as did Buonaiuti in 1946. Before his death in 1944 Murri made a retraction. Loisy entirely abandoned the Christian Faith. But no sect arose. Hardly ever before in the history of the Church was a heresy overcome so rapidly and so completely.

Over and above such derailments, which, after all, stirred intellects only temporarily, serious theological research proceeded on its way throughout the nineteenth century. Much that was excellent was accomplished in the fields of Church History, patristics, and historical theology. Here the Germans may claim a place of honor. Beside the unfortunate Döllinger stand others whose names are familiar to the historical scholarship of all nations: Johann Adam Möhler (✝1838), Josef Hergenröther (✝1890, a cardinal), Karl Josef Hefele (✝1893), Franz X. Kraus (✝1901), Franz X. Funk (✝1907), Johannes Janssen (✝1891), Pius Gams, O.S.B. (✝1892), Heinrich Schrörs (✝1928), Ludwig von Pastor (✝1928), Nikolaus Paulus (✝1930), Hartmann Grisar, S.J. (✝1932), Albert Erhard (✝1940), Franz Josef Dölger (✝1940), and Karl Bihlmeyer (✝1942). In the investigation of Scholasticism great merit belongs to Karl Werner (✝1888), Heinrich Denifle, O.P. (✝1905), Klemens Bäumker (✝1924), Franz Ehrle, S.J. (✝1934, a cardinal), and Martin Grabmann (✝1949). Worthy of special mention are: among French historians, Cardinal Pitra, O.S.B. (✝1889), Louis Duchesne (✝1922), Pierre Batiffol (✝1928); the Belgian Bollandist Hippolyte Delehaye (✝1940); the Italians, Cardinal Angelo Mai (✝1854), Luigi Tosti, O.S.B. (✝1897), Achille Ratti (✝1939 as Pope Pius XI), and Pio Franchi de' Cavalieri.

In Rome the discoveries and exemplary publications of the layman, John Baptist de Rossi (✝1894), led to a flowering of

Christian archaeology. The great finds in the catacombs, such as the discovery of the papal crypt with sepulchral inscriptions of the third century—of Pontian, Fabian, Cornelius, and others—came just at the right time, when historical skepticism, become almost a mania, threatened to scrap all of primitive Christian history. They strengthened the shaken confidence in the sources. De Rossi's work was continued by Orazio Marucchi, Josef Wilpert, Anton de Waal, John Peter Kirsch, Paul Styger, and Enrico Josi.

A broad field opened up for biblical scholarship. It was necessary to acquire familiarity with the unquestionably great achievements of philology, textual criticism, and Oriental archaeology and thereby to erect a dam against destructive criticism. Here too German scholars acquired merit: Paul Schanz (✝1905), Johannes Belser (✝1916), the Jesuits Cornely (✝1908) and Knabenbauer (✝1912), and Leopold Fonck (✝1930) and Augustin Merk (✝1945), who were members of the Pontifical Biblical Institute in Rome, founded in 1909. In France Vigouroux published the *Dictionnaire de la Bible* (Paris, 1891). Epoch-making was the work of the French Dominican, Lagrange (✝1938), who also established the Ecole Biblique et Archéologique Française in Jerusalem.

The advances made in the historical field were of profit to speculative theology. The arguments from Scripture and Tradition became richer and more reliable. The certain and the hypothetical could be more clearly distinguished. Among the systematizers of the nineteenth century, in addition to the neo-Scholastics already mentioned, the following were also prominent: in dogmatic theology Mathias Josef Scheeben (✝1888), Josef Pohle (✝1922), Christian Pesch (✝1925), and Louis Billot (✝1931); in moral theology Antonio Ballerini (✝1881), Augustin Lehmkuhl (✝1918), Hieronymus Noldin (✝1922).

EDUCATION OF PRIESTS

Quite special solicitude was devoted in the nineteenth century to the training of recruits for the priesthood, whose numbers had grown rapidly since the mid-century. Questions concerning education and schools stood everywhere in the foreground. This was a legacy of the *Aufklärung,* and the Church on the one hand had to wage a persistent fight against the especially conspicuous effort on the part of states to regulate the pedagogical field, while on the other hand she could profit by the many accomplishments in educational methods, which without any doubt were among the most worthwhile things that the *Aufklärung* had produced. In the confusion of the revolutions and secularizations major seminaries had to a great extent collapsed and had to be revived, while minor seminaries had to be established almost everywhere. Today nearly every larger diocese possesses both seminaries. Where the diocesan territories are too small to support institutions of their own, as in Ireland and especially in Italy, regional seminaries were established.

The scholarly demands which were made on candidates for the priesthood and on professors of theology increased very much in the course of the nineteenth century. Pius XI's regulation of studies in 1931 (*Deus Scientiarum Dominus*) goes very far in this respect. Many professors of theology are formed in Rome itself, where almost every nation has its college. The students earn the academic degrees at the Gregorian University or equivalent institutes, such as the Angelicum of the Dominicans and the Ateneo Lateranense, as well as at the specialized schools of biblical scholarship, Oriental theology, archaeology, and ecclesiastical music.

RELIGIOUS INSTRUCTION

Catechisms, that is, brief summaries of Catholic teaching

554

in the form of question and answer for the purpose of instructing children and adults, had long existed. Those prepared by Saint Peter Canisius in Germany (1555) and by Saint Robert Bellarmine in Italy (1598) were widely used. These were not intended as school texts but for purposes of instruction in the church. Religious instruction as a school subject was an achievement of the nineteenth century. In this regard the pioneer can be considered to have been the Silesian Augustinian Canon, Ignaz Felbiger (✝1788), who was called to Austria by Maria Theresa, where among other things he composed a catechism for the Austrian states in 1777. In Germany the Westphalian priest and teacher, Overberg (✝1826), did the same. As an inheritance from the pedagogical ideas of the *Aufklärung,* as wide a departure from Scholastic theological methods as possible made itself felt also in catechetics, as the catechism published in 1842 by the Tübingen professor, Hirscher, shows. In 1847 the Jesuit, Deharbe, turned again to Scholastic methods. His catechisms, translated into other languages, long dominated the field, until in recent times they were replaced by school texts which seek to adapt themselves more to the intellectual grasp of children. All these efforts, however, only show how very serious the nineteenth century was with regard to basic religious instruction. The teaching of catechism to children, regarded in previous centuries as a work of humility, became an honorable function. In struggles between Church and state and at the concluding of concordats, the right of children to religious instruction in the school often played the first role.

RELIGIOUS EDUCATION OF THE PEOPLE

It cannot be denied that the religious education of the Catholic people was improved all along the line in the nineteenth century. This pastoral work of its nature never comes to an end, for it is a question of forming each generation anew. And even with the mere impressing of the truths of Faith by methods of instruction, indispensable as that is, not everything is done. The Catholic must not only know the truths of salvation, but also the life of the Church, her institutions, her destinies. In what concerns this well-rounded Catholic "training," the Catholics of the United States are at present models, thanks to their splendid school organization. Of the greatest importance for this is also the Catholic press, not so much the great political dailies as the countless and quietly operating periodicals, weeklies, and diocesan and parish newspapers. These now exist even in the remotest regions of the *diaspora*.

THE CO-OPERATIVE MOVEMENT

The co-operative movement in the Church reaches back in its origins to the Third Orders of the thirteenth century and the confraternities of the later Middle Ages. But it did not acquire its more recent form until the nineteenth century. The enormous growth of population and the corresponding increase in pastoral activity on the one hand, and the spoliation of the Church through secularization on the other, made it necessary to find new funds by means of private collections. Thus arose the countless collecting associations for the support of every facet of pastoral work, above all for the foreign missions. The Lyon Mission Society, founded in 1822 by Pauline Jaricot, remained throughout the nineteenth century the financial basis of the missions. Since 1922 its headquarters have been in Rome. Other such associations were the German Franz-Xaver-Verein (Aachen, 1841), the Society of the Holy Childhood, founded at Paris in 1843 and later spread especially among the German children, the Missionsverein Katholischer Frauen und Jungfrauen Deutschlands (1893), the Sodality of Saint Peter Claver for the African missions (1894), and a host of collecting societies in all countries, which usually support particular missions or missionary institutes. The alms for the missions, resulting mostly from modest contributions, were estimated in 1913 at from 16,000,000 to 20,000,000 marks.

Collecting associations in Germany for special purposes comprised the Borromäus-Verein for the spread of good books, founded at Bonn in 1845; the Bonifatiusverein (Paderborn, 1849) for the spiritual care of the *diaspora*; the Raphaelsverein for emigrants (1871); the Görresgesellschaft for the support of scholarly efforts and of Catholic scholars (1876). Associations of this sort are, of course, not mere financial enterprises; at the same time they foster in their members interest in the great tasks of the Church and give them the opportunity to exercise their Christianity in practice. This is especially the case with the many charitable associations, in which the work of the individuals is more important than their financial contributions. In this respect the models are the Saint Vincent de Paul Conferences, established at Paris in 1833 by Frédéric Ozanam, which have spread all over the Catholic world.

The charitable associations and institutes were usually grouped into diocesan units. The Caritasverband, founded by Lorenz Werthmann in 1897 and having its headquarters in Freiburg, was established for the whole of Germany. The Church maintains her right to practice charity even against the tendency of modern states to draw all relief into their own spheres. The Church practices charity because activity springing from love of neighbor belongs to Christianity, not for propaganda purposes and even less from any fear of defections or of movements of social revolution.

From the Piusverein, founded at Mainz in 1848 by Franz Adam Lennig, arose the annual meetings of the Catholics of Germany. These "Catholic Days," which were imitated in

557

many other countries, helped to strengthen the sentiment of unity among the faithful.

The first Catholic student associations in Germany arose at the University of Bonn (Bavaria, 1844), Breslau (Winfridia, 1849), and Munich (Aenania, 1851). The three largest units had a combined membership of 152 clubs with 6,905 students in 1913. Despite definite drawbacks, these associations gave a firm footing to the Catholic students in the predominantly unbelieving atmosphere of the universities and strengthened the Catholic sense of honor, which too often left much to be desired in the *intelligentsia*. Their great importance is seen also in the fact that they were copied successfully in many countries outside Germany.

The Gesellenvereine founded in 1849 by Adolf Kolping, a priest of Cologne, were of importance for the creation of a Christian laboring class. In 1905 they comprised 72,000 crafts-men and conducted 347 hospices.

Every country has its own associations and types of organization. In North America the Holy Name Society for men exists in every parish. The women belong to the Sodality of Our Lady or to the Congregation of Mary; the students, to the Sodality of Mary or to the Students' Mission Crusade. A very strong organization is the Knights of Columbus, copying the lodges of the Freemasons, even with a certain amount of secrecy and initiation rites, but in other respects by no means fearing the light. Of specialized organizations there are, among others, the National Catholic Rural Life, especially in the Mid-West, for the support of rural pastoral work, which is very difficult in the United States; Labor Schools; evening schools for workers; and Catholic Workers' Groups. The schools, especially the great Catholic colleges and universities, almost all have their own organizations of supporters. Differing from the German, the American does not feel such a need of combining all possible organizations into general secretariates and all-embracing organizations. Still, there exists in Washington the National Catholic Welfare Conference for the general organization of affairs.

France is very rich in Catholic societies, or *oeuvres*, not to mention the fact that some of those that now exist everywhere, such as the Saint Vincent de Paul Conferences and the great mission associations, had their origin in France.

NINETEENTH CENTURY SAINTS

Canonization is not to be interpreted as though it were a distribution of rewards, and accordingly one may not compute statistically from the list of canonizations in what region and at what time the spiritual life flourished most. The tribunal of canonization, which since the sixteenth century has been the Congregation of Rites, is independent and non-partisan in its judgment, but the selecting of candidates depends upon many things, including chance situations. The tribunal does not look for candidates, but merely judges those presented to it. Thus it happens that places where a greater interest in canonization prevails, for example Italy, show especially numerous canonized saints, but it is not to be inferred from this that there is a higher percentage of sanctity in the places in question. Furthermore, the processes last so long, sometimes for centuries, that no conclusive judgment can be reached in regard to a determined period from the completed processes.

Just the same, the course of Church history, at least in its great outlines, is reflected in canonizations. It is no mere accident that Spain displays so many saints in the sixteenth century, France in the seventeenth, and that throughout the Middle Ages Germany counts so many, whereas for long after the Reformation it had almost none and did not again have any canonized saints until the nineteenth century.

In the nineteenth century, especially its first half, France had an extraordinarily large number of saintly women religious. Many of them have already attained to the honors of the altar, among them the religious founders, Jeanne Antide Thouret (✝1826), Sophie Barat (✝1825), Euphrasia Pelletier (✝1868), Thérèse Soubiran (✝1889), and Emilie de Vialar (✝1856). Others are the Sacred Heart Sister Philippine Duchesne (✝1852), the Sister of Charity Catherine Labouré (✝1876), Bernadette Soubirous of Lourdes (✝1878), and the famous twenty-four-year-old Carmelite Thérèse of the Child Jesus (✝1897). Among men saints are the religious founders, André Hubert Fournet (✝1834), Pierre Julien Eymard (✝1868), and Michel Garicoits (✝1863). Best known is the Curé of Ars near Lyon, Saint Jean-Baptiste Vianney (✝1859).

Italy cannot boast so many, but it did produce saints of a pronounced individuality. Before it rushed into anti-clerical policies Piedmont possessed a triple constellation in Cottolengo (✝1842), one of the great charity workers of recent times, Don Bosco (✝1888), the incomparable educator of youth and religious founder, and his teacher and confessor, Cafasso (✝1860). A second Saint Aloysius appeared in the holy Passionist cleric, Gabriel Possenti (✝1862). Outstanding among Italian missionaries was Blessed Justin de Jacobis (✝1860), vicar apostolic of Abyssinia; among women two religious foundresses, Blessed Magdalena of Canossa (✝1835) and Saint Francesca Cabrini (✝1917), and the holy serving-girl, Saint Gemma Galgani of Lucca (✝1903). An interesting personality is Blessed Contardo Ferrini (✝1902), professor at the University of Pavia, who acquired international fame from his works on the history of Roman law.

The German-speaking countries gave the Church two

saints, one at the beginning of the nineteenth century, Saint Clement-Maria Hofbauer (✝1825), who can be called the second founder of the Redemptorists, and one at the end, the holy Capuchin lay brother, Conrad von Parzham (✝1894). Canonization processes have been introduced for, among others, Franziska Schervier (✝1876), foundress of the Poor Sisters of Saint Francis, Katharina Kaspar (✝1898), foundress of the Sisters of Dernbach, Maria Droste zu Vischering (✝1899), who died among the Sisters of the Good Shepherd in Portugal, and most recently for the Benedictine lay brother of Einsiedeln, Meinrad Eugster (✝1925).

It is clear that in the nineteenth century the types of saints were numerous and multiform. This is not to be understood as though "cloister piety" had lost its leading role, as is sometimes asserted, and that beside it or even in its place a new lay sanctity had arisen. In the Church this is not possible, for the evangelical counsels will always remain the norm for every ideal of holiness. Here there is question, not of a break, not of new ways of spirituality, but of a richer unfolding of the same ideal in varied conditions of life.

Thus it can be said that the recent age has formed the youth in a special type of holiness or of parish activity. The first communicant, the big city altar boy, the secondary school sodalist, the modern German, the Scout de France, the Jocist (*Jeunesse Ouvrière Catholique*), the American college boy, have become mere types, with often splendid individual representatives. At a more mature age we find the Catholic working girl, the Catholic teacher, the parish social worker, the Saint Vincent de Paul member, already active at secondary school age, the Catholic journalist, politician, and statesman. Of course, not all these types originated in the nineteenth century. The Catholic physician, teacher, and artist are types that in part go far back, and all the more is this true of the Catholic

561

farmer and artisan. New and more frequent than is commonly supposed, is, on the contrary, the saintly industrial worker. The process of canonization of the Irish industrial worker, Matt Talbot, who died in 1925, has been introduced.

the present.
the mission countries

THE PERIOD from the outbreak of World War I in 1914 to the present is too brief to justify its being regarded as a special epoch of history. It may really form the introduction to a new age, just as the revolutions and wars between 1789 and 1814 inaugurated the nineteenth century.

It is now quite apparent that Europe has lost its leading role. World War I began as a struggle among the European powers for world domination; it ended with universal exhaustion. World War II has shown that Europe is now only an object over which America and Asia will fight in the future.

The Church entered into this terrible crisis far better prepared than she had been at the time of the political and social upheaval that began with the French Revolution. Of course, the Church too was severely hurt by the enormous destruction of human life and values which were the concomitants and results of both world wars. But her inner structure, so far as can now be seen, suffered no collapse. She does not have to start over again; she is the only social structure in the world that has remained unaltered in the unprecedented cataclysms of the last thirty years. This is asserted, and with amazement, even by her enemies, who have not decreased but rather have multiplied.

In the individual countries Church and state affairs were not substantially different in their general character from those of the nineteenth century. The Church witnessed the usual oscillation of governments between *Kulturkampf, modus vivendi,* concordat, and renewed rupture. Pastoral work continued without any serious breakdown.

The changes on the political map after World War I were not entirely favorable to the Church. The Catholics of Germany suffered a diminution in numbers by the detachment of Alsace-Lorraine, West Prussia, Poznan, and Upper Silesia, which were for the most part Catholic. On the other hand, the Weimar constitution of August 11, 1919, was not disadvantageous to the Church. And while the division of the Austro-Hungarian monarchy into three small independent states brought to an end what had been at least in name a Catholic great power, the three new states, Austria, Hungary, and Czechoslovakia, remained predominantly Catholic. The neighboring countries of Italy and Poland, which received portions of the old monarchy, were also Catholic. Partly Catholic Transylvania went to Rumania, with which a concordat was concluded in 1927. The Catholic South Slavs— Slovenes, Croats, Slavonians, Bosnians—were joined to the Serbs in the kingdom of Yugoslavia and for a time enjoyed comparative religious freedom, even though a concordat did not materialize.

Poland, which in 1930 counted 31,000,000 inhabitants, of whom almost 20,000,000 were Latin Catholics and 3,500,000 were Catholic Ruthenians, concluded a concordat with the Vatican in 1925. Lithuania, too, with 2,300,000, was for the most part Catholic; the concordat dates from 1927.

Through the separation of Ireland from England in 1921 there arose a new Catholic state, though, of course, it may be asked whether this was an advantage for the Church. The political position of the Catholics in England was weakened by the loss of Ireland, and the Catholics in Ireland themselves, who had hitherto played a great role in the Anglo-Saxon world, fell, so to speak, into a voluntary isolation.

THE LATERAN TREATY

The most important ecclesiastical-political happening between the two world wars was the reconciliation of Italy with the Holy See. The desire for this had been fundamentally present on both sides from 1870. On the part of the Church it was understood that a restoration of the former Papal State was neither possible nor desirable. On the other hand, a solution had to be found whereby, in regard to the kingdom of Italy, the pope would not be placed in a position similar to that of the popes in Avignon in regard to France.

From 1922 Italy was ruled by Benito Mussolini, prime minister and *duce* of the Fascist party. Personally without any internal relationship to the Church, but filled with the idea of raising Italy to the position of a leading world power, he wanted to eliminate the Roman Question as an open wound in the body politic. After difficult negotiations there came into existence on February 11, 1929, an agreement known as the Lateran Treaty, from the papal Lateran Palace where the signing took place. The signatories were Mussolini as Italian prime minister and Cardinal Gasparri as papal secretary of state. The pope renounced all territorial claims to the former Papal State. Italy recognized the territory of the Vatican Palace and Saint Peter's basilica as a sovereign state with diplomatic representation, passport system, post, and coinage. A whole series of papal buildings and institutes in Rome acquired extraterritoriality of varying degrees. Italy paid a single indemnity of 1,750,000,000 lire. Simultaneously, in regard to the ecclesiastical situation in Italy there was concluded a

565

concordat which the pope had made the condition of his acceptance of the Lateran Treaty.

Only the later writing of history will be in a position, on the basis of experience, to determine the good or evil consequences of the Lateran Treaty.[1] However, it will be difficult to discover another path Pius XI could have taken. The tiresome Roman Question had to be removed from the world eventually. Of course, what the pope attained in 1929 was a minimum: at bottom it was not much more than had been offered in 1871 by the Law of Guarantees, which Pius IX had so energetically rejected. At that time an expressive protest against the spoliation of the Church had been necessary. But to protest forever is worthless. What the Church needs is the pope's independence of any political power, and this was secured by the Lateran Treaty. Some, it is true, would have desired an international guarantee. Italy refused such an arrangement, and Pius XI did the right thing in not demanding it. Undoubtedly, an international guarantee, as, for example, through the League of Nations, would have once more involved a sort of tutelage, as in the days of the Holy Alliance. In addition to this drawback, an international pledge of fidelity would have been worthless. So long as Italy remains steadfast, the pope does not need any guarantee from the other powers; and a guarantee would be of no avail against an intentional violation of right and the use of force.

PERSECUTIONS

In Spain and Mexico the Church underwent violent persecutions and bloodshed. In Spain the persecution began with the establishment of the republic in 1931 and assumed a frightful character with the outbreak of civil war in 1936. The

[1] See Arnold J. Toynbee, *A Study of History*, IV (London: 1939), 220 f. (Translator's note.)

number of murdered bishops is reckoned at twelve, of priests at over 6,000; to these were added many clerics and lay brothers of different Orders. Many of these deaths were accompanied by bestial cruelties, and in a large number hatred of religion and of the priesthood must be regarded as the inciting motive, so that it is a question of real martyrdoms. The preliminary investigations for a future process of canonization are in progress. Peace has again prevailed since the end of the civil war in 1939.

In Mexico the presidency of Carranza (1915–1920) produced a storm, followed by a more severe one under Calles (1924–1928). After a temporary *modus vivendi*, the persecution erupted again in 1931. Pius XI impressively raised his voice against the conspiracy of silence that was observed by the world press in regard to the shocking happenings in Mexico.

NATIONAL SOCIALISM IN GERMANY

A persecution of a special kind was launched in Germany by National Socialism. The National Socialist movement was at first joyfully welcomed by Catholics, because they saw in it no danger for religion but only a counterpoise to the Social Democratic Party, which had become too powerful since World War I. In reality, National Socialism only gradually became a *Weltanschauung* and finally almost a religion. There flowed into it the strange propaganda which General Ludendorff had begun soon after World War I against "Jews, Jesuits, and Freemasons," the scientific and especially the historical ideas of Rosenberg, gathered from the anti-Christian literature of recent decades, and Haushofer's anthropological racial doctrine and geopolitical theories, interpreted in a nationalistic vein. A fertile soil was provided by the deep resentment which had seized upon wide circles of the population following the Treaty of Versailles and its sad consequences. The position of Catholics became unusually difficult. Some believed that the policy of the National Socialists should be at least partly approved, while at the same time their *Weltanschauung* could be rejected. The prohibitions against joining the party, issued by the bishops, produced difficult conflicts of conscience.

The world economic crisis, beginning in 1930, and the consequent increasing impoverishment and embitterment of the masses caused the National Socialist party, as the party of the dissatisfied, to grow enormously. The foreign powers were blind to the danger. On January 30, 1933, President von Hindenburg named Adolf Hitler chancellor, and in the following elections to the Reichstag the party obtained forty-four percent of all the votes. Since the new government at once declared its desire to maintain religious peace and even concluded a concordat with the Holy See on July 20, 1933, the bishops could hardly do otherwise than lift their prohibition.

Later it was often asked how Pius XI and his secretary of state, Pacelli, who had an exact knowledge of the German situation, could have accepted a concordat which was regarded by the government as a mere chess move and which it hardly intended to observe. It is certain that the arrangement was not easy for the pope to make. But the pope cannot refuse a treaty on the ground that it can later be broken. He could not give the government the opportunity to say, "We have extended the hand of peace, but the pope has declined it." Furthermore, at this moment there existed a definite, if not great, likelihood that the National Socialist party, once in power, would turn to lawful paths. The constitution was still in force. The head of the state, with whom the pope had made the concordat, was not Hitler but von Hindenburg. The great powers later concluded treaties with Hitler when the constitution had been shelved and the prospect of a return of a lawful state of affairs was non-existent.

For the Church in Germany there now began an extremely difficult time. That the Center had to disband caused hardly any setback, for the Reichstag had been rendered powerless. But almost all Catholic organizations and associations were also dissolved or brought into line. Thereby much Catholic influence was lost. Monasteries were suppressed; priests were imprisoned on the most varied accusations or even without any, and were put into concentration camps. The number of priests executed or killed in some other way between 1933 and 1945 is not insignificant. Preaching and religious instruction were supervised; Catholic newspapers and parochial bulletins, insofar as they were still permitted to appear, had to accept tendentious articles without being allowed to indicate the pressure that was being exerted on them. Anti-religious school texts were prescribed. The party press, submerging everything, was allowed to print blasphemous satires, such as the notorious "Black Corps." There were even public demands for Catholics to withdraw from the Church, often accompanied by strong moral pressure. In order to destroy respect for the clerical and religious states the so-called morality trials were staged and given the widest publicity. It was deeply to be regretted that in Germany, formerly so rightly proud of its blameless judiciary, were to be found jurists who were a party to all this.

It was painful to German Catholics that in foreign countries, even in Catholic lands, the opinion persisted that in Germany there was no persecution of the Church. Germany was completely closed off from the outside world. Only edited news crossed the frontiers. Even within Germany it was hard to form a correct picture. Of course not only Catholics were oppressed and imprisoned, but also believing Protestants,

Jews, and Communists in great number. It might appear that the governing circles sought, cruelly, it is true, but without distinction or partisanship, to get rid of all elements "hostile to the state," without being particularly influenced by hatred of religion or hatred of the Church. In especially crude cases it would always be stated that such things were due to regrettable excesses on the part of subordinates. The encyclical *Mit Brennender Sorge* of March 14, 1937, acted in this regard like an exposure. In it the pope spoke of "machinations which from the start knew no other goal than a struggle of annihilation," of "a thousand forms of organized religious slavery," of the "unheard-of distress of conscience of faithful Christians," of "treaty reinterpretation, treaty evasion, treaty undermining, treaty violation." In regard to the demand for withdrawal from the Church, the pope said:

Among the spokesmen there are many who, by reason of their official position, seek to create the impression that leaving the Church, and the disloyalty to Christ the King which it entails, is a particularly convincing and meritorious form of profession of loyalty to the present state. With cloaked and with manifest methods of coercion, by intimidation, by holding out the prospect of economic, professional, civic and other advantages, the loyalty of Catholics and especially of certain classes of Catholic officials to their faith is put under a pressure that is as unlawful as it is unworthy of human beings.[2]

The conduct of the Catholics was, on the whole, admirable. The broad masses of the Catholic people stood firm. As during the ancient Christian persecutions in Roman times, their

2 *The Church in Germany: Encyclical Letter of His Holiness, Pope Pius XI*, Vatican Press Translation (Washington: 1937), p. 16. (Supplied by Translator.)

constancy cannot be measured merely by the number of those who attained to bloody martyrdom, although such were not wanting. In foreign countries it was occasionally asked why the Catholics, and especially the bishops, did not offer a more active resistance. But how could they have done so? Violent resistance in a country that bristled with weapons would have been perfectly hopeless and directly criminal. A legal way did not exist. The numerous notes and protests from the ecclesiastical superiors disappeared, usually unanswered, in the offices. Bishops, especially, had to keep in mind that any measures of theirs would be answered with reprisals against clergy and people. The most courageous bishop will hesitate to stake the property, liberty, and perhaps the lives of his flock on a hopeless heroic gesture. Thus nothing was left, as in all real persecutions, except to hold out, to preserve what there was to preserve, and for the rest to hope that the storm would not last too long.

THE POPES SINCE 1914

BENEDICT XV (1914–1922)

When Pius X died in August, 1914, Italy was still neutral, and thus the cardinals, even those from the belligerent nations, could meet in conclave. Giacomo Della Chiesa was elected as Benedict XV. He had been undersecretary of state under Leo XIII, then archbishop of Bologna, and only recently had become a cardinal. It was very difficult for the pope to maintain the strict neutrality required by his office, since both sides were convinced of the justice of their cause and took it amiss that the pope did not declare for it. On the other hand, it was apparent that the pope's political prestige must increase by reason of his neutrality. England and Holland, which were hitherto unrepresented at the Vatican, established legations in

1914. This made Italy once more apprehensive. A few days before its entry into the war, Italy, in the secret pact of London of April 26, 1915, had its allies promise that the pope would remain excluded from the future peace negotiations.

On August 1, 1917, Benedict XV directed a diplomatic note to all the belligerents with an invitation to a peace settlement. Some of the governments did not acknowledge it at all, others replied evasively. The pope now endeavored at least to alleviate the sufferings of war and in this he actually accomplished a great deal.

In the internal affairs of the Church Benedict XV's name is linked with the establishing of two new congregations of cardinals, that for studies at seminaries and universities (1915) and that for churches with Oriental rites (1917). He also brought to a conclusion the great work of his predecessor, the codification of the entire *corpus* of ecclesiastical law, by the publication in 1917 of the *Codex Juris Canonici*. The new code was at once appraised by legal specialists as a masterpiece of legislation.

Benedict XV was not so brilliant a personality as Leo XIII, but was a thoroughly noble and balanced character and in addition very intelligent and completely unselfish. For the hard years of World War I and the succeeding period of distress the Church could scarcely have wanted a more capable head. Always in poor health, he died unexpectedly on January 22, 1922.

pius xi (1922–1939)

For almost a century unusually outstanding popes had occupied Saint Peter's Throne, and it seemed doubtful whether it would again and again be possible to discover a really great personality for this highest office on earth. Some thought of Gasparri, the actual creator of the new code, who had been

572

secretary of state under Benedict XV; others, of Pius X's secretary of state, Merry del Val, who, however, had numerous opponents. Finally, a *novus homo* was elected—Achille Ratti, who had just recently become archbishop of Milan and a cardinal. As a scholar, Achille Ratti was by no means a *novus homo*. He had been prefect of the Ambrosian Library in Milan and then of the Vatican Library in Rome; he was in contact with many scholars, was acquainted with foreign lands, and spoke fluent German.

Pius XI had about him much that recalled the great reform popes of the sixteenth century—their vitality and industry, their broad view, their love of building. When, through the treaty with Italy, the finances of the Holy See had become more secure, he subjected the whole complex of the Vatican Palace to a radical restoration, which it badly needed, erected the Vatican Pinacotheca and several other buildings in the Vatican City, including the radiobroadcasting station, and a number of central ecclesiastical institutions in Rome. For those closest to him he was not always an easy-going chief, for he required much, but he inspired confidence. His secretary of state in the first half of his pontificate was Gasparri; from 1930 it was Pacelli, who he hoped would be his successor.

In the great work of reconciliation with Italy Pius XI, a match for the highly gifted and forceful Mussolini, was just the man. He refused to be intimidated. When in 1938 Hitler came to Rome and was received by Mussolini with royal pomp, he expressed the desire to visit the pope; but Pius XI went to his villa at Castelgandolfo and had the Vatican museums locked.

Of the numerous encyclicals of Pius XI, the most outstanding were those on Christian marriage (*Casti Conubii*, 1930) and the social order (*Quadragesimo Anno*, 1931); the latter commemorated the fortieth anniversary of the appearance of

Leo XIII's *Rerum Novarum*. His care for Catholic Action, which he conceived as a stronger organization of the lay apostolate, was not attended by the desired success. In some non-Italian countries, where the Catholic laity was already too much organized, Catholic Action was understood as a sort of blanket organization, broken down into diocesan and parish groups, whereby not only were the already existing larger bodies interfered with here and there, but also, in place of the wished-for lay apostolate, there resulted a stronger binding of the lay organizations to the hierarchical offices.

In addition to the ordinary jubilee year of 1925, Pius XI had two extraordinary jubilees celebrated, in 1929 and 1933; of these, the last especially brought to Rome unprecedented throngs of pilgrims. Pius XI loved great celebrations and saw to it that they were conducted with the utmost dignity. But he did not seek popularity. In Rome he was perhaps less popular than some of his predecessors, but he was highly respected. This appeared at his death. For days people, a million of them, passed by the corpse lying in state in Saint Peter's, and 5,000 soldiers, sent by the Italian government, hardly sufficed to maintain order in the square.

PIUS XII (1939–   )

For the first time in history all the then living cardinals were able to attend the conclave. In the third scrutiny Cardinal Pacelli, who had been secretary of state, was elected. His election had been universally expected. Pius XII knew almost all the leading statesmen personally. He had been in North and South America, and he spoke many languages, including German with hardly a trace of a foreign accent. The Romans were especially glad that after a long period a son of the Eternal City had once more become pope.

But there was for the pope himself no cause for joy.

Scarcely six months after his election the long expected Second World War broke out.

In consequence of the Lateran Treaty the pope's position this time was more favorable than in the previous war. Then Italy on its entry into the war had compelled the Vatican envoys of the Central Powers to leave Rome. Now the diplomatic corps remained, but the representatives of states at war with Italy had to move into the Vatican. The president of the United States, which had no envoy at the Holy See, sent a personal representative to the pope.[3] The Vatican was, to be sure, kept under close observation, but, apart from individual encroachments, the pope's sovereign position remained inviolate. Moreover, he now had better means, especially through the radio, of keeping in contact with all of Christendom than had been the case under Benedict XV.

Mussolini was overthrown in July, 1943. In September the Italian government agreed to an armistice with the Allies. The king left Rome and the German troops occupied the city after a brief bombardment. Even at this time, apart from a few unsuccessful attempts to destroy the Vatican radio station by bombing, nothing serious was undertaken against the pope. How far the plans of the German command went is as yet unknown. In any case, the pope was determined to remain in Rome. He worked through diplomatic channels to prevent the Allies from bombing Rome, though the city swarmed with German troops. He succeeded in having the actual city spared, even if the suburbs had to endure heavy air attacks. When, finally, in June, 1944, the Allies marched into Rome, the pope received huge ovations from the grateful people.

During the entire war the pope admonished the human race, through diplomatic channels and by radio, in regard to

3 Myron Taylor held this post from 1940 till his resignation in 1950. (Translator's note.)

the conduct of war. When the Germans had occupied half of Europe, he repeatedly cautioned against a too harsh treatment of the conquered countries. At the Vatican he organized a series of relief agencies, among them an office for tracing prisoners which was able to give news of 8,000,000 missing persons. Especially with the entry of the Allies into Rome, gifts flowed in from all sides, notably from North and South America and Spain, and the papal motorcades and railroad cars rolled unceasingly throughout Italy and far beyond the frontiers with food and clothing.

The customary pilgrimages to Rome ceased during the war, but in their place hundreds of thousands of soldiers marched through the city, and these used their often brief stay for seeing the pope; at first it was the Germans, and later the Allies from all over the world. The pope tirelessly granted audiences, dispensed with all ceremonial, and spoke with the men in all tongues. The majority were not Catholics, and many came from places where the darkest prejudices against all things Catholic still prevailed. The impression which they received of the unpretentious friendliness of the head of the Church was always profound.

During the war the pope named no new cardinals. In February, 1946, he created thirty-two at one time, among them the bishops of Habana, Lima, Santiago de Chile, Rosario in Argentina, São Paulo in Brazil, Utrecht, Lourenço Marques in Portuguese Africa, Peking, Sydney, Toronto in Canada, and, in the United States, Saint Louis, Detroit, Chicago, and New York. Even defeated Germany received three new cardinals: Frings of Cologne, von Preysing of Berlin, and Galen of Münster; the last-named died a few weeks later. By these nominations the pope desired, after the destructive struggle of nations, to express vividly the universality of the Church.

Curiously enough, such a pope is the object of the coarse

anti-clerical agitation which was allowed to spread in Italy directly after the end of the war. In Rome on every street corner there are on sale newspapers with vulgar affronts and caricatures of pope and clergy.[4]

The pontificate of Pius XII has fallen in the most trying period of Church History since the struggle with Napoleon. In some ways the years since the conclusion of World War II in 1945 have been even more difficult than his first years, principally because of the rapid spread of Communism. Not only has the Soviet Union absorbed a number of neighboring countries or aided in putting Communist regimes in control, but the Communist party has made alarming gains in several countries of Western Europe and in Asia and Africa. In the general parliamentary elections in Italy in 1948, the civic committees of Catholic Action helped bring about the victory of the Christian Democratic Party, but the situation there and in France remains tense. Esthonia, Latvia, Lithuania, and parts of Germany, Finland, Poland, and Rumania have been swallowed up, while Poland, East Germany, Czechoslovakia, Hungary, Yugoslavia, Albania, Rumania, Bulgaria, China, Outer Mongolia, North Korea, and North Viet-Nam are Communist-dominated; in other words, about one-third of the total population of the world is under Communist rule.

The Church has suffered in varying degrees in these lands. In 1946 Archbishop Stepinac of Zagreb in Yugoslavia was tried and condemned to sixteen years' imprisonment. In 1949 occurred the equally sensational trial and imprisonment of the primate of Hungary, Cardinal Mindszenty and the removal of Archbishop Beran of Prague from office by the government. The whereabouts of the last-named prelate have been clouded in obscurity since his banishment, but the other two sufferers

---

[4] The five following paragraphs, bringing the reign of Pius XII to the present, have been added by the translator.

have already been released from prison, though they are still impeded in the exercise of their office. The pope's reply was the excommunication of all members of the Communist Party and all who aid or abet it. The Communist victory in China in 1949, three years after the establishment of the hierarchy, resulted in the expulsion or imprisonment of all foreign-born missionaries and in the imprisonment or death of all native clerics and religious. The Polish hierarchy remained relatively secure for a few years, but its efforts to come to an agreement with the Communist government failed and since 1953 the primate, Cardinal Wyszinski, has been unable to govern his flock. In these and other countries several other bishops and many priests have suffered cruelly for their loyalty to the Holy See, and government-sponsored schismatic movements have had only limited success.

The jubilee of 1950 afforded great consolation to the Holy Father. Several million pilgrims visited the Eternal City and a brilliant series of events took place, including numerous beatifications and canonizations. The canonization of Saint Maria Goretti, the youthful martyr of chastity, on June 24 was attended by such a multitude that the rites were conducted outside Saint Peter's. On August 12 the pope issued one of his most important encyclicals, *Humani Generis,* in which he discussed various false opinions of the present day. The climax of the jubilee came on November 1, when in the presence of thirty-six cardinals and 450 bishops, the Assumption of Our Lady was solemnly defined. The year 1954 was declared a special "Mary Year," in honor of the centenary of the definition of the Immaculate Conception. Throughout the world special devotions took place in honor of the Mother of God, but nowhere with such *éclat* and good taste as in the Eternal City. The chief event of the year was the proclamation

578

of Our Lady's queenship on October 11 and the establishment of a special feast under this title, to be celebrated on May 31.

In 1953 twenty-four cardinals were created. To the great joy of the Catholic world this number included the heroic Archbishops Stepinac of Zagreb and Wyszynski of Gniezno and Warsaw.

On March 2, 1956, occurred the pontiff's eightieth birthday and the seventeenth anniversary of his election. The period from March 2 to March 12, the anniversary of his coronation, was observed by Catholics everywhere as a time of special prayer and other events in honor of the occasion, and tokens of filial love and esteem poured into the Vatican.

INTERNAL MOVEMENTS IN THE CHURCH

On the whole, the interior life of the Church displays an uninterrupted advance on all sides in the twentieth century. Much that had been started modestly in the nineteenth century reached its full development only in the twentieth: increasing reception of the sacraments, growth of vocations to the priesthood and the religious life, religious instruction in the schools, preaching, literature, charitable work, missionary zeal.

The unprecedented cataclysms of the two world wars, however, did not fail to leave their traces on the interior life of the Church. Not that they weakened it; but they did cause a definite restlessness and tension. Under the repeated blows of fate, Catholics became just as nervous as the rest of mankind.

During World War I and still more after it, it became, so to speak, the fashion "to explore one's conscience," "to readjust oneself." Many Catholics found the Church to blame for everything, claiming that she had failed. There was much talk of inner warmth, of the spirit of primitive Christianity to which the road back must be found. Trust in the hierarchical

579

sacramental care of souls was shaken in many. Hence, there arose in clerical circles a frantic search for the most modern pastoral methods. One often heard that the priest must go out to "the people," to "the workers," and even that he must himself become a laborer. Christian moral principles, especially in regard to the right of ownership, must be revised.

In such trains of thought there lay much idealism and also much anxiety. This was partly the attitude of zealots who, in the depths of their hearts, believed they were serving a lost cause, fighting feverishly a last stand to hold off ruin.

THE LITURGICAL MOVEMENT

A real enrichment resulted from the efforts to familiarize the laity more than hitherto with the liturgical texts and ceremonies and thus to bring them to a more willing participation in the divine worship. Such endeavors reach far back into the nineteenth century. The French Benedictine, Prosper Guéranger, abbot of Solesmes (✝1875), can be regarded as the founder. In Germany the practical missals of Anselm Schott (✝1896), a Benedictine of Maria Laach, spread widely, especially among students. The Mainz circle around Bishop Ketteler also worked in this direction. At least since the beginning of the present century, catechists in Germany have striven for a more impressive organization of worship in the schools. Meanwhile, the scholarly resources became richer and richer, and from the second decade of the twentieth century we can speak of a real liturgical movement. Unfortunately, our century has a passion for pushing valuable ideas too far and for rushing them to death. Liturgy became fashionable. A critical tendency invaded the movement. The best pastors often had to endure the reproach that they were not liturgical enough. Many zealots lost a sense of proportion: while the whole world was in flames, they were minutely discussing whether and how this or that ceremony ought to be changed. But on the whole the movement has certainly created much that is good, and even those who, half-jokingly, complained of a liturgical terror were unable to escape its beneficent influence.[5]

In the first decades of the twentieth century Belgium, Holland, Germany, and France were almost the only countries where the liturgical renaissance had taken hold, but in them it was actively sponsored by the hierarchy and the clergy. This revival is actually only one phase of a threefold contemporary movement centering in the doctrine of the Mystical Body, which has been found to be the most effective method of presenting Christianity to the modern world. In its theological aspect, the movement expounds the doctrine of the Mystical Body; in its liturgical aspect, it calls for a more active participation in the corporate worship of the Mystical Body; in its apostolic aspect, it urges all to Catholic Action for the building up of the Mystical Body.

In the United States as elsewhere the liturgical movement has had its extremists, but in recent years these are becoming less prominent and the worthwhile facets of the revival are in the foreground, that is, the effort to bring the Mass, especially, to the people and to have them assist at it in the most profitable way by as active a participation as possible.

The movement really began in the United States with the launching of the periodical *Orate Fratres* in December, 1926. The editor, Virgil Michel, O.S.B., a monk of Saint John's Abbey, Collegeville, Minnesota, was the recognized leader until his death in 1938. His successor, Godfrey Diekmann, O.S.B., has followed faithfully in his footsteps, securing the services of excellent contributors and keeping his readers

---

[5] The five following paragraphs, treating recent developments in the liturgical movement and its progress in the United States, have been added by the translator.

abreast of all new developments. Meanwhile, the *Leaflet Missal* was inaugurated in 1930. The Liturgical Arts Society was founded in 1932; its *Liturgical Arts Quarterly* spreads the idea that the church edifice must be properly suited for official corporate worship. The National Liturgical Days, held in 1929, 1930, and 1931, were humble harbingers of the National Liturgical Week that has been enthusiastically observed since 1940. The Pius X Institute of Liturgical Music, at Manhattanville College of the Sacred Heart in New York City, has done pioneer work in restoring the Gregorian Chant to the people. Numerous school texts, for the elementary grades, high school, and college, have been published, as well as several other periodicals in addition to *Orate Fratres*, which, since the December, 1951, number, is known as *Worship*. The monks of Saint John's and other Benedictine abbeys are still active, but they have no monopoly of the movement, for eager and capable leaders are found in most other Orders and among the diocesan clergy.

Everywhere one of the chief points of the program is the widest possible use of the vernacular in the liturgy. The Holy See has shown itself quite willing to allow copious use of the vernacular in the administration of the sacraments and sacramentals. Vernacular rituals have already been obtained by Poland, Austria, France, Germany, various missionary lands, and, since 1954, the United States.

Pope Pius XII, while disapproving of the extravagances of the extremists and of those who presumed, on their own authority, to celebrate Mass in the vernacular, is deeply interested in the liturgical movement and has done more for its growth than any of his predecessors. The celebrated encyclical, *Mystici Corporis* of 1943, prepared the ground by a profound treatment of the doctrine of the Mystical Body. In 1944 a new translation of the psalter from the original texts appeared. In 1947 in the encyclical *Mediator Dei* the pope discussed the true meaning of the liturgy and, while censuring those who had gone too far, had high praise for the movement. In 1951, by way of a five-year experiment, he allowed the transfer of the Holy Saturday rites to the night hours preceding Easter Sunday, thereby restoring the ancient Paschal Vigil. In 1953 he mitigated the strictness of the Eucharistic fast and made provision for evening Masses. On March 23, 1955, he issued a sweeping simplification of the rubrics of the missal and breviary, and on November 16 he completely revised all the rites of Holy Week in order to make them more accessible to the laity. Finally, on December 25, 1955, he published the encyclical *Musicae Sacrae Disciplina*, treating of sacred music. None of the changes sprang from any tendency toward archaeologism; their essential motivation is the pope's fatherly solicitude to see clergy and laity pervaded with what Pius X called "the primary and indispensable source of the true Christian spirit."

IRENIC ENDEAVORS

Another current, which likewise became a sort of movement right after World War I, might be likened to a peace or reconciliation crusade. The separated Eastern Churches were regarded with growing understanding and sympathy. The liturgical movement contributed much to this. Not only was there an increased study of Eastern controversial theology, which since 1931 has been prescribed in seminaries as a special field, but there were not a few priests and clerics who voluntarily adopted the Byzantine Rite in order thereby to be better qualified to work for reunion.[6]

6 In 1930 the submission of Mar Ivanios and Mar Theophilus, bishops of the Jacobite Church of Malabar, with some of their clergy and laity, aroused quite a stir; in a short time many other Malabarese followed them. For this now flourishing group the Syro-Malankarese Rite was instituted. (Translator's note.)

More especially, there arose in many the desire for closer contact with Protestants of the various denominations. The more it appeared that public life was becoming non-Christian and wide circles were turning from all Faith, the more appealing seemed an amalgamation of all who still regarded themselves as Christians.

Among Protestants conferences and congresses were organized to insure co-operation within their own ranks and, as far as possible, with the Orientals too. The organization "Life and Work," whose soul was the Swedish Archbishop Nathan Söderblom (✝1931), arranged the conferences of Stockholm (1925) and Oxford (1937); the organization "Faith and Order," those of Lausanne (1927) and Edinburgh (1937). Both organizations then established at Utrecht in 1939 a provisional committee for a "World Council of Churches." The work was interrupted by the war, but in 1946 a new meeting took place in Geneva.

The Catholic Church always refused to participate. Pius XI explained this attitude, which was painful to some Catholics, in the encyclical *Mortalium Animos* of 1928. The much quoted words of Christ "that there may be one flock and one shepherd" do not apply to the future. The unity of Christians exists in the Catholic Church. Everyone who wishes to join her is welcome. But there is no higher unity of a universal Christendom to which the Church can join herself.

The Church has not objected to discussions, such as those which the archbishop of Mechlin, Cardinal Mercier, held with the Anglican Lord Halifax in 1921, which created a definite stir, or to the reunion conferences between Slavic Catholics and Orthodox, which occurred rather often at Velehrad in Moravia from 1907. To a most courteous inquiry of the above-mentioned provisional committee of 1939 the Holy See replied through the apostolic delegate in England that nothing stood in the way of a private contact with the delegate or with the bishops.[7]

NATIONALISM

Nineteenth century nationalism fired many countries to the boiling point during the present century, especially since World War I. The nation is basically a cultural community, especially a community of language and custom. When political rights and claims are turned aside from this cultural community we speak of nationalism; that is, when politically dependent national groups raise the demand for independence or politically dominant groups the demand for the denationalization of subjected minorities. Nationalism can also exist where national community and state coincide and it expresses itself chiefly in pride and megalomania. This national sensitivity and arrogance are sometimes the greater, the smaller and weaker the state in question.

Although nationalism sets up dividing barriers among men, especially those of an emotional sort, it has until now inflicted less harm upon the Church than upon the states. The unity of the Church consists essentially in the union of the members with the head and only through that in the union of the members with one another. At all events, it does not result from individual Catholics extending their hands across state and language barriers. The unity of the Church is not destroyed if there exists no lateral communication among her members. Hate and hostility among individual Catholics, as among Catholic peoples, are, it is true, combated by the Church as

[7] In 1908 Paul James Francis, an Anglican clergyman in the United States, inaugurated the Church Unity Octave, a period of special prayer from January 18 to 25 for the reunion of Christendom. In October, 1909, seventeen members of his Society of the Atonement entered the Catholic Church. In December, 1909, Pope Pius X sanctioned and blessed the octave, and in 1916 Benedict XV extended it to the whole Church. It is now known as the Chair of Unity Octave. (Translator's note.)

un-Christian and sinful, but they do not abolish the sacramental-juridical unity of the Church. The Church is something quite different from a world-friendship society or an inter-state organization.

In fact, experience has shown, especially the experience gained during the two world wars, that the unity of Catholics is strong, even emotionally. They really raised weapons against one another, but the preaching of hatred always found little response in Catholic populations. In succoring countries hurt by war Catholics were foremost. After World War I both Americas, Spain, Holland, Switzerland were most generous. The same is now being repeated after World War II.

This does not mean that modern state nationalism has brought with it no burden for the Church or that it even represents something desirable. Thus, for example, the strong supra-national attitude in regard to the pope has become more difficult since the reconciliation with the Italian state. The important thing is not whether the pope is a born Italian, but whether the Italian Catholics of the future will show the necessary sense of responsibility and the necessary self-denial not to push the pope, who dwells in their midst, into their state nationalism. Hitherto the Catholics of all countries have with pride termed themselves Roman, that is, papal, Catholics. In the mouths of some Italian writers "Romanità" is used at present in a somewhat different sense, as though not the pope but rather the Italian nation occupied in the Church a kind of central position.

LOSSES AND DANGERS

No one can deny that in most countries the prestige of the Church has grown since the beginning of the twentieth century. Now little is heard of the proverbial inferiority of Catholics in the nineteenth century. However, the number of the Church's enemies has not for that reason become smaller, but larger. Likewise, it can be said that the care of souls has become more intensive all along the line. But losses and defections have not thereby ceased. The twentieth century has seen formal movements of separation from the Church in particular countries, as in Czechoslovakia after 1918 and in Germany after 1933. Such agitation never, of course, achieved the desired or feared result, but it produced painful losses. In some countries conversions are numerous, as in North America, where they range from 50,000 to 70,000 annually, and in England, where there are some 10,000 a year, but great losses occur yearly from mixed marriages. And we should not be disheartened by the fact that the general increase of humanity at present is more rapid than the numerical growth of the Church. This is not a reason for pessimistic reflections on the future, but it does show that for the Church there is no rest, no golden age.

THE MISSIONS

The spread of the Church over the entire earth, which we see reaching its completion today, has seemingly occurred in fits and starts. In reality, however, it is not determined by chance, but by internal and external laws. The exterior frame is the geographical horizon of mankind, which has constantly widened and really only since the nineteenth century has encompassed the whole earth. The interior law is a certain tension, which, since the days of the apostles, has characterized the Church's urge to press into new countries beyond the geographical horizon.

Human culture first arose around the eastern Mediterranean basin: Mesopotamia, Egypt, Greece. When Christianity entered the world, the cultural center of gravity still lay in this region, but the culture itself had already pushed far westward and circled the whole Mediterranean. When in the seventh century Islam spread over the old original countries in the East with a new but less valuable culture and at the same time reared a frontier through the entire length of the Mediterranean, the ancient and by now Christian culture became an exclusively European and Western culture.

For a long time it appeared as though the Church would remain confined to Europe. But her dynamic interior tension was unchecked. The Church had hardly filled the entire space of Europe when the impulse to expansion expressed itself in the crusading movement. First conceived as a religious war with arms in the European mediaeval manner, it was transformed by the preaching of the Mendicant Orders into a movement of expansion, gropingly at first, in the manner of an experiment, and without lasting success. Nevertheless, the Franciscans not only established themselves in the Holy Land under Turkish rule, but at the beginning of the fourteenth century they penetrated into the interior of Asia as far as China.

The crusading idea, the concept of military and political conquest for Christendom, was kept alive on the Iberian peninsula in the *Reconquista* and, when this was finished, was transformed at the time of the discoveries into the *Conquista*. The herald of the Gospel joined the movement of conquest and displayed his pastoral activity in the subjugated New World under the protection of Spanish and Portuguese colonial power. Thus the European circle was broken in the sixteenth century and the greater part of America was won for the Church.

But in the modern period the situation of the Church in regard to the secular power changed. Longest of all, the Spanish kings still held to the idea of the Christian prince, who stood for the spread of God's kingdom. As a rule, however, there appeared in the place of the Christian prince the state, which more and more pursued its own interests, from which the Church had to make herself independent to achieve her own work of saving souls.

Significantly, a new name for the spreading of the Faith originated in the sixteenth century—mission. The word comes from the vocabulary of Saint Ignatius Loyola, who placed his religious at the pope's disposal for any sort of "mission" and strengthened their willingness for this by a special vow of obedience. The most conspicuous of these "missions" were now those to distant heathen lands, and thus people became accustomed to understand by "mission" the sending of a priest to the pagans and finally the actual work of converting them. In this new word lies a deep historical meaning: no longer does the Christian conqueror invite the Church to follow him, but the Church, the pope, sends his own messengers wherever new possibilities show themselves. Only in this way did a participation of all Catholic peoples in the spread of the Faith become possible. Out of the so-called unconscious expansion impulse, which was never lacking to the Church, there grew a conscious missionary desire, not only on the part of superiors, but of subjects as well, a stage which was reached only in the nineteenth century.

For even if the Church had long expanded beyond Europe —America, especially, had been opened up to her—still the greatest part of her task, even in America, remained incomplete and one can almost say that it was the missionary will of the nineteenth century that first made the Church a really world Church.

INDIA

In 1498, six years after Columbus had set out on the first voyage to America, Vasco da Gama, coming from Portugal

589

around the Cape of Good Hope, landed at Calicut on the western coast of South India. Still farther to the south the Portuguese occupied Cochin in 1502, landed on Ceylon in 1505, conquered Goa to the north in 1510, established themselves in 1532 on the peninsula of Salsette, opposite modern Bombay, and in 1536 took possession of Diu on the coast of Gujerat.

India is not a country, but a continent, like North or South America. But whereas America was almost uninhabited in the age of the Spanish, Portuguese, and English conquerors, the Portuguese in India came upon a world of rich culture, powerful states, and long political history. The Portuguese conquests played only a minor role in the internal history of India. The Portuguese capital, Goa, brilliant as it was for a time, was never in any sense the capital of India.

The Christianization of India is still a vastly more difficult task than was the Christianization of Europe, for which the Church needed a thousand years. Hence, it is not to be wondered at that it has still not made much progress after four and one-half centuries.

Vasco da Gama brought along two Trinitarians, one of whom died on the way, while the other was later murdered. In 1500 Cabral brought eight Franciscans and several secular priests. The first Dominicans came to India in 1503. But one can hardly speak of a real missionary endeavor, especially in the interior.

Of the greatest significance was the arrival of Saint Francis Xavier (really Javier), who landed at Goa in 1542 after a passage of thirteen months. Xavier came from Navarre and, with Ignatius Loyola, was one of the founders of the Jesuits. He did his missionary work south of Goa on the fishing coasts and in Travancore, then went to Ceylon, and still farther eastward in 1545. Goa remained his headquarters, even though he returned there only temporarily. He died in 1552 on the island of Sancian off the South China coast, not yet forty-seven years old. He became almost immediately a mythical figure among the sailors in the Far East and later also in Europe. People related unheard-of miracles—the gift of tongues, raising of the dead, and conversions of heathens by the hundreds of thousands. The reports which he and his companions sent faithfully to Europe contain none of this. Xavier's importance lies, not in mass conversions, but in the organization of the mission work. Like Saint Paul, he went through the mission field, tried out methods, created small centers, and had them cared for by co-workers trained by him. That after his early death there were not lacking missionaries to continue his work was due to his letters, which were at once spread throughout Europe and evoked an indescribable missionary enthusiasm. In the latter fact lies the second significance of this extraordinary man.

Success, however, remained less than expected. Outside the very restricted Portuguese sphere of influence, the Faith gained no footing. Goa, a see since 1533, became an archbishopric in 1558, with Cochin as suffragan. In 1606 there was added the see of Mylapore near Madras on the east coast, where the tomb of the Apostle Thomas was venerated. The so-called Thomas Christians on the west coast, communities with the Nestorian Syrian Rite, whose ancient origin is shrouded in darkness, were to some extent reunited to the Church in 1599, and the archbishopric of Cranganore was erected for them.

In addition to the deplorable example of the Europeans, which hindered Christianization in India as well as in all other overseas countries, the chief obstacle to successful missionary activity among the natives of India was the unfamiliar appearance of the missionaries. To the savages of America, even the half-civilized Aztecs, the Spaniards with their horses and fire-arms had seemed like gods; on the culturally proud, arrogant, and self-sufficient Hindus, the Portuguese, together with their missionaries, made the impression of a casteless rabble.

The Jesuit missionary, Roberto Nobili, a nephew of Saint Robert Bellarmine, withdrew, with the consent of his superiors, from all other Europeans, even from his own confreres, and from 1606 was found in Madura in the dress and manner of life of a Brahman scholar. He studied Sanskrit and was the first to discover its relationship with the European languages. He left no doubt as to his character as a Christian priest and made conversions among the Brahmans, but his work was not continued.

In general, the seventeenth century brought only reverses. The Jesuit missionaries for a time fixed their hopes on the friendly attitude of the Emperor Akbar (1556–1605) and his son, Schahangir. In 1637 a vicariate apostolic was erected for the north, but mass conversions failed to materialize. More-over, there occurred unending conflicts between the Portu-guese, who claimed the patronage over even the churches outside their own territories, and the Congregation of Propa-ganda. The Portuguese district in the south and west and on Ceylon was restricted by the Dutch, who were everywhere hostile to the missions. In addition there arose quarrels among the missionaries as to how far one might proceed in accommo-dating oneself to the civil customs of the natives. The Aposto-lic Delegate Tournon, sent from Rome to investigate the question, condemned in 1704 the Jesuits' practice of accom-modation, which seemed to him to go too far. On the other hand, the archbishop of Goa protested the infringement of Portuguese sovereignty by the delegate. In 1744 Benedict XIV definitively condemned the practice of accommodation and the Jesuits submitted, but they were now expelled by the Portuguese government.

With the suppression of the Society of Jesus mission work in India seemed to have come to an end. At first the still existing Portuguese claims to patronage stood in the way of a resumption in the nineteenth century. Since nothing could be hoped for on this side, Gregory XVI on his own authority established the vicariates of Madras and Calcutta in 1834 and those of Pondicherry and Ceylon in 1836, and in 1838 declared the patronage abolished. Thereupon occurred among the Portuguese clergy the so-called Goa Schism, which was not ended till 1886.

Meanwhile, more and more European missionaries were coming to India, which was not only pacified by English rule but even experienced a significant cultural upsurge. The Jesuits and other Orders instituted higher schools. Even in the north missions were now undertaken, notably by the Capuchins. The Belgian Jesuit, Lievens, succeeded from 1885 in bringing about in Chota-Nagpur, north of Calcutta, a mass movement which in a few years was responsible for more than 100,000 conversions. In 1886 Leo XIII established the Indian hierarchy, with at first eight archbishoprics and twenty-nine bishoprics.

In 1868 India counted 1,500,000 Catholics; today there are 5,000,000. This figure is still small in a land of more than 360,000,000 inhabitants, but the situation has changed very much in favor of the Catholics. The main body of Catholics still lives in South India, which is on the whole the culturally more advanced part. Here they play a role in public life. The reunited Thomas Christians in Malabar, who have grown to almost half a million, are not foreign groups but take an active share in ecclesiastical life. In the north there are still wide stretches of pure *diaspora*, apart from some large cities, such as Karachi in the west and Calcutta in the east. On the other hand, there are more conversions in the north than in the south.

The political independence of India ought on the whole to cause no harm to the Church. She is already sufficiently well-established and the former idea that Christendom is identical with Europeanism is disappearing more and more. Of the 5,000 priests laboring at present in India three-fourths, including many bishops, are natives; the same is true of 7,000 of the 10,000 Sisters. Nothing more is heard of the old questions of accommodation and rite. The caste system, which formerly caused so much trouble, is hardly noticed any more in ecclesiastical life.

To be sure, in this vast land an enormous field of labor still confronts the Church. And the Church in India is far from independent of recruits from Europe or America. But she is no longer a mission Church in the sense that pioneer work must first be done.[8]

CHINA

China too, compared with the European standard, is not a country but a continent; however, differing from India, it has formed a national and political unity from time immemorial. In the days of the Portuguese and Spanish sea voyages, China was a locked world, a fabled kingdom everywhere talked about as more powerful and more cultured than even Japan, but one not to be entered. Francis Xavier had understood that China is, for the missions, the key to the entire Far East, but he died on the threshold of this vast land without having set foot in it.

In 1557, five years after his death, the Portuguese suc-

[8] In 1953 Archbishop Valerian Gracias of Bombay became India's first cardinal. At present the position of the Church is rather difficult in India because of anti-Christian agitation. (Translator's note.)

ceeded in establishing themselves on the island of Macao. Macao lies near the place where Xavier died, at the gateway to Canton, the capital of South China. The spot was well chosen. Macao could soon compete with Goa. Today its importance has passed to Hong Kong lying opposite it, which was occupied by the English in the nineteenth century.

From Macao and the nearby Philippines Franciscans, Augustinians, and Dominicans several times tried vainly to penetrate China, which was closed to all foreigners. Only in 1583 did two Italian Jesuits, Ruggieri and Ricci, succeed. Ricci went about as a Chinese scholar, but, like his confrere Nobili in India, with no intention of deceiving. He spoke and wrote classical Chinese and was able, by his knowledge of mathematics, astronomy, and geography, to make himself so useful to the government that the spreading of the Christian Faith was not forbidden him. He settled permanently at Peking in 1601 and died there in 1610. The Jesuits sent missionaries from Europe with special scholarly and technical training to continue Ricci's work. Adam Schall of Cologne, who occupied Ricci's position from 1631, was able to maintain himself when in 1644 the Manchus took Peking and overthrew the old dynasty. Schall was a mandarin of the first rank. The Jesuits hoped, through their influence over the emperor, to be able to bring the entire Empire to Christianity at one time. This hope for a new Constantine proved to be vain, but just the same there were in China in 1650, despite many a persecution, 150,000 Christians.

The Dominicans too began to work in China from 1632, the Franciscans from 1633, and later also Augustinians and priests of the Paris seminary. To many of these new missionaries it seemed that the Jesuits were going to extremes in their toleration of Chinese customs, such as the ceremonies in honor of the ancestors and of Confucius, and hence there gradually developed the unfortunate "Quarrel over Chinese Rites," which obstructed missionary work. This was not mere jealousy between Orders; the questions were really difficult, and within the particular Orders, even among the Jesuits, opinions differed. In Europe, of course, as the war against the Society of Jesus became more and more violent, the affair was often unduly exaggerated and, to accusations of lax moral doctrine, wealth, and love of power, were also added idolatry and disobedience to the pope.

The first condemnation of the Jesuits' practice of accommodation came from Innocent X in 1645. By means of explanatory reports they succeeded in obtaining some mitigations. The Apostolic Delegate Tournon, who had already come out against the local accommodation in India, came to China in 1707 and expressed himself severely against the practice of the Jesuits. The succeeding delegate, Mezzabarba, made some concessions in 1720, but they were not approved in Rome. Finally, in 1744 Benedict XIV gave the definitive condemnation. However, when modern historians of the missions state that he thus gave the "deathblow" to the Chinese mission, they are certainly overdoing it. In 1726 there were 300,000 Christians in China, and in spite of many persecutions this number maintained itself into the nineteenth century. The suppression of the Society of Jesus did more damage to the progress of the missions than did all the decrees on rites.

At first, the sole bishopric for China was Macao from 1575. In 1659 the Propaganda erected two vicariates apostolic in Tonkin and Cochin China, to which were attached several Chinese provinces, and in 1680 the vicariate apostolic of Fukien for all of South China. Thereby came friction with the Portuguese patronage, and in 1690, to satisfy the Portuguese, the pope established Peking and Nanking as dioceses, which were placed under the archbishop of Goa.

The first Chinese priest was a Dominican, who was ordained at Manila in 1656 and was later named vicar apostolic of Nanking. As such, he ordained three Chinese Jesuits. It is due especially to the native priests that Christianity maintained itself in China during the difficult decades around 1800, when no further recruits came from Europe. Furthermore, in 1811 a violent and long-lasting persecution broke out. Not until 1844 did France enforce free exercise of religion; this was renewed in the treaties of Tientsin in 1858 and Peking in 1860. Around 1850 the Catholics numbered 320,000, with 135 Chinese and eighty-four foreign priests. The great upsurge now began under the French protectorate. The Franciscans, Dominicans, Lazarists, and priests of the Paris seminary, who were already laboring in the country, were joined by the Jesuits in 1842, priests of the Milan seminary in 1858, missionaries of Scheut in 1865, Christian Brothers in 1870, missionaries of Steyl in 1879, and others. In 1847 came the first Daughters of Charity, in 1860 the Italian Sisters of Canossa, in 1867 the Little Sisters of the Poor. Today all the larger religious communities take part in the Chinese mission. The number of Chinese Catholics climbed to 742,000 in 1900, and to 3,183,000 with 655,000 catechumens in 1940, so that now, with an annual increase of 100,000, it has exceeded the four-million mark. The number of Chinese priests rose from 135 at the middle of the nineteenth century to 400 in 1900 and to 2,113 in 1940. In 1926 Pius XI personally conferred episcopal consecration on six Chinese priests, and in 1946 Pius XII named the first Chinese cardinal. In the same year he elevated the former vicariates apostolic to diocesan rank, so that now China has twenty archbishoprics and seventy-nine bishoprics.

The unremitting persecutions, civil wars, and guerilla warfare could not stop the missionary work. Thirty thousand Christians lost their lives in the Tientsin Blood Bath of 1870.

In the Boxer Rebellion of 1900 forty-five missionaries, nine Sisters, and many lay Christians were killed. The revolution of 1911 and the overthrow of the monarchy did not disturb the missions, but the succeeding and still continuing wars did. Again and again the missionaries had to flee or were held for ransom by guerilla bands, and churches and schools were destroyed. But the country is so large that always only particular districts were affected and it is comparatively easy to again make good the property damage. After the most recent events too, in 1949, it once more seemed as though a great part of the mission work would be destroyed. However, Chinese missionary history till now has taught that such reverses are never lasting.

On the whole, China, in spite of the relatively small number of Catholics, is one of the most promising lands for the Church and it is really possible that the Church's center of gravity, which at present has shifted from Europe to America, may in later centuries come to rest in China. The "Yellow Peril," of which there was so much talk among European politicians of the nineteenth century, is for the Church a "Golden Hope."

JAPAN

The history of the Church in Japan is a long chain of disappointments. In 1549, coming from Goa and Malacca, Francis Xavier landed in Japan, moved through a great part of the island empire, and investigated the missionary possibilities. When he returned to Goa in 1551, he left behind his confrere Torres. Soon came other Jesuit missionaries. The number of Christians rapidly increased. In 1571 there were 30,000; thirty years later, 750,000. Conversions were frequent among the nobles and the territorial princes. Valignani, superior of the Jesuits, was a first-class organizer and at the same time a

598

resolute opponent of Europeanism in missionary activity. An embassy from four Christian princes went to Europe in 1582, was honorably received by the pope, and on its return in 1590 told of the greatness of the Church and of the brilliance of the West.

It was not, however, until 1596 that the first bishop came to Japan. In 1601 he ordained the first Japanese priests, two Jesuits and a secular priest. Today it is very difficult to fathom why so little care was later taken to provide a native clergy. However, it may have been more than a mere "inexcusable neglect" on the part of the Jesuits, as a recent mission historian puts it. In any case, decline was brought about not in that way but by force on the part of the government. From 1592 other religious missionaries also came to Japan, mostly Spaniards from the Philippines.

As early as 1587 the Shogun Taikosama, as the missionaries called him, issued the first persecuting decree. Later he showed himself favorable, but in 1597 he had six Franciscans, three Jesuits, and seventeen other Christians put to death. These are the famous martyrs of Nagasaki, canonized by Pius IX in 1862. Under Taikosama's successor, Diafusama, the persecution grew worse. Dutchmen and Englishmen incited him against the Portuguese and Spaniards, and hence against Catholics. From 1612 one decree after another appeared, and martyrdoms multiplied. In 1625 the number of Christians in Japan was still estimated at 600,000, but there was no longer any possibility of bringing in priests. Dominicans, Franciscans, Augustinians, and Jesuits made fruitless attempts. Most of them were quickly discovered and killed. The last Jesuits landed in 1643. In the eighteenth century the priest, Sidotti, who had come to China with the delegate, Tournon, reached the Japanese coast, but he died in prison in 1715. Three Jesuits who traveled to Japan in 1749 disappeared.

599

Only in 1858 did Napoleon III obtain that the few French living in the country could have divine services, but even now any missionary activity remained proscribed. In 1865 the Vicar Apostolic Petitjean discovered a remnant of the old Japanese Christians, who cautiously ascertained whether he recognized the pope, practiced celibacy, and honored Our Lady. For a long time a valid form of baptism had not been used among them. Though Petitjean was successful in recalling only a small part of them to the true Faith, he did, at least, establish the beginnings of a future community. In 1875 the government granted religious toleration, and now the number of Christians slowly rose from 20,000 in 1879 to 54,000 in 1898. Today they are little more than 120,000, most of whom live in the district of Nagasaki, the territory of the earlier Christians. Individual conversions from the educated circles are not rare. The Church enjoys indisputable prestige, and this finds expression in the presence of a Japanese envoy at the Holy See. But on the whole Japan is still among the most sterile of mission lands.

THE PHILIPPINES

Between the three great Asiatic realms of India, China, and Japan on the one hand and the Australian continent on the other lie huge land masses intersected and surrounded by inlets: the Indo-China peninsula and the largest island group on earth, stretching from Sumatra to the Philippines and New Guinea. Missionary centers for this world, comparable in square dimensions to Europe, were in the sixteenth century partly Malacca, occupied by the Portuguese in 1511, and partly the Philippine Islands, seized by the Spaniards in 1559 and named for Philip II. Francis Xavier went from Malacca to the Moluccas in 1546 and preached in Amboina and Ternate. In the Portuguese sphere were Siam and Cambodia, where missionary attempts were made in the seventeenth century. The Catholic missions on the Sunda Islands were annihilated, except for a small remnant, by the advance of the Dutch, who in 1641 took Malacca and gradually occupied the entire archipelago. Only on Timor, which remained Portuguese, did a somewhat large Catholic community maintain itself. Today it numbers about 70,000. It was not until 1807 that Catholic priests could come to the Dutch islands, at first only for the care of the Catholic Europeans. Real mission work did not begin again until 1859; since the turn of the century it has been making great progress, but in the meantime Islam had taken possession of all the Dutch islands.

The Philippines were made Spanish and Christian exactly as were the Spanish colonies in America. The missionaries, who came by way of Mexico, were at the same time protectors of the natives. At first they were Augustinians, but later principally Franciscans. In 1592 the Dominicans erected a special province, and the Jesuits did the same in 1606. Manila, a see since 1578, became an archbishopric in 1595 with Nueva Segovia, Nueva Caceres, and Cebu as suffragans. Around the middle of the seventeenth century there were 2,000,000 Christians.

The colony remained almost untouched by events in the rest of the world. Its isolation was still further accentuated by the fact that the only route of commerce and communication was that *via* Mexico to Spain. Not until 1814 was Manila opened to international trade. In the epoch of the *Aufklärung* and of liberalism anti-clericalism and freemasonry were imported, just as in America, from Spain. Here as there, it was a disadvantage that the Spanish government could not make up its mind to name natives as bishops. Even when Spain lost the colony in 1898, there was among the bishops not a single Filipino.

601

The occupation by the United States seemed at first harmful to the Church. In addition to other achievements of civilization, the Americans introduced their non-religious public schools. Protestant sects displayed a zealous activity. However, a greater pastoral effort established itself, partly because of the care of American religious. The number of dioceses was increased from five to fifteen. World War II, with the Japanese occupation of 1942–1944, caused great property damage and brought death to more than 100 priests.

As in other Catholic countries of Europe or South America, there are in the Philippines many Catholics who are indifferent or even hostile to the Church. The dearth of priests is especially painful. There are only about 2,000, whereas the United States has almost 49,000 for slightly more than twice the number of Catholics. In recent years, incidentally, vocations have gratifyingly increased. The Philippines, with their 16,-000,000 Catholics, remain a Catholic country, the only one in the eastern hemisphere. Anyone who comes to this island group from China or from Japan gets this impression. By their mere existence the Philippines help to make the Church at home in Asia. The International Eucharistic Congress of 1937 at Manila was an event for East Asia and a great help toward making European Catholics aware of the islands. For while the Filipino speaks Spanish, he has not become a European. His is essentially an Asiatic country. The European, who can hardly distinguish Japanese and Chinese superficially, regards him as one of these.

INDO-CHINA

From the Philippines in the sixteenth century went Spanish Franciscans to the Celebes, Borneo, and Sumatra, but without achieving permanent success. Tonkin and Cochin China also received their first missionaries from Manila. In addition to

Dominicans from Manila, priests from the Paris seminary labored in Tonkin. In spite of persecutions there were 250,000 Catholics with a native clergy at the end of the seventeenth century. Cochin China, Annam, and Tonkin had to endure severe persecutions in the nineteenth century as well, especially under Emperor Tüdük, who put to death five bishops, 115 priests, and thousands of the faithful. The political and religious struggles ended in 1886 with the occupation of all Indo-China by France. The Catholics there number well over 1,000,000, more than five percent of the population, and thus proportionately more than in China.

KOREA

The Korean peninsula has a unique mission history, for a Christian community was formed there before a missionary entered the country. Korea was a vassal state of China and wholly inaccessible to Europeans. But over the frontiers came Christian Chinese books, which were read eagerly. A member of the annual tribute-bearing embassy to Peking had himself baptized there in 1784. Having returned home, he collected a community of 4,000 Christians. Soon it had to endure persecutions, and even martyrdoms occurred. Not until 1794 could a disguised Chinese priest visit the Christians. From 1831 the Paris missionaries tried to get in, but in 1866 the vicar apostolic and several missionaries were put to death. From the time that Korea came under Japanese protectorate in 1895, bloody persecutions at least ceased. The number of Catholics has grown to more than 100,000.

Thus, then, monsoon Asia, or the entire expanse of India, Indo-China, China, Japan, and the southeast island world, has a Catholic Christianity of about 25,000,000, almost as large as that of the United States. But the picture is quite different.

603

Half of humanity lives in monsoon Asia, and Catholics are almost swallowed up. North America has long ceased to be a mission land. In the United States the Church is no longer on the receiving but on the giving end. The Church in Asia, on the contrary, does not by any means stand everywhere on her own feet. Many regions still depend on recruits, especially priests, from without. But the Church is gaining ground in Asia, especially in the two most important lands, India and China. She has become native to Asia; there is a Catholic Christianity of an Asiatic type. The "brown" or "yellow" priest and bishop are common sights in Rome. The Church has no race anxieties.

AUSTRALIA

In Australia, the last continent to be discovered and settled, the history of the Church begins with the year 1787. It was then that the first shipment of convicts was brought from England to Botany Bay, where later the city of Sydney arose. Among the convicts, whose numbers were soon increased by other shipments, were also political prisoners, including Catholic Irishmen. In 1817 an Irish Cistercian obtained permission from the government to go to Australia in order to undertake the spiritual care of the exiles, but he was not admitted by the colonial governor. Not until 1821 could two priests enter Australia. They found 2,000 Catholics. Ecclesiastically, Australia then formed a part of the vicariate apostolic of the island of Mauritius. Since the anti-Catholic laws had been abolished in England in 1829, the English Benedictine, Ullathorne, sent to Australia as vicar general in 1833, could organize the care of souls. He discovered 20,000 Catholics but only one church and two chapels with four priests, one of whom lived in Tasmania. In 1834 another Benedictine, John Polding, was named first vicar apostolic of Australia.[9] As early as 1842 Sydney was erected as an archbishopric, and simultaneously Hobart became a bishopric for Tasmania. Other dioceses were quickly established—Adelaide in 1843, Perth in the west in 1845, Melbourne in 1847. Today there are in Australia five archdioceses with fourteen suffragans and three vicariates apostolic. The number of Catholics has grown to 1,500,000, almost one-fourth of the total population.

Australia is a country of the whites. The natives, for whom the missions exist, number only a few thousand. The Catholics enjoy a position of respect. They have their schools and colleges, and the religious communities have their special Australian provinces. Whether Australia can permanently maintain its artificial isolation, its prohibition of Asiatic immigration, remains to be seen. Just the same, the Church's position in Australia is sufficiently strong so that she scarcely needs fear external crises. Of course, the Australian continent is very remote and, furthermore, turns its back, so to speak, on the rest of the world—since the larger settlements are concentrated in the southeast—so that this country, despite its favorable religious situation, will hardly ever play a leading role in the Church. This is even more the case with the approximately 100,000 Catholics of New Zealand.

THE ISLAMIC COUNTRIES

Tropical monsoon Asia is separated from Europe by a broad belt of arid regions which, in regard to Europe, are called the Near East—Anatolia, Syria, Mesopotamia, Persia, Arabia. With respect to geographical character this area includes all of North Africa and also the districts to the east of

9 Ullathorne and Polding were members of the English Congregation of Benedictines. In 1845 other Benedictines, from Compostela in Spain, began work in Australia and established the abbey of New Nursia. (Translator's note.)

the Caspian Sea, known as Central Asia, which toward the north changes imperceptibly into equally arid North Asia. It is a land of steppes and deserts, which, almost everywhere more than 2,000 kilometers wide, stretches from Cape Verde on the Atlantic Ocean to the Gobi Desert. This strip is the world of Islam. Together with all North Asia, it forms the great white spot on the map of the Church. It is not only that the number of Catholics in this entire region is very small and dwindling, but that almost nowhere can any missionary progress be noted. Included, too, in this belt are lands, such as Algeria, Egypt, Syria, and Asia Minor, which in antiquity were flourishing Catholic countries.

Two small states with a Christian majority lie like islands surrounded by the world of Islam—Abyssinia and, independent since 1946, the Lebanese Republic. Since the sixteenth century Jesuits, Franciscans, and Capuchins have repeatedly labored for the reunion of the schismatic Abyssinians, and several of them lost their lives in the effort. Today there are scarcely 30,000 Catholic Abyssinians, most of whom live in the colony of Eritrea. The new republic of Lebanon, with Beirut as capital, has somewhat over 1,000,000 inhabitants, most of them Christians, and of these about 40,000 are Catholics. At present Beirut is the residence of the two patriarchs of the Catholic Armenians and the Catholic Syrians, both of whom are cardinals, and also of the papal nuncio. The patriarch of the Maronites resides in Bekerkeh.

The Catholics of all rites living in the rest of the vast Islamic area do not number so much as 2,000,000. Most of them belong to French North Africa, including Tunisia, and are almost all of European origin.

The reason why the Church has up to now not been able to penetrate this "white spot" does not lie in any want of a universal missionary intention or in any impossibility of con-

verting individual Moslems, but rather in the absolute in-
tolerance of Islamic society. Whatever may be the laws of the
country in question, a Moslem who receives baptism, or who
approaches a missionary for this purpose, infallibly incurs the
ostracism of society and often puts his life in danger. In India
and in predominantly Islamic countries many Moslem students
attend the Christian higher schools. The missionaries have to
dread the conversion of one of them to Christianity, for this
will usually almost certainly mean the end of the school and
of missionary activity. Outside his environment the Moslem is
no harder to convert than others. Social pressure brings it
about that conversions to Christianity are extraordinarily rare.

Here lies the Church's greatest task for the future, a task
which generally she has not yet assumed. Unless she does so,
she can hardly be termed the world Church in the geographical
sense. At least a beginning has been made everywhere; in the
most important lands of the future, India, China, and perhaps
central Africa, it is more than a beginning. The Islamic world
has long ceased to be a barricade that confines the Church to
Europe, as in the Middle Ages; it is outflanked on all sides.
But it is still a world which is inaccessible to the Church and
there are in existence no indications that it will be otherwise
in the near future.

AFRICA

South of the Sahara Africa is a new missionary land. Old
dioceses exist on the Atlantic islands in the west—Las Palmas
on the Canaries goes back to the fifteenth century, Funchal
was erected in 1514, Cape Verde in 1532, the Azores in 1534.
On these islands about 1,000,000 Catholics live today. Of the
Portuguese possessions on the mainland only Angola in the
west and Mozambique in the east are still preserved. Angola
became a bishopric in 1596 and is divided today into several

vicariates apostolic. Lourenço Marques in Mozambique became a see in 1612; its present bishop is a cardinal. Of the islands in the Indian Ocean, Mauritius and Réunion today count more than 100,000 Catholics; the Seychelles, the Admiralty Islands, and Zanzibar, only a few thousand.

On the large island of Madagascar, which in its geographical character belongs to Asia rather than to Africa, a vicariate apostolic was erected in 1848. The missions have flourished unusually well, so that today there are on the island more than 500,000 Catholics, with a numerous native clergy.

The whites of South Africa are mostly Protestants. The Boers have been anti-Catholic from time immemorial. The Catholics of the Union of South Africa, some 350,000 in number, are to a great extent converted negroes.

The rest of the continent, "Dark Africa," was, until around the middle of the nineteenth century, well-known only along the coasts. Relations with the interior were for the most part not established until the twentieth century. The missions are almost all of a modern and very recent date. At present there are more than 100 vicariates and prefectures apostolic and mission districts, which are constantly increasing through partitions. Many of these missions are very promising. There are vicariates in which the number of catechumens, that is, of those preparing for baptism, far exceeds the number of baptized. The largest centers are Uganda and the Belgian Congo, where entire districts are Catholic. Naturally, the competition of the Protestant and, in the north, of the Islamic missions is keen. The hope of some missionaries that within a few decades all of the interior of Africa will be Catholic will not be so quickly realized. Nevertheless, some 5,000,000 have already been converted and every year several hundreds of thousands are added. If this movement of conversion continues for a time, there will arise here a Negro Church which will be of decisive significance for the future of Africa.

conclusion

C AN it be said that the Church is on the point of conquering the whole world? Certainly not, in the sense that the Church is a colonial power, an *imperium*. She never was such, she never will be such, she does not want to be such. The Church has never, even in the Middle Ages, had the intention of turning the whole world into a gigantic Church-State. Today the Church desires only what Saint Paul and the first apostles desired—to preach the Faith everywhere, to show to as many men as possible the way to salvation. For this goal— freedom to preach the Faith and to minister to souls—she will always fight, even with political means. Here she does not shrink from conflict with any world power. For the rest, she is unconcerned about who rules in India, China, Australia, or central Africa, what sort of constitutions the peoples there have, how they fashion their political and economic life. The Church profited by the colonial era from the sixteenth century and was grateful to the colonial governments when they fostered her pastoral work. But the end of the colonial system that we are now experiencing only indirectly concerns her.

Still another question, the basic question of all Church History, obtrudes itself here: is the Catholic Church of today still the Church of Christ and of the apostles? Today the Church is an enormous structure with a code of law, administrative machinery and property, press and diplomatic representation. Is she still the Church of the fishermen on the Lake

609

of Genesareth, of the tentmaker of Tarsus, the Church of the first Pentecost and of the catacombs?

She is. At all events, in the sense that all her present-day bishops can trace back their ordination and power of jurisdiction to the apostles in an uninterrupted series, and especially that the pope is the two-hundred and sixty-third successor of the Apostle Peter. Her Faith and her doctrine are no less and no more than the teaching of Christ and the apostles. The Church is today still occupied with carrying out the Lord's command: Go and teach all nations, baptizing them in the Name of the Father and of the Son and of the Holy Spirit. Yes, only today she is in a position to carry out this command in the full extent of its meaning. The Church today still celebrates the great bequest of the Lord, the Eucharist, the source of life and unifying bond of Christianity, but today, instead of the Twelve Apostles in the room of the Last Supper, there are almost 400,000, who, scattered over the whole world, daily offer the Sacrifice of the New Covenant. The Church can proudly say: If she has carried out any command of her divine Founder, surely it is the one that He gave her at that most holy hour, "Do this in commemoration of Me."

BIBLIOGRaphy

Acta Sanctorum. Edited by J. Bollandus and others. Antwerp: in progress since 1643. New edition, Paris: in progress since 1863.

American Benedictine Review, The. The American Benedictine Academy. Newark: 1950—.

American Historical Review, The. The American Historical Association. Richmond: 1895—.

Americas, The. Academy of American Franciscan History. Washington: 1944—.

Ancient Christian Writers. Edited by Johannes Quasten and J. C. Plumpe. Westminster (Md.): in progress since 1946.

Ante-Nicene Christian Library, The. Edited by A. Roberts and J. Donaldson. 24 vols. Edinburgh: 1866–1872. New impression, edited by A. Coxe. 8 vols. Buffalo: 1884–1886. Supplements by A. Menzies and A. Coxe, 1887. Additional volumes to the original series, edited by A. Menzies. Edinburgh: 1897.

Bardenhewer, O. *Geschichte der altkirchlichen Literatur.* 2d edition. 5 vols. Freiburg-im-Breisgau: 1913–1932.

Bardenhewer, O. *Patrologie.* 3d edition. Freiburg-im-Breisgau: 1910. English translation from the 2d edition: by J. J. Shahan, *Patrology: The Lives and Works of the Fathers of the Church.* Freiburg and Saint Louis: 1908.

Bihlmeyer, Karl. *Kirchengeschichte.* Neubesorgt von Hermann

Tüchle. Vol. I, 14th edition, Paderborn: 1955; Vol. II, 14th edition, Paderborn: 1955; Vol. III, Section 1, 11th and 12th edition, Paderborn: 1955; Vol. III, Section 2, in preparation.

Caspar, Erich. *Geschichte des Papsttums.* 2 vols. Tübingen: 1931–1933.

Catholic Encyclopedia, The. 17 vols. New York: 1907–1922.

Catholic Historical Review, The. The American Catholic Historical Association. Washington: 1915—.

Catholic University of America Patristic Studies, The. Washington: since 1922.

Catholic University of America Studies in Mediaeval and Renaissance Latin Language and Literature, The. Washington: since 1933.

Catholic University of America Studies in Mediaeval History, The. New series. Washington: since 1938.

Cayré, F. *Précis de patrologie et d'histoire de la théologie.* 2 vols. Paris: 1927–1930. English translation: by H. Howitt, *Manual of Patrology and History of Theology.* 2 vols. Tournai: 1936–1940.

Dictionnaire apologétique de la foi catholique. Edited by A. d'Alès. 4th edition. 4 vols. Paris: 1914–1922.

Dictionnaire d'archéologie chrétienne et de liturgie. Edited by F. Cabrol, H. Leclercq, H. Marrou. Paris: in progress since 1907.

Dictionnaire de droit canonique. Edited by A. Villien, E. Magnin, and R. Naz. Paris: in progress since 1924.

Dictionnaire de spiritualité ascétique et mystique. Edited by M. Viller. Paris: in progress since 1932.

Dictionnaire de théologie catholique. Edited by A. Vacant, E. Mangenot, E. Amann. Paris: in progress since 1899.

Dictionnaire d'histoire et de géographie ecclésiastiques. Edited by A. Baudrillart, A. Vogt, M. Rouziès, A. de Meyer, E. van Cauwenbergh. Paris: in progress since 1912.

Enchiridion Fontium Historiae Ecclesiasticae Antiquae. Edited by J. M. C. Kirch. 6th edition. Barcelona: 1947.

Enchiridion Patristicum. Edited by M. J. Rouet de Journel. 14th edition. Barcelona: 1946.

Enchiridion Symbolorum, Definitionum, et Declarationum de Rebus Fidei et Morum. Edited by H. E. Denzinger, C. Bannwart, and J. B. Umberg. 25th edition. Barcelona: 1948.

English Historical Review, The. London: 1886—.

Fathers of the Church, The. Edited by Ludwig Schopp and others. New York: in progress since 1947.

Funk, F. X. *Lehrbuch der Kirchengeschichte.* Edited, from the 6th edition, by Karl Bihlmeyer. 10th edition. Paderborn: 1936. English translations: by Luigi Cappadelta, *A Manual of Church History,* 2 vols. (from the 5th edition), London: 1910; by P. Perciballi and W. H. Kent, *A Manual of Church History,* 2 vols., London: 1914.

Garraghan, Gilbert J. *A Guide to Historical Method.* Edited by Jean Delanglez. New York: 1946.

Guilday, Peter. *An Introduction to Church History.* Saint Louis: 1925.

Hefele, Karl Josef. *Conciliengeschichte.* 7 vols. Freiburg-im-Breisgau: 1855–1874. 2d edition, 6 vols., 1873–1882. Continued by Josef Hergenröther, Vols. VIII and IX, Freiburg-im-Breisgau: 1887–1890. French translation, corrected and augmented: by Henri Leclercq, *Histoire des conciles d'après les documents originaux.* 8 vols. Paris: 1907–1921. Vols. IX-XIV by C. de Clercq, A. Michel, P. Richard, in progress.

Histoire de l'église depuis les origines jusqu'à nos jours. Publiée sous la direction de Augustin Fliche et Victor Martin. To comprise 26 vols. Paris: in progress since 1934. English translation of Vols. I-III: by Ernest C. Messenger, *The History of the Primitive Church,* 2 vols., New York: 1949;

613

The Church in the Christian Roman Empire, 2 vols., New York: 1953.

Historical Bulletin, The. Saint Louis University. Saint Louis: 1922—.

Hughes, Philip. *A History of the Church*. 3 vols. London and New York: 1934–1947. Vols. I and II revised in 1948.

Hughes, Philip. *A Popular History of the Catholic Church*. New York: 1949.

Kirsch, J. P. (editor). *Kirchengeschichte*. Unter Mitwirkung von Andreas Bigelmair, Josef Greven, und Andreas Veit. 4 vols. Freiburg-im-Breisgau: 1930–1933.

Lexikon für Theologie und Kirche. 10 vols. Freiburg-im-Breisgau: 1930–1938.

Lortz, Joseph. *History of the Church*. Adapted from the 5th and 6th German editions by Edwin G. Kaiser. Milwaukee: 1939.

Mann, Horace K. *The Lives of the Popes in the Middle Ages*. 18 vols. in 19. Saint Louis: 1902–1932. The first five volumes read: *in the Early Middle Ages*.

McSorley, Joseph. *An Outline History of the Church by Centuries*. Saint Louis: 1944.

Mid-America. Loyola University. Chicago: 1918—.

Mourret, Fernand. *Histoire générale de l'église*. Revised edition, 9 vols. Paris: 1914–1921. English translation: by Newton Thompson, *A History of the Catholic Church*. Saint Louis: in progress since 1930.

Pastor, Ludwig. *Geschichte der Päpste seit dem Ausgang des Mittelalters*. 16 vols. in 21. Freiburg-im-Breisgau: 1886–1933. English translation: by F. I. Antrobus, R. F. Kerr, E. Graf, and E. F. Peeler, *The History of the Popes from the Close of the Middle Ages*. 40 vols. Saint Louis: 1899–1953.

Patrologiae Cursus Completus. Edited by J. P. Migne. Series

Latina, 221 vols., Paris: 1844–1864; Series Graeca, 161 vols., Paris: 1857–1866.

Poulet, Charles. *Histoire de l'église.* 2 vols. Paris: 1926. English translation: by Sidney A. Raemers, *A History of the Catholic Church.* 2 vols. Saint Louis: 1934–1935.

Poulet, Charles. *Initiation à l'histoire ecclésiastique.* 3d edition. Paris: 1944.

Quasten, Johannes. *Patrology.* 2 vols. Westminster (Md.): 1950–1953.

Revue bénédictine. Maredsous: 1884—.

Revue d'histoire ecclésiastique. The Catholic University of Louvain: 1900—.

Sacrorum Conciliorum Nova et Amplissima Collectio. Edited by J. D. Mansi. 31 vols. Florence and Venice: 1757–1798. New edition and continuation, 56 vols. Paris: 1901–1924.

Schmidlin, Josef. *Papstgeschichte der neuesten Zeit.* 3 vols. München: 1933–1936.

Select Library of Nicene and Post-Nicene Fathers of the Christian Church, A. Edited by Ph. Schaff. 14 vols. New York: 1887–1893. Second series, edited by Ph. Schaff and H. Wace. 14 vols. New York: 1890–1900.

Speculum. The Mediaeval Academy of America. Cambridge (Mass.): 1926—.

index

Abélard, Peter, noted as Scholastic theologian, 247

Abyssinia, beginning of Christianity in, 134

Acacius (of Constantinople)
and *Henoticon*, 141
excommunication of, 141

Act of Supremacy, and the Church, 409

Acta Apostolicae Sedis, official organ of Curia, created, 537

Acts of the Apostles, noted as historical source, 8–9

Adrian VI, Pope, 349–350

Aeterni Patris (encyclical) noted, 551

Africa
and Christianity, 4th century, 146–147
missionary work in, 607–608

Agape, 43–44

Agapitus II, Pope, and ecclesiastical organization of Saxony, 185

Agapius, Bp., martyrdom, noted, 81

Agatho, St., constitution of, noted, 172

Ailly, Pierre d', Cardinal, and Council of Constance, 307

Akoimetoi (monks), 120

Alberic II (Prince of Rome), 185

Albigenses, 237–238

Albornoz, Aegidius, Cardinal, and uprisings in Rome (1354), 297–298

Alembert, Jean le Rond d', *Encyclopédie*, 482

Alexander II, Pope, 208–209

Alexander III, Pope, 269–271

Alexander IV, Pope, 279–280

Alexander V, anti-pope, 306

Alexander VI, Pope, 306, 334–336
and papal state, 338–339
and struggle for Naples, 336–337
excommunication of Savonarola by, 340–341

Alexander VII, Pope, 443

Alexander VIII, Pope, 445

Alexandria, School of, 22–23

Alexius IV (Byzantine Emperor) and the crusades, 261–262

Alfonso VI (Asturias) and Cluniac reform, 195

All Souls, Commemoration of, feast of, 196

Alphonsus Liguori, St., founder of Redemptorists, 438

Ambrose, St., 111
and Western monasticism, 121
influence on St. Augustine, 114

America
Church in, 446–480
colonization of, 451–459
European powers in, 17th century, 449
political occupation of, 449–451
population
at time of discovery of America, 451–452
in 1956, 540

American Institute of Management, studies on Holy See, 529n

American Protective Association, in U. S., noted, 508

Anacletus II, anti-pope, 266–267

Anagni (Papal residence) attack by Philip the Fair on, 287–288

Anchieta, José de, S.J., apostle of Brazil, 474–475

Andrew II (Hungary) and crusades, 262

Andronicus (Emperor of Greece) and the Venetians, 261

Angevins (dynasty) and Naples, 282–283

Anglican Orders, 410–411

Annates, 294

Anomoians, 100

Anselm, St., founder of Scholasticism, 246

A NOTE ON THE TYPE

IN WHICH THIS BOOK WAS SET

This book has been set in Weiss, an interesting face created by E. R. Weiss of Germany, who prefers to be called a painter. While he has studied almost every known letter in the world and copied inscriptions from Roman monuments, Renaissance capitals and fantastic baroque letter-forms from gravestones, he still remains a painter. The Weiss types, while traditional letters, are the product of our own time. Lines of text take on a gracious air—an easy limpid flow when set in this modern type design. Weiss types have good color and create dignity whenever one sees them, either in a book or advertisement. This book was composed and printed by the York Composition Company, Inc., of York, Pennsylvania, and bound by Moore and Company of Baltimore. The design and typography are by Howard N. King.